THE TRANSMISSION OF SCHIZOPHRENIA

The Transmission of Schizophrenia

Proceedings of the Second Research Conference of the
Foundations' Fund for Research in Psychiatry,
Dorado, Puerto Rico, 26 June to 1 July 1967

Editors

DAVID ROSENTHAL, Ph.D.

and

SEYMOUR S. KETY, M.D.

THE QUEEN'S AWARD,
TO INDUSTRY 1966

PERGAMON PRESS

OXFORD · LONDON · EDINBURGH · NEW YORK
TORONTO · SYDNEY · PARIS · BRAUNSCHWEIG

Pergamon Press Ltd., Headington Hill Hall, Oxford
4 & 5 Fitzroy Square, London W.1

Pergamon Press (Scotland) Ltd., 2 & 3 Teviot Place, Edinburgh 1

Pergamon Press Inc., Maxwell House, Fairview Park, Elmsford, New York 10523

Pergamon of Canada Ltd., 207 Queen's Quay West, Toronto 1

Pergamon Press (Aust.) Pty. Ltd., 19a Boundary Street, Rushcutters Bay, N.S.W. 2011, Australia

Pergamon Press S.A.R.L., 24 rue des Écoles, Paris 5ᵉ

Vieweg & Sohn GmbH, Burgplatz 1, Braunschweig

First edition 1968
Reprinted 1969

Library of Congress Catalog Card No. 69–14242

Printed in Great Britain by Page Bros. (Norwich) Ltd.

08 013018 6

CONTENTS

IV. STUDIES EXAMINING THE INTERACTION BETWEEN GENETIC AND EXPERIENTIAL FACTORS

V. RECAPITULATION AND CRITICAL OVERVIEW

FOREWORD

By the end of the nineteenth century Emil Kraepelin's concept of dementia praecox had gained wide acceptance throughout the psychiatric world, although a number of people criticized the prognostic assumption in which it was grounded, and many diagnoses had to be revised years after they had originally been made. Kraepelin believed he had defined a unitary metabolic disorder, and in the first decade of this century he assumed the leadership of a vigorous psychiatric research institute in Munich with the intention of discovering the root cause of that disorder. As part of the concentrated effort, he brought Ernst Rüdin from Switzerland to develop an intensive program of research into the genetics of dementia praecox and manic-depressive insanity. Rüdin and his colleagues marshalled a massive body of evidence that was consistent with a genetic interpretation of both disorders, but they could not agree on the mode of genetic transmission. Moreover, the various searches for the metabolic error repeatedly led into blind alleys or developed basic knowledge that had application only to other diseases. Although the elusiveness of the metabolic error was disappointing, the investigators took compensatory comfort in the continually reinforced belief that dementia praecox was a genetic disease.

Meanwhile, Sigmund Freud promulgated concepts of mental functioning and symptom formation that seemed to have relevance even to the most serious functional psychotic disorders. Eugen Bleuler, building on Freud's ideas, found meaning in the symptoms of his psychotic patients, and came to look on dementia praecox somewhat differently. He changed the name of the disorder to schizophrenia, but saw the latter as *a group* of disorders that were founded less on the concept of a deteriorative end-state and more on symptoms that he called fundamental and accessory. In the process, the concept of the disease was broadened considerably, and one could validly direct one's interest to the study of life experiences that seemed to lead to the peculiar speech, thought, feeling and behavior that were so prominent in the disorder.

From these divergent beginnings arose two schools of thought whose approach to and understanding of schizophrenia contrasted markedly with each other. In one, the clinical picture reflected metabolic disturbances; in the other, it reflected an attempt to resolve severe intrapsychic and interpersonal conflicts and disturbances. Although the two views need not be mutually exclusive, the fact was that for decades neither school concerned itself seriously about the other. As a matter of fact, at times the divided feelings erupted into recriminations and expressions of hostility, as each side accumulated further evidence to support its view of the genesis of the disorder.

In the late 1950's and early 1960's a few investigators began to build bridges across the gulf between the two approaches to schizophrenia. These bridges took the form of critical examination of one's own views, serious concern and criticism of the other side's evidence, and the development of new conceptual and methodological approaches to the study of schizophrenia. By the mid-1960's it became clear that the earlier dialectically opposed views were ready for some kind of synthesis. The synthesis could be a long time in coming about, but it could be facilitated and expedited by a direct confrontation of leading exponents of the opposed views. To be effective, such a confrontation should be personal rather than literary and must rest on presentations of hard data that can stand the test of rigorous criticism.

Against this background and in this context was conceived the idea of a confrontation conference in which many of the world's foremost scientists who had marshalled important, recent research evidence and who advocated different views of the role of genetic and environmental factors in the etiology of schizophrenia could be brought together to present their respective positions and the data on which they based them. Not all such scientists could be invited. Distinguished investigators from Scandinavia, Japan, Germany, Britain, U.S.A. and elsewhere were reluctantly omitted, but it was hoped that their basic views would be represented by other participants in the Conference.

The Conference itself lasted five and a half days. The days were long. Paper presentations provided the springboard to open, vigorous exchanges of views and penetrating criticisms. Animated discussions continued outside the conference room itself. By the week's end most investigators had come to know one another personally and to develop a healthy respect for contrasting positions and bodies of data.

Although the focus of the Conference was etiological, we used the word "transmission" rather than "etiology" to designate the core topic, since the relevant evidence to date is concerned with how schizophrenic disorder is passed on to members of a family, class or culture rather than with immediate and specific causes.

This Conference is the second in a series of three Psychiatric Research Conferences which the Directors of the Foundations' Fund for Research in Psychiatry agreed to sponsor as a contribution to psychiatric research. The editors wish to express their appreciation to them for the concept and the support which made this Conference possible, to Drs. Fredrick C. Redlich, Howard F. Hunt and Clark J. Bailey, who, with the editors, planned the program and selected the participants, and to the participants themselves who provided the substance and shared the spirit of the Conference. It is gratifying to have these proceedings first appear in the *Journal of Psychiatric Research*.

DAVID ROSENTHAL
SEYMOUR S. KETY

PARTICIPANTS

Yrjö A. Alanen

Gordon Allen

E. James Anthony

Manfred Bleuler

John A. Clausen

Leon Eisenberg

L. Erlenmeyer-Kimling

Norman Garmezy

William Goldfarb

Irving I. Gottesman

David Hamburg

Leonard L. Heston

Howard F. Hunt

Jon L. Karlsson

Seymour S. Kety

Melvin L. Kohn

Einar Kringlen

Theodore Lidz

Gardner Lindzey

Brian MacMahon

Sarnoff A. Mednick

Elliot G. Mishler

H. B. M. Murphy

William Pollin

David Reiss

Lloyd Rogler

David Rosenthal

Fini Schulsinger

James Shields

Margaret T. Singer

Eliot Slater

Pekka Tienari

Paul H. Wender

Lyman C. Wynne

I. INTRODUCTION

A 23-YEAR LONGITUDINAL STUDY OF 208 SCHIZOPHRENICS AND IMPRESSIONS IN REGARD TO THE NATURE OF SCHIZOPHRENIA

MANFRED BLEULER

Psychiatrische Universitätsklinik Burghölzli, Zürich

I HAVE been asked to present to you in the short space of 45 minutes, first, some of the results of my research work with schizophrenics, and, secondly, my purely personal ideas with regard to the genesis and origin of schizophrenic psychoses. The first and the second part of my presentation have, therefore, to be strictly distinguished one from the other: the first consists in mentioning facts and in discussing them briefly; the second consists in summarizing personal convictions—my favourite fancies, if you will.

The research work on schizophrenics, to which my remarks will mainly be confined, deals with 208 of 216 schizophrenics who were admitted to my Clinic Burghölzli in Zürich after I became its Head in 1942. I lost sight of 8 of them in the course of the years. The large majority, however, 208 admitted schizophrenics, I was able to follow up from the years 1942 or 1943 together with all their parents, siblings, and children until their death or until the end of this study in 1963–5. This was possible because Switzerland was quite isolated during the Second World War, during which time its population remained constant, and even after the war fluctuations were much rarer than in most other civilized countries.* The study of these 208 schizophrenics is, of course, not my only experience with schizophrenics. I have studied and published many other investigations. In 1941, for instance, I published a comparison of psychotic evolution with the original personality of schizophrenics and with the personalities of 8776 relatives of theirs. I made particular studies of schizophrenics who fell sick in advanced age, who were treated successfully or unsuccessfully, and of schizophrenics with endocrine peculiarities and other particular groups. In co-operation with other physicians of my clinic, I summarized several thousand publications on schizophrenia. During the greater part of my life I have lived in hospitals which cared mostly for severe cases of schizophrenia, and from babyhood on through my whole childhood, gravely sick schizophrenics even lived in my parents' family. You might, therefore, criticize harshly the interpretations of my experience, you might even find them foolish, but please do not reproach me for never having seen severe cases of schizophrenia, as was done in a recent discussion.

When I speak of schizophrenia, I mean a real psychosis. I excluded from the study border-line cases, as for instance pseudoneurotic patients who had never been psychotic in the social sense of the conception. I am sure that clinicians all over the world would agree

---

* This study has been supported by the Foundations' Fund for Research in Psychiatry, New Haven.

3

with the diagnosis of schizophrenia in all or nearly all the patients to whom I refer today as schizophrenics. It was easy to make such a selection because our clinic is—and aims to be— a clinic specializing in severe psychotics; for this reason mild border-line cases are rarely admitted.

Firstly, I should like to pick out some findings with regard to the *long courses* of schizophrenic psychoses. They can be classified in an easy and natural way. Firstly, a straight direct evolution has to be distinguished from a phasic evolution. Secondly, the outcome after many years has to be considered, and I distinguished between most severe chronic psychoses, mild chronic psychoses, and recovery. These distinctions result in the subdivision of psychotic evolutions into seven different patterns:

Straight evolutions:
  (1) acute onset followed immediately by chronic severe psychosis (catastrophe schizophrenia);
  (2) chronic onset leading slowly to chronic severe psychosis;
  (3) acute onset followed immediately by chronic mild psychosis;
  (4) chronic onset leading slowly to chronic mild psychosis.
Phasic evolutions:
  (5) several acute episodes leading to chronic severe psychosis;
  (6) several acute episodes leading to chronic mild psychosis;
  (7) one or several acute episodes with outcome in recovery.

Over 90% of all schizophrenias observed for many years fit into one or other of these patterns. Only a small remainder of about 5% evolves atypically; for instance, there might be acute episodes after a long-standing chronic episode or rare cases of recovery after chronic evolution.

From the descriptions of Kraepelin as well as from the experience of my father at the Burghölzli Clinic, we have an idea of the frequencies of these different patterns of evolution at the beginning of the century. In a study which I published 25 years ago, I determined the percentages shown in Fig. 1. (Here we see the maximum and minimum values as determined in different groups of schizophrenics.) I can now compare the impressions of Kraepelin and of my father with my statistics of patients treated until 1942 and my statistics with patients treated until 1963.

This comparison shows firstly that catastrophe-schizophrenia is dying out. Kraepelin and my father did not mention their percentage, but it must be concluded from their descriptions that they found it very frequently. By 1941 the rate had gone down to 5–18%. Ever since then, this most terrible form of schizophrenia has become increasingly rare. In my material not a single psychosis beginning after 1942 has developed in this way.

A second very impressive observation concerns the proportion between most severe and milder chronic psychoses many years after onset: the milder chronic conditions have increased, the severe chronic conditions have decreased within the last decades. It seems very likely that such an improvement has much to do with our therapy. I am less certain if it is mainly due to our active therapy or rather to the fact that patients are no longer mishandled, that isolation in isolation rooms and neglect to discharge patients at the right moment do not occur any longer.

The findings mentioned are encouraging. There are, however, other observations which are rather discouraging. While the most malignant *acute* schizophrenias are under control now, the most malignant *chronic* schizophrenias are not. The percentage of chronic onset leading slowly to chronic severe psychoses has remained nearly the same within the last 25 years. This seems to be the nuclear group of severe schizophrenia. A further finding is also disappointing: it was not possible to increase the percentage of recoveries much over one-third of all cases. I cannot prove statistically that recoveries are more frequent than before. When some 30 years ago the shock treatments of schizophrenia were introduced, it was

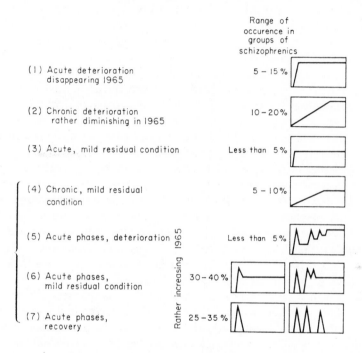

FIG. 1. Long courses of the schizophrenias according to my catamneses of 316 schizophrenics completed in 1941.

maintained that they could cure the majority of patients if applied early after onset of the psychosis. Statistics by other authors and by myself show clearly that such optimism is not justified. Many patients seemingly cured by the great somatic therapies relapsed into their psychosis later on, and after some years the number of recoveries among the somatically treated and the untreated patients is the same.

I have to come to the conclusion that up to now modern therapy has proved capable of extinguishing the most malignant acute schizophrenias and improving all chronic schizophrenic psychoses. However, in spite of modern therapy there still exists the sad chronic evolutions to severe chronic conditions, and it is doubtful whether modern therapy has been able much to increase the number of total, life-long recoveries.

B

During my study I became more and more fascinated by the late course of schizophrenic psychosis, in the further progress after 20, 30 and more years after onset. Generations of psychiatrists felt that schizophrenia was a process psychosis always progressing to complete deterioration, if life was long enough to allow the process to come to an end. There was a general impression that the outcome of schizophrenia was a "final state" (*Endzustand*), and that this final state could only progress or remain unchanged, but never improve. I am certain today that the contrary is true. More than 20 or 30 years after the onset of a severe schizophrenic psychosis the general tendencies are towards an improvement. This improvement is by no means only apathy, it is not due mainly to a loss of energy and activity, it is not a burning-out, as it was formerly supposed to be. It is true that it is mostly a partial improvement, but it consists of a real reappearance of both healthy intellectual life and very warm-hearted, very human emotional life in certain situations and in contact with certain persons. I should like to give you only a few pertinent figures.

I consider the group of patients who did not recover and who did not die soon after the psychosis had started. Their psychosis had lasted between 25 and 60 years. A quarter of them did not reach a stable condition, but still showed acute episodes during the last years of observation, these improving again very much. Of the patients who seemed to have reached a final state and who would have been considered as petrified, incorrigible, hopeless cases, at least one-third (58 of 150) again showed a definite improvement in this very late phase of the psychosis. Only 4 were still deteriorating after several decades of a psychotic life.

The lack of a trend towards further deterioration 20, 30, 50 years after the onset of the psychosis is also demonstrated by the number of hospitalized patients many years after the beginning of the psychosis. The 208 schizophrenics studied were collected as hospital admissions. In 1942/3 all were hospitalized. Five years later only 40% were still hospitalized. This percentage remained stable until the end of the observation period. At this time the psychosis had started between 22 and 61 years before, yet again only 40% of the patients were hospitalized in psychiatric hospitals. Of these 40%, a minority did not even need hospitalization for their psychosis but had become physical (particularly senile) invalids or the hospital had become their home and they no longer wanted to leave it.

In what do the improvements consist, decades after the onset of the disease, when it has seemed that a long and unchangeable stage has been reached? Many times the patients started to speak normally and to show very natural and fine feelings towards certain visitors, certain doctors or certain nurses. Or they started to show quite their original personality on some occasions, during work, during visiting hours, during physical diseases, during festivities, or during group psychotherapy. Others became milder, friendlier, more coherent, not only on particular occasions but in their general attitude in the hospital wards or in foster-families.

We also tried to elicit the reasons, if possible the psychodynamics of the late improvements. In this respect it was easy to show the coincidence of some influences with the improvement as regards time, but it always remained uncertain if we could postulate a causal relationship when the relationship as regards time was given. The most probable explanation of many late improvements was old age. My observation in this respect is in accordance with the work of Christian Müller, published at our clinic. He studied old schizophrenics and found a good many of them much improved. In some few cases of my study late improvements followed physical sickness, loss of a close relative, or change of environment. What seems most important—in some cases new therapeutic endeavours were successful even in these late stages of the psychosis. The therapeutic techniques proving successful were different. Mostly they consisted in group psychotherapy.

The cases I counted as not improving during the close of the observation represented, however, no deterioration in the old and absolute sense of the word. These conditions have nothing to do with the grave deterioration in severe atrophy of the brain. Even in the worst chronic cases, signs of normal intellectual and emotional life hidden behind the psychotic attitude could be demonstrated. During the study of his childhood I discovered, for instance, that one of the most chronic schizophrenics showing no improvement had loved animals in his childhood. In spite of his being in a backward ward, I therefore gave him a guinea-pig. Ever since then it has been touching to see how he loves it. He speaks with it in the natural and warm way a child speaks with his pet animal. He takes great care that other patients are kind to it. He was brought with a group of other patients to see a circus down-town. He was lost in the crowd and everyone was anxious about what would happen to him. However, the patient, who had not been outside the hospital for many years, found his way back in the dark night, although the way there is rather complicated.

It is certainly a wonderful experience to watch these late, unexpected improvements. However, there are also depressing observations to be mentioned. Late improvements have been seen in all patterns of the evolution of the psychosis except in one pattern: patients whose psychosis had started chronically and had slowly deteriorated to a chronic, most severe psychosis have not been seen to improve at the end of the observation period. This group of schizophrenics resists therapy both in the early and in the late phase of the psychosis. The late improvements were seen in patients in whom the psychosis had developed in acute phases and in those chronic cases who had never reached severe deterioration. We again come to the conclusion: the most chronic progressive cases are the ones resisting therapy as far as therapeutic successes can be demonstrated statistically. It is a tremendous task for the future to seek more effective therapy just in these cases, whereas we are already proud of good therapeutic results in all the other cases.

Leaving aside the long course of schizophrenic psychoses, I should like to mention *some of the other findings* in my latest study of the 208 schizophrenics already described.

On an average, *familial environment during childhood* was worse in female than in male schizophrenics. Several years ago Rosenthal demonstrated that among schizophrenic twins two sisters are more frequent than two brothers. He also demonstrated that two schizophrenic siblings are more frequently sisters than brothers and that schizophrenic siblings of the same sex are relatively more frequent than schizophrenic siblings of different sex. This is also true among my schizophrenic families. Rosenthal believes that these findings are best explained by the assumption that early familial influences can cause a predisposition to schizophrenia and, if so, more frequently or to a higher degree in girls than in boys. I found in my study much evidence in favour of such an assumption.

I calculated the incidence of broken homes, not only of the 208 schizophrenic probands, but also of 724 other schizophrenics, of 2008 individuals of the average population, and of patients with alcoholic and neurotic difficulties. I am aware that broken-home statistics have to be handled with much caution. I was impressed, for instance, that the number of broken homes in the average population showed a significant difference in the city of Zürich compared with the villages near Zürich. This difference was greater than the differences among groups of schizophrenics, on the one hand, and groups of representatives of the general population described in the literature, on the other. There was no significant difference between the number of broken homes of my male schizophrenics and of the average population. However, the number of broken homes in the anamnesis of female schizophrenics was greater than in the anamnesis of male schizophrenics and greater than in the general population. The latter difference was significant.

If we do not consider the broken homes alone, but also most miserable emotional conditions of a child living with both parents, the same difference between the two sexes holds good: female schizophrenics have been brought up under unfavourable childhood conditions more frequently than male schizophrenics.

Of the 4160 years by schizophrenics lived altogether before they reached their 20th birthday, their childhood environment is known for 4144 years. I calculated how many years the male and female schizophrenics lived together with schizophrenic parents and with step-parents. The female schizophrenics lived more years with schizophrenic parents and with step-parents than the male schizophrenics. The difference is more marked with regard to step-mothers than to step-fathers.

Totally different findings point in the same direction. In both sexes the relationship to the parent of the same sex is worse than the relationship to the parent of the opposite sex. Particularly bad was the relationship of the girls to their mothers. This relationship became worse during adolescence.

Not all of these findings are statistically significant, but some of them, and all point towards the same assumption: that early familial disturbances in the childhood of girls might cause a disposition to schizophrenia. There is no statistical proof that this is also true for boys. I do not know which environmental stresses are more active in boys than in girls. Up to now we only can speculate in this respect.

Time prevents my discussing even shortly other findings of my study. I should like to mention the following:

(1) The majority of schizophrenics who had suffered under unfavourable familial conditions in their childhood had also demonstrated schizoid traits already in childhood. It seems that the pathogenetic influence of unfavourable childhood conditions at first induces an unfavourable personality disposition in the sense of a schizoid personality. This latter is again a predisposition for the schizophrenic psychosis. On the other hand, it is not statistically demonstrated that early influences in childhood cause a predisposition to schizophrenia without a preliminary schizoid personality development.

(2) The erotic and sexual activities of schizophrenics are, on an average, much diminished. They also remain single more frequently than the average population. They have much less offspring than healthy people. The much diminished fertility of schizophrenics compared with the average population was established in 1956 by Essen-Moeller and in 1938 by Kallmann. It is again confirmed for the present time in my study. The earlier authors thought that increasing birth control might put a stop to this difference. This is not the case. I think that the demonstration of a reduced fertility of schizophrenics is important for the theories of schizophrenia. I shall discuss this point later.

(3) The frequency of schizophrenic psychoses among the relatives of schizophrenics is very similar in my new study to my earlier studies and to many other studies of the Munich school of Ruedin. It is particularly interesting that the number of schizophrenics among the parents of schizophrenics has been found in most varying groups of schizophrenics to be near 7%.

(4) The social and intellectual level in the families of schizophrenics is not reduced from generation to generation. It is, on an average, maintained, in spite of the terrible burden a schizophrenic is for many families.

(5) I tried to find out what distinguishes a schizophrenic in his childhood from his brothers and sisters who never became psychotic. The future patient has, indeed, frequently a much more difficult position in his parent's family than his siblings. I agree with Lidz and Alanen and other authors with regard to this finding. In my study, however, the particular burden on the future schizophrenic sibling is of a most varying type. It may happen that he is more attached to a morbid parent than his siblings. This, however, is not the rule. More frequently the future schizophrenic is intellectually more or less gifted than the other members of the family and is isolated on this account.

I shall now summarize *my ideas with regard to the genesis and nature of schizophrenic psychoses.*

It is safe to state: Up to now a somatic background of schizophrenia has not been discovered, neither a brain lesion nor a pathology of metabolism. I do not disagree with any somatic theories of schizophrenia on account of philosophic speculations or on account of over-generalizations of psycho-analytical theories as others do. I disagree with them just because I am attached to biology and to general medicine. As far as I can see, all the somatic theories of schizophrenia are open to most severe criticism from biologists. As a physician, I feel that we are not allowed to diagnose a somatic disease without somatic findings. It seems not to be good medical policy to maintain that schizophrenia is a symptom of a somatic disturbance, if we cannot demonstrate this somatic disturbance, just as a conscientious physician is not allowed to treat any complaint as a cardiac disease if there is no cardiac symptomatology to be demonstrated. My personal studies with regard to potential somatic backgrounds of schizophrenia have been made in the fields of psycho-endocrinology. They have led to the simple observation: most schizophrenics are endocrinologically healthy and most endocrine patients are not schizophrenic. We can even go further and state: Any psychopathological complications of somatic disturbances are not schizophrenic psychoses.

I have discussed the frequency of improvements many years after the onset of the psychosis. It is difficult to explain it if schizophrenia is an error of metabolism or any brain atrophy.

Since we are unable to find somatic backgrounds of schizophrenic psychoses, we must seriously consider the possibility that the development of schizophrenia is similar in nature to all other human developments whose somatic background we are unable to perceive. The neurotic, the psychopathic and the normal personality development under the influence of inherited dispositions and the environment continue without any intelligible correlations in the body. It is possible and probable that schizophrenic developments follow similar pathways remote from any understood, ascertainable and perceptible somatic processes.

The lack of significant somatic findings in schizophrenia is not the only hint that schizophrenia must be understood as a psychological process. There are other observations pointing in the same direction. In schizophrenics the healthy life is never simplified and finally extinguished as in progressive organic psychoses. The most complicated and the most normal intellectual and emotional life of schizophrenics is only hidden behind the psychosis, but it still continues. Neither is the schizophrenic way of life anything new in a psychotic. Hidden schizophrenic life goes on in the healthy, in dreams, day-dreams, mysticism, in autistic, archaic, and magical thinking, in the creations of artists and so on. The schizophrenic psychosis can neither be characterized by the final loss of any function nor by the production of any new morbid process. It must be characterized by a loss of equilibrium of two different, in themselves normal ways of living. One tendency is to form a fantastic inner world as a picture of conflicting, contradictory human wishes and human fears, as a picture of contradictory human nature. This form of life is hidden in the healthy and it overwhelms all obstacles in the schizophrenic. In his every-day life the healthy man has to overcome and to fight the disharmony of his nature. He has to harmonize and to integrate his different moods, drives and interests in order to arrive at useful decisions and to secure his existence.

The background of neurotic, psychopathic and normal personality development is given first by inborn dispositions and second by environmental influences, particularly by the world of human relations. Research on the genesis of schizophrenia has been successful in demonstrating that schizophrenic developments, too, have much to do with just the same two influences: the influence of inherited dispositions and the influence of life experience, particularly experience in social life. No other significant roots of schizophrenia have been demonstrated. It seems to me that we are obliged to try out the hypothesis that schizophrenic developments are mainly due to the collective action of inherited dispositions of the personality development, and to environmental, particularly interhuman experiences.

Many observations which I have not mentioned as yet are hints in the direction of such a conception. For instance: there are no limits between morbid personality development in the sense of an induced psychosis and schizophrenic psychoses, no limits between schizophrenic reactions and so-called real schizophrenic psychoses, no limits between severe schizoid personality development and development into schizophrenic psychoses. There are, however, fairly distinct limits between chronic organic brain syndromes and schizophrenic syndromes, at least in the great majority of cases.

Neither heredity alone nor environment alone is sufficient to explain the morbid development into a schizophrenic psychosis. We must assume a collective activity, an interplay of both. Among the many observations in this respect I want only to mention shortly the most evident ones. Human environment must play an important role because we can observe its influence on the patient during social and psychological therapy as in an experiment. If you know the life history of schizophrenics in intimate detail, you always find close temporal connections between environmental circumstances and the psychotic evolution. Furthermore, schizophrenics feel that these disturbances are the logical reaction to unhappy life experience. This is, of course, not a proof for the psychologic background of schizophrenic development. It is, however, a hint in the direction of the significance of psychodynamic processes. Up to now, we cannot assert that psychodynamics explain schizophrenic developments without an unfavourable heredity. Nobody has discovered that psychological stress situations in the life history of schizophrenics are of a specific nature and of another type from stress situations which many people can stand without becoming schizophrenic. By no means can schizophrenia, on the other hand, be explained by hereditary influences alone. This is one of the clear consequences of twin research.

It therefore seems most probable that the interdependence of hereditary tendencies and of life experience form the background of schizophrenic psychoses.

Of what nature are they?

I cannot admit that hereditary disposition consists of the morbidity of one or two or three genes which are altered by mutation. Among other reasons, two observations speak against this old hypothesis. Firstly, no family research was able to demonstrate that the occurrence of schizophrenia follows any Mendelian law. The results of family research suggested the most different and complicated Mendelian transmissions, but all of them can easily be criticized. Secondly, the fertility rate of schizophrenics is very much reduced and, in spite of this, schizophrenia remains a very frequent psychosis. If we assert that mutation of a gene is the main background of schizophrenia, we must conclude that the mutation rate is very high. As a matter of fact it would have to be much higher than any known mutation rate. If no morbid genes for schizophrenia exist, the hereditary background of schizophrenia is most probably a disharmony, an insufficient interplay of different pre-dispositions of the personality. It is, indeed, just this disharmony of the personality which has been observed again and again as the personal disposition for schizophrenia; the schizoid personality type, which has been described so carefully by many earlier clinicians, is nothing but a personality which has difficulties in harmonizing its drives and interests and in forming a clear and definite attitude and will, a strong ego, as the Americans call it. As far as constitutional physical dispositions of schizophrenia could be elicited, they have to be summarized as physical disharmonies running parallel to the personal disharmonies.

If no specific morbid gene to schizophrenia exists, no specific psychological stress situation exists either. I cannot see that such a stress situation has been discovered as yet. Most different stress situations are to be found in the life history of schizophrenics and most different stress situations might disturb the harmony of the personality.

While we cannot find exactly the same definite hereditary insufficiency and exactly the same definite environmental stress during careful psychological and social study of every schizophrenic, we find reasons to assert that the discordances of personality of an individual kind elicit discordances of the human environment of an individual kind. Each schizophrenic development takes a unique, individual course, just as any personality is a unique individual with his unique individual life experience. As no two men are alike, no two psychotic developments are alike either. All of them have in common the disharmony of both inborn traits of the personality and life experience.

We have also to consider our knowledge of the therapy of schizophrenics when trying to understand the nature of their psychoses. No specific therapy of schizophrenia has been discovered. There is neither a specific somatic treatment of schizophrenia, nor a specific psychotherapeutic technique. What is effective in the treatment of schizophrenics is also effective in the development of the healthy: clear and steady personal relations, and sudden confrontation with new responsibilities or with dangers threatening life. The same forces restraining the overflowing of a prelogical, unrealistic, disordered, disrupted form of life in the healthy are effective in the therapy of schizophrenics.

We might therefore venture a formulation as follows. Schizophrenic life is characterized by dissociation, by splitting, by lack of harmony. Hereditary dispositions to schizophrenia consist in disharmonic tendencies for personality development. Such a disposition impairs the world of human relationships. The disrupted and ambitendent relationships with others increasingly disturb the personality development of the future patient. He comes to a breaking point when he is supposed to deal with a new stress. The therapy of schizophrenics has to utilize just the same influences developing and strengthening the healthy: steady human relationships and confrontation with responsibility and danger.

This is, of course, a preliminary conception. It is in accordance with present-day knowledge. Future discoveries may lead to other conceptions. For the moment, however, it may be right to build up conceptions which summarize our present knowledge and not to take into account morbid processes which have never been demonstrated.

REFERENCES

BLEULER, M., *Krankheitsverlauf, Persönlichkeit und Verwandtschaft Schizophrener und ihre gegenseitigen Beziehungen,* Thieme, Leipzig, 1941.

BLEULER, M., Forschungen und Begriffswandlungen in der Schizophrenielehre 1941–1950, *Fortschr. Neurol.,* **19**, 385–452 (1951).

BENEDETTI, G., KIND, H., und MIELKE, F., Forschungen zur Schizophrenielehre 1951–1955, *Fortschr. Neurol.,* **25**, 101–79 (1957).

BENEDETTI, G., KIND, H., und JOHANSSON, A. S. (unter Mitarbeit von P. F. GALLI), Forschungen zur Schizophrenielehre 1956–1961, *Fortschr. Neurol.,* **30**, 341–505 (1962).

BENEDETTI, G., KIND, H., und WENGER, VERENA, Forschungen zur Schizophrenielehre 1961–1965. Uebersicht (Teil I), *Fortschr. Neurol.,* **35**, 1–34 (1967).

BENEDETTI, G., KIND, H., und WENGER, VERENA, Forschungen zur Schizophrenielehre 1961–1965. Uebersicht (Teil II), *Fortschr. Neurol.,* **35**, 41–121 (1967).

MÜLLER, CHR., *Ueber das Senium der Schizophrenen,* Bibl. Psychiat. Neurol., Fasc. 106, S. Karger, Basel, 1959.

II. GENETIC STUDIES

A REVIEW OF EARLIER EVIDENCE ON GENETIC FACTORS IN SCHIZOPHRENIA

ELIOT SLATER

Psychiatric Genetics Research Unit, Institute of Psychiatry, Maudsley Hospital, London

EDITH ZERBIN-RÜDIN, daughter of famed Ernst Rüdin, has recently reviewed the work done on hereditary factors in the endogenous psychoses for an important section of 132 pages in the fifth volume of *Humangenetik*. This review will no doubt prove an authoritative reference.

In the part given to schizophrenia, Zerbin-Rüdin finds it necessary to begin by giving a clinical description of schizophrenia. I feel that it is necessary to follow that excellent example. There is a moderate amount of agreement, though one that is far from fully satisfactory, between psychiatrists of Britain, Germany and all western European countries about what is and what is not to be called schizophrenia; but it seems to be the case that in the North American continent a much wider concept is employed. Some American authorities, I believe, consider it not only a misleading and futile exercise to make a diagnosis of "schizophrenia", but regard the whole clinical practice of trying to make a diagnosis, i.e. to allocate the individual patient to what may be a mythical nosological entity, as an obsolete approach.

The individual is in himself unknowable, and we can only begin to learn something about him by comparing him with other men. In so far as he resembles all mankind without exception, we can learn nothing about him that we do not already know about mankind in general. If in any respect he is absolutely unique, we can learn nothing about the causes of that uniqueness. However, if he differs from the majority of mankind in a respect in which others also differ, we can learn something about him from a study of the deviant group. Diagnostic classification comes under this logical principle. There are respects in which schizophrenics differ from others, and it is incumbent on us to define these respects and to come to some agreement about our definitions. Whether schizophrenia is a nosological entity or not, we must give it an operational definition. If, at this conference, we are going to be able to communicate with one another, we must have an agreed delimited field of discourse.

For the European psychiatrist, schizophrenia is an illness affecting the mind and the personality of the patient in a way which is seldom completely resolved; after an attack of illness there is nearly always some degree of permanent change of personality, and if there are several attacks this change will become more and more marked. This change is one that de-individualizes and dehumanizes the patient, and leaves him, above all, with impaired capacities for normal affective responses. While an attack of illness is proceeding there will be one or more of a series of distinctive symptoms: hallucination in a clear state of consciousness, passivity feelings, primary delusional experiences, and rather typical forms of thought disorder. After recovery, often only partial, some of these symptoms may persist; but the principal disabilities will be in the form of various psychological defects.[1] It is illnesses of these kinds which have been made the subject of the investigations reviewed by Zerbin-Rüdin, and which I propose to discuss. Excluded from consideration, as far as I am concerned, are all non-progressive deviations of personality, pseudoneurotic schizophrenia, and other nebulous entities.

It is a fact of considerable importance that "schizophrenia", using the European conception roughly formulated above, is approximately equally frequent in all countries where adequate investigations have been made. This is shown in Table 1, in which the data are

TABLE 1. EXPECTATION OF SCHIZOPHRENIA FOR THE
GENERAL POPULATION

Date	Country	N	Expectation (%)	S.E.
1931	Switzerland	899	1·23	0·368
1936	Germany	7,955·5	0·51	0·088
1942	Denmark	23,251	0·69	0·054
1942	Finland	194,000	0·91	0·021
1946	Sweden	10,705	0·81	0·087
1959	Japan	10,545	0·82	0·088
1964	Iceland	4,913	0·73	0·121

taken from Zerbin-Rüdin, and from Kishimoto (1959), dates in the left-hand column being the means of the years in which the investigations were reported, and N being given in life-risks. It will be seen that there is no general move upwards in the course of time, which might have been expected, since with improving health services, over the course of decades the chance of receiving hospital treatment for a psychiatric disorder will increase. In England the Registrar-General's figures show an increase in hospitalizations for psychiatric disorder, but the biggest part of it is in the neurotic-psychopathic diagnoses. In England, on the 1960 returns, one can calculate the expectation of a man being admitted to a health service hospital with a diagnosis of schizophrenia as 1·13% by the age of 55, the expectation for a female being 1·08%.

It is difficult to explain this constancy from one country to another, when countries differ very much in social organization and modal patterns of intrafamilial relationships, without hypothesizing a genetical predisposition fairly evenly distributed over Europe and very likely over the world. Genetic variation does of course occur. Some markedly deviant estimates of schizophrenia expectation have been found in some regions, e.g. Garrone's (1962) estimate of 2·4% for Geneva and Böök's (1953) estimate of 2·85% for an isolated region of Sweden north of the Arctic Circle. There is likely to be a variation in gene frequencies in Böök's small isolated highly inbred sample; but whether this is also the case

[1] Professor Bleuler in his paper gives a picture of schizophrenia which is rather different in its emphasis. He draws attention to the capacity for improvement even of the long-standing schizophrenic, and the more favourable outcome we see today compared with a generation ago. The formulation I have given stresses the fact that, even after satisfactory recovery from an attack of schizophrenia, there will often, even usually, be some change in personality, perhaps only obvious to the psychiatrist who has known the patient from of old, or the patient's family or his closer friends. Professor Bleuler and I have discussed the formulation given above, and find no difference of opinion between us.

with Garrone's Genevese is more doubtful. It is possible that Garrone's diagnostic criteria differ a little from the general European pattern.

THE RELATIVES OF SCHIZOPHRENIC PATIENTS

About 25 independent investigations have been summarized by Zerbin-Rüdin to give estimates of the expectancy of schizophrenia in various degrees of relatives of schizophrenic patients. Her tables are rather complicated, and the salient facts have been expressed in a simplified form in Table 2. Here I have included only the "certain" schizophrenics; if doubtful ones had been added, these figures would have been increased by about 25%.

TABLE 2. EXPECTATION OF SCHIZOPHRENIA FOR RELATIVES OF SCHIZOPHRENICS

Relationship	N	Schizophrenic	Expectation (%)
Parents	6,331	243	3·8
Sibs	7,571	659	8·7
Children	1,149·5	138	12·0
Uncles and aunts	3,376	68	2·0
Half-sibs	311	10	3·2
Nephews and nieces	2,315	52	2·2
Grandchildren	713	20	2·8
First cousins	2,438·5	71	2·9

Perhaps the first point to be noted is the very considerable numbers of persons investigated in nearly all degrees of relationship, with the exception perhaps of the half-sibs. We may then note that expectations are higher in the first-degree relationships than in the second-degree relationships. The figure is about the same for all four types of second-degree relationship, between two and three times the expectation for the general population. Rather surprisingly first cousins of schizophrenics, i.e. the children of uncles and aunts, have an expectation no lower than theirs (actually higher in the table). This slightly anomalous finding can probably be attributed to such things as sampling errors and differences between diagnosticians, on the one side, and, on the other side, the fact that we are getting fairly close to the general population expectation.

While the difference in expectation between first-degree and second-degree relationships is compatible with genetical causation, it could also be caused, in part at least, by environmental factors. What is peculiar, from the theoretical genetical point of view, is the big differences between parents, sibs and children. However, are they real differences? The figure for children is 38% up on the figures for sibs, but over half the material comes from Kallmann, who tended to get higher expectations than other workers. I would be inclined to say that there is no reliable evidence that the expectation in children of schizophrenics actually is higher than in their sibs. The figure for the expectation in parents, on the other hand, is conspicuously low. However, there can be little doubt that the method of ascertainment of schizophrenia in parents of schizophrenics leads to artificially low figures. This has been investigated by Essen-Möller (1955). He argues that the parents of probands do not really enter into observation until precisely the moment of birth *of the proband*; and making adjustments for this considerably decreases the number of life-risks observed. If these corrections are made, the expectation of schizophrenia in the parents of schizophrenics is estimated by Essen-Möller as about 11%, i.e. at about the same figure as for sibs and children.

The similarity between the three estimates of risk in parents, sibs and children seems to me to be important evidence of a genetical factor. It is what we would expect either on a polygenic theoretical basis, or on a hypothesis involving dominance; it does not fit in well with genetical theories involving recessivity, as in such a case the risk in sibs should be higher than in either parents or children. On the other hand, I find it very difficult to imagine environmental factors extending over three generations which would tend to make the parents of patients, the sibs of patients and the children of patients resemble the patients themselves all to about the same degree.

A point of crucial importance emerges when we consider what is the sex of the parent involved, when both a parent and a child have suffered from schizophrenic illnesses. When one proceeds from schizophrenic probands upwards into the antecedent generation one finds more schizophrenic mothers than schizophrenic fathers; and this circumstance has been regarded as an indication of the intrafamilial tensions to which the later schizophrenic has been subjected in childhood, and therefore as a demonstration of the effectiveness of psychic causes. However, Essen-Möller (1963) has demonstrated how the surplus of mothers can probably be accounted for by the fact that women tend to marry and produce their children at earlier ages than men, and, if they become schizophrenic, to do so at a later age. By proceeding from a proband to his parents, we observe about twice the number of risk-lives in the mothers as in the fathers.

This is in entire conformity with the finding that the risk of schizophrenia is just the same for the child of a schizophrenic whether the schizophrenic is a father or a mother. Data extracted from Kallmann's tables 34–37 (Kallmann 1938), as shown in Table 3, exhibit this

TABLE 3. INCIDENCE OF (DEFINITE) SCHIZOPHRENIA IN THE CHILDREN OF SCHIZOPHRENICS, BY SEX OF PROBAND (AFTER KALLMANN, 1938)

	Children of					
	Female probands			Male probands		
Proband	N	Sch	%	N	Sch	%
Hebephrenic } Catatonic }	241·5	42	17·4	130·5	24	18·4
Paranoid } Simple }	194·5	17	8·7	112·0	11	9·8

very clearly. Manfred Bleuler in his own extensive investigations has also found that the risk of schizophrenia for the children of schizophrenic mothers is no greater than for the children of schizophrenic fathers. This is in accordance with genetical expectations but is difficult to reconcile with environmentalist theories. Mothers are no closer to their children genetically than are fathers, though psychologically so much closer.

The same line of thought is suggested when we make use of Zerbin-Rüdin's classification of the sib data into families in which the parents were free from schizophrenia and those in which one parent was schizophrenic. The accumulated data are shown in Table 4. Here it is a matter for surprise that the risk for the sibs of schizophrenics is only about 40% higher where one of the parents is schizophrenic than where neither is. I would like to reserve my

TABLE 4. EXPECTATION OF SCHIZOPHRENIA FOR SIBS OF SCHIZOPHRENICS

Parentage	N	Schizophrenic	Expectation (%)
Neither parent schizophrenic	6,293	544	8·6
One parent schizophrenic	569	69	12·1

opinion whether this fits in well with a polygenic theory, though I think it would be found compatible. Obviously it goes quite well with the hypothesis of a dominant or partially dominant gene. The schizophrenic patient would have to have received such a gene from one or other parent, and it would not greatly affect the chances of other children these parents would have had, whether the gene manifested itself in the parent or did not. On the other hand, it is again not easy to suggest environmental mechanisms which would cause very great enhancement of the general population risk for the sib of a schizophrenic, but very little additional risk with schizophrenia affecting a parent as well. Theories of the psychic contagion type do not go well with this.

THE CHILDREN OF TWO PARENTS BOTH SCHIZOPHRENIC

If two individuals both schizophrenic are mated with one another, nature is conducting an experiment of a rather crucial kind for the geneticist. A simple dominant theory would lead to an expectation of 75% schizophrenia in the children of the cross, a simple recessive theory to an expectation of 100%—either figure being liable to reduction if the rate of manifestation of genotype as phenotype is less than 1. The hypothesis of an intermediate gene leads to an expectation a good deal lower than either simple dominance or recessivity, but one still much higher than the expectation of schizophrenia in the children of a mating between a schizophrenic and a non-schizophrenic (Slater, 1958). The mating of two schizophrenics is a far from frequent phenomenon, so that the series reported by individual workers are always small. Fortunately we have an excellent review by David Rosenthal of the results of this work, and from the data he provides I have constructed Table 5. To enter Kallmann's (1938) data in this table, I took the age distribution he shows in table 58 of his book, and gave the members of the sample weights appropriate to their ages as shown in table 5 of Rosenthal's paper. This gives us a *Bezugsziffer* of 28·9491. It will be seen that the estimate of the risk run by the children of an affected pair by this method of calculation comes out a good deal lower than the 55·3%, alternatively 68·1%, which Kallmann calculated, and is much nearer to the Kahn–Schulz–Elsässer–Lewis figure—so close in fact as to be not significantly different ($0.30 > p > 0.20$). Perhaps the best estimate we could make would be to take the summed data of all the investigations, as shown in the final row of my Table 4.

TABLE 5. EXPECTATION OF SCHIZOPHRENIA FOR CHILDREN OF
PARENTS BOTH SCHIZOPHRENIC

Investigator	N	Schizophrenic (a)	? Schizophrenic (b)	Expectation (%)	
				(a)	(a+b)
Kahn Schulz Elsässer Lewis	105·1	36	10	34·3	43·8
Kallmann	(?) 28·9	13	3	44·9	55·3
Total	134·0	49	13	36·6	46·3

It is perhaps surprising that the risk of schizophrenia for the children of two schizo-phrenics should be as low as 36%, alternatively 46%. In his paper Rosenthal draws attention to the relative lowness of the risk, bearing in mind that the environment of a child with two schizophrenic parents would probably be inimical. On environmentalist theories one might have thought that a child coming from such an environment would stand no chance at all, and that the risk would have proved to be 100%. From the genetical point of view, this figure fits in very well with the hypothesis of a single major gene, intermediate between dominance and recessivity. I think it quite possible that a polygenic theory might also prove compatible with this finding; but this would require demonstration.

THE EARLIER TWIN INVESTIGATIONS

It is natural enough that twin investigations in schizophrenia have aroused much more interest than any other kind of genetical investigation. The information that such studies provide is as important for environmental as for genetical analysis. Given access to both twins, the determination of zygosity is possible with very low margins of error; and even when one has only reasonably reliable information about the degree of physical resemblance, fewer errors are likely to be made about zygosity than, say, about clinical diagnosis. Differ-ences within monozygotic pairs can be used to determine how important environmental differences are in furthering or preventing the onset of psychosis, and a careful examination of these differences may show what the environmental factors are which should be taken into account. The difference between the concordance rates, or degree of resemblance, shown by MZ and by same-sexed DZ twins respectively give us some idea of the genetical contribution to causation. Twin investigations, however, are of little help in trying to decide whether one mode of inheritance or another is involved.

The next table (Table 6) summarizes the data from the earlier twin series. The figures have been taken from the synoptic table prepared by Gottesman and Shields (1966) which has important advantages, if one wants to present data in their simplest and most trans-parently honest form and avoid quibbling arguments. Age corrections, which have the effect of increasing concordance rates, have not been used; and the analysis is in terms of pairs observed, and not in terms of the proband method which demands the double entry of pairs in which both members have been independently ascertained. The table ends with Inouye, 1961, and has been cut at this point because representatives of nearly all the modern investigations (Tienari, Kringlen, Gottesman and Shields, Fischer) are here with us to present their own data.

TABLE 6. THE EARLIER TWIN SERIES (AFTER GOTTESMAN
AND SHIELDS, 1966)

Investigator	Date	MZ pairs			SS DZ pairs		
		N	C	%	N	C	%
Luxenburger	1928	19	11	58	13	0	0
Rosanoff	1934	41	25	61	53	7	13
Essen-Möller	1941	11	7	64	27	4	15
Kallmann	1946	174	120	69	296	34	11
Slater	1953	37	24	65	58	8	14
Inouye	1961	55	33	60	11	2	18

What is noteworthy about the figures of Table 6 is the remarkably good agreement between investigators extending over a generation in time and over three continents and five countries. Taking all the results together, we have 220 pairs concordant out of 337 MZ pairs, i.e. 65%; and 55 pairs concordant out of 458 DZ pairs, i.e. 12%. The DZ figure is about what could have been expected of pairs of sibs, and does not appear to have been much enhanced by the communalities in environment due to being born into a family at the same time. The MZ figure is many times greater, and gives great evidential weight to the genetical hypothesis.

The early twin reports have been subjected to criticism from many sides and to the most thorough-going re-examination, above all by Rosenthal in a series of papers (1959, 1960, 1961, 1962a, 1962b).

One criticism is that if the same observer makes the diagnosis and examines the twins for zygosity, the diagnosis may be subjectively influenced. Knowledge that the pair was mono-zygotic might lead to a looser diagnosis of schizophrenia in the co-twin, and to a spurious finding of concordance. Actually it is not very difficult for an honest worker, aware of the trend of his opinions, to maintain objectivity; and he can secure himself against criticism if he supplies the critic with full clinical details. Then it is up to the critic to revise the diagnoses if he wishes, and construct his own tables of concordance. There are, of course, very good practical reasons for carrying out all necessary inquiries, psychiatric and biological, on a single occasion, and most economically by a single worker. I know of no evidence that in any of the major twin investigations diagnoses have been slanted to inflate concordance rates. The results obtained by the earlier workers are, in fact, supported and validated by the new investigations reported in this conference (Kety, Rosenthal, Schulsinger, Wender).

The public image of Kallmann's work particularly suffered from criticism from this angle. With the help of Dr. Seymour Kety, and with the support of Dr. John Rainer, Dr. Erlenmeyer-Kimling and Dr. Arthur Falek, three of us, Dr. Gottesman, Mr. Shields

c

and I (1967), were put in a position to examine Kallmann's data in such a way as to establish what his criteria of diagnosis were. This is shown in Table 7. Kallmann used only the cases

TABLE 7. CUMULATIVE PAIRWISE CONCORDANCE AS A FUNCTION OF VARIOUS CRITERIA

"Second" twin	MZ		DZ		Total schizophrenic "second" twins so diagnosed
Had mental hospital diagnosis of schizophrenia when Kallmann first investigated pair	87/174	50·0%	31/517	6·0%	118
Had mental hospital diagnosis of schizophrenia by end of study	95/174	54·6%	32/517	6·2%	127
In mental hospital diagnosed by Kallmann as schizophrenia	100/174	57·5%	41/517	7·9%	141
Diagnosed by Kallmann as definite schizophrenia	103/174	59·2%	47/517	9·1%	150
Diagnosed by Kallman as schizophrenia, inclusive of suspected schizophrenia	120/174	69·0%	53/517	10·3%	173

he diagnosed as "definite" schizophrenics for the calculation of morbidity risks, and of the 150 cases so diagnosed 141 or 94% has been treated in mental hospitals. The way in which numbers increase as criteria are broadened shows every indication of proportionality between MZ and DZ cases. Personally, I am of the opinion that the suspicions of Kallmann's objectivity which have been voiced are now entirely discredited.

Another criticism which has been made, and still is made, is that one may not get a fair selection of twins by ascertaining twinship from such sources as the information provided by relatives. What one should do is to go back to birth registers. This point was made long ago by Luxenburger; and in his own series, as also in the well-known series of epileptic twins reported by Conrad, ascertainment of twinship was carried out in this way. However there is no evidence at all that, if one does rely on family knowledge, one gets a biased sample. One must miss some pairs of twins in this way, but there is no reason to think that among them there is an excess of psychiatrically discordant ones. If that were the case one would expect to find an excess of MZ pairs, for instance, in such series as that of my own, an excess which does not exist.

Rosenthal has made a number of other interesting points:

(1) Schizophrenia is commoner in the families of concordant pairs than in the families of discordant pairs.
(2) The affected member of a discordant pair had a more benign psychosis than the members of concordant pairs (male pairs).
(3) These differences were big enough to suggest that there might be two groups of schizophrenic illnesses, one in which the genetical contribution is considerable, one in which it is minimal.
(4) Concordance rates are distorted by selection of cases from hospital resident popula-

tions. This distortion occurs in two ways. The resident population consists of relatively severe cases, and there are reasons for thinking that the severer the psychosis, the larger the part that is probably played by genetical predisposition. The resident population also includes an undue proportion of females, and concordance rates run higher in female pairs than in male ones.

After all his criticisms, Rosenthal validated the twin method of investigation and concluded that "despite their difficulties and errors, the twin studies probably have contributed our most reliable data regarding the inheritance of schizophrenia". At the time when he was doing this work of retro-analysis, Rosenthal was already involved with the unique Genain quadruplets, which do not come within my purview; they must have brought home to him with great vividness the probability of there being some genetical contribution to schizophrenia.

Let me briefly refer to some of Rosenthal's criticisms. It is an unfortunate fact that, if you improve methods of investigation in one respect you are likely to impair them in another. It is now desirable, as Rosenthal maintains, to make our schizophrenics selected for study as representative as possible of schizophrenics as they are to be met in the general population. In doing so we are likely to lose certainty in diagnosis. I think myself it was no disadvantage of the early series that hospital resident populations were sampled; in doing so index cases were ascertained in which the diagnosis of "schizophrenia" was in most cases beyond dispute. It is only against the background of information obtained in this way that we are now encouraged to go forward into genetical investigations into the families of patients suffering from border-line conditions.

Gottesman and Shields (1966) have found support for Rosenthal's view that concordance within pairs is positively correlated with severity of psychosis. However, further material will be needed before this can be regarded as established. Whether or not it is confirmed, the information will not be more than peripheral to the understanding of genetic-environmental interaction.

Rosenthal's suggestion that the core group of schizophrenias may break down into two sub-groups, in which the genetical contribution is respectively important and minimal, seems to me unlikely to prove correct, though it provides an interesting idea for the planning of future work. There is no sound evidence at present that paranoid schizophrenias are genetically distinct from catatonic–hebephrenic schizophrenias; and the observational evidence which Rosenthal adduced for concluding that secondary cases of schizophrenia may be found in the families of concordant MZ pairs but not in the families of discordant MZ pairs is not in agreement with the observations of Luxenburger, Tienari and Kringlen. The Schulz–Leonhard study (1940) showed less schizophrenia in the parents of patients suffering from schizophrenias of a typical and deteriorating kind, than in the parents of atypical cases.

Another speculation by Rosenthal with some evidential basis and urgently needing more, is that concordance rates are higher in pairs of female twins than in pairs of male twins. If this is confirmed, one might well conclude that the environmental contribution to causation could be responsible. In most societies males occupy the entire span of variation in modes of life and types of environment, while the majority of women lead a more domestic existence which is to a large extent much the same thing everywhere. Anything which tends to diminish environmental variance will tend to magnify the apparent contribution made by heredity, and this will show up in twin concordance rates just as much as in other measures. I think it quite possible that this may be a part-cause of the difference between the findings of Scandinavian twin investigations and investigations elsewhere. Considering the great climatic variation between, say, north and south Sweden, this land must offer a greater variety of bio-environments than, say, England; on the other hand, it seems quite likely that there is greater genetic variability in England than in Sweden.

This may be the point at which to comment on the fact that more recent twin investigations in schizophrenia have produced lower concordance rates in MZ pairs than the earlier investigations shown in Table 2. It may be that with milder psychoses bringing about admission to hospital nowadays, and with more effective treatment masking the most typically schizophrenic syndromes and long-term histories, we are now seeing some degree of dilution of genetical by non-genetical cases, or, on the polygenic model, ascertaining cases in which the genetical component is quantitatively less.

TWINS BROUGHT UP APART

When we compare the concordance rates in pairs of MZ twins with the concordance rates in same-sexed DZ twins, we are observing the results of a natural experiment in which the genetic factor is massively varied, while the environmental factor is to a considerable extent held constant. We can take the experiment one stage further, and see what happens when the genetical factor is held constant and there is a massive change in the environmental factor. Nature performs this experiment for us when two MZ twins are brought up apart. Table 8, from a paper by Shields and Slater (1967) shows what is on record about such pairs.

TABLE 8. MZ TWINS REARED APART, ONE OR BOTH OF THEM SCHIZOPHRENIC

Investigation	Age at separation	Number of pairs		Source
		Concordant	Discordant	
Kallmann, Germany, 1938	Soon after birth	1	—	Daughters of schizophrenic proband
Essen-Möller, Sweden, 1941	7 years	1	—	In consecutive series of schizophrenic twins, Followed up by Kaij (1960)
Craike and Slater, U.K., 1945	9 months	1	—	Single case report
Kallmann and Roth, U.S.A., 1956	Not stated	1	—	Index pair in series of childhood schizophrenics
Shields, U.K., 1962	Birth	1	—	From consecutive series of Maudsley Hospital twins
Tienari, Finland, 1963	3 years and 8 years	—	2	All twin births
Kringlen, Norway, 1964	1 year, 10 months	—	1	Index case in twin series
Mitsuda, Japan, 1965	Infancy	5	3	All investigated twins with psychiatric illness

All but one of these cases were ascertained in the course of twin investigations carried out with other aims in view. That is, there was no bias in favour of observing or reporting either concordance or discordance. The exception is the Craike–Slater pair, picked up as a clinical observation. It is noteworthy that the Japanese material forms 50% of the total, i.e. half of both the concordant and the discordant pairs. It seems that, in Japan, there is much less adverse feeling to separating a pair of twins than in other countries we know. The concordance rate in this series is 63%, or 60% if the Craike–Slater pair is omitted, which fits quite well with concordance rates observed in MZ pairs brought up together.

It is above all in twin investigations that we shall hope to see the effects of environmental differences. Our findings warn us that these effects will be most difficult to uncover. So far the likeliest-looking environmental causes of a schizophrenic or schizophrenic-like illness belong in the organic field: intoxications, vitamin deprivation, brain damage, epilepsy, etc. These factors affect the individual himself, and do not involve solely or even primarily inter-personal relationships. Labhardt's very thorough work (1963) on psychogenic psychoses suggests that schizophrenia-like states are only produced by interference with diencephalic and mesencephalic function.

On the genetical side I would come to practically the same view as that of Gottesman and Shields, at the end of a chapter in which they review previous twin studies and report an important new study of their own. They conclude: "It seems reasonable to postulate that genetic factors are largely responsible for the specific nature of most of the schizo-phrenias and that these factors are necessary but not sufficient for the disorder to occur." One may repeat, largely responsible but not wholly responsible, and most of the schizo-phrenias but not all—at least if one takes schizophrenia simply as a syndrome in clinical descriptive terms. I am myself convinced that in special circumstances typical schizophrenic dysfunction and typical schizophrenic symptoms can appear in an individual endowed with no more in the way of a genetical predisposition to schizophrenia than is shared by the average member of the general population. Patients with schizophrenia-like epileptic psychoses had no excess of schizophrenics among their relatives (Slater and Glithero, 1963). It is probably true, though it has not yet been shown, that the schizophrenia-like psychoses of amphetamine poisoning (Connell, 1958) also require no raised level of genetical pre-disposition. Such disturbances are, however, usually of short or limited duration. They may stand in the same relation to the general run of schizophrenias as the focal epilepsies do to primary centrencephalic epilepsy. In tackling the vast range of problems with which schizophrenia confronts us, the Gottesman–Shields hypothesis is surely the best-supported working hypothesis; it is certainly one that can be adapted to the needs of the research worker whatever his chosen approach.

REFERENCES

Böök, J. A. (1953) Schizophrenia as a gene mutation, *Acta genet. (Basel)* **4**, 133–9.

Connell, P. H. (1958) *Amphetamine Psychosis,* London.

Essen-Möller, E. (1955) The calculation of morbid risk in parents of index cases, as applied to a family sample of schizophrenics, *Acta genet. (Basel)* **5**, 334–42.

Essen-Möller, E. (1963) Über die Schizophreniehäufigkeit bei Müttern von Schizophrenen, *Schweiz. Arch. Neurol. Psychiat.* **91**, 260–6.

Garrone, G. (1962) Étude statistique et génétique de la schizophrénie à Genève de 1901 à 1950, *J. Génét. hum.* **11**, 89–219.

GOTTESMAN, I. I. and SHIELDS, J. (1966) Contributions of twin studies to perspectives on schizophrenia, in *Progress in Experimental Personality Research 3* (ed. Maher, B. A.), New York, Academic Press.

GOTTESMAN, I. I., SHIELDS, J., and SLATER, E. (1967) Kallmann's 1946 schizophrenic twin study in the light of new information, *Acta psychiat. scand.* (in press).

KALLMAN, J. (1938) *The Genetics of Schizophrenia,* New York, J. J. Augustin.

KISHIMOTO, K. (1959) A study on the population genetics of schizophrenia, *2nd Internat. Congress for Psychiatry,* vol. II, pp. 20–8, Zürich.

LABHARDT, F. (1963) *Die Schizophrenieähnlichen Emotionspsychosen: ein Beitrag zur Abgrenzung schizophrenieartiger Zustandsbilder,* Berlin.

ROSENTHAL, D. (1959) Some factors associated with concordance and discordance with respect to schizophrenia in monozygotic twins, *J. Nerv. Ment. Dis.* **129**, 1–10.

ROSENTHAL, D. (1960) Confusion of identity and the frequency of schizophrenia in twins, *Arch. Gen. Psychiat.* **3**, 297–304.

ROSENTHAL, D. (1961) Sex distribution and the severity of illness among samples of schizophrenic twins, *J. Psychiat. Res.* **1**, 26–36.

ROSENTHAL, D. (1962a) Problems of sampling and diagnosis in the major twin studies of schizophrenia, *J. Psychiat. Res.* **1**, 116–34.

ROSENTHAL, D. (1962b) Familial concordance by sex with respect to schizophrenia, *Psychol. Bull.* **59**, 401–21.

ROSENTHAL, D. (1966) The offspring of schizophrenic couples, *J. Psychiat. Res.* **4**, 169–88.

SCHULZ, B. and LEONHARD, K. (1940) Erbbiologish-klinische Untersuchungen an insgesamt 99 im Sinne Leonhards typischen beziehungsweise atypischen Schizophrenien, *Z. ges. Neurol. Psychiat.* **168**, 587–613.

SHIELDS, J. and SLATER, E. (1967) Genetic aspects of schizophrenia, *Hospital Med.* **1**, 579–84.

SLATER, E. (1958) The monogenic theory of schizophrenia, *Acta. genet.* (*Basel*), **8**, 50–6.

ZERBIN-RÜDIN, E. (1967) Endogene Psychosen, in *Humangenetik,* vol. II (ed. Becker, P. E.), Stuttgart, Thieme.

SCHIZOPHRENIA IN MONOZYGOTIC MALE TWINS

PEKKA TIENARI

Oulu University, Oulu, Finland

THE main results of the study to be reviewed in this paper have been published earlier (Tienari, 1963, 1966, 1967), but owing to some criticisms, and also misunderstanding as regards sampling and diagnostic classification, I will give some detailed information on these points.

THE STARTING MATERIAL

The starting material of my study consisted of all the same-sexed male twins born in Finland from 1920 to 1929. This population was collected by the Finnish Foundation for Alcohol Studies for their own study on the drinking habits of twins (Partanen *et al.*, 1966). In Finland, birth statistics are collected either by the parishes or in some instances by other population register authorities. In the 1920's this information about the number of births was sent to the Finnish Central Statistical Office. From the records kept by the Central Statistical Office, information was available on the number of multiple births and on the total number of births for each local register. According to these data, the number of live births totalled 794,958 in the years 1920–9; of these 1·5%, or 11,910, were multiple births.

Unfortunately, the number of male twin births could not be obtained separately. After locating the twin births in each population register in this manner, the Finnish Foundation for Alcohol Studies sent a letter to every local register requesting certain data on each male twin pair born between 1920 and 1929. In most cases the register authorities themselves provided this information, but in some large cities local branches of the State Alcohol Monopoly were requested to collect data from the registers. By November 1957, information from each register, sometimes after several contacts, was gathered. Thus a total of 2933 twin pairs were listed (female and opposite-sexed pairs were not included in this figure). Having gathered the names of the twins, their actual addresses had to be obtained. The National Pensions Institute kept a complete register of the Finnish population until 1 January 1954. Through this register it was checked whether the twins were still alive, and information was collected on changes of addresses. After that, inquiries were sent to the local census authorities in order to obtain addresses as of 1 January 1958.

On the basis of data thus obtained, it was found that in 1787 pairs one or both of the twins had died or lived abroad. These were considered unsuitable for a sociological interview study. The remaining pairs (1146) were supposedly alive and residing in Finland in the beginning of 1958. A card index was made. In each pair the twin whose Christian name preceded the name of the other in alphabetical order was termed the A-twin and his twin brother was termed the B-twin. In 1958, an attempt was made by the Finnish Foundation for Alcohol Studies to interview each of the twins personally. In 903 pairs it proved possible to interview both of the twins, and in a further 60 pairs one of the twins (Table 1). Through

TABLE 1. THE STARTING MATERIAL

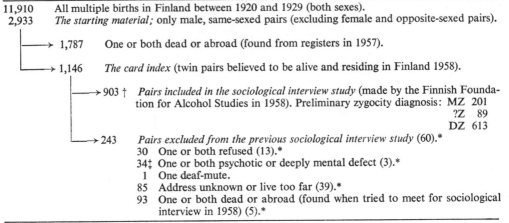

11,910	All multiple births in Finland between 1920 and 1929 (both sexes).
2,933	*The starting material;* only male, same-sexed pairs (excluding female and opposite-sexed pairs).
→ 1,787	One or both dead or abroad (found from registers in 1957).
→ 1,146	*The card index* (twin pairs believed to be alive and residing in Finland 1958).
→ 903 †	*Pairs included in the sociological interview study* (made by the Finnish Foundation for Alcohol Studies in 1958). Preliminary zygocity diagnosis: MZ 201 ?Z 89 DZ 613
→ 243	*Pairs excluded from the previous sociological interview study* (60).*
30	One or both refused (13).*
34‡	One or both psychotic or deeply mental defect (3).*
1	One deaf-mute.
85	Address unknown or live too far (39).*
93	One or both dead or abroad (found when tried to meet for sociological interview in 1958) (5).*

* The number of pairs where one of the twins was interviewed.

† The final number of the sample of FFAS was 902 because one of the interviewed pairs was excluded from their study (being drunk during the interview).

‡ I have included in this figure the 5 pairs excluded from the card index of FFAS because they, according to the parishes, were psychotic.

these interviews, biographical data on the subjects, and data related to the social psychology of twins and to the subjects' drinking habits, were gathered. In addition, the subjects were asked whether *he or his twin brother* had had any of a number of specified illnesses (e.g. psychoses, nervous troubles, insomnia, some psychosomatic diseases), and they were asked whether they had been under treatment in a hospital or under medical care for any other illnesses. In connection with the interviews, polysymptomatic traits were recorded for the purposes of a zygocity diagnosis, which was later checked serologically (Sammalisto, 1961).

THE SAMPLE OF THE PRESENT STUDY

I decided to use these data previously acquired by the Finnish Foundation for Alcohol Studies as my starting point for a study of schizophrenia in MZ male twins. In Finland we do not have any psychosis register covering the whole country. My intention was to confine the study to those pairs where I was able to study both twins personally. As there was available a twin material in whose selection age and sex had been the sole criteria, the formation of a smaller group suitable for use in psychiatric investigation formed a problem of its own. Two objectives .were settled on: first, to trace and personally investigate the highest possible number of MZ pairs of psychiatric interest; and, second, to investigate, in addition a wholly unselected group of MZ pairs. The pairs for the present study were chosen from among the twin pairs of the starting material as follows.

A. *Pairs included in the previous sociological interview study* (903 pairs)

(1) MZ pairs (201). Every MZ twin pair residing in a specified geographical area (82 Finnish-speaking pairs) was investigated. As regards the MZ twins remaining outside the specified geographical area, all those who had in the previous interview study complained of psychic or nervous troubles, had been in a hospital for psychiatric reasons, all excessive drinkers, all abstainers, all in whom peptic ulcer had been suspected, and all who had been apart during childhood were investigated (44 pairs). Thus 126 pairs belonging to the MZ group of the starting material (or 70% of the total Finnish-speaking twin population, numbering 180 in all) were included in the present study. A number of 15 pairs that had been previously regarded as MZ according to the preliminary zygocity diagnosis, proved serologically dissimilar. This left 111 MZ pairs.

(2) Pairs with doubtful zygocity (89 pairs). The zygocity diagnoses of the pairs of doubtful zygocity that were residing within the specified area were checked (26 pairs), and the MZ pairs thus discovered (9) were also investigated.

(3) Hospital records were collected in every case where persons belonging to the DZ or doubtful zygocity group had told in the previous interview study that he had been in treatment in a psychiatric hospital.

B. *Pairs excluded from the previous sociological interview study* (243 pairs)

Using the registers of central mental hospitals, an attempt was made to discover whether either twin among pairs in the refusal group (30 pairs) had been in mental hospital treatment. Two cases of psychosis were discovered in this way. All pairs that had been left outside the previous sociological interview study because of mental illness or deep mental deficiency were traced (34 pairs). Of the 36 twin pairs that had had psychosis or deep mental defect, 11 proved to be MZ and were included in my sample.

In 39 pairs from among the 85 pairs that had been excluded from the previous study because their addresses were unknown or because they lived too far, it had been possible to interview one of the twins. Thus only 46 pairs were left where information about psychosis was not available (not considering the twin pairs where death or emigration had been the reason for exclusion).

Considering the total starting material (2933 pairs), it had been previously found that in 1880 pairs, one or both of the twins was dead or lived abroad. The remaining pairs (1053) were supposedly alive and residing in Finland. Information about psychosis was available in the latter group in 1007 pairs (903+104), whereas no information was available in 46 pairs. The final MZ sample consisted of 131 pairs (111+9+11). Of these, 125 pairs were personally investigated. This happened mainly in 1960. More than two-thirds of them were re-examined in 1962–3.

The psychiatric interviews were semistructured, and particular attention was devoted to the establishment of contact with the person to be interviewed. The psychiatric interview was supplemented by psychological tests. The tests were scored and interpreted by clinical psychologists exclusively on the basis of the test records, without any other information about the subjects at their disposal. The parents of the twins (or, if they were not available, the older siblings) were interviewed in most cases. The case histories of schizophrenic, psychopathic and neurotic cases have been published previously (Tienari, 1963). The cases of psychosis and mental defect are presented in Table 2.

TABLE 2. THE PSYCHOTIC CASES

	MZ	DZ
Schizophrenia or schizophreniform psychoses	16	21 (23?)
Affective psychoses	—	5
Reactive psychoses	1	3
Deep mental defect	—	12

SCHIZOPHRENIC CASES

The 16 schizophrenic cases are presented in Table 3. Clinical subtype was hebephrenic in 5 cases, catatonic in 3, paranoid in 6; 1 case was atypical, and in 1 case the patient was

TABLE 3. THE SCHIZOPHRENIC CASES
(only identical pairs)

Case	Subtype of diagnosis	Age of onset	Deterioration	Familial incidence of sch.
881	Hebephrenic	22	Extreme	Yes
152	Hebephrenic	30 (?)	Medium	Yes
608	Hebephrenic	30 (?)	Medium	No
1080	Hebephrenic	18	Extreme	Yes
1143	Hebephrenic	24	Medium	No
728	Catatonic	25	Extreme	Yes
954	Catatonic	24	Medium	Yes
406	Catatonic	28	None (?)	Yes (?)
32	Paranoid	34	Mild (org.?)	No
74	Paranoid	29	Mild (?)	Yes
989	Paranoid	29 (?)	Mild (?)	No
349	Paranoid	32	None (?)	Yes (?)
1142	Paranoid	31	None	No
462	Paranoid (?)	30	Medium (org.?)	No
67	Atypical	34	None	Yes
821	Border-line	33	None	Yes

considered as border-line schizophrenic. In all the cases the illness had set in at a relatively young age. An extreme or medium degree of deterioration was discernible in 8 cases; 3 were slightly deteriorated, whereas no deterioration was present in 5 cases. Eight or ten cases had a positive family history of schizophrenia. The zygocity diagnoses were confirmed serologically in 15 pairs. The 16 pairs included 2 (152, 608) in which the zygocity diagnosis was subject to reservations.

In 9 cases the hospital diagnosis was schizophrenia (Table 4); in 2 cases it was schizophreniform psychosis, and, in 1 case, schizo-affective psychosis. In 1 case the hospital

Table 4. Hospital Diagnoses of Schizophrenic Cases

881	Schizophrenia	32	Schizophreniform psychosis (sch.?)
152	Schizophrenia	74	Paranoid psychosis
608	Schizophrenia	989	(Never hospitalized)
1080	Schizophrenia	349	Psychosis
1143	Schizophrenia	1142	Schizophrenia
728	Schizophrenia	462	Schizophreniform psychosis
954	Schizophrenia	67	Schizo-affective psychosis
406	Schizophrenia	821	(Never hospitalized)

Cases 32 and 462 are brain-injured.

diagnosis was paranoid psychosis. The Case 349 had been under care at a ward for psychotics in a communal home. In 2 cases the patient had not been hospitalized.

Shields (1965) has regarded 4 of the above cases as organic. In 2 cases, arguments in support of such view might be presented. In pair 462, both twins had suffered a traumatic brain injury; moreover, the twin who developed schizophrenic symptoms manifested a high degree of mental deterioration. It should be noted that the psychotic symptoms did not set in until 8 years after the injury; prior to the onset of these symptoms, the patient had been able to work for years. As for pair 32, psychotic symptoms set in 15 years after the injury; the brain injury was not a severe one; no dementia was present; and before becoming psychotic the patient had been wholly capable of work. The psychotic symptoms set in shortly after his marriage had ended in divorce. Since 1964 the patient has been able to work regularly, although psychotic symptoms have persisted (the most recent items of information date from May 1966). Therefore, case 462 might be considered a psychosis where organic factors have played a role, whereas in case 32 it is unlikely that such factors have been of much significance. In the other 2 cases (608, 74) there is no reason to suspect the presence of an organic psychosis. Both are typical functional psychoses.

In May 1967 inquiries concerning the 32 twins were addressed to every psychiatric hospital to which they might have been admitted according to their places of residence. Six of the sixteen schizophrenics mentioned above were under mental hospital treatment (881, 152, 608, 728 and 1080 had been continuously in hospital, 1143 had been re-admitted). In addition, case 1142 was hospitalized for a short period for a relapse in January–February 1967. None of the others had been in a hospital since 1963. According to the information provided by his relatives, case 67 has been symptom-free since 30 September 1963, when he was discharged from the psychiatric clinic.

CO-TWINS OF THE SCHIZOPHRENIC CASES

In 1963 none of the 16 co-twins was psychotic, even though 3 (608, 74, 989) might be said to have some border-line features. None of them could, however, be regarded as a border-line schizophrenic. In May 1967 the inquiries sent to psychiatric hospitals revealed that one of the co-twins (67) was in a mental hospital for a depressive psychosis with some schizophreniform traits. Another co-twin (608) had in August 1964 stayed for a month in a neuropsychiatric department for examination and observation; no psychiatric diagnosis, apart from feeblemindedness, was established; the patient's psychic condition had apparently improved somewhat after my last examination. None of the other co-twins had been under mental hospital treatment.

Furthermore, I have carefully scrutinized each of the case histories anew, classifying them with a view to an extensive and strict concordance study. A classification of the co-twins based upon the most recent data, and their ages at present are seen in the Table 5.

TABLE 5. CO-TWINS OF THE SCHIZOPHRENIC CASES

Case	Age	
881	45	Mild character neurosis (introvert)
152	46	Neurasthenic neurosis (border-line features?)
608	46	Neurosis (border-line?). Feeblemindedness
1080	39	Healthy (introvert)
1143	42	Healthy (with mild neurotic traits)
728	43	Healthy (introvert, eccentric)
954	38	Healthy
406	40	Healthy (introvert)
32	41	Mild character neurosis (introvert)
74	41	Character neurosis (border-line features?)
989	43	Character neurosis (border-line features?)
349	47	Healthy (introvert)
1142	45	Healthy (primitive)
462	44	Brain injury; blindedness.
67	38	Schizo-affective psychosis
821	44	Healthy (introvert)

It will be noted that pair 67 must be regarded as concordant beyond doubt. In addition, there were 4 pairs (152, 608, 74 and 989) which, in a *very broad sense* might be considered concordant; in each case, the co-twins possibly had some border-line features. None of them had, however, exhibited psychotic symptoms. None of them can be classified as border-line schizophrenic either.

The length of time elapsed since the falling ill of the schizophrenic twin is 11 years or more in 14 cases, and 8 years in 1 case.

CONCORDANCE FIGURES

Using a strict concept of concordance, the concordance rate is one-sixteenth (6%) if all the cases are taken into account; and it is one-tenth (10%) if only the schizophrenia diagnoses established in hospitals are taken into consideration, and the 2 cases suspected to be brain-organic are excluded. Employing a broad concept of concordance, the concordance rates are five-sixteenths (31%) and three-tenths (30%) respectively. The highest concordance rate, five-fourteenths (36%), is obtained when only pairs 32 and 462 are excluded; that is where the presence of brain-organic factors has been suspected. Employing varied concordance concepts and diagnostic criteria, the concordance rate consequently varies between 6% and 36%.

HAVE ALL CASES OF SCHIZOPHRENIA IN THE STARTING MATERIAL BEEN DISCOVERED?

In collecting the starting material, each of the twins was interviewed personally (by FFAS)—provided it was possible to meet him and that there was no prior information indicating that he was psychotic or deeply feebleminded (considered unsuitable for a social interview study). Each of the interviewed persons was directly asked whether *he or his twin brother* has been suffering from psychosis or had had nervous symptoms, or whether he had been under hospital treatment or had been cared for by a doctor. Thus only where information was deliberately withheld could an interviewed pair have been disregarded. Moreover, 70% of the MZ pairs in the starting material of the Foundation were also interviewed by me once or twice, and the picture thus obtained was supplemented by the results of the psychological tests and by the recorded data available on the subjects. I did not come across a single case where an attempt would have been made to keep information secret. As regards the identified 16 cases of schizophrenia, 2 (1142, 1143) were revealed by the data supplied by the parishes; 8 (881, 152, 608, 1080, 728, 954, 989, 462) were discovered on the basis of the information obtained from the social welfare authorities or relatives, at the stage when attempts were being made to meet the twins. One case (74) was identified when the list of those who refused to co-operate was compared with the hospital patient registers; and 2 (406, 349) reported during the sociological interview that they had been in hospital for psychiatric reasons. Two (32, 67) who belonged in my sample, fell ill with psychotic symptoms only after the sociological interview, and were discovered and referred to hospital by me. One case (821) was discovered in connection with the study of the regional group (border-line schizophrenia, not treated in a hospital).

It seems probable, therefore, that the subjects' age might be one factor responsible for unidentifiable cases. When the sociological interview study of the Foundation took place (1958), the subjects were between 27 and 38. Thus, they had only survived a part of the risk age of schizophrenia. Among the MZ pairs of the starting material $(201 - 126 = 75)$ not included in the series dealt with in the present study, there may, of course, have been persons who have fallen ill after 1959 (when they were last met). My series included 183 persons (74%) who were over 35 years of age, but no more than 52 (20%) who were over 40, when I most recently interviewed them personally. Thus, the possibility of fresh cases is not excluded in this group either. Judging from the results of previous studies, however, the fresh cases that may emerge are likely to be discordant since the age of onset for concordant pairs has generally been quite low.

Another possible source of error derives from the pairs that remained outside of the study. As shown in Table 1, all male pairs numbered 2933. The pairs for which it proved possible to secure rather reliable information on the occurrence of psychoses totalled 1007 (Table 6). The schizophrenic cases encountered in this group (consisting of 2014 individuals) numbered 37, the corrected morbidity risk being $2 \cdot 24 \pm 0 \cdot 36 \%$. The relatively high figure may mean that the number of unidentified cases is not high. There remains $(2933 - 1007 =)$ 1926 pairs, and I began to analyse these cases in 1967. Later on, I intend to acquire recorded data on all those in the total population who have survived until the risk age for schizophrenia. A preliminary scrutiny of the population has revealed that, in 1501 pairs, one or

TABLE 6. THE TWIN PAIRS WHO SURVIVED UNTIL THE RISK AGE OF SCHIZOPHRENIA,
AND THE AVAILABILITY OF INFORMATION ON PSYCHOSES

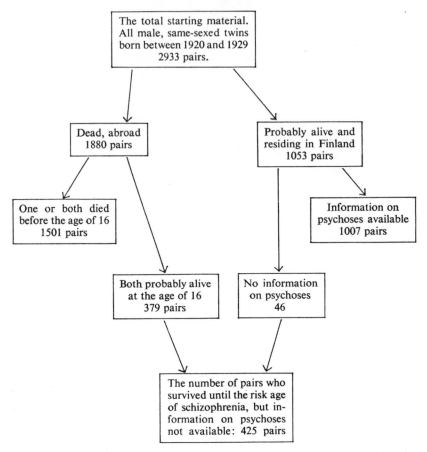

both twins died before reaching the age of 16 (i.e. before the risk age for schizophrenia). In addition, there are 295 pairs in which at least one twin had died but both have probably reached the age of 16; and there are 78 pairs in which one or both of the twins are living abroad. Consequently, the number of pairs not covered by my study who have survived until the risk age for schizophrenia is (1926 − 1501 =) 425. In a large majority of these cases, however, at least one of the twins has already died. (The unknown address group may also include cases of death.) The number of possible MZ twin schizophrenics in this group appears difficult to estimate in advance, since both the fact of being a MZ twin and the fact of being admitted to a mental hospital may involve selective factors regarding mortality (the high tuberculosis mortality rates previously characteristic of mental hospitals; the higher mortality rates for MZ twins; their higher proneness to be exposed to similar dangers —e.g., infections or death during the war—owing to the fact that they are together with each other more than are DZ twins).

If we take the total twin population where both twins probably have survived until the risk age of schizophrenia, we get $(1007 + 425 =)$ 1432 pairs, or 2864 individuals. The number of schizophrenic cases discovered until now is 38 (including the co-twin who became ill later) which gives the relative frequency number of 1.33% (without age correction). This relatively high number does not support the assumption that the pairs who remained outside of my sampling must have many concordant pairs.

INTRAPAIR DIFFERENCES IN THE SCHIZOPHRENIC GROUP

Earlier I focused my attention upon intrapair differences in the group of 16 MZ pairs discordant for schizophrenia (Tienari, 1963), since such differences must reflect environmental factors. It appeared that the twin who became schizophrenic had probably had disturbances in his father relationship in 13 cases. Seven of the twins who later developed schizophrenia had a poorer father relationship than their co-twins; the opposite did not seem to be true for any of the pairs. In 8 cases the sick twin had been more dependent upon his mother, as compared with his co-twin; the opposite was the case with none of the pairs. In 14 cases the twin who developed schizophrenia had been submissive to his co-twin even in childhood, and he had been dominant only in 2 cases. Moreover, the twin who fell ill had been the "spokesman" more rarely than his co-twin; as a rule, he had done worse at school, had been more well-behaved and sensitive in childhood; he began to be employed and left the home later; and he also married later than his co-twin. On the other hand, the differences in birth weight and birth order, physical development and superiority in physical undertakings during childhood did not correlate with the falling ill with schizophrenia.

INTRAPAIR DIFFERENCES IN THE REGIONAL MZ GROUP

It has been claimed that both prenatal and natal factors may make for intrapair differences in the case of MZ twins. This is to say that they may constitute a source of error, causing the part played by postnatal environmental factors to appear greater than it actually is compared with the genetic ones. This was why I attempted to analyse the intrapair differences in the above-mentioned unselected group of MZ twins, formed on a regional basis (80 pairs), which included not only normal persons but also persons suffering from personality disturbance varying in degree, and including schizophrenia. Judging from the statistical relationship between birth order or differences in birth weight and other variables, birth in itself did not seem to be of any particular significance for psychic or social differences observed later in life (Tienari, 1966). Among early differences, psychic dominance correlated most distinctly with the later differences studied. Each of the various aspects of dominance (physical strength, psychic dominance, and the role of a spokesman) spanned in factor analysis a factor of its own (referred to as physical superiority, leadership and temper, respectively). Leadership was the factor that emerged first, and it accounted for a larger proportion of the common-factor variance than did any other factor; it obtained loadings in most of the variables measuring psychic or social advantage. The temper factor had appreciable loadings exclusively in the childhood variables. As for the physical superiority factor, it obtained loadings in physical differences during childhood and in two variables pertaining to youth: age at leaving home and getting married. A further factor, termed an achievement of independence factor was also obtained. It was independent of the childhood differences, and had loadings in variables related to youth and in certain adulthood variables indicating social and intellectual achievements or (degree of absence of) psychic disturbance. Leadership and the achievement of independence factor were the only factors with noteworthy loadings in variables indicating differences in adulthood. Thus the results did not support the view that prenatal and natal factors or differences in physical development during childhood are among those with a distinct bearing upon the differences during adolescence and adulthood that reflect psychic or social superiority.

CONCLUSIONS

I have made an attempt to trace and diagnose all the persons belonging to specified age groups in a Finnish population of same-sexed male twins (those born in 1920–9) through an epidemiological investigation. Thus far, a total of 17 cases has been found in which 1 of the 2 MZ twins is or has been schizophrenic and has a surviving co-twin available for study. In this group, the concordance rate for schizophrenia varied from 6 % to 36 %, depending upon the concordance concept and the diagnostic criteria employed. The possibility exists that the population concerned also includes cases of schizophrenia which have not yet been discovered. In my opinion, concordance figures are not so significant in themselves as they have perhaps sometimes been considered to be. The twin studies undertaken in recent years have suggested that, in the case of MZ twins, discordant outnumber concordant pairs with respect to schizophrenia. Therefore, the centre of emphasis in research should be shifted to the intrapair variability encountered in symptomatology and personality disorders, as well as in the other aspects of personality development.

REFERENCES

PARTANEN, J., BRUUN, K., and MARKKANEN, T. (1966) Inheritance of drinking behaviour. A study on intelligence, personality, and use of alcohol of adult twins, *The Finnish Foundation for Alcohol Studies*, vol. 14, Helsinki, pp. 1–157.

SAMMALISTO, L. (1961) The determination of zygocity in a study of Finnish twins, *Acta genet. (Basel)* 11, 251–64.

SHIELDS, J. (1965) Book review, *Brit. J. Psychiat.* 111, 777–81.

TIENARI, P. (1963) Psychiatric illnesses in identical twins, *Acta psychiat. scand.* 39, suppl. 171, pp. 1–195.

TIENARI, P. (1966) On intrapair differences in male twins with special reference to dominance-submissiveness, *Acta psychiat. scand.* 42, suppl. 188, pp. 1–166.

TIENARI, P. (1967) Concordance and discordance for schizophrenia in twins, *The Fourth World Congress of Psychiatry, Proceedings* 2, 1082–6.

SEVERITY/CONCORDANCE AND DIAGNOSTIC REFINEMENT IN THE MAUDSLEY–BETHLEM SCHIZOPHRENIC TWIN STUDY

Irving I. Gottesman*

Department of Psychology and Graduate Training Program in Behavior Genetics,
University of Minnesota, Minneapolis, Minnesota

By looking more closely at the similarities and differences among the recently initiated studies on schizophrenic twins by Tienari (1963), Kringlen (1966, 1967), and ourselves (Gottesman and Shields, 1966a, b; 1967) we may, as a result of the discussion at this Conference, harvest a set of facts that are wheat, a set of presumed facts that are chaff, and a set of data that current winnowing techniques do not permit being neatly separated into wheat and chaff. Let me review briefly the sampling procedures and earlier results of the Maudsley–Bethlem Schizophrenic Twin Study conducted by Shields and myself and then supplement such information with details about the ages and diagnoses of our material as well as some extensions of our results.

From the beginning of 1948 a register of all twins treated at the Maudsley and Bethlem Royal Joint Hospital has been kept. The Hospital is a short-stay post-graduate psychiatric teaching facility in Southeast London with a large outpatient department handling more than 2000 new adults and more than 300 children each year. The social class of patients is similar to that of London as a whole. Sample representativeness is enhanced by the absence of Veterans' Hospitals, the scarcity of private psychiatrists and private hospitals, the excellent reputation of the Hospital, and the widespread acceptance of socialized medicine. The vast majority of patients come from the immediately surrounding geographical area. On admission to any department of the Hospital every patient is routinely asked whether he was born a twin; the answer is recorded on the "face sheet" and later punched onto cards for the official triennial reports. When our register was closed on 31 March 1964, 392 adult patients with twins of the same sex who had survived to age 15 were listed. We believe ascertainment to be virtually complete for all twins among an estimated starting material of 45,000 psychiatric patients seen consecutively during a 16-year period. A close check of a large subsample of patients (25,867) showed that 2·19% of all adult outpatients and 2·56% of inpatients were twins. About 2·39% of persons *born* in the United Kingdom are twins according to vital statistics. From the latter and the Weinberg method, 28·6% of all United Kingdom twins would be expected to be monozygotic (MZ) as would be 26·3% of all Maudsley twins; zygosity proportions of our twins do not depart from expectation (42%

* The research reported herein was done in collaboration with my colleague James Shields, MRC Psychiatric Genetics Research Unit, Maudsley Hospital, London. Support for the project comes from USPHS grants MH–13117–02 and T1–MH–10679–02.

of same sex pairs are MZ). Our 57 schizophrenic index pairs consisted of 24 MZ and 33 same sex DZ pairs; 5 pairs, 4 MZ and 1 DZ, had both twins registered, yielding 62 official probands, 31 males and 31 females. Twenty-one of the probands had not received a diagnosis of schizophrenia at the Maudsley but at some other hospital during another admission. Only a few of the reasons for extending the series in this way need be noted. The symptoms of schizophrenia are protean enough so that the disorder may resemble many other types of psychiatric impairment, especially early in the course. We had observed that some twins diagnosed as say, anxiety reaction, on their first admission to the Maudsley received un-ambiguous diagnoses of schizophrenia on their next admission to the Maudsley. Had they gone elsewhere for subsequent hospitalization, the cases would have been missed. In a follow-up study of patients under age 30 diagnosed as depressives at the Maudsley (Clark and Mallett, 1963), one-third received diagnoses of schizophrenia when readmitted to any hospital. Finally, we knew we could perform our data analyses with or without the 21 added probands to see whether it made any difference. ·

Although our twins need not have been hospitalized to be registered, all were at some point; time in hospital ranges from 6 weeks to 750 among the probands, one co-twin has been in for a total 1383 weeks. Only 6 MZ probands and 5 DZ had been hospitalized prior to the start of the register in 1948 so that most probands were first admissions or "fresh" cases. The twins were born between 1893 and 1945. Median age on last information was 37, range 19–65. The age of the material meant that almost all were alive at the time of our follow-up 1963–5. Of the 48 MZ twins, 42 (88%) have been seen personally by one or both of us. Four of the others had previously been seen on our behalf by Unit staff, and the remaining 2 were specifically seen by their GP before they disappeared from sight. Of the 66 DZ twins, 49 (74%) were seen by one or both of us and 3 by colleagues; of the remaining 14, 4 were dead, 4 abroad, 1 untraceable, and 5 uncooperative. All discordant pairs of twins have been followed for over 3 years from the onset of illness in the proband.

Although our method of sampling was different from that of Tienari and Kringlen, it would be incorrect to conclude that it was less adequate for the task at hand. Tienari started with a birth register of all male twins born in Finland between 1920 and 1929 and set himself the difficult task of identifying all who later became schizophrenic. Death, emigration, and difficulties in tracing persons 35 or more years after birth with an intervening World War took their toll on the sample. Of the 2288 pairs of male twins in the starting material only 903 (39%) remained; of these only 22% to 32% were MZ against an expecta-tion of about 45% of same sex pairs. Kringlen also started with a birth register of twins and had the additional advantage of a national register for psychoses. Of the 25,000 pairs of twins born in Norway between 1901 and 1930, 342 pairs had one or both members hospital-ized for a functional psychosis after the age of 15, of whom 233 had a schizophrenic (180) or schizophreniform (53) psychosis. As a result of Kringlen's careful personal investigation of cases he was able to conclude (1967) that about 20% of the co-twins found to have been psychotic were not in the register of psychosis, "either because they had never been hospital-ized or because of unsatisfactory reporting". In the *absence* of mortality and other attenuat-ing factors such as emigration, and given a lifetime morbid risk for schizophrenia of 1%, one might have expected to come across 500 cases of schizophrenia in a material of 50,000 unselected twins by the end of the risk period. Neonatal mortality alone would have reduced the number of intact pairs by about 6250 (Karn, 1953) at the end of the first month of life. Kringlen found 198 cases of "strict" schizophrenia and 73 further cases of schizophreniform psychoses. Kringlen's sampling was as near to ideal as anyone is likely to come. The point of these comments is that all three studies, like all studies of schizophrenia, have inevitable kinds of selection operating to make samples less than ideal. It will be important to keep in mind the possible effects of the selective factors on the results (Gottesman and Shields, 1966b).

Just as there is no perfect sample, there is no perfect way of communicating the results of a study of schizophrenic twins with *the* concordance rate. The intricacies of concordance rates in twin studies have been discussed at length by Allen *et al.* (1967); fortunately two of the authors are here today. The simplest but not necessarily the truest view of concordance comes from simple direct pairwise counting with no correction for age; the criteria for a diagnosis of schizophrenia should be uncontaminated by a knowledge of zygosity. Using as a criterion of schizophrenia a psychiatrist's diagnosis, at any point in the career of the co-twin (i.e., Grade I) and at or after registration at the Maudsley for the proband, and uninfluenced by our own hindsight, we found a MZ concordance rate of 42% and a DZ rate of 9%. A probandwise method of counting yields rates of 50% (14/28) for MZ and 12% (4/34) for DZ pairs. Using the formula recommended by Allen (1965) that halves the number of index cases from concordant pairs, our rates become 33% MZ and 6% DZ. When the conventional Weinberg abridged method for age correction is applied to our pairwise rates of 42% and 9% with a risk period of 15 to 40, the concordance rates go up considerably to 65% and 17%. Most of us are agreed that some form of correction for age is necessary for all conditions with a variable age of onset, but the Weinberg method makes assumptions that are not met in samples of schizophrenic twins. Ideally, only pairs where the co-twin is either schizophrenic or past say age 45, could be used in the calculations. Such a procedure requires a large enough sample to insure stability; Kallmann's (1946) material was not analyzed in this fashion but Kringlen's (1967) was with no appreciable change in the uncorrected rates.

TABLE 1. AGE DISTRIBUTION MZ PAIRS AT TIME OF DX SC SECOND TWIN OR
LAST INFORMATION

Concordant pairs	Age at Dx Sc in 2nd twin	15 20* 22 19*		29* 33 35* 37 30 33		
Discordant pairs	Age at last infor. 2nd twin	20	24 25 32 26	37 39 42 46 47 40 44 46 50		

* Doubly represented pairs. Note no bias in favor of both becoming probands only when both Dx Sc at about same time.

It is obvious that the age distribution of each sample at the time of study as well as the intrapair correlation in age of onset of schizophrenia determine what effects corrections for age have on the uncorrected rates. Table 1 gives the age at first diagnosis of schizophrenia (i.e. not onset of symptoms nor necessarily first hospitalization) in the second member of a pair to be so diagnosed for the 10 concordant (Grade I) MZ pairs in our sample. It also shows the age at last information of the 14 discordant MZ co-twins. It can be seen in Table 1 that 8 of the discordant identicals are already beyond the latest age (37) at which any Grade I pairs became concordant.

Table 2 compares the 2 groups of MZ twins with respect to the intrapair differences in time between diagnoses of schizophrenia or between diagnosis of schizophrenia and age at last information of the co-twin. From Table 2 it can be seen that 9 of 10 MZ pairs became concordant in less than 5 years, and half of the discordant pairs have been so for longer than 5 years; all but one of the 14 discordant MZ pairs (Grade I criterion) have been so for 3 years or longer. Although we cannot completely assume that the past pattern for becoming concordant will hold in the future, the fact remains that a considerable number of the co-twins of identicals diagnosed as schizophrenic have enjoyed long periods of mental health. In Slater's (1953) series one pair became concordant after 31 years, and 4 of 28 after 17 years. Essen-Möller's well investigated series of 7 MZ probands showed none fully concordant when reported in 1941, but one was reported in 1960 (Kaij) and another became fully concordant only recently (Essen-Möller, 1967, personal communication).

TABLE 2. MZ INTRAPAIR DIFFERENCES (YEARS) IN AGE AT DX SC SECOND TWIN OR LAST INFORMATION

		0	1*	2	3	4*	7	8	9	12*	13	14	17
Concordant pairs	Years between Dx of Sc	0	1*	2	3	4*				12*			
		0	1*										
		0	1										
Discordant pairs	Years between Dx of Sc and co-twin age at last information		1		3	4	7	8	9		13	14	17
					3	4						14	
					3								
					3								

* Doubly represented pairs. Note no bias in favor of both becoming probands only when both Dx Sc at about same time.

I should now like to discuss briefly the effects of diagnostic refinement on our concordance data. Rather than rely solely on the crude criterion of having ever been diagnosed at least once as schizophrenic, we are in the process of having judges make diagnoses from case histories that do not reveal zygosity or information about the co-twin and which focus on psychopathology and status at the time of follow-up. So far the histories have been judged by British, American and Japanese psychiatrists leading to little variability in the final concordance rates. I will only present data based on the decisions of Judge A,[1] a senior British psychiatrist with considerable experience with schizophrenics and whose diagnostic standards are aligned with traditional Continental psychiatry and thus more strict than those of American diagnosticians. Among our 48 MZ twins we had earlier found 34 cases with a chart diagnosis of schizophrenia. Eight of the cases were diagnosed blindly by Judge A as other than schizophrenia, although one of these was called a symptomatic schizophrenia (i.e. organic psychosis mimicking schizophrenia) and two had alternative diagnoses of ? schizophrenia. Among our 66 DZ twins we had 36 Grade I cases of schizophrenia of whom 3 were diagnosed blindly as other than schizophrenia; one of the 3 had a secondary diagnosis of ? schizophrenia.

[1] We are indebted to Dr. Eliot Slater, Director of the Psychiatric Genetics Research Unit, for bringing his wisdom to bear on our case histories.

What then were the effects of this refinement of diagnoses on the originally reported concordance rates? First the number of index pairs was reduced from 24 MZ to 17 and from 33 DZ to 30. The simple pairwise concordance rates using Judge A's decisions were 41% (7/17) for the identicals and 10% (3/30) for the fraternals, virtually identical with the results using only chart diagnoses. Since the probands were independently ascertained and blindly diagnosed, the probandwise concordance rates are also of interest. The rates become 52% (11/21) MZ and 13% (4/31) DZ, again little change from before. Allen-type rates for the refined sample were 34% MZ and 7% DZ.

SUBTYPE CONCORDANCE AND THE QUESTION OF SPECIFICITY

The question arises of how the Kraepelinian subtypes may be related to one another genetically. Kallmann (1938) favored a hypothesis of the biological unity of schizophrenia as a whole. He considered that the form of the illness was determined by a series of factors other than the special hereditary predisposition. In light of the significant though far from complete resemblances in clincial picture between pairs of affected relatives, Slater (1947) suggested that these resemblances were attributable to the action of modifying genes. Our view (Gottesman and Shields, 1967) is similar in that it suggests that most instances of schizophrenia could be conceptualized as biologically related. It might nevertheless be argued that some of the subtypes represent phenotypes of discrete genotypes. Unfortunately, the few studies done on the children of dual mating schizophrenics (Rosenthal, 1966), do not provide sufficient data for conducting standard types of segregation analyses. What clinical evidence there is casts doubt on the isomorphism of the schizophrenias seen in parent-child dyads. In the particular case of the Genain quadruplets, Rosenthal (1963, p. 519) said that to the extent that genotype could be implicated in subtype patterning it led to a catatonic–hebephrenic sequence. He went on to say that if catatonia and hebephrenia represented discrete genotypes in the general population, we would be left positing three discrete genotypes; he rejected this hypothesis as "hardly parsimonious". I should like to raise the possibility that the hebephrenic features noted in 3 of the 4 quads were phenocopies, i.e. not a reflection of a genotype associated with hebephrenia. Within a diathesis-stress framework the net effect on the phenotypes of schizophrenia will be the same for, say, 4 units of diathesis and 6 units of environmental stress as it would be for 6 units of diathesis and only 4 units of stress. Both the pregnancy history and the EEG abnormality of the quads leaves open the possibility of minimal brain damage contributing stress units. Hester and Iris in whom hebephrenic features were most prominent had the lowest birth weights and the worst premorbid history (e.g., circumcision). Myra, with the best premorbid history and the best outcome, had the least severe schizophrenia of the 4 and was never noted to have had hebephrenic features. Such speculations as these are also hardly parsimonious, but parsimony may not always be our best master.

The comparison of MZ twin intrapair resemblances should permit the discovery of any subtypes of schizophrenia that may be either more under genetic control than others or free of such control. The concept of modifying genes cannot enter the picture since they would be matched in a pair of identicals. Kallmann (1946) did not follow the pattern of analyzing his twin data in terms of subtypes as he had done earlier (1938) with his family data; the early data suggested familial association for hebephrenic and catatonic but not for paranoid schizophrenia. Although Slater (1953) did not analyze MZ concordance by subtype, he reported a significant resemblance in concordant identicals for catatonic signs and passivity feelings. Rosenthal's (1959) reanalysis of Slater's male MZ twins led him to observe that discordant pairs were predominantly paranoid with a negative family history. Kringlen (1967) has given us the first specific analysis of concordance by subtype. He concluded that his data lent no support to the idea that one type of schizophrenia was more genetically determined than others. His analysis also permitted him to say that ". . . if both twins in a monozygotic pair develop schizophrenia, they tend to be of the same subtype, which may support the hypothesis of heritability of subtype. It must, however, also be admitted that concordance in subtype can be explained by social factors in terms of identification processes". Kringlen found that among his 14 concordant MZ pairs (schizophreniform psychoses omitted), 13 had the same subtype diagnosis, surely a remarkable finding in support of genetic specificity. Seven of the 14 pairs were both concordant for what Kringlen called "catatonic-paranoid" schizophrenia which makes it difficult to compare with our own data analyzed along similar lines. Table 3 presents a probandwise analysis of concordance-discordance by schizophrenic subtype for our 21 MZ pairs, using the blind diagnoses of Judge A.

TABLE 3. SCHIZOPHRENIC SUBTYPE SPECIFICITY IN 21 MZ PROBAND PAIRS BLINDLY DIAGNOSED BY JUDGE A

Index twin	Co-twin					Total
	Discordant	Hebephrenic	Catatonic	Atypical	Paranoid	
Hebephrenic	1*	7				8
Catatonic	1†					1
Atypical	5				1	6
Paranoid	3			1	2	6
Totals	10	7	0	1	3	21

* Proband has equivocal neurological signs, his co-twin is normal.
† Co-twin Dx "recurrent endogenous depression".

Some important findings emerge from this kind of analysis of our data. As with Kringlen's data, when both twins are schizophrenic they tend to be of the same subtype, i.e. 9 of 11 pairs. Unlike Kringlen's data the subtypes do not appear to be equally under genetic control. Hebephrenic cases, with one exception, have only hebephrenic co-twins. The one exception is noteworthy since the co-twin is fairly normal and was one of our Grade IV twins (Gottesman and Shields, 1966a). The index twin in this pair, diagnosed blindly as hebephrenic, has equivocal neurological signs. He is completely deaf and therefore difficult to interview. An EEG showed slow delta waves in the left frontal area, but the co-twin's EEG was also abnormal. Only the index twin was a prisoner-of-war, during which time he experienced severe malnutrition in a Japanese camp. His hebephrenia may also, in part, be merely phenotypic, as I suggested for Hester: the proband had been continuously in hospital for 690 weeks by the end of our observation period in 1964 and is still in today. For the time being the pair represents an exception in our material. We had only one catatonic index twin and her co-twin was discordant for schizophrenia but was diagnosed blindly as psychotic–recurrent endogenous depression. The six atypical schizophrenic index twins show one example of crossing over (to paranoid schizophrenia), but, more importantly, no other co-twins concordant for a schizophrenic illness. The 6 paranoid schizophrenic index twins have 3 MZ co-twins free of definite schizophrenia, 2 with the same subtype and 1 with an atypical schizophrenia.

Our provisional analysis of Judge A's subtype diagnoses leads us to suggest that hebephrenic, paranoid and atypical schizophrenias all show fairly high degrees of *specificity,* but only hebephrenic and paranoid subtypes are shown by our material to have high *heritability.* Some atypical schizophrenics would most likely be called schizo-affectives in the USA while others presented mixtures of symptoms from the subtypes. Our material does not permit a conclusion about catatonic schizophrenia but Kringlen's data and earlier findings suggest to us as much specificity and almost as much heritability as for the hebephrenic subtype. We leave open for the moment the issue of whether the subtypes of schizophrenia are best thought of as polymorphic or as clusters on a dimension; the former implies discontinuity of genotype, the latter does not.

SEVERITY AND CONCORDANCE AND COMMENTS ON A POLYGENIC THEORY

Severity is as vague and ambiguous a term as *concordance.* The varying operational definitions of these terms is often not made explicit and since such definitions may not correlate highly with each other, the literature has become clouded by seemingly inconsistent views. The situation is not unlike that in learning theory where the use of different criteria for the strength of a learned response led to conflicting views about the value of learning theories. Among the criteria used so far for severity of schizophrenia have been age at onset of symptoms, age at first hospitalization, intensity of symptoms, equating nuclear cases (hebephrenic and catatonic) with severe, course and outcome of the illness, number of attacks, time in hospital, and Phillips Scale ratings of premorbid history to get "process" schizophrenics. Kringlen (1967) has used an *ad hoc* 7 point mental health rating scale of unknown reliability and validity to obtain a measure of severity; it appears to combine information on symptoms and outcome.

Rosenthal (1966) concluded from his analysis of the age at first admission of the offspring from dual mating schizophrenics that severity was influenced primarily by environmental factors, a point he had made earlier (1963) from his observations on the Genain quadruplets. Kringlen (1967) has found "no evidence of hereditary factors influencing the course and outcome". His statement was based in part on finding 1 hebephrenic and 4 catatonic[2] MZ index twins with normal co-twins (4 normal co-twins had index twins with

---

[2] The equating throughout the literature on schizophrenia of hebephrenic and catatonic cases with an inevitably deteriorating outcome seems to be based on a misunderstanding of E. Bleuler (1950). Even in the period 1898–1905 at Burghölzli Hospital, 60% ($N = 307$) of schizophrenics could return to society and *earn a living* after their first hospitalization. By subtype 43% of catatonics showed medium or severe deterioration, as did 42% of hebephrenics and 35% of paranoids. Bleuler remarked, "...it is noteworthy how small the differences really are" (p. 259). Mitsuda (1967) showed how important for prognosis was the distinction between typical and atypical catatonics. Among a series of 48 catatonics, 20 recovered, all were atypical and 14 of these 20 showed no deterioration. Twenty-three other than typical catatonics had full remissions or social remissions after ECT. Of 20 hebephrenics, none recovered, all had a chronic course, and all showed deterioration.

"extremely severe" ratings of 7 points, while 10 normals had twins with 6 point ratings). We (Gottesman and Shields, 1966b, 1967), on the other hand, have suggested that severity is determined in the first instance by the number of genes in a posited polygenic system. Our suggestion derived from the analyses we had made of the relationship between concordance and severity, the latter defined first in terms of weeks hospitalized and then in terms of work status at the time of follow-up. We said,

> If the diathesis (to schizophrenia) takes the form of a polygenic system, having a large proportion of the genes predisposes a person to developing schizophrenia by lowering his threshold for coping with stress, and, at the same time, tends to make for a poor prognosis. In this instance we could infer that a proband with a good outcome had had few of the genes in the system, and we would expect his co-twin to have a much lower probability of decompensating than the co-twin of a severe schizophrenic. This explanation would hold whether or not one assumed with Slater (1958) and others that a further single gene was essential for the development of most schizophrenias, or whether one espoused a broader polygenic model for both etiology and course or outcome. [1966b, p. 70.]

Let me review briefly our findings on severity and then go on to examine more closely whether they might have been due to one artifact or another. In our first reports (1966a, b) we used three indicators of severity of schizophrenia in the proband and with each found a striking difference in the proportion of MZ co-twins who were also schizophrenic depending on whether the proband fell into a "mild" or "severe" category:

INDICATOR OF SEVERITY IN PROBAND

Degree of impairment	(1) ≥1 year in hospital	(2) ≥2 years in hospital	(3) Not working, <6 months out of hospital
Mild	20% (2/10)	29% (4/14)	17% (2/12)
Severe	67% (12/18)	71% (10/14)	75% (12/16)

At that time we saw no gross differences in age or type of treatment between the mild and severe cases that might have accounted for the results.

In our new analyses we first made allowance for the possibility that severe cases might have been observed longer from the time of their first hospitalization than mild cases. If it were true, it would have led to classifying pairs as mild and discordant that might eventually have become severe and concordant. Allowance was made by simply expressing total length of hospitalization in the proband as a per cent of total time elapsed since first hospitalization. The figures for MZ probands ranged from 1 to 90% with a median of 26%. Probandwise concordances for mild and severe cases were calculated as before, using criterion cutting points of 15, 20, 25, 30, 50 and 75% of elapsed time in hospital. The results were very consistent and I shall only report findings based on a hopefully reasonable definition of severity, namely, 20% of elapsed time since first hospitalization as a psychiatric inpatient. Using this criterion (4) we found that 33% of the co-twins of mild schizophrenics had a hospital diagnosis (Grade I) of schizophrenia as did 62% of co-twins of severe MZ probands.

There still remains the possibility that the difference between the co-twins of mild and severe schizophrenics may be exaggerated by the inclusion of pairs followed up for a relatively short time. A concordant pair followed for the first 5 months after hospitalization with the proband spending only the first month in hospital would yield a pair classified as severe and concordant; if the proband's remission were permanent, longer follow-up would yield a pair classified as mild and concordant. Furthermore, mild cases observed for a short time might subsequently accumulate enough time to be called severe. To test this idea we simply omitted all MZ pairs from our sample who had been followed for less than 5 years since first hospitalization, thus losing 6 pairs. Table 2, already showed that within 5 years concordance would usually have become manifest for MZ twins and by then degree of impairment should be obvious in most cases. Using criterion (4) with this reduced sample followed for more than 5 years, we obtain another set (5) of concordances for co-twins of mild and severe probands—40 and 75% respectively; the overall probandwise concordance for analysis (5) was 59%.

Just in case the lack of a common denominator for the amount of time followed up beyond the first 5 years was distorting our results, analysis (5) was repeated but only the per cent time hospitalized during the *first 5 years after initial hospitalization* was used. The range for 22 MZ probands was 8–92% with a median of 27%. The results for analysis (6) were exactly the same as with (5)—40% concordance in the co-twins of mild probands, 75% for the severe.

As a further step in the refinement of our data on severity and concordance we simultaneously removed all probands not followed for longer than 5 years and those that Judge A had called other than schizophrenic. Our sample of MZ probands was reduced to 18. We looked at the results for both total time followed up (analysis 7) and for a common denominator of just per cent time in hospital during the first 5 years subsequent to initial hospitalization (analysis 8). The results were the same for (7) and (8), again using as a criterion of severity 20% time in hospital. Thirty-eight per cent of the co-twins of mild MZ probands were diagnosed as schizophrenic by Judge A as were 80% of the co-twins of the severe probands. The overall probandwise concordance for both analyses was 61%, a figure that makes

TABLE 4. SUMMARY OF RELATIONSHIP BETWEEN SEVERITY AND
CONCORDANCE IN MZ PAIRS

Analytic criterion	Concordance in co-twin of mild proband	Concordance in co-twin of severe proband
(1) In hospital ≥1 year	20% (2/10)	67% (12/18)
(2) In hospital ≥2 years	29% (4/14)	71% (10/14)
(3) Not working, in hospital within past 6 months	17% (2/12)	75% (12/16)
(4) In hospital ≥20% F.U. time	33% (4/12)	62% (10/16)
(5) In hospital ≥20% F.U. time and followed 5 years	40% (4/10)	75% (9/12)
(6) In hospital ≥20% in 1st 5 years and followed 5 years	40% (4/10)	75% (9/12)
(7) In hospital ≥20% F.U. time, followed 5 years and Dx Sc by Judge A	38% (3/8)	80% (8/10)
(8) In hospital ≥20% in 1st 5 years, followed 5 years and Dx Sc by Judge A	38% (3/8)	80% (8/10)

provision for both diagnostic refinement and a kind of correction for age. To help follow this recitation of 8 variations on a theme, the results have been gathered together in Table 4.

Our conclusion from the above findings is that the previously reported association between severity and concordance was not biased by either length of follow-up or diagnostic accuracy. Severity assessed by outcome (3 above) and concordance was also little affected by eliminating the 6 pairs followed for less than 5 years; the mild and severe rates were 25% and 79% respectively, overall, 60%. So far the calculations above have been based on the proband method. If the probands in some concordant pairs are not "truly" independently ascertained, the method provides overestimates of the real state of affairs. We should like to present just one pairwise analysis of data on severity assessed by outcome. Twin A is classified as severe or mild (in pairs with 2 probands, the first to be registered is arbitrarily termed A) and we then determine whether Twin B is schizophrenic (Grade I) or not. The results are given in Table 5. We obtain the remarkable finding of a zero per cent concordance

TABLE 5. PAIRWISE ANALYSIS OF OUTCOME AND CONCORDANCE

B-twin status	A-twin status at follow-up		
	Mild: working and out of hospital	Severe: poorer outcome	Total
Schizophrenic	0	10	10
Non-schizophrenic	10	4	14
Total	10	14	24
Per cent concordance	0%	71%	42%

for MZ pairs where Twin A happened to be working and out of hospital for 6 months or more at the time of follow-up while 71% (10/14) of the B twins of severely ill identicals had been hospitalized and diagnosed as schizophrenic. Strömgren (1965) has said that when one does research on schizophrenia, one must be prepared for anything!

It would be fruitful to link our results as well as those of other twin and family studies of schizophrenia to the large body of data on the process-reactive distinction in schizophrenia. Garmezy (1965) has provided a masterful and scholarly review of the concepts and issues involved. Among his conclusions was the following:

> All told, the evidence suggests that greater reliance can be placed on the reduction of subject variability through procedures that separate subjects on the basis of prognostic rather than symptom criteria.

Our use of simple prognostic criteria support his conclusion. Garmezy was pessimistic about the power of the Phillips Premorbid Scale to reduce the resulting heterogeneity in process and reactive ratings *within* diagnostic subtypes: in his own data, hebephrenic, catatonic and paranoid cases were widely distributed along the process-reactive dimension. I would like to suggest that our simple and objective criteria be tried for the task of reducing within subtype variability. One of the other points at issue was whether the distinction was best viewed as a continuum or as a dichotomous typology. Garmezy favored the former from his review of the literature and we believe our data above support the idea that the process-reactive dimension is a continuum, and further, that the continuum reflects multiple aspects of severity. More support for the view that the distinction is quantitative and not qualitative comes from the mean MMPI profiles, both zygosities and sexes combined, of 25 severe probands and 21 mild probands determined by our outcome criterion. The profile shapes were virtually identical, with the severe probands being 10 T-score points or more higher on Scales *F, Depression, Psychasthenia, Schizophrenia,* and Welsh's *A,* and more than 10 points lower on Barron's *Ego-strength Scale.* Schaefer (1965), as reported by Garmezy, found no important differences between the MMPIs of schizophrenics classified as process and reactive by the Phillips Scale.

CONCLUSIONS

Our attempt to bring about the demise of our earlier findings has been unsuccessful. At this juncture we see no compelling reasons to revise our earlier statements which were in support of a diathesis-stress model and of a polygenic theory. The latter, at any rate, does not require very high levels of concordance in identical twins to generate appreciable estimates of the heritability of a threshold character (Falconer, 1965; Gottesman and Shields, 1967). As with pyloric stenosis, diabetes mellitus and club foot, incidences in relatives far below those found for characters inherited in a Mendelian fashion are sufficient to support a polygenic theory. Polygenic theory, while still in need of a great deal of refinement and specificity, has the power to encompass the diverse findings from both environmental and genetic points of views. This leads inevitably to a well-worn closing statement—the genes resulting in schizophrenia are necessary but they are not very often sufficient for the occurrence of the disorder.

REFERENCES

ALLEN, G. (1965) Twin research: problems and prospects, in A. G. Steinberg and A. G. Bearn (eds.), *Progress in Medical Genetics,* Vol. IV, New York, Grune & Stratton, pp. 242–69.

ALLEN, G., HARVALD, B., and SHIELDS, J. (1967) Measures of twin concordance, *Acta Gen. Stat. Med.* **17**, 475–81.

BLEULER, E. (1950) *Dementia Praecox or the Group of Schizophrenias,* New York, International University Press.

CLARK, J. A. and MALLETT, B. L. (1963) A follow-up study of schizophrenia and depression in young adults, *Brit. J. Psychiat.* **109**, 491–9.

FALCONER, D. S. (1965) The inheritance of liability to certain diseases, estimated from the incidence among relatives, *Ann. Hum. Genet. (London)* **29**, 51–76.

GARMEZY, N. (1967) Process and reactive schizophrenia: some conceptions and issues, in M. Katz and J. Cole (eds.), *The Role and Methodology of Classification in Psychiatry and Psychopathology,* Washington, D.C. Government Printing Office, pp. 419–66.

GOTTESMAN, I. I. and SHIELDS, J. (1966a) Schizophrenia in twins: sixteen years' consecutive admissions to a psychiatric clinic, *Brit. J. Psychiat.* **112**, 809–18.

GOTTESMAN, I. I. and SHIELDS, J. (1966b) Contributions of twin studies to perspectives on schizophrenia, in B. A. Maher (ed.), *Progress in Experimental Personality Research,* Vol. 3, New York, Academic Press, pp. 1–84.

GOTTESMAN, I. I. and SHIELDS, J. (1967) A polygenic theory of schizophrenia, *Proc. Nat. Acad. Sci.* **58**, 199–205.

KAIJ, L. (1960) *Alcoholism in Twins,* Stockholm, Almqvist & Wiksell.

KALLMANN, F. J. (1938) *The Genetics of Schizophrenia,* New York, Augustin.

KALLMANN, F. J. (1946) The genetic theory of schizophrenia: an analysis of 691 schizophrenic twin index families, *Am. J. Psychiat.* **103**, 309–22.

KARN, M. N. (1953) Data of twin births occurring in two English metropolitan hospitals, *Acta Genet. Med. Gem.* **2,** 152–63.

KRINGLEN, E. (1966) Schizophrenia in twins, an epidemiological–clinical study, *Psychiatry* **29,** 172–84.

KRINGLEN, E. (1967) Hereditary and social factors in schizophrenic twins, Paper read at *First Rochester International Conference on Schizophrenia, Rochester, New York.*

MITSUDA, H. (1967) Clinico-genetic study of schizophrenia, in H. Mitsuda (ed.), *Clinical Genetics in Psychiatry,* Kyoto, Bunko-Sha, pp. 49–90.

ROSENTHAL, D. (1959) Some factors associated with concordance and discordance with respect to schizophrenia in monozygotic twins, *J. Nerv. Ment. Dis.* **129,** 1–10.

ROSENTHAL, D. (ed.), *et al.* (1963) *The Genain Quadruplets,* New York, Basic Books.

ROSENTHAL, D. (1966) The offspring of schizophrenic couples, *J. Psychiat. Res.* **4,** 169–88.

SCHAEFER, SARAH (1965) MMPI profiles of good and poor premorbid schizophrenic patients, Summa cum Laude thesis, University of Minnesota.

SLATER, E. (1947) Genetical causes of schizophrenic symptoms, *Mschr. Psychiat. Neurol.* **113,** 50–8.

SLATER, E. (1953) *Psychotic and Neurotic Illnesses in Twins,* London, Her Majesty's Stationery Office.

SLATER, E. (1958) The monogenic theory of schizophrenia, *Acta Gen. Stat. Med.* **8,** 50–6.

STRÖMGREN, E. (1965) Psychiatrische Genetik, in H. W. Gruhle *et al.* (eds.), *Psychiatrie der Gegenwart,* Vol. 1/1A, Berlin, Springer, pp. 1–69.

TIENARI, P. (1963) Psychiatric illnesses in identical twins, *Acta Psychiat. Scand.,* Suppl. 171.

AN EPIDEMIOLOGICAL–CLINICAL TWIN STUDY ON SCHIZOPHRENIA

EINAR KRINGLEN

Institute of Psychiatry, University of Bergen,
Haukeland Sykehus, Bergen, Norway

IN THIS paper I have chosen to be rather summary in my presentation of methods and concordance rates and instead focus attention on some data which might be new to the majority of the audience.

In a previous study I found no significant difference in concordance rates for monozygotic and dizygotic schizophrenic male twins (Kringlen, 1964). As the sample in that study was relatively small, a more comprehensive study has been conducted, in which all twins recorded in the Norwegian birth register from 1901 to 1930—in all about 50,000 twins—have been checked against the Central Register of Psychosis. This has provided a relatively large, and what is more important, an unselected sample of psychotic twins.

The study had three principal aims. First, to obtain representative concordance figures for all types of functional psychoses; second, to study problems pertaining to nosology; and third, to study a larger sample of discordant pairs in order to clarify crucial environmental factors.

In other words the aim was to conduct a combined hereditary and environmental study of the functional psychoses, with the main emphasis on schizophrenia.

METHODS

The checking of the Twin Register against the Register of Psychosis resulted in 519 pairs of twins. After exclusion of some diagnostic categories, such as organic psychosis and severe mental deficiency, and all pairs where the co-twin had died before the age of 15, a sample of 342 pairs of twins was left. These twins were in the age group 35–64 years, and one or both had at some time been hospitalized in Norway for functional psychosis, i.e. schizophrenia, manic depressive illness, or reactive psychosis.

Zygosity diagnosis was arrived at by blood and serum grouping, as well as information about identity confusion as children. Seventy-five pairs were classified as monozygotics (MZ) and 257 pairs as dizygotics (DZ), whereas ten pairs of the same sex had unknown zygosity.

As many as possible of the families of the MZ pairs, including parents and siblings, were personally investigated. Personal interviews were obtained with the MZ twins within the schizophrenic group in 82%, the rest being twins who had died prior to follow-up, had

49

left the country, or simply refused to see me. Forty-two pairs of DZ of the same sex were also personally investigated but not their families.

RESULTS

The frequency of functional psychoses in twins

Owing to the uniqueness of the twin relationship, particularly in MZ pairs, twins face special problems during childhood and adolescence, and it would seem not unlikely that twins might have a higher frequency of mental illness than the normal population.

After considering admission rates to Norwegian hospitals, I have been unable to demonstrate any difference between twins and the general population in frequency of functional psychosis combined or for sub-groups of schizophrenia, manic-depressive illness, and reactive psychosis. The calculations were carried out for males and females separately.

These findings have implications for theory. First of all, higher concordance rates in MZ twins cannot be explained away by postulating that the twinship in itself predisposes to schizophrenia or other psychoses. The findings furthermore cast doubt on Jackson's (1960) "confusion of ego identity theory" of schizophrenia. Jackson in a thought-provoking article tried to give an environmental interpretation for increased concordance rates with respect to schizophrenia in MZ twins. The author maintained that the identity problem of the schizophrenic patient could find no better nidus than in the inter-twining of twin identities, "in the ego fusion that in one sense doubles the ego since the other is felt as part of the self, and in another halves it, since the self is felt as part of the other".

Rosenthal analysed the twin investigations published by Luxenburger (1928) and Essen-Möller (1941) and could not support this theory of Jackson. He found that the proportions of twins with schizophrenia and manic-depressive psychoses correspond quite closely to the proportions of twins in the population.

Tienari (1963), on the other hand, found higher, but not statistically significant, morbidity figures of schizophrenia for the twin-population than for the general population. The figures were also higher for MZ twins than for DZ. According to the author, this might be due to methodological factors.

In the main, it should be possible to conclude safely that the evidence available from my own material and the literature gives very little support to the hypothesis that functional psychosis is more frequent in twins than in non-twins. If differential rates do occur, they would seem to be of a negligible nature and of no practical importance.

Survey of the sample by age, sex and zygosity

The ages of the twins are evenly distributed between 35 and 64 years with a mean of 49 years. This refers to the year 1965 when the field work was completed.

Table 1 gives a summary of the sample and a comparison of the zygosity of the twins observed with the expected number according to Weinberg's method.

The 126 pairs of twins of opposite sex are without further ado dizygotics. Roughly speaking, there ought to be the same number of dizygotics of the same sex. According to

TABLE 1. SURVEY OF THE SAMPLE

	Observed			Expected total
	Male	Female	Total	
MZ	37	38	75	90
DZ, same sex	65	66	131	126
Unknown zygosity, same sex	6	4	10	—
DZ, opposite sex	—	—	126	126
Total pairs	108	108	342	342
Siblings of MZ twins	166	163	329	—

Weinberg's differential method, the number of monozygotics is then obtained by subtracting the double number of opposite-sex dizygotics from the total of all twins (Stern, 1960). There are fewer in this group found to be monozygotics than expected. The difference is not, however, statistically significant.

As shown in Table 1, there is the same number of male and female pairs of the same sex. In most previous studies there has been an excess of female pairs, most likely due to shortcomings in sampling.

Concordance figures

There are at least two methods of computation of concordance rates, the pairwise method and the proband method. The pairwise concordance method has been employed in the present study. This method is simple; one just calculates the percentage of concordant pairs in a twin population. If, for example, we have 100 pairs of twins and there is concordance in 50 pairs, the concordance rate is 50%.

The definition of concordance, however, may vary. A pair of twins may be concordant for certain personality traits, for certain symptoms, for diagnosis. As we move forward I will define in each case what I mean by concordance.

Table 2 gives an overall picture of the concordance rates with the three main diagnostic groups—schizophrenia, reactive psychosis, and manic-depressive illness—lumped together. A pair is classified as concordant in this connection if both partners have received a hospital

TABLE 2. CONCORDANCE FOR ALL TYPES OF "FUNCTIONAL PSYCHOSIS"*

	Number of pairs	Concordant pairs	Discordant pairs	Per cent concordance
MZ	75	18	57	24
DZ, same sex	131	8	123	6
Unknown zygosity	10	0	10	0
DZ, opposite sex	126	8	118	6

* These figures are arrived at by checking the twin register against the register of psychosis. The figures are without age correction.

diagnosis of functional psychosis. In other words, if one twin is schizophrenic and the other is suffering from a reactive psychosis, the pair is classified as concordant. The figures were arrived at by checking the twin register against the register of psychosis and the figures are without age correction.

The concordance rates are significantly different for MZ and DZ, but the difference is less than usually reported.

The concordance figures for "strict"—that is strictly defined schizophrenia—plus the group of schizophreniform psychoses are presented in Table 3.

TABLE 3. CONCORDANCE FOR SCHIZOPHRENIA AND SCHIZOPHRENIFORM PSYCHOSES BASED ON REGISTERED HOSPITALIZED CASES

	Number of pairs	Concordant pairs	Discordant pairs	Per cent concordance
MZ	55	14	41	25
DZ, same sex	90	6	84	7
DZ, opposite sex	82	8	74	10
Unknown zygosity	6	0	6	0

Table 4 shows the concordance figures when a rather wide concept of concordance is used, and it is based on personal investigation as well as hospitalization. A pair is grouped as concordant if the index case has a diagnosis of schizophrenia or schizophreniform psychosis and the co-twin has either the same diagnosis or a diagnosis of reactive psychosis or border-line. Personal knowledge was utilized for half of the schizophrenic DZ group of the same sex. The opposite-sex dizygotics were not personally seen at all.

TABLE 4. CONCORDANCE FOR SCHIZOPHRENIA AND SCHIZOPHRENIFORM PSYCHOSES BASED ON PERSONAL INVESTIGATIONS

	Number of pairs	Concordant pairs	Discordant pairs	Per cent concordance
MZ	55	21	34	38
DZ, same sex (estimated)	90	9	81	10

As Table 4 shows, even if a rather wide concept of concordance is used, the concordance rates are still low. There is some increase for both monozygotics and dizygotics. The estimated concordance rates for same-sex dizygotics are perhaps too low (cf. the concordance figures for opposite-sex twins without personal investigation, Table 3).

Table 5 gives the concordance rates for typical schizophrenia, excluding the so-called schizophreniform psychosis. Regardless of school of thought, most clinicians should be able to agree on a diagnosis of schizophrenia for these cases. The findings are based on hospitalized registered cases, but personal investigation did not change Table 5 significantly.

Table 6 gives a summary of the incidence of schizophrenia in different genetic and social groups, namely monozygotic co-twins, dizygotic co-twins and siblings of monozygotics.

As Table 6 shows, there is first of all a clear difference in morbidity rates (concordance rates) for MZ co-twins compared with the other groups. The rates for dizygotics and siblings are rather similar; we observe, however, that there is a difference, rates for DZ being higher, although not statistically significant (the difference is 1·1 times the standard error of the two proportions when the calculations are based on hospitalized registered cases of schizophrenia and schizophreniform psychoses). From a genetical point of view

TABLE 5. CONCORDANCE FOR "STRICT" SCHIZOPHRENIA, BASED ON
REGISTERED HOSPITALIZED CASES

	Number of pairs	Concordant pairs	Discordant pairs	Per cent concordance
MZ	45	12	33	27
DZ, same sex	69	3	66	4
Unknown zygosity	2	0	2	0
DZ, opposite sex	64	3	61	5

one should expect to find the same morbidity rate in co-twins of dizygotics as in siblings. We have to make one qualification, that we are dealing with two populations, siblings of MZ twins and co-twins of DZ twins. Ideally we should like to compare the morbidity rate in these co-twins with that of siblings of DZ twins. Most likely, however, this objection is theoretical in nature. I do not see in what way these populations should be different. They are for instance similar in terms of social class, sex and age.

TABLE 6. INCIDENCE OF SCHIZOPHRENIA IN DIFFERENT GENETIC
AND SOCIAL GROUPS

	Typical schizophrenia		Schizophrenia and schizophreniform psychosis	
	H.R. (%)	P.I. (%)	H.R. (%)	P.I. (%)
MZ co-twins (one twin index case)	26·7	31·0	25·4	38·2
DZ same-sexed co-twins (one twin index case)	4·3	—	6·7	10·0 (?)
DZ opposite-sexed co-twins (one twin index case)	4·7	—	9·8	—
Sibs of MZ twins (one twin index case)	3·4	4·8	5·2	6·2

H.R. = hospitalized registered. P.I. = personally investigated.

It is natural to attach significance to these observed differences, and to ascribe the higher morbidity figures in co-twins of DZ twins, compared with the morbidity rates in siblings, to the twinship itself.

E

Table 7 gives a summary of the results obtained in various studies as regards morbidity figures in twins compared with siblings.

TABLE 7. MORBIDITY RISK IN SIBLINGS OF SCHIZOPHRENICS, BASED ON TWIN POPULATIONS

Studies compared			Relation to index-case		
Investigator	Year	Country	MZ co-twins (%)	DZ co-twins (%)	Full sibs (%)
Luxenburger	1935	Germany	54·0	14·0	11·8
Kallmann	1946	USA	69·0 (85·8)	10·3 (14·7)	10·2 (14·3)
Slater	1953	England	68·3 (76·3)	11·3 (14·4)	4·6 (5·4)
Kringlen	1967	Norway	25·4 (38·2)	8·1 (10–12)	5·2 (6·8)

The percentages in parentheses refer to age-corrected figures with respect to Kallmann's and Slater's studies. The figures in parentheses with respect to my own study refer to percentages based on personal investigation and employment of a wide concept of concordance.

Sex and concordance

In previous studies there is a considerable difference between the concordance rates in schizophrenia for women and those for men, the latter being markedly lower. This is apparent in the studies of Luxenburger (1928), Rosanoff *et al.* (1934), and Slater (1953). Kallmann (1940, 1950), and Inouye (1961) did not give breakdowns of their concordant and discordant pairs by sex. Tienari (1963) and Kringlen (1964a, b) studied only male pairs. Table 8 gives an overall picture of the concordance rates for the two sexes separately, with the three main diagnostic groups—schizophrenia, manic-depressive psychosis and reactive psychosis—lumped together.

As Table 8 clearly shows, there is no significant difference in concordance rates for male

TABLE 8. CONCORDANCE WITH RESPECT TO FUNCTIONAL PSYCHOSIS IN MALE AND FEMALE TWINS, BASED ON HOSPITALIZED AND REGISTERED CASES

	MZ		DZ Same sex		DZ Opposite sex
	Female	Male	Female	Male	Female/Male
Number of pairs	38	37	66	65	126
Concordant pairs	9	9	5	3	8
Discordant pairs	29	28	61	62	118
Per cent concordance	23·7	24·3	7·6	4·8	6·3

and female. In monozygotics there is in fact a slightly higher concordance rate in males. Within the same-sexed DZ group there is a slight difference in the expected direction, but statistically it is not significant. The difference in concordance rates between the DZ females and the DZ of the opposite sex is quite negligible.

Table 9 gives the concordance figures for males and females with respect to schizophrenia and schizophreniform psychoses combined. We find here higher concordance figures for females both in monozygotics and dizygotics of the same sex; the differences are, however, statistically insignificant. Important is, however, the fact that the concordance figure for dizygotics of the opposite sex is higher than for the DZ females.

TABLE 9. CONCORDANCE WITH RESPECT TO SCHIZOPHRENIA AND SCHIZOPHRENIFORM PSYCHOSES IN MALE AND FEMALE MZ AND DZ TWINS. THE FIGURES ARE BASED UPON HOSPITALIZED AND REGISTERED CASES

	MZ		DZ Same sex		DZ Opposite sex
	Female	Male	Female	Male	Female/Male
Number of pairs	24	31	35	55	82
Concordant pairs	7	7	3	3	8
Discordant pairs	27	24	32	52	74
Per cent concordance	29·2	22·6	8·6	5·5	9·8

Table 10 gives the concordance figures for males and females in monozygotics with respect to schizophrenia and schizophreniform psychoses combined. These rates are based on personal examination, and a rather wide concept of concordance is used. The con-

TABLE 10. CONCORDANCE WITH RESPECT TO SCHIZOPHRENIA AND SCHIZOPHRENIFORM PSYCHOSES IN MALE AND FEMALE MZ TWINS, BASED UPON PERSONAL INVESTIGATION AND USING A WIDE CONCEPT OF CONCORDANCE

	MZ		
	Female	Male	Total
Number of pairs	24	31	55
Concordant pairs	8	13	21
Discordant pairs	16	18	34
Per cent concordance	33	42	38

cordance rates are higher in males, in other words, in the unexpected direction. The difference is not, however, statistically significant.

In conclusion it may be said that the study does not show any differences in concordance rates in the two sexes, and this diverges from the rather uniform findings of previous studies. We will revert to this question in the general discussion.

Alanen (1958), in an excellent review of twin studies, drew attention to the differential concordance rates in the two sexes, and Jackson (1960), in his critique, discussed the same phenomenon, maintaining that the difference might be explained in terms of twin closeness and identification. Later on Rosenthal (1961, 1962) also discussed this problem in some detail and noted that there was an excess of female twins obtained in the three largest of the major twin studies. This was especially pronounced in Rosanoff et al.'s study with a female:male ratio 4:1, but also in Slater's study the sample was dominated by females with a ratio 2:1. Rosenthal ascribed this to the fact that these authors had sampled from resident hospital populations. Women were thus more likely to become inhabitants of the chronic wards than men, according to Rosenthal (1961).

Table 11 gives the concordance with respect to schizophrenia for the two sexes separately, based on several investigations. One must bear in mind that the percentages are based in

TABLE 11. CONCORDANCE WITH RESPECT TO SCHIZOPHRENIA IN MALE AND FEMALE MZ AND DZ TWINS*

		MZ		DZ Same sex		DZ Opposite sex
		Female (%)	Male (%)	Female (%)	Male (%)	(%)
Luxenburger	(1928)†	88	67	0	0	0
Rosanoff et al.	(1934)	78	42	14	9	6
Essen-Möller	(1941)†	75	67	18	9	—
Slater	(1957)	73	45	16	10	5
Mitsuda	(1957)	50	50	—	—	—
Inouye	(1961)†	62	58	—	—	—
Gottesman and Shields	(1966)	45	38	12	6	—
Kringlen	(1967)‡	29	23	9	6	10
		33	42	—	—	—

* Kallmann (1946) and Harvald and Hauge (1965) did not break down the figures according to sex, but from Kallmann's figures for same-sexed and opposite-sexed pairs one can compute that the ratio is 17·6 to 11·5. From Inouye's (1961) report it was only possible to compute percentages for the MZ group.

† Included doubtful schizophrenic co-twins (Luxenburger), reactive psychotic co-twins (Essen-Möller), and schizophrenic co-twins (Inouye).

‡ Schizophreniform psychosis included. First row is based upon hospitalized registered cases. Second row is based on personal investigation.

many cases on an extremely small number of MZ pairs. This is particularly the case for the studies by Essen-Möller and Mitsuda.

Clearly brought out by the literature is a trend toward higher concordance rates in females, both in MZ and DZ same-sexed twins. Furthermore there is a higher concordance rate in same-sexed dizygotics than in opposite dizygotics in the studies where such figures are available. The differences, however, seem to disappear in more recent studies; particularly is this true for my own study, where I could find no differences when the data were based on more intensive studies with personal follow-up.

It is difficult to explain this tendency. Sampling could be one factor, but according to Rosenthal (1962) this is unlikely, and the tendency is apparent also in samples based on consecutive admission, with twinship established from the birth registers (Essen-Möller and Luxenburger).

If the psychological hypothesis is valid why should this tendency not prevail in all studies, and more specifically why not in the present one?

One might speculate if the phenomenon under discussion might have some relation to time and culture. Higher female concordance could be explained in terms of closeness and identification. The reason why this phenomenon was more marked in earlier studies could be that the girls in former days were more strictly brought up with less opportunity for social contact than boys were. Girls might be more restricted in their activities outside the home, they might stay more at home and work as domestic servants, whereas the boys migrated more frequently and earlier, and became more exposed to varying social influences. Most boys have at least to enter military service so even boys who tended to stay at home would move from home at the age of 19–21 for shorter or longer periods of time. Furthermore, close ties between sisters do not carry the opprobrium that they might do with brothers (Jackson, 1960).

With an increasing female emancipation this sex difference in upbringing and attitudes towards boys and girls has vanished. This could offer an explanation of the fact that the higher female concordance rates are disappearing in more recent studies.

Today one would expect higher female concordance to be particularly pronounced in cultures where girls and women are more restricted in their activities, whereas the phenomenon should vanish in cultures where females enjoy equal rights with males. If the general impression that girls are brought up more independently and liberally in Norway than in many other countries is correct, the findings of my own study become meaningful.

Those were speculations which cannot be refuted or supported by empirical studies. Only replications of twin studies in other cultures, using the same technique, can give us more firm answers.

Comparison between the schizophrenic concordant and discordant cases

From a genetic point of view one might think that hereditary cases of schizophrenia would be disproportionately represented among the concordant cases, whereas the environmentally determined cases would be more frequently represented among the discordant pairs (Allen, 1954; Rosenthal, 1959).

In this study no marked difference was found between the concordant and discordantly affected schizophrenics in the MZ group with respect to family incidence of schizophrenia, clinical picture, and outcome. In other words the analysis gave no indication that the concordant pairs were more hereditarily determined than the discordantly affected pairs, findings which agree with Luxenburger (1936) and Tienari (1963).

From an environmental point of view, however, one could contend that concordance could be partly due to a commonality of milieu, in terms of similar upbringing, stress and identification.

The analysis of the data gives some evidence for the environmental hypothesis. The concordant pairs have apparently experienced a somewhat more stressful or pathogenic childhood, reflected in lower social class and more frequent social isolation. The concordant pairs have furthermore been more close to each other and have been less influenced by extrafamilial social contacts, thus having had less opportunity for individual development and growth. These differences were, however, not statistically significant at the 5% level.

Nosology and subtype of schizophrenia

Let us now take a look at the co-twins of schizophrenics. As can be seen from Table 12, the co-twins of typical chronic schizophrenics display a broad range of psychopathological conditions.

In only 31% both twins show the same psychopathology. In another 9% the co-twin of schizophrenics has either been affected with a reactive psychosis or can be described as a border-line case. Our three border-line patients have never presented a clear-cut picture of psychosis; thus none of them has ever been hospitalized. However, they show certain personality traits that are more of a psychotic than a neurotic nature. One of them, for instance,

TABLE 12. CLASSIFICATION OF THE CO-TWINS OF MZ-INDEX CASES
WITH TYPICAL SCHIZOPHRENIA (SCHIZOPHRENIFORM EXCLUDED)

Psychopathology of MZ co-twin	Number	Percentage
Typical schizophrenia	14	31
Reactive psychosis	1	2
Border-line states	3	7
Neurosis	13	29
Normality	14	31
Total co-twin	45	100

is rather suspicious and withdrawn, with slight thinking disturbances, and the two others are extremely schizoid. Some would most likely classify these border-line cases as ambulatory or pseudo-neurotic schizophrenics.

In the group of neurotic co-twins, we find a broad spectrum of clinical symptoms, namely character disorders, anxiety states, depressive neuroses, somatic neuroses, and one case where alcohol was the main problem.

Table 13 shows the range of pathology in co-twins of schizophreniform psychotics.

TABLE 13. CLASSIFICATION OF THE CO-TWINS OF MZ-INDEX CASES
WITH SO-CALLED SCHIZOPHRENIFORM PSYCHOSIS

Psychopathology of MZ co-twins	Number	Percentage
Schizophreniform psychosis	3	30
Neurosis	4	40
Normality	3	30
Total co-twins	10	100

The numbers here are too small for any definite conclusion, but there is no indication that the picture is different from the typical schizophrenic group.

There are few pure hebephrenic, catatonic, or paranoid syndromes. Usually one finds a combination of syndromes. In concordant cases, however, the same syndrome is usually present in both partners. In Table 14 is tabulated the relationship between the syndromes in concordant pairs.

As can be seen, there is a clear tendency, with the qualification that the numbers are small, towards the same subtype of schizophrenia in both twins.

TABLE 14. SUBTYPE ASSOCIATION IN MZ CONCORDANT SCHIZOPHRENIC PAIRS
(SCHIZOPHRENIFORM EXCLUDED)

	Co-twins					Total
	Heb.	Cat.	Par.	Cat. par.	Others	
Hebephrenic	2					2
Catatonic		1			1	2
Paranoid			2			2
Catatonic-paranoid				7		7
Others, mix syndrome					1	1
Total number of concordant pairs						14

Our next question is: Are all of the so-called normal or neurotic co-twins more or less randomly paired with various subtypes of schizophrenia and the various degree of severity this disease presents? Would for instance a case of malignant schizophrenia—believed by many to be of a genetic origin—be more aptly paired with a psychotic who shows either the same type of psychosis or a border-line type with marked schizoid traits, while, on the other hand, would a case of benign schizophrenia—believed to be of a non-genetic type—be paired with a merely neurotic co-twin or even with a normal co-twin?

Table 15 shows that the normal co-twin may be paired with any type of schizophrenia.

TABLE 15. SUBTYPE OF SCHIZOPHRENIA PAIRED WITH NORMAL
MZ CO-TWINS (SCHIZOPHRENIFORM EXCLUDED)

Subtype of MZ index cases	Total number	Number of clinically normal co-twins
Hebephrenia	6	1
Catatonia	7	4
Paranoid type	13	2
Mixed syndromes	19	7
Total	45	14

The data show furthermore that the normal co-twins may be paired not only with moderately severe cases of schizophrenia but even with extremely deteriorated partners.

The data lend no support to the idea that some subtypes of schizophrenia are considerably more genetically determined than others; furthermore there is no clear evidence of hereditary factors influencing the course and outcome.

On the other hand, if both twins in a MZ pair develop schizophrenia, they tend to be of the same subtype, which may support the hypothesis of hereditability of subtype. It must, however, also be admitted that concordance in subtype can be explained by social factors.

Premorbid personality

In the main, the results show that birth order, birth weight, difficult birth, physical strength in early childhood, and psychomotor development during the first years of life are of practically no significance for later schizophrenic development. On the other hand, there is a clear correlation between some personality factors in childhood and later schizophrenia.

Table 16 shows the relationship between personality factors in childhood such as loneliness, reserve, obsessive behaviour, dependency, and schizophrenia.

TABLE 16. RELATIONSHIP BETWEEN CHILDHOOD FACTORS AND LATER SCHIZOPHRENIC DEVELOPMENT IN CONCORDANT AND DISCORDANT MZ AND DZ TWIN PAIRS

	Schizophrenia and schizophreniform psychosis											
	MZ								DZ			
	Concordant				Discordant				Discordant			
	A	B	Equal	Not known	A	B	Equal	Not known	A	B	Equal	Not known
More reserved and lonely	15	3	1	2	18	2	7	7	16	7	3	3
More sensitive	6	5	2	8	14	5	5	10	8	4	4	13
More "sweet" and obedient	8	5	1	7	8	5	10	11	7	2	4	16
More obsessional	4	3	1	13	11	3	3	17	9	2	0	18
More dependent	5	3	4	9	20	1	2	11	9	2	4	14
More nervous	7	3	6	5	17	2	11	4	12	4	8	5

In both MZ and DZ groups the schizophrenic one has been significantly more often the more submissive, reserved and lonely, obsessive, and the more dependent. The same tendency is present with traits like sensitivity and obedience. Furthermore, in both MZ and DZ twins the schizophrenic has been significantly more often the more nervous in childhood.

The schizophrenic twin had fewer friends of both sexes premorbidly and was more passive sexually than the non-schizophrenic twin, and also more frequently unmarried. The schizophrenic twin also had a lower social status than the non-schizophrenic twin.

I have demonstrated a relationship between some personality factors and development of schizophrenia. In discordantly affected pairs of schizophrenic twins personality differences were already discernible in childhood. These differences in personality can be ascribed to environmental factors, since they are present not only in dizygotics, but also in monozygotics. These premorbid traits could be forerunners of later manifest schizophrenia; most likely, however, they are just general predispositions to mental illness. Many children are introverted, obsessive, and dependent, and do not develop schizophrenia.

Relationship to twin and parents

In the discordantly affected pairs the schizophrenic twin has more frequently been the submissive partner in the twin relationship. The difference is highly statistically significant for both MZ and DZ pairs.

These findings are in accordance with the result of previous studies (Slater, 1953; Tienari, 1963; Kringlen, 1964b; Pollin et al., 1965). Tienari found that the schizophrenic twin had been more submissive in practically all cases, namely 14 against 1.

The data show that more schizophrenics had a difficult relationship to their father in childhood. Further, more schizophrenics have been close to their mother. In both MZ and DZ discordant groups the mother has been more often over-protective of the twin that was later to become schizophrenic.

In the main, the figures are small and do not reach statistical significance, but the trend is in the expected direction and thus supports more than contradicts the observations of family research in schizophrenia.

GENERAL DISCUSSION AND CONCLUSIONS

I have previously discussed the sources of error inherent in this study (Kringlen, 1966, 1967a, b). In conclusion it might be said that the sources of error which relate to sampling, zygosity diagnosis, and risk period are of no practical importance.

In the main, the concordance figures for schizophrenia are found to be 25–38 % in monozygotics and 4–10 % in dizygotics, according to whether the concordance rates are based on registered hospitalized cases or personal investigations, and whether a wide or a strict concept of schizophrenia is employed.

For a more detailed discussion of previous twin studies in schizophrenia in relation to my own findings, you are referred to my monograph (Kringlen, 1967b).

My own investigation and earlier studies clearly show that the clinical picture found in the non-schizophrenic co-twins is rather variable, since it ranges from a duplication of the schizophrenic psychosis to neurosis, or even clinical normalcy. The normal co-twin may be paired with any of the Kraepelinian subtypes of schizophrenia. Further, the normal co-twin may be matched not only with a milder case of schizophrenia but even with a very severely affected partner.

The onset of schizophrenia may be in adolescence or later. It would appear, however, that various personality characteristics which were correlated with later development of schizophrenia are laid down in childhood. Usually the more introverted, the more submissive, the more dependent and the more obsessive twin is more likely to develop schizophrenia. In other words, schizophrenia development is clearly related to premorbid personality development. We are, however, not facing any rigid determinism; sometimes the apparently more healthy twin falls ill with schizophrenia.

The significant difference in concordance rates for MZ and DZ twins with respect to schizophrenia supports a genetic factor in the etiology of schizophrenic illness. However, how much of the difference between MZ and DZ groups is attributable to heredity and how much to the special condition of being a MZ twin is still open to question.

What then is inherited? It is certainly not the symptoms that are inherited, nor a distinct type of personality; more likely it is certain developmental potentials.

It seems to me that an unspecific polygenic mode of inheritance can best account for the facts available. A polygenic inheritance can best explain the gliding transition from normality to severe mental illness, found in siblings and parents.

A polygenic inheritance can make intelligible the great variation of clinical pictures found in families of schizophrenics and the fact that the number of patients with so-called clinical "forme-frustes" are larger than the number of manifest schizophrenics (cf. Alanen, 1966). This is just what one should expect in conditions which are the expression of variations of normal traits. Some might object that schizophrenia, at least the severe cases, are qualitatively different from normal personality development. They agree that there is no clear-cut distinction between clinical normalcy and neurosis, but they feel it more difficult to think of schizophrenia as extremes on a continuum. I think, however, that most psychiatrists who have worked therapeutically with schizophrenics will favour the idea of grades of personality disorganization. There are degrees of suspiciousness, there are grades of withdrawal and aloofness, and there are, in particular, degrees of thinking disturbances (Lidz et al., 1961; Singer and Wynne, 1963). Furthermore, one should bear in mind that a quantitative variation may present itself to the investigator as a qualitative difference, when the margin of adjustment is overstepped. The low concordance figures in MZ twins with respect to schizophrenia shows, however, that the environmental contribution to the etiology is considerable. Human beings with the same hereditary equipment as schizophrenic twins have a 60% chance of escaping the illness. The broad range of psychopathology which we have encountered in human beings with the same genotype shows also the significance of environmental factors in the etiology of mental illness.

Our analysis has shown that the environmental factors are probably not of a somatic, but of a social character.

We have not, however, been able to demonstrate convincingly the specific nature of any social factor. This is comprehensible, first of all because my study, even if I had the opportunity to investigate several family members, has to be looked upon as a crude study from a dynamic environmental point of view. Secondly, these factors may be difficult to discover by the retrospective method. Finally, these environmental factors are certainly difficult to evaluate and determine if they are due to interpersonal disturbances in social systems where cause and effect is interwoven in a series of multiple interactions. Only observation of family communication on the spot over periods of time may be able to give us a more firm answer.

If our hypothesis is correct, that the genetic disposition is an unspecific polygenic one, furthermore that the environmental factors play a significant role in the etiology of schizophrenia, then the so-called solution of the schizophrenia riddle will not come from any simple biochemical breakthrough, as there are no simple biochemical answers to the problem of variation in height and weight, epileptic disposition, or variation in blood-pressure.

REFERENCES

ALANEN, Y. O. (1958) The mothers of schizophrenic patients, *Acta psychiat. scand.,* Suppl. 124.
ALANEN, Y. O. (1966) The family in the pathogenesis of schizophrenic and neurotic disorders, *Acta psychiat. scand.,* Suppl. 189.

ALLEN, G. (1954) Discussion, in Proceedings of the conference on problems and methods in human genetics, *Amer. J. Hum. Genet.* **6**, 162–4.

ESSEN-MÖLLER, E. (1941) Psychiatrische Untersuchungen an einer Serie von Zwillingen, *Acta psychiat.*, Suppl. 23.

GOTTESMAN, I. I. and SHIELDS, J. (1966) Schizophrenia in twins: 16 years' consecutive admissions to a psychiatric clinic, *Brit. J. Psychiat.* **112**, 809–18.

INOUYE, E. (1961) Similarity and dissimilarity of schizophrenia in twins, *Proc. Third World Congress Psychiatry*, Montreal, University of Toronto Press, Vol. 1, 524–30.

JACKSON, D. D. (1960) A critique of the literature on the genetics of schizophrenia, in *The Etiology of Schizophrenia*, (ed. D. D. Jackson), Basic Books, New York.

KALLMANN, F. J. (1946) The genetic theory of schizophrenia. An analysis of 691 schizophrenic twin index families, *Am. J. Psychiat.* **103**, 309–22.

KALLMANN, F. J. (1950) The genetics of psychoses; an analysis of 1232 twin index families, *Congr. Intern. Psychiat. Paris*, VI, 1–40.

KRINGLEN, E. (1964a) Discordance with respect to schizophrenia in monozygotic male twins, *J. Nerv. Ment. Dis.* **138**, 26–31.

KRINGLEN, E. (1964b) *Schizophrenia in Male Monozygotic Twins*, University Press, Oslo; and *Acta psychiat. scand.*, Suppl. 178.

KRINGLEN, E. (1966) Schizophrenia in twins. An epidemiological–clinical study, *Psychiatry* **29**, 172–84.

KRINGLEN, E. (1967a) Hereditary and social factors in schizophrenic twins; an epidemiological–clinical study, presented at the First Rochester International Conference on Schizophrenia, March 1967.

KRINGLEN, E. (1967b) *Heredity and Environment in the Functional Psychoses. An Epidemiological–Clinical Twin Study*, University Press, Oslo and Heinemann, London.

LIDZ, T., WILD, C. et al. (1961) Thought disorder in the parents of schizophrenic patients, *J. Psychiat. Res.* **1**, 193–200.

LUXENBURGER, H. (1928) Vorläufiger Bericht über psychiatrische Serienuntersuchungen an Zwillingen, *Z. g-s. Neurol. Psychiat.* **116**, 297–326.

LUXENBURGER, H. (1934) Die Manifestationswahrscheinlichkeit der Schizophrenie im Lichte der Zwillingsforschung, *Z. psych. Hyg.* **7**, 174–84.

LUXENBURGER, H. (1936) Untersuchungen an Schizophrenen Zwillingen und ihren Geschwistern zur Prüfung der Realität von Manifestations-Schwankungen, *Z. ges. Neurol. Psychiat.* **154**, 351–94.

MITSUDA, H. (1957) Klinisch-Erbbiologische Untersuchungen der endogenen Psychosen, *Acta genet.* (*Basel*) **7**, 371–7.

POLLIN, W., STABENAU, J. R., and TUPIN, J. (1965) Family studies with identical twins discordant for schizophrenia, *Psychiatry* **28**, 60–78.

ROSANOFF, A. J., HANDY, L. M., PLESSET, I. R., and BRUSH, S. (1934) The etiology of so-called schizophrenic psychoses with special reference to their occurrence in twins, *Am. J. Psychiat.* **91**, 247–86.

ROSENTHAL, D. (1959) Some factors associated with concordance and discordance with respect to schizophrenia in identical twins, *J. Nerv. Ment. Dis.* **129**, 1–10.

ROSENTHAL, D. (1961) Sex distribution and severity of illness among samples of schizophrenic twins, *J. Psychiat. Res.* **1**, 26–36.

ROSENTHAL, D. (1962) Familial concordance by sex with respect to schizophrenia, *Psychol. Bull.* **59**, 401–21.

SINGER, M. T. and WYNNE, L. C. (1963) Differentiating characteristics of parents of childhood schizophrenics, childhood neurotics, and young adult schizophrenics, *Am. J. Psychiat.* **120**, 234–43.

SLATER, E. (1953) *Psychotic and Neurotic Illnesses in Twins*, Her Majesty's Stationery Office, London.

STERN, C. (1960) *Principles of Human Genetics*, Freeman, San Francisco.

TIENARI, P. (1963) Psychiatric illnesses in identical twins, *Acta psychiat. scand.*, Suppl. 171.

STUDIES ON THE OFFSPRING OF TWO SCHIZOPHRENIC PARENTS*

L. Erlenmeyer-Kimling

Department of Medical Genetics, New York State Psychiatric Institute,
College of Physicians and Surgeons, Columbia University, New York, N.Y.

It is now generally agreed that both heredity and environment are important in producing schizophrenia. Indeed, this is so well recognized that, as Kringlen (1967) has recently pointed out, the conclusion is a "trivial" one. The key to schizophrenia, therefore, may be understood to lie in the nature of the interaction between genic products and environmental factors. The question to be asked is not "What are the relative contributions of heredity and environment", but rather "What kinds of environmental input trigger manifestations of the disorder in genotypically vulnerable persons, and why are these important, in a psychophysiological sense?"

If schizophrenia were a disease occurring in self-reproducing plants, it would only be necessary to submit the clones to a spectrum of environments to obtain an index of the range of reaction of the genotype—or series of genotypes if different clones were found to express the disease under certain conditions. As it is, there are at least two approaches to the problem of interaction in schizophrenia. One is a retrospective approach that seeks to analyze interaction through intensive historical probing of the environmental dissimilarities experienced by genotypically identical individuals, i.e., monozygotic twins, who are discordant for the manifestation of schizophrenia (Allen, 1954; Pollin et al., 1966). The second is a prospective design. It involves developmental studies of high-risk populations in which the attempt is made to chart, in medias res, the impact of environmental factors upon the course of behavioral maturation and to correlate these longitudinally with mental status outcome in later years. High-risk populations for developmental studies are, by definition, children with schizophrenia in one or both parents. There are, to my knowledge, two longitudinal investigations on high-risk populations now active, viz. those of Mednick and Schulsinger in Denmark and of Rosenthal and colleagues in Israel.[1] These studies deal chiefly with the children of one affected parent.

In this paper I should like to consider the offspring of two schizophrenic parents (dual matings) as candidates for longitudinal research and to present, in a tentative way, a design

* Research reported in this paper is supported by a grant (MH–03532) from the National Institute of Mental Health, U.S. Public Health Service and a grant from the Scottish Rite Committee on Research in Schizophrenia. Pilot work in progress is supported by General Research Support Grant 5560, National Institutes of Health, to the New York State Psychiatric Institute.

[1] Two other studies should be mentioned. One is Sobel's (1961) investigation of infants born to schizophrenic mothers; this study is no longer active. The second is the research being carried out by B. Fish and colleagues (1966); although this work is not based specifically on high-risk populations of the type considered here, it is yielding a great deal of valuable longitudinal data.

that has seemed to me to offer interesting possibilities for the analysis of gene-environment interaction. Any research design, of course, is laid out to deal with questions that seem important within the designer's own conceptual framework of the problem. I should like, therefore, to discuss briefly also my own current way of thinking about schizophrenia.

DUAL MATINGS AND THEIR OFFSPRING

If the offspring of dual mating couples are to be offered as candidates for developmental studies, several questions should be considered. These have to do with: (1) the probability that such children will manifest schizophrenia, (2) the expectancy of locating dual mating cases through sampling procedures, and (3) the likelihood that a reasonable number of the children of dual mating parents will be useful for developmental research.

Schizophrenia risk

Data from the 5 investigations on dual mating children may be used in evaluating the schizophrenia risk. These are the studies of Elsässer (1952), Kahn (1923), Kallmann (1938), Lewis (1957) and Schulz (1940). All were retrospective and were concerned chiefly with the estimation of morbidity risk figures. The 5 studies have been amply reviewed, most recently and thoroughly by Rosenthal (1966), and the reader is referred to that paper for more complete details. Table 1 summarizes data from the previous studies and shows the crude percentage of definite schizophrenic cases among the children aged 15 or over in each study. For all of the material combined, the crude percentage is 25·2%.

TABLE 1. SUMMARY OF FIVE STUDIES OF OFFSPRING OF TWO SCHIZOPHRENIC PARENTS

		Children				
Investigator	Total families*	Ever-born†‡	Surviving to age 15 and over†‡	Schizo-phrenia§	Crude (%)	Questionable schizophrenia
Kahn, 1923	8	26	17	7	41·1	2
Kallmann, 1938	12	55	35	13	37·1	3
Schulz, 1940	23	92†	59†	13	22·0	5
Elsässer, 1952	15	72	56	12	21·4	3
Lewis, 1957	7	27‡	27‡	4	14·8	0
Total	65	272	194	49	25·2	13

* Excludes infertile marriages and those discarded by investigators because children were too young or because children could not be traced.
† One child of doubtful paternity (and also doubtful schizophrenia) excluded by Schulz in his calculations is also excluded here.
‡ Lewis does not give number ever-born and includes only those children who were age 20 or over at investigation.
§ Per investigators, not reassessed.

Age-corrected morbidity risk estimates vary according to the method of calculation. Estimates reported by the original investigators range from 36·1 % (Elsässer's figure for his own material using the Strömgren method) to 55·3% (Kallmann's estimate for definite schizophrenia in his cases, using the abridged Weinberg method—Kallmann's well-known figure of 68·1% includes the three questionable cases). Rosenthal (1966) has made several calculations of morbidity expectancy rates on the combined material, excluding the Kallmann study. These are: 34·3% for the Strömgren method, 43·6% for the abridged Weinberg method with the risk period taken as ages 15–45, and 35·7% for the unabridged Weinberg method (excluding Lewis as well as Kallmann).

In presenting the foregoing calculations, Rosenthal has carefully discussed the problem of handling the individuals classified as "questionable schizophrenia", as well as those with other psychiatric conditions. He rightly points out that inclusion of both of these groups would substantially increase the risk estimates but that the grounds for their inclusion are doubtful. On the other hand, the validity of including them with the "normal" cases is doubtful also. It might be best to use a method of differential weighting at least for the cases classified as "questionable schizophrenia". Schulz (1940), for example, considered counting the questionable cases as one-half in the schizophrenia-risk estimates. If this were done with the combined material of the 4 studies considered by Rosenthal, however, the estimates would be increased by only about 5%.

For the record, the Kallmann data should be included in the composite analysis. The Strömgren and the unabridged Weinberg methods cannot be used for all 5 studies, but computations may be carried out with the abridged Weinberg method as in Table 2. Without differential weighting of the questionable cases, the morbidity risk estimate for all 5 studies combined is 39·2%; with the 13 questionable cases counted as one-half, the estimate rises to 44·4%.

TABLE 2. CALCULATION OF MORBIDITY RISK, BY THE ABRIDGED WEINBERG METHOD, FOR OFFSPRING OF DUAL MATINGS IN THE FIVE PREVIOUS STUDIES

Age	Kahn (1923)			Kallmann (1938)			Schulz (1940)			Elsässer (1952)			Lewis (1957)			Combined		
	N	S	Q	N	S	Q	N	S	Q	N	S	Q	Tot.	S	Q	Tot.	S	Q
under 15	9	—	—	20	—	—	34	—	—	16	—	—	—	—	—	79	—	—
15–44	10	3	—	23	7	1	42	12	3	42	9	—	*	**	—	117*	31**	4
45 and over	7	4	2	12	6	2	16	1	2	14	3	3	*	**	—	49*	14**	9
Total	26	7	2	55	13	3	92	13	5	72	12	3	27	4	0	245 (+L.) 272	45 (+Lewis) 49	13

N=total number in the age group, including nonsurvivors.
S=definite cases of schizophrenia according to the investigator.
Q=questionable cases of schizophrenia.
* Distribution unknown. Age corrected = 17·5.   ** Distribution unknown.

It is clear, therefore, that the overall calculations of morbidity risk for the dual mating children remain in the neighborhood of 35–44%, depending upon the method used for computation, the studies included and the treatment of questionable cases. Although the final figures are well below the often-quoted 68%, the dual mating children are still, as might be expected, the group with the highest risk for developing schizophrenia, with the exception of MZ cotwins.[2]

On the basis of schizophrenia risk, then, the children of two schizophrenic parents are an ideal group for prospective research. Follow-up of a sizeable sample of such children should yield a sufficiently large number of subjects in whom the effects of gene-environment interaction may be observed and statistically analyzed. Moreover, Rosenthal's analysis (1966) of the ages at first admission among the children in 4 of the studies (Kallmann's excluded) shows that over 75% of those who are eventually hospitalized will be admitted by their mid-twenties. Thus follow-up studies need not be extended throughout the entire risk period (upper limit usually set arbitrarily at age 45–50) to obtain maximum information about the children.

Probability of ascertainment

Although children with one schizophrenic parent have a lower expectancy of manifesting schizophrenia—9–16% (cf. Kallmann et al., 1964)—they are more readily available as subjects than are dual mating children. For example, a recent fertility study shows that more than 33% of schizophrenic women (in New York State) will have at least one child by the time of first admission (Erlenmeyer-Kimling et al., in press). Despite the greater opportunity of observing the unfolding of interaction patterns pertinent to schizophrenia in dual mating children, this group will be of no use for research if samples of adequate size cannot be collected. Four of the five previous studies present a gloomy outlook with respect to the probability of ascertainment. While the investigators do not state the numbers of schizophrenic admissions from which the dual mating cases were drawn, it is clear that the handful of acceptable cases in each study was culled from a large number of admissions over a period of many years. Kallmann is known to have considered the dual mating families to be very rare: he used to say that for a number of years he had offered a dollar (which he had increased to 5 with inflation) to anyone who would notify him of a fertile marriage between two diagnostically verifiable schizophrenic patients.

The frequency of dual mating cases may be roughly estimated from Kallmann's 1938 data. The total sample contained 1087 schizophrenic probands. Among these 14 dual mating couples were located. Of these, 12 were fertile, and evidently 3 of the marriages were between two probands (p. 165), so that the effective number for a frequency count would be 9. The expectancy of locating a fertile dual mating case in a population of schizophrenic patients would thus, on the basis of Kallmann's material, be about 1 : 121. The expectancy of

---

[2] In contrast to the uncorrected schizophrenia rate of 25·2% found for the offspring of two schizophrenic parents, calculations on the pooled data for the 11 major twin studies give an uncorrected concordance rate of 58·7%, or if the studies are weighted to equalize their contributions to the combined total, 52·4%. The weighting procedure gives disproportionate emphasis to the smaller studies which tend to show lower concordance rates. The weighted figure, however, does not diverge greatly from the unweighted, thus lending support to the claim made by Gottesman and Shields (1966) that the various twin studies constitute replications of the same experiment. Figures are based on: Essen-Möller, 1941; Gottesman and Shields, 1966; Harvald and Hauge, cited by Gottesman and Shields; Inouye, 1961; Kallmann, 1946; Kallmann and Roth, 1956; Kringlen, 1966; Luxenburger, 1928; Rosanoff et al., 1934; Slater, 1953 (resident and consecutive series); Tienari, 1963.

ascertaining a MZ twin (whose cotwin survived to adulthood) in a population of schizo-phrenic patients has been estimated by Rosenthal (1960) as about 1 : 210.[3] The chance of obtaining a dual mating case for study would thus seem to be considerably better than the chance of obtaining a useful MZ twin! The 11 studies (cited in footnote 2) carried out on MZ twins include a total of 441 pairs, in contrast to the 5 studies of dual mating families with a total of 65 couples.

The frequency of dual matings obtained through sampling will vary for time and place according to changing marriage and fertility patterns. Further calculations regarding the frequency of marriages between two schizophrenics may be obtained from a newer collection of cases.[4] A brief report on this collection has appeared elsewhere (Kallmann et al., 1964); since that time 6 additional cases, with a total of 15 children, have been ascertained. The collection consists of 3 groups. One of them (Group S) qualifies as a legitimate series of cases ascertained through sampling procedures. The Group S cases were located in the course of an investigation of marriage and fertility trends among schizophrenic patients admitted to 11 of the New York State hospitals in 1934–6 or 1954–6. Patients in the main study were obtained by sampling and diagnostically reviewing consecutive admissions to the 11 hospitals during each period. Only those cases with verifiable diagnoses of schizophrenia (and who were over the age of 15 at admission) were retained for investigation. Detailed des-criptions of the sampling and diagnostic verification procedures, as well as follow-up of psychiatric histories of the relatives of the patients, in the main study are reported elsewhere (Erlenmeyer-Kimling et al., 1966, and in press). Information was sought on the psychiatric histories of all spouses. Those classified as acceptable dual mating spouses had had at least one admission to a mental hospital and had received a hospital diagnosis of schizophrenia which was independently confirmed on the basis of clinical records by at least two psy-chiatrists on our staff. As it happens, no patients in the main study were married to each other. Three fertile matings that occurred between schizophrenic patients in hospital (i.e., between an index case and another schizophrenic patient) are included in the group.

The other 2 groups in the current collection are not useful for estimating the frequency of dual mating cases ascertainable through sampling. Group I was obtained through inquiries with ward and social service personnel at the hospitals sampled in the fertility study. Strictly speaking, it is not a sample. Diagnostic criteria for both spouses, however, were the same as for Group S. The 41 pairs (32 fertile) in Group I were retained out of a total of 145 cases reported, the remainder having failed to meet stringent diagnostic criteria. Group P, consisting of 4 sets of parents of index cases in the main fertility study, is even less appro-priately termed a sample, although both parents in each set had received hospital diagnoses of schizophrenia. In total, the collection includes 66 fertile matings with 169 children surviving to age 15 or over. The number of children in each group, as well as age and sex distributions of survivors, is given in Table 3.

[3] Rosenthal points out that this probability would vary for time and place according to the frequency of twin births and to the infant mortality differential for MZ twins compared to single-born persons. He reports as observed ratios 1 : 542 for Essen-Möller's Swedish material (1941) and between 1 : 121 to 1 : 229 for Luxenburger's German material (1928).

[4] This collection was started in 1961 by Dr. Franz J. Kallmann. Credit for much of the work on this material as well as the initial analyses, goes to Dr. Arthur Falek (now Chief, Division of Human Genetics, Georgia Mental Health Institute, Atlanta, Georgia).

F

Table 3. Statistical Description of Dual Mating Cases included in the Present Study
(see text for explanation of groups)

	Group S	Group I	Combined	Group P
Number pairs*	35*	41	76	4
Fertile pairs*	30*	32	62	4
Children:				
Ever-born	79	81	160	25
Stillbirths,† deaths before age 15	13	2	15	1
Surviving to age 15 or older, or under 15 and living	66	79	145	24
Ages at last information‡				
<15 (living)	20 (30%)	41 (52%)	61 (42%)	—
15–19	9 (14%)	17 (22%)	26 (18%)	—
20–44	29 (44%)	16 (20%)	45 (31%)	—
45 and over	8 (12%)	5 (6%)	13 (9%)	—
Male	27 (41%)	42 (53%)	69 (48%)	10 (42%)
Female	38 (58%)	37 (47%)	75 (52%)	14 (58%)
Sex unknown	1 (1%)	0	1 (<1%)	0

* Includes three fertile in-hospital matings.
† Minimum figures obtained for stillbirths.
‡ Mean year of last information 1964.

For purposes of estimating the expectancy of locating dual mating cases, only Group S may be considered. As seen in Table 4, one out of every 151 patients studied in the earlier survey period of the fertility investigation had offspring by another schizophrenic individual.

Table 4. Fertile Dual Mating Cases ascertained in a Study of Marriage and Fertility Trends among Samples of Schizophrenic Patients admitted to 11 State Hospitals in New York during the Survey Years 1934–6 and 1954–6

	Survey period 1934–6			Survey period 1954–6		
	Male	Female	Total	Male	Female	Total
Total schizophrenic patients sampled*	878	934	1812	660	695	1355
White	815	860	1675	565	580	1145
Nonwhite	63	74	137	95	115	210
Dual mating patients†	5	7	12	7	11	18
White	5	7	12	6	8	14
Nonwhite	—	—	—	1	3	4
Ratio—d.m. to total	1:176	1:133	1:151	1:94	1:63	1:75
Ratio—d.m. white to total white	1:163	1:123	1:140	1:94	1:73	1:82

* Excludes 170 patients for whom no history was available.
† Fertile only. Includes 3 in-hospital matings between verified schizophrenic patients.

For the later period, the figure rises to one in 75, or one in 82 if nonwhite cases are omitted. The proportion would increase further to about 1 : 40, if unmarried persons in the total patient population were screened out. Based on the more current sample, then, the expectancy of locating a fertile dual mating is between 2·5 to 5 times as great as the expectancy of locating a schizophrenic MZ twin with surviving cotwin. There does not seem to be any *a priori* reason for treating the offspring of two schizophrenic parents as an inaccessible population.

Ages of dual mating parents and children

There may be other factors that argue against the feasibility of doing developmental studies with dual mating children. For example, the family does not become "officially" a dual mating case until both parents have been hospitalized. By the time that the second parent is admitted, however, the family members might be too old to be useful as subjects for research that has as its goal the evaluation of gene-environment interaction over the course of development.

The previous studies suggest that this may be a problem. Lewis (1957) stated that a sample of dual mating parents "will contain a higher proportion of patients whose illness began in middle life" (p. 363), and it would follow that the children would probably be past the ages of interest before the family could come to attention. Rosenthal's analysis (1966) of the combined material of Kahn, Schulz and Elsässer shows that the average ages at first admission were 36·6 years for fathers and 37·6 years for mothers in the dual mating couples. These are certainly older than the first admission ages of schizophrenic patients in general, and, as Rosenthal notes, significantly older than the admission ages of the children.

Again, reference to the newer collection of cases is of interest. Data for Groups S and I have been pooled in Table 5, as there are no significant differences between the 2 groups.

TABLE 5. Mean Ages of the Spouses in Groups S and I
(pooled data for 59 pairs)*†

Age (in years)	Husband		Wife	
	Mean	S.E.	Mean	S.E.
Onset of psychosis (estimate)	27·9	1·41	25·7	1·12
First admission	32·9	1·21	29·9	1·39
Marriage (to d.m. partner)	27·5	0·75	23·8	0·70
Birth of first child (d.m.)	29·6	0·69	26·0	0·77

* Groups S and I do not differ significantly with respect to these characteristics.
† The three in-hospital matings from Group S are omitted.

Mean ages at first admission are $32·9 \pm 1·2$ years for husbands and $29·9 \pm 1·4$ years for wives; $31·42 \pm 0·9$ years for both sexes combined. These cases are significantly younger at first admission than the dual mating partners in the previous investigations (for both sexes $t = 4·35$, $p < 0·001$; for males, $t = 2·05$, $p < 0·05$; for females, $t = 3·85$, $p < 0·002$).

The difference in admission ages may be due to changes in patterns of hospitalization, marriage and fertility between the time of collection of the old and the new materials. There is, however, a marked difference in the criteria used in selection of cases for the previous investigations and the present one. The earlier studies were concerned with morbidity-risk estimates. The investigators specifically discarded families that did not contain at least one child aged 20 or over, as well as families in which children could not be traced for psychiatric evaluation. Their reported cases, therefore, are representative of that portion of the available material that met the foregoing criteria, and not of dual mating cases generally. It is not claimed that Group I, or the combined material for S and I, is representative either (although S alone is), but the cases were unselected with respect to ages of the children and to the possibility of tracing them.

Exactly how selection for age of the children could affect the observed admission ages of the parents is not clear. Nevertheless, some such relationship may exist in the previous material. Analogous findings are observed for the current Group P where at least one child (the fertility-study index case) had to have reached the age of risk for schizophrenia. Only 2 of the 8 parents in Group P were younger than age 39 at first admission. Group P, though, may underrepresent the number of dual matings among parents of index cases. Parents hospitalized during the early part of an index case's life have the greatest chance of being lost; possibly these would also be the parents with younger admission ages. The fertility study includes, for example, 16 index cases who were adopted in early childhood. Information is available on only one of the natural parents of these cases: a hospitalized schizophrenic father. There may, or may not have been dual mating couples among the missing parents. The point is that, in attempting to trace two generations retrospectively as the previous studies did and as has been done with Group P, the cases that may be most easily lost are those in which hospitalization of the parents totally disrupts the home early in the child's life. The parents in these cases may be admitted at an earlier age. This is rather tortuous reasoning, but it is one way of accounting for the differences among the various sets of data.

A further comment should be added about the ages at admission and the issue of severity of schizophrenia in the parents. Kallmann (1953), and apparently Lewis, expected that dual mating parents would show mild forms of the disease. If age at admission is used as an index of severity (Rosenthal, 1966), the parents in the previous studies qualify as being mildly affected. Study of the histories, however, shows that subsequent course was quite poor in many of the parents. In the present Group P, at least 5 of the 8 parents qualify as severe cases on the basis of their postadmission histories. In a study of sibling pairs hospitalized for schizophrenia (Erlenmeyer-Kimling, in press), age at admission bears no relationship to final outcome, and data from the main fertility study suggest that persons admitted at younger ages are more likely to be discharged within a given period of time than persons admitted at older ages (Erlenmeyer-Kimling et al., in press). The use of admission age as an index of severity may be questioned, therefore, as may the hypothesis that dual mating parents tend to be only mildly affected.

For the purposes of this paper, the parental ages at first admission are of interest chiefly in so far as they may be correlated with the expectancy of locating young children whose parents have both already been identified as schizophrenic. Table 6 shows, for Groups S and I, the age distribution of living children at the time of the second parent's hospitalization, as well as the numbers of children born during and after hospitalization. The average age of living children at the time of the second parent's hospitalization was 7 years; approximately 68% of these children were aged 10 or younger. Of all children surviving to adolescence, 23% were born during or after the second parent's hospitalization. Longitudinal

Table 6. Birth of Children in Relation to Hospitalization of Parents and Age Distribution at Time of Second Parent's Admission

Group and ages of children	Born by admission of second parent	Born during hospitalization of second parent	Born after admission of second parent	Total children*
Group S	49 (75·4%)	5 (7·7%)	11 (16·9%)	65 (100·0%)
Group I	62 (78·5%)	2 (2·5%)	15 (19·0%)	79 (100·0%)
Combined total:	111 (100·0%)	7	26	144
Ages 0–6	56 (50·5%)	—	—	—
Ages 7–10	20 (18·0%)	—	—	—
Ages 11–14	12 (10·8%)	—	—	—
Ages 15 and over	23 (20·7%)	—	—	—

* Surviving children. Birth of one case unknown in relation to hospitalization of parents.

follow-up of parents like the ones in these groups would thus yield a respectably large sample of children in age ranges appropriate for a developmental study.

Childhood placement histories

One final question about the dual mating offspring may be evaluated from the data on the current collection. What happens to the children during their formative years? Table 7 shows the placement histories of the children up to the age of 15. Only 21·6% remained in continuous residence at home with one or both parents during childhood; approximately 16% were reared by relatives. More than 38% were placed in foster homes or agency care, and thus away from the influence of the biological family altogether. Unfortunately, the

Table 7. Childhood Placement Histories of the 182 Children of Two Schizophrenic Parents—All Three Groups Combined
(adapted from Tables 6 and 7, Kallmann et al., 1964)

Children	Continuous home care	Deceased or undetermined as to placement*	Placed with relatives	Otherwise placed out of home
Number	40	45	29	71
%	21·6	24·3	15·7	38·4

* 15 deceased in childhood; 32 histories are unclear.

recording of exact ages at separation from the family is inadequate, although it is probable that most of the separations occurred before the child was 10 years old. It also seems apparent from scrutiny of the family histories that very few of the children were given out for adoption during infancy.

Whether these histories are representative of the offspring of dual mating children in general remains to be seen. The data do provide an alert to the kinds of environmental disruptions that must be anticipated in planning a longitudinal investigation. If adopted children are desired as subjects, they should be obtainable in adequate supply, although not necessarily with separation from the affected parents dating from the earliest years. Fewer children may be available for a continuously home-reared group, and even those that do remain at home will probably experience major upheavals during the course of childhood as one or both parents undergo readmissions to hospital. Control for such factors is seen as one of the major problems in designing effective developmental investigations with the high-risk population.

In summary the cumulative data on dual mating families show: (1) That the morbidity expectancy for the offspring is in the neighborhood of 35–44%, depending upon how the cases are counted. While the figures are lower than sometimes reported, they are sufficiently high that a substantial number of the children to be studied may be expected to manifest schizophrenia eventually. (2) That the frequency of fertile dual mating couples ascertainable through sampling should be moderately high. (3) That the age of dual mating partners at first admission is, at least in current samples, not as high as previously reported, and that a large proportion of the children are either in the preadolescent age range when the second parent is admitted to hospital for the first time, or are born after that hospitalization. Thus, children in the younger age groups may be more accessible than had been indicated by the earlier studies. (4) That problems of maintaining contact with the children and of analyzing the effects of major disruptions of environmental surroundings upon the child's subsequent behavioral patterns represent critical points to be foreseen and accounted for in the design of research.

Despite the latter difficulties, the overview of the data encourages the idea that the offspring of schizophrenic parents can be drawn upon as an effective population for longitudinal study.

CONCEPTUAL FRAMEWORK

Genic errors are assumed to underlie all true cases of schizophrenia as well as certain marginal conditions. Phenocopying may occur also and such cases should be distinguished be several features (e.g. absence of family history of schizophrenia, presence of irritative lesions of the CNS or of chemical or physical trauma or of extreme psychological stress preceding onset of the schizophreniform disorder). It is currently not possible to isolate these cases with certainty, but it is probable that phenocopies account for a relatively small proportion of the schizophrenic population.

A distinction should be made between genes and their primary products on the one hand and the intermediary mechanisms that constitute the predisposition to schizophrenia on the other hand. Gene action is responsible for setting up a physiological imbalance. The pathways between genes and the intermediary mechanisms are probably very little influenced by external environment, although interaction with other genes out of the total genotypic milieu is quite likely. At the level of the intermediary mechanisms, however, environmental interaction undoubtedly plays a large role.

The degree of predisposition varies. There are two possible models to explain this. One is the polygenic-threshold model suggested by Edwards (1960), by Gottesman and Shields (1966, 1967) and others. Essentially, this model states that the predisposition is determined by a complex of genes acting together and that a given degree of allelic loading surpassing a threshold cut-off point is necessary for the manifestation of schizophrenia. Expression or not-expression and gradations in severity are thus seen in terms of quantitative loading in relation to the threshold, as well as environmental shaping. Since Gottesman and Shields will summarize the evidence for the polygenic theory most elegantly, it is unnecessary to say more here, except to agree that the model can be used to explain various aspects of the cumulative data on familial risk distributions quite well.

A second possible model is one in which schizophrenia is regarded as a heterogeneous collection of entities stemming from a number of different, independently acting genic errors (cf. Erlenmeyer-Kimling and Paradowski, 1966; Planansky, 1955), analogous to the situation for mental deficiency (Jervis, 1962; Morton, 1960), to the group of diseases known as Fanconi syndrome (cf. discussion by Sutton, pp. 291–3, 1962) and to several other disease groups. According to this model, a number of different primary enzymatic defects could feed into a final common pathway or intermediary mechanism. The extent to which the final pathway is disrupted might be different, however, depending upon the route taken in reaching it, so that variations in predisposition could exist between the different genotypes. Multiple allele series at given loci are also possible—with different alleles producing different degrees of effect. The activity of the various genes will, furthermore, be modulated by the total genotypic background against which the alleles are placed. Interaction at the genotypic level, however, does not necessarily imply a specific system of modifiers or suppressors as suggested in Kallmann's theory (1946). Finally, both the degree of predisposition and the influences of environmental factors will cooperate to determine whether schizophrenia, psychological disturbances of lesser sorts, or perhaps no symptomatology becomes manifest at the behavioral level.

Although implications of the two models are not the same, it is presently difficult to distinguish between them. The heterogeneity model, like the polygenic one, is capable of explaining discordance in MZ twins and the fact that morbidity expectancy in the children of 2 schizophrenic parents is lower than would be required under straightforward single gene models. Both have better possibilities of explaining the maintenance of schizophrenia in populations over the evolutionary course of history than do single gene models (Erlenmeyer-Kimling and Paradowski, 1966; Gottesman and Shields, 1967).[5]

With either of these two models, it is easy to see why a specific biochemical error has thus far failed to be established on firm ground. Of the two, the heterogeneity model perhaps holds forth more optimism with regard to an ultimate biochemical solution to schizophrenia —or rather group of solutions—since with properly designed family studies, it may be possible to delimit a series of specific errors. Primary biochemical deficiencies would be extremely difficult to identify, however, if, for example, the enzymes upon which the genes

---

[5] It may be noted that some of the differences in family-risk data obtained in the Scandinavian studies and those conducted elsewhere could be due, quite apart from the usual diagnostic problems, to population differences in degree of severity. Estimated overall incidence could be the same although proportions of severe and mild cases might differ. The two models discussed here could explain such variations without resorting to environmental differences. In the polygenic model, it would be postulated that allelic frequencies differ in the populations in question, so that the probability of recombinations quantitatively sufficient for severe forms would be increased in some, decreased in other, populations. In the heterogeneity model, it is only necessary that the frequency of alleles at different loci varies across populations. It would be of interest to compare United States subpopulations of comparatively unmixed descent, with uniform diagnostic criteria to determine whether differences in severity exist among them.

have their basic effects were important only in embryonic or early developmental stages in the formation of nervous tissue, later becoming inactive.

In attempting to study gene-environment interaction, however, we are concerned to a greater extent with the intervening psychophysiological mechanisms into which primary gene products are translated, rather than the primary products themselves. I should like to pursue one line of speculation, out of the many possible ones, about the nature of the intervening mechanisms. Differences in sensory and perceptual processes from person-to-person seem to provide a clue to much of psychological individuality in the normal range of behavior (Erlenmeyer-Kimling *et al.,* 1963), and it is tempting to consider that excessive responsivity to sensory input with resulting distortions of perceptualization may underlie schizophrenic disturbances. Miller (1960) suggested that information input overload might be a possible antecedent of psychopathology; he pointed out that beyond a certain level of input, output decreases in a "confusional state" and that costs (e.g. the amount of energy required to transmit an average bit of information) at very high rates of input are probably much greater than at low rates. Miller's information input overload may be seen as corresponding to sensory input overload.

The idea that perceptual distortions are associated with schizophrenia is certainly one that has been expressed many times and that has been documented by a very large amount of experimental data (cf. Venables, 1964). Hoffer and Osmond (1966) have made the point, however, that relatively few theoretical views of schizophrenia seem to have placed the observed difficulties in perception on the "cause", rather than the "effect", side of the ledger. Hoffer and Osmond themselves emphasize perceptual changes as being causative. McGhie and Chapman (1961) also conclude that much of the symptomatology of schizophrenia may be interpreted as reaction to perceptual change. Their data include self-reports made by acute schizophrenic patients which indicate that the experience of sensory swampage is a real one.

On the basis of their data, McGhie and Chapman and several other investigators, have turned to consideration of the reticular system as the possible mechanism through which schizophrenic disorders are mediated. Lindsley (1961) has noted that the ascending reticular formation (possibly with descending influences as well as corticofugal and centrifugal controlling influences) may be a common basis for the behavioral and subjective phenomena encountered in sensory deprivation, sensory overload and sensory distortion. "Because of its strategic location at the crossroads for incoming and outgoing messages and its apparent ability to sample all such activity and to develop from it a more lasting influence in a form of alerting and attention, the reticular system appears to provide a common mechanism for the foregoing sensory conditions and their effects" (Lindsley, 1961, p. 175). Kornetsky and Mirsky (1966) document the case for reticular system involvement in schizophrenia with evidence from pharmacological and EEG studies which, in their opinion, suggest that "schizophrenic patients are in a state of chronic hyperarousal . . . (resulting) from a dysfunction in those areas of the brain concerned with the maintenance of arousal and attention . . ." (p. 317).

F. Fish (1961, 1962, 1963), in particular, has formulated a detailed theory of the neurophysiological basis of schizophrenia in which overactivity of the reticular system is seen as producing abnormal domination of thought processes by the sensory input. Fish hypothesizes how various stages in the intensification of reticular activity may affect cortical processes and suggests how the degrees of overactivity may be related to paranoid delusions, hallucinatory experiences, catatonia, and hebephrenic behavior. His theory allows for the possibility of checks and reversals of the process to account for remission, as well as for the establishment of self-perpetuating circuits leading to chronic states. The reticular overactivity itself, he notes (1963, p. 166) could be the product of any of several pathways, namely: (1) a biochemical disorder existing within the reticular system; (2) a lesion of the reticular system produced by chemical or physical trauma; (3) focal overactivity in a structure which normally causes reticular activity—this in turn, although Fish does not say so, could presumably be effected either through biochemical deficiencies or irritative lesions; (4) abnormalities or excesses of hormones affecting the adrenergic system which influences the reticular system; (5) failure of inhibitory influences from the cerebral cortex. Other possibilities could undoubtedly be added, for example, high membrane permeability within the reticular system.

It may readily be seen that all except the second possibility in Fish's list could result from gene-controlled defects; the trauma-induced lesion could account for some phenocopies. If the polygenic model of schizophrenia is taken, it will be assumed that the gene complex works along only one of these pathways. If the heterogeneity model is considered, different genes may be expected to work their effects through different pathways, all leading to the common end-result of reticular overactivity. Indeed, in summarizing the case for his theory, Fish (1963) states that "it is highly probable that there are many different kinds of schizophrenia due to many different causes" (p. 167).

Certainly, the reticular system seems to offer good possibilities as the intermediary mechanism in schizophrenia. Behavioral phenomena following from the experience of sensory overload may be seen as a branching chain, with all of the ramifications observed in the various forms of schizophrenia being possible. At the first level of the chain are perceptual distortions, thought disorder and attempts at defensive coping with, or screening out of, the excess input. Anxiety is a function of perceptual distortion at least and may follow from other points in the chain as well. Anxiety may either link into a positive feedback to reticular overarousal, thereby intensifying the entire process, or in moderate degree may provide support for maintenance of the defensive screen.

The success in building and maintaining a defensive screen will be contingent partially upon the genetically mediated severity of the fundamental dysfunction (predisposition) and partially upon environmental factors. Stressful environments which break down a defensive screen or prevent one from being adequately constructed will have the effect of recircuiting the behavior chain into higher and higher levels of overarousal. Environmental situations containing low stress may permit defensive screens to be preserved successfully for longer periods of time or even permanently. Maintenance of a screening mechanism, which probably includes selective inattention and selective withdrawal, however, may be achieved at relatively high cost to the individual in terms of expenditure of energy, so that personality deficits result. Indeed, marginal states in general may be the reflection of various permutations of degree of predisposition and degree of environmental stress. Rosenthal (1963) has pointed out the intensity of potential environmental stressors, like the degree of inherited predisposition, may be continuously graded, and that the severity of expression would depend upon both. It will be the purpose of developmental studies of high-risk populations, such as the one tentatively outlined in the following section, to attempt to isolate the relationship between behavioral change, particularly at the perceptual level, and specific kinds and intensities of incoming environmental stresses.

TENTATIVE RESEARCH PLAN

The research plan outlined here is a tentative one, with many specific details still to be filled in. In essence, the design is one that permits both longitudinal and cross-sectional comparisons of behavioral and physiological developmental patterns in groups of high-, intermediate-, and low-risk children. The main goals of such a study would be related to the conceptual framework discussed in the previous section, although a family of working hypotheses could be tested simultaneously.

The study would: explore intensively in the area of sensory and perceptual processes; look for possible indicators of abnormal or unusual changes in these over time; look for possible relationships between environmental events and perceptual change, and between perceptual change and changes in other areas of behavior (e.g. learning, personality characteristics and social behavior); look wherever possible for neurophysiological signs correlating with behavioral change. In particular, it would be hypothesized that subjects showing an intensification of perceptual change over time would be those with the greatest probability of manifesting schizophrenia in later years, while those showing moderate perceptual change with little intensification of the process might manifest marginal disorders. It would be important to analyze the ways in which environmental stress influences behavior immediately, as well as longitudinally, and to attempt to classify what constitutes "stress". Similarly, the study would seek to define what constitutes "support", and how stress and support may differ among the various risk groups.

The design in its final form would be arranged to allow for a number of contingencies such as probability of loss of subjects through death, through major disruption of the home, through failure to retain cooperation on a longitudinal basis, etc. Some of the contingencies are included here in the tentative outline. It may be noted that the design is envisaged as providing data of interest to a number of problems in human behavior genetics, in addition to the primary questions centered around the mechanisms of gene-environment interaction in schizophrenia.

Subject groups

Table 8 shows the subject groups that would be included in this design. The three main groups are: a high-risk group consisting of children of two schizophrenic parents; an intermediate-risk group consisting of children of one schizophrenic parent—these will probably be consistently limited to children of schizophrenic mothers; a low-risk group, consisting of children of two nonschizophrenic parents. Each group is divided into home-reared and adopted subgroups and these are further separated into three age groups.

The numbers entered into the various cells of the table are for illustration only. The relative sizes of the cells are selected with certain contingencies in mind. For example, the

TABLE 8. OUTLINE OF RESEARCH GROUPS IN A PROPOSED STUDY OF THE CHILDREN OF SCHIZOPHRENIC PARENTS
(numbers in cells are for illustration only)

Age-group at beginning of study	Children of two schizophrenic parents		Children of one schizophrenic, one "normal" parent		Children of two normal parents	
	Home-reared	Adopted	Home-reared	Adopted	Home-reared	Adopted
Birth–2 years	30	20	30	20	60	40
5–7 years	25	15	25	15	50	30
10–12 years	20	15	20	15	40	30
Subgroup total	75	50	75	50	150	100
Group total	125		125		250	

cells for the children of nonschizophrenic parents contain twice as many subjects as do cells for the other two main groups. This is because each child in the high- and intermediate-risk groups will be matched by a child with nonschizophrenic parents. The ideal format, however, if the pool of children with one schizophrenic parent proves sufficiently large, will be to match dual mating children with one intermediate-risk and two low-risk children. The design would thus yield quartets of children representing three degrees of genetic loading and matching for a number of macro-environmental variables. If the pool of intermediate-risk children is not large enough for choice, the design is capable of falling back on matched pairs rather than quartets.

Matching characteristics will include, in addition to sex, age and home status: ethnic background; educational levels of the parents or long-term guardians; socioeconomic rating of the home; sibship size and structure at initiation of the study. In the adoptive subgroups, at least one further matching criterion will be approximate length of residence in the adoptive home.

The adoptive subgroups are included for two reasons. The obvious one is the attempt to divorce the environmental and hereditary contributions of the biological family. A less apparent reason is the need to meet the problem of disruption of the parental home in the home-reared subgroup of dual mating children (and, to a lesser extent, the children of one schizophrenic parent). As was pointed out in an earlier section, about 21 % of the dual mating children in a current collection of cases remained in continuous residence at home. The remainder were placed out at various times during childhood—about 38 % going to adoptive, foster or agency care. A smaller proportion of the children with one schizophrenic parent may also be expected to experience disruptions of the parental home. Although a fair amount of environmental chaos will have to be anticipated for the children of schizophrenic parents whether they remain in or leave the parental home, total displacement will destroy the efficiency of matches between these children and the children of nonschizophrenic parents. While the displaced children may be followed for descriptive purposes, the matched pair may be lost for the longitudinal analysis of variance. With this in mind, the sizes of the home-reared subgroups are purposely set higher than the adoptive subgroups, which are expected to be relatively stable once they are initially located. The adopted children are expected to be harder to obtain, especially in the youngest age group, but easier to retain.

The home-reared subgroups are also included for two reasons: first, because it will be of importance to know what kinds of environmental surroundings the schizophrenic parents actually provide and how they are perceived by the children over time; second, because the natural parents themselves should be tested. In particular, biochemical and neurophysiological measures will be attempted with the schizophrenic parents. If the genotypic heterogeneity model of schizophrenia has any validity, within-family analyses will be the only way to approach biochemical research. If possible, within-family analyses should be performed by various teams of investigators that currently hold firm hypotheses regarding biochemical factors relating to schizophrenia.

Course of the study and age-groups

The study is planned in 5-year segments. Within one 5-year segment, the youngest age group (birth–2 years) moves into the age range of the middle age group (5–7 years) at the start of the study, the middle age-group moves into the age range of the oldest group (10–12 years) at the start of the study, and the oldest group moves into the beginning of the schizophrenia risk period. The 5-year segments are designated with the specific purpose of blocking out intervals at which reassessment of progress must be carried out. The thought is to provide natural stopping-points in the hope of avoiding some of the pitfalls that have plagued longitudinal studies in the past.

The initial age groups are selected for the following reasons. The youngest group (birth–2 years) is chosen for the purpose of observing the earliest developmental stages, which, as B. Fish *et al.* (1966) suggest, may have high relevancy for the prediction of future pathological outcome. Literature on early experience factors in other mammals also suggests that this may be the critical period for the development of later behavioral patterns (cf. Scott, 1963). The middle age group (5–7 years) is selected because it represents the period when the children will be just entering school and embarking upon a broadened course of social contact outside the family. This may be seen as a second "critical" period within the child's life. The oldest age group (10–12 years) is at the threshold of a third "critical" period. These children will be entering into the turbulent adolescent years that some authors regard as the decisive time for triggering latent potentialities of schizophrenia. It is expected that follow-up of the oldest group may be maintained at relatively low cost for additional 5-year segments to bring the subjects into the maximum risk years for manifestation of schizophrenia.

The choice of age groups in conjunction with the 5-year plan means that it will not only be possible to study the behavioral and physiological development of each group at a given critical period, but that each of the two younger groups will be brought forward to the point of testing them on the same measures used for the subsequent age group at the beginning of the study.

Types of measurements

Only broad categories of measurements are indicated here. Obviously, these will vary across age groups. It is hoped, however, that it will be possible to assemble test batteries and experimental procedures that are relevant for each age group while giving continuity across ages. This will permit assessments of maturation, as well as test–retest reliability.

For the parents (natural and adoptive) the following measures are planned: diagnostic evaluation by a panel of psychiatrists and psychologists as part of the ascertainment procedure before the children can be included into the study; life history inventories; marital adjustment scales; ratings of the emotional tone of the home; ratings of the child's behavior and development; standardized intelligence and personality tests; concept formation and figure-ground measures. Diagnostic re-evaluation will be carried out periodically during the course of the study and parental or guardian ratings of the emotional tone of the home and of the child's behavior will be collected at yearly intervals (more frequently in families undergoing periods of stress). Natural parents, in addition, will have physical, biochemical and neurophysiological measurements.

For the children (age dependent), the following measures are planned: diagnostic evaluation as part of the ascertainment procedure; standardized intelligence and personality tests; motor development; experimental procedures concerned with sensory and perceptual processes (including information processing analyses, cross-modality comparisons, and games designed to elicit information about the subject's ongoing perceptual organization); concept formation; social maturity and social responsiveness (including peer group relationships); school records and teachers' ratings of behavior; anthropometric, biochemical and neurophysiological measures.

Data evaluation will take the form of analyses of variance in a number of directions. They will include comparisons across the main groups, or more specifically, across the matched quartets of children over time. Comparisons of adopted and home-reared children within the high- and intermediate-risk groups will also be of prime importance. Since the conceptual framework discussed in the previous section would suggest that perceptual and physiological changes should be observable in pre-schizophrenic individuals, it will be of particular interest to evaluate intra-individual variability over the course of the study. Within-session lability may also be worth comparing in the different groups of subjects. Possible correlations between environmental variables, as assessed through data on the parents and the home, and behavior will also be sought.

CONCLUDING COMMENTS

A plan for the developmental study of high-, intermediate- and low-risk children is laid out in sketchy fashion here, but it is hoped that the general outline may be of some interest for thinking about research into the problems of gene-environment interaction in schizophrenia.[6]

[6] A study that is being conducted by Dr. E. James Anthony in St. Louis first came to my attention during the course of this Conference. There are many points of similarity between the research outline discussed here and Dr. Anthony's study which is actually in progress, although the latter does not include children of two schizophrenic parents.

Many aspects of the design have not been discussed. One is the problem of sampling. Pilot work is now underway to determine: (1) how this should be done; (2) whether it *can* be done in a locale like the New York Metropolitan area; and (3) whether a sample can actually be retained for follow-up in such an area. Information drawn from the current collection of cases will give some guidelines for the pilot work itself. I hope that the pilot work will also be useful for standardizing interview techniques, developing some of the experimental procedures, and establishing systematic ways for maintaining frequent contact—and making it attractive to the families!

Other problems that have not been discussed have to do with the criteria for selection of the families, details relating to the diagnostic classification and especially the problem of evaluation of the missing natural parents of adoptive children, paternity determinations in doubtful cases, and the ensurance of objectivity on the part of the researchers. I mention these issues here to indicate that they must all be handled before research of this type can proceed. These problems are, of course, equally troublesome in retrospective studies, and it seems possible that the key to the nature of interaction in schizophrenia may be best understood through prospective analysis of developing processes.

ACKNOWLEDGEMENTS

I should like to express my great appreciation to four people for their constant assistance. Miss Elyse vanden Bosch worked long and patiently to update the material on the current collection of dual mating cases. She carried out most of the analyses and helped with the bibliography. Miss Susan Nicol, as always, helped in a variety of ways with the last-minute crisis of completing the manuscript. Mrs. Anne Moscato, as always, gave generously of her time and patience in typing the manuscript. Mrs. Laine Ruut prepared and typed the tables.

REFERENCES

ALLEN, G. (1954) Discussion in Conference on problems and methods in human genetics, *Am. J. Hum. Genet.* **6**, 162.

EDWARDS, J. H. (1960) The simulation of Mendelism, *Acta genet. Statist. med.* **10**, 63.

ELSÄSSER, G. (1952) *Die Nachkommen geisteskranker Elternpaare,* Stuttgart, Thieme.

ERLENMEYER-KIMLING, L. (1968) The sibships of schizophrenics, in (Vandenberg, S., ed.) *Progress in Human Behavior Genetics,* Baltimore, Johns Hopkins Univ. Press.

ERLENMEYER-KIMLING, L., JARVIK, L. F., and KALLMANN, F. J. (1963) Genetics and psychological individuality, Paper read at XVII Internat. Cong. Psychol., Symposium on *Behavior Genetics,* Washington, D.C.

ERLENMEYER-KIMLING, L., NICOL, S., RAINER, J. D. and DEMING, W. E. (in press) Changes in fertility rates of schizophrenic patients in New York State.

ERLENMEYER-KIMLING, L. and PARADOWSKI, W. (1966) Selection and schizophrenia, *Am. Nat.* **100**, 651.

ERLENMEYER-KIMLING, L., RAINER, J. D., and KALLMANN, F. J. (1966) Current reproductive trends in schizophrenia, in (Hoch, P. and Zubin, J., eds.) *Psychopathology of Schizophrenia,* New York, Grune & Stratton.

ESSEN-MÖLLER, E. (1941) Psychiatrische Untersuchungen in einer Serie von Zwillingen, *Acta psychiat. (Kbh.),* Suppl. 23.

FISH, B., WILE, R., SHAPIRO, T., and HALPERN, F. (1966) The prediction of schizophrenia in infancy: II. A ten-year follow-up report of predictions made at one month of age, in (Hoch, P. and Zubin, J., eds.) *Psychopathology of Schizophrenia,* New York, Grune & Stratton.

FISH, F. (1961) A neurophysiological theory of schizophrenia, *J. Ment. Sci.* **107**, 828.

FISH, F. (1962) The functional psychoses in the light of Hebb's theory, *Confin. psychiat. (Basel)* **5**, 130.

FISH, F. (1963) The unitary psychosis—a neurophysiological model, *Confin. psychiat. (Basel)* **6**, 156.

GOTTESMAN, I. I. and SHIELDS, J. (1966) Schizophrenia in twins: 16 years' consecutive admissions to a psychiatric clinic, *Brit. J. Psychiat.* **112**, 809.

GOTTESMAN, I. I. and SHIELDS, J. (1967) Polygenic theory of schizophrenia, *Abst. NAS Sci.* **156**, 537.

HOFFER, A. and OSMOND, H. (1966) Some psychological consequences of perceptual disorder and schizophrenia, *Internat. J. Neuropsychiat.* **2**, 1.

INOUYE, E. (1961) Similarity and dissimilarity of schizophrenia in twins, *Proc. Third World Congress Psychiatry, Montreal*, Vol. 1, 524, Univ. of Toronto Press and McGill Univ. Press.

JERVIS, G. A. (1962) Genetic aspects of mental deficiency, in (Kallmann, F. J., ed.) *Expanding Goals of Genetics in Psychiatry*, New York, Grune & Stratton.

KAHN, E. (1923) Studien über Vererbung und Enstehung geistiger Störungen. IV. Schizoid und Schizophrenie im Erbgang, *Monogrn. Gesamtgeb. Neurol. Psychiat.* **36**.

KALLMANN, F. J. (1938) *The Genetics of Schizophrenia*, New York, Augustin.

KALLMANN, F. J. (1946) The genetic theory of schizophrenia: an analysis of 691 schizophrenic twin index families, *Am. J. Psychiat.* **103**, 309.

KALLMANN, F. J. (1953) *Heredity in Health and Mental Disorder*, New York, Norton.

KALLMANN, F. J., FALEK, A., HURZELER, M., and ERLENMEYER-KIMLING, L. (1964) The developmental aspects of children with two schizophrenic parents, in (Solomon, P. and Glueck, B. C., eds.) *Recent Research on Schizophrenia*, Washington, D.C., Psychiatric Research Report No. 19, American Psychiatric Association.

KALLMANN, F. J. and ROTH, B. (1956) Genetic aspects of preadolescent schizophrenia, *Am. J. Psychiat.* **112**, 599.

KORNETSKY, C. and MIRSKY, A. (1966) On certain psychopharmacological and physiological differences between schizophrenics and normal persons, *Psychopharmacologia (Berl.)* **8**, 309.

KRINGLEN, E. (1966) Schizophrenia in twins: an epidemiological–clinical study, *Psychiatry* **29**, 172.

KRINGLEN, E. (1967) Hereditary and social factors in schizophrenic twins: an epidemiological clinical study, Paper read at First Rochester International Conference on Schizophrenia, Rochester, New York.

LEWIS, A. J. (1957) The offspring of parents both mentally ill, *Acta genet. Statist. med.* **7**, 349.

LINDSLEY, D. B. (1961) Common factors in sensory deprivation, sensory distortion and sensory overload, in (Solomon, P. *et al.*, eds.) *Sensory Deprivation*, Cambridge, Harvard Univ. Press.

LUXENBURGER, H. (1928) Vorläufiger Bericht über psychiatrische Serieuntersuchungen an Zwilligen, *Z. ges. Neurol. Psychiat.* **116**, 297.

MCGHIE, A. and CHAPMAN, J. S. (1961) Disorders of attention and perception in earlier schizophrenia, *Brit. J. Med. Psychol.* **34**, 103.

MILLER, J. G. (1960) Information input overload and psychopathology, *Am. J. Psychiat.* **116**, 695.

MORTON, N. E. (1960) The mutational load due to detrimental genes in man, *Am. J. Hum. Genet.* **12**, 348.

PLANANSKY, K. (1955) Heredity in schizophrenia, *J. Nerv. Ment. Dis.* **122**, 121.

POLLIN, W., STABENAU, J. R., MOSHER, L., and TUPIN, J. (1966) Life history differences in identical twins discordant for schizophrenia, *Am. J. Orthopsychiat.* **36**, 492.

ROSANOFF, A. J., HANDY, L. M., PLESSET, I. R., and BRUSH, S. (1934) The etiology of so-called schizophrenic psychoses with special reference to their occurrence in twins, *Am. J. Psychiat.* **91**, 247.

ROSENTHAL, D. (1960) Confusion of identity and the frequency of schizophrenia in twins, *Arch. Gen. Psychiat.* **3**, 297.

ROSENTHAL, D. (1963) Theoretical overview: a suggested conceptual framework, in (Rosenthal, D., ed.) *The Genain Quadruplets*, New York, Basic Books.

ROSENTHAL, D. (1966) The offspring of schizophrenic couples, *J. Psychiat. Res.* **4**, 169.

SCHULZ, B. (1940) Kinder schizophrener Elternpaare, *Z. ges. Neurol. Psychiat.* **168**, No. 1–3, 332.

SCOTT, J. P. (1963) The process of primary socialization in canine and human infants, *Monogr. Soc. Res. Child Develpm.* **28**, No. 1.

SLATER, E. (with the assistance of SHIELDS, J.) (1953) Psychotic and neurotic illnesses in twins, *Med. Res. Counc. Spec. Rept. Ser.* No. 278, London, Her Majesty's Stationery Office.

SOBEL, D. E. (1961) Children of schizophrenic patients: preliminary observations on early development, *Am. J. Psychiat.* **118**, 512.

SUTTON, H. E. (1962) Metabolic defects in relation to the gene, in (Burdette, W. J., ed.) *Methodology in Human Genetics*, San Francisco, Holden-Day.

TIENARI, P. (1963) Psychiatric illnesses in identical twins, *Acta psychiat. (Kbh.)*. Suppl. 171.

VENABLES, P. H. (1964) Input dysfunction in schizophrenia, in (Maher, B. A., ed.) *Progress in Experimental Personality Research*, Vol. 1, New York, Academic Press.

GENEALOGIC STUDIES OF SCHIZOPHRENIA

JON L. KARLSSON

Department of Pediatrics, School of Medicine,
University of California, San Francisco

IT WOULD appear from material already presented that the evidence in support of a hereditary basis for schizophrenia can be considered sufficiently strong to justify advancing the direction of genetic studies from the question of whether hereditary factors are involved to the next phase of how the genetic transmission occurs. This view is consistent with the conclusions reached by all authorities in genetics who have evaluated the available data.[1, 2, 3] Their assessment does not deny that environmental factors may also be operative, but emphasizes that geneticists are satisfied that hereditary factors have been established to play a role and are prepared to proceed with further research on the genetic aspects of the problem and attempt to define the hereditary mechanisms involved.

One fruitful approach to study the mode of transmission is to investigate families with known psychotic members born more than a century ago. According to the principles of genetics, a continuity of mental disease should be seen in the subsequent generations, and the distribution of the disorder within large kindreds must be consistent with the Mendelian laws. Personality characteristics of non-psychotic relatives of schizophrenics are of special interest, as there are indications that genes involved in schizophrenia may in different combinations influence normal personality traits. This author has proposed that schizophrenics are heterozygous for a gene which is also carried by persons of superior intellect or leadership ability.[3] This hypothesis can be further tested by genealogic studies.

METHODS AND RESULTS

In a previous paper the author has presented extensive pedigrees on an Icelandic kindred whose complete genealogy could be traced for seven generations.[4] Schizophrenia was first encountered in a woman born in 1735, and psychosis occurred in each subsequent generation, usually transmitted through non-psychotic members. It was mentioned that many gifted persons belonged to this kindred and that it might be of interest to determine their positions in the genealogic tree in relation to the occurrence of mental illness. Such a study can at present be done most satisfactorily on persons who were born over 100 years ago. With index cases of more recent origin, the available material would be insufficient.

If gifted persons are selected who were born into the above kindred before the year 1860, an attempt can be made to determine whether they possessed the "dominant" gene felt to be involved in schizophrenia.[3] One can assume that the gene would have existed in one of the parents to be present in an index case. The probability of the full sibs of the index case also having received the gene would be 50%. If there are several sibs who produce children, an accidental loss of the gene is unlikely. By tracing the descendants of the entire sibship for two additional generations, one would hope to gather a sufficient number of persons to be able to judge whether an increased risk of schizophrenia is present and whether the total pattern is similar to that previously described. Because the mental hospital in Reykjavik did not exist until 1907, the earlier generations in such pedigrees are not likely to have had hospital treatment. Precise diagnosis is most likely to have been established for the more recent generations. It must be realized that with available resources not all psychotic cases are identified.

Individuals born before 1860 belong mostly to generations I–V as traced from the original parents.[5] Approximately 1000 persons belong in these generations. In a country

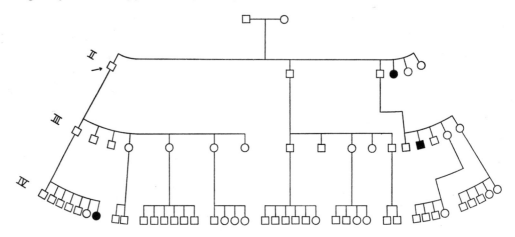

Fig. 1. Family tree of a member of the Icelandic Parliament, marked by an arrow, who was born in 1731. Squares indicate males, circles females. Psychotic persons are shown in black. Individuals who died before age 15 years are eliminated.

composed until recently mostly of farmers, one would not expect to encounter a large fraction of highly gifted individuals who were successful in finding a significant expression for their talents.

A survey covering the entire kindred has led to the identification of 7 persons among the members born before 1860 who can be considered gifted in the sense of being scholars (2), political leaders (2), or financially successful community officials (3). All of these individuals turn out to have psychotic relatives. The first case is a man in generation II who became a representative for his district in the Icelandic Parliament. His pedigree is shown in Fig. 1. The second gifted person, a member of generation III, turns out to be the son of the first case. His family is traced in Fig. 2. Three gifted individuals are encountered in generation IV, two of them being grandchildren of the gifted index case in generation II. Figures 3, 4, and 5 show their pedigrees. No highly distinguished person is known in generation V, but in generation VI a person appears who emigrated to America, became an electrical engineer and organized civic activities, including the establishment of two newspapers. This man is probably the most creative person in the early generations of the kindred, having among

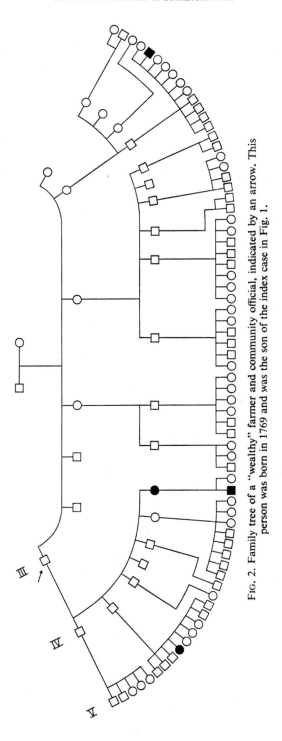

FIG. 2. Family tree of a "wealthy" farmer and community official, indicated by an arrow. This person was born in 1769 and was the son of the index case in Fig. 1.

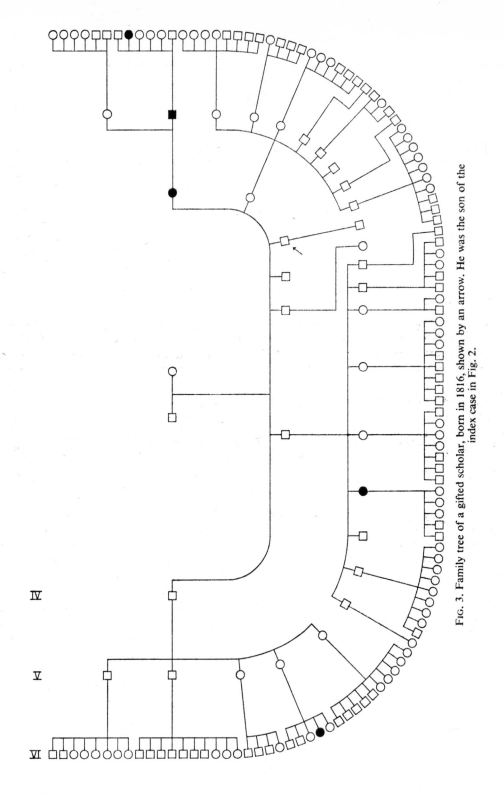

IV   V   VI

FIG. 3. Family tree of a gifted scholar, born in 1816, shown by an arrow. He was the son of the index case in Fig. 2.

other things developed a plan for the electrification of Reykjavik before the turn of the century. A pedigree comparable to the ones shown cannot be established for the latter individual, as he had no full sibs and produced no children. However, he was the grandson of the psychotic sister of the index case in Fig. 3 and also had a psychotic half-sister.

It should be emphasized that this survey embraces all highly distinguished persons who could be identified among the early descendants in all the branches of the kindred. It turns out that most such persons are located in the same branch which in previous studies was shown to have the highest incidence of mental illness.

Figure 1 traces the family of a gifted farmer, born in 1731, who served as a representative for his district in the Icelandic Parliament. Mental illness is seen in his sister as well as in his granddaughter and a nephew.

Figure 2 shows the family of the only gifted person identified in generation III, which includes approximately 100 persons. This man, born in 1769, is described as highly successful

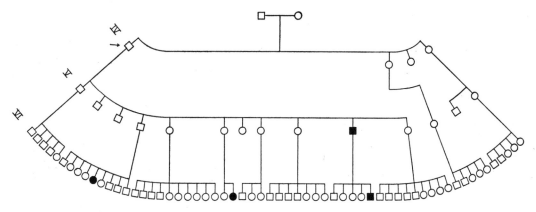

FIG. 4. Family tree of a member of the Icelandic Parliament, who was born in 1813, marked by an arrow. He was a grandson of the index case in Fig. 1.

financially and was an official in his community. Again a pattern of mental illness is seen, affecting his daughter and two grandchildren.

Figure 3 traces the genealogy of the only accomplished scholar, besides the engineer already mentioned, who was born into the kindred before 1860. This man, a son of the index case in Fig. 2 and a grandson of the index case in Fig. 1, was born in 1816. He became a renowned linguist, taught at the Latin College in Reykjavik, wrote textbooks, and translated many works from Latin and Greek. Mental illness obviously exists around this person, the closest psychotic relative being his sister, whose severe illness is well documented. As mentioned above, the grandson of that sister was highly gifted.

Figure 4 traces the family of a person in generation IV, born in 1813, who, like his grandfather, became a member of the Icelandic Parliament. Mental illness is seen in his son as well as in 3 of his grandchildren.

Figure 5 shows the family of a farmer, born in 1841, who was referred to as "wealthy" because of his material success. He also held a public office in his locality. Mental illness

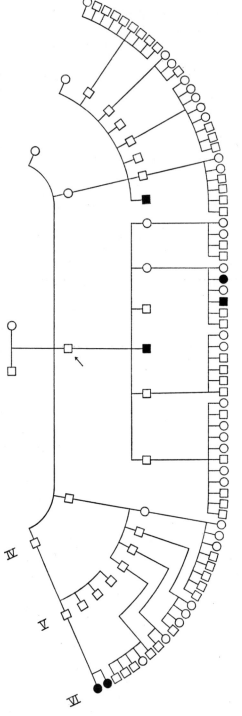

Fig. 5. Family tree of a "wealthy" farmer and community official, born in 1841, marked by an arrow. This pedigree comes from a different branch of the kindred than do the previous figures.

abounds in this pedigree, which comes from a different branch of the kindred than the previous families.

One other person in the kindred who also was designated "wealthy", like the index cases in Figs. 2 and 5, similarly had mentally ill relatives, but he was an only child and did not leave a pedigree comparable to the ones shown.

The favorite media of creative expression in Iceland have for a long time been poetry and writing. Unfortunately, no eminent poets or authors belong in the kindred under study. This writer is aware of several successful poets born during the period of study into other kindreds who had mentally ill relatives, but a systematic study has not been completed. Several eminent musicians born after 1860 are clustered within the pedigree shown in Fig. 5.

DISCUSSION

Although the index cases in the present study were gifted rather than psychotic, the pattern of schizophrenia is similar to that illustrated in previously published pedigrees, which dealt exclusively with schizophrenia.[3, 4] The distribution of the disorder has been found to be consistent with a mechanism of modified "dominant" inheritance. The specific mechanism proposed by this author involves a basic gene designated S, with a mutant counterpart designated s. The frequency of the s gene has been estimated as 0·03. The genotype Ss leads to a different phenotype than the genotype SS, but in most instances no disease results from the presence of the s gene. A separate gene, designated P, with a mutant allele designated p, is perhaps metabolically related to the S gene, but the two are inherited independently. The p gene is estimated to occur in a frequency of 0·4, and it

TABLE 1. PERSONALITY TYPES ASSOCIATED WITH TWO
IDENTIFIABLE SEPARATELY INHERITED GENES

Percentage frequency	Genotype formula	Personality type
79	*SSPP* or *SSPp*	Normophrenic
15	*SSpp*	Tensiphrenic
5	*SsPP* or *SsPp*	Superphrenic
1	*Sspp*	Schizophrenic
0·1	*ssPP* or *ssPp*	Retarded or autistic
0·01	*sspp*	

shows classical recessive inheritance, PP and Pp individuals being phenotypically indistinguishable and only the pp genotype showing abnormal characteristics. Given these basic premises, one can compute the frequency of occurrence of the different theoretical gene combinations involving the two genetic loci. It should be emphasized that the figures can only be considered approximations at this time, subject to further population studies and clarification of diagnostic criteria.

In addition to the calculated frequency of the different possible gene combinations at the S and P loci, Table 1 lists the basic personality characteristics felt to be associated with each genetic constitution. The terms in the last column are used to designate the corresponding genotypes, and variations in phenotype would exist within each category as well as occurring with each individual in terms of time. Thus an individual with the genotype *Sspp* is termed schizophrenic, but no more than 80% of such persons seem to develop symptoms diagnosable as psychosis, with many of them suffering only episodic illnesses. It is assumed, however, that the *Sspp* constitution influences the personality of the individual throughout his life.

Apart from the system of personality types determined by the *S* and *P* genes, there appears to exist an independent system which is related to extroversion and introversion.[6] There are also some indications that the latter characteristics may be dependent on the output of steroid hormones, the person who produces more steroids tending to become extroverted and self-confident as well as having a round face. Presumably there are still additional variables which influence personality patterns, allowing for considerable variability within each of the groups listed in Table 1.

The group designated *normophrenic* is estimated to account for 79% of all persons, and by definition this type represents the average or ordinary man. No definitive studies have been made of this group, but it would not include persons of exceptional ability or persons who are grossly psychopathic. At this time there is no way of specifically identifying individuals belonging in this group, but a person picked randomly would be likely to belong here. Just how the extroversion–introversion factors would modify the personality of a normophrenic remains an open question, but it seems likely that the extroverted members would tend toward weight gain and a jovial disposition.

The *tensiphrenic* group according to the calculations includes 15% of all persons. This type of individual is potentially identifiable in certain pedigrees. The mating of two psychotic persons would lead to only schizophrenic and tensiphrenic offspring among their normally developed children. Other families with a high manifest risk of schizophrenia in the children would also include members of this type. This writer has studied several families of the latter kind, and the conclusion that the *SSpp* genotype leads to nervous tension is based mainly on the results of that study.[3] From other available data it seems possible that tensiphrenic persons may develop sociopathic tendencies.[7] It should be stressed, however, that more data are needed to confirm these preliminary findings. In what manner the extroversion–introversion factors may modulate the tensiphrenic type is entirely unknown.

The *superphrenic* group, with the genotype *SsPP* or *SsPp,* accounts for 5% of all persons, and this type of individual appears to be identifiable in several ways. A healthy person who is known to have a psychotic parent or a psychotic sib as well as having himself produced a psychotic child would most likely have the genotype *SsPp*. The index cases in the pedigrees in this paper may also be assumed to carry the *s* gene. Certain psychologic procedures, referred to as object sorting tests, likewise appear to identify carriers of a "dominant" gene.[8] Since the responses of such carriers on the tests differ from those of the "normal" person and resemble those of schizophrenics, their performance has been felt to represent a "thought disorder", but it is apparent that the implied value judgment may have to be reassessed. The rating of the test performance is carried out so as to reward replies which are considered to be quite solid and highly logical. For example, a person achieves a high score if he groups together all objects made of the same or closely related materials, such as metals, or all objects that serve a similar purpose, such as all eating utensils. Individuals who apply more imagination to the test, for example grouping together all objects that burn or unrelated objects that under special circumstances might be used together, are penalized according to the degree of "irrelevance" judged to be shown by such responses. However, since the subject is unaware of the rating system, the test does not in reality determine whether he can give more "relevant" replies, rather whether he prefers to. It seems probably that under such circumstances a subject would be penalized for a vivid imagination and more particularly for trying to play games with the examiner, while so-called "concrete" thinking is rewarded. An entirely different type of evidence gathered by this writer, including that presented in this paper, suggests that in actual life, individuals with the superphrenic genotype are often highly productive, tending to assume leadership in cultural or social affairs. It was on the basis of such evidence that the suggestion was made that rather than suffering from a thought disorder the carrier of the *s* gene may in reality be more gifted than the ordinary person. Independent evidence, giving further support to this view, was described recently in a follow-up of 47 children born to schizophrenic mothers, but reared in foster homes.[9] Several gifted persons existed in this material, while no individuals of superior performance were encountered in a control group consisting of 50 foster-reared persons born to non-schizophrenic mothers.

Considerable variation is seen within the superphrenic group. The superphrenic extrovert may well be the type generally recognized as the round faced, highly confident and very outgoing social leader. Such persons are commonly encountered as politicians, business men, or other professionals. This writer has identified several socially eminent persons in Iceland who are so placed in pedigrees as to have to be assigned the genotype *SsPp*. It is possible that the superphrenic introvert may be more inclined to follow intellectual pursuits rather than selecting a profession requiring contact with people. In contrast to the extroverted type, he seems to shun social competition. He is also of a more lean body habitus.

According to the figures in Table 1, 99% of all persons would be normophrenic, tensiphrenic, or superphrenic. The remaining 1% would consist mainly of individuals with the gentotype *Sspp*, who are designated *schizophrenic*. The majority of such persons may become overtly psychotic during some part of their lives, but they should not be assumed to be necessarily inferior to the types that manifest more resistance to stress. There is strong evidence that the "schizophrenic" group includes persons who become the most highly creative members of society. The risk of psychosis appears to be exceedingly high among the most creative persons in various artistic or scholastic pursuits. In his extensive study of the world's greatest men of creative genius, Lange-Eichbaum[10] found their risk of psychosis to be of the same order as that seen in relatives of schizophrenics with the highest risk, namely monozygotic cotwins. According to the proposed system, any person who develops definite psychotic symptoms must all along have had the genotype *Sspp*. The obvious conclusion is that the schizophrenic genotype leads not only to reduced resistance to stress, but also to a potential for creativity and superior judgment, although the potential may come to fruition in only a few persons.

The extroversion–introversion dimension appears to manifest itself in persons prone to psychosis. The schizophrenic extrovert is likely to be diagnosed as manic depressive, while the schizophrenic introvert seems to represent the typical dementia praecox type.

The data presented in this paper give support to the view that a person cannot be highly gifted without being heterozygous at the S locus. This can be considered an example of heterosis or hybrid vigor, a well-known phenomenon in other organisms. No gifted individuals were identified in the kindred under study without the evidence for the Ss constitution appearing in their pedigrees. The total evidence supports the view that a gifted person must have the superphrenic genotype, $SsPP$ or $SsPp$, while a high creative potential seems more likely to be associated with the constitution $Sspp$. Schizophrenia is perhaps a state of overstimulation, which in most instances leads to a toxic condition, but in a few individuals results in the type of creativity on which mankind is dependent for scientific and cultural progress.

There is evidence that the system of personality types proposed in Table 1 is biochemically related to the production of adrenalin related compounds and involves the arousal system of the brain.[3] An elucidation of a hereditary basis for this system is an example of how the field of genetics may help to pave the way for biochemical studies and define the groups which likely will be found to be chemically distinct.

There is no intention in the present work to deny that environmental factors exert their influence on the development of personality patterns. The participation of genetic influences should not be ignored either, and efforts need to be made to define their exact nature. The conclusions described in this paper are not seen as the final word on the subject, but rather as an illustration of one kind of approach which may turn out to be useful in the total attack on the problem of personality differences. The relationship of the proposed human types to the systems of classification described earlier by Kretschmer[11] and by Sheldon[12] also needs to be clarified.

REFERENCES

 1. HUXLEY, J., MAYR, E., OSMOND, H., and HOFFER, A., Schizophrenia as a genetic morphism, *Nature* **204**, 220–1 (1964).
 2. BÖÖK, J. A., A genetic and neurophsyciatric investigation of a North-Swedish population, *Acta genet.* **4**, 1–100 (1953).
 3. KARLSSON, J. L., *The Biologic Basis of Schizophrenia*, C. C. Thomas, Springfield, Ill., 1966.
 4. KARLSSON, J. L., The longitudinal family distribution of schizophrenia, *Hereditas* **52**, 127–38 (1964).
 5. JONSSON, G., *Bergsaett I–III*, Holar, Reykjavik, 1966.
 6. JUNG, C. G., *Psychological Types*, Harcourt, Brace & Co., New York, 1923.
 7. ROBINS, L. N., *Deviant Children Grown Up*, Williams & Wilkins, Baltimore, 1966.
 8. MCCONAGHY, N., The use of an object sorting test in elucidating the hereditary factor in schizophrenia, *J. Neurol. Neurosurg. Psychiat.* **22**, 243–6 (1959).
 9. HESTON, L. L., Psychiatric disorders in foster home reared children of schizophrenic mothers, *Brit. J. Psychiat.* **112**, 819–25 (1966).
10. LANGE-EICHBAUM, W., *The Problem of Genius*, Kegan Paul, Trench, Trubner, London, 1931.
11. KRETSCHMER, E., *Physique and Character*, Harcourt, Brace & Co., New York, 1926.
12. SHELDON, W. H. and STEVENS, S. S., *The Varieties of Temperament*, Harper & Bros., New York, 1942.

SUMMARY OF THE GENETIC EVIDENCE

JAMES SHIELDS

Medical Research Council Psychiatric Genetics Research Unit,
Institute of Psychiatry, Maudsley Hospital, London, S.E. 5

INTRODUCTION

The speakers on the genetic panel[1-6] are to be congratulated on the clear way in which they have presented their papers. We have listened to a wide range of opinions. If anyone, on the basis of his own work alone, would be justified in dismissing the relevance of genetics to the schizophrenia problem, it is surely Dr. Tienari. Yet nowhere in his paper does he specifically do this. The furthest he goes is to say that factors other than genetic may to some extent make for similarity between identical twins, a view with which few would venture to disagree. Professor Bleuler believes heredity is important but non-specific. In his view the genes contribute physical disharmonies that run parallel to disharmonies of personality of many kinds. Dr. Kringlen, on the evidence of his most recent work, seems to be moving from a rather sceptical position as to the importance of genetic factors to a more positive acceptance of their role; his position is now closer to that of Dr. Gottesman, at least in so far as he speaks of polygenic inheritance.

The other three speakers are more committed to a specific role played by genetics, and they have expressed views as to the most likely mode of transmission or how its part in development might be studied. Dr. Slater favours the view that a single gene is a common factor to most schizophrenia. Dr. Erlenmeyer-Kimling is inclined to think of heterogeneity in the sense of a number of alternative specific genes. Dr. Gottesman believes there are merits in a polygenic theory, or the combined effect of many genes. None of them seeks to deny the contribution of the environment.

The task I have been allotted is to make a comprehensive statement about *all* the major evidence for genetic transmission, and not to restrict myself to a discussion of the papers that have been read. My chief, Dr. Slater, has made my task easier by having already given an excellent account of the earlier work. What I propose to attempt is to highlight or expand some of the points he made. I shall then discuss the recent twin studies. The point I shall try to make here is that these should be regarded as complementing the older studies—confirming, refining or improving them—and not as discrediting them. Finally, I shall discuss some of the views as to how schizophrenia might be transmitted and their relevance to the question of genetic–environmental interaction to which most of us at least pay lip service. At what I hope will be appropriate places, I shall discuss points raised by the speakers on the panel.

Before reviewing the main evidence, it is worth while stressing some rather obvious points that are apt to be overlooked. The knowledge or presumption of internal psychological processes of development or of external physical or social influences on a trait is no reason to assume that differences of heredity are of no effect. Knowledge about psychopathology need be no more reason for excluding genetics in schizophrenia than, say, knowledge about biochemistry would be in phenylketonuria. And to say that phenylketonuria is caused or prevented by an environmental factor, nutrition, makes it no less a genetic disorder of metabolism. Again, if no biochemical error is identified or no simple Mendelian ratios occur, this is still no reason for saying a trait is not influenced by genetic factors. We do not expect to find a clear-cut biochemical distinction between tall men and short men or expect that stature will segregate in man as it did in Mendel's sweet peas. Influenced by nutrition though it is, we have no problem about recognizing the relevance of genetic differences here.

All characters are acquired, and heredity and environment interact in the development of all of them. When we speak of a genetic transmission of an illness we are not addressing ourselves to the unreal problem of whether it is caused by heredity *or* by environment. But it is not an unreal problem to ask how far differences in the genotype and differences in the environment contribute to the development of an illness—even if that illness be schizophrenia. Provided genetic differences make a contribution it is important to try to find out what we can about their nature. This holds however much or however little we know about environmental factors. And, of course, the converse holds. The better one factor is studied, the more the ground is delimited in which the effects of other factors can be sought.[7]

EVIDENCE FOR GENETIC TRANSMISSION

The first ground, then, for thinking that genetic factors play a part in schizophrenia is a general one. Man is genetically extremely diverse. Morphological and physiological traits, growth rates, resistance to diseases occurring at any time of life—many of these are under some degree of genetic influence. So, too, are intelligence and some temperamental traits, notably social introversion. It would be surprising if schizophrenia were altogether exempt from genetic influence, even if this influence should turn out to be slight. So far no environmental factor has been found that is common to all schizophrenia and affects all genotypes equally. Until it is, the presumption is that genetic variability plays a part in etiology.

Slater in his paper presented the main factual evidence, collected and confirmed in many studies in many parts of the world. His first point was that the incidence of schizophrenia, strictly defined, was similar in most countries, despite great social variations. His second was that the raised incidence in families was in accord with a genetic hypothesis. The distribution of cases within families was more consistent, he thought, with segregation of the genes than with differences in the environment. This was particularly evident when concordance rates were found in the earlier twin studies to be four or five times higher in MZ pairs than in same-sexed DZ pairs reared together. Even MZ twins reared apart were concordant and discordant in about the same frequency as in parallel studies of MZ twins reared together.

Sibling risk and abnormality in parent

Let us now look again at some of the studies of siblings and children, bearing the total picture in mind. How far could the common family environment account for the findings?

When neither parent is schizophrenic the best estimate of the risk of schizophrenia in the sib of a schizophrenic is about 8% or 9%. When one parent is schizophrenic it rises, but only to 12%; but when both parents are schizophrenic the risk shoots up to over 35%. If it is objected that this rise might be accounted for by the extremely chaotic environment provided by such a family, it can be pointed out that in what must be an almost equally chaotic environment—that in which one parent is schizophrenic and the other psychopathic —the sibling risk, according to Kallmann[8]; is only 15%. Furthermore, Elsässer[9] showed that 70% of the non-psychotic children of two schizophrenics are quite normal. These findings are in keeping with the importance of genetic factors.

Dual mating studies

This may be the appropriate point at which to comment on the studies of dual matings. All who have examined the data—Elsässer[9] in his 1952 monograph, Rosenthal[10] in his recent paper and at this meeting Slater and Erlenmeyer-Kimling—are agreed as to the likely order of risk to offspring of two schizophrenics. Besides the studies already referred to, two others may be mentioned. Böök[11] and Hallgren and Sjögren[12] in their respective Swedish population surveys, between them reported three dual matings. Of the 11 children, 5 were schizophrenic. The crude rate of 45% is consistent with the range of figures between 34% and 46% that have been cited.

Erlenmeyer-Kimling has told us about her scientifically extremely neat plan for the investigation of the children of dual matings, and we must all hope that some day the fictitious figures in her tables will be replaced by real ones. It is in keeping with current ideas that her investigation is planned prospectively, studying the development of eventual psychosis and doing so under varying environmental conditions. It came as a surprise to learn that dual matings of schizophrenics are now likely to be as frequent as schizophrenics with MZ twins. In some respects the thought of their frequency is a disturbing one. There will no doubt be problems in capitalizing on the existence of such families for research, which will make them more difficult to study than twins; but if the adopted and fostered children of two schizophrenics can be traced and followed up, the solution of these difficulties will bring compensating advantages.

A question of some interest is whether schizophrenics from such matings differ in any way from others. On most genetic and environmental theories one might perhaps expect that some at least would be extremely severely affected. Nothing spectacular in the direction of more severe cases among the offspring has been observed. Rosenthal,[10] however, has noted that age at first admission tends to be lowered in female schizophrenics from dual matings. According to the preliminary results of the New York Group[13] a few years ago, 16 children of two schizophrenic parents had been hospitalized with verified "schizophrenia after pubescence" in a group of 170 whose mean age was only 15·7 years. One wonders whether the tendency noted by Rosenthal is being confirmed and whether the sexes are affected differently. So far there has been no mention of cases of childhood schizophrenia occurring.[1]

Work on dual matings is being carried out from yet another angle. According to the report of a WHO group,[14] tissue culture experiments are being made on embryonic material derived from foetuses obtained from interrupted pregnancies when both parents were schizophrenic. This work is being carried out by Professor Vartanian of Moscow (personal communication from Dr. D. W. Kay, Rapporteur of the WHO Group) but details of the results are not yet known.

Environmental influences on incidence in siblings

Various studies have been made to see whether there is a tendency for affected sibs to come close together in a family, as might be expected if the family environment were more noxious over certain periods of time than others. There is evidence that this may be so in juvenile delinquency,[15] but not in schizophrenia according to analyses made by Schulz[16] and others. Reports have from time to time been made, investigating the point whether certain places in the sibship, such as first or last born, were particularly at risk. Many findings have been negative, others inconsistent.

The best evidence of a statistical kind showing the importance of environmental factors in schizophrenia derived from family studies comes from three sets of findings: the higher incidence in DZ twins than in sibs, in same-sexed sibs than in opposite-sexed sibs and in female relatives than in males. In each case it is understandable that this should be so, though there are possible sources of bias, suggesting that some of the reported difference may be exaggerated.

The higher incidence in DZ twins than in sibs was present in studies that investigated both, as Kringlen showed in his paper. The difference was small in Kallmann's[17] work (morbid risks: 15% DZ twins, 14% sibs), it was larger in Slater's[18] (morbid risks: 14% DZ twins, 5·4% sibs) and moderate in Kringlen's uncorrected rates: (8·1% DZ twins and 5·2% sibs). Some of the difference might be due to the fact that the twin partners are investigated more thoroughly than the sibs, and not entirely to the greater similarity of the environments of twins.

The pooled crude concordance rates in six studies of 430 DZ pairs of opposite sex is only 5·6%,[7] which is about half the concordance rate usually reported in DZ pairs of the same sex, and the difference is consistent in all studies except Kringlen's. Once again it could be partly due to the more thorough investigation of same-sex pairs.

The hypothesis that sex-role indentification might lead to a greater resemblance in psychosis between relatives of the same sex within the nuclear family is one which Rosenthal[19] considered merited attention, and views are sometimes put forward by psychodynamic thinkers attributing most of the resemblance between relatives to factors of this kind. Similar explanations have been put forward for the frequently observed tendency for pairs of female relatives to be affected more often than males, supported by the observation

---

[1] Dr. Erlenmeyer-Kimling tells me there were two cases of childhood schizophrenia in the New York study (onsets at 4 and 8 years) but none of infantile autism.

that *folie-à-deux* occurs more frequently in female than in male pairs of subjects. All the evidence, however, does not go in the same direction.

In 1959 Hallgren and Sjögren[12] published a thorough population-based family study of schizophrenia in two typical rural Swedish islands. Table 1 shows that they found 84 pairs of psychotic relatives; 42 of the secondary cases of psychosis among parents and sibs were females and 42 males; 43 pairs of affected relatives were of the same sex and 41 of

TABLE 1. SEX OF PROBAND AND SEX
OF RELATIVE

(data taken from Hallgren and Sjögren[12])

Schizophrenic proband	Psychotic parent or sib		
	Male	Female	Total
Male	23	22	45
Female	19	20	39
Total	42	42	84

43 pairs same sex, 41 pairs opposite sex

opposite sex. Kringlen's twin study[5] did not show the predicted relationship between sex and concordance (33% in female MZ, 42% in male MZ pairs, using a wide conception of concordance and based on personal investigation); and in the Maudsley twin study 11 pairs of schizophrenic proband and severely abnormal parent or sib were persons of the same sex and 17 persons of different sex (unpublished observation). Some of the studies in which the association was strongest, such as that by Zehnder,[20] were based on pairs of relatives in the same hospital, and the excess of female pairs observed there may have been influenced by a tendency for male schizophrenics to migrate more from their place of origin. Moreover, it may be easier to obtain information about abnormal females than males. For instance, females consult their doctors for psychiatric illness nearly twice as often as males.[21] Most of the earlier twin studies contain an excess of female probands so that if female relatives are more easily discovered, an excess of female pairs would result. I shall refer to the twin studies in more detail later on and suggest that the higher concordance in females is to a large extent likely to be an artefact of sampling.

Certainly the effects of sex and of place in the family are well worth exploring as a means of detecting environmental causes of resemblance between relatives. However, deviations from randomness in some studies do not lead to the conclusion that nothing of relevance to schizophrenia is transmitted genetically.

Discussion of the validity of MZ vs. DZ comparisons

The strongest evidence for genetics comes from twin studies. If the family milieu, the time of birth into such a milieu and the sex of the child are the main factors accounting for the raised incidence in families, there should be little or no difference between the incidence in MZ co-twins and DZ co-twins of the same sex as the proband. Except for the study of Tienari,[22] in which the MZ co-twins were schizoid rather than schizophrenic, significantly higher concordance rates have been observed in MZ pairs. For the moment let us take it as established that the MZ co-twins of schizophrenics are at least twice as often and, in many types of samples, 4 or 5 times as often schizophrenic as DZ co-twins of the same sex. This difference will be accounted for by influences from two sources: by the effects of the greater genetic similarity of MZ twins, and by any greater similarity in environmental factors relevant to schizophrenia shared by MZ twins and not by DZ twins. How important are the latter?

Three ways in which environmental factors might contribute are sometimes put forward: the risks of monozygosity, the effects of identification and the sharing of a more similar environment.

1. It is said[23] that MZ twins *per se* may be at special risk for schizophrenia on account of problems such as confusion of identity and weak ego formation. If this were so, one would expect to find more MZ twins among samples of schizophrenics than in the population as a whole. This has not been found. Rosenthal[24] has reviewed the careful work done on this by Luxenburger and Essen-Möller; and other workers—early and recent—have found the same.

2. A second way in which environmental factors might contribute to the higher MZ concordance rates is the identification of one twin with the other. Theoretically, this could work in either direction. A potential schizophrenic could be stopped from becoming psychotic by strong ties with his normal twin; and a twin who might otherwise have escaped might be driven into psychosis by the illness of his twin. The identification theory thus need not imply an excess of MZ twins, though if it were true one might have expected more cases of *folie-à-deux,* in the sense of shared delusions or identical symptoms, among concordant MZ pairs than one finds in practice.

It is true that twins in concordant pairs tend to fall ill within two or three years of one another rather than at intervals spread at random, or at decreasingly frequent intervals, over the period of risk. This observation may be open to the interpretation that one twin has affected the other as to time of onset or that both have responded to the same stress.[25] Yet some pairs become concordant after a lapse of many years. In Slater's series differences of up to 31 years in age of onset were observed.

All those who are interested in schizophrenic twin studies will be pleased to learn that Professor Essen-Möller, when he retires later this year, is intending to follow up the twins whose histories he published in 1941.[26] Over the course of the years at least two pairs have become concordant in respect of typical schizophrenia, several years apart.

A further argument against the identification theory comes from a study of pairs of sibs by Tsuang[27] where both were treated in the same hospital for any psychiatric disorder. Though the predicted excess of females and same-sex pairs was observed, these pairs were no more alike in diagnosis than male or opposite-sex pairs.

3. A third way in which the environment might contribute to the higher concordance of MZ pairs arises from the possibility that MZ twins might be more likely to be exposed together to a predisposing environment than DZ twins. In particular (or so it might be argued) MZ twins may have been treated more alike within the family. For example, both

might be picked upon by a morbid parent. Kallmann[17] reported a somewhat higher concordance rate in pairs that had been living together for 5 years or more before the onset than in pairs who had been separated during this period.

The strongest argument against both the identification and the common environment theories as major causes of the higher MZ concordance comes from studies of twins reared apart and differing in the critical points: first, that they did not have the same opportunity for identifying with one another; and secondly that they were reared by mothers of different personality in families of different structure. The fact that their homes may sometimes have been of the same socio-economic level or that neither home may have been ideal is irrelevant to the present argument. Studies by Shields[28] and by Juel-Nielsen[29] of normal twins reared apart show that personality resemblance in MZ twins is not to be accounted for wholly or even mainly by subtleties of the shared environment. Reported cases of twins brought up apart where one or both are schizophrenic have been infrequent, at least in Western cultures, but as Slater showed in his paper they are quite often concordant despite their not having shared the same critical environment. A further case might also have been mentioned: the pair of MZ twins reported by Rosanoff et al.[30] which these authors called both manic-depressives but which sound from the published case histories as if they might both have been schizophrenics.[31] A younger brother was a hospitalized hebephrenic. The mother had an involutional melancholia. The twins were separated when a few months old, one remaining in the home, and the other living 200 miles away in a very different socio-cultural environment.

So far, studies by Heston[32] and Karlsson[33] of persons reared apart from schizophrenic members of their biological family speak in the same direction as those of twins brought up apart. It is not appropriate for me to anticipate what they, and others who have been studying this question, may say about their work later in this Conference.[2]

The above discussion of the confusion of identity, identification and common family environment theories is not intended to imply that environmental causes of schizophrenia are non-existent or even minimal. It does, however, support the view that genetic factors account in the main for the higher MZ concordance rates. There is therefore plenty of evidence from family and twin studies to allow us to entertain genetic ideas about schizophrenia as much as ideas of any other kind.

[2] Since Dr. Karlsson's paper in these Proceedings does not address itself to this aspect of his Icelandic study we may add the relevant findings here. He obtained data about the sibs (over the age of 15) of schizophrenic patients who were children of parents one of whom was psychotic or suspected of psychosis. Of these sibs 102 were reared by their parents, and of them 12 became schizophrenic; 8 were reared by relatives, of whom 2 became schizophrenic; 9 were reared by non-relatives, 3 becoming schizophrenic. In 8 cases in which an individual who eventually became schizophrenic had been brought up in a foster family it was possible to compare the incidence of schizophrenia in the biological and in the foster sibs; of 29 biological sibs, 6 became schizophrenic, of 28 foster sibs none. There is no evidence that institution or foster-home reared children of non-schizophrenic parentage have an increased risk of schizophrenia such as would account for Heston's and Karlsson's findings. It may also be pointed out that foster studies of twins or other relatives do not of themselves provide genetic evidence; they merely give evidence as to the effect or lack of effect of specific environments.

H

RECENT TWIN STUDIES

The current Danish study

Perhaps the greatest obstacle to accepting this kind of argument comes from the results of recent twin studies.

Before turning to the significance of the Finnish, Norwegian and English studies, the findings of which have been presented, allow me to refer briefly to the provisional results of a Danish twin study by Dr. Margit Fischer.[34] Dr. Fischer has generously given me her permission to mention this work. It is based in the first place on Harvald and Hauge's[35] register of all twins born in Denmark between 1870 and 1910 who had survived until the fifth year of life and is now extended to include most twins born up to 1920. The sample is therefore an old one. Inquiries by questionnaire and by record searching were made for all twins, followed by personal investigation of the psychiatric sample. Since 1938 there has been a register of psychiatric patients in Denmark, and for the latter part of the period names on the twin register could be checked against names on the psychiatric register, much as was done in Norway by Kringlen. It was realized that some cases of schizophrenia will have been missed, particularly from the early period, but the sample appeared to be representative. Sixty-six pairs of like sex were found in which at least one twin met the strict Danish criteria for schizophrenia.

Table 2 shows that zygosity could not be decided in 11 pairs, including some where both

TABLE 2. DANISH TWIN STUDY OF SCHIZOPHRENIA
(PRELIMINARY FINDINGS)
(data taken from Fischer[34])

Zygosity	Number of pairs	Pairs concordant	
		I Strict schiz.	I + II Schiz. Other psychosis
MZ	16	3 (19%)	9 (56%)
DZ	34	2 (6%)	5 (15%)
Uncertain	11	1 (9%)	3 (27%)

twins had died. MZ pairs were more alike than DZ. Although only 3 out of 16 MZ pairs were concordant when a diagnosis of strict schizophrenia in the co-twin was taken as the criterion, 6 further co-twins had been psychotic, bringing concordance for psychosis up to 56%. Dr. Fischer informs me that the "other psychoses" in the co-twins "varied from atypical psychosis, over paranoid psychosis to episodic schizophreniform psychosis", and she believes that most of them would have been diagnosed as schizophrenic in the USA. She regards them as representing a milder form of classical process schizophrenia. Since all co-twins were over 46, the question of age correction did not arise. The sexes were approximately equally represented in the material, and concordance was somewhat higher in female pairs: for example, concordance in respect of psychosis occurred in 4 out of 9 male and in 5 out of 7 female MZ pairs. Fischer considers her results to be similar to those of Essen-Möller,[26] Kringlen[36] and Gottesman and Shields.[37]

Comparison of recent twin studies with one another

I do not propose to summarize the presentations[3-5] of the findings of the other three recent twin studies separately. Their sampling methods all have much to recommend them, but they differ in detail.

Tienari started with all male twins born in Finland between 1920 and 1929 and set himself the hard task of identifying all that had been, or were, in any way psychiatrically abnormal. Personal investigation was centred on the identical twins, and their case histories have been published.

Kringlen in effect started with a defined psychiatric population, namely all persons in the Norwegian psychosis register; and from among those born between 1901 and 1930 he identified twins by checking names against a register of all twin births. Personal investigation was confined to pairs of like sex, but information from records was available on pairs of unlike sex too. Kringlen's is the largest of the recent studies.

In Great Britain, as in most countries, there is no national psychosis register or register of twin births, or official means of tracing persons to their current address. The sample which Gottesman and I obtained was also based on a defined psychiatric population, namely all patients attending a large out-patient clinic and short-stay psychiatric hospital over a 16-year period, where twinship had been systematically ascertained, not retrospectively, but

TABLE 3. RECENT TWIN STUDIES IN SCHIZOPHRENIA
MZ SIMPLE CONCORDANCE RATES
(reported at FFRP Conference, Puerto Rico, 1967)

Investigation (country)	No. of pairs*	Range of concordance reported in respect of schizophrenia or possibly related disorder	Nature of possibly related disorder included in upper limit shown
Tienari (Finland)	16 (10)	6–36%	Borderline features
Fischer (Denmark)	16	19–56%	Psychosis
Kringlen (Norway)	55 (45)	25–38%	Schizophreniform or borderline
Gottesman and Shields (U.K.)	24 (17)	41–46%	Diagnosed "?schizophrenia"

* In parentheses number of pairs after exclusion of index cases not regarded as strict schizophrenia.

at the time of admission. Investigation was restricted to pairs of like sex. Distinctive features are the blind diagnostic evaluations and the psychological testing of relatives.

Table 3 endeavours to summarize the findings in the four recent studies in so far as they concern MZ pairs. All the later investigators, as did Essen-Möller, required a flexible concept of concordance to do justice to their data. This was on account of the variety of psychiatric abnormalities that might legitimately be regarded as severely schizoid or atypically psychotic or in some other way related to schizophrenic psychosis, and which occurred even among the identical co-twins of conservatively diagnosed cases. This was most notable in the Finnish and Danish studies. (Concordance rates would be raised to a higher level still if one were to add schizoid personalities: Tienari regarded 75% of his co-twins as psychotic, borderline or schizoid, and Gottesman and I would include as schizotypic at least one personality-disordered co-twin on the basis of his MMPI profile. The table, however, does not include such cases.)

When comparing these findings with those of the earlier studies, the new facts available about Kallmann's 1946 study[38, 2] may be relevant: simple pairwise concordance there ranged from 50% (where both MZ twins had a hospital diagnosis of schizophrenia at the start of the study) to 69% (inclusive of "suspected schizophrenia"—Kallmann's classification).

The difference as compared with earlier work is, of course, most marked in the Finnish study. Despite thorough field work and a further follow-up, only one strictly concordant male pair could be found in the entire *living* twin population studied. It looks as if Dr. Tienari or Dr. Alanen, if they should wish to locate concordant pairs for intensive family studies of schizophrenia in Finland, would have greater difficulty finding them than would Dr. Pollin or Dr. Lidz in an urban American population of the same size. In the Finnish study concordance shows up at 36% only when borderline states are included and organic schizophreniform psychoses excluded.

Concordance is somewhat higher in the other studies, and they show a fair amount of agreement generally. There are differences, however. Concordance in respect of psychosis was lower in the Norwegian than in the Danish study, though resemblance in clinical picture among pairs where both twins were psychotic was closer in the Norwegian, where, as Kringlen has shown, it was extremely close. (According to the data presented, schizophreniform psychosis in one twin was matched with schizophreniform psychosis in the other in three pairs, and with psychoses of other kinds in none. In no fewer than 13 out of 14 pairs where both twins had a typical schizophrenia, clinical sub-type was the same. The psychotic co-twin of the remaining typical case had a reactive psychosis.) In the Danish sample, on the other hand, typical schizophrenias were more often matched with transient psychoses, as was the case in Essen-Möller's earlier Swedish series.

Concordance for strict schizophrenia was highest in the English study. (The eleventh case included within the upper limit shown is a co-twin who has not consulted a psychiatrist but whose history has been diagnosed as possibly schizophrenic by two judges.) Within concordant pairs, sub-type resemblance, according to the independent blind classification, was close, though not so close as in the Norwegian study. The crude incidence of psychosis of any kind in co-twins was similar to that found in the Danish study, if a little lower. However, if allowance were to be made for the younger age of the English twins, the concordance rate would approach those of the older studies. Among the newer studies, only in the London and Norwegian samples can the incidence of schizophrenia in the co-twin be seen to rise with increasing morbidity of the proband.

We are therefore left with the picture of a fair degree of variability, both within so-called concordant twin pairs and between centres. Instead of asking which concordance rates are the correct ones, we should perhaps be trying to identify schizophrenic equivalents and asking why potentially schizophrenic genotypes manifest themselves at different levels in different populations or samples.

EVALUATION OF CONCORDANCE RATES, OLD AND NEW

A few years ago critics were understandably asking whether the reported concordance rates for schizophrenia in MZ twins might not be misleadingly high. It may be worth while now to review these criticisms and, in the light of recent work, to ask also whether in some respects concordance rates may not sometimes be misleadingly low.

The points I have listed in Table 4 are over-formalized, and except for the first two

TABLE 4. REPORTED CONCORDANCE RATES FOR SCHIZOPHRENIA IN MZ PAIRS

Too high?	Too low?
1. Illegitimate use of proband method.	1. Proband method not used.
2. Unrealistic correction for age.	2. No allowance made for age.
3. Preferential reporting of concordant pairs.	3. Potentially concordant co-twins missed through mortality, etc.
4. Discordant MZ pairs diagnosed as DZ.	4. Inclusion of nongenetic varieties among probands.
5. Too loose a criterion of schizophrenia, especially for MZ co-twins.	5. Inherited abnormality need not imply deterioration; too strict a criterion used for co-twin.
6. Female schizophrenia concordant largely for psychogenic or environmental reasons; samples over-weighted with females.	6. Division of role in twins makes MZ pairs less alike than they would otherwise have been.
7. Concordance in co-twin related to severity of proband; samples over-weighted with severe cases.	7. Genetic heterogeneity of populations

they do not balance each other logically; but it may be a help to set them out in this way. I cannot attempt within the scope of this paper to give anything approaching a complete account of any of them.

Concordance rates too high?

1. The first reason why some have thought concordance rates to be too high is that the proband method may have been used when this was not justified, and several concordant pairs counted twice. This objection has been taken into account in all the tables that have been presented here. In fact, only Luxenburger and Slater applied the proband method, and this had the effect of increasing their crude MZ concordance rates only from 58% to 64%, and from 65% to 68%, respectively. Kallmann did not use the proband method in this way.

2. The second reason is the method of age correction. Kallmann's much-quoted rate of 86% was derived by a procedure which has been criticized as inapplicable to twins.

(Gottesman referred to this point.) In fact only Kallmann and Slater used age correction. It is the uncorrected figures that have been reported here.

3. A third reason is the possibility of a preferential reporting of concordant MZ pairs in studies where the twinship of all patients could not be reliably checked, either by direct inquiry at the time of admission when informants are available, or retrospectively from birth records. This possibility is difficult to exclude when dealing with an old case material; but if it had occurred to a significant extent one would have predicted the finding of a relative excess of MZ over DZ pairs in the samples, and this was not found. Slater has reminded us that he obtained his cases in the first instance by direct personal inquiries of relatives. There is unlikely to have been a bias caused by hearing about concordant pairs in the same hospital; in only 2 out of 24 concordant MZ pairs and in 1 out of 10 concordant DZ pairs were both twins in the same hospital at the time of inquiry. There is the further possibility that discordant pairs are more easily missed than concordant pairs, since the latter have two chances of being ascertained. In Slater's series this source of bias cannot have had much effect since in only 4 out of 24 MZ and in 3 out of 10 DZ concordant pairs were both twins ascertained as probands.

4. The next two considerations arise from the possibility of unconscious observer bias in the form of contaminated diagnosis. First, there is the possibility that several discordant MZ pairs have been mistakenly diagnosed as DZ. Zygosity diagnosis is in fact more reliably made than some critics have thought.[39] But supposing this form of bias had operated in Kallmann's study, Gottesman and Shields[40] have estimated that it would not have reduced his raw concordance rate of 69% to one below 60%. Most studies have employed blood-grouping or finger-printing as objective aids in zygosity determination.

5. The other kind of contaminated diagnosis is related to the question of looseness of diagnosis of schizophrenia, and it might be thought to occur rather easily if the investigator knows he is dealing with a MZ co-twin. Kallmann laid himself open to criticisms of this kind on account of the way he presented his data. The new information shows that he did not change more MZ than DZ diagnoses in favour of schizophrenia, and that most twins called schizophrenic by him had been hospitalized. Slater and Essen-Möller published case histories which have proved invaluable to later workers. In our current study at the Maudsley Hospital we are having histories judged blind by psychiatrists of different schools of thought.

6. A sixth reason for thinking that concordance rates in the earlier studies were too high was that samples were over-weighted with females, and that female pairs tended to be more often concordant than males for psychological reasons. Evaluation of this objection is difficult, since it is so closely linked with other problems of sampling, such as chronicity of the samples. It is true that in all studies but Kringlen's (as he has pointed out) concordance was higher in females, though in some the difference was very slight and quite insignificant statistically. However, Kallmann did not report the sexes separately, but stated there was no sex difference in concordance. Tienari studied male pairs only.

Table 5 divides the remaining eight studies into two: first, those that were based upon consecutive admissions to hospitals or to psychosis registers, and where twinship could be checked either on admission or from birth records; and, secondly, the remainder. The latter studies were based mainly on resident hospital populations, which contain an excess of

TABLE 5. SEX, SAMPLING AND CONCORDANCE

(data taken from Gottesman and Shields[40] and papers presented at this Conference)

Studies investigating both sexes and reporting results separately	Concordance for schizophrenia in MZ twins by sex and source		
	Male	Female	
Based on consecutive admissions, twinship checked*	27/59 (46%)	25/53 (47%)	n.s.
Not so based†	28/55 (51%)	60/84 (71%)	$p < 0.02$
All studies	55/114 (48%)	85/137 (62%)	

* Essen-Möller,[26] Slater[18] (consecutive sample), Kringlen,[5] Gottesman and Shields,[37] Fischer.[34]

† Luxenburger,[41] Rosanoff et al.,[42] Slater[18] (resident sample), Inouye.[43]

females and severe cases and many old cases where there might no longer be reliable information about the co-twin; or where availability of both twins was a condition of inclusion;[43] or where they relied on second-hand information, the reliability of which is difficult to assess.[42] The Slater series has been divided into its resident and consecutive sections,[40] though he admitted that in the consecutive section the check on twinship was haphazard rather than complete. In the Scandinavian samples concordance has been taken at the level of psychosis or borderline psychosis in the co-twin.

The results show that in the more completely investigated samples the sexes were equally represented and, what is more, there was virtually no tendency for female pairs to be more often concordant than males. The higher concordance in females is accounted for entirely by the possibly less representative samples. It could equally well have arisen through concordant or partially concordant male pairs having been missed as through any liability of females to suffer from induced schizophrenia. The hypothesis of a decreasing risk to females in the post-Ibsen world[5] may be unnecessary. If there is, or was, a tendency for female pairs to be more alike, it is probably a slight one and could be accounted for by the greater environmental variability in male pairs.

7. The last reason, and possibly the main one, why the earlier concordance rates were so high is that the samples on which they were based were heavily weighted with severe or chronic cases, and that such cases may be more likely than others to have affected twins. The evidence for the association between severity and concordance, first put forward by Rosenthal,[44] comes from several of the twin studies: Luxenburger[41] commented that early hebephrenic and catatonic illnesses were the most concordant, paranoid illnesses being more variable within pairs. This observation is in keeping with the lower incidence of schizophrenia in relatives of paranoid cases than those of hebephrenics and catatonics, which was found by Kallmann[8] and by Hallgren and Sjögren;[12] and also with the results of Rosenthal's[45] analysis of Slater's case histories. Kallmann[17] reported that non-schizophrenic co-twins were matched with non-deteriorating index cases. Inouye[43] found that concordance was lowest with cases of "mild chronic or transient schizophrenia". Finally, in the Maudsley Hospital series the association stood up to various types of

analysis, as you heard,[4] including Judge A's independent diagnoses—it was not accounted for by mild cases not being "true" schizophrenias. The association need not hold at all times or in all populations. It would disappear if we could cure malignant schizophrenia. It does not hold to the same degree in the Scandinavian studies, where severe cases of the process type are not often matched with schizophrenic co-twins.

Concordance rates too low?

I now come to possible reasons why the reported concordance rates may in some respects underestimate the significance of genetic factors. The first two reasons are the reverse sides of the first two reasons previously mentioned, namely that the proband method was *not* used and *no* allowance was made for the age of the co-twins.

1. For a comparison with population incidences of schizophrenia we need to know the incidence in co-twins of cases (that is to say in the co-twins of a representative series of probands). It is this rate that should be compared with the incidence in other classes of person. For example, in order to appreciate the full significance of Kringlen's findings it may be necessary to convert the simple pairwise concordance rate, which he so rightly reports initially, into the percentage of affected co-twins of registered cases. The effect of such a recalculation would be to raise his range of concordance from between 25% and 38% pairwise to between 40% and 50% probandwise. It is this probandwise (casewise) rate that should be compared with the expectation of schizophrenia of something over 1% in Norway. And it is this casewise rate which may be transformed to give an indirect estimate of the pairwise rate in the population.[46]

2. It is unlikely that Kringlen's sample or Fischer's needs much correction for age, but this is not true for younger samples, as previously mentioned.

3. A third possibility is the missing of concordant co-twins through death, emigration or failure to trace the twin. This is admittedly conjectural only, but could arise if any of these variables were relatively frequent among schizophrenics or pre-schizophrenics, which is not unlikely. A single concordant pair missed in Tienari's sample for any of these reasons would bring his concordance rate more into line with those of other recent studies.

4. A fourth reason might be an over-representation of non-genetic varieties of schizophrenia in samples showing low concordance rates. This was a possible source of bias in the Maudsley series, where we deliberately cast our net widely. It seems that misdiagnosed cases, or too loosely diagnosed cases, of schizophrenia in probands from discordant pairs were balanced by atypical cases among the co-twins of strict schizophrenic probands. Judge A's diagnoses did not appreciably alter the previously reported concordance. Tienari has now calculated concordance rates both with and without inclusion of probands who possibly had an organic psychosis or who did not have a verified hospital diagnosis of schizophrenia.

5. A fifth possibility is the failure to diagnose mild or atypical schizophrenia in co-twins. It could well be that it is not so much a deteriorating psychosis that is inherited as some other abnormality at present not easily detected. If such a genetic abnormality were an essential prerequisite for the development of most schizophrenias, and it were relatively infrequent, concordance rates in respect of strict deteriorating schizophrenia would under-

estimate the importance of the genetic factor. A related possibility has been suggested by Allen.[47] Once MZ twins undergo differentiation even from trivial environmental factors, their growth or behaviour may come under control of different genes, present in both but effective only in one.

6. The next possibility is a psychosocial one, arising from the tendency for MZ twins in general to cast themselves or to be cast by their parents in different roles. This tendency would make twins less alike than they would otherwise have been. If, given the genetic predisposition, it is the more submissive, mother-dependent twin who has a critically greater risk of falling ill, the chances are that if MZ twins did not so consistently differ in this way they would more often both have remained well or both have become psychotic.

7. My final reason why some concordance rates may be lower than others is that populations may differ in their genetic structure. This is admittedly a conjectural possibility but one that might account for the apparently genuinely lower frequency of strictly con- cordant pairs in the Scandinavian countries than in other countries where twin studies have been carried out.[3] If a gene or genes predisposing to schizophrenia had also, at some period, had some advantage for survival in certain environments, populations in those environments might through natural selection have become relatively uniform genetically in respect of other genes which prevented the more undesirable manifestations of what we now loosely term the schizophrenic genes. By reason of genetic uniformity, environmental factors would therefore contribute most of the observed variance, as Slater remarked. This, if true, might also account for the lack of association between concordance and severity in the Scan- dinavian twin studies as well as for the lower level of concordance. For Scandinavian populations would be more uniform in respect of those segregating polygenes which in other populations might explain the association between severity and concordance.

Of course, there are many parts of the world in which twin studies of schizophrenia have not been made, so we are in no position to say whether Mediterranean countries, for instance, would follow the New York or the Helsinki pattern, or quite a different one.

Let me attempt to summarize what I have been trying to say about reasons for the differences in the reported concordances in MZ twins. If one takes into account the small size of some of the samples and certain key dimensions, some of the discrepancies may be more apparent than real. Biased case-finding techniques and diagnostic contamination, combined with dubious statistical procedures, probably account for only a small part of the differences. The sex difference in concordance may be largely an artefact. The populations sampled, the psychiatric classification adopted and the severity of the starting cases are likely to be of greater importance. In some populations—in some cultures, if you like—concor- dance may show up at different levels than in others. Viewed in perspective, schizophrenic twin studies are variations on the same theme, replications of the same experiment:[40] MZ co-twins of schizophrenics are more like their partners than DZ co-twins in respect of strict schizophrenic psychosis and related disorders; and this is primarily on account of their greater genetic similarity. While no one would wish to deny environmental influences,

[3] It may be noted[48] that Kallmann's reported morbidity risks in his Berlin [8] and New York[17] studies for the sibs and the children of schizophrenics are about twice those of Hallgren and Sjögren[12] in their Swedish study, and the range of the simple crude MZ concordance rate in Kallmann's 1946 twin study (50–69%) is about twice that reported from Norway by Kringlen (25–38%).

we are nevertheless justified in continuing to think about schizophrenia along genetic lines; and the recent twin studies may help us in doing so.

M. BLEULER AND GENETIC-ENVIRONMENTAL INTERACTION

Before turning to the nature of the genetic transmission, now may be the appropriate place at which to summarize and discuss Manfred Bleuler's contribution to the Conference.

Professor Bleuler has given us a fascinating account of the evolution of schizophrenia under increasingly humane and therapeutically hopeful conditions. His account was based on long observation, immense experience and an obvious desire to understand each one of 208 patients and their families.

My comments on his paper must be restricted to the genetic aspects. After the surprise of the reports from other centres of a zero concordance in identical twins[22] and of 60% of schizophrenics having at least one more-or-less schizophrenic parent,[49] it comes as something of a relief to learn that Bleuler is finding that the morbid risks for relatives in the new study are very close to those reported by the Munich school and of the order shown to us in Slater's paper. Bleuler has collected valuable empirical data on sibs that will need little correction for age, and one looks forward to their publication. It will also be of considerable interest to see to what extent he has confirmed the tendency for female relatives and those of the same sex as the patient to be at greater risk, in view of the lack of such an association in the Norwegian and London twin studies and in the Swedish population-based investigation of Hallgren and Sjögren. The long period of observation of Bleuler's families— over 20 years— raises hopes of some useful information about morbidity among the children of schizophrenics. However, numbers will probably be small, since the 1942–3 Swiss cohort was not yet narrowing the large gap in fertility between schizophrenics and the general population. In New York a decade later, Kallmann's group[50] showed that this gap was beginning to close.

As far as the genetic transmission of schizophrenia is concerned, Bleuler's theory offers no specific hypothesis that can easily be tested. If it is a disharmony of genes that is at fault, rather than a specific gene or an excess of genes having a particular effect, and moreover if the basis on which schizophrenia develops is unique in each case, it is difficult to see why it runs in families at all: one might expect it to be more randomly distributed or at most slightly raised in sibs. If Professor Bleuler merely took the view that the genotype contributed in a quite non-specific way, one would hope to look for something specific about the milieu which was common to most schizophrenics. But he takes the view that the unfavourable aspects of the environment are quite non-specific too. Thus he offers no way of discovering what is reacting with what. His paper makes one only too aware that there may be no easy answer.

When discussing the interplay of inherited predisposition and experience, Bleuler made the important point that this is a two-way process. Not only do unsatisfactory environments make living more difficult for the endangered personality, but "discordances of personality elicit discordances of the human environment". It may therefore well be that pre-schizophrenic personalities elicit so-called schizophrenogenic behaviour in parents. For instance, indecision might invite a "double-bind" as much as the converse. But, whichever cause of "schizophrenogenic" behaviour one regards as primary—mother or child or some kind of incompatibility—there is the question of the etiological contribution of the resulting disturbed personal relationships.

Bleuler drew attention to the poorly integrated nature of the schizoid personality. If we take the view that schizophrenia usually develops out of a schizoid personality, how much difference does it make to a schizoid youth whether he is brought up by a vague, nebulous mother who leaves him to his own devices without "confronting him with his responsibilities" or by a rigid, impervious, insensitive mother, and how much better does he in fact fare with a warm, understanding, accepting mother? The longitudinal study of a high risk group such as the Burghölzli families may offer some clues as to what kind of régime suits the schizoid personality best.

A further thought arises from a consideration of Bleuler's views. If it is predicted that the genetic predisposition to schizophrenia finishes with whatever it might contribute to the schizoid nature of the personality, a group that would be worth following-up would be children showing symptoms of withdrawal and daydreaming, and not selected by reason of having close relatives who are schizophrenic. Morris et al.[51] followed up 54 such children 16–24 years after they had been seen in a child guidance clinic. Only one was schizophrenic and another psychiatrically ill but unhospitalized; most were satisfactorily adjusted adults. It would appear that such children as a whole are not at serious risk of becoming schizophrenic and that the schizoid personality is not necessarily the most critical predisposing factor in schizophrenia. And more than a schizoid personality may be involved genetically.

THE NATURE OF THE GENETIC TRANSMISSION

The Munich school, empirical risk figures, major genes

I turn now to the nature of the genetic transmission. It is largely on the work of the pre-war Munich school and its pupils in other countries that one's opinion has to be based, for the simple reason that few others have collected relevant data.

There are many strong points about this work. It was based on fairly uniform diagnostic standards. It did not lump all behaviour disorders together as part of a hereditary neuropathic taint. Patients were not simply divided into those with and those without a positive family history of an ill-defined kind. Instead, workers of this school calculated the incidence of specific disorders, whether hospitalized or not, among the total number of specified relatives of defined index cases. An attempt was generally made to distinguish between definite and doubtful cases among relatives, not all of whom would be available. These workers were more sensitive than any others in the psychiatric field to problems of sampling, and on the statistical side they were advised by one of the big names in genetics, Wilhelm Weinberg. Strong links were forged with psychiatric epidemiology, especially in the Scandinavian countries, since it was important to compare empirical risk figures for relatives of patients with those for the general population. The work has been comprehensively summarized by Zerbin-Rüdin.[52]

Ideas in psychiatry have changed and it is easy to point out that the Munich school paid little attention to internal psychological processes or to interpersonal relationships which may or may not be relevant to etiology.

One of the chief conclusions of the Munich school was to establish the essential genetic independence of typical schizophrenia and typical manic–depressive psychosis. This conclusion held in general, provided typical cases were chosen. By restricting themselves to diagnostically clear starting cases in an attempt to secure genetic as well as clinical homogeneity, they may have underestimated the incidence of other disorders in relatives and overestimated the genetic distinctness of clinical syndromes. It is possible that some of the workers were over-confident of their diagnoses and unaware of the dangers of contaminated diagnosis, though the Schulz–Leonhard study[53] was an early and instructive exercise in double-blind experiment.[48]

When workers started from a total sample of psychiatric cases, not all typical ones, more diagnostic overlap was found. In Slater's[18] twin series, nearly as many sibs of 158 schizophrenics (including atypical schizophrenics) had affective disorders as schizophrenia, and there were actually more parents with affective psychosis than schizophrenia—16 as against 12; 78 parents had other abnormalities (mostly personality disorders). When Ødegaard[54] took successive admissions and compared them with their psychotic first degree relatives, he confirmed that there was a significant excess hospitalized with the same diagnosis, although there was also considerable overlapping in diagnosis between pairs of relatives. Other methods of classification were tried, but Ødegaard concluded that "evidently it is not easy to improve upon Kraepelin's nosological stroke of genius". Since affected second-degree relatives did not show a significant resemblance in psychosis of the same kind, he considered that the clear genetic background of the Kraepelinian classification was likely to be multifactorial.

Table 6 shows the results of Ødegaard's study and of similar studies by Mitsuda[55] and by Tsuang[27] which also found a significant but far from complete resemblance in diagnosis

TABLE 6. PAIRS OF RELATIVES BOTH HOSPITALIZED FOR PSYCHIATRIC DISORDER
(based on Tsuang[27])

Resemblance between relatives as to diagnosis of schizophrenia

Investigation	No. of pairs	Relationship	Method of diagnosis	Schizophrenia diagnosed in			Significance level†
				Both relatives	One only	Neither	
Mitsuda,[55] Japan	163	Not specified	Investigator	101	27	35	***
Ødegaard,[54] Norway	197	1st degree	Hospital	55	65	77	***
Tsuang,[27] U.K.	71	Sibs	Ever diagnosed	28	17	24	***
			Final hospital	13	25	33	*
			Independent	9	27	35	n.s.

† From χ^2 (1-tail).

*** $= p < 0.00025$.

* $= p < 0.05$.

between pairs of hospitalized relatives where one of them was schizophrenic. In the last and smallest of these studies the resemblance in diagnosis failed to reach statistical significance when it was made blind from a summary of the case notes.

It is instructive to recall Rüdin's[56, 48] pioneer study of the genetics of schizophrenia, published in 1916, which endeavoured to apply the principles of Mendel to the families of over 700 schizophrenics, many of them diagnosed by Kraepelin. Rüdin himself noted that psychoses of other kinds occurred in sibs nearly as frequently as dementia praecox itself; and the presence of psychoses of other kinds in a parent increased the risk of schizophrenia in a sib. A single Mendelian gene did not fit. Two independent recessive gene pairs gave a better fit, but Rüdin was not altogether satisfied with this two-gene theory and he considered the possibility that inheritance was more complex and recessive only in the sense that factors on both sides of the family were involved. This theory is not unlike some of the polygenic theories that came to be formulated later. Rüdin also studied step- and half-sibs and investigated birth order. He thought environmental factors clearly played a part in schizophrenia but their nature and importance could not be determined. Many of the problems that faced Rüdin are still with us.

It is understandable that at that time Rüdin should have started with the assumption that schizophrenia might turn out to be a simply inherited Mendelian trait, and that when Mendelian ratios did not fit, he and members of his school should think at first in terms of two or three major genes, each of which was thought to be necessary, or of single genes with reduce penetrance, or of genetic heterogeneity in the sense of a number of different major genes, any one of which might produce schizophrenia. Bruno Schulz[57] came eventually to consider this last the most likely possibility.

To some modern ears main genes and the additional assumptions of reduced penetrance and modifying genes may sound like what Medawar[58] has termed "geneticism", or the application to human affairs of a genetic knowledge or understanding which is assumed to be very much greater than it actually is. I do not believe that all who think in these terms fall into this error. Slater,[59] for instance, regards his elegant monogenic theory not as proved but as a suggestion that, despite appearances to the contrary, it might still be worth while looking for a single biochemical factor underlying most cases of strictly diagnosed schizophrenia, however much other constitutional and environmental factors also contribute. The fact that no such common cause has been discovered is not to say that it does not exist. If such a factor were identified, it would offer a reasonable hope of understanding how schizophrenia develops, and perhaps of preventing its more distressing manifestations. On monogenic theory as calculated by Slater nearly all schizophrenics will be heterozygous, only about one heterozygote in four will develop the psychosis, and there may therefore be much scope for rational environmental intervention. Since the reduced fertility of schizophrenics would eliminate more genes from one generation to the next than could easily be made up by fresh mutation, a single-gene theory would predict a hitherto unidentified balancing process, affording schizophrenic gene-carriers some selective advantage.[60]

Broad polygenic theory with spectrum of specificity

An alternative working hypothesis, and one which may seem more in keeping with our ignorance, is to start with a broad multifactorial theory in which both genetic and environmental factors are involved and in which the genetic factors are polygenic in the sense that more than one gene contributes to the end result. This would be something like retaining the old modifying genes and throwing out the hypothesis of the main gene until it has been proved essential or can be identified in the great majority of carriers. Developments in genetics over the years have stressed more and more the interaction of genes with one another in development and their interaction with the environment at all stages of life. Most genes may have specific functions, which in theory could be detected if one knew the right test. For instance, the blood group genes are detected in the laboratory by use of the appropriate anti-sera. Otherwise the direct effect of the ABO genes comes to light only in the form of a transfusion reaction. However, the ABO genes have indirect effects, if small ones, on the incidence of duodenal ulcer, cancer of the stomach and other diseases. A common assumption is that a gene affects many traits and a complex trait is influenced by many genes. A one-to-one relationship between gene and diagnosis might be thought unlikely when we are dealing with a disorder developing not until early adult life and recognized only by psychological symptoms.

But if many genes combine in the genetic predisposition to schizophrenia they may do so with different degrees of specificity. Some might be related rather closely to the development of the primary symptoms. Those who think that abnormalities of perception are basic in schizophrenia might ask whether these may be mediated in part by genes which regulate the feed-back of information. Erlenmeyer-Kimling's hopes lie in this direction.

Some of those who believe that progress in the understanding of schizophrenia may lie in the study of cognitive disturbances have also thought along genetic lines. McConaghy's[61] hypothesis was that the object sorting test might identify the heterozygotes on a recessive theory of schizophrenia; and the Lidz group,[49] who are inclined to dismiss the evidence for genetic factors in schizophrenia as out of date, make an exception when they allow the possibility of a genetic predisposition to symbolic distortion. However, from our own findings in the Maudsley schizophrenic twins and their familes I doubt whether the object sorting test will provide a simple answer.

If factors such as a low threshold for anxiety arousal are thought to be important in schizophrenia,[62] the additive effects of genes influencing the physiology of anxiety manifestations might contribute towards the schizophrenic diathesis. At a less specific level, genes contributing to an introverted temperament might play an important part. Other genes or groups of genes would play a still more indirect role, modifying the manifestation one way or another or contributing to the disharmonies of development which Bleuler believes to be of such importance.

Thus we may envisage a wide spectrum of genes varying in specificity and shading off into the genetic background as a whole. The more specific genes would tend to be the rarer of the alleles at a particular locus, or else recessive to their alternative allele. The genes in such a system would also vary somewhat as to which aspects of the illness they most affected. Generally speaking, however, the more of the predisposing genes that are inherited from among those in the system, the more likely would schizophrenia be to develop. In some cases a schizophrenic illness would be more or less inevitable, whatever the environment, and of a kind that in our present state of knowledge would carry a poor prognosis. (One thinks of Bleuler's chronic malignant schizophrenia.) In other cases, perhaps the majority, the illness would only develop under an appropriate stress (which might vary from individual to individual) and such cases might possess a better capacity for recovery. Such a theory would predict the observed tendency for some degree of resemblance in Kraepelinian sub-type, though an imperfect one, between affected first-degree relatives and a closer one between MZ twins. It would also predict a higher risk for a sib of a schizophrenic when one parent is affected than when neither is affected, and the occurrence among relatives of schizoid personalities, of borderline psychoses and of illnesses that do not fit the conventional diagnosis of schizophrenia. It would also be consistent with the tendency found in several twin studies for concordance to be higher when the illness of the proband was severe— i.e. when, other things being equal, the genotype is likely to be one containing many of the genes in the system. The difficulty to which Bleuler and Erlenmeyer-Kimling referred of how it is that the genetic elements in schizophrenia are maintained in the population despite the reduced fertility of schizophrenics is less acute under the polygenic theory, since the load is spread and the response to negative selection slower. It is conceivable that in some environments some of the contributory genes are at a selective advantage.[32, 33, 63]

A special case of a broad polygenic theory is that a major gene with low manifestation together with modifying genes might account for a high proportion of schizophrenia. This, of course, is the monogenic theory in another guise. The effects of a theory of this kind and of a simpler additive polygenic theory are similar. Evidence as to whether the major gene theory is correct could be obtained if one studied heavily loaded families with three or more affected persons in earlier generations and with good information about the more remote relatives.[64] The attempt is one that would be worth making and would be one of the tasks to be done if the broad polygenic theory is to be made more precise. It is possible that Karlsson's[33] genealogical study in Iceland adds support to a specific gene theory of some kind.

The broad theory would also allow the possibility of some heterogeneity in the sense that some cases of schizophrenia might be caused by much rarer genes with high penetrance, much as is the case in mental subnormality. Other cases might be environmental pheno-copies. The existence of such genes has been suspected but not proved, since, if they exist, they are probably not distinctive in their clinical effects. Cases of atypical schizophrenia with good recovery run true in some families. One such was recently described by Kaij,[65] suggesting the presence of a dominant gene. Elsässer's[9] work suggested that while some cases of atypical psychosis may run true to type, others are related genetically either to typical schizophrenia or to manic-depressive psychosis. Newton Morton[66] and the WHO group of experts[14] that reported recently on "Genetics in Psychiatry" have suggested that studies of the offspring of cousin marriages where both parents are normal and of certain racial crossings would help to detect whether rare recessive genes with high penetrance contributed much to the totality of psychosis. Several neurological disorders, such as the muscular dystrophies and retinitis pigmentosa, separate themselves out into several discrete genetic types.[67] Even haemophilia has been shown to consist of two sex-linked disorders, not one. But such conditions are all much rarer than schizophrenia. Probably the great mass of cases of schizophrenia would defy analysis along such lines.

Various other possibilities exist, which are consistent with current trends in genetics. Some authorities, Stern[68] among them, think that multiple alleles may well be involved in several traits. Lerner[69] discusses other possibilities such as blocks of polygenes. His chapter on polygenic inheritance is subtitled "This is an extremely intricate subject".

Simple additive polygenic system

The polygenic model I have outlined is broad but not, I hope, too vague to be helpful. A simpler if narrower version is more easily tested and has the advantage that it allows estimates to be made of the heritability of schizophrenia. The simpler polygenic model assumes that all the genes in the system are additive, that is to say they do not exhibit dominance and recessivity; they all have approximately equal effects on the trait, one allele in each pair predisposing development in a schizophrenic direction, the other in a non-schizophrenic direction; no one gene contributes substantially more than any other.[70] A large number of different gene combinations and hence different genetic pathways could produce the same end-result. Previously such models were applied only to normally distributed quantitative traits, such as stature and intelligence. More recently they have been applied to apparently all-or-none traits, such as certain diseases, for instance malignant hypertension, where disease with its secondary complications supervenes once a certain threshold in an underlying predisposing trait such as blood pressure has been passed.

Edwards[71] and Falconer[72] have put forward statistical models for calculating the proportion of first-degree relatives that would be affected if the underlying but not directly measurable predisposition were genetically determined by a simple polygenic system with a threshold effect. These estimates take the frequency of the disorder in the general population into account. The rarer the trait the nearer will the threshold be to the tail end of the distribution and the less likely that a relative will be affected. Edwards thought that the square root of the population incidence was a good approximation to the expected incidence in first-degree relatives. Thus, with a population frequency of schizophrenia taken to be 1 in 100, 1 relative in 10 will be affected without any allowance made for environmental effects. Falconer's method estimates 100% heritability when incidence in first-degree relatives is about 15%. Using the Falconer method an attempt can be made to estimate what proportion of the variance of the trait in the population studied is determined by additive genes. Heritabilities can be calculated for different relatives, taking the degree of genetic resemblance into account. These estimates should agree if all the assumptions are met. If they do not agree, the comparison of h^2 from different relatives enables one, at least in theory, to see which assumptions are not being met. Gottesman and Shields[73] have applied the method to some of the twin and family data in schizophrenia, including second-degree relatives; and estimates made from different relatives all give substantial heritabilities for the underlying liability to schizophrenia. So far as we can judge there are no significant dominance effects among the polygenes, and estimates from MZ and DZ twins agree well—for instance heritability estimates were 87% and 86% respectively in the Maudsley series and 82% and 86% in Kringlen's[36] Norwegian study. (Calculations here were in terms of co-twins of probands, counting schizophreniform psychoses, but not borderline states, as schizophrenia.) The heritabilities derived from the older twin studies gave impossibly high values of over 100% which indicated that all the assumptions of the simple polygenic model did not apply. Among various possibilities it may be that the assumption of the normal distribution of the underlying predisposition is not met. This would be so if a major dominant gene played a large part in determining liability. Major specific environmental effects of an all-or-none kind mimicking the segregation of a dominant gene could have the same effect, but not environmental influences common to whole families.

Similar estimates of heritability are obtained in diabetes, a condition that has certain parallels with schizophrenia, in so far as its incidence in the population and in families is concerned and the variety of possible genetic explanations that have been put forward. On a polygenic model, incidences of the disorder in relatives that appear to be low absolutely, but high in relation to the population incidence, are compatible with a high degree of genetic control.

SOME POSSIBILITIES FOR FURTHER GENETIC RESEARCH

An estimate of heritability derived from a simple polygenic model (or for that matter of the manifestation rate on a monogenic model), though perhaps a valuable first step, is not something we should be satisfied with for long. One of the tasks should be to identify contributing genetic factors and explore how they combine or interact with one another and the environment.

One approach already mentioned that may be fruitful is to make genetic studies of perceptual, cognitive or other personality measures that might contribute to part of the underlying predisposition; and another is to carry out further studies on the illnesses of pairs of affected relatives to find out which aspects of psychosis have the highest heritability.

In recent years an increasing number of genetic polymorphisms have been discovered, not only blood groups but also plasma proteins and red-cell enzymes.[74, 75] We have the position, on the one hand, of polymorphisms in search of diseases to which one of the genes confers some degree of protection, and, on the other hand, of diseases in search of major genes with identifiable effects that make a minor contribution to their etiology. For instance, it is known that duodenal ulcer is more likely to occur in persons of blood group O and in non-secretors of ABO substances in the saliva than it is in other persons; but Fraser Roberts[76] has estimated that only 3% of the degree of resemblance between brothers in respect of duodenal ulcer is to be ascribed to their sharing genes at these two loci. These major genes would therefore be contributing a small part towards the underlying multifactorial basis of duodenal ulcer. A suggestive provisional report by Camps and Dodd[77] revealed a significant excess of non-secretors belonging to blood group A in a sample of 218 alcoholics. It might be worth while looking at the distribution of the new enzyme polymorphisms in schizophrenia.

Psychiatric disorders of other kinds such as occur to excess in the families of schizophrenics may be studied independently to learn whether there is an excess of schizophrenia in the relatives of an unselected sample of persons suffering from these disorders. In this way the genetic relationship between the various psychiatric syndromes may be explored.

I

A number of conditions other than process schizophrenia have been studied in which the risk of schizophrenia in a sib has been found to be considerably raised above that in the general population but lower than that generally found in the sibs of schizophrenics. Table 7

TABLE 7. SOME DISORDERS POSSIBLY RELATED GENETICALLY TO
TYPICAL SCHIZOPHRENIA

Nature of illness in proband	Risk of schizophrenia in sibs (%)
Recovered schizophrenia (Wittermans and Schulz)[78]	3·3
Late paraphrenia (Kay and Roth)[79]	3·4
Involutional psychosis (Kallmann)[80]	4·2
Delusional climacteric psychosis (Knoll)[81]	4·7–6·5
Schizophrenic reaction (Rohr)[82]	5·3
Mixed psychosis (manic-depressive/schizophrenic) (Angst)[83]	7·1
Paranoia (Kolle)[84]	2·9–8·6

shows some where the risk lies between 3% and 8%. The work of Rohr[82] and Angst[83] was done in Bleuler's department. Where two figures appear these are the risks for definite schizophrenia and for schizophrenia inclusive of doubtful cases. Schizophrenia precipitated by head injury entailed a schizophrenia risk for sibs of 2·9%[85] and is not shown. Benign schizophreniform psychosis as studied by Welner and Strömgren[86] entailed a total psychosis risk of 4·9% for the sibs, but surprisingly the risk for strictly diagnosed schizophrenia was only 1·3%. So far as I know there have been no genetic studies of borderline states or of pseudoneurotic schizophrenia.

In those conditions that show a raised schizophrenia risk for relatives, one possibility is heterogeneity: a proportion may be genetically the equivalent of typical schizophrenics and the remainder unrelated genetically to schizophrenia. This is the explanation that comes to mind if one thinks along monogenic lines. Another possibility, in accord with a polygenic model, is that most sufferers from these conditions share to a greater extent than the average person but to a lesser extent than most typical schizophrenics genes which contribute to the polygenic system.

Evidence that schizophrenia is not merely an environmentally determined exaggeration of neurosis comes from studies which start with neurotic patients. Ernst[87, 88] found no excess of schizophrenia in the families of neurotics except in the minority of cases where the neurotic patient was found on follow-up to have developed schizophrenia himself. The most distinctive feature of the genetic investigations in schizophrenia is therefore the big relative increase in the families in the incidence of the same infrequent disorder, schizophrenia, rather than the lower relative increase in the incidence of neuroses or minor character disorders which are common.

If there is a genetic connection between schizophrenia and giftedness, it is unlikely in general to be a close one. Juda studied 294 men of genius and Zerbin-Rüdin 412 first-class university entrants. In neither group was there a significant excess of schizophrenia in the subjects themselves or in their parents, sibs or children.[89]

It is probably to the distinctive quality of the personality disorder in abnormal relatives that considerable attention should be devoted, as the earlier workers realized when they tried to distinguish schizoid psychopathy from other abnormalities. By using control groups consisting of the families of other kinds of patient and employing appropriate tests and observations, one would hope to define more clearly what personality characteristics should be called schizoid or schizotypic and what psychiatric disorders be regarded as forming part of the schizophrenic *Kreis,* spectrum or continuum of psychopathology.

Light on some of the constitutional characteristics predisposing to schizophrenia might also be shed by the comparison of schizophrenics with their healthy same-sexed sibs. Yet a further step to be taken is called for whenever any promising biochemical lead is discovered. Many biochemical abnormalities found in schizophrenics may be attributable to the effects of the illness or of drugs or of hospital diet. Any tendency for the levels of untreated relatives to be raised in respect of the same abnormality would rule out the effect of illness, drugs and diet and throw light on the nature of the genetic predisposition. Leads in this direction[90, 91] have yet to be confirmed.

It is clear that classical twin and foster child studies comprise only a part of psychiatric genetics.

INTERACTION WITH ENVIRONMENT

An account of the genetic evidence would be incomplete without any mention of the role of environmental factors. Since these, and the nature of their interaction, are to be discussed in the following sessions, I will restrict myself to a discussion of questions that have been raised by speakers on the genetic panel—first, the environmental aspect of diathesis–stress theory and its relationship to severity and concordance; and secondly, the lessons that can be learned from studies of discordant MZ twins.

Diathesis–stress theories and severity

Diathesis–stress types of theory, in which the genetic and environmental factors contributing to a disorder are each thought of as being essentially graded, have been ably put forward by Rosenthal[92] in respect of schizophrenia, by Slater and Slater[93] in their heuristic theory of neurosis, and by Freud. In 1937 Freud[94] wrote: "The aetiology of all neuroses is a mixed one . . . Generally there is a contribution of the two factors: the constitutional and the accidental. The stronger the constitutional factor the more readily will a trauma lead to fixation, with its sequence in a disturbance of development; the stronger the trauma the more certain is it that it will have injurious effects even when the patient's instinctual life is normal." In the same paper Freud made it clear that by constitutional he meant genetic. "It does not imply a mystical overvaluation of heredity", so he believed, "if we think it credible that, even before the ego exists, its subsequent lines of development, tendencies and reactions are already determined." Those who have formulated diathesis–stress theories have generally regarded them as potentially helpful in planning treatment and predicting outcome.

Gottesman[4] analysed in some detail the rather striking association between severity of schizophrenia in the proband and presence of schizophrenia in the co-twin which came to light in the Maudsley twin series. He interpreted it in terms of a polygenic theory. Theoretically, however, it is only one side of the picture to observe that persons suffering from a severe or chronic form of a disorder to which a diathesis–stress model applies will be those in whom the genetic predisposition was strong. Provided that there are some environmental variables that generally tend to facilitate the development of the disorder and that the role they play is not entirely insignificant compared with that of heredity, then severe intractable cases will tend to score higher in respect of these variables than milder cases. This is best demonstrated when heredity is controlled. In the unique case of the Genain quadruplets,[91] identical in their heredity and all of them schizophrenic, the four sisters between them spanned a wide range of severity; and by dint of a uniquely thorough investigation it could be shown how differences in severity and in premorbid personality were related to the different life experiences of the quadruplets, notably those arising from the different personal relationships that developed in an extremely disturbed family environment.

However, no corresponding association across potentially schizophrenic genotypes has so far been clearly demonstrated. One would predict that the shared premorbid backgrounds of concordant MZ pairs would be more noxious than those of discordant pairs. Kringlen[5] has looked at this point and is cautious about his findings. Gottesman and I have also examined the Maudsley study from this point of view, so far without conspicuous success. This is not to say that differences between the backgrounds of concordant and discordant pairs do not exist. But the higher the heritability of schizophrenia the more difficult will they be to detect.

The initial assumption as regards symptoms, on the one hand, and severity, on the other, is the unhelpful one that heredity and environment each influences both the nature of the psychiatric disorder and its severity. On the whole, however, evidence seems to favour the view that in some respects heredity is rather more important for the type of reaction, whereas its occurrence and severity are more dependent on environmental stresses. This was one of the conclusions of a Maudsley Hospital study[95] of 192 neurotic and personality disordered twin pairs. And in families containing a schizophrenic, it is schizophrenia and related disorders that are revealed by means of twin and family studies as being influenced genetically, rather than the presence or absence of abnormality of *any* kind. Again, within pairs where both twins are definitely schizophrenic, resemblance as to sub-type is marked, as the Norwegian, the Maudsley and the Genain studies show, whereas many twin pairs are discordant and several differ in severity.

Discordant MZ pairs

It has been the hope of all investigators of schizophrenic twins that the histories of discordant MZ pairs would lead to the identification of critical environmental events for the development of the psychosis. Unfortunately their attempts have tended to be submerged in the heated nature–nurture controversy.

There are difficulties, however, in interpreting the observations on discordant pairs from the point of view of environmental causes of schizophrenia. There is the possibility, particularly if the twins are young, that the pair will eventually become concordant; there is the possibility that the illnesses of a sizeable proportion of twins with unaffected partners may represent different varieties of schizophrenia from the illnesses of twins with concordant partners, and consequently that conclusions from the one group may not be applicable to the other; and thirdly, the difference between the twins may be rather small, if (for example) one is a reactive schizophrenic and the other a compensated schizotype with borderline features, leaving relatively little difference to account for.[40]

What may perhaps be more misleading is that, if genetics plays a major and specific role, the environmental factors associated with the affected twin may be interaction effects only, i.e. they may operate only on the relatively few genetically predisposed individuals, and have little or no influence as independent causes of schizophrenia over the population as a whole. Whether this is so or not would need to be decided by investigation of the schizophrenia-risk for persons who have been exposed to the suspect environmental variable but who are not selected because they are close relatives of schizophrenics. While no one would wish to deny the importance of discovering the nature of precipitating factors, it might be misleading to suppose that one had necessarily thereby discovered factors that were etiological in their own right. This would be an example of the error Thoday [96] has termed "environmentalism". Furthermore, the factors differentiating the future schizophrenic from his co-twin may highlight prematurity and dominance–submissiveness in a manner that might be less relevant in the singly born than in twins.

In their papers Tienari and Kringlen reported some of the premorbid features in which the future schizophrenic tended to differ from his twin. They agreed in finding him to have been submissive to his twin and somewhat more dependent on his mother, to have had a poorer relationship with his father and to have had a less active sex life. Birth weight and physical development in childhood were not so clearly related to schizophrenia. Particularly in the matter of dominance, there was general agreement in the Maudsley and Slater twin studies too. Inouye also found the schizophrenic or the more severely affected schizophrenic to have been the more passive and asocial twin. The intra-pair differences noted do not appear to be specific for schizophrenia, however. Kringlen commented that the future schizophrenic showed a greater general predisposition to mental illness. Tienari[22] found similar intra-pair differences to distinguish twins discordant in respect of neurosis. And there were no differentiating features in Slater's study that were distinctive for the schizophrenic group.

The Twin and Sibling Unit at the NIH has been reporting interesting findings from their intensive investigation of a young and specially selected sample of discordant pairs. As a crude example of what I mean by the need to test out environmental hypotheses on persons not selected by reason of their genetic relationship to a schizophrenic, I have attempted to relate the environmental variables found by the Pollin group to the total sample of Finnish twins reported in detail by Tienari.[97]

Pollin et al.[98, 99] found that in MZ pairs discordant for schizophrenia the future schizophrenic had generally been consistently inferior to his co-twin in a number of ways, including birth weight, submissiveness and school achievement. It might be considered that such factors were cumulative in their effect. With each taken singly, there might be a tendency for the poorer twin in respect of a variable to have somewhat poorer psychiatric adjustment, though there would be many exceptions, inferiority in some variables being balanced by superiority in others; but (or so it might be argued), when all occur together in the same twin, this twin would surely be at greater risk for psychiatric disorder than twins as a whole—in a high proportion of cases such twins would be so "battered" psychologically that they might become psychotic. The superior twin, spared these relevant stresses, should be healthier than most. Whether or not the inferior twin was schizophrenic or merely neurotic or delinquent would no doubt depend upon the quality of the family environment, or whether the inferior twin had identified with the psychologically sicker parent, according to current psychodynamic views.[49, 100]

Tienari[96] studied personally all available identical male twins, born 1920–9, normal and abnormal, living in a defined region of Finland, and he assessed them according to a number of intra-pair differences, including birth weight, three aspects of dominance-submissiveness, and school achievement.

TABLE 8. INTRA-PAIR DIFFERENCES AND PSYCHIATRIC ABNORMALITY: EFFECT OF CUMULATIVE DIFFERENCES IN BIRTH WEIGHT, DOMINANCE (3 ASPECTS) AND SCHOOL ACHIEVEMENT
(data taken from Tienari,[97] all identical twins in Finnish regional group)

Psychiatric classification (Tienari)	Pairs in which the same twin is inferior in all variables			Twins from other pairs	All twins
	(1) Inferior twin	(2) Expected*	(3) Superior twin	(4)	(5)
Normal	10	(10)	11	52	73
Deviant personality	5	(8)	7	46	58
Neurotic or psychopathic	4	(2)	3	12	19
Psychotic	3	(2)	1	6	10
Total persons	22	(22)	22	116	160

* Calculated (to nearest whole number) from col. (5).

TABLE 9. CUMULATIVE INTRA-PAIR DIFFERENCES AND PSYCHIATRIC ABNORMALITY
(IDENTICAL TWINS IN REGIONAL GROUP)
(data taken from Table 8)

Investigator's psychiatric classification	Twins differing consistently from partner in birth weight, dominance (all aspects) and school achievement (22 pairs)		
	Inferior twin	Expected (derived from all 80 pairs in group)	Superior twin
Normal	10	10	11
Not normal	12	12	11
Alternative division			
Normal or deviant	15	18	18
Neurotic, psychopathic or psychotic	7	4	4

Twenty-two out of eighty pairs of identical twins differed in such a way that the same twin was inferior in all five variables. Let us now see how the 22 "inferior" and 22 "superior" twins, thus defined, differ from one another and from twins as a whole in their psychiatric adjustment. Table 9 (which is derived from Table 8) shows the sample divided into "normal" and "abnormal" groups in two different ways, first into those classified by Tienari as "normal", on the one hand, and as deviant personality, neurotic, psychopathic or psychotic, on the other. On the basis of the total of 160 twins one would expect in a sample of 22 to find about 10 normal and 12 abnormal persons. This is precisely the distribution observed among the 22 inferior twins. The latter are just as often normal as Finnish twins as a whole.

The lower part of the table shows an alternative grouping. When deviant personalities are classed with normals there is now a tendency for the inferior twin to be more often abnormal than in the population as a whole—the figures are 7 abnormal observed as against 4 expected—but the "superior" twins, whom one would expect to have a low risk, have their full share of abnormality. This suggests that low birth weight plus submissiveness plus low achievement are not the chief determinants of psychiatric abnormality over the twin population as a whole.

I may have sounded cautious about the prospects of advances in our study of environmental factors, in the strict sense, through the study of the twins of schizophrenics or other high-risk groups. And it may be, as Bleuler believes, that the stresses may be too variable from person to person to allow any generalization. But one hopes not. The belief that, in our present state of knowledge, genetic factors are likely to be paramount, does not make it any less important to try to identify the kind of environments which, at the physiological, sociological or inter-personal level, facilitate or prevent the most malignant manifestations of schizophrenic disorder in persons predisposed to it. On the contrary, any line of investigation is to be encouraged that will enable the genetic–environmental interaction to be better understood and rational prophylactic measures to be adopted. One hopes that, by whatever means, an environmental factor or constellation of factors will be identified which will predict schizophrenia. It may not do so with the same likelihood as is predicted by being the identical twin of a schizophrenic, whether reared in the same home or not; but perhaps some factor may be found which would predict schizophrenia with a likelihood approaching that of the risk incurred (say) by the sib of a schizophrenic. Perhaps the later sessions of the Conference will provide some clues.

REFERENCES

1. BLEULER, M., A 23-year longitudinal study of 208 schizophrenics and impressions in regard to the nature of schizophrenia. These Proceedings, p. 3.
2. SLATER, E., A review of earlier evidence on genetic factors in schizophrenia. These Proceedings, p. 15.
3. TIENARI, P., Schizophrenia in monozygotic male twins. These Proceedings, p. 27.
4. GOTTESMAN, I. I., Severity/concordance and diagnostic refinement in the Maudsley–Bethlem schizophrenic twin study. These Proceedings, p. 37.
5. KRINGLEN, E., An epidemiological–clinical twin study on schizophrenia. These Proceedings, p. 49.
6. ERLENMEYER-KIMLING, L., Studies on the offspring of two schizophrenic parents. These Proceedings, p. 65.
7. SHIELDS, J. and SLATER, E., Genetic aspects of schizophrenia, *Hosp. Med. (Lond.)* **1,** 579 (1967).
8. KALLMANN, F. J., *The Genetics of Schizophrenia,* New York, Augustin, 1938.
9. ELSÄSSER, G., *Die Nachkommen geisteskranker Elternpaare,* Stuttgart, Thieme, 1952.
10. ROSENTHAL, D., The offspring of schizophrenic couples, *J. Psychiat. Res.* **4,** 169 (1966).

11. Böök, J. A., A genetic and neuropsychiatric investigation of a north-Swedish population, *Acta genet.* (*Basel*) **4**, 1 (1953).
12. HALLGREN, B. and SJÖGREN, T., A clinical and genetico-statistical study of schizophrenia and low-grade mental deficiency in a large Swedish rural population, *Acta psychiat.* (*Kbh.*), Suppl. 140 (1959).
13. KALLMANN, F. J., FALEK, A., HURZELER, M., and ERLENMEYER-KIMLING, L., The developmental aspects of children with two schizophrenic parents, *Psychiat. Res. Rep. Amer. Psychiat. Assoc.* **19**, 136 (1964)
14. WHO, *Research on Genetics in Psychiatry*, report of a WHO Scientific Group, *Wld. Hlth. Org. Techn. Rep. Ser.* **346** (1966).
15. COWIE, J., COWIE, V. A., and SLATER, E., *Delinquency in Girls*, London, Heinemann (in press).
16. SCHULZ, B., Zur Frage der Erblichkeit in der Schizophrenie, *Acta genet.* (*Basel*) **6**, 50 (1956).
17. KALLMANN, F. J., The genetic theory of schizophrenia: an analysis of 691 schizophrenic twin index families, *Am. J. Psychiat.* **103**, 309 (1946).
18. SLATER, E. (with the assistance of SHIELDS, J.), *Psychotic and Neurotic Illnesses in Twins*, Medical Research Council special report series, No. 278, London, Her Majesty's Stationery Office, 1953.
19. ROSENTHAL, D., Familial concordance by sex with respect to schizophrenia, *Psychol. Bull.* **59**, 401 (1962).
20. ZEHNDER, M., Über Krankheitsbild und Krankheitsverlauf bei schizophrenen Geschwistern, *Mschr. Psychiat. Neurol.* **103**, 230 (1941).
21. SHEPHERD, M., COOPER, B., BROWN, A. C., and KALTON, G. W., *Psychiatric Illness in General Practice*, London, Oxford University Press, 1966.
22. TIENARI, P., Psychiatric illnesses in identical twins, *Acta psychiat.* (*Kbh.*), Suppl. 171 (1963).
23. JACKSON, D. D., A critique of the literature on the genetics of schizophrenia, in D. D. Jackson (ed.), *The Etiology of Schizophrenia*, New York, Basic Books (p. 37), 1960.
24. ROSENTHAL, D., Confusion of identity and the frequency of schizophrenia in twins, *Arch. Gen. Psychiat.* **3**, 297 (1960).
25. ABE, K., The morbidity rate and environmental influence in monozygotic co-twins of schizophrenics, *Brit. J. Psychiat.* (in press).
26. ESSEN-MÖLLER, E., Psychiatrische Untersuchungen an einer Serie von Zwillingen, *Acta psychiat.* (*Kbh.*), Suppl. 23 (1941).
27. TSUANG, M. T., A study of pairs of sibs both hospitalized for mental disorder, *Brit. J. Psychiat.* **113**, 283 (1967).
28. SHIELDS, J., *Monozygotic Twins Brought up Apart and Brought up Together*, London, Oxford University Press, 1962.
29. JUEL-NIELSEN, N., Individual and environment, a psychiatric–psychological investigation of monozygotic twins reared apart, *Acta psychiat.* (*Kbh.*), Suppl. 183 (1965).
30. ROSANOFF, A. J., HANDY, L. M., and PLESSET, I. R., The etiology of manic-depressive syndromes with special reference to their occurrence in twins, *Am. J. Psychiat.* **91**, 725 (1935).
31. PRICE, J. S., The genetics of depressive behaviour, in A. Coppen and A. Walk (eds.), *Recent Advances in Affective Disorders*, London, Roy. Med.-psychol. Assoc. (in press).
32. HESTON, L. L., Psychiatric disorders in foster home reared children of schizophrenic mothers, *Brit. J. Psychiat.* **112**, 819 (1966).
33. KARLSSON, J. L., *The Biologic Basis of Schizophrenia*, Thomas, Springfield, Ill., 1966.
34. FISCHER, M., Preliminary report of a Danish twin study on schizophrenia (in preparation).
35. HARVALD, B. and HAUGE, M., Hereditary factors elucidated by twin studies, in J. V. Neel, M. W. Shaw and W. J. Schull (eds.), *Genetics and the Epidemiology of Chronic Diseases*, Washington, D.C., US Department of Health, Education and Welfare (p. 61), 1965.
36. KRINGLEN, E., Schizophrenia in twins, an epidemiological–clinical study, *Psychiatry* **29**, 172 (1966).
37. GOTTESMAN, I. I. and SHIELDS, J., Schizophrenia in twins: 16 years' consecutive admissions to a psychiatric clinic, *Brit. J. Psychiat.* **112**, 809 (1966).
38. SHIELDS, J., SLATER, E., and GOTTESMAN, I. I., Kallmann's 1946 schizophrenic twin study in the light of new information, *Acta psychiat.*, (*Kbh.*), **43**, 385 (1967).
39. JABLON, S., NEEL, J. V., GERSHOWITZ, H., and ATKINSON, G. F., The NAS–NRC twin panel: methods of construction of the panel, zygosity diagnosis, and proposed use, *Am. J. Hum. Genet.* **19**, 133 (1967).
40. GOTTESMAN, I. I. and SHIELDS, J., Contributions of twin studies to perspectives on schizophrenia, in B. A. Maher (ed.), *Progress in Experimental Personality Research*, Vol. 3, New York, Academic Press (p. 1), 1966.
41. LUXENBURGER, H., Vorläufiger Bericht über psychiatrische Serienuntersuchungen an Zwillingen, *Z. ges. Neurol. Psychiat.* **116**, 297 (1928).

42. ROSANOFF, A. J., HANDY, L. M., PLESSET, I. R., and BRUSH, S., The etiology of so-called schizophrenic psychoses with special reference to their occurrence in twins, *Am. J. Psychiat.* **91**, 247 (1934).

43. INOUYE, E., Similarity and dissimilarity of schizophrenia in twins, *Proceedings, Third World Congress of Psychiatry 1961*, **1**, 524, Montreal, University of Toronto Press, 1963.

44. ROSENTHAL, D., Sex distribution and the severity of illness among samples of schizophrenic twins, *J. Psychiat. Res.* **1**, 26 (1961).

45. ROSENTHAL, D., Some factors associated with concordance and discordance with respect to schizophrenia in monozygotic twins, *J. Nerv. Ment. Dis.* **129**, 1 (1959).

46. ALLEN, G., HARVALD, B., and SHIELDS, J., Measures of twin concordance, *Acta genet. (Basel)* **17**, 475 (1967).

47. ALLEN, G., Twin research: problems and prospects, in A. G. Steinberg and A. G. Bearn (eds.), *Progress in Medical Genetics, IV,* New York, Grune & Stratton (p. 242), 1965.

48. SHIELDS, J., The genetics of schizophrenia in historical context, in A. Coppen and A. Walk (eds.), *Recent Developments in Schizophrenia, A Symposium,* London, Roy. Med.-psychol. Assoc. (p. 25), 1967.

49. LIDZ, T., FLECK, S., and CORNELISON, A. R., *Schizophrenia and the Family,* New York, International Universities Press, 1966.

50. ERLENMEYER-KIMLING, L., RAINER, J. D., and KALLMANN, F. J., Current reproductive trends in schizophrenia, in P. H. Hoch and J. Zubin (eds.), *Psychopathology of Schizophrenia,* New York, Grune & Stratton (p. 252), 1966.

51. MORRIS, D. P., SOROKER, E., and BURRUSS, G., Follow-up studies of shy, withdrawn children—1: Evaluation of later adjustment, *Am. J. Orthopsychiat.* **24**, 743 (1954).

52. ZERBIN-RÜDIN, E., Endogene Psychosen, in P. E. Becker (ed.), *Handbuch der Humangenetik,* Vol. V/2, Stuttgart, Thieme (p. 446), 1967.

53. SCHULZ, B. and LEONHARD, K., Erbbiologisch-klinische Untersuchungen an insgesamt 99 im Sinne Leonhards typischen beziehungsweise atypischen Schizophrenien, *Z. ges. Neurol. Psychiat.* **168**, 587 (1940).

54. ØDEGAARD, Ø., The psychiatric disease entities in the light of genetic investigation, *Acta psychiat. (Kbh.),* Suppl. 169, 94 (1963).

55. MITSUDA, H., Klinische-erbbiologische Untersuchung der endogen Psychosen, *Acta genet. (Basel)* **7**, 371 (1957).

56. RÜDIN, E., *Zur Vererbung und Neuentstehung der Dementia Praecox,* Berlin, Springer, 1916.

57. SCHULZ, B., Die Schizophreniegefährdung der verwandten Schizophrener, *Ärztl. Monatshefte f. berufl. Fortbild.* **5**, 299 (1950).

58. MEDAWAR, P., *The Future of Man,* London, Methuen, 1960.

59. SLATER, E., The monogenic theory of schizophrenia, *Acta genet. (Basel)* **8**, 50 (1958).

60. HUXLEY, J. A., MAYR, E., OSMOND, H., and HOFFER, A., Schizophrenia as a genetic morphism, *Nature (London)* **204**, 220 (1964).

61. MCCONAGHY, N., The use of an object sorting test in elucidating the hereditary factor in schizophrenia, *J. Neurol. Neurosurg. Psychiat.* **22**, 243 (1959).

62. MEDNICK, S. A. and SCHULSINGER, F., A longitudinal study of children with a high risk for schizophrenia: a preliminary report, in S. G. Vandenberg (ed.), *Methods and Goals in Human Behavior Genetics,* New York, Academic Press (p. 255), 1965.

63. GOTTESMAN, I. I., Personality and natural selection, in S. G. Vandenberg (ed.), *Methods and Goals in Human Behavior Genetics,* New York, Academic Press (p. 63), 1965.

64. SLATER, E., The expectation of abnormality on paternal and maternal sides: a computational model, *J. Med. Genet.* **3**, 159 (1966).

65. KAIJ, L., Atypical endogenous psychosis: report on a family, *Brit. J. Psychiat.* **113**, 415 (1967).

66. MORTON, N. E., The detection of major genes under additive continuous variation, *Am. J. Hum. Genet.* **19**, 23 (1967).

67. PRATT, R. T. C., *The Genetics of Neurological Disorders,* London, Oxford University Press, 1967.

68. STERN, C., Population genetics—statement by the moderator, *Proc. World Population Conf.* **1**, 114 (1965).

69. LERNER, I. M., *The Genetic Basis of Natural Selection,* New York, Wiley, 1958.

70. MATHER, K., *Human Diversity,* Edinburgh, Oliver & Boyd, 1964.

71. EDWARDS, J. H., The simulation of Mendelism, *Acta genet. (Basel)* **10**, 63 (1960).

72. FALCONER, D. S., The inheritance of liability to certain diseases, estimated from the incidence among relatives, *Ann. Hum. Genet. (Lond.)* **29**, 51 (1965).

73. GOTTESMAN, I. I. and SHIELDS, J., A polygenic theory of schizophrenia, *Proc. Nat. Acad. Sci.* **58**, 199 (1967).

74. HARRIS, H., Inherited variations of human plasma proteins, *Brit. Med. Bull.* **17,** 217 (1961).
75. PRICE, J., Human polymorphism, *J. Med. Genet.* **4,** 44 (1967).
76. ROBERTS, J. A. F., ABO blood groups, secretor status, and susceptibility to chronic diseases: an example of a genetic basis for family predispositions, in J. V. Neel, M. W. Shaw, and W. J. Schull (eds.), *Genetics and the Epidemiology of Chronic Diseases,* Washington, D.C., US Department of Health, Education and Welfare (p. 77), 1965.
77. CAMPS, F. E. and DODD, B. E., Increase in the incidence of non-secretors of ABH blood group substances among alcoholic patients, *Brit. Med. J.* **i,** 30 (1967).
78. WITTERMANS, A. W. and SCHULZ, B., Genealogischer Beitrag zur Frage der geheilten Schizophrenien, *Arch. Psychiat. Nervenkr.* **185,** 211 (1950).
79. KAY, D. W. and ROTH, M., Environmental and hereditary factors in the schizophrenias of old age ("late paraphrenia") and their bearing on the general problem of causation in schizophrenia, *J. Ment. Sci.* **107,** 649 (1961).
80. KALLMANN, F. J., The genetics of psychoses: an analysis of 1232 twin index families, *Congrès International de Psychiatrie,* Rapports VI: Psychiatrie Sociale, Paris, Hermann (p. 1), 1950.
81. KNOLL, H., Wahnbildende Psychosen der Zeit des Klimakteriums und der Involution in klinischer und genealogischer Betrachtung, *Arch. Psychiat. Nervenkr.* **189,** 59 (1952).
82. ROHR, K., Beitrag zur Kenntnis der sogenannten schizophrenen Reaktion, *Arch. Psychiat. Nervenkr.* **201,** 626 (1961).
83. ANGST, J., *Zur Ätiologie und Nosologie endogener depressiver Psychosen,* Monogr. Gesamt. Neurol. und Psychiat. 112, Berlin, Springer, 1966.
84. KOLLE, K., *Die primäre Verrücktheit,* Leipzig, Thieme, 1931.
85. SCHULZ, B., Zur Erbpathologie der Schizophrenie, *Z. ges. Neurol. Psychiat.* **143,** 175 (1932).
86. WELNER, J. and STRÖMGREN, E., Clinical and genetic studies on benign schizophreniform psychoses based on a follow-up, *Acta psychiat. (Kbh.),* **33,** 377 (1958).
87. ERNST, K., *Die Prognosen der Neurosen, 120 jahrzehntelange Katamnesen poliklinischer Fälle,* Monogr. Gesamt. Neurol. und Psychiat. 85, Berlin, Springer, 1959.
88. ERNST, K. and ERNST, C., 70 zwanzigjährige Katamnesen hospitalisierter neurotischer Patientinnen, *Schweiz. Arch. Neurol.* **95,** 359 (1965).
89. ZERBIN-RÜDIN, E., Psychiatrische, soziologische und genetische Aspekte der Begabung, *Praxis,* **54,** 1435 (1965).
90. ARNOLD, O. H. and HOFFMANN, G., Ergebnisse einer biochemischen Untersuchungsmethode der Schizophrenie und ihres Erbhintergrundes, *Wien. klin. Wschr.* **75,** 593 (1963).
91. FESSEL, W. J., HIRATA-HIBI, M., and SHAPIRO, I. M., Genetic and stress factors affecting the abnormal lymphocyte in schizophrenia, *J. Psychiat. Res.* **3,** 275 (1965).
92. ROSENTHAL, D. (ed.) *et al., The Genain Quadruplets,* New York, Basic Books, 1963.
93. SLATER, E. and SLATER, P., A heuristic theory of neurosis, *J. Neurol. Psychiat.* **7,** 49 (1944).
94. FREUD, S., Analysis terminable and interminable, *Collected Papers,* 5, London, Hogarth (p. 316), 1937.
95. SHIELDS, J. and SLATER, E., La similarité du diagnostic chez les jumeaux et le problème de la spécificité biologique dans les névroses et les troubles de la personnalité, *L'Évolution Psychiatrique* 31, 441 (1966).
96. THODAY, J. M., Geneticism and environmentalism, in J. E. Meade and A. S. Parkes (Eds.), *Biological Aspects of Social Problems,* Edinburgh, Oliver & Boyd (p. 92), 1965.
97. TIENARI, P., On intrapair differences in male twins, *Acta psychiat. (Kbh.),* Suppl. 188 (1966).
98. POLLIN, W., STABENAU, J. R., and TUPIN, J., Family studies with identical twins discordant for schizophrenia, *Psychiatry* **28,** 60 (1965).
99. POLLIN, W., STABENAU, J. R., MOSHER, L., and TUPIN, J., Life history differences in identical twins discordant for schizophrenia, *Am. J. Orthopsychiat.* **36,** 492 (1966).
100. MOSHER, L. R., POLLIN, W., and STABENAU, J., Identification, cognitive style and psychopathology in identical twins, Paper presented at annual meeting of Amer. Psychiat. Assoc., Atlantic City, N.J., May 1966.

III. SOCIAL, CULTURAL AND INTERPERSONAL STUDIES

DOES SCHIZOPHRENIA DISORGANIZE THE FAMILY?
THE MODIFICATION OF AN HYPOTHESIS

LLOYD ROGLER

Department of Sociology, Yale University,
New Haven, Connecticut

ABOUT 2 years ago Professor Hollingshead and I published *Trapped: Families and Schizophrenia.*[1] This book reported the findings of an intensive, controlled case study of 40 families who live in the slums and public housing developments of the San Juan metropolitan area of Puerto Rico. To gather data for the study, from 35 to 40 visits were made to each family over a 4- to 7-month period. The husbands and wives were interviewed separately on these visits but with identical schedules. We have data also from observations made in the homes and neighborhoods of the families. Repeated visits were necessary to observe interpersonal relations in the families and to secure the personal, intimate information we needed.

The third source of data comes from a 2-hour psychiatric examination made by professionally trained Puerto Rican psychiatrists to determine the mental health status of each husband and wife. In 20 of the families neither the husband nor the wife was afflicted with a psychotic disorder. In the other 20 families at least one spouse was diagnosed as schizophrenic: specifically, in 7 families the husband but not the wife was schizophrenic; in 9 families the wife but not the husband was afflicted with this disorder; and in 4 families both spouses were schizophrenic.

The 20 families with at least one spouse who was schizophrenic were screened from those persons who had solicited psychiatric aid at the local clinics and hospital or who had been referred there for treatment. The 20 families in which neither spouse was afflicted with schizophrenia were drawn from a pre-listed census of households in the residential areas where the afflicted families lived. All 40 families resided in the San Juan metropolitan area. The spouses lived in the same household and were between 20 and 39 years of age. All the families were in the Class V group which is the lowest socioeconomic group according to Hollingshead's Two Factor Index of Social Position (August B. Hollingshead, *Two Factor Index of Social Position,* New Haven, Connecticut: privately printed, 1957).

Today I would like to present to you some observations and second thoughts about schizophrenia as it may affect the lower-class Puerto Rican family. One purpose of our research was to study the impact of schizophrenia on the family. The working hypothesis was that schizophrenia would have a marked and pronounced disruptive effect upon the family. We thought a severe mental disorder, such as schizophrenia, could be expected to

[1] Lloyd H. Rogler and August B. Hollingshead, *Trapped: Families and Schizophrenia,* John Wiley, New York, 1965.

rupture the unity of the family, bring chaos and confusion, and create bitterness between the husband and wife. In brief, the effect would be disorganization within the family. This thinking had its roots in a broad discursive assumption that pervades much of the literature in the behavioral sciences, namely that personal and social disorganization are interrelated.

Another source of the hypothesis came to light as we interviewed the mentally sick persons about their illness. The schizophrenic persons viewed their illness as a wicked intrusion that had caused them great suffering, and they wanted to rid themselves of the torment it brought to their lives. To explain the illness, they blamed problems at work and in the family; physical illnesses and the deaths of family members; starvation; bewitchment through evil spirits; physical beatings; violence; and so on through the painful vicissitudes of life at the bottom rung of the socioeconomic ladder. Practically all of the causes they cited have a common property: they are bad or wrong in a moral sense. Thus, underlying the sick person's thoughts about his illness is an assumption that bad effects must have had bad causes. But many theoretical speculations in social psychiatry—whether they deal with the causes or effects of mental illness—are not free of this assumption, as I think could be shown by an examination of the variables which are often considered to be relevant. As researchers, we were no exception to this point. We expected that family disorganization would result from the schizophrenia of the spouses both because of theory and because of our tacit value stance. My comments will focus upon the working hypothesis, and I will explain how our ideas were modified as a result of the data collected in the study.

To examine the hypothesis that more sick than well families would show evidences of disorganization, we divided the families into 2 groups and made a series of comparisons. The 20 families in which both spouses were free of psychotic disorders were compared to the 20 families in which either one or both spouses were schizophrenic. In the comparisons, the replies to questions in the interviews from *both* husbands and wives were analyzed. For example, each spouse was asked a series of questions to determine whether or not his expectations towards his marriage had been fulfilled. Each person was asked also to report how frequently he argued with his spouse. The respondents were asked whether or not they would choose the same spouse if life could be lived anew. Probes were made to determine how the person evaluated his spouse's behaviour in relation to his own definition of ideal family roles. In brief, a variety of items were used to compare the sick and well families.

The result of the comparisons were surprising. Although in the well families relations were more often harmonious and spouses more often satisfied than in the sick families, the differences were not statistically significant. According to our hypothesis, there should have been marked differences, indeed compelling differences. How could a family cope with the severe psychotic disorder of the husband, or the wife, or both, and not differ notably from a family free of such mental health problems? We began to wonder if the working hypothesis should be completely abandoned.

The next sequence of analyses provided clues to solve our puzzle. The sick families were divided into 3 groups: families with a schizophrenic wife, families with a schizophrenic husband, and families in which both spouses suffered from this mental illness. A series of comparisons were then made, including the 20 families that had spouses who were not afflicted with a psychotic disorder. The replies to the questions in the interviews that had been used before were used again. These comparisons indicated significant differences when the 40 families were divided into 2 groups according to whether or not the wife was schizophrenic. On the other hand, the effect of the husband's mental health status appeared to be negligible.

Thus, empirical patterns that had been obscured before were now revealed: families in which only the husband was schizophrenic resembled the families with spouses free of psychotic disorders. However, the families with wives who were schizophrenic, whether the husbands were sick or well, fulfilled the conditions of the working hypothesis, namely that schizophrenia would disorganize the family. In these families, husbands and wives were more often disillusioned with marriage, enveloped in conflict, and unwilling to choose each other as mates if life could be lived anew; they had unfavorable opinions of each other's comportment in the family.

In his efforts to arrive at "significant" findings the researcher typically is attuned to the observation of differences between the groups being compared. Such differences often serve as a point of departure for the subsequent analysis of data, and an effort is made to reconstruct the social arrangements and processes that produce the differences. The observation which indicated the importance to the family of the psychiatric status of the wife was a clear invitation to undertake this task.

But data are sometimes not so openly hospitable. While an invitation is extended to further analysis, it is in a reserved manner. The similarity between families free of psychotic illness and those in which only the husband was schizophrenic offered such an invitation. Thus, a lack of difference between the groups being compared can also be taken as a point of departure for further analysis. One is likely to pursue such a course when expectations have failed to materialize in the data. The expectations are held strongly, and one is heavily committed to them. Also, there is always the possibility that 2 groups may resemble each other according to a set of measures yet have substantially different social processes that determine the outcome of the measures.

At this point in the analysis of the data, the assumption that schizoprenia has a uniformly disorganizing effect upon the family could be challenged. The psychiatric status of the wife but not of the husband was relevant to the family, at least the measures used had so indicated. Why should this be the case? To answer this question, all of the data in the study, gathered during 35–40 visits to each family, were assembled. Many questions were then developed and used to examine the large amount of data on the families. The questions dealt with cultural norms, the organization of roles in the family, the spouses' performance of the roles, and the relevance of schizophrenia to family roles.

Cultural norms in Puerto Rican society stipulate that females are or should be reserved, conforming, and modest. In marriage, these norms converge upon another set of norms associated with the role of wife and mother. An important theme in this complex of norms is that of self-sacrifice. A wife and mother ought to be all-giving, expecting little in return. It is her lot in life to bear the pain of economic hardship, the sicknesses of the children, the occasional ingratitude of relatives. An unmistakable tone of the sacred, of the martyr, infuses her world of "oughts". Anguish provides the test of a saintly life. But if Christian martyrdom requires a tight-lipped stoicism of quiet suffering, it is at this point that the lower-class Puerto Rican wife and mother departs from the role. Conversations with acquaintances, friends, and relatives often consist of mutual efforts to invite a sympathetic response by reciting a personal history of suffering. "¡Ay bendito! ¡Que mucho ella ha sufrido!" ("Oh poor one! How much she has suffered!")—is an exclamation that punctuates many such conversations. To be the object of this attitude provides the married woman with a source of emotional support and rationalizes the problems she confronts in family life.

Whereas females are sexually innocent and weak, males are thought to be sexually malicious and strong. This distinction is relevant to the masculinity complex—or *machismo*—which pervades the culture. To act like a *macho* the man must make the appropriate response to a variety of challenges. A sexual opportunity must be used. During sexual intercourse, the man must sustain his desire and capacity beyond those of his partner. Physical courage is stressed. A man must not weep if injured. An affront from another man—such as a touch on the face or buttocks—requires the restitution of honor, often through retaliation. No real *macho* would tolerate open efforts by his wife to control or boss him. She should be kept in her place. The antithesis of the *macho* is the *pendejo,* the inconsequential pubic hair, or the man who acts like a dummy manipulated by his wife, the ventriloquist. Thus, the world of the *macho* is populated by opponents, both men and women, who must be overcome in the process of asserting one's masculine identity. The *macho* complex orients the husband towards his male peers in the street-corner groups that abound in the slums and public housing developments of the city.

Marriage, however, imposes a new set of obligations upon the husband. He is the main source of economic support and the symbolic head of the household. His role is devoid of the sacred overtones attached to that of the woman, but it is his responsibility to impose respect and order in the family. Typically, the wife wants him to spend more time at home and to show a proper amount of concern for her and the children. When she suspects that he is being unfaithful, she erupts in anger. But the husband feels pressured to behave according to the imperatives of the *macho* role that he be independent and not submit to his wife's efforts to curtail the freedom he enjoyed as a single man. Being part of the home and part of the "street", the husband maintains an uneasy balance in responding to conflicting expectations. The dilemma the husband confronts creates tension in the marriage.

With this overview of family and sex roles, let us turn now to the families to describe briefly what we found beginning with the spouses who do not have a psychotic illness. In these families, a clear-cut division of labor between the husband and wife governs every-day activities. The husbands provide economic sustenance for their families by working away from home as construction workers, janitors, kitchen assistants, handy-men, ambulatory barbers, and small businessmen selling fruits and vegetables. At home the wife endeavors to make the husband comfortable. She serves his meals and has clean clothes ready for him. The wife is restricted to the home doing housework and taking care of the children. This gives the husband the advantage of observing or inferring how well she has done her duties as a wife and mother. If she has been derelict, he punishes her. In contrast, the wife knows little about what the husband does when he leaves to spend long hours away from home, an arrangement which favors the husband over the wife.

The wife, however, is by no means powerless, and the marital relationship is not one of an authoritarian husband incessantly dictating to a subservient wife. The long absences of the husband from the home during the day, and often during the evenings, enables the wife to control much of what occurs in the family. She can maintain a great deal of autonomy in the management of the household and family. However, early in the field work we discovered that it was unwise to interview wives late in the afternoon. At that time of the day the wife cooks and prepares for her husband's arrival home from work. As long as she can satisfy her husband's desire for an orderly and comfortable life at home, he does not subject her to demanding and provoking questions. The wife is aware of this and usually makes resolute efforts to keep things as they should be at home.

Most household details and decisions about running the family from day to day are defined in the culture as feminine. For this reason, they do not readily invite intrusions from the husband. Nor is the husband as involved as the wife in the lives of relatives. Confined to the home and restricted to contacts with blood and affinal relatives, the wife orients herself towards the nuclear and extended family. The solution of interpersonal problems in the family is her specialty, as are problems associated with the health of members of the family. She is deeply enmeshed in the communicative structure of the broader family and is more active than the husband in keeping the bonds of kinship alive and viable. The family comprises practically her entire life space.

Thus, families with no psychotic members are maintained as a cohesive force. With minor variations, each spouse plays his role according to the expectations of the culture.

However, the data of the study demonstrate very clearly that schizophrenia incapacitates the person, whether it be the husband or the wife, to perform the customary social roles. Along with the confusing and tormenting symptoms of the illness, the sick person suffers excruciating anxiety. The energy he expends in bracing himself from imaginary threats, attacks, and injuries causes him to feel fatigued. He has little left of himself to do the work that is expected. When he tries to work, the course he pursues is erratic, random, and diffused. To associates, friends, and relatives, the sick person's behavior is idiosyncratic and foolish.

Schizophrenic husbands experience many difficulties at work. They are unable to respond adequately to the demands of employment. Moreover, it is not long before the sick man is identified by associates at work as a person who behaves in strange and unpredictable ways. Often he becomes the object of jokes and taunts. In brief, he has begun to be labeled a *loco* and treated accordingly. Overwhelmed by distressing symptoms and assigned to a deviant role heavily charged with a stigma, the sick man withdraws from work. For many of the same reasons he also moves away from the circle of friends and associates that are so central to participation in the masculine world.

As the sick man becomes unemployed and removes himself from the demands of the *macho* role, he imbeds himself in the family. The onus then falls upon his unafflicted wife. She moves to cope with the economic hardships resulting from the husband's unemployment by working away from home. Her efforts to support the family, at first erratic, soon become organized as she secures full-time employment. Many household tasks defined in the culture as feminine are then performed by the sick husband.

A number of changes accompany this role reversal between husband and wife. The sick husband becomes the wife's patient. She seeks to alleviate his symptoms, calm his anxieties, and to assure him that the illness is transitory. Better times will come. He depends upon

J

her for social support. The skills that the wife has acquired at cementing the socio-emotional bonds in the family come into wide play; and, if the efforts she makes to cope with her husband's illness are a drain on her physically and emotionally, she is nonetheless rewarded by the idea that she is sacrificing herself. Her sense of martyrdom is confirmed by her husband who repeatedly expresses his gratitude. The wife also appreciates the fact that her sick husband no longer goes out "to the street"; his allegiance is now to the home.

Thus the sick husband's family develops solidarity through the mutual efforts of the spouses to deal with problems associated with the illness. The new role relationship between the husband and the wife differs markedly from that of families in which neither spouse is schizophrenic. Although a deviant arrangement, it nonetheless serves to maintain a balance of satisfaction between the spouses comparable to that experienced by the husbands and wives who do not have a psychotic illness.

Families with schizophrenic wives married to sick or well husbands differ notably from the foregoing two groups of families. Perhaps it is sufficient to describe this difference in general terms, as much of what needs to be said can already be anticipated.

Very much like the sick husband, the sick wife is unable to function adequately in her customary roles. The requirements of household chores, of caring for the children, and of providing the order and tranquillity in the home desired by the husband, exceed her capacity to respond. Her home is dishevelled and chaotic, showing repeated but incomplete efforts to manage the routines of housekeeping. Her interpersonal competence in the family is attenuated, as is her capacity to provide social support for relatives who are in need. Although the husband perceives the wife as sick of the nerves, he feels this does not justify her misbehavior and downright rebelliousness. His efforts to correct her by indifference, by sharp reprimand, and physical violence are fruitless. The wife counters by attacking him, by denying him sexual relations, and often by retaliating with physical violence. Neither spouse can coerce the other into more acceptable conduct. Both are involved in a circle of mutual recrimination and hatred. In response, the husband projects himself more and more into the masculine world of street-corner activities. He solves the dilemma of the married man by withdrawing from the home. This, in turn, accentuates the marital problems associated with the *macho* role.

In the double schizophrenic families the husband plants himself in the home and engages his wife in a continuous round of bitter arguments. But, regardless of the husband's mental health status, when it is the wife who is sick, neither spouse can cope with the problems associated with schizophrenia by reorganizing their relationship in more satisfying terms. This inability contributes to the lack of solidarity in the family.

The hypothesis that schizophrenia disorganizes the family can now be examined in relation to the experience acquired in this study. The data indicate that the effect of schizophrenia on the family depends upon the sex role of the family member who is afflicted. When only the husband is sick, the customary arrangement of the roles of the husband and wife changes, and the family reorganizes itself to cope with the problems stemming from the illness. A new form of organization emerges. Husbands and wives reverse work roles, and the wife expands upon the therapeutic functions which are already a part of her role in the culture. The cultural image of the female martyr supports her efforts. The activities of the husband and of the wife complement each other, and the spouses experience mutual satisfaction. No such complementarity is to be found in the families with schizo-phrenic wives, regardless of the husband's psychiatric status. Instead, the wife withdraws from the requirements of her family roles, and the husband does not attempt to compensate for her many incapacities. Family life is chaotic, disorderly, and conflict ridden. The hypothesis, therefore, applies to the families in which the wife is schizophrenic but not to the families in which only the husband is afflicted with this mental illness.

It is clear now that there was a bias built into the interview questions which were used to compare the diagnostic family groups in the first part of the analysis. The questions dealt primarily with the feelings and attitudes the husbands and wives had towards each other and towards their marriage. The questions alone tell us little about the processes that mediate and condition the linkage between schizophrenia and the unity of the family. To fill this gap we need to know how roles are modified as the family confronts problems and how social control in the family operates as each person tries to change or reinforce the deviant or customary behavior of his partner. Carefully designed field research is needed to study this problem. We need also to develop field techniques for measuring those explicit and implicit interpersonal arrangements and processes that define the family as a social institution.

CULTURAL FACTORS IN THE GENESIS OF SCHIZOPHRENIA

H. B. M. Murphy

Department of Psychiatry, McGill University, Montreal, Canada

Any review of empirical data touching possible sociocultural influences on the genesis of schizophrenia must face serious difficulties, since such influences are overlapping continua, not simple dichotomies of presence or absence, and will almost certainly have interacted elaborately with each other before producing the final result. It is not to be thought, for instance, that the experience of a migrant is the same regardless of the social class he moves i., or that patterns of intrafamilial behavior are unaffected by the cultural expectations of the surrounding society. Accordingly, there are a host of concomitant variables which theoretically need to be allowed for when we seek to assess the relevance of any one, and since there is no study which has been able to handle them all the reviewer of such literature has continually to draw inferences from inadequate evidence. It is in some ways much easier to write a theoretical paper in this field, selecting hypotheses and suggesting means of testing them, than to write a descriptive one, when so much of what one would like to describe has never been filled in.

These problems apply to any sociocultural approach to schizophrenia and to most other approaches as well, but one is probably more aware of them when considering specifically cultural influences, since culture interpenetrates all other aspects of social life. Culture, in the sense used in transcultural psychiatry, consists of the values, beliefs and patterns of behavior which a society teaches to its members, with a view to equipping them better for the task of life. In traditional societies we are accustomed to think of these beliefs and practices as maintaining an existence of their own with very little reasoned relationship to actual living conditions, but they did not start out that way, and beyond a certain point they do not persist in that way either, if they become inappropriate to actual conditions and if the society is making any attempt to adjust. The obvious analogy, though one which must not be pushed too far, is with habits of eating, walking, writing, etc., which are learnt by children and maintained throughout life with no rational reconsideration until some change, physiological or environmental, forces the person to examine whether the development of different habits might be more satisfactory. To discuss a particular culture without reference to the conditions to which it was a response can thus be as senseless as to discuss the sailor's rolling walk without considering conditions at sea, especially if these conditions are no longer present. Accordingly, in evaluating a culture medically or in seeking the cultural determinants of disease, the conditions under which the culture developed are usually relevant, whether these conditions persist or whether they have changed, and although we may occasionally meet an association which persists despite the setting, it is logical to expect that it is the combination of culture and conditions which is pathogenic, rather than either alone.

There are two questions which this paper is expected to tackle. The first is whether there is sufficient evidence to justify the belief that cultural factors can affect not only the symptomatology of schizophrenia, but its incidence and course. For this, what is required is merely the demonstration of an association between the two variables, plus supporting evidence to suggest that that association is not caused by some third, extraneous factor such as genetic or social selection. If such a demonstration is possible, then even though one cannot say how the two are connected, cultural factors must be kept in mind in discussing the genesis of schizophrenia, whereas if it is not possible then it is better that we put them out of mind since the fewer possibilities we have to juggle with the better. The second question is whether, should an association be found, there is any evidence as to how this might be operating. Here it may be permissible to use less concrete data provided these offer clues to the intervening links in the causal chain.

The first of the two questions sounds relatively easy to answer, since we have a world full of widely different cultures to choose from, and if an association can be established between cultural factors and schizophrenia for any one of these then, theoretically at least, the association becomes potentially present in all the rest. Ideally, however, any such demonstration must in some way manage to exclude such potentially competing explanations as genetic loading of a population, social selection by migration, the stresses of social change and the adverse effects of low or minority status; and this is extremely difficult. It might be thought that the easiest way would be to find some remote and exotic people in whom schizophrenia, if not entirely absent, was at least extremely rare. Apart from the problem of excluding a genetic explanation in such a case, however, there is a much greater problem which faces one when one attempts to study schizophrenia in non-westernized peoples, namely the problem of diagnostic criteria. Among such peoples, regardless of continent but with possible exceptions for specific cultures, acute short-lasting psychoses form a major part of all recognized mental disorder, and there is no agreement on where these lie in our current diagnostic classifications. Some psychiatrists include most such cases under schizophrenia on the grounds of their delusional or hallucinatory elements and of the fact that a few of these acute states, indistinguishable from the rest initially, develop into typically chronic schizophrenia later. Other workers, however, call them organic psychoses, incriminating one of the various infections or infestations which nearly every patient in these countries has. Still others regard them as something different from either. The relative number of such conditions is too high for us to treat them as we do borderline schizophrenias in North America, by pretending that they do not make a real difference one way or the other, and their short duration creates serious difficulties for field surveys, which are usually forced to deduce incidence on the basis of prevalence. (This problem will face the Sarawak survey which the Foundations' Fund is supporting.) Study of the longer-term prognosis of these acute states could cast new light on the nature of the functional psychoses, and we are carrying out research into this question at the present time. But the fact remains that until better agreement is reached on the criteria for diagnosing schizophrenia in such peoples, an epidemiological approach to that disorder among them is almost impossible.

That sends us back to the examination of relatively lesser differences in rates between population samples whose clinical pictures are more typical. An abundance of potentially useful material exists, but there are virtually no discussions of the comparative merits of the different possible explanations for their findings, so that it has been necessary to do original research for this paper on the more promising sources, research which has unfortunately not usually enabled me to resolve the existing ambiguities. I propose to summarize the evidence on the three peoples regarding whom the case for a cultural influence seems most plausible and then go on to some new data which I am only now working out but which seem to constitute the strongest argument for a cultural influence so far available. I must apologize for the fact that in two of the three illustrations the original work was in part my own, for it is the task of a review paper to give wide coverage to other people's work. It happens, however, that very few researchers have tackled this question systematically, and it is easier for me to assess the influence of extraneous factors in a group which I know than in one which I do not. The three illustrations will all relate to higher-than-average rates of schizophrenia, not to lower-than-average, for the simple reason that the former are fairly self-evident whereas with the latter there is always the suspicion that cases have been missed, and extra work needs to be done to allay that suspicion. There is one well-known instance of a below-average rate of schizophrenia where the extra work had been done and where cultural factors are properly explored, namely the Hutterite survey of Eaton and Weil.[5] Unfortunately, since the original genetic stock of these communities was quite narrow ("In 1950 there were only fifteen patronyms in the entire sect", *op. cit.*, p. 32), the possibility of an unusually healthy genetic base cannot be excluded even though the researchers show that the treatment of mentally disturbed people in this culture is tolerant and supportive. Also, I have calculated the 1961 schizophrenia admission rate for the Mennonites and Hutterites combined, from Canada's prairie provinces, and that rate is not significantly below average. Hence although this last finding does not exclude a low rate for the Hutterites alone (Canadian census data do not permit their differentiation from the Mennonites) it makes the attribution of a protective cultural factor doubtful.

The three groups we will be considering are the Tamilians of South India, the southern Irish, and the people of north-west Croatia.

THE TAMIL-SPEAKING PEOPLE OF SOUTH INDIA AND CEYLON

The most incontroversial evidence of an excess liability to schizophrenia in this people comes from data on the student population at the University of Singapore. The upper part of Fig. 1 shows the relative incidence of the disorder in the three main ethnic groups attending that institution, as calculated by Z. N. Kadri for 1958–63[8] and by myself for a previous 5-year period. My own rates are based on too few cases to be significant, but they show the same trend as Kadri's data, where the differences are quite significant. Since the students were given free medical attention, since any failure to attend courses had to be explained to the university authorities with medical certificates being passed to Dr. Kadri or myself for checking, and since abnormal behavior or abnormal academic performance on the part of any student usually led to him being referred to the health service, I believe that these differences are not distorted by concealment of non-Indian cases or by other interference with ascertainment. Failure to recognize schizophrenia remains a possible source of error, of course, but this was much more likely with Indian than with Chinese patients owing to the more hysterical quality of the former. In my own first years in Singapore I made this mistake, diagnosing as hysterical neuroses patients who later proved to have schizophrenia.[1]

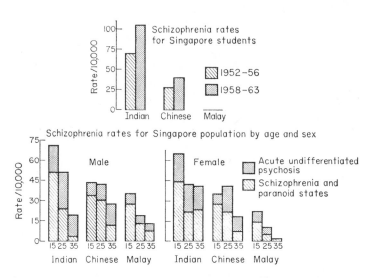

Fig. 1(a). Incidence of schizophrenia in students at the University of Singapore; for two 5-year periods. (Z. N. Kadri[8] and present author.)

(b). First admission rates to mental hospital, 1950–4, for Indian, Chinese, and Malay sections of the population of Singapore; by age and sex; cases diagnosed as schizophrenia, paranoid state and acute undifferentiated psychosis only. (Cases over the age of 44 have been exluded since the "undifferentiated psychosis" group tend after that age to have a more obviously organic basis.)

The excess of Indian over Chinese and Malay rates of schizophrenia among university students is reflected, though to a lesser degree, in the general Singapore population, whether or not one adds to the cases diagnosed as schizophrenia those which we might call the acute undifferentiated psychoses. (In Singapore at that time they were labeled as toxic psychoses, but a specific toxic element was very rarely implicated and discussions with the hospital doctors revealed that they were using this term for any case that showed initial confusion.) However, as the lower part of Fig. 1 shows, there is an interesting point about the age distribution of the Indian and other cases, for the Indian rate is especially high only in the youngest age group and in males drops off very sharply thereafter. Furthermore, when rates are calculated both by age and social class, as I have done for total hospital admissions in an earlier paper,[11] then for younger men (15–29) the curve is the reverse of the expected, with the highest rates in the highest class and the lowest in class III. This

---

[1] My original paper[10] on the Singapore students was written before that realization was made, so that the hysterical quality of Indian psychopathology was stressed there and their liability to schizophrenia overlooked. The original comment on the schizoid character of the Chinese patients remains valid as referring to introversion and seclusiveness, but not if it is thought to imply a liability to schizophrenia.

fits with our university findings and might be explained in two very different ways. On the one hand Kadri has shown that virtually all of his Indian cases derived from a particular subgroup of Tamilians, those coming to Singapore not directly from India but from Ceylon, where their ancestors had migrated some centuries previously. These Ceylonese Tamils, as they are called, are found particularly in administrative and professional sections of the middle class and they tend to marry among themselves, so that if there were an inherited liability to schizophrenia in this narrowly based subgroup it could account for some of the peculiarities of schizophrenia distribution. However, that would not explain the differences in the male and female age curves for schizophrenia in the Singapore Indians as a whole or for other peculiarities in the distribution of schizophrenia by occupational group among them. These peculiarities, and the other points remarked on, appear better explained on the basis of the marked and culturally produced difficulties which Tamil youth, from India and from Ceylon alike, have in handling relations with authority. (These difficulties are described in the earlier paper.[10]) Moreover, a genetic predisposition to schizophrenia in the small Ceylonese Tamil group, while quite possible, would not explain why in the Indian Army the Tamil-speaking people in the south exhibited a greater predisposition to schizophrenia than the peoples of other regions and subcultures.

This picture of the mental disorder rates in the Indian Army has to be gathered from a number of sources all of which have some limitations since, as with most wartime military papers, one does not meet accurate data on patients and on the size of the population-at-risk in the same paper. However, from Bhattacharjya,[2] Singh[17] and in particular from Hyatt Williams,[21] it is clear that the south Indian had more mental disturbance than soldiers from other regions, more difficulties with discipline and authority, and proportionately more schizophrenia in cases coming to psychiatric attention. Hyatt Williams, for instance, found a highly significant difference, as Table 1 shows. The difference could still be genetically based, of course, since the southerners are mainly of Dravidian and the northerners of

TABLE 1. PERCENTAGE DISTRIBUTION OF INDIAN ARMY PATIENTS, BY DIAGNOSIS, FOR THOSE FROM SOUTH INDIA AND FOR ALL OTHERS (from Williams[21])

Psychiatric cases seen on the Arakan (Burma) front	Indian Army regional groups	
	South	All others
(N)	(86)	(273)
Schizophrenia	19·8%	7·7%
Affective psychoses	14·0%	12·1%
Confusional psychoses	17·4%	12·8%
Hysterical states	38·3%	31·1%
Anxiety states	7·0%	29·3%
Personality disorders	3·5%	7·0%
	100·0%	100·0%

($\chi^2 = 16\cdot7$; $n = 1$; $p = 0\cdot001$ for schizophrenia v. rest.)

Aryan stock, but the army drew from such a wide population (Madras state alone has 30 million inhabitants) that the odds seem in favour of the sociocultural explanation.

The Indian Army, like Singapore, was westernized in its social structure, and the question may still be asked whether in a more traditional social setting these same Indian groups would have shown the same excess of schizophrenia, There are some indications that in village India, south or north, the risk of schizophrenia is less, although in large cities like Madras it is not. However, the evidence here is too slight to argue from. What can be said is that Indians regardless of region appear to have difficulty in adjusting to Western conditions. For instance, university health services in the United States, Britain and Australia see more serious disturbance in Indian students than in other Asian or African visitors.[2] But there are too many possible explanations for this to disentangle here. It is sufficient to say that in the conditions described, Tamilians and perhaps other Indians show an excess of schizophrenia with characteristics which cannot easily be accounted for by genetic or other selection, which are not exhibited by other peoples under the same conditions, and which seem easiest explained on the basis of a combination of cultural and social factors.

THE PEOPLE OF NORTH-WESTERN CROATIA

The evidence for an excess of schizophrenia in the people of this region has been accumulated by European psychiatrists since the 1930's and is summarized for the English reader by Crocetti et al.[3] Mainly, this evidence derives from hospital data but statistics from military service tribunals show that the rate of rejection by reason of schizophrenia is twice as high for the relevant population as it is for the rest of the country. Those interested in the detailed checks which Crocetti and his colleagues carried out on their material are referred to the original paper, but it can be broadly summarized by stating that although that material was in many ways incomplete, no evidence could be found to indicate that the difference between the specified population and the rest of Croatia was other than genuine.

A number of possible explanations for the observation have been explored, in each case with negative results. Thus, it was initially believed that the excess might derive from a few isolated and inbred communities, but the researchers have shown that it has a much wider distribution. Then it was thought that since the area had seen much migration, the excess might derive from the immigrants. Analysis of cases, however, showed that they derived much more from the non-migrant than from the migrant group. No one to my knowledge has previously proposed a cultural explanation for the findings, and at first thought this would appear unlikely, since the finding relates not to the total population of Croatia or to a recognized subcultural minority, but to a geographic sector. A limited reading of the history of the region,[6] however, led me to realize that the reported boundary between the high and lower rate areas coincides roughly with a geographic and historical division which I believe, on the basic of discussions with Yugoslav colleagues, to have produced sociocultural differences as well.

Briefly, the affected area of Istria and the country round Rijeka (which some of us may recognize better under its former Italian name of Fiume) is that part of Yugoslavia which

[2] Various personal communications.

has the strongest ties to the west of Europe and the weakest ties to the rest of the country. A long history of links, first to Venice, then to the Hapsburgs, and then by conquest to Mussolini's Italy, have made the people of this part, so I am told, more "European" and more "civilized" by their own way of thinking than the rest of their countrymen. Moreover, it is this part of Croatia which can be inferred to have been most affected by the historic conflict of loyalties and identities which arose from the Croats being Roman Catholics caught up in national and pan-slavic movements which Rome was opposed to.[3] (In Central Croatia Rome was felt to be further away, and there was until after WWII a greater admixture of Serbian Orthodox influence.) Today this corner of the country is still the one which has the strongest ties to western Europe through tourism, is still the most "civilized" in terms of material riches and property values,[7] and still apparently doubtful about its attachment to the centers of national political power, since its officials are the most reluctant to leave their home area for the capital[7] This long-standing sociocultural ambivalence, if it still persists, could offer a hypothetical link to schizophrenia, as I will attempt to indicate later. Regardless of that hypothesis, however, the fact remains that there are some sociocultural differences between the sector with the high schizophrenia rates and the rest of Croatia, and as long as other explanations for the high rate cannot be found these sociocultural differences have to be accepted as potentially relevant.[4]

THE IRISH CATHOLICS

Evidence suggesting that schizophrenia is unusually frequent in this people can be found on both sides of the Atlantic, and stretches from last century to the present decade, although always the picture is somewhat confused by their much more striking liability to the alcoholic psychoses. The first reference which I have traced in my preparation for this paper is by Spitzka from New York in 1880.[18] There he noted that acute melancholia was particularly frequent in German immigrants, hebephrenia in Jewish ones, and "terminal dementia" in the Irish. By the last term he presumably means chronic schizophrenia, but chronic organic states might also have been included. Each few years more writers present a similar picture, and by 1913 both Pollock for New York[15] and Swift for Massachusetts[19] give sufficiently detailed information to make it almost certain that Irish rates for mental hospital admission were considerably higher than those for other immigrant groups even after alcoholic psychoses had been excluded.

Swift recognized the relevance both of considering the second generation of immigration and of allowing for the age distribution of the different populations but he had no sound means of doing either. Pollock, for the period around 1920,[16] and Malzberg for that around 1930,[9] did have these means, and in both writers we find the earlier impressions of an Irish liability to schizophrenia confirmed, though the frequency of the disease in the

---

[3] A good description of this problem from an Anglo-Saxon viewpoint is given in Rebecca West's once-famous book *Black Lamb and Grey Falcon*.[20]

[4] Since the above was written I have learnt that the excess morbidity in this people applies not only to schizophrenia but to a wide variety of somatic illnesses, and that nutritional factors are now being investigated. While the facts presented above remain correct, therefore, it seems unwise to cite this population as an example of an association between culture and schizophrenia.

so-called "new" immigration from eastern and southern Europe is beginning to overshadow this. Pollock, for instance, now shows the Irish to have the highest frequency of schizophrenia from among eleven immigrant groups from north-western Europe (roughly, the "old" immigration) but to be overshadowed by many from the "new" groups, the Poles especially.[16] Malzberg, as the figures in Table 2 show, found that although the Irish were

TABLE 2. FIRST ADMISSION RATES FOR
SCHIZOPHRENIA, NEW YORK, 1929–31, BY
CULTURE OF ORIGIN
(Malzberg[9])

Cultural origin	Immigrants (age-standardized rates)		Native-born of immigrant parents (crude rates)
	Male	Female	Combined sexes
Irish	29·6	37·4	25·2
English	28·5	23·4	15·9
German	44·8	27·1	21·0
Italian	34·4	26·7	12·2
Scandinavian	40·5	27·8	19·7
Polish	31·7	35·4	not given
Russian	33·9	25·8	not given

still the most vulnerable of the cultural groups studied by him from among the second generation of immigration, and still the most vulnerable of female immigrant groups, they were no longer the most vulnerable in the male immigrant population. However, it must be remembered that by the 1920's and 1930's the Irish had a considerable advantage over most other immigrant peoples in New York State, since they were English-speaking and had already gained a solid foothold of political power.

After 1931 the US lost interest in European immigrants and their countries of origin, but the story can be taken up elsewhere. First, in Ireland itself it had recently been rediscovered that Ireland had double the number of patients in mental hospitals per 1000 population, that England and Wales has.[14] I say rediscovered rather than discovered, for back at the beginning of the century it had been noticed that the rate of insanity in Ireland was 4·7 per 1000 as compared to 3·3 in England, although the latter had the better medical services.[5] In the recent report, however, the matter is taken further, for it is pointed out that Ireland has not only double the English bed occupancy rate, but double the admission rate of England as well, with the proportion diagnosed as schizophrenia among these admissions again being higher than in England.[14] Until new evidence comes in, therefore, we must assume that schizophrenia is genuinely more frequent among the Irish in Eire today than among their English-speaking neighbors, just as it was among the Irish immigrants to the US, and as it proves to be among people of Irish Catholic origin in Canada, when

---

[5] Noted by Swift in 1913[19] and discussed from a different angle by O'Doherty.[14] An investigation into the current picture of Eire is being planned and may already have been commenced by Dermott Walsh.

compared with those of other English-speaking origin. In the Canadian provinces whose rates I am currently studying they have the highest schizophrenia rate of any origin group from western Europe, and are exceeded only by the Russians and Poles when one looks more widely.[6] These Canadian statistics refer not to the first or to the second generation of immigration only, but to the whole population regardless of how many generations they had been in Canada, and on that basis one would have expected the Irish, with their long settlement, to have been at a definite social advantage over peoples like the Dutch and Scandinavians who arrived later.

The fact that schizophrenia is found with unexpected frequency both in that part of the population that emigrated and in the ancestors of that part that stayed at home, suggests strongly that social selection is not an explanation for the foregoing findings, although the social experiences leading up to and deriving from the migration may have some relevance, since O'Doherty has shown that it is the Irish counties with the highest schizophrenia rate that produced the highest emigration. The possibility remains that the whole Irish people have a genetic predisposition to the disease, but this is argued against by two factors. One is that the mean age of marriage is late among the southern Irish,[(1)] so that there is less likelihood of the schizophrenic getting married; the other is that while there is this liability among the Roman Catholic southern Irish, there is no evidence of a corresponding tendency in the Protestant northerners. On the last point it must be admitted that the Protestant northerners contain a very much greater admixture of Anglo-Saxon stock than the southerners, but one would have still expected some signs of an inherited racial liability, if such existed. From north Ireland I can trace no reference to this and in Canada, though it has not been possible to calculate rates for this subgroup of the total population,[7] the rural survey which will be referred to below did permit the identification of a large Irish Protestant community, and this had the lowest schizophrenia prevalence rate of all the 14 communities studied. Accordingly, while once again an association between culture and schizophrenia cannot positively be established here, it is difficult to think of any characteristic of the Irish which could explain the steady excess of schizophrenia which they have shown and which does not at least partly involve some aspect of their cultural heritage. I do not intend at this point to say what aspect of that heritage I myself suspect may be schizophrenogenic, but there are elements of their family tradition which could be inculpated, and another aspect will be touched on briefly later.[8]

---

[6] Italians have a higher female rate than the Irish in the provinces studied, but there is reason to believe that this is atypical and that if the Niagara peninsula with its heavy Italian settlement had been included the Italian female rate would have been much lower.

[7] The above references to the Irish Catholic picture in Canada strictly speaking refer to the picture for the Catholic population of British origin, since this was the only way in which a reliable differentiation could be made. However, the very great majority of Canadians belonging to the Roman Catholic Church and claiming British origin are of Irish descent, so that the groups are approximately equivalent.

[8] During the discussion of this paper Dr. Elliot Mishler raised the question whether the higher Irish rates could be related to the fact that Irish mothers are on average later in commencing child-bearing than mothers in other cultures. The standard texts on schizophrenia all suggest (at least by omission) that there is no association between maternal age and the risk of schizophrenia in the offspring so that this would seem to answer the question. However, although probably not of much relevance to the Irish, there would seem to be grounds for a re-examination of maternal age as a variable, with greater allowance for birth rank. See Moran, P. A. P.: *Ann. Hum. Genetics*, **28,** 269 (1965).

THE ROMAN CATHOLICS IN CANADA

In the foregoing section there had to be an unsatisfactory equating of "peoples" with "cultures", the reason being that official statistics do not usually acknowledge cultural divisions in any other way, and we have needed to use official sources in order to measure large populations and hence eliminate local vagaries. The concept of a "people", however, implies a sharing of a gene pool quite as much as it does a sharing of cultural traditions, and even though I have tried to cite only instances where there are features difficult to explain on a genetic basis, it may be felt that the evidence is inconclusive. There have recently come into my hands, however, data which while not covering any one complete culture, nevertheless involve a cultural element shared by many peoples and not parallelled genetically.

With the Irish and with the Croatians it was noted that the high schizophrenia rates were found in the Catholic sections of a population and were apparently not repeated in the Protestant and Eastern Orthodox sections. In both it was a point of doubtful significance, since the non-Catholics tended to be of different or more mixed ethnic stock. Among the Singapore Indians I could also have offered rates suggesting that schizophrenia was more frequent in Christians, Catholics in particular, than in the remainder of that population, but there were too many other questions that would have had to be disentangled for this to be worth while. When Canadian mental hospitalizations for schizophrenia are analyzed by origin and by religion, however, a result is obtained which seems to permit of only one explanation, namely that there is some element of Roman Catholic tradition which is more conducive to schizophrenia in Canada than the corresponding aspect of Protestant tradition.

Figure 2 presents the relevant comparisons. It will be seen that in every single one of the cultural subgroups of Canadian society in which there is a sufficient proportion of Roman Catholics for their mental hospitalization rates to be worth while calculating, the Catholic rate exceeds the non-Catholic with respect to schizophrenia in males. In female schizophrenics the same difference is of doubtful significance, being present in 5 out of the 8 groups only, and in the affective disorders it is absent. Since every patient whose religion is not recorded is assumed to be non-Catholic for this calculation the actual differences in hospitalization rates are probably greater than those shown, and field survey data suggest that if non-hospitalized cases had been included the rates would be wider apart still.[9] The question now is: what does this difference mean and, more pertinently for this paper, can we infer there to be some underlying cultural influence or an influence of a different sort?

The easiest way to approach that question is by asking what alternative hypotheses exist. The idea of a common genetic pool which would be shared by the Catholics from all these different backgrounds but not by the Protestants can be rejected, but there are selective processes which could produce such a result without really implying much relationship to the specific cultural features of the Catholic Church. Thus, mentally disturbed individuals seeking help for their condition sometimes turn to religions other than their own, and certain sects or churches go out of their way to offer such help, thereby increasing the apparent rate of mental disturbance among their members. This is the case with the Jehovah's Witnesses today, and formerly with the Salvation Army, but I have no evidence to suggest

---

[9] In the "Fourteen Communities Survey" Catholics were found to be less ready to seek psychiatric help than Protestants were, and to have a higher proportion of never-hospitalized mental patients.

that the shift to Catholicism by disturbed individuals in Canada is greater than the shift away from it, so that this does not appear to be the reason for these findings. Another type of shift, namely into the religion of the upper class "establishment", could affect our results in a different way, for this tends to take place in the successful and upwardly mobile, thus increasing the proportion of the healthy in the high-prestige church or sect and reducing that proportion in the churches which the upwardly mobile came from.[10] Such a shift does take place in Canada, with the United Church of Canada being the main recipient, but the shift occurs more strongly away from the smaller Protestant sects than it does from the Roman Catholic Church, and the latter has a higher overall rate for schizophrenia than all

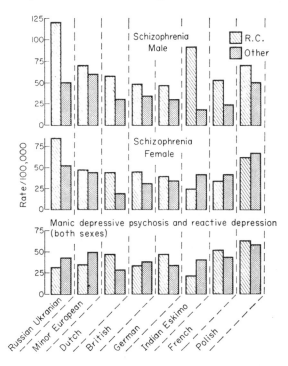

FIG. 2. Comparative age-standardized rates of mental hospitalization for schizophrenia and affective disorders, in Roman Catholic and other sections of the Canadian population, 1961, analyzed by culture of origin. (Data are for 7 provinces only; origin groups with insufficient Roman Catholics for calculation of representative rates have been excluded; those reporting either Jewish religion or Jewish origin have been excluded also, otherwise all patients and all population not specifically reporting themselves to be Roman Catholic have been included under the category of "other".)

but one of the Protestant sects, the exception being the Jehovah's Witnesses mentioned above. Yet a third type of selection is through migration, and if recent immigration to Canada (specifically, to the seven provinces to which Fig. 2's data apply) had been predominantly Catholic while earlier migration had been predominantly Protestant within each of the relevant subcultures, then a higher rate of schizophrenia in the Catholics would be

[10] This type of shift becomes questionable if one allows for the possibility, suggested by other contributors to this symposium, that there is a genetic association between schizophrenia and creativity.

expected. There is no evidence to that effect,[4] however, and post-war immigration has in any event been mainly to the cities of Toronto and Montreal,[4] which had to be excluded from the analysis for Fig. 2, owing to incomplete reporting by their hospitals.

These essentially extraneous explanations being rejected, is there any plausible explanation which involves the cultural traditions of the Catholic Church more directly, bearing in mind that the difference applies to males much more than to females? A first point that needs to be remembered here is that cultural attitudes can affect marriage and reproduction and thereby affect the transmission of defective genes. For instance, late marriage, as in the Irish, will tend to reduce the genetic transmission of schizophrenia by restraining some schizophrenia-prone from bearing children before the disease has had time to become manifest. Marriage arranged by parents, as in parts of Asia, may have the same effect, since it is usual to investigate the family history of a prospective spouse quite carefully. However, this is not relevant here, since the only recognized influence of this kind among the 8 sub-cultures, namely that in the Irish, could be expected to operate in the opposite direction, and in any case such an influence would be expected to show its effect equally on men and on women. A second point which needs to be considered, since the common cultural element is religious affiliation, is whether the specifically religious teachings of one church are more schizophrenogenic than that of another; but here again we would need to ask why the effect should show itself more in males than in females. Certainly there are religions whose tenets give more support to one sex than to the other, but this does not seem to be the case with Catholicism and Protestantism. However, when we move from the purely religious domain to differences of custom and of broad value orientation, then there are two ways in which Catholicism and Protestantism differ and which might be expected to affect the sexes differently.

One of these differences concerns the celibacy of the priesthood and the fact that in the Catholic Church an important adult male model held before the eyes of a boy is one which excludes marriage and sexuality. Depending on what theory one holds on the genesis of schizophrenia, one can see this as creating problems for the schizophrenia-prone male or as offering him a socially accepted mode of escape from the threats which sexuality and the intimacies of marriage may appear to pose. Hence a hypothesized relation to the incidence of schizophrenia in the two sexes is difficult to propose on that basis. (And moreover, the celibacy of nuns presents girls with similar problems and solutions, though probably to a lesser degree.) The other difference concerns orientations towards independence, work, and social competition. Protestantism stresses independence, private problem-solving and work, while tacitly approving of material acquisitiveness. Catholicism stresses communality, obedience, and greater attention to intangibles. This difference and the subsequent argument that the Protestant ethic is better geared to modern competitive capitalism may appear worked to death, but it still holds some relevance for us here since the Catholic orientation is to some extent in conflict with the wider cultural beliefs of North American society, whereas the Protestant orientation is less so. The Catholic could therefore be said to be faced with greater difficulties in reconciling the expectations impinging on him than the Protestant does, and the male Catholic can be expected to face more such difficulties than the female, since it is in wider society rather than in the home that the conflict is likely to arise.

Whether or not this last point is relevant to the higher incidence of schizophrenia in Catholic males cannot be established at present; I know of simply no evidence on the matter. The fact remains, however, that Catholic males do have a higher incidence of schizophrenia than Protestant ones, whether we take the hospitalization data for 7 provinces or the field survey data for 14 rural communities, and this difference does not seem to be explainable in any way which would enable us to disregard the cultural teachings of the two groups.

MODES OF OPERATION

These four illustrations offer the strongest evidence presently available for the theory that culture can influence the genesis of schizophrenia. I believe myself that that evidence is sufficient to justify the theory and, furthermore, that it points to culture having an evocative effect rather than merely a distributive one. The illustrations, with the exception of the last, concerned whole peoples and not merely particular strata into which schizophrenia-prone individuals could be expected to drift or to be pushed. However, with the Croatians, the Canadian Catholics and more doubtfully with the Tamils the point was made that their cultural heritages and their present social situations were to some extent in conflict, echoing the earlier remark that we must expect an interaction of sociocultural influences rather than the discovery of constant and independent causal factors. Because cultural traditions are adaptive, any part of such tradition that is strongly evocative of schizophrenia or another mental disorder is likely to become modified, and this is probably one of the reasons why differences in schizophrenia incidence between cultural groups are usually much less than differences between component parts of any one of them.

But now, what evidence is there as to the way in which cultural influences operate with the disease? While there have been some theories on the subject, there are virtually no studies which appear to have investigated the matter, particularly if we confine ourselves to schizophrenia and disregard studies of mental disorder in general. Of course, in one sense all studies into social factors in the genesis of schizophrenia could be cited, since all take place within a particular cultural setting and the social characteristics are never independent of it. This is particularly clear in those studies which have attempted to elucidate the psycho-dynamics of schizophrenia in the North American Negro. Behind the dramatic foreground action of such studies looms the heavy backdrop of US Anglo-Saxon cultural traditions. Even with such an apparently universal phenomenon as the relation of schizophrenia to social class one can detect a cultural influence. In Singapore quite different associations between schizophrenia and social class appear in the three major peoples, and I suspect that differences which have appeared between British and US findings here may reflect a cultural difference in the way in which class structure is accepted. But with the exception of some US Negro data, where we would still have some difficulties in deciding which culture we were relating them to—the Negro or the White—the cultural element is not sufficiently explicit for such material to be easily used. Hence, with new apologies for reverting to my own data, I propose to ignore the general literature on social factors and to focus on a single illustration where the relative significance of cultural and other variables was specifically investigated.

The illustration derives from our "Fourteen Communities Survey", which was a field

K

investigation of the key informant type focusing mainly on the active prevalence of psychosis regardless of whether psychiatric care had been received or not. The communities were chosen to represent various cultural traditions and levels of social organization, and attention was especially paid to community–patient relationships. Six of the communities were French-Canadian, three of them chosen to represent the traditional culture and three to represent "border" conditions where that tradition had less hold. The three traditional communities proved to have an extremely high prevalence of schizophrenia in women (13·1 per 1000 adults) and the same phenomenon appeared in each, although they were in different counties and had virtually no recent intermarriage. A review of case material revealed the following features.

The main excess of female cases was found in married women who showed signs of publicly recognizable disorder only after the age of 35. Of the 8 such cases, only 1 was in hospital although several were deteriorated to the extent that made such care desirable. All but one had four or more children and in most instances the oldest child had left home or was about to leave. Almost all exhibited delusions of reference and focused these delusions on husband and children. Some had attempted to break with their home and husband by running away (in which case they were hospitalized but soon brought back to look after their children); the others did not make any such "avoidance" gesture but instead accused their husbands or children of misbehavior, attempts at poisoning, etc., and these, since they continued to fulfil their household duties after a fashion, were never hospitalized. In the males of these same communities and in the females of the other communities studied, this picture in this age group was quite rare.

The other excess of female cases was of a more familiar type, occurring in young unmarried women. However, once again the clinical picture was remarkably uniform and quite different from what was shown by the male cases in the same communities. Onset is gradual, with no history of sexual deviancy or of intended marriage but sometimes with a history of the girl trying to establish an independent career in teaching, etc. The career, if embarked on, is abandoned; the girl stays in her parents' home, becomes increasingly withdrawn or increasingly hypochondriacal, and thus slides gradually into a chronic sick-role which may never involve naming the illness and which usually evokes no disapprobation. Some of the women remain in this state, dependent on their parents, keeping apart from community affairs but conforming to its prescribed sick-role behavior, and never being sent to hospital or getting treatment for the psychiatric condition. More usually, however, there is a rebellion against the prescribed role, an exhibition of behavior that is socially disapproved, hospitalization relatively soon after that occurs, and thereafter usually a failure of such attempts as the hospital makes to get the patient back to her family. In the three communities there are eight patients who fit this picture, and what differentiates them from the early-starting male schizophrenics in the same communities is that the males mostly either reintegrate themselves with the community and gradually lose their symptoms or leave it entirely, whereas the females do neither.

Contrasting with these pictures, we found almost no schizophrenia in younger married women, although this was common in the other three French-Canadian communities, and almost none in older single women, although this also was to be found in some other communities.

When the social background to this phenomenon was investigated with the aid of a French-Canadian sociologist, the following was found. The three traditional communities still depict the ideal woman as one who gets married early, has many children, is hardworking, patient, diligent and submissive to her husband. Motherhood is envisaged as a highly rewarding role, and the idea of an independent career for women outside of the religious orders is only now being accepted as a possibility. About a generation ago, however, more schooling became available locally, and since the boys were often taken away to work in the fields while their sisters were left to their classes, the girls became more educated than their brothers and potential husbands. Furthermore, local orders of nuns provided post-school courses in practical nursing, typing, domestic science, etc., and imbued the girls with the idea that this knowledge was there to be made use of, while for the boys local opinion was still maintaining that farming did not require education. For the controlling, organizing type of woman this situation could be and was quite gratifying, for they could marry men less educated than themselves and use their own education to control first their families and then, through their husbands, the male domain of public affairs, while still receiving community approval because they maintained a façade of submission. Such behavior could not be publicly taught or recognized in this male-oriented Catholic society, however, and neither would it satisfy those women who sought a husband to love and respect or those others who were not attracted to marriage at all. A conflict can thus be inferred to have arisen in the minds of many women regarding how to pursue both the ideal of womanhood which the tradition taught and the modern goal of a life which would permit them more use of their new education and more individuality. We find this conflict reflected in the comments of our women informants and in the expressed desire of present-day mothers that their daughters should be able to escape and make a life for themselves. More importantly, however, I believe that we find this conflict reflected in the symptomatology of the female schizophrenics attempting to avoid, to escape from or to destroy the type of marriage which their society sought to tie them to. It is noteworthy that during the early years of marriage and motherhood, when the woman can apply her education to the bringing-up of her young children and can thereby ignore the problems of daily life with an inarticulate and narrow-sighted husband, no schizophrenia makes itself known; only before the decision to marry is made or after the main joys of motherhood are past.

The problem which this generation of women in these villages has been facing might be coloring the symptomatology of the schizophrenics without being at all relevant to the genesis of their disorder. However, in view of the fact that the female rate is double that of the male there and almost double that of the female rate in the "new" French-Canadian villages where a career outside of marriage is much easier to pursue for women, it seems reasonable to believe that the conflict is relevant to the genesis of the disease and not just to its appearances. Moreover, when one looks at the data from the other communities then similar though less striking associations between a conflict of expectations and the onset of schizophrenia appear. That is to say, in the Polish and in the Irish Catholic cases from this survey one can detect a clustering of pathology in sections of the communities that are particularly affected by some cultural inconsistency or conflict of expectations, and a relative absence of schizophrenia in other sections of the population whom the culture either demands very little from or guides very clearly. Details of these other situations can be found in a recent paper;[12] here I wish to indicate what I think they have in common.

The situation in the traditional French-Canadian villages could be described as one of role conflict, but such conflict is too common to be in itself the mediating link we are seeking. Therefore it must be asked what more is present in that situation and in the others. In my opinion one finds the following: a problem of choice which affects the individual deeply; pressure by the community or culture to make some choice; contradictions or confusion in the guidance which the culture provides; chronicity in the sense that the problem persists until a decision is taken. It will be seen, I think, that the type of confrontation which appears to be schizophrenia-evoking in these communities has some similarities to the types of confrontation which are believed to be schizophrenogenic within families and some similarities also to the situations of the peoples cited earlier in this paper. I have suggested elsewhere[13] that it has also similarities to conditions which have been demonstrated in the laboratory to induce pathological thought processes in already schizophrenic subjects. These considerations, however, go beyond the assigned scope of this paper. It is sufficient to say in conclusion that the demonstration of a probable relationship between culture and schizophrenia need not and should not be taken as merely adding one more variable to the already excessive number that apparently must be taken into consideration before schizophrenia can be understood properly. Culture in itself should not be thought of as a factor in the disease; rather it should be thought of as one of a host of variables which can confront the schizophrenia-prone individual with a particular class of experience able to evoke his disease. What is important is to define the characteristics of that class, not to catalogue its innumerable sources.

REFERENCES

1. ARENSBERG, C. M. and KIMBALL, S. T., *Family and Community in Ireland,* Cambridge, Massachusetts, 1940.
2. BHATTACHARJYA, B., On the wartime incidence of mental diseases in the Indian Army, *Ind. J. Neurol. Psychiat.* **1,** 51 (1949).
3. CROCETTI, G. M. *et al.,* Selected aspects of the epidemiology of schizophrenia in Croatia (Yugoslavia), *Milbank Mem. Fund Q.* **42,** 9–37 (1964).
4. DOMINION BUREAU OF STATISTICS (CANADA), *Census of Canada,* 1961 (section 92–562), Ottawa, 1964.
5. EATON, J. W. and WEIL, R. J., *Culture and Mental Disorders,* Illinois, 1955.
6. ETEROVICH, F. H. and SPALATIN, C., *Croatia: Land, People, Culture,* Toronto, 1964.
7. FISHER, J. C., *Yugoslavia—A Multinational State,* San Francisco, 1966.
8. KADRI, Z. N., Schizophrenia in the university students, *Singapore Med. J.* **4,** 113–18 (1963).
9. MALZBERG, B., *Social and Biological Aspects of Mental Disease,* Utica, 1940.
10. MURPHY, H. B. M., Cultural factors in the mental health of Malayan students, in D. H. Funkenstein, (ed.), *The Student and Mental Health: An International View,* World Federation for Mental Health, 1959, pp. 164–222.
11. MURPHY, H. B. M., The epidemiological approach to transcultural psychiatric research, in de Reuck and Porter (eds.), *Transcultural Psychiatry, A Ciba Foundation Symposium,* London, 1965, pp. 303–27.
12. MURPHY, H. B. M., Canadian rural communities and their schizophrenic patients, Paper presented at a Basic Conference on Human Behavior, McGill University, Montreal, 1967.
13. MURPHY, H. B. M., Sociocultural factors in schizophrenia: a compromise theory, to be published in Freyhan and Zubin (eds.), *Social Psychiatry,* American Psychopathological Association 1967 volume.
14. O'DOHERTY, E. F., The high proportion of mental hospital beds in the Republic, (abstracted in) *Transcult. Psychiat. Res.* **2,** 134–6 (1965).

15. POLLOCK, H. M., A statistical study of the foreign-born insane in New York state hospitals, *State Hospitals Bull.* 10–27 of special number (1913).
16. POLLOCK, H. M., Frequency of schizophrenia in relation to sex, age, environment, nativity and race, *Schizophrenia* (Assn. Res. Nerv. Ment. Dis., vol. 5), New York, 1928.
17. SINGH, K., Psychiatric practice among Indian troops, *Ind. Med. Gazette* **81,** 394 (1946).
18. SPITZKA, E. C., Race and insanity, *J. Nerv. Ment. Dis.* **7,** 342–8 (1880).
19. SWIFT, H. M., Insanity and race, *Am. J. Insanity* **70,** 143–54 (1913).
20. WEST, R., *Black Lamb and Grey Falcon,* New York, 1941.
21. WILLIAMS, A. H., A psychiatric study of Indian soldiers in the Arakan, *Brit. J. Med. Psychol.* **23,** 131 (1950).

SOCIAL CLASS AND SCHIZOPHRENIA:
A CRITICAL REVIEW

MELVIN L. KOHN

Laboratory of Socio-environmental Studies,
National Institute of Mental Health, Bethesda, Maryland

MY INTENT in this paper is to review a rather large and all-too-inexact body of research on the relationship of social class to schizophrenia, to see what it adds up to and what implications it has for etiology.[1] Instead of reviewing the studies one by one, I shall talk to general issues and bring in whatever studies are most relevant. It hardly need be stressed that my way of selecting these issues and my evaluation of the studies represent only one person's view of the field and would not necessarily be agreed to by others.

Before I get to the main issues, I should like to make five prefatory comments:

1. When I speak of schizophrenia, I shall generally be using that term in the broad sense in which it is usually employed in the United States, rather than the more limited sense used in much of Europe. I follow American rather than European usage, not because I think it superior, but because it is the usage that has been employed in so much of the relevant research. Any comparative discussion must necessarily employ the more inclusive, even if the cruder, term.

2. I shall generally not be able to distinguish among various types of schizophrenia, for the data rarely enable one to do so. This is most unfortunate; one should certainly want to consider "process" and "reactive" types of disturbance separately, to distinguish between paranoid and non-paranoid, and to take account of several other possibly critical distinctions.

Worse yet, I shall at times have to rely on data about an even broader and vaguer category than schizophrenia—severe mental illness in general, excluding only the demonstrably organic. The excuse for this is that since the epidemiological findings for severe mental illness seem to parallel those for schizophrenia alone, it would be a shame to ignore the several important studies that have been addressed to the larger category. I shall, however, rely on these studies as sparingly as possible and stress studies that focus on schizophrenia.

3. Social classes will be defined as aggregates of individuals who occupy broadly similar positions in the hierarchy of power, privilege and prestige.[2] In dealing with the research literature, I shall treat occupational position (or occupational position as weighted somewhat by education) as a serviceable index of social class for urban society. I shall not make any distinction, since the data hardly permit my doing so, between the concepts "social class" and "socio-economic status". And I shall not hesitate to rely on less than fully adequate indices of class when relevant investigations have employed them.

4. I want to mention only in passing the broadly comparative studies designed to examine the idea that mental disorder in general, and schizophrenia in particular, are products of civilization, or of urban life, or of highly complex social structure. There have been a number of important studies of presumably less complex societies that all seem to indicate that the magnitude of mental disorder in these societies is of roughly the same order as that in highly urbanized, Western societies. I refer you, for example, to Lin's study in Taiwan,[3] the Leightons' in Nova Scotia,[4] Leighton and Lambo's in Nigeria,[5] and Eaton and Weil's of the Hutterites.[6] For a historical perspective within urban, Western society, Goldhamer and Marshall's study in Massachusetts[7] is the most relevant; it indicates that the increasing urbanization of Massachusetts over a period of 100 years did not result in any increase in rates of functional psychosis, except possibly for the elderly.

These data are hardly precise enough to be definitive, but they lead one to turn his attention away from the general hypothesis that there are sizeable differences in rates of mental disorder between simpler and more complex social structures, to look instead at differences within particular social structures, where the evidence is far more intriguing. I do not argue that there are no differences in rates of schizophrenia among societies, only that the data in hand are not sufficient to demonstrate them.[8] We have more abundant data on intra-societal variations.

5. One final prefatory note. Much of what I shall do in this paper will be to raise doubts and come to highly tentative conclusions from inadequate evidence. This is worth doing because we know so little and the problem is so pressing. Genetics does not seem to provide a sufficient explanation,[9] and, I take it from Kety's critical review, biochemical and physiological hypotheses have thus far failed to stand the test of careful experimentation.[10] Of all the social variables that have been studied, those related to social class have yielded the most provocative results. Thus, inadequate as the following data are, they must be taken seriously.

It must be emphasized, however, that there are exceedingly difficult problems in interpreting the data that I am about to review. The indices are suspect, the direction of causality is debatable, the possibility that one or another alternative interpretation makes more sense than the one I should like to draw is very real indeed. These problems will all be taken up shortly; first, though, I should like to lay out the positive evidence for a meaningful relationship between class and schizophrenia.

I. EVIDENCE ON THE POSSIBLE RELATIONSHIP OF SOCIAL CLASS TO RATES OF SCHIZOPHRENIA

Most of the important epidemiological studies of schizophrenia can be viewed as attempts to resolve problems of interpretation posed by the pioneer studies, Faris and Dunham's ecological study of rates of schizophrenia for the various areas of Chicago[11] and Clark's study of rates of schizophrenia at various occupational levels in that same city.[12] Their findings were essentially as follows:

Faris and Dunham: The highest rates of first hospital admission for schizophrenia are in the central city areas of lowest socio-economic status, with diminishing rates as one moves toward higher-status peripheral areas.[13]

Clark: The highest rates of schizophrenia are for the lowest status occupations, with diminishing rates as one goes to higher status occupations.

The concentration of high rates of mental disorder, particularly of schizophrenia, in the central city areas[14] of lowest socio-economic status has been confirmed in a number of American cities—Providence, Rhode Island;[15] Peoria, Illinois;[16] Kansas City, Missouri;[17] St. Louis, Missouri;[18] Milwaukee, Wisconsin;[19] Omaha, Nebraska;[20] Worcester, Massachusetts;[21] Rochester, New York;[22] and Baltimore, Maryland.[23] The two ecological studies done in European cities—Sundby and Nyhus's study of Oslo, Norway[24] and Hare's of Bristol, England[25]—are in substantial agreement, too.

The concentration of high rates of mental disorder, particularly of schizophrenia, in the lowest status occupations has been confirmed again and again. The studies conducted by Hollingshead and Redlich in New Haven, Connecticut,[26] and by Srole and his associates in midtown, New York City,[27] are well-known examples; a multitude of other investigations in the United States have come to the same conclusion.[28] Moreover, Svalastoga's re-analysis of Strömgren's data for northern Denmark is consistent,[29] as are the Leightons' data for "Stirling County", Nova Scotia,[30] Ødegaard's for Norway,[31] Brooke's for England and Wales,[32] Stein's for two sections of London,[33] Lin's for Taiwan,[34] and Steinbäck and Achté's for Helsinki.[35]

But there are some exceptions. Clausen and I happened across the first, when we discovered that for Hagerstown, Maryland, there was no discernible relationship between either occupation or the social status of the area and rates of schizophrenia.[36] On a re-examination of past studies, we discovered a curious thing: the larger the city, the stronger the correlation between rates of schizophrenia and these indices of social class. In the metropolis of Chicago, the correlation is large, and the relationship is linear: the lower the social status, the higher the rates. In cities of 100,000 to 500,000 (or perhaps more), the correlation is smaller and not so linear: it is more a matter of a concentration of cases in the lowest socio-economic strata, with not so much variation among higher strata. When you get down to a city as small as Hagerstown—36,000—the correlation disappears.

Subsequent studies in a number of different places have confirmed our generalization. Sundby and Nyhus, for example, showed that Oslo, Norway, manifests the typical pattern for cities of its half-million size: a high concentration in the lowest social stratum, little variation above.[37] Hollingshead and Redlich's data on new admissions for schizophrenia from New Haven, Connecticut, show that pattern, too.[38]

There is substantial evidence, too, for our conclusion that socio-economic differentials disappear in areas of small population. The Leightons found that although rates of mental disorder do correlate with socio-economic status for "Stirling County", Nova Scotia, as a whole, they do not for the small (population 3000) community of "Bristol".[39] Similarly, Buck, Wanklin, and Hobbs, in an ecological analysis of Western Ontario, found a high rank correlation between median wage and county first admission rates for mental disorder for counties of 10,000 or more population, but a much smaller correlation for counties of smaller population.[40] And Hagnell found no relationship between his admittedly inexact measures of socio-economic status and rates of mental disorder for the largely rural area of southwestern Sweden that he investigated.[41]

I think one must conclude that the relationship of socio-economic status to schizophrenia has been demonstrated only for urban populations. Even for urban populations, a linear relationship of socio-economic status to rates of schizophrenia has been demonstrated only for the largest metropolises. The evidence, though, that there is an unusually high rate of schizophrenia in the lowest socio-economic strata of urban communities seems to me to be nothing less than overwhelming. The proper interpretation why this is so, however, is not so unequivocal.

II. THE DIRECTION OF CAUSALITY

One major issue in interpretating the Faris and Dunham, the Clark, and all subsequent investigations concerns the direction of causality. Rates of schizophrenia in the lowest socio-economic strata could be disproportionately high either because conditions of life in those strata are somehow conducive to the development of schizophrenia, or because people from higher social strata who become schizophrenic suffer a decline in status. Or, of course, it could be some of both. Discussions of this issue have conventionally gone under the rubric of the "drift hypothesis", although far more is involved.

The drift hypothesis was first raised as an attempt to explain away the Faris and Dunham findings. The argument was that in the course of their developing illness, schizophrenics tend to "drift" into lower status areas of the city. It is not that more cases of schizophrenia are "produced" in these areas, but that schizophrenics who are produced elsewhere end up at the bottom of the heap by the time they are hospitalized, and thus are counted as having come from the bottom of the heap.

When the Clark study appeared, the hypothesis was easily enlarged to include "drift" from higher to lower-status occupations. In its broadest formulation, the drift hypothesis asserts that high rates of schizophrenia in the lowest social strata come about because people from higher classes who become schizophrenic suffer a decline in social position as a consequence of their illness. In some versions of the hypothesis, it is further suggested that schizophrenics from smaller locales tend to migrate to the lowest status areas and occupations of large metropolises; this would result in an exaggeration of rates there and a corresponding underestimation of rates for the place and class from which they come.

Incidentally, the drift hypothesis is but one variant of a more general hypothesis that any differences in rates of schizophrenia are the result of social selection—that various social categories show high rates because people already predisposed to schizophrenia gravitate into those categories. This has long been argued by Ødegaard, but with data that are equally amenable to social selection and social causation interpretations.[42] Dunham has recently made the same point, but I think his data argue more convincingly for social causation than for social selection.[43] Intriguing though the issue is, it is presently unresolvable; so it would be better to focus on the more specific question, whether or not the high concentration of schizophrenia in the lowest socio-economic strata is the result of downward drift.

One approach to this problem has been to study the histories of social mobility of schizophrenics. Unfortunately, the evidence is inconsistent. Three studies indicate that schizophrenics have been downwardly mobile in occupational status,[44] three others that they have not been.[45] Some of these studies do not compare the experiences of the schizophrenics to those of normal persons from comparable social backgrounds. Those that do are nevertheless inconclusive—either because the comparison group was not well chosen, or because the city in which the study was done does not have a concentration of schizophrenia in the lowest social class. Since no study is definitive, any assessment must be based on a subjective weighing of the strengths and weaknesses of them all. My assessment is that the weight of this evidence clearly indicates either that schizophrenics have been no more downwardly mobile (in fact, no less upwardly mobile) than other people from the same social backgrounds, or at minimum, that the degree of downward mobility is insufficient to explain the high concentration of schizophrenia in the lowest socio-economic strata.

There is another and more direct way of looking at the question, however, and from this perspective the question is still unresolved. The reformulated question focuses on the social class origins of schizophrenics; it asks whether the occupations of fathers of schizophrenics are concentrated in the lowest social strata. If they are, that is clear evidence in favor of the hypothesis that lower class status is conducive to schizophrenia. If they are not, class might still matter for schizophrenia—it might be a matter of stress experienced by lower class adults, rather than of the experience of being born and raised in the lower class—but certainly the explanation that would require the fewest assumptions would be the drift hypothesis.

The first major study to evaluate the evidence from this perspective argued strongly in favor of lower class origins being conducive to mental disorder, although perhaps not to schizophrenia in particular. Srole and his associates found, in their study of midtown New York, that rates of mental disorder correlate nearly as well with their parents' socio-economic status as with the subjects' own socio-economic status.[46] But then Goldberg and Morrison found that although the occupations of male schizophrenic patients admitted to hospitals in England and Wales show the usual concentration of cases in the lowest social class, their fathers' occupations do not.[47] Since this study dealt with schizophrenia, the new evidence seemed more directly in point. One might quarrel with some aspects of this study —the index of social class is debatable, for example, and data are lacking for 25% of the originally drawn sample—but this is much too good a study to be taken lightly. Nor can one conclude that the situation in England and Wales is different from that in the United States, for Dunham reports that two segments of Detroit show a similar picture.[48]

There is yet one more study to be considered, however, and this the most important one of all, for it offers the most complete data about class origins, mobility, and the eventual class position of schizophrenics. Turner and Wagonfeld, in a study of Monroe County (Rochester), New York, discovered a remarkable pattern: rates of first treatment for schizophrenia are disproportionately high, both for patients of lowest occupational status and for patients whose fathers had lowest occupational status, but these are by and large not the same patients.[49] Some of those whose fathers were in the lowest occupational class had themselves moved up and some of those ending up in the lowest occupational class had come from higher class origins. Thus, there is evidence both for the proposition that lower class origins are conducive to schizophrenia and for the proposition that most lower-class schizophrenics come from higher socio-economic origins. No wonder partial studies have been inconsistent!

The next question one would want to ask, of course, is how the schizophrenics' histories of occupational mobility compare to those of normal people of comparable social class origins. Turner and Wagonfeld have not the data to answer this definitively, for they lack an appropriate control group. They are able, however, to compare the mobility experiences of their schizophrenics to those of a crosss-section of the population, and from this they learn two important things. More schizophrenics than normals have been downwardly mobile. This downward mobility did not come about because of a loss of occupational position that had once been achieved, but reflected their failure ever to have achieved as high an occupational level as do most men of their social class origins.

This argues strongly against a simple drift hypothesis—it is not, as some have argued, that we have erroneously rated men at lower than their usual class status because we have classified them according to their occupations at time of hospitalization, after they have suffered a decline in occupational position. It is more likely that a more sophisticated drift hypothesis applies—that some people genetically or constitutionally or otherwise predisposed to schizophrenia show some effects of developing illness at least as early as the time of their first jobs, for they are never able to achieve the occupational levels that might be expected of them. If so, the possibilities of some interaction between genetic predisposition and early social circumstances are very real indeed.

One direction that further research must take is well pointed out by the Turner and Wagonfeld study. The question now must be the degree to which the correlation of class and schizophrenia results from a higher incidence of schizophrenia among people born into lower-class families, the degree to which it results from schizophrenics of higher class origins never achieving as high an occupational level as might have been expected of them —and why.

For the present, I think it can be tentatively concluded that despite what Goldberg and Morrison found for England and Wales, the weight of evidence lies against the drift hypothesis being a sufficient explanation. In all probability, lower-class families produce a disproportionate number of schizophrenics, although perhaps by not so large a margin as one would conclude from studies that rely on the patients' own occupational attainments.

Parenthetically, there is another important question involved here, the effects of social mobility itself. Ever since Ødegaard's classic study of rates of mental disorder among Norwegian migrants to the United States,[50] we have known that geographic mobility is a matter of considerable consequence for mental illness,[51] and the same may be true for social mobility.[52] But we have not known how and why mobility matters—whether it is a question of what types of people are mobile or of the stresses of mobility—and unfortunately later research has failed to resolve the issue.

III. THE ADEQUACY OF INDICES

The adequacy of indices is another major issue in interpreting the Faris and Dunham, the Clark, and all subsequent investigations. Most of these studies are based on hospital admission rates, which may not give a valid picture of the true incidence of schizophrenia. Studies that do not rely on hospital rates encounter other and perhaps even more serious difficulties, with which we shall presently deal.

The difficulty with using admission rates as the basis for computing rates of schizophrenia is that lower-class psychotics may be more likely to be hospitalized, and if hospitalized to be diagnosed as schizophrenic, especially in public hospitals. Faris and Dunham tried to solve this problem by including patients admitted to private as well as to public mental hospitals. This was insufficient because, as later studies have shown, some people who suffer serious mental disorder never enter a mental hospital.[53]

Subsequent studies have attempted to do better by including more and more social agencies in their search for cases; Hollingshead and Redlich in New Haven,[54] and Jaco in Texas,[55] for example, have extended their coverage to include everyone who enters any sort of treatment facility—Jaco going so far as to question all the physicians in Texas. This is better, but clearly the same objections hold in principle. Furthermore, Srole and his associates have demonstrated that there are considerable social differences between people who have been treated, somewhere, for mental illness, and severely impaired people, some large proportion of them schizophrenic, who have never been to any sort of treatment facility.[56] So we must conclude that using treatment—any sort of treatment—as an index of mental disorder is suspect.

The alternative is to go out into the community and examine everyone—or a representative sample of everyone—yourself. This has been done by a number of investigators, for example Essen-Möller in Sweden,[57] Srole and his associates in New York,[58] the Leightons in Nova Scotia.[59] They have solved one problem, but have run into three others.

1. The first is that most of these investigators have found it impossible to classify schizophrenia reliably, and have had to resort to larger and vaguer categories—severe mental illness, functional psychosis, and such. For some purposes, this may be justified. For our immediate purposes, it is exceedingly unfortunate.

2. Second, even if you settle for such a concept as "mental illness", it is difficult to establish criteria that can be applied reliably and validly in community studies.[60] For all its inadequacies, hospitalization is at least an unambiguous index, and you can be fairly certain that the people who are hospitalized are really ill. But how does one interpret the Leightons' estimate that about a third of their population suffer significant psychiatric impairment,[61] or Srole's that almost a quarter of his are impaired?[62]

Personal examination by a single psychiatrist using presumably consistent standards is one potential solution, but usable only in relatively small investigations. Another possible solution is the further development of objective rating scales, such as the Neuropsychiatric Screening Adjunct first developed by social scientists in the Research Branch of the US Army in World War II[63] and later incorporated into both the Leightons' and Srole's investigations, but not developed to anything like its full potential in either study. The limitation here is that such scales may be less relevant to the measurement of psychosis than of neurosis.

To make significant further advances, we shall have to break free of traditional methods of measurement. Epidemiological studies still largely rely on a single, undifferentiated overall assessment. Even when such an assessment can be demonstrated to be reliable within the confines of a single study, it has only limited use for comparative studies and is questionable for repeated application in studies designed to ascertain how many new cases arise in some given period of time. At minimum, we must begin to make use of our developing capacities at multivariate analysis. One obvious approach is to try to differentiate the several judgments that go into clinical diagnoses, develop reliable measures of each, and examine their interrelationship. At the same time, it would be well to develop reliable measures of matters conventionally given only secondary attention in epidemiological research—for example, the degree of disability the individual has sustained in each of several major social roles.[64] A third path we might try is the further development of objective measures of dimensions of subjective state (such as anxiety, alienation, and self-abasement) thought to be indicative of pathology. All these and others can be measured as separate dimensions, and then empirically related to each other and to clinical assessments.

Whether or not these particular suggestions have merit, I think the general conclusion that it is time for considerable methodological experimentation is indisputable.

3.   The third problem in community studies is that it is so difficult to secure data on the incidence of mental disturbance that most studies settle for prevalence data.[65] That is, instead of ascertaining the number of new cases arising in various population groups during some period of time, they count the number of people currently ill at the time of the study. This latter measure—prevalence—is inadequate because it reflects not only incidence but also duration of illness. As Hollingshead and Redlich have shown, duration of illness—in so far as it incapacitates—is highly correlated with social class.[66]

Various approximations to incidence have been tried, and various new—and often somewhat fantastic—statistical devices invented to get around this problem, but without any real success. Clearly, what is needed is repeated studies of the population, to pick up new cases as they arise and thus to establish true incidence figures. (This is what Hagnell did, and it was a very brave effort indeed.) The crucial problem, of course, is to develop reliable measures of mental disorder, for without that our repeated surveys will measure nothing but the errors of our instruments. Meantime, we have to recognize that prevalence studies use an inappropriate measure that exaggerates the relationship of socio-economic status to mental disorder.

So, taken all together, the results of the studies of class and schizophrenia are hardly definitive. They may even all wash out—one more example of inadequate methods leading to premature, false conclusions. I cannot prove otherwise. Yet I think the most reasonable interpretation of all these findings is that they point to something real. Granted that there isn't a single definitive study in the lot, the weaknesses of one are compensated for by the strengths of some other, and the total edifice is probably much stronger than you would conclude from knowing only how frail are its component parts. A large number of complementary studies all seem to point to the same conclusion: that rates of mental disorder, particularly of schizophrenia, are highest at the lowest socio-economic levels, at least in moderately large cities, and this probably isn't just a matter of drift or inadequate indices or some other artifact of the methods we use. In all probability, more schizophrenia is actually produced at the lowest socio-economic levels. At any rate, let us take that as a working hypothesis and explore the question further. Assuming that more schizophrenia occurs at lower socio-economic levels—Why?

IV. ALTERNATIVE INTERPRETATIONS

Is it really socio-economic status, or is it some correlated variable that is operative here? Faris and Dunham did not take socio-economic status very seriously in their interpretation of their data. From among the host of variables characteristic of the high-rate areas of Chicago, they focused on such things as high rates of population turnover and ethnic mixtures and hypothesized that the really critical thing about the high-rate areas was the degree of social isolation they engendered. Two subsequent studies, one by Jaco in Texas,[67] the other by Hare in Bristol, England,[68] are consistent in that they, too, show a correlation of rates of schizophrenia to various ecological indices of social isolation. The only study that directly examines the role of social isolation in the lives of schizophrenics, however, seems to demonstrate that while social isolation may be symptomatic of developing illness, it does not play an important role in etiology.[69]

Several other interpretations of the epidemiological evidence have been suggested, some supported by intriguing, if inconclusive, evidence. One is that it is not socio-economic status as such that is principally at issue, but social integration. The Leightons have produced plausible evidence for this interpretation.[70] The problems of defining and indexing "social integration" make a definitive demonstration exceedingly difficult, however, even for the predominantly rural populations with which they have worked.

Another possibility is that the high rates of schizophrenia found in lower-class populations are a consequence of especially high rates for lower-class members of some "ethnic" groups who happen to be living in areas where other ethnic groups predominate. In their recent study in Boston, for example, Schwartz and Mintz showed that Italian–Americans living in predominantly non-Italian neighborhoods have very high rates of schizophrenia, while those living in predominantly Italian neighborhoods do not.[71] The former group contribute disproportionately to the rates for lower-class neighborhoods. (The authors suggest that this may explain why small cities do not show a concentration of lower-class cases: these cities do not have the ethnic mixtures that produce such a phenomenon.)

Wechsler and Pugh extended this interpretive model to suggest that rates should be higher for any persons living in a community where they and persons of similar social attributes are in a minority.[72] Their analysis of Massachusetts towns provides some surprisingly supportive data.

Other possibilities deal more directly with the occupational component of socio-economic status. Ødegaard long ago showed that rates of schizophrenia are higher for some occupations that are losing members and lower for some that are expanding.[73] His observation was correct, but it explains only a small part of the occupational rate differences. Others have focused on alleged discrepancies between schizophrenics' occupational aspirations and achievements,[74] arguing that the pivotal fact is not that schizophrenics have achieved so little but that they had wanted so much more. The evidence is limited.

One could argue—and I see no reason to take the argument lightly—that genetics provides a quite sufficient explanation. If there is a moderately strong genetic component in schizophrenia, then one would expect a higher than usual rate of schizophrenia among the fathers and grandfathers of schizophrenics. Since schizophrenia is a debilitating disturbance, this would be reflected in grandparents' and parents' occupations and places of residence.

In other words, it could be a rather complex version of drift hypothesis. The only argument against this interpretation is that there is no really compelling evidence in favor of it; one can accept it on faith, or one can keep it in mind while continuing to explore alternatives. Prudence suggests the latter course of action.

There are other possibilities we might examine, but since there is no very strong evidence for any of them, that course does not seem especially profitable. One must allow the possibility that some correlated variable might prove critical for explaining the findings; it might not be social class, after all, that is operative here. Until that is demonstrated, however, the wisest course would seem to be to take the findings at face value and see what there might be about social class that would help us to understand schizophrenia.

V. CLASS AND ETIOLOGY

What is there about the dynamics of social class that might affect the probability of people becoming schizophrenic? How does social class operate here; what are the intervening processes?

The possibilities are numerous, almost too numerous. Social class indexes and is correlated with so many phenomena that might be relevant to the etiology of schizophrenia. Since it measures status, it implies a great deal about how the individual is treated by others—with respect or perhaps degradingly; since it is measured by occupational rank, it suggests much about the conditions that make up the individual's daily work, how closely supervised he is, whether he works primarily with things, with data, or with people; since it reflects the individual's educational level, it connotes a great deal about his style of thinking, his use or non-use of abstractions, even his perceptions of physical reality and certainly of social reality; furthermore, the individual's class position influences his social values and colors his evaluations of the world about him; it affects the family experiences he is likely to have had as a child and the ways he is likely to raise his own children; and it certainly matters greatly for the type and amount of stress he is likely to encounter in a lifetime. In short, social class pervades so much of life that it is difficult to guess which of its correlates are most relevant for understanding schizophrenia. Moreover, none of these phenomena is so highly correlated with class (nor class so highly correlated with schizophrenia) that any one of these facets is obviously more promising than the others.

This being the case, investigators have tended to pursue those avenues that have met their theoretical predilections and to ignore the others. In practice, this has meant that the interrelationship of class, family, and schizophrenia has been explored, and more recently the relationship of class, stress, and schizophrenia, but the other possibilities remain largely unexamined. Given the inherent relevance of some of them—class differences in patterns of thinking, for example, have such obvious relevance to schizophrenia—this is a bit surprising.

But let me review what has been done. The hypothesis that stress is what is really at issue in the class–schizophrenia relationship is in some respects especially appealing, in part because it is so direct. We have not only our own observations as human beings with some compassion for less fortunate people, but an increasingly impressive body of scientific evidence,[75] to show that life is rougher and rougher the lower one's social class position.

The stress explanation seems especially plausible for the very lowest socio-economic levels, where the rates of schizophrenia are highest.

There have to my knowledge been only two empirical investigations of the relationship of social class to stress to mental disorder. The first was done by Langner and Michael in New York as part of the "Midtown" study.[76] This study, as all the others we have been considering, has its methodological defects—it is a prevalence study, and many of the indices it uses are at best questionable—but it tackles the major issues head-on, and with very impressive and very intriguing results. It finds a strong linear relationship between stress and mental disturbance, specifically, the more sources of stress, the higher the probability of mental disturbance. It also finds the expected relationship between social class and stress. So the stress hypothesis has merit. But stress is not all that is involved in the relationship of social class to mental disorder. No matter how high the level of stress, social class continues to be correlated with the probability of mental disturbance; in fact, the more stress, the higher the correlation.[77] Thus, it seems that the effect of social class on the rate of mental disorder is not only, or even principally, a function of different amounts of stress at different class levels.

In a more recent study in San Juan, Puerto Rico, Rogler and Hollingshead ascribe a more important role to stress.[78] Theirs was an intensive investigation of the life histories of a sample of lower-class schizophrenics, along with comparable studies of a well-matched sample of non-schizophrenics. Rogler and Hollingshead found only insubstantial differences in the early life experiences of lower-class schizophrenics and controls; they did find, however, that in the period of a year or so before the onset of symptoms, the schizophrenics were subjected to an unbearable onslaught of stress. In effect, all lower-class slum dwellers in San Juan suffer continual, dreadful stress; in addition to this "normal" level of stress, however, the schizophrenics were hit with further intolerable stress which incapacitated them in one or another central role, leading to incapacitation in other roles, too.

The picture that Rogler and Hollingshead draw is plausible and impressive. It is not possible, however—at least not yet—to generalize as far from their data as one might like. Their sample is limited to schizophrenics who are married or in stable consensual unions. These one would assume to be predominantly "reactive" type schizophrenics—precisely the group whom one would expect, from past studies, to have had normal childhood social experiences, good social adjustment, and extreme precipitating circumstances. So their findings may apply to "reactive" schizophrenia, but perhaps not to "process" schizophrenia. In addition, for all the impressiveness of the argument, the data are not so unequivocal. Their inquiry was not so exhaustive as to rule out the possibility that the schizophrenics might have had different family experiences from those of the controls. Furthermore, the evidence that the schizophrenics were subjected to significantly greater stress is not so thoroughly compelling as one might want. Thus, the case is not proved. Nevertheless, Rogler and Hollingshead have demonstrated that the possibility that stress plays an important role in the genesis of schizophrenia is to be taken very seriously indeed. Certainly this study makes it imperative that we investigate the relationship of class to stress to schizophrenia far more intensively.

At the same time, we should investigate some closely related possibilities that have not to my knowledge been studied empirically. Not only stress, but also reward and opportunity,

L

are differentially distributed among the social classes. The more fortunately situated not only are less beaten about, but may be better able to withstand the stresses they do encounter because they have many more rewarding experiences to give them strength. And many more alternative courses of action are open to them when they run into trouble. Might this offer an added clue to the effects of class for schizophrenia?

More generally, what is there about the conditions of life of the lowest social strata that might make it more difficult for their members to cope with stress? One can think of intriguing possibilities. Their occupational conditions and their limited education gear their thinking processes to the concrete and the habitual; their inexperience in dealing with the abstract may ill-equip them to cope with ambiguity, uncertainty, and unpredictability; their mental processes are apt to be too gross and rigid when flexibility and subtlety are most required. Or, a related hypothesis, the lower- and working-class valuation of conformity to external authority, and disvaluation of self-direction, might cripple a man faced with the necessity of suddenly having to rely on himself in an uncertain situation where others cannot be relied on for guidance.

These hypotheses, unfortunately, have not been investigated; perhaps it is time that they were. The one hypothesis that has been studied, and that one only partially, is that lower- and working-class patterns of parent–child relationships somehow do not adequately prepare children for dealing with the hazards of life. Now we enter what is perhaps the most complicated area of research we have touched on so far, and certainly the least adequately studied field of all.

There has been a huge volume of research literature about family relationships and schizophrenia,[79] most of it inadequately designed. One has to dismiss the majority of studies because of one or another incapacitating deficiency. In many, the patients selected for study were a group from which you could not possibly generalize to schizophrenics at large. Either the samples were comprised of chronic patients, where one would expect the longest and most difficult onset of illness with the greatest strain in family relationships, or the samples were peculiarly selected, not to test a hypothesis, but to load the dice in favor of a hypothesis. In other studies, there have been inadequate control groups or no control group at all. One of the most serious defects of method has been the comparison of patterns of family relationship of lower- and working-class patients to middle- and upper-middle-class normal controls—which completely confounds the complex picture we wish to disentangle. In still other studies, even where the methods of sample and control-selection have been adequate, the method of data-collection has seriously biased the results. This is true, for example, in those studies that have placed patients and their families in stressful situations bound to exaggerate any flaws in their interpersonal processes, especially for people of lesser education and verbal skill who would be least equipped to deal with the new and perplexing situation in which they found themselves.[80]

Still, some recent studies have suggested respects in which the family relationships of schizophrenics seem unusual, and unusual in theoretically interesting ways—that is, in ways that might be important in the dynamics of schizophrenic personality development. Work by Bateson and Jackson on communication processes in families of schizophrenics[81] and that by Wynne and his associates on cognitive and emotional processes in such families,[82] for example, are altogether intriguing.

But—and here I must once again bring social class into the picture—there has not been a single well-controlled study that demonstrates any substantial difference between the family relationships of schizophrenics and those of normal persons from lower- and working-class backgrounds. Now, it may be that the well-controlled studies simply have not dealt with the particular variables that do differentiate the families of schizophrenics from those of normal lower- and working-class families. The two studies that best control for social class—Clausen's and my study in Hagerstown, Maryland[83] and Rogler and Hollingshead's in San Juan[84]—deal with but a few aspects of family relationship, notably not including the very processes that recent clinical studies have emphasized as perhaps the most important of all. It may be that investigations yet to come will show clear and convincing evidence that some important aspects of family relationships are definitely different for schizophrenia-producing families and normal families of this social background.

If they do not, that still does not mean that family relationships are not important for schizophrenia, or that it is not through the family that social class exerts one of its principal effects. Another way of putting the same facts is to say that there is increasing evidence of remarkable parallels between the dynamics of families that produce schizophrenia and family dynamics in the lower classes generally.[85] This may indicate that the family patterns of the lower classes are in some way broadly conducive to schizophrenic personality development.

Clearly these patterns do not provide a sufficient explanation of schizophrenia. We still need a missing X, or set of X's, to tell us the necessary and sufficient conditions for schizophrenia to occur. Perhaps that X is some other aspect of family relationships. Perhaps lower-class patterns of family relationships are conducive to schizophrenia for persons genetically predisposed, but not for others. Or perhaps they are generally conducive to schizophrenia, but schizophrenia will not actually occur unless the individual is subjected to certain types or amounts of stress. We do not know. But these speculative considerations do suggest that it may be about time to bring all these variables—social class, early family relationships, genetics, stress—into the same investigations, so that we can examine their interactive effects. Meantime, I must sadly conclude that we have not yet unravelled the relationship of social class and schizophrenia, nor learned what it might tell us about the etiology of the disorder.

VI. CONCLUSION

Perhaps, after so broad a sweep, an overall assessment is in order. There is a truly remarkable volume of research literature demonstrating an especially high rate of schizophrenia (variously indexed) in the lowest social class or classes (variously indexed) of moderately large to large cities throughout much of the Western world. It is not altogether clear what is the direction of causality in this relationship—whether the conditions of life of the lowest social classes are conducive to the development of schizophrenia, or schizophrenia leads to a decline in social class position—but present evidence would make it seem probable that some substantial part of the phenomenon results from lower class conditions of life being conducive to schizophrenia. It is not even certain that the indices of schizophrenia used in these studies can be relied on, although there is some minor comfort in that studies using several different indices all point to the same conclusion. Perhaps it is only an act of faith that permits me to conclude that the relationship of class to schizophrenia is probably real, an act of faith only barely disguised by calling it a working hypothesis.

This working hypothesis must be weighed against a number of alternative interpretations of the data. Many of them are plausible, several are supported by attractive nuggets of data, but none is more compelling than the most obvious interpretation of all: that social class seems to matter for schizophrenia because, in fact, it does.

When one goes on to see what this might imply for the etiology of schizophrenia, one finds many more intriguing possibilities than rigorous studies. There is some evidence that the greater stress suffered by lower-class people is relevant, and perhaps that lower- and working-class patterns of family relationships are broadly conducive to schizophrenia—although the latter is more a surmise than a conclusion.

Finally, it is clear that we must bring genetic predisposition and class, with all its attendant experiences, into the same investigations. That, however, is not the only sort of investigation that calls for attention. We have reviewed a large number of hypotheses, several major conflicts of interpretation, and many leads and hunches that all cry out to be investigated. The most hopeful sign in this confusing area is that several of the recent studies have gone far beyond seeing whether the usual stereotyped set of demographic characteristics correlate with rates of schizophrenia, to explore some of these very exciting issues.

REFERENCES AND NOTES

1. The *raison d'être* of this review, aside from its being momentarily current, is in its effort to organize the evidence around certain central issues and to make use of all studies relevant to those issues. There are no definitive studies in this field, but most of them contribute something to our knowledge when placed in perspective of all the others. For an alternative approach, deliberately limited to those few studies that meet the reviewers' standards of adequacy, see MISHLER, ELLIOT G. and NORMAN A. SCOTCH, Sociocultural factors in the epidemiology of schizophrenia: a review, *Psychiatry* 26, 315–51 (1963). Dunham has recently argued for a more radical alternative; he disputes the legitimacy of using epidemiological data to make the types of social psychological inference I attempt here and insists that epidemiological studies are relevant only to the study of how social systems function. This seems to me to be altogether arbitrary. But see DUNHAM, H. WARREN, *Community and Schizophrenia: An Epidemiological Analysis,* Detroit, Wayne State University Press, 1965, and Epidemiology of psychiatric disorders as a contribution to medical ecology, *Archives of General Psychiatry* 14, 1–19 (1966). Some other useful reviews and discussions of issues in this field are: DUNHAM, H. WARREN, Current status of ecological research in mental disorder, *Social Forces* 25, 321–6 (1947), FELIX, R. H. and R. V. BOWERS, Mental hygiene and socio-environmental factors, *The Milbank Mem. Fund Quart.* 26, 125–47 (1948); DUNHAM, H. WARREN, Social psychiatry, *Am. Sociol. Rev.* 13, 183–97 (1948); CLAUSEN, JOHN A., *Sociology and the Field of Mental Health,* New York, Russell Sage Foundation, 1956; CLAUSEN, JOHN A., The ecology of mental illness, *Symposium on Social and Preventive Psychiatry,* Walter Reed Army Medical Center, Washington, D.C., 97–108 (1957); CLAUSEN, JOHN A., The sociology of mental illness, in Robert K. Merton *et al.* (ed.), *Sociology Today, Problems and Prospects,* New York, Basic Books, 1959; HOLLINGSHEAD, AUGUST B., Some issues in the epidemiology of schizophrenia, *Am. Sociol. Rev.* 26, 5–13 (1961); DUNHAM H. WARREN, Some persistent problems in the epidemiology of mental disorders, *Am. J. Psychiat.* 109, 567–75 (1963); and SANUA, VICTOR D., The etiology and epidemiology of mental illness and problems of methodology: with special emphasis on schizophrenia, *Ment. Hyg.* 47, 607–21 (1963). The present review leans heavily on my earlier paper, On the social epidemiology of schizophrenia, *Acta Sociol.* 9, 209–21 (1966), but is more complete in its coverage and represents—for all its similarities to the earlier paper—a thorough re-assessment of the field.
2. WILLIAMS, ROBIN M., JR., *American Society: A Sociological Interpretation,* New York, Knopf, 1951, p. 89.
3. LIN, TSUNG-YI, A study of the incidence of mental disorder in Chinese and other cultures, *Psychiatry* 16, 313–36 (1953).

4. This study is reported in three volumes: LEIGHTON, ALEXANDER H., *My Name is Legion: Foundations for a Theory of Man in Relation to Culture,* New York, Basic Books, 1959; HUGHES, CHARLES C. with MARC-ADELARD TREMBLAY, ROBERT N. RAPOPORT and ALEXANDER H. LEIGHTON, *People of Cove and Woodlot: Communities from the Viewpoint of Social Psychiatry,* New York, Basic Books, 1960; LEIGHTON, DOROTHEA C. with JOHN S. HARDING, DAVID B. MACKLIN, ALLISTER M. MACMILLAN, and ALEXANDER H. LEIGHTON, *The Character of Danger: Psychiatric Symptoms in Selected Communities,* New York, Basic Books, 1963.

5. LEIGHTON, ALEXANDER H., T. ADEOYE LAMBO, CHARLES C. HUGHES, DOROTHEA C. LEIGHTON, JANE M. MURPHY, DAVID B. MACKLIN, *Psychiatric Disorder among the Yoruba,* Ithaca, Cornell University Press, 1963 and Psychiatric disorder in West Africa, *Am. J. Psychiat.* **120,** 521–5 (1963).

6. EATON, JOSEPH W. in collaboration with ROBERT J. WEIL, *Culture and Mental Disorders: A Comparative Study of the Hutterites and Other Populations,* Glencoe, Illinois, Free Press, 1955. This volume includes a valuable comparison of rates of psychosis in a variety of different cultures, from an arctic fishing village in Norway to Baltimore, Maryland to Thuringia to Formosa to Williamson County, Tennessee. It must be noted that although Eaton and Weil find the rate of functional psychosis among the Hutterites to be roughly comparable to that for other societies, they find the rate of schizophrenia to be low (and that for manic-depressive psychosis to be correspondingly high). There is, however, reason to doubt the validity of their differential diagnosis of schizophrenia and manic-depressive psychosis.

7. GOLDHAMER, HERBERT and ANDREW W. MARSHALL, *Psychosis and Civilization,* Glencoe, Illinois, Free Press, 1953.

8. For further documentation of this point, see also MISHLER and SCOTCH, *op. cit.*; DUNHAM, *Community and Schizophrenia, loc. cit.*; DEMERATH, N. J., Schizophrenia among primitives, in Arnold M. Rose (ed.), *Mental Health and Mental Disorder,* New York, W. W. Norton, 1955.

9. Some of the principal recent studies that bear on this point are: ROSENTHAL, DAVID, Problems of sampling and diagnosis in the major twin studies of schizophrenia, *J. Psychiat. Res.* **1,** 116–34 (1962); TIENARI, PEKKA, Psychiatric illnesses in identical twins, *Acta psychiat. scand.* **39,** Suppl. 171 (1963); and KRINGLEN, EINAR, Discordance with respect to schizophrenia in monozygotic twins: some genetic aspects, *J. Nerv. Ment. Dis.* **138,** 26–31 (1964); *Schizophrenia in Male Monozygotic Twins,* Oslo, Universitetsforlaget, 1964, 76 pp.; and Schizophrenia in twins: an epidemiological–clinical study, *Psychiatry* **29,** 172–84 (1966).

10. KETY, SEYMOUR S., Recent biochemical theories of schizophrenia, in Don D. Jackson (ed.), *The Etiology of Schizophrenia,* New York, Basic Books, 1960.

11. FARIS, ROBERT E. L. and H. WARREN DUNHAM, *Mental Disorders in Urban Areas: An Ecological Study of Schizophrenia and Other Psychoses,* Chicago, University of Chicago Press, 1939.

12. CLARK, ROBERT E., The relationship of schizophrenia to occupational income and occupational prestige, *Am. Sociol. Rev.* **13,** 325–30 (1948); and Psychoses, income, and occupational prestige, *Am. J. Sociol.* **54,** 433–40 (1949).

13. The pattern is most marked for paranoid schizophrenia, least so for catatonic, which tends to concentrate in the foreign-born slum communities (FARIS and DUNHAM, *op. cit.,* pp. 82–108). Unfortunately, subsequent studies in smaller cities dealt with too few cases to examine the distribution of separable types of schizophrenia as carefully as did Faris and Dunham.

14. There are some especially difficult problems in interpreting the ecological findings, which I shall not discuss here because most of the later and crucial evidence comes from other modes of research. The problems inherent in interpreting ecological studies are discussed in ROBINSON, W. S., Ecological correlations and the behavior of individuals, *Am. Sociol. Rev.* **15,** 351–7 (1950) and in CLAUSEN, JOHN A. and MELVIN L. KOHN, The ecological approach in social psychiatry, *Am. J. Sociol.* **60,** 140–51 (1954).

15. FARIS and DUNHAM, *op. cit.,* pp. 143–50.

16. SCHROEDER, CLARENCE W., Mental disorders in cities, *Am. J. Sociol.* **48,** 40–8 (1942).

17. *Ibid.*

18. DEE, WILLIAM L. J., An ecological study of mental disorders in metropolitan St. Louis, unpublished M.A. thesis, Washington University, 1939; SCHROEDER, *op. cit.*; QUEEN, STUART A., The ecological study of mental disorders, *Am. Sociol. Rev.* **5,** 201–9 (1940).

19. SCHROEDER, *op. cit.*

20. *Ibid.*

21. GERARD, DONALD L. and LESTER G. HOUSTON, Family setting and the social ecology of schizophrenia, *Psychiat. Quart.* **27,** 90–101 (1953).

22. GARDNER, ELMER A. and HAROUTIN M. BABIGIAN, A longitudinal comparison of psychiatric service to selected socio-economic areas of Monroe County, New York, *Am. J. Orthopsychiat.* **36,** 818–28 (1966).

23. KLEE, GERALD D., with EVELYN SPIRO, ANITA K. BAHN, and KURT GORWITZ, An ecological analysis of diagnosed mental illness in Baltimore, in Monroe, Russell R., *et al.* (eds.), *Psychiatric Epidemiology and Mental Health Planning*, Psychiatric Research Report No. 22, the American Psychiatric Association, April, 1967.

24. SUNDBY, PER and PER NYHUS, Major and minor psychiatric disorders in males in Oslo: an epidemiological study, *Acta psychiat. scand.* **39**, 519–47 (1963).

25. HARE, E. H., Mental illness and social conditions in Bristol, *J. Ment. Sci.* **102**, 349–57 (1956).

26. HOLLINGSHEAD, AUGUST B. and FREDERICK C. REDLICH, *Social Class and Mental Illness*, New York, John Wiley, 1957.

27. SROLE, LEO, with THOMAS S. LANGNER, STANLEY T. MICHAEL, MARVIN K. OPLER, and THOMAS A. C. RENNIE *Mental Health in the Metropolis: the Midtown Manhattan Study*, volume 1, New York, McGraw-Hill, 1962.

28. See, for example, LOCKE, BEN Z., with MORTON KRAMER, CHARLES E. TIMBERLAKE, BENJAMIN PASAMANICK and DONALD SMELTZER, Problems of interpretation of patterns of first admissions to Ohio State public mental hospitals for patients with schizophrenic reactions, in Benjamin Pasamanick and Peter H. Knapp (eds.), *Social Aspects of Psychiatry*, the American Psychiatric Association (Psychiatric Research Reports No. 10), 1958; FRUMKIN, ROBERT M., Occupation and major mental disorders, in Arnold Rose (ed.), *Mental Health and Mental Disorders*, New York, W. W. Norton, 1955; DUNHAM, *Community and Schizophrenia, loc. cit.*; LEMKAU, PAUL, with CHRISTOPHER TIETZE and MARCIA COOPER, Mental hygiene problems in an urban district: second paper, *Ment. Hyg.* **26**, 1–20 (1942); FUSON, WILLIAM M., Research note: occupations of functional psychotics, *Am. J. Sociol.* **48**, 612–13 (1943); TURNER, R. J. and MORTON O. WAGONFELD, Occupational mobility and schizophrenia, an assessment of the social causation and social selection hypotheses, *Am. Sociol. Rev.* **32**, 104–13 (1967). Relevant, too, are some early studies whose full significance was not appreciated until later. See, for example, WILLIAM J. NOLAN, Occupation and *dementia praecox*, *(New York) State Hospitals Quart.* **3**, 127–54 (1917); ØDEGAARD, ØRNULV, Emigration and insanity: a study of mental disease among the Norwegianborn population of Minnesota, *Acta psychiatr. neurol.*, Suppl. 4, esp. pp. 182–4 (1932); GREEN, HOWARD W., *Persons Admitted to the Cleveland State Hospital, 1928–37*, Cleveland Health Council, 1939. One puzzling partial-exception comes from Jaco's study of Texas. He finds the highest incidence of schizophrenia among the unemployed, but otherwise a strange, perhaps curvilinear relationship of occupational status to incidence. Perhaps it is only that so many of his patients were classified as unemployed (rather than according to their pre-illness occupational status) that the overall picture is distorted. See JACO, E. GARTLEY, Incidence of psychoses in Texas, *Texas State J. Med.* **53**, 1–6 (1957), and *The Social Epidemiology of Mental Disorders*, New York, Russell Sage Foundation, 1960.

29. SVALASTOGA, KAARE, *Social Differentiation*, New York, David McKay, 1965, pp. 100–1.

30. LEIGHTON, *et al., The Character of Danger, loc. cit.*, pp. 279–94.

31. ØDEGAARD, ØRNULV, The incidence of psychoses in various occupations, *Int. J. Soc. Psychiat.* **2**, 85–104 (1956); Psychiatric epidemiology, *Proc. Roy. Soc. Med.* **55**, 831–7 (1962); and Occupational incidence of mental disease in single women, *Living Conditions and Health*, **1**, 169–80 (1957).

32. As reported in MORRIS, J. N., Health and social class, *The Lancet*, 7 February 1959, pp. 303–5.

33. STEIN, LILLI, 'Social class' gradient in schizophrenia, *Brit. J. Prev. Soc. Med.* **11**, 181–95 (1957).

34. LIN, *op. cit.* and LIN, TSUNG-YI, Mental disorders in Taiwan, fifteen years later: a preliminary report, Paper presented to the Conference on Mental Health in Asia and the Pacific, Honolulu, March 1966.

35. STENBÄCK, ASSER and K. A. ACHTÉ, Hospital first admissions and social class, *Acta psychiat. scand.* **42**, 113–24 (1966).

36. CLAUSEN, JOHN A. and MELVIN L. KOHN, Relation of schizophrenia to the social structure of a small city, in Pasamanick, Benjamin (ed.), *Epidemiology of Mental Disorder*, Washington, D.C., American Association for the Advancement of Science, 1959. In that paper, the data on occupational rates were incompletely reported. Although we divided the population into four occupational classes, based on US Census categories, we presented the actual rates for only the highest and lowest classes, leading some readers to conclude, erroneously, that we had divided the population into only two occupational classes. In fact, the average annual rates of first hospital admission for schizophrenia, per 100,000 population aged 15–64, were:

      (a) professional, technical, managerial, officials and proprietors: 21·3
      (b) clerical and sales personnel: 23·8
      (c) craftsmen, foremen, and kindred workers: 10·7
      (d) operatives, service workers, and laborers: 21·7

Our measures of occupational mobility, to be discussed later, were based on movement among the same four categories.

37. SUNDBY and NYHUS, *op. cit.*

38. HOLLINGSHEAD and REDLICH, *Social Class and Mental Illness, loc. cit.,* p. 236.

39. LEIGHTON, D. C. with J. S. HARDING, D. B. MACKLIN, C. C. HUGHES, and A. H. LEIGHTON, Psychiatric findings of the Stirling County study, *Am. J. Psychiat.* **119**, 1021–6 (1963); and LEIGHTON *et al., The Character of Danger, loc. cit.,* pp. 308–21.

40. BUCK, CAROL with J. M. WANKLIN and G. E. HOBBS, An analysis of regional differences in mental illness, *J. Nerv. Ment. Dis.* **122**, 73–9 (1955).

41. HAGNELL, OLLE, *A Prospective Study of the Incidence of Mental Disorder,* Stockholm, Svenska Bokförlaget, 1966.

42. ØDEGAARD, Ø., Emigration and insanity, *loc. cit.*; Psychiatric epidemiology, *loc. cit.*; Occupational incidence of mental disease in single women, *loc. cit.*

43. DUNHAM, *Community and Schizophrenia, loc. cit.*

44. Evidence that schizophrenics have been downwardly mobile in *occupational* status has been presented in SCHWARTZ, MORRIS S., The economic and spatial mobility of paranoid schizophrenics and manic depressives, unpublished M.A. thesis, University of Chicago, 1946; LYSTAD, MARY H., Social mobility among selected groups of schizophrenic patients, *Am. Sociol. Rev.* **22**, 288–92 (1957); TURNER and WAGONFELD, *op. cit.* In addition, there has been some debatable evidence that the ecological concentration of schizophrenia has resulted from the migration of unattached men into the high-rate areas of the city. See GERARD, DONALD L. and LESTER G. HOUSTON, Family setting and the social ecology of schizophrenia, *loc. cit.*; HARE, E. H., Family setting and the urban distribution of schizophrenia, *J. Ment. Sci.* **102**, 753–60 (1956); DUNHAM, *Community and Schizophrenia, loc. cit.* (Dunham's data, however, show that when rates are properly computed, rate-differentials between high- and low-rate areas of Detroit are just as great for the stable population as for in-migrants).

45. Evidence that schizophrenics have not been downwardly mobile in occupational status is presented in HOLLINGSHEAD, AUGUST B. and FREDERICK C. REDLICH, Social stratification and schizophrenia, *Am. Sociol. Rev.* **19**, 302–6 (1954), and *Social Class and Mental Illness, loc. cit.,* pp. 244–8; CLAUSEN and KOHN, Relation of schizophrenia to the social structure of a small city, *loc. cit.*; and DUNHAM, *Community and Schizophrenia, loc. cit.*; and Social class and schizophrenia, *Am. J. Orthopsychiat.* **34**, 634–42 (1964). Evidence that the ecological concentration of schizophrenia has not resulted from in-migration or downward drift is presented in LAPOUSE, REMA with MARY A. MONK and MILTON TERRIS, The drift hypothesis and socioeconomic differentials in schizophrenia, *Am. J. Public Health* **46**, 978–86 (1956); HOLLINGSHEAD and REDLICH, Social stratification and schizophrenia, *loc. cit.*; and, as noted in the preceding note, DUNHAM, *op. cit.*

46. SROLE *et al., Mental Health in the Metropolis, loc. cit.,* pp. 212–22.

47. GOLDBERG, E. M. and S. L. MORRISON, Schizophrenia and social class, *Brit. J. Psychiat.* **109**, 785–802 (1963).

48. DUNHAM, Social class and schizophrenia, *loc. cit.*; and DUNHAM, H. WARREN, PATRICIA PHILLIPS and BARBARA SRINIVASAN, A research note on diagnosed mental illness and social class, *Am. Sociol. Rev.* **31**, 223–7 (1966). See also JAMES W. RINEHART's Communication, *Am. Sociol. Rev.* **31**, 545–6 (1966).

49. TURNER and WAGONFELD, *op. cit.*

50. ØDEGAARD, ØRNULV, Emigration and mental health, *Ment. Hyg.* **20**, 546–53 (1936). See also ASTRUP, CHRISTIAN and ØRNULV ØDEGAARD, Internal migration and disease in Norway, *Psychiat. Quart. Suppl.* **34**, 116–30 (1960).

51. See TIETZE, CHRISTOPHER with PAUL LEMKAU and MARCIA COOPER, Personality disorder and spatial mobility, *Am. J. Sociol.* **48**, 29–39 (1942); LEACOCK, ELEANOR, Three social variables and the occurrence of mental disorder, in Leighton, Alexander H., John A. Clausen and Robert N. Wilson (eds.), *Explorations in Social Psychiatry,* New York, Basic Books, 1957; MISHLER and SCOTCH, *op. cit.*

52. KLEINER, ROBERT J. and SEYMOUR PARKER, Goal-striving, social status, and mental disorder: a research review, *Am. Sociol. Rev.* **28**, 189–203 (1963). See also MYERS, JEROME K. and BERTRAM H. ROBERTS, *Family and Class Dynamics in Mental Illness,* New York, Wiley, 1959; and PARKER, SEYMOUR and ROBERT J. KLEINER, *Mental Illness in the Urban Negro Community,* New York, Free Press, 1966.

53. See, for example, KAPLAN, BERT with ROBERT B. REED and WYMAN RICHARDSON, A comparison of the incidence of hospitalized and non-hospitalized cases of psychosis in two communities, *Am. Sociol. Rev.* **21**, 472–9 (1956); see also all of the major community studies of mental illness.

54. HOLLINGSHEAD and REDLICH, *Social Class and Mental Illness, loc. cit.*

55. JACO, *The Social Epidemiology of Mental Disorders, loc. cit.*

56. SROLE et al., Mental Health in the Metropolis, loc. cit., esp. pp. 240–51.
57. ESSEN-MÖLLER, E., Individual traits and morbidity in a Swedish rural population, Acta psychiat. neurol. scand., Suppl. 100, 1–160 (1956); ESSEN-MÖLLER, ERIK, A current field study in the mental disorders in Sweden, in Hoch, Paul H. and Joseph Zubin (eds.), Comparative Epidemiology of the Mental Disorders, New York, Grune and Stratton, 1961; HAGNELL, op. cit.
58. SROLE et al., Mental Health in the Metropolis, loc. cit.
59. LEIGHTON et al., The Character of Danger, loc. cit.
60. See DOHRENWEND, BRUCE P. and BARBARA SNELL DOHRENWEND, The problem of validity in field studies of psychological disorder, J. Abnormal Psychol. 70, 52–69 (1965).
61. LEIGHTON et al., Psychiatric findings of the Stirling County study, loc. cit., p. 1026.
62. SROLE et al., Mental Health in the Metropolis, loc. cit., p. 138.
63. STAR, SHIRLEY, The screening of psychoneurotics in the army, in Stouffer, S. A. with L. Guttman, E. A. Suchman, P. F. Lazarsfeld, Shirley A. Star, and J. A. Clausen (eds.), Measurement and Prediction, Princeton, NJ, Princeton University Press, 1950.
64. See JOHN A. CLAUSEN's incisive analysis, Values, norms and the health called 'mental': purposes and feasibility of assessment, Paper presented to the Symposium on Definition and Measurement of Mental Health, Washington, D.C., 16 May 1966, mimeographed.
65. See KRAMER, MORTON, A discussion of the concepts of incidence and prevalence as related to epidemiologic studies of mental disorders, Am. J. Public Health, 47, 826–40 (1957).
66. HOLLINGSHEAD and REDLICH, Social Class and Mental Illness, loc. cit.
67. JACO, E. GARTLY, The social isolation hypothesis and schizophrenia, Am. Sociol. Rev. 19, 567–77 (1954).
68. HARE, Mental illness and social conditions in Bristol, loc. cit.
69. KOHN, MELVIN L. and JOHN A. CLAUSEN, Social isolation and schizophrenia, Am. Sociol. Rev. 20, 265–73 (1955); see also CLAUSEN and KOHN, The ecological approach in social psychiatry, loc. cit.
70. LEIGHTON, DOROTHEA C., et al., The Character of Danger, loc. cit.; Psychiatric findings of the Stirling County study, loc. cit.
71. SCHWARTZ, DAVID T. and NORBETT L. MINTZ, Ecology and psychosis among Italians in 27 Boston communities, Social Problems 10, 371–4 (1963); see also their more extended discussion in "Urban ecology and psychosis: community factors in the incidence of schizophrenia and manic-depression among Italians in Greater Boston", mimeographed, 1963.
72. WECHSLER, HENRY and THOMAS F. PUGH, Fit of individual and community characteristics and rates of psychiatric hospitalization, Paper presented to the Sixth World Congress of Sociology, Evian, September, 1966.
73. ØDEGAARD, The incidence of psychosis in various occupations, loc. cit.
74. KLEINER and PARKER, op. cit.; MYERS and ROBERTS, op. cit.
75. DOHRENWEND, BARBARA SNELL and BRUCE P. DOHRENWEND, Class and Race as status-related sources of stress, in Sol Levine and Norman A. Scotch (eds.), The Study of Stress, Chicago, Aldine, in press.
76. LANGNER, THOMAS S. and STANLEY T. MICHAEL, Life Stress and Mental Health, New York, The Free Press of Glencoe, 1963.
77. The latter finding is in part an artifact of the peculiar indices used in this study, and reflects differences not in the incidence of illness but in type and severity of illness in different social classes at various levels of stress. At higher stress levels, lower-class people tend to develop incapacitating psychoses and middle-class people less incapacitating neuroses.
78. ROGLER, LLOYD H. and AUGUST B. HOLLINGSHEAD, Trapped: Families and Schizophrenia, New York, John Wiley, 1965.
79. See the references in KOHN, MELVIN L. and JOHN A. CLAUSEN, Parental authority behavior and schizophrenia, Am. J. Orthopsychiat. 26, 297–313 (1956), in Clausen, John A. and Melvin L. Kohn, Social relations and schizophrenia: a research report and a perspective, in Don D. Jackson (ed.), The Etiology of Schizophrenia, New York, Basic Books, 1960, and in SANUA, VICTOR D., Sociocultural factors in families of schizophrenics: a review of the literature, Psychiatry 24, 246–65 (1961).
80. For a more complete discussion, see CLAUSEN and KOHN, Social relations and schizophrenia, loc. cit., pp. 309–16.
81. BATESON, GREGORY with DON JACKSON, JAY HALEY and JOHN WEAKLAND, Toward a theory of schizophrenia, Behav. Sci. 1, 251–64 (1956). See also MISHLER, ELLIOT G. and NANCY E. WAXLER, Family interaction processes and schizophrenia: a review of current theories, Merrill-Palmer Quart. Behav. Development 11, 269–315 (1965).
82. WYNNE, LYMAN C. with IRVING M. RYCKOFF, JULIANA DAY and STANLEY I. HIRSCH, Pseudo-mutuality in the family relations of schizophrenics, Psychiatry 22, 205–20 (1958); and RYCKOFF, IRVING with JULIANA

DAY and LYMAN C. WYNNE, Maintenance of stereotyped roles in the families of schizophrenics, *AMA Arch. Psychiat.* **1,** 93–8 (1959). See also MISHLER and WAXLER, *op. cit.*

83. KOHN and CLAUSEN, Parental authority behavior and schizophrenia, *loc. cit.*
84. ROGLER and HOLLINGSHEAD, *op. cit.*
85. KOHN, MELVIN L., Social class and parent–child relationships: an interpretation, *Am. J. Sociol.* **68,** 471–80 (1963); PEARLIN, LEONARD I. and MELVIN L. KOHN, Social class, occupation, and parental values: a cross-national study, *Am. Sociol. Rev.* **31,** 466–79 (1966).

THE FAMILY, LANGUAGE, AND THE TRANSMISSION
OF SCHIZOPHRENIA

THEODORE LIDZ

Department of Psychiatry,
Yale University School of Medicine, New Haven, Connecticut

IT HAS long been my belief that our understanding of the nature and etiology of schizophrenia has been blocked by the deficiencies in our grasp of personality development and
integration. At the recent international conference on the etiology of schizophrenia in
Rochester, I tried to convey in broad outline an approach to both personality development
and to the study of schizophrenia that seems—to me—to take into account our current
knowledge and also provides hypotheses to direct future studies (Lidz, 1967). I do not wish
to repeat what many at this Conference heard in Rochester. The essence of what I said is
simple and may even seem obvious to some. For an infant to grow up—even one that is
properly endowed genetically—and develop into a reasonably well-integrated and competent individual, he requires positive direction and guidance in a suitable interpersonal
environment and social system. However, the developmental theories used in psychiatry,
including psychoanalytic theory, implicitly or explicitly consider that a normal infant will
develop into a functioning and reasonably stable adult as a concomitant of his physical
maturation unless he receives very faulty nurturance in his first few years, or he is seriously
traumatized. Indeed, innate sources of libidinal fixation—unknown and undemonstrated
but readily hypothesized—are invoked as explanations of various types of psychopathology
by analytically oriented psychiatrists as readily as other psychiatrists fall back on hypothetical genetic anomalies and metabolic impairments of brain functioning in schizophrenia.
The extent and complexity of the positive forces required to mold the personality and equip
the child with essential adaptive techniques have largely been overlooked because they are
built into the institutions and mores of all societies which could not survive if they were
not—and into the omnipresent family which everywhere has the implicit task of carrying
out the basic socialization and enculturation of the new generation. Man's biological make-up
requires that he grow up in a family—or some planned substitute for it—not simply for his
protection and nurture during his lengthy immaturity, but to be directed into an integrated
person who possesses the techniques, knowledge, and roles he requires for survival and for
adaptation in that physical and social environment in which he happens to grow up.

I discussed the requisites that the family must provide a child under four overlapping
and somewhat arbitrary headings.

1. The parental nurturant functions: how parents must meet the child's changing
needs and supplement his immature capacities in a different manner at each phase of his
development. The influence of the nature of the nurture on the individual's emotional

security, his development of initiative and autonomy, and upon the quality of his basic trust in himself and his world was considered.

2.   The family organization: how the dynamic structure of the family provides a framework for integrating the child's developing personality, channeling drives, providing conflict-free areas into which to develop, guiding into the proper gender identity and away from incestuous and stultifying erotic entanglements, etc.

3.   The family as the basic unit of society: the family as the primary social system in which the child learns the cardinal social roles and institutions of his society. It was noted how *roles* which are units of *social systems* become part of the *personality*; and how institutions enter motivation, as well as how both roles and institutions are fundamental to communication.

4.   The family as an enculturating agency: the family inculcates the child in the basic instrumental techniques of the culture, including the language. Enculturation is considered separately from socialization, concerned with what is transmitted symbolically across the generations rather than what is carried out by societal organizations—though there is considerable overlap.

Today I shall focus upon the process of enculturation—the inculcation of the instrumental techniques of the culture, and, indeed, only upon one aspect of it, the transmission of language upon which virtually all ego functioning depends; and upon how faulty linguistic abilities relate to the transmission of schizophrenia. Despite such limitation, I shall only be able to discuss a few aspects of the problem, for as I started to prepare this paper I soon realized that any reasonably comprehensive presentation would require a monograph.

All psychoses involve gross failures of ego functioning; that is, a loss of the capacity to guide the self into the future. The failure may be due to damage or dysfunction of the brain with disorganization of perception or cognition; or because severe affective disturbances color and distort thinking and motivation in the direction of the mood. The essence of schizophrenia—the critical attribute of schizophrenia—lies in the distortions of mentation that occur without degradation of intellectual potential. The nature of the essential thought disorder in schizophrenia has been variously defined in such terms as loss of capacity to think abstractly, failures of categorization, overinclusiveness, derailment of associations, impaired ability to exclude the irrelevant, etc. Eugen Bleuler realized that virtually all other manifestations of the condition or conditions he named schizophrenia could follow as a consequence of the disordered associations. However, he considered the disordered patterns of association to be a manifestation of some unknown "process" affecting the functioning of the brain—probably a toxic disorder (Bleuler, 1911).

The question that confronts us is whether the cognitive disorder is a manifestation of some malfunction of the brain or if it is essentially what is wrong with the schizophrenic patient. Are aberrant ways of thinking necessarily a reflection of brain dysfunction or rather of the ways in which a child has been taught meanings and reasoning—or of how a person has been forced to distort his perception or his internalized version of his world to gain some spurious resolution of untenable conflicts? Is the nonsense that enters my room through the television set the fault of the apparatus? I believe that an understanding of linguistic and cognitive development permits the hypothesis that we promulgated in our paper, "The Transmission of Irrationality" (Lidz. *et al.*, 1958). It is that some individuals who have failed to achieve or maintain a workable personality integration can, when en- suing conflicts become untenable, withdraw from social living into an internalized world and gain some resolution and room for living by breaking through the confines imposed by the culture's meaning system and logic. It is not a way open to all but perhaps only to those who in childhood had a faulty grounding in the culture's meanings and ways of thinking. The condition tends to perpetuate itself because the patient ceases to test the validity of his thinking by how it helps him master his environment or promotes collabora- tion with others.

One of the major breakthroughs in the study of schizophrenia that has followed the focus on the disturbed family environments in which the patients grew up has been the realization that the thought disorder does not arise *de novo* in the patient, but is a reflection, an outgrowth, or a reaction to the severely disturbed thought processes—both stylistic and ideational, of the parents.

Thus, I wish to consider two aspects of the problem. One, the relationship between language, ego functioning, and schizophrenia; and then the indications that the dis- ordered language and thought of the schizophrenic derives from the patient's interrelations with his parents rather than from some metabolic dysfunction.

The importance of language to thought and to human functioning in general extends beyond the problem of schizophrenia but it is crucial to the study of schizophrenia. The uniquely human techniques of adaptation, indeed the emergence of the human organism, depended upon the evolution of a brain and neuromuscular system that permitted the use of tools and the development of that uniquely human tool, the word. By means of language man transmitted what he learned to subsequent generations and gradually built up and institutionalized techniques of adaptation that each child must acquire. Even as the fetus recapitulates the genetic evolution of the species, the child after emerging from the womb must assimilate an organized filtrate of the experiences of his forebears as they evolved into a culture. Physiologically, man can, as other organisms, adapt to relatively limited environmental conditions, but by using tools and the techniques transmitted through the culture he can modify environments to meet his physiological requirements. He needs language to discover or invent these techniques, to transmit them to others and to acquire them from others as he grows up.

A person also needs language to adapt to new situations. In order to direct his life into the future he must acquire the verbal tools that permit him to build up an internalized symbolized version of his world which he manipulates imaginatively before committing himself to irrevocable action. Of course, thinking uses visual imagery and visual symbols as well as other sensory modalities, but words are the pivotal points that permit selective recall and enable a person to project a future toward which he can strive. The orientation toward future goals releases from primary motivation through drive impulsion and from learning primarily through conditioning. Without a capacity to conceptualize a future, man cannot direct himself toward it, and there can be no ego functioning.

If a person's meaning system and syntactical usage is muddled, ego functioning will be seriously handicapped. Now, we must realize that a person's experience unfolds in a cease- less flow. In order to perceive, understand, think about, and talk about his experience, it must be divided into categories. There are innumerable ways of dividing experience into categories, even though in contrast to Whorf, I believe that man everywhere will divide certain aspects of his environment into very much the same categories (Whorf, 1956). Each culture tends to categorize experience somewhat differently and some cultures extremely differently. The child cannot learn from scratch what took millennia to learn, but must learn his culture's system in order to think and communicate coherently. The vocabulary of a language is, in essence, a catalogue of the categories into which the culture divides its world and its experiences. In learning the language the child is learning to categorize. Now, categories are formed by selecting common attributes of things or events to bestow some degree of equivalence to experiences that can never be identical. Chairs can be sat upon; balls will roll, etc. Each thing or event can be classified in a multiplicity of ways according to the attributes utilized; e.g. a soccer ball can be grouped with objects that are "round", or "brown", or "leather covered", or are "sports equipment". One factor in intelligence depends upon the capacity to classify the same experience in many ways—to grasp its relationship to a variety of different events. To a very marked degree, such capacities depend upon having the words available to designate the various potential categorizations.

Now, it is such categorizing that permits abstraction from the concrete, never to be repeated, single experience. Indeed, single experiences are never precisely repeated, and we would never learn from experience if we did not abstract attributes that could apply to other experiences. Unless we categorize we cannot form expectancies, and without expectancies we cannot be intelligent. Herein lies a vital characteristic of words—they have a predictive value that permits the utilization of experience—and makes reflective thinking possible. A child who has learned that candy is something sweet and good to eat, will, when given something he is told is candy expect to find it sweet, even though it is dissimilar from any candy he has previously encountered. The predictive value of words often provides direction and precludes much of the necessity for trial-and-error learning.

The trustworthiness of the expectation produced by a word depends upon the critically defining attributes of the word. If the word "mother" is defined as a "married woman who loves her children", some children are led into erroneous expectations that a more critical definition, "a female parent" would avoid. Indeed, many schizophrenic patients have distorted their perception of reality because they have been taught that "love for her child" was a critical attribute of the word "mother".

The categorizing of experiences through the abstraction of common attributes, the labeling of categories by words, and the attainment of meanings by defining the critical attributes designated by the word are all essential to ego development and to ego functioning. Through the categories provided by language, the world in which a person lives, his own needs, and the behaviour of others gain some degree of order and predictability.

I have made rather short shrift of a very complicated and highly pertinent topic. I wish to draw attention to one other consequence of forming categories. A category serves as a filter that permits attention to essentials and eliminates the intrusion of non-essentials into the train of thought. If I think of "trees", I leave out other plant life—bushes, grass, flowers—though associations to these categories remain available because they are, along with "trees", a subordinate category of the superordinate category of "vegetable matter". Even though the boundary separating these types of plant life are somewhat arbitrary, our society finds the differentiations useful—and the names serve to screen out and focus thinking to what is pertinent. The failures of persons to sustain focal attention, to be flooded by stimuli, to have derailment of associations, to suffer from over-inclusive thought processes, etc., can be related to deficiencies in the categorization through words—a process which serves as a filter in a different manner than does the reticular activating system of the brain.

Now the vocabulary and its meanings—how usefully and accurately words are used in their categorizing functions and how the words are joined syntactically—are taught the child by his elders, largely by members of his family. This subtle and involved process is subject to many conscious and unconscious influences. The child uses words to solve problems. Meanings are learned rapidly or slowly, accurately or inaccurately, precisely or vaguely according to how effectively and consistently proper usage attains objectives for the child. It depends upon the interaction between child and tutors, the consistency between teachers, the cues they provide, to what they respond and to what they remain oblivious; the meanings they reward and those they ignore. The process of learning a meaning is a lengthy process as we learn from studying Piaget, and depends upon overcoming egocentricity, developing capacities to move beyond preoperational thought to become capable of classifying and then of thinking in categories. It involves the increasing experience with the word and what it designates.

The child's experiences within his family play a critical role in learning meanings and syntax. Do some children, because of the faulty meanings held by their parents and the parents' difficulties in communicating, fail to learn properly the culture's ways of categorizing and communicating and thus lack adequate means of relating to others, for understanding their experience, for gaining useful expectations? Do they develop aberrant or confused meanings that distort perception of events and impede efforts at problem solving? Can the ensuing impairments in adaptive capacities and in ego functioning make them prone to schizophrenic disorganization? These are critical questions that have moved into the forefront of research concerning schizophrenia, and concerning the functioning of the family.

Over the past 10–12 years a number of observers and investigators have produced evidence that the schizophrenic patient grows up in a family environment which is either not conducive to inculcating a firm grounding in meanings and syntax, or which teaches distorted meanings and reasoning. I can only consider several of these studies. Bateson, Jackson, and coworkers focused on the so-called double-bind situation in which the child is habitually subjected to conflicting messages or demands on different levels (Bateson *et al.*, 1956). The double-bind concept has become somewhat obscured, but in brief, the child, in seeking to gain approval or to avoid punishment, is damned if he does and damned if he doesn't—and is cognitively and emotionally torn apart by the conflicting messages. Sometimes one parent sets the bind and in other situations the child cannot meet the conflicting and irreconcilable demands and needs of the two parents.

Taking another approach, my colleagues and I (Lidz *et al.*, 1958) drew attention to the difficulties that ensue because one or both parents can maintain their own precarious integration only under sharply circumscribed conditions. They seek to delimit the environment, particularly the family environment, to establish and maintain conditions that permit them to maintain the one limited role they can perform. Reality cannot alter nor new circumstances modify the conception of themselves and the family they hold and must hold to maintain their precarious emotional equilibrium. The parents' delimitation of the environment and their insistence on altering the family members' perceptions and meanings, creates a strange family milieu filled with inconsistencies, contradictory meanings, and denial of what should be obvious. Facts are constantly altered to suit emotionally determined needs. The children in such families subjugate their own needs to the parents' defenses, and their conceptualization of experiences are in the service of solving parental problems rather than in mastering events and feelings. The acceptance of mutually contradictory experiences requires paralogical thinking. We drew attention to how a parent's imperviousness to a child's needs and a parent's needs to mask the true nature of intrafamilial situations derive from defenses of his equilibrium and distort the child's meanings and reasoning. The inability of a parent, usually the mother, to establish boundaries between herself and the child, using him to complete her own life also accounts for the imperviousness and intrusiveness of such parents and creates profound confusions in the child as to what are his needs and perceptions and which his mother's, and often leads to despair over the usefulness and validity of communication as a means of solving problems. In the same article we also drew attention to the fact that the majority of schizophrenic patients had at least one parent who was more or less schizophrenic or paranoid, and taught the children strange or delusional ideas and often frank distrust of the motives of persons outside the family or even of the other parent. Some patients grew up in what we termed a *folie en famille*.

Wynne and Singer have advanced our understanding of the problem greatly by drawing attention to the styles of communication of parents of schizophrenic patients (Wynne and Singer, 1963a, 1963b; Singer and Wynne, 1965). Through the study of protocols of projective tests and also of samples of conjoint family therapy sessions, they have demonstrated the parents' amorphous or blurred and fragmented or disruptive styles, with inability to focus attention selectively on shared percepts or feelings, or to keep internal and external states discrete making meaningful communication within the family almost impossible. Further, the lack of closure of what those parents seek to communicate reflects a pervasive meaninglessness and pointlessness that does not permit clear-cut concepts to develop or stand— making it difficult for a child to learn conceptual thinking. The parents' inability to take and maintain an appropriate distance is reflected in their language by a concrete literalness with switches to vague, overgeneralized syncretic responses. As is often the case, Singer and Wynne drew attention to something that is obvious *after* it has been pointed out—something that had long plagued psychiatrists who sought to communicate with parents of schizophrenic patients—but which had remained undefined. Our group rapidly confirmed Wynne and Singer's findings and applied them to the Object Sorting Test, and Dr. Cynthia Wild developed a reliable scoring technique that clearly differentiated a highly significant proportion of parents of schizophrenic patients from controls (Wild *et al.,* 1965).

Now, it may at first seem that these various studies, though interesting, have come up with some very different findings. Bateson and Jackson's group are concerned with the impact—largely the emotionally disorganizing impact—of the bind in which the patients are placed by their parents. Wynne and Singer specifically state that they consider parental style more important than content. Our group has spoken of the transmission of irrationality.

However, I believe that if we but look behind the scenes, so to speak, we will realize that these difficulties center around common problems of parents of schizophrenic patients.

A large proportion of the parental difficulties in communication seem to be related to and perhaps to derive from the parents' diffuse ego boundaries or from the parents' needs to limit the environment and distort the perception of experiences in order to maintain their precarious emotional equilibrium. These two conditions interrelate and may be facets of the same personality difficulties.

As Cynthia Wild has pointed out (Wild, 1965), various aspects of the disordered styles of communication of the parents taking the Object Sorting Test reflect the loss of boundaries between the person taking and giving the test—the schizophrenic parent imbuing both tester and test with his own thoughts and feelings. He is upset because the tester does not know what the testee is thinking, or he changes the rules as if he were the tester, says "you" when he means "I", etc. Then, too, he considers the objects being sorted egocentrically in terms of how he would use them, or how they fit into some story involving him—as if they could only be sorted and understood as part of his own life. Similarly the difficulties in maintaining a proper distance which Wynne and Singer pointed out as obfuscating communication may be considered as a difficulty in maintaining boundaries—the parent becomes intrusively close or flees to extreme distance in an attempt to maintain separateness. Singer and Wynne have emphasized the failure of such parents to maintain focal attention; including difficulties in keeping distinct the same representation of objects over time—leading to puzzling negations and denials of previously given responses; and difficulties in separating one's own thoughts and feelings from those of others. These involve boundary problems, and as Schachtel (Schachtel, 1959) has pointed out, a failure to move beyond childhood egocentricity to enable the subject to decenter and realize that objects have an existence and permanence separate from one's own involvement with them. Indeed, these parents constantly relate to their children as if they only existed in relationship to the parent and the parent's needs.

Now, considered differently, these amorphous and fragmented, and otherwise vague and diffuse ways of communicating represent deficiencies in forming categories. When objects are treated as unique, one-time experiences, they cannot be categorized, for as I noted earlier, categorizing involves selecting out common attributes from non-identical experiences. To think categorically, to enter into Piaget's stage of formal operations, a person must move beyond an egocentric orientation, beyond considering things and experiences as only part of the self. It is of interest to us that the English anthropologist Edmund Leach (Leach, 1966) has also pointed out that each culture divides experience into categories which it labels with words. As the experience which is categorized is continuous, boundaries must be established between categories by placing a taboo on (or as a psychiatrist would say—by repressing) what lies between the categories. He notes that a fundamental task of the child is to differentiate the self and the non-self—that is to establish ego boundaries. He believes this is so vital that every culture has placed a taboo on what is simultaneously self and non-self to foster formation of ego boundaries—notably on all body secretions and excretions (other than tears) which are part of the self and become non-self. We might also consider the taboo placed on sexual intercourse and nursing at the breast, which have to do with fusion of the self and another, and also upon what might confuse the

M

differentiation between maleness and femaleness. The parents of schizophrenic patients have not established such boundaries between self and non-self—and perhaps this has a global influence upon the ability to form discrete and useful categories. If the self becomes mixed into all objects—if everything is perceived egocentrically, perhaps discrete separations required for categorization cannot be maintained.

In an article on the symbiotic needs of schizophrenic patients written in 1951, Dr. Ruth Lidz and I pointed out (Lidz and Lidz, 1952) that it is the failure of the mother to establish ego boundaries between herself and the child and her treating the child as an extension of herself—or as someone who will live out her wishes and needs—that leads to the symbiotic needs of the schizophrenic patient. We can now indicate that a child who grows up with such parents amidst such confused communication will have grave difficulties decentering, in learning coherent meanings, in becoming able to form categories, in selecting out critical attributes, in gaining predictabilities from meanings, and will thus have impaired capacities for ego functioning.

The culture places taboos on certain behaviors, perceptions, topics for conversation and conscious thought, taboos that are conveyed to each child by his parents—and also in part through having words to think about the permissible but not for certain tabood ideas that should be repressed. There is, as Freud noted clearly, a relationship between verbalizing and making conscious. With failure to inculcate proper categorization, the child is not only deprived of an essential means of filtering out the extraneous and inappropriate, but may spend much time preoccupied with the material that *lies between categories*. May I suggest that the perceptions and associations that lie between categories may be considered as the world of *anti-categories*? It concerns—let us posit—material concerning the fusion between the self and the mother, the childhood polymorphous perverse wishes and fantasies, the cannibalistic impulses, the dream-like notions of being of the opposite sex or hermaphroditic, and other such material that is eliminated from awareness as a child grows up, and can have little conscious representation for which no clear-cut categorization can exist. It is in this anti-category world that the schizophrenic patient spends much of his time: a world into which we, as therapists, have grave difficulty in penetrating and about which we have but fragmentary glimpses, but which erupts into his talk and his associations as from another world. It is not just the eruption of his internalized version of reality that is somewhat akin to ours, but more of a nether world, a world that is antipodal, composed of what we have learned even to keep out of most of our fantasies and perhaps even out of our dreams. Am I just talking of the unconscious in different terms? Perhaps, but I think not quite, at least this is but one aspect of the unconscious. In any event I am trying to think about this topic and cannot yet think about it clearly.

Now what of the delusional nature of the orientation that many of these parents have concerning their environment which they convey as reality to their children? Paranoid projections can also be regarded as manifestations of faulty ego boundaries. The person attributes his own feelings to others—unable to differentiate clearly what is within and without the self. He also may project superego dictates onto the environment—extrojecting poorly internalized introjects; or gaining support against repressed impulses by hallucinating threats of punishment. As it is the parents who interpret reality to the child, directly or indirectly informing the child how the world should be seen and understood, the parents' delusional and paralogical concepts often seriously influence the child's meaning and value systems.

Another major source of difficulty and distortion in a child's learning a consistent and coherent system of meanings arises in these families from the parents' needs to limit the environment and to force upon the family erroneous perceptions to maintain their own precarious emotional equilibrium. The child is taught erroneous percepts and concepts and is placed in a bind of being rejected unless he accepts the distortion. Perhaps, I first became aware of such difficulties many years ago when a schizophrenic youth said to me, "The one thing I can be sure of is that my mother loves me." Having heard the mother's qualified acceptance of her son, and her bitter rejection of him unless he lived to complete her frustrated existence, I know that for the patient to accept the axiom that his mother loved him, he needed to distort his entire grasp of interpersonal relationships, and to negate the emotions he perceived in his mother and felt in himself. The child may also be placed in a double bind when mutually exclusive expectations and demands are made of him—and there is no way out of the impasse except flight. As he is in a symbiotic tie or still highly dependent, the flight may be intrapsychic rather than geographic—into fantasy or into that nebulous room that exists between categories.

Although I have been seeking to focus on the family's task of transmitting the culture's linguistic tools to the child, and have neglected the family's nurturant tasks and its role in structuring the child's personality and in socializing the child, it has become clear, I believe, that the nature of the nurture influences language learning. A mother who cannot establish ego boundaries will have serious difficulties meeting the changing needs of the child, and keeps the child from a range of experience needed to decenter. Further, verbal learning has its roots in the preverbal mutuality between mother and child. More specifically, if we study the work of Roger Brown (Brown and Fraser, 1964), Susan Ervin (Ervin, 1966), and others on the actual process of language learning, we appreciate the subtleties of the mother–child interaction in teaching and learning language. When the baby can use the single sentence word such as "water"—only a person who intimately knows the child and his behavioral patterns can know if "water" means "I am thirsty", "Let me play with water", "I want the shiny object like the water glass", or "I am bored and want company". The mother in filling the need begins to define the word and its use—often without knowing it—saying "Baby wants water", "Baby drink water", "Baby play with glass", etc., as appropriate. Brown has demonstrated how mothers are constantly expanding the little child's syntax by amplifying just beyond what the child can express but may be able to understand. Such constant and appropriate linguistic interchange seems essential to the proper learning of language and the child's cognitive development. But what happens when—as was the case with many mothers of schizophrenics we studied—the mother is in a postpartum depression, or is otherwise so preoccupied with her own needs and woes that she can scarcely pay attention to the child, or when she is responding to her needs and not the child's.

The structure of the family as a social system also influences the development of meanings. Clear role allocations and relationships serve at the same time to obviate the need for certain verbal clarifications and form the foundations upon which considerable intrafamilial communication rests. Certain assumptions are taken for granted when a child makes a request of his father rather than his mother; or when the mother talks to her son in contrast to her daughter. When, to take a brief example, the customary gender roles are reversed and the father stays at home, shopping, cooking, and cleaning; while the mother is the chief breadwinner—then even though the child calls the female parent "mother", the attributes and associations connected with the word diverge markedly from the cultural norm.

My topic has been too ambitious, and I must end leaving unmentioned very much that I have been seeking to think through. I have primarily been trying to convey the inherent connection between schizophrenia and the linguistic and cognitive disturbances that are critical attributes of the condition. Ego functioning depends upon language and the ability to abstract common attributes in experiences and categorize them by the appropriate words. The capacity to use language is a uniquely human capacity which all undamaged infants possess; but learning language is a highly involved process that depends largely on the nature of the tutelage and the tutors in the family. It is not a skill learned in isolation but involves and reflects the entire process of personality development. I have tried to indicate some of the ways in which parents of schizophrenic patients are deficient tutors and how the family they create is an inappropriate milieu for teaching the child his cardinal adaptive tool. I have sought to illustrate both how poor grounding in linguistic abilities prepares the way for schizophrenic withdrawal and also how distorted meanings and ways of thinking become an inherent part of the offspring in such families.

REFERENCES

BATESON, G., JACKSON, D., HALEY, J., and WEAKLAND, J. (1956) Toward a theory of schizophrenia, *Behav. Sci.* **1**, 251–64.

BLEULER, E. (1911) *Dementia Praecox or the Group of Schizophrenias,* New York, Int. Univ. Press, 1950.

BROWN, R. and FRASER, C. (1964) The acquisition of syntax, in *The Acquisition of Language,* Monographs of the Society for Research in Child Development, Ser. No. 92, Vol. 29, No. 1, Eds. U. Bellugi, and R. Brown, Cambridge, Massachusetts, Society for Research in Child Development, Inc.

ERVIN, S. (1966) Imitation and structural change in children's language, in *New Directions in the Study of Language,* Ed. Eric H. Lenneberg, pp. 163–88, Cambridge, Massachusetts, the M.I.T. Press.

LEACH, E. (1966) Anthropological aspects of language: animal categories and verbal abuse, in *New Directions in the Study of Language,* Ed. Eric H. Lenneberg, pp. 23–63, Cambridge, Massachusetts, the M.I.T. Press.

LIDZ, R. W. and LIDZ, T. (1952) Therapeutic considerations arising from the intense symbiotic needs of schizophrenic patients, in *Psychotherapy with Schizophrenics,* Eds. E. Brody and F. Redlich, New York, Int. Univ. Press, reprinted in *Schizophrenia and the Family.*

LIDZ, T. (1967) The family, personality development and schizophrenia (to be published).

LIDZ, T., CORNELISON, A., TERRY, D., and FLECK, S. (1958) Intrafamilial environment of the schizophrenic patient: VI. The transmission of irrationality, *Arch. Neurol. Psychiat.* **79**, 305–16.

SCHACHTEL, E. (1959) The development of focal attention and the emergence of reality, in *Metamorphosis: On the Development of Affect, Perception, Attention and Memory,* New York, Basic Books.

SINGER, M. T. and WYNNE, L. C. (1965) Thought disorder and family relations of schizophrenics: IV. Results and implications, *Arch. Gen. Psychiat.,* **12**, 201–12.

WHORF, B. (1956) *Language, Thought and Reality: Selected Writings of Benjamin Lee Whorf,* Ed. John Carroll, New York, M.I.T. Press and Wiley.

WILD, C. (1965) Some implications, in *Schizophrenia and the Family,* New York, Int. Univ. Press, Chap. XXII, Pt. II.

WILD, C., SINGER, M., ROSMAN, B., RICCI, J., and LIDZ, T. (1965) Measuring disordered styles of thinking in the parents of schizophrenic patients on the object sorting test, in *Schizophrenia and the Family,* New York, Int. Univ. Press, Chap. XXII, Pt. I.

WYNNE, L. C. and SINGER, M. T. (1963a) Thought disorder and family relations of schizophrenics: I. A research strategy, *Arch. Gen. Psychiat.* **9**, 191–8.

WYNNE, L. C. and SINGER, M. T. (1963b) Thought disorder and family relations of schizophrenics: II. A classification of forms of thinking, *Arch. Gen. Psychiat.* **9**, 199–206.

METHODOLOGIC AND CONCEPTUAL ISSUES IN THE STUDY OF SCHIZOPHRENICS AND THEIR FAMILIES*

LYMAN C. WYNNE

Adult Psychiatry Branch, National Institute of Mental Health,
Bethesda, Maryland

I

DURING the past dozen years, my colleagues and I at the National Institute of Mental Health have engaged in a series of clinical, observational and experimental studies of possible links between individual psychopathology, especially schizophrenia, and family functioning. In this paper I shall comment on only certain selected aspects of this research program, emphasizing those points which may be methodologically and conceptually relevant to the special problem of the origins and development of schizophrenic illness.

From the beginning of this program, we have explicitly included in our thinking the likelihood that *both* gene-determined and environmental factors may contribute to the development of schizophrenic disorders. Environmental factors include psychological experience and non-hereditary biologic factors. We have felt that the traditional concepts and methodology of genetics research on schizophrenia are especially inadequate for the evaluation of the psychologic experiential factors. For example, concordance of diagnoses for more than one member of a given family has been used by some investigators as evidence for a gene-determined etiology with little consideration of alternative hypotheses. Such conclusions have too often been based either on ignorance of alternative hypotheses about how such concordance could appear or on consideration of only the most naïve and oversimplified versions of non-genetics hypotheses. We have tried to develop a conceptual frame of reference and series of research procedures which will be relevant to detailed evaluation of non-genetics hypothesis, but which can and should, as a scientific principle, be combined with an equally careful consideration of genetics hypotheses.

Let me begin with a brief summary of some of the main concepts which we feel need to be added to the formulations of genetics if experiential factors are to be adequately considered. I also shall include comments on how these concepts have helped shape our empirical research methods.

First, it is basic to our frame of reference that behavior be examined from a transactional viewpoint. This concept, derived from the formulations of Dewey and Bentley (1949), has a number of implications with complex consequences: (a) The meaning of behavior, symptomatic and otherwise, derives in considerable part from its context. This is fully in accord with the 1911 views of Eugen Bleuler, who emphasized that "the individual symptom in

---

* This paper reviews the research approach that has been developed collaboratively with Dr. Margaret Thaler Singer.

itself is less important than its intensity and extensiveness, and *above all, its relation to the psychological setting*" (E. Bleuler, 1911, p. 295). However, much traditional psychiatry tends in practice, and sometimes also in theory, to identify symptoms as if they were things in themselves apart from the setting or context. This traditional viewpoint is especially inadequate when one aims to understand the relation of intrafamilial communication and other interpersonal processes to the experience and behavior of psychiatric patients. From the research standpoint, a methodologic consequence of adopting a transactional viewpoint is that clinical or test descriptions of an individual's behavior should be evaluated only together with the context of instructions, comments, and inquiries made by others before or during the behavior. Thus, Rorschach responses, for example, are not viewed as a purely intrapsychic, in-the-head stream of projections and associations, but as bits of communication behavior embedded in a transactional process with another person. The extent to which the two or more persons share the same frame of reference, set, or role-relationship, and also share and communicate about the same percept, ideas, or feelings then becomes the subject matter to be evaluated.

(b) The transactional viewpoint also specifically emphasizes that persons undergo internal change as a result of interchange with one another. (Strictly speaking, the term "interaction" refers to interchange which does not result in internal change of the participants. Rather, persons in interaction are viewed as coming in contact like billiard balls and separating without significant internal change through or across each of them. The psychological inadequacy of this viewpoint is the main reason for our preference for the term "transaction" over "interaction".) In a long-term view of family and individual development, this implies that both parents and their offspring undergo change as a result of their transactions with one another, and that their characteristics have to some degree emerged as responses adaptive to one another. The extent to which individuals are enduringly shaped as a result of transactional processes is obviously a matter of degree and a matter of the developmental phase or stage in which the transactions begin and continue. There presumably are aspects of both bone structure and psychological structure which become quite rigid as one grows up, but the likelihood of deformities developing is presumably greater in childhood and early life than later. Again it should be stressed that this is a matter of degree. Dr. Singer and I have emphasized repeatedly that, from the transactional frame of reference, there are no one-way streets in family life. We do not suggest that all of the effects of family members on one another are in the direction of parent upon child.

(c) At the same time, the transactional viewpoint should not be misunderstood as implying a global, undifferentiated picture of family relationships. To the contrary, particular aspects of behavior must be specified and delineated in order for analysis of transactional data to be possible.

A second, closely related concept in our work is the family as a small social system: In general terms, a system is formed by two or more units—persons, molecules, or whatever—which are in interdependent transactions with each other. Further, systems tend to maintain an equilibrium, a stable overall state ("homeostasis") even though the persons or other units making up the system may change. Theoretically, systems may be closed and self-sufficient, but biologic and social systems are always open and linked to other systems. The conditions under which families function as systems is an empirical question which can be examined experimentally, for example, with the approaches described at this conference by Drs. Mishler and Reiss. In recent years, I have become quite interested in understanding more about the circumstances in which the family system and family homeostatis concepts are not applicable. Nevertheless, these formulations have been highly provocative in stimulating both family research and the conjoint psychotherapeutic treatment of family units.

One specific application of the system concept which we have used is based upon the following reasoning: to the extent that there has been an enduring complementarity in the relationships of family members with one another, certain characteristics and behavior of any one family member should be predictable from the characteristics and behavior of the rest of the family. Dr. Margaret Singer, other colleagues, and I have explicitly made use of this hypothesis in a series of studies (Loveland *et al.,* 1963; Morris and Wynne, 1965; Singer, 1967; Singer and Wynne, 1963, 1964, 1965a, 1965b, 1966; Wynne, 1967, 1969; Wynne and Singer, 1963a, 1963b, 1966).

It should be noted that the characteristics of intrafamilial relationships make such predictions hypothetically possible for *any* family which has been enduringly intact, not just for families which contain a schizophrenic member. Working blindly, without direct data from or about a given individual family member, but only with data from other family members, we have been able to deduce accurately and in detail characteristics of the index individual member. Although we have especially emphasized in published reports how this deductive or predictive effort applies to diagnostic characteristics, the principles involved go beyond particular symptoms such as those of schizophrenics.

This leads into another major concept—that of epigenesis. An epigenetic view assumes that the interchanges or transactions at each developmental phase build upon the outcome of earlier transactions; this means that constitutional and experiential influences recombine in each developmental phase to create new biological and behavioral potentialities which then help determine the next phase. If the transactions at any given developmental phase are distorted or omitted, all the subsequent developmental phases will be altered because they build upon a different substrate. We hypothesize that the family environment needs to provide certain kinds of influence in each maturational phase of the individual. What is appropriate and what may have pathological consequences thus varies over time and must always be considered in this developmental context.

This formulation implies that there is a continuing series of transactions in which the "fit" between the person's innate and learned equipment and the kind of stimulation and responsiveness received from the environment are both critical to the developmental process. For example, in early infancy a reciprocal relatedness between mother and infant on a nonverbal basis appears to influence the later development of communicative language. By noting where parents seem to have marked difficulties, for example, in engaging in interpersonal relationships or in language usage, one can predict where there will be difficulties in a "fit" even with a child who is biologically relatively normal. Thus, developmental difficulties of the offspring become predictable if one has data about highly deviant environmental influences, even though these difficulties may be partially corrected through unusually positive biologic capacities of the child. Similarly, behavioral disorders are predictable if data is available about severe biological deviances of a child, given an ordinary range of possible "fits" with persons in the rearing environment.

Thus, the "predictive" research conducted by Dr. Singer and I, together with other colleagues, makes use of the concept of a "fit" or "misfit" between family members, beginning with biologic dispositions but evolving, epigenetically through time, in recurrent transactional patterns. A few comments about "prediction" as a method are in order here. We have used the term "prediction" in a sense proposed by John Benjamin (1959). The central methodologic principle of prediction research is that the investigator examines one set of data and hypothesizes or predicts the characteristics of another set of data unknown to him at the time of the prediction, either because the other data were independently obtained, or are yet to be obtained. In time, predictions may be prospective and longitudinal, or they may be cross-sectional or horizontal (that is, involve data independently obtained at a given point in time).

As Benjamin has stressed, the predictive method stimulates the explication of the criteria and the sharpening of concepts and procedures through which the predictions are being made. It also can sharpen the search for contaminating variables and for suitable controls. Usually, in a field as complex as family research, it is not practicable to eliminate in a single study all possible contaminants which might account for predictive success or predictive error. However, this research strategy can stimulate one to become more cognizant of potential sources of contamination and to set up a series of studies in which these possible difficulties are examined one after another.

The use of predictive methods leads into the question of another major concept, namely that of the structural, stylistic or formal features of individuals and of families. I refer here to those features which predictably endure or recur in a variety of situations and are not newly formed in response to each new circumstance or stimulus. We have assumed that in the long-term relationships which occur in family life there will be certain transactional patterns that will have occurred with high frequency. Such patterns are likely to have differing influences upon different individual family members because their susceptibility to formative change inevitably varies both constitutionally and experientially, depending upon such factors as stage of individual maturation and development and role within the family. We have been especially interested in those aspects of family life which appear to be patterned and recurrent, that is, "structural" or "stylistic".

Similarly, with respect to those persons who are diagnosed as schizophrenic, we have felt that it was especially crucial to deal with structural or core features of the schizophrenic disorder, those aspects of the illness which seem to recur under a variety of circumstances, even in periods of remission from florid symptoms. For example, the so-called "formal" aspects of schizophrenic thinking disorders appear to be based upon relatively enduring response dispositions of the individual. Therefore, we have attempted to define and delineate the diverse varieties of thought disorders but have found it necessary to go beyond conventional clinical formulations of thought disorder in order to make this concept operationally useful for research purposes (see Wynne and Singer, 1963b, 1966).

This effort has led us into another pair of concepts: focal attention and shared focal attention. We have described these concepts in detail elsewhere (Wynne and Singer, 1966). The use of these concepts has led us directly to a variety of specific research methods for studying both individual schizophrenic thought disorder and family communication patterns. The concept of focal attention is concerned with how a person attends to internal and external stimuli, modulates their intensity, and organizes them into perceptual and response patterns that may alternatively be sustained or flexibly altered in the course of a variety of transactions with the environment. The more or less repetitive patterns in which persons attend to stimuli have been described and measured in recent years in terms of dimensions which emerge from the factor analysis of performance scores on a variety of psychophysiologic, perceptual and cognitive laboratory tests. These dimensions have been termed attentional, perceptual, and cognitive response dispositions, or cognitive control principles. They share the formal, stylistic and structural characteristics which I have been describing above. (See Silverman, 1964 and 1967; Wynne and Singer, 1966; Wynne, 1967.) These dimensions of behavior include such features as field dependence–independence, extensiveness of scanning control, stimulus intensity control, and leveling–sharpening, and are also closely related to psychophysiologic and neurophysiologic measures, such as the cortical evoked response (Buchsbaum and Silverman, 1968).

The concept of response dispositions provides a promising approach to the study of schizophrenics and their families for several reasons. First, available evidence suggests that these response dispositions are to some extent stable, "built-in" aspects of an individual's functioning, but there is no prejudgment as to *how* they were built in, whether on an innate, inherited basis or on the basis of recurrent and perhaps intense experiential factors.

Second, the fact that experimental methods exist for studying the cognitive control dimensions provides another way of looking at similar phenomena which are manifest in clinical data and in the communication samples obtained with the Rorschach and related techniques. How a person organizes language and attends to particular percepts, ideas and feelings in an interpersonal transaction should be related to how the same person focuses attention in experimental situations.

Third, the use of these dimensionalized concepts makes possible the study, with the same methods, both of schizophrenics and of other family members who are not symptomatically schizophrenic but who may have some characteristics in common with the overtly schizophrenic family member. If one only relies exclusively upon the traditional concept of schizophrenia as a symptomatic entity which at least in theory is discrete and delimited, then one finds that most members of the families of schizophrenics, even parents and siblings, have not been given a diagnosis of schizophrenia in the course of ordinary contacts with psychiatric facilities. We have found, as has Lidz *et al.* (1965) and others, that many of these family members have severe disturbances for which there would be no psychiatric evaluation except on a research basis. More commonly, eccentricities have been noted in the relatives of schizophrenics to which a vague label such as "schizoid" has been applied. However, "schizoidness" is not a clear or unified concept (Planansky, 1966) and does not lend itself to systematic research comparisons of individuals from the same family or from different families. In contrast, the conceptual paradigm of a series of dimensions of response dispositions provides a basis for specific comparisons of each and every family member who is studied.

Thus, as an overriding methodologic principle of our work, we have attempted to convert the concepts used into measurable component features. A closely related objective in our research is to evaluate specifically the reliability with which our procedures can be used. We have sought to simplify and clarify the procedures sufficiently so that they are usable by any intelligent assistant or researcher. Our assumption is that until the methods can be used equally well by a number of investigators, the details and criteria of the procedures have not been adequately communicated. Such reliability has now been achieved with the special scoring methods used by Dr. Singer with Rorschach protocols from family members. Even bright undergraduates can score these protocols with an inter-rater reliability of above 80%. For those features for which we have developed evaluation methods that are reliable and that are reasonably satisfactory conceptually, we are now going ahead as rapidly as possible to evaluate the degree to which the various features are correlated within the same individual, between individuals of the same family, and between family system variables and individual variables. Later, these methods can be applied to longitudinal studies of individuals and families and to detailed studies of special samples, such as adoptive families, which should help clarify etiologic questions. However, further basic methodologic work and correlational studies are first necessary before these approaches can be applied efficiently to special samples.

II

One variety of study which we have now used with several hundred families involves the prediction of symptom patterns of the index family member from data obtained from other family members seen individually and conjointly. Various portions of this material have been published (e.g. Singer and Wynne, 1963, 1965b). Although the results have been consistently highly significant statistically, we are continuing to refine our criteria and scoring procedures. For this reason, it would be premature to attempt a comprehensive summary of this work. However, it may be of interest for me to make a few tentative generalizations at this time.

In families containing one or more late adolescent or young adult offspring, the presence and severity of thought disorder can be independently evaulated in each family member by means of individually administered procedures such as the Rorschach, the Proverbs Test, and the Object-sorting Test. These test protocols have been evaluated blindly for two different sets of features. First, the protocols have been rated for features suggesting "schizophrenicness", that is evidence of thinking disorders and other deviances which would ordinarily be regarded as signs of schizophrenic illness in the person himself or herself. Second, the transactions in the verbatim protocols have also been rated for what very, very loosely, for convenience of expression only, might be called "schizophrenogenicness", that is features of communication which hypothetically would be expected to induce difficulties in focusing attention and handling meaning in the listener.

If an offspring is schizophrenic, the "schizophrenic" set of features can be used to measure concordant similarities between the overt schizophrenic and other family members. Such similarities could have been transmitted from parents to offspring either through shared genetic equipment or shared experience with one another, or they could have arisen in parallel through similar but unshared environmental factors, either physical or psychosocial.

The "schizophrenogenic" set of features only in part overlap with the first and are organized from a quite different frame of reference, namely the transactional impact on the other person in an interchange. These features have not been selected because of the likelihood that they have been transmitted in a similar form from parents to offspring, but because they might link parents and offspring who have had a prolonged relationship with one another. "Schizophrenogenic" features include (a) varieties of behavior which are in more than one family member and, also, (b) features which differ in the form shown in members of the same family. These features, whether similar or different, are linked together in an over-all family pattern or system which is interpersonally and psychologically meaningful as a whole.

Empirically, the distinction between "schizophrenicness" and "schizophenogenicness" makes possible the comparison of alternative sets of criteria, the one based upon the presumed transmission of concordant similarities and the other based upon specific kinds of predictable complementarities between family members, involving both similarities and differences. Unfortunately, the fact that similarities between parents and offspring can arise either through heredity or through the transactions of psychological identification processes means that when such comparisons are carried out with intact families who already have a schizophrenic offspring, the question of the origin of the similar features remains. Longitudinal studies and other special studies such as those with adoptive families are needed for an evaluation of this question, if such studies are designed so it is possible to consider whether the similarities are independent of actual intrafamilial transactions or existed prior to these transactions.

Meanwhile, evidence is accumulating that better "cross-sectional" predictive accuracy about the characteristics of offspring is possible if we use transactional, "schizophrenogenic" criteria than if we look only for concordant similarities. In addition to our work at NIMH, this distinction has been studied by the Yale group using the Object-sorting Test. Lidz et al. (1963), replicating an experiment by McConaghy (1959), used a scoring technique developed by Lovibond (1953) for use with the Object-sorting Test. This scoring method was a direct measure of "schizophrenicness". Later, these same Object-sorting protocols, plus additional records, were re-scored with a scoring technique developed by Dr. Margaret Singer which emphasizes transactional principles and which tries to measure "schizo-phrenogenicness".

When the Yale group introduced rigorous controls for blindness of the raters and for educational level of the subjects, they found that the Lovibond scoring method did not make a very sharp discrimination between the parents of schizophrenics and the parents of normal controls (Rosman, et al., 1964). However, when the Singer scoring method was used, an improved discrimination was made, at a high level of statistical significance (Wild et al., 1965). In accord with what we have hypothesized about the importance of how family members combined together, the distinction between the parents of patients and the parents of controls was especially striking when the scores for the parents were summed for couples compared to data analysis of individual parents.

We have obtained similar findings in scoring parental Rorschachs. We have studied parental Rorschachs extensively using a scoring manual that evaluates transactional "schizophrenogenicness" in terms of 41 categories of communication defects and deviances (Singer and Wynne, 1966). Statistically, 22 of these categories were both frequent in occurrence and highly discriminatory in a sample of families different from those on whom the manual was devised (Singer, 1967; Wynne, 1967). This scoring of the parental Rorschachs, it should be emphasized, was done entirely blindly, without any knowledge by the raters concerning the diagnoses of the offspring, and inter-rater reliability was also high.

Further, the particular variety of thinking disorder in the schizophrenic offspring, classified as "amorphous", "fragmented", or "constricted", as well as a number of other features about the offspring, such as depressive and apathetic tendencies, can be predicted from the frequency of certain defects and deviances shown in parental communication samples.

Let me reiterate for purposes of emphasis and clarity: When we use a transactional viewpoint in scoring Rorschach and other records, we do not intend to evaluate evidence of schizophrenic illness in the parent but, rather, what are the effects upon the listener of this kind of communication. This then leads more directly into criteria which are relevant to making predictions about offspring who have been in long transactional contact with these parents.

In scoring these records, we have made heavy use of the concept of sharing foci of attention and of sharing sets and role relationships. To what extent does the speaker join in a common task-orientation or set with the listener? Does he raise questions and make comments to discover whether or not the listener is following him and understanding? Does he select a focus of attention which is differentiated and clearly communicated? Is the set taken about a particular focus sustained or is he readily distracted so that his ideas are not spelled out or elaborated? Does he continue until some kind of closure about a given focus or topic has been achieved? Also, when he does not understand what the other person is suggesting or saying, does he attempt to find out what the other person's frame of reference or focus of attention is, or does he assume shared understanding despite repeated questions or expressions of perplexity by the listener?

The features which have statistically proved to be most highly differentiating of the parents of schizophrenics involve problems of closure and peculiarities of speech and language usage which are mostly not of the kind found in overt schizophrenics. It has been our over-all impression that the parents of schizophrenics who are not themselves overtly or symptomatically schizophrenic, speak in communication patterns which are maximally befuddling to a listener who is trying to share a focus of attention or set with these parents. Tentatively, our data suggest that the parents of schizophrenics show these features in a considerably more pervasive and frequent fashion than the same features are found in communication of schizophrenics themselves. Schizophrenics show other kinds of disorders, ordinarily features which are more easily identified as "crazy" and therefore can be dismissed or not "heard". However, the parents of schizophrenics tend to communicate in such a way that the listener tries to understand, but ends up distrusting his own understanding.

In the NIMH material, test and interview data of several kinds have now been obtained from about 280 families. In 122 families there was a young adult schizophrenic or a childhood psychotic. In the 158 comparison families, the offspring included non-schizophrenic psychiatric patients, medical patients, and normal controls. Quite consistently, in each sample that has been carefully studied and statistically analyzed, 85–95% of the families have been correctly differentiated as to the diagnosis of offspring based upon the parental communication samples. These differentiations are consistently significant at $p=0.01$ and better. Several papers have reported the details of these studies which will not be repeated here. (See, for example, Singer and Wynne, 1963, 1965b; Singer, 1967; Wynne, 1967.)

Sample selection: Obviously, the meaning of these findings hinges to a considerable extent upon the nature of the samples of families studied. I shall summarize some aspects of the sample characteristics in order to help indicate the present scope of this research and some of the directions that we believe the work should take in the future.

(a) *Diagnosis and diagnostic subtype of index family members*

Table 1 gives a summary picture of the main samples of families to which I will refer in this discussion. They are classified according to the gross diagnosis of the index family member. It should be noted that the data from the various sources is not uniform in the

TABLE 1. SAMPLES OF FAMILIES BY GROSS DIAGNOSIS OF INDEX MEMBER

	Adolescent and adult schizophrenics	Adolescent and adult non-schizophrenics	Child psychotics	Child non-psychotics
Bethesda, NIMH	55	45		
Houston	19	40		
Japan	18	3	10	10
San Francisco			20	60
	92	88	30	70
		180		100
			280	

ways in which it was obtained. Although each sample was quite homogeneous in itself, the different samples are not directly comparable with one another except in terms of certain selected aspects.

In the Bethesda sample, nearly all the families have been studied with the following procedures: individual diagnostic interviews, individual Rorschach, TAT, Object-sorting Test, MMPI, Proverbs Test, and Consensus or Relation Rorschachs, especially with the parents as a couple in the Spouse Rorschach (Loveland *et al.,* 1963; Loveland, 1967). Small subsamples have also been studied with excerpts from tape recordings of family therapy interviews, with structured research interviews with the parents as a couple, and with experimental procedures, especially the Revealed Differences technique. During the past year, the patients and now family members are being tested with an extensive battery of psychophysiologic, perceptual and cognitive procedures (Dr. Julian Silverman). The NIMH families have also been regularly evaluated with individual and conjoint art procedures in which the interaction while working together on a series of art tasks has been evaluated (Mrs. H. Kwiatkowski). Individual and conjoint family therapy and extensive history taking, with home visit observations in many instances, have contributed to a clinical picture obtained in some depth. However, the clinical data have not been used in the predictive studies described here.

The sample from Houston, made available by Dr. Seymour Fisher, consists of individual Rorschachs from the parents, with clinical and demographic data about all of the family members. Most of the data from San Francisco was obtained at the Langley Porter Children's Service and was made available to us by Drs. Jeanne Block, Virginia Patterson, and S. A. Szurek. This material consisted of Rorschachs and TATs from the parents and extensive clinical descriptions of the child patients.

The Japanese data are being studied collaboratively with Professor S. Kuromaru in Kobe, working with a sample of families of child-patients and normal controls, and in Osaka and Kyoto with Professor M. Murakami, Dr. Kenji Sakamoto, and Dr. Y. Kasahara. The data in this work consist particularly of individual Rorschachs from both parents and patients and descriptive clinical data about the patient and family members.

Not included in Table 1 is a very interesting sample of families recently studied by Drs. Alan Rosenthal and Manfred Behrens (1968) of St. Elizabeth's Hospital in Washington, D.C. They have used the Family Rorschach technique to make blind ratings about three kinds of families: 11 lower class white schizophrenics and their families, 17 lower class Negro schizophrenics and their families, and 11 lower class Negro control families. Although these investigators were able to distinguish the white and Negro families on the basis of language dialect differences, when they used transactional criteria such as rating how adequately the family members shared foci of attention, the families of schizophrenics differentiated from the lower class Negro control families at a level of significance of $p < 0.001$. This study indicates that the communication disorders associated with the existence of a schizophrenic family member are not the same as communication patterns associated with low socioeconomic status in itself.

It should be noted that the schizophrenics in these various samples have a wide range of degree of severity of illness. Patients are included both with an insidious onset and other features generally ascribed to "process" schizophrenia, as well as patients with acute onset and so-called "reactive" features.

Among the families of the adolescent and the young adult patients, the age range of the index offspring was generally 15–28 years, with a relatively small number of patients having a later onset. This has meant that the sample has an under-representation of coherent, integrated paranoids. Unfortunately, from the standpoint of family studies, many late-onset, coherently paranoid patients have detached themselves from their familes of origin some years ago and, in some cases, have established families of their own, making difficulties in comparing these data with those from younger patients and their families.

One of the most interesting aspects of this work is that the criteria for the parents of the schizophrenics with different forms of thinking seem to differ. In addition, as reported previously, characteristics of the parents of childhood psychotic patients are quite markedly different from the parents of the schizophrenics who become ill in adolescence or young adulthood (Singer and Wynne, 1963).

With respect to the non-schizophrenics, similar subtype distinctions can be made, illustrating the point that the principles involved in making these differentiations are not dependent upon unique characteristics of individual schizophrenics nor unique effects of schizophrenic illness upon the parents or other family members. Rather, the systematic ways in which the characteristics of individual family members relate to one another can, judging from our research experience, be evaluated in any family, at least for those family members who have had enduring experience with one another. As a further indication of this point, Dr. Singer has been able to match patients with the specific family from which they come, and has also matched a relatively small number of "well" siblings with their families (Singer and Wynne, 1965b). This matching seems to be equally possible for the families of non-schizophrenics and for the families of schizophrenics, again suggesting that principles of family relationships and organization are involved rather than anything idiosyncratic for schizophrenia as a disease entity.

(b) *Diagnosis of parents and other family members*

In all of the samples except for the NIMH series, the parents were uniformly selected because they were themselves free from overt, symptomatic psychiatric illness. In the NIMH work, we have also studied a sub-sample of families in which there is a parent or a sibling who is psychotic in addition to the index offspring. However, as I mentioned above, the features in which we are most interested do not depend upon the presence of overt craziness in the parent or sibling. Families with overtly psychotic parents are, if anything, only mildly different from the other families with schizophrenic offspring, who do not have overtly psychotic parents.

(c) *Social competence of family members*

Presently, we are organizing our data for a computerized analysis of such questions as whether certain selected features of the Rorschach scores, for example, are related to factors of social competence, such as educational and occupational levels. What we have done already is to show that when the families of schizophrenics and non-schizophrenics are matched with respect to social class variables such as occupation and education, the families of the schizophrenics and non-schizophrenics can nevertheless be differentiated. It should be noted that the entire series of 59 families from Houston was a lower-class and lower-middle-class group with an average parental education of eighth grade. The group studied by Drs. Alan Rosenthal and Behrens at St. Elizabeth's Hospital is an extremely lower-class group, slum dwellers with very little education and essentially no occupational skills. It is especially striking that Drs. Rosenthal and Behrens were able to differentiate these lower-class families of the schizophrenics from lower-class normal controls at a level of accuracy of 85 % (Behrens and Rosenthal, 1968).

Interpersonal competence, an aspect of social competence different from educational and occupational level, deserves evaluation and control in studies of schizophrenics and their families, since there is often such severe and chronic impairment in this respect. We are currently working on procedures for rating such matters more reliably.

Another aspect of social competence which is important is the degree of chronicity of illness and particularly the duration of hospitalization. In part of our material, we have matched schizophrenics and controls with respect to duration of hospitalization by working with non-schizophrenic psychiatric patients who are hospitalised for other psychiatric reasons. There are limitations to the extent to which such matchings can take place when one deals with chronic patients. Therefore, we have tried to compare patients relatively soon after the first psychiatric admission, but would prefer, of course, to work prospectively with families in which the overt symptomatic disorder has not yet emerged. As one technique of controlling for chronicity which I would like to try on a more extended basis in the future, we have applied the Revealed Differences technique (Strodtbeck, 1958) to a sample of twenty families in which the schizophrenics were matched in terms of acuteness and chronicity with a comparison group of medical patients whose illness had disrupted their ordinary social role performance, but was not life-threatening. Patients with various kinds of metabolic and orthopedic problems fell into this comparison group.

(d) *Cultural groups*

In the portion of the sample from the white American, middle-class NIMH families, preliminary data inspection has not revealed any particular differences associated with national origins or religious affiliations. However, Drs. Rosenthal and Behrens at St. Elizabeth's Hospital in Washington, in their comparison of lower-class Negro families with lower-class white families, have been able to find distinctive differences associated with this subcultural distinction, which, however, did not submerge or obscure the differences associated with diagnostic groups (Behrens and Rosenthal, 1968; Rosenthal and Behrens, 1968). This finding also fits with observations we are in the process of making collaboratively in Japan in which we find that there are interesting cultural differences compared to the American sample, but that the similarities associated with the presence of a schizophrenic offspring stand out very strikingly nonetheless. By further analysis of specific categories of communication deviances in these cross cultural samples, we hope to learn a good deal more in the future about similarities and differences associated on the one hand with different kinds of psychopathology and on the other hand with cultural variations. Data from a smaller sample of families studied in rural Lebanon also support these observations.

(e) *Family role structure and family boundaries*

It is very important to recognize that most of the families studied were intentionally intact families with both biologic parents available. This obviously represents a skewed sample of families.

However, in the St. Elizabeth's series, working with very lower-class families, it was not possible to work with both biologic parents, so Drs. Rosenthal and Behrens selected at least two adults who had been important in the rearing experience of the child. Sometimes, for example, this was a grandmother and the mother, sometimes a stepfather and a mother, sometimes an aunt and a mother. As indicated above, the families could nevertheless be differentiated.

In field work in Lebanon, I was particularly interested in the problem of family boundaries and the question of how to study families in which there are several generations living together in extended families and lineages. Future work should match families with respect to the extent that there are contacts with extended family members and also with respect to the family's position in the community in which they live. There seem to be differences in patterns of families which are peripheral or marginal to the main values and social structure of a community compared to those who are in the main stream. At this time I mention this only to indicate that there are a considerable number of potentially important social variables which deserve much more investigation in the future in relation to their possible relevance to psychopathology in particular family members. We have by no means been able to control for all of them yet. However, as I have discussed in more detail elsewhere, the family can serve as a strategic research focus because of its intermediary size between the individual and broader units of the culture and social structure (Wynne, 1969).

A particular type of family structure which we have not yet studied but which is of very great interest is the family in which there are two sets of parents, the biologic parents and the adopting or foster parents. In principle, the methods which we have developed for scoring specific categories of communication behavior, for example, can be used to distinguish groups of specific features which may be correlated differentially for biologic versus rearing parents. I hope that data of these kinds can be obtained with the kind of families Drs. Kety, Rosenthal, and Wender are now studying in Denmark. Dr. Singer has made one trip to Denmark to explore these possibilities with Dr. Rosenthal.

III

CONCLUDING COMMENTS

I hope it is quite clear that I have been describing research which has been intended from the beginning to pass through a series of stages. The earliest phase of this work consisted of exploratory clinical studies, with emphasis upon hypothesis formation and concept formulation. Second, we moved into work in which we have used horizontal or cross-sectional prediction studies to evaluate hypotheses about links within families and as a heuristic technique for sharpening concepts and procedures used. Third, after working with a rather narrow sample of middle-class white American families, we have substantially expanded the kind of samples studied in order to evaluate the generalizability of the procedures and concepts. We feel that this work is of value and interest in its own right, and the specific question of the relevance to the origin and development of schizophrenic illness has not been directly studied thus far. We have, however, selected our procedures in such a way that they pertain to central rather than peripheral features of schizophrenic illness. Also, we have looked at aspects of family patterns which appear to have enduring characteristics and are not ordinarily subject to conscious recognition or control but are abiding, automatic, and unconscious ways of behaving and relating. Considerably more work needs to be done on this methodologic and conceptual level, some of which we can do with data now at hand but not yet analyzed. A study in which we are particularly interested is the correlation between types of communication defects and deviances and patterns of psychophysiologic, perceptual, and cognitive response dispositions. In studying both communication patterns and experimentally derived cognitive and perceptual variables, the central concept in our formulations is attention—how one takes a set toward incoming stimuli, how one organizes and sustains responses to the stimuli and how one shares foci of attention with other persons in ongoing transactions. Response dispositions seem to be

N

stable through a considerable variety of contexts and represent tendencies which, in the case of individuals, appear to be quite enduring and may even be related to neonatal response dispositions. On the level of family and group transactions, there also seem to be rather stable characteristics of transactional processes which, as the work of Drs. Mishler, Reiss, and others, has suggested, have "system" characteristics that persist despite shifts of performance of the individuals who make up the systems.

As a principle of research strategy, we have felt that refinement of methods for studying these various features of individual and family functioning, together with clarification of some of the potential contaminating variables, has been important before it is possible to know what to emphasize and measure in developmental and etiologic studies. It is our belief that the recent and ongoing work on these methodologic and conceptual details will in the fairly near future be at a point where the application of these methods to special samples and longitudinally studied samples will be worth-while and fruitful. It is well recognized that one of the great problems with longitudinal studies has been that they have been undertaken before the investigator has a very clear idea of what he wants to measure in relation to future outcomes, so that he works out his methods only after the baseline data have been obtained.

Finally, I wish to conclude with a few general points which Dr. Singer and I have made in several places previously, but which perhaps deserve underlining. None of the forms of behavior which we have observed in the families of schizophrenics is unique to these families. Rather, the differences are a matter of frequency of behavior. The differences hold up with a variety of kinds of data and despite a number of diagnostic, social, and cultural variations which might be expected to blur the distinctions associated with diagnosis but which, in fact, do not. Also, it should be noted that the horizontal predictions which we have made have not been in relation to symptom content, and they have not been concerned with the nature of the stress or other circumstances precipitating a particular episode of illness. Rather, we have been interested in those factors which are likely to have been predisposing rather than precipitating, enduring rather than only immediate. We have assumed that a variety of factors, both familial and nonfamilial, precipitate acute episodes of psychiatric disorder. We have, in short, been interested in those structural or stylistic features which might lead to an increased vulnerability to a number of possible precipitating circumstances.

REFERENCES

BEHRENS, M. I., ROSENTHAL, A. J., and CHODOFF, P. (1968) Communication in lower-class families of schizophrenics: II. Observations and findings, *Arch. Gen. Psychiat.* (in press).

BENJAMIN, J. D. (1959) Prediction and psychopathological theory, in L. Jessner and E. Pavenstedt (eds.), *Dynamic Psychopathology in Childhood,* New York, Grune & Stratton, pp. 6–77.

BLEULER, E. (1911) *Dementia Praecox or the Group of Schizophrenias,* transl. by Joseph Zinker, 1950, New York, International Univ. Press.

BUCHSBAUM, M., and SILVERMAN, J. (1968) Stimulus intensity control and cortical evoked response, *Psychosom. Med.* **30,** 12–22.

DEWEY, J. and BENTLEY, A. F. (1949) *Knowing and the Known,* Boston, Beacon Press.

LIDZ, T., FLECK, S., and CORNELISON, A. (1965) *Schizophrenia and the Family,* New York, International Univ. Press.

LIDZ, T., WILD, C., SCHAFER, S., ROSMAN, B., and FLECK, S. (1963) Thought disorders in the parents of schizophrenic patients: a study utilizing the Object-sorting Test, *J. Psychiat. Res.* **1**, 193–200.

LOVELAND, N. T. (1967) The relation Rorschach: a technique for studying interaction, *J. Nerv. Ment. Dis.* **145**, 93–105.

LOVELAND, N. T., WYNNE, L. C., and SINGER, M. T. (1963) The family Rorschach: a new method for studying family interaction, *Family Process* **2**, 187–215.

LOVIBOND, S. H. (1953) The Object-sorting Test and conceptual thinking in schizophrenia, *Aust. J. Psychol.* **5**, 52–70.

MCCONAGHY, N. (1959) The use of an Object-sorting Test in elucidating the hereditary factor in schizophrenia, *J. Neurol. Neurosurg. Psychiat.* **22**, 243–5.

MORRIS, G. O. and WYNNE, L. C. (1965) Schizophrenic offspring and parental style of communication, *Psychiatry* **28**, 19–44.

PLANANSKY, K. (1966) Conceptual boundaries of schizoidness: suggestions for epidemiological and genetic research, *J. Nerv. Ment. Dis.* **142**, 318–31.

ROSENTHAL, A. J., BEHRENS, M. I., and CHODOFF, P. (1968) Communication in lower-class families of schizophrenics: I. Methodological problems, *Arch. Gen. Psychiat.* **18**, 464–70.

ROSMAN, B., WILD, C., RICCI, J., FLECK, S., and LIDZ, T. (1964) Thought disorders in the parents of schizophrenic patients: a further study utilizing the Object-sorting Test, *J. Psychiat. Res.* **2**, 211–21.

SILVERMAN, J. (1964) The problem of attention in research and theory in schizophrenia, *Psychol. Rev.* **71**, 352–78.

SILVERMAN, J. (1967) Variations in cognitive control and psychophysiological defense in the schizophrenias, *Psychosom. Med.* **29**, 225–51.

SINGER, M. T. (1967) Family transactions and schizophrenia: I. Recent research findings, in *The Origins of Schizophrenia, Excerpta Medica International Congress Series,* No. 151, pp. 147–64.

SINGER, M. T. and WYNNE, L. C. (1963) Differentiating characteristics of parents of childhood schizophrenics, childhood neurotics, and young adult schizophrenics, *Am. J. Psychiat.* **120**, 234–43.

SINGER, M. T. and WYNNE, L. C. (1964) Stylistic variables in family research, Presented at a symposium Milwaukee Psychiatric Hospital and Marquette University, Wisconsin, Department of Psychiatry.

SINGER, M. T. and WYNNE, L. C. (1965a) Thought disorder and family relations of schizophrenics: III. Methodology using projective techniques, *Arch. Gen. Psychiat.* **12**, 187–220.

SINGER, M. T. and WYNNE, L. C. (1965b) Thought disorder and family relations of schizophrenics: IV. Results and implications, *Arch. Gen. Psychiat.* **12**, 201–12.

SINGER, M. T. and WYNNE, L. C. (1966) Principles for scoring communication defects and deviances in parents of schizophrenics: Rorschach and TAT scoring manuals, *Psychiatry* **29**, 260–8.

STRODTBECK, F. L. (1958) Family interaction, values, and achievement, in D. C. McClelland, A. L. Baldwin, V. Bronfenbrenner, and F. L. Strodtbeck (eds.), *Talent and Society,* New York, Van Nostrand.

WILD, C., SINGER, M. T., ROSMAN, B., RICCI, J., and LIDZ, T. (1965) Measuring disordered styles of thinking, *Arch. Gen. Psychiat.* **13**, 471–6.

WYNNE, L. C. and SINGER, M. T. (1963a) Thought disorder and family relations of schizophrenics: I. A research strategy, *Arch. Gen. Psychiat.* **9**, 191–8.

WYNNE, L. C. and SINGER, M. T. (1963b) Thought disorder and family relations of schizophrenics: II. A classification of forms of thinking. *Arch. Gen. Psychiat.* **9**, 199–206.

WYNNE, L. C. and SINGER, M. T. (1966) Schizophrenic impairments in sharing foci of attention: a conceptual basis for viewing schizophrenics and their families in research and therapy, Presented as the Bertram H. Roberts' Memorial Lecture, Yale University, New Haven, Connecticut, 26 April.

WYNNE, L. C. (1967) Family transactions and schizophrenia: II. Conceptual considerations for a research strategy, in *The Origins of Schizophrenia, Excerpta Medica International Congress Series,* No. 151, pp. 165–78.

WYNNE, L. C. (1969) The family as a strategic focus in cross-cultural psychiatric studies, in Caudill, W. and Lin, T. (eds.), *Mental Health Research in Asia and the Pacific,* East-West Center Press, Honolulu (in press).

FROM THE MOTHERS OF SCHIZOPHRENIC PATIENTS TO INTERACTIONAL FAMILY DYNAMICS

Yrjö O. Alanen

Psychiatric Clinic, University of Helsinki, Helsinki, Finland

THE following is a concise recapitulation of certain findings and views associated with my own investigations concerning the transmission of schizophrenia. The title of this paper indicates the direction in which my views have developed.

I. THE MOTHERS OF SCHIZOPHRENIC PATIENTS

The discussions I had with my principal and teacher, Professor Martti Kaila, in Helsinki during 1952 first interested me in these questions. My own intention was to investigate what had become of boys who had grown up without a father. Kaila regarded this as too difficult, suggesting three alternatives instead. One was the study of the childhood family environments of schizophrenic patients. He had been in the United States a few years previously and become acquainted with the views held in America concerning the psychodynamics of schizophrenia. He did not believe that such a grave illness was psychologically understandable, and he mainly expected that my investigation would confirm this opinion. In the course of my work I was led to different conceptions. Nevertheless, though my teacher's views remained reserved at bottom, he retained an especially positive and constructive attitude toward my work. I find it opportune to express my gratitude to my teacher at this particular Conference for two different reasons. First, because he will retire on pension this year; and, secondly, because two of the European students invited to attend this Conference are his pupils.

Descriptive findings

Despite the fact that I had taken an interest in the part played by fathers, I initially confined my study to the mothers of schizophrenic patients and to the mother–child relationships, because the psycho-analytic views on schizophrenia regarded these as the most important points. Employing the psychiatric interview, I investigated the mothers of 100 schizophrenic patients, and the mothers of 20 neurotic patients and 20 normal persons formed the control series. It goes without saying that I also became acquainted with the patients themselves. At the same time I became permanently interested in the psychotherapy of schizophrenic patients, and this greatly influenced the development of my views. The Rorschach test was administered to 92 of the mothers of schizophrenic patients and to all 40 mothers in the control series.

The interviews with the mothers of schizophrenic patients shortly revealed that a majority of them manifested distinct psychopathological features. In a preliminary report presented in 1955 (Alanen, 1956) I placed particular stress upon the following features of the mothers of schizophrenic patients: many of them were embittered, aggressive and devoid of natural warmth; they were anxious and insecure, often with obsessive features; despite their insecurity, they were characterized by a dominating, rather than submissive, pattern of interpersonal relationships, and this was particularly so for their relationships with the children who fell ill. I also paid attention to the fact that the mothers' bitterness was particularly intense as regards their own emotionally stern childhood and youth and their unhappy and conflict-ridden marriages; as well as to the fact that in many cases their difficulties had apparently been especially pronounced at the time of the birth and during the early years of that particular child who later became psychotic.

For the monograph on "The mothers of schizophrenic patients", published in 1958, I classified the mothers that I had studied into clinical categories on a unidimensional scale. This classification was based both upon the interview findings and upon the Rorschach test results, scored and analysed by R. O. Viitamäki, Ph.D. The testing supplemented the picture obtained of the mothers particularly in the following respect: in addition to certain manifestly psychotic mothers, there were many whose schizoid or borderline psychotic features attracted my attention. Moreover, there were several mothers who were not characterized by the classical features of a schizoid personality, but who nevertheless manifested a very accentuated blockage or constriction of affective life, poor self-control, and an inability to feel themselves into the inner life of other people. These findings made me convinced that the mothers in question had to be regarded as suffering from disorders graver than the "ordinary" psychoneuroses. Looked at this way, more than half the mothers of schizophrenics were affected by disorders exceeding the psychoneurotic level.

Table 1 illustrates the distribution of mothers according to clinical category.

Mother–child relationships

Also, the picture I then received of the psychodynamic mother–child relationship in schizophrenia was coloured mainly by the mothers who were characterized with attributes such as "schizoid", "emotionally defective", and "lacking in empathic ability". Particularly characteristic of the mothers of schizophrenics was what I termed a "schizoid pattern of interpersonal relationships"; they were dominating, lacked understanding and did not respect the child as an independent person. It was natural to consider that the psychological effects caused to the child by the mother's disorders influenced the child's development even during the earliest mother–child relationship. The fact, already mentioned above, that the time surrounding the birth of the child that later fell ill had been particularly difficult for many a mother also spoke for an early developmental disturbance, emphasized by psycho-analytic investigators. There were other findings, however, speaking against the view that only this stage would be decisive. To mention one of these findings, it seemed to me that visible signs of an oral frustration were not sufficiently frequent; for example, there was no difference between the schizophrenia series and the control series in the duration of breast-feeding. Though aggressive, these mothers could not be characterized

TABLE 1. DISTRIBUTION OF MOTHERS OF SCHIZOPHRENICS, NEUROTICS AND NORMAL
PERSONS BY CLINICAL CATEGORY

Group	A	B	C	D	Total A+B+C+D	E
Sch. I	1	1	6	3	11	2
Sch. II	6	4	21	6	37	4
Sch. III	1	1	3	2	7	5
Sch. IV	4	3	9	10	26	3
Sch. V	—	2	1	—	3	2
Total Sch.	12	11	40	21	84	16
Neurotics	—	1	1	7	9	11
Normal	—	—	1	5	6	14

Groups Sch. I and Sch. II included the mothers of the patients suffering from typical ("process") schizophrenia: groups Sch. III and Sch. IV consisted of the mothers of the patients who had reactive, prognostically more benign "schizophreniform psychoses", and group Sch. V comprised the mothers of the patients whose disease pictures were complicated by some serious organic illness or injury. The letters refer to the following categories. A, mothers who had been manifestly psychotic. B, other mothers whose ego was very weak, giving rise to a tendency to unbearable anxiety and to unrealistic thought and behaviour patterns bordering on the psychotic. C, other mothers whose disturbances were more serious than psychoneurotic. D, psychoneurotically disturbed mothers. E, mothers who only manifested slight neurotic disturbances or were completely healthy. In this monograph, as well as in the monograph I published later, statistical methods were employed only in the analysis of the psychological test results. But they were not applied to the interview findings, since classifications based on such findings are somewhat inexact by necessity. According to Dr. Viitamäki, the mothers of schizophrenic patients in my series were, in the light of the Rorschach variables:

1. In possession of a greater amount of schizoform traits than the control mothers;
2. More aggressive, on the average, than the controls;
3. More anxious than the controls; and
4. Less able to have affective-emotional and, also, intellectual contacts than the controls.

All these differences were statistically significant.

As I am convinced that my present audience will neither overestimate nor underestimate the importance of statistical significance calculations, I propose to present such concerning Table 1 also. When mothers were divided into disturbed persons (groups A, B, C, and D) and non-disturbed persons (group E) and the difference between the schizophrenia series and the control series was tested for statistical significance by means of the chi-square test, the difference proved highly significant ($\chi^2 = 29 \cdot 8$; $p < 0 \cdot 001$). The difference was of course still more pronounced when groups A, B, and C, on the one hand, and groups D and E, on the other, were combined. It was also found that disorders more serious than neurotic (groups A, B, and C) were almost significantly more frequent in the mothers of typical schizophrenics than in the mothers of patients with schizophreniform psychoses ($\chi^2 = 4 \cdot 43$; $p < 0 \cdot 05$). It will be noted that the difference was due to the considerably higher frequency of mothers of process schizophrenics in group C, as compared with the mothers of patients affected by schizophreniform psychoses.

as rejecting. On the contrary, many of them had had a very possessive attitude toward the child from the outset. To these mothers, the child had clearly meant compensation for earlier frustrations. It became clear to me that, in these cases, the child meant exceptionally much to the mother, from the viewpoint of the gratification of her own emotions and needs— a point also emphasized by Lewis B. Hill (1955). Observations like these, also confirmed by my psychotherapeutic experience, suggested that, in the pathogenesis of schizophrenia, a disturbed mother–child relationship is a factor that continually influences the child's development, rather than one which only has a bearing during the earliest phase (cf. also Alanen, 1960a, b).

Firmly and aggressively dominating attitudes toward the child were definitely more frequent in the mothers of typical ("process") schizophrenics, compared with the mothers in the schizophreniform ("reactive") psychosis group, where warmer, more softly over-protective mother–child relationships were more common. This speaks against the view that only reactive schizophrenias, but not process schizophrenias, are psychologically understandable. There was a distinct difference between the attitudes of the male schizo-phrenics' and the female schizophrenics' mothers: the attitudes of the former I characterized as "possessively protective" and those of the latter as "inimically protective".

II. INTERACTIONAL FAMILY DYNAMICS

The obvious disturbedness of the fathers of many patients whose mothers I investigated, as well as the family constellations marked by marital conflicts or by a disproportionate dominance of one spouse, already attracted my attention to pathogenic factors other than those associated with the mother–child relationship in a narrow sense. Here I was also influenced by the studies conducted by Theodore Lidz's group, at Yale University, with which I became acquainted at the time when my monograph approached completion. In listening to the presentation of Lidz at the International Congress for Psychiatry in Zurich in 1957 (Lidz *et al.*, 1958), and in reading the papers published by the Yale group (Lidz *et al.*, 1957a, b), I was continually faced with matters similar to those I had encountered myself in the interviews, but which I had not been capable of formulating in an equally clear manner. The influence upon my views of Lidz's group naturally grew stronger when I had the opportunity to participate in its work personally for a 12 month period in 1959–60.

One question with which I was particularly preoccupied was this. Why do some of the children of a particular family fall ill with schizophrenia, whereas others do not? Is this due to genetic factors, constitutional differences, or to differences between the children as regards the position they have in the family dynamics? Observations on several families spoke for the importance of the last-mentioned factor. All this amounted to a stimulus to further investigations, which were no longer confined to the patients' mothers alone but were concerned with the entire familial network. A new project, made possible through a research grant that Foundations' Fund for Research in Psychiatry awarded me in 1960, was concerned with the study of the families of orientation of 30 schizophrenic and 30 neurotic patients. (15 male and 15 female patients included in both groups.) This study was under-taken in Helsinki in the form of team-work by a group of psycho-analytically oriented psychiatrists. Inclusion in the series was unselected but based upon given diagnostic criteria —only typical schizophrenias with primary symptoms and rather typical cases of neurosis were admitted—and upon the availabliity of at least one parent for investigation. It was postulated, in addition, that each family was to have 2–4 children, including the index patient, aged between 15 and 40 years. The results of this investigation were published last year in a monograph entitled "The family in the pathogenesis of schizophrenic and neurotic disorders" (Alanen *et al.*, 1966).

Descriptive findings

Let us again first mention some of the descriptive findings. As regards the parents of schizophrenic patients, both our interviews and the psychological testings carried out by Kalevi Takala, the psychologist of our team, confirmed the earlier findings concerning the disturbedness of mothers. They also revealed, however, that disorders in the fathers were not less marked. A clinical classification similar to—though not completely identical with—the one employed in the study of mothers was applied. It again turned out that a majority of the parents of the schizophrenic patients had to be assigned to categories representing disorders graver than neurotic. On the other hand, neurotic-level disorders, most of which were sub-clinical, predominated in the group of parents of neurotic patients. Also, the siblings of schizophrenic patients were definitely more seriously disturbed than the siblings of neurotic patients, but the disorders of the former represented greater variability, as compared with the disorders of schizophrenic patients' parents: apart from schizophrenic, borderline schizophrenic and schizoid disturbances, a wide variety of psychopathic and neurotic disorders was encountered, and a considerable proportion of these siblings were considered "normal". There was a tendency for the siblings of the same sex as the patient to be more ill than the opposite-sexed siblings were, and this was particularly so for disorders graver than neurotic. We felt that the explanation of this finding was to be based upon the psychodynamic family constellations: some of the families in our schizophrenia series were, it seemed to us, more pathogenic for the development of the sons, while others were more pathogenic for the daughters.

Tables 2 and 3 illustrate the distribution of the parents and the siblings of the schizophrenic and neurotic patients according to diagnostic category.

TABLE 2. DISTRIBUTION OF PARENTS OF SCHIZOPHRENIC AND NEUROTIC
PATIENTS BY CLINICAL CATEGORY

Sub-series	Degree-of-disturbance category						
	?	VI	V	IV	III	II	I
Fathers of sch. p.	4	1	6	14	5	—	—
Mothers of sch. p.	1	3	6	12	7	1	—
Parents of sch. p. (total)	5	4	12	26	12	1	—
Fathers of neur. p.	4	—	—	6	10	8	2
Mothers of neur. p.	2	—	1	4	15	8	—
Parents of neur. p. (total)	6	—	1	10	25	16	2

The diagnostic categories employed were the following:
VI   Schizophrenic psychosis.
V   Functional psychoses other than schizophrenic, borderline conditions with psychotic traits.
IV   Disorders more serious than ordinary psychoneuroses, but without psychotic traits.
III Psychoneurosis, psychoneurotic personality.
II   Normal with mild disorder traits.
I   Normal without disorder traits.

TABLE 3. DISTRIBUTION OF SIBLINGS OF SCHIZOPHRENIC AND NEUROTIC PATIENTS
BY CLINICAL CATEGORY

Sub-series	Degree-of-disturbance category					
	VI	V	IV	III	II	I
Same-sexed siblings of sch. p.	2	5	7	5	9	—
Opposite-sexed siblings of sch. p.	2	1	3	6	9	—
Siblings of sch. p. (total)	4	6	10	11	18	—
Same-sexed siblings of neur. p.	—	—	1	11	11	2
Opposite-sexed siblings of neur. p.	—	—	3	6	13	2
Siblings of neur. p. (total)	—	—	4	17	24	4

A unidimensional scale like this is, of course, open to the criticism, for instance, that qualitatively dissimilar disorders fall within the same category if they represent, quantitatively, the same level of disturbance. Category IV is particularly heterogeneous: the most typical diagnoses belonging to it were, in our series, schizoid and paranoid character disorders, alcoholism, psychopathies and extremely severe character neuroses; other syndromes in this category included drug addictions and sexual perversions. As I see it, this kind of classification is nonetheless justifiable where the intention is to obtain a general picture in a comparative study, especially when problems associated with the proneness to psychosis are concerned: a common characteristic of the disorders in category IV, and simultaneously one distinguishing these from the neuroses, is the presence of comparatively grave disturbances in the functions of the ego. In our series, the line of demarcation between the disorders characteristic of the schizophrenia families and those characteristic of the neuroses families ran in fact between categories IV and III, and this can be regarded as an indication of the clinical importance of the classification. Borderline psychotic traits (category V) are, in turn, an indication of still more serious disturbances of the ego; that is, disturbances which already imperil reality testing. It would probably be advisable—in epidemiological studies, for example, where use is made of a classification like this—to assign not only schizophrenic but also other manifest functional psychoses to category VI.

Senile deterioration and other kinds of organically based deterioration of the psychic functions naturally formed a problem. We made an attempt to eliminate the effects of these from our scale through assigning each of the parents in the category corresponding to his psychic situation during his most central years of adulthood. Nevertheless, the subjects who had suffered from a schizophrenic or other functional psychosis ending in remission were placed in category VI or category V.

Statistical analysis revealed that disorders graver than neurotic were highly significantly more frequent in schizophrenic patients' parents than in neurotic patients' parents ($\chi^2 = 34 \cdot 35$; $p < 0 \cdot 001$). A similar, highly significant difference was also found between the siblings of schizophrenic patients and those of neurotic patients ($\chi^2 = 14 \cdot 12$; $p < 0 \cdot 001$). On the other hand, when neurotic-level disturbances were also taken into account, the emerging difference was only almost significant ($\chi^2 = 4 \cdot 11$; $p < 0 \cdot 05$). The difference between the same-sexed and the opposite-sexed siblings of schizophrenic patients failed to reach a statistically significant level, owing to the limited number of subjects. On the other hand, certain significant differences between these groups were found in the psychological test results. Perhaps the most interesting of these—it was discovered by Mr. Takala only afterwards—was the one between series of siblings in our schizophrenia families which only included children of one sex and those consisting of children of both sexes. He found that in the latter, i.e. in mixed series of siblings, the average ego strength, according to the Rorschach test, was almost significantly better, as compared with the former series (Becker's Ego Strength Scale: $\chi^2 = 6 \cdot 07$; $p < 0 \cdot 02$).

Chaotic and rigid families. Comments on environmental versus genetic transmission

Our investigation strongly supported the view that—when the problem of schizophrenia is being approached from a psychodynamic aspect—attention must be given to the entire interactional dynamics of the family network rather than to the mother–child relationship alone. That this is so was already suggested by the gravely disturbed marriages of our patients' parents: our findings confirmed those of Lidz *et al.* concerning the "schismatic" or "skewed" nature of these marriages. Compared with the marriages of the parents of our schizophrenic patients, those of the parents of our neurotics appeared "well integrated"; i.e. they were characterized by mutual solidarity, in spite of the spouses' disorders and even conflicts.

The study of the marital disturbances of the parents of schizophrenic patients revealed, however, that these were traceable to frustrations and developmental inhibitions that had already begun in their own childhood homes and to their persistent infantile and dependent strivings, which the other, equally immature partner of the marital union was unable to meet. The result was a vicious circle of mutual, additional emotional frustrations and dilapidation, completed and perpetuated by ungratified dependent needs, which easily led to the parent to seek gratification from the offspring. This pathogenic train of disturbed emotional relationships, proceeding from generation to generation, is a phenomenon very familiar to those with experience in the family therapy of schizophrenics.

In investigating the general atmosphere in the families of schizophrenics—as an environment for the children to grow up in—we encountered two predominant patterns, that clearly differed from those met in our neurotic patients' families, which were either better organized or were marked by lesser disorders of emotional relationships. We termed these families in our schizophrenia series chaotic and rigid respectively. The atmosphere of predominantly chaotic families was incoherent and irrational, often disproportionately dominated by one parent's psychotic or borderline-level thought and behaviour disorders. As for the rigid families, typical of them was an atmosphere coloured by an extreme inelasticity of role constellations and emotional impoverishment, and by the unbending nature of the attitudes and expectations that one or both parents directed on to the children. Ten of our thirty families were chaotic and 11 were rigid; 6 families formed an intermediary group, exhibiting features characteristic of both main types; and 3 remained outside of this classification or were "untypical", approximating, however, to the "rigid" group.

This classification has to do with the two basic components of normal parental functions. Parents are important for their children's development as persons from whom the children learn things and as the children's earliest emotional objects. Gross disturbances of the former function were particularly pronounced in chaotic families, whereas disturbances of the latter were characteristic of rigid families—though it must be added that in many families in our schizophrenia series both functions were disordered.

When the situation was looked at from the children's standpoint, it seemed legitimate to assume that, in chaotic families, they had "learned" and adopted their parents' disturbed behaviours through identification. And, perhaps more important, the children's possibilities of learning from their parents' skills and abilities adequate for good inward adjustment and adjustment to the extra-familial social environment were very defective. In the rigid families, on the other hand, the parents' intrusive and dominating—and often mutually incompatible —need expectations, based upon their own frustrations, seemed to be particularly noxious to the children: they tied the child to a pathogenic circle, from which it was difficult for him to rid himself, thus "driving" him to a failure of individuation and to an autistic or symbiotic regression.

It should be emphasized that intrusive parents were also met in the chaotic families. And though these parents were perhaps not as consistently strict as those encountered in the rigid families, they were persons who were governed by very deviant need projections and whose self-boundaries regarding the child were in many cases wholly undifferentiated. The chaotic families of this kind differed most clearly from the rigid ones, in that they were characterized not only by disturbed emotional relationships but also by a network of persistent paralogic patterns. In certain of these families, it was apparently the patient child that was the most definitely perplexed member and the one whose attempts to build an identity of his (or her) own had failed most totally.

Almost all of the patients' siblings whom we regarded as "normal", as well as the neurotic siblings, came from rigid or atypical families, whereas a majority of the siblings who exhibited borderline psychotic features or were psychopaths were members of chaotic families. This observation, the significance of which is of course limited by the smallness of our series, is very compatible with the assumption that the preconditions for an adequate ego development are particularly poor in chaotic families. On the other hand, the positions of the various siblings in the family dynamics differed most clearly in the rigid families. There, the patient had invariably been fettered more by the pathogenic family dynamics than had the other children; for example, the patient had become the other member of a symbiosis induced by the mother, or, in the case of schismatic families, the patient had been traumatized particularly badly by the parents' chronic conflicts. In several cases the position of the healthier siblings had been quite different. The differences among the sibling positions were particularly conspicuous in the families where the healthy siblings were not of the same sex as the patient. In the rare cases where the patients from rigid families also had gravely disturbed siblings, the latter had been subject to much the same parental attitudes as the patient had been.

The concept of heterogeneity among the families of different kinds of schizophrenics has also been recently emphasized by Wynne and Singer (1963) and Singer and Wynne (1965). Though we did not approach this question from quite the same aspect as they did, one similarity between our observations is worth mentioning here. There are schizophrenics who, apparently owing to identification processses, manifest disorders very similar to those exhibited by their parents; and there are others who are very dissimilar to their parents but, through disordered behaviour, meet their parents' expectations, so as to be complementary to them. Investigation of the background of patients of the latter type generally leads to the discovery of a very dominating parent, who has developed a symbiotic relationship with the patient, the patient being an "extension" of the parent, rather than a person with an independent identity. It was of some interest to note that this was so for several rigid families with no earlier family history of psychosis.

In this context I propose to present a few comments on the interrelation between genetic and environmental transmission patterns, suggested by our series. According to our findings, there can exist both genetic and environmental transmission mechanisms. We encountered two main patterns of environmental transmission, one of which was associated with the faulty identifications, in the chaotic families, the other bound with the pathogenic emotional relationships especially characteristic of the rigid families. As can be expected, a more specific, genetic transmission of schizophrenia—if there is such a transmission—and a transmission of psychotic patterns through faulty identifications overlap in chaotic families. The schizophrenic parents and a majority of the patients' schizophrenic second-degree relatives too were found in the chaotic family group. Thus it seems possible to assume that the occurrence of schizophrenia in these families is more closely associated with a hereditary predisposition than it is in rigid families. This is an open question and one of the points which the study of schizophrenic parents' children who have grown up in a non-schizophrenic environment might better elucidate.

The fact that neurotic and psychopathic disorders were more frequent than schizophrenic psychoses in the siblings of schizophrenic patients speaks against the view that schizophrenia is a disorder specifically different from other psychic disturbances. Rather, the emergence of schizophrenia seems to be the gravest expression of the family's general tendency toward mental disorders (Alanen *et al.,* 1963). Our own views are supported in this respect by, for example, the findings of Atkinson *et al.,* of Newcastle, in a study on which a preliminary report was presented at the Madrid Congress in 1966; this is so, despite the fact that the diagnostics employed by these investigators were obviously far more conservative than those applied by us in Finland. Results pointing in the same direction have also been obtained in the twin studies by Tienari (1963) and Kringlen (1964), who have been led to emphasize the relative nature of the genetic predisposition and the importance of the factors associated with the family dynamics.

In my opinion, it is natural to think that both sets of factors affecting the development of the human personality, that is, his hereditary endowment, consisting of the genes, and the experiential influences associated with his environment of growth, also bear the disturbances in the development of the personality. This view found support in the findings, for instance, which we made in analysing the reasons for differences in the development of children in the same family. As already mentioned, we discovered psychological factors associated, for example, with parental attitudes determined by the child's sex and with the child's identification opportunities. The stress situation encountered by the mother at the time surrounding the child's birth, and the effects of these upon her later relationship with the child, retained their place as a component of the over-all picture. Yet it appeared highly probable that structural (genetically based) psychological factors—though they are very difficult to distinguish from the later influences—also had played an important part in many families. An illustrative example of these is provided by a child who is innately more passive than his siblings, and who, owing to this very fact, is selected by the mother as the child on to whom she most definitely directs her own dependent needs. Let us specify this hypothesis as follows: It is possible to think that, in a disturbed family environment, a greater innate passivity or inclination to introversion in some particular child would act as one of the selective factors predisposing to later schizophrenic development.

Findings of family studies and psycho-analytic theory

From the very outset I was interested in the relationship between family study findings and psycho-analytic theory. The gist of the matter was the disproportionate stress that the psycho-analytic authors I had read placed upon the early oral frustrations and fixations, as compared with other factors involved in the family dynamics. As the last part of my presentation, I would like to propose some points dealing with the integration of family studies with psycho-analytic conceptions.

The first point which I wish to emphasize is this: The "classical" psycho-analytic hypotheses concerning schizophrenia are fallacious in that they rest too exclusively upon the libido psychology, disregarding the fact that schizophrenia is a regressive illness of the ego, viz. of the adaptive functions of the personality. This point may seem self-evident, but, in the revision of psycho-analytic theory, it has not been attended to sufficiently (to be sure, one attempted revision has been made by Arlow and Brenner, 1964).

Secondly, in the disturbed ego development, enough attention must be devoted not only to the early stage of differentiation of the ego—which is also important—but also to the subsequent phase of the individuation of the self, during which the future schizophrenic patient does not achieve sufficient independence but remains in a heightened dependence upon his parents. Our investigations suggested that—judging from the patient's and their siblings' sex identifications as reflected in the interests and personality traits revealed by the psychological tests—a stable identification with the parents was clearly in an inverse relation to the remaining dependence upon the parents. Lidz *et al.* have also recently (1965) given attention to the fact that "the deficiency in a sense of autonomy" forms a critical aspect if schizophrenia; and that "the patient does not feel capable of guiding his own life but seeks direction and decision from others" (including hallucinated or delusional extrojects). I share this view, although it seems to me that the characterization of schizophrenia as a deficiency disease is not very felicitous, since this name does not pay enough attention to the aspects associated with the interactional point of view, the mutual need dynamics and relationship between parents and children (cf. also the "pathologic need complementarity" emphasized by Boszormenyi-Nagy, 1962).

The third point to which I wish to call attention is that the problems associated with the disturbances of the oedipal phase also have a considerable bearing on schizophrenia—even though it has been customary to emphasize them in connection with neurotic rather than psychotic disorders. Although a tendency towards regression is based to a large extent upon earlier fixations, leading to autistic tendencies, one cannot help realizing, in becoming acquainted with these family environments, how enormously problematic—it is anxiety and guilt-provoking—many of them are from the viewpoint of this particular phase. The son of a possessive mother, whose father is either passive or paranoidally jealous—and this was quite a common constellation in the families of our male schizophrenics—is especially prone to develop unresolvable ties with his mother, incestuous anxieties, guilt problems and a disturbed sexual identity. The same applies to the daughter in a schismatic family whose mother is very jealous of her daughter for the affection the daughter receives from her father. In the case of our neurotic patients, the preconditions for the mastery of oedipal problems appeared far better, owing to the parents' more balanced mutual relationship.

The general chaotic or rigid nature of the families of the schizophrenic patients should, of course, also be invariably kept in mind.

It seems to me that one of the reasons why the ego development of schizophrenic patients is disturbed lies in the conflicting needs and emotions they direct toward their different parents. This conflict culminates at the oedipal stage: it is not at all possible for them to integrate and neutralize these strivings, which still remain drifting in their world of fantasy leading to later psychosexual disorders and to a heightened inclination to regression. More than one of my schizophrenic psychotherapy patients has stated that his father and mother relationships are separate, mutually incompatible matters. A defective integration of the ego functions at this stage probably also plays a part in the general difficulty to master interpersonal relationships involving more than one object, which is characteristic of schizophrenic patients.

In my opinion, this kind of view concerning the development of the ego is very compatible with what psycho-analytic ego psychology, in the form represented by Rapaport, for example, maintains about the significance of the neutralization processes for the development of the defensive apparatus of the ego (Rapaport, 1951). In schizophrenic patients these processes of neutralization have remained defective and the underlying infantile instinctual strivings chaotically uncontrolled.

The last point which I propose to make is as follows. In many schizophrenic patients the autistic tendencies, which, in my opinion, are predominantly regressive, come to occupy an important position even during the infantile development. In other patients, a regression takes place suddenly, during adolescence, when the flimsy integration of the ego gives way under the pressure of the person's inward instinctual drives—often at a stage when the protective dependency ties with the parents have been weakened (Alanen et al., 1965). These patients in particular feel an intense need for new identifications, which would help them towards improved ego mastery—but similar needs, though more latent, are also observable in patients of the former type.[1] The existence of such needs supports the view that disturbances in both the early and the later ego development play a role in the pathogenesis of schizophrenia. These needs for identification—which I termed the ego's dependency needs in my monograph—are one of our strongest allies in the psychotherapy of schizophrenia. They are interesting from the viewpoint of psycho-analytic theory and they are in need of further study.

REFERENCES

ALANEN, Y. O. (1956) On the personality of the mother and early mother–child relationship of 100 schizophrenic patients, *Acta psychiat. neurol. scand.* **31**, Suppl. 106, 227–34.

ALANEN, Y. O. (1958) The mothers of schizophrenic patients, *Acta psychiat. neurol. scand.* **33**, Suppl. 124.

ALANEN, Y. O. (1960a) Über die Familiensituation der Schizophrenie–Patienten, *Acta psychother.* **8**, 89–104.

ALANEN, Y. O. (1960b) Some thoughts of schizophrenia and ego development in the light of family investigations, *Arch. Gen. Psychiat. (Chicago)* **3**, 650–6.

ALANEN, Y. O., J. REKOLA, A. STEWEN, M. TUOVINEN, K. TAKALA, and E. RUTANEN (1963) Mental disorders in the siblings of schizophrenic patients, *Acta psychiat. scand.* **39**, Suppl. 169, 167–75.

---

[1] These strivings for identification are, depending on the level of the ego functions, "primary" in nature, in that the line of division between object and self remains vague, and/or "secondary", bearing a resemblance to the way in which a normal child constructs his ego (cf. the discussion of these types of identification in Sandler, 1960).

ALANEN, Y. O., J. K. REKOLA, A. STEWEN, K. TAKALA, and M. TUOVINEN (1965) On factors influencing the onset of schizophrenia in the light of a family study, *Confin. Psychiat.* **8,** 1–8.

ALANEN, Y. O., in collaboration with J. K. REKOLA, A. STEWEN, K. TAKALA, and M. TUOVINEN (1966) The family in the pathogenesis of schizophrenic and neurotic disorders, *Acta psychiat. scand.* **42,** Suppl. 189.

ARLOW, J. A. and C. BRENNER (1964) *Psychoanalytic Concepts and the Structural Theory,* Internat. Univ. Press, New York.

ATKINSON, M. W., D. W. KAY, D. ROMNEY, and R. F. GARSIDE (1966) A preliminary report of enquiries into the contribution of hereditary and environmental factors in the aetiology of schizophrenia, Paper read at the IVth World Congress of Psychiatry in Madrid.

BOSZORMENYI-NAGY, I. and J. L. FRAMO (1962) The concept of schizophrenia from the perspective of family treatment, *Family Process* **1,** 103–13.

HILL, L. B. (1955) *Psychotherapeutic Intervention in Schizophrenia,* Univ. of Chicago Press, Chicago.

KRINGLEN, E. (1964) Schizophrenia in male monozygotic twins, *Acta psychiat. scand.* **40,** Suppl. 178.

LIDZ, T., A. R. CORNELISON, S. FLECK, and D. TERRY (1957a) The intrafamilial environment of the schizophrenic patient: I. The father, *Psychiatry* **20,** 329–42.

LIDZ, T., A. R. CORNELISON, S. FLECK, and D. TERRY (1957b) Marital schism and marital skew, *Am. J. Psychiat.* **114,** 241–8.

LIDZ, T., A. CORNELISON, D. TERRY, and S. FLECK (1958) The transmission of irrationality, *AMA Arch. Neurol. Psychiat.* **79,** 305–16.

LIDZ, T. and S. FLECK (1965) Family studies and a theory of schizophrenia, in T. Lidz, S. Fleck, and A. R. Cornelison, *Schizophrenia and the Family,* Internat. Univ. Press, New York.

RAPAPORT, D. (1951) The autonomy of the ego, *Bull. Menninger Clinic* **15,** 113–23.

SANDLER, J. (1960) On the concept of superego, in the *Psychoanalytic Study of the Child,* Vol. XVII.

SINGER, M. T. and L. C. WYNNE (1965) Thought disorders and family relations of schizophrenics: III–IV, *Arch. Gen. Psychiat. (Chicago)* **12,** 187–212.

TIENARI, P. (1963) Psychiatric illnesses in identical twins, *Acta psychiat. scand.* **39,** Suppl. 171.

WYNNE, L. C. and M. T. SINGER (1963) Thought disorder and family relations in schizophrenia: I–II, *Arch. Gen. Psychiat. (Chicago)* **9,** 191–206.

FAMILY INTERACTION AND SCHIZOPHRENIA: ALTERNATIVE FRAMEWORKS OF INTERPRETATION

ELLIOT G. MISHLER and NANCY E. WAXLER

Massachusetts Mental Health Center and Harvard Medical School,
Boston, Massachusetts

WE HAVE recently completed an intensive study of relationships between schizophrenia and family interaction. Rather than reporting our findings in detail, we would like to discuss a problem that came to be of critical importance in our work particularly at the late stages of data analysis and interpretation. It is a problem that has received far too little attention, systematic or otherwise, from other investigators in this area, and it would seem particularly appropriate that we begin to repair this neglect at a conference concerned with the transmission of schizophrenia. I am referring to the problem of interpretation, that is, of how to interpret the findings of our own and others' empirical studies that there are consistent differences in patterns of interaction between the families of schizophrenic patients and other types of families. It will be evident, as we proceed, that the issues involved bear more than a passing resemblance to those raised and reviewed in several other papers presented at the conference, particularly those that focused on alternative genetic models as explanations of concordance studies.

The type of family used for comparison purposes varies from study to study depending upon the inclinations and interests of different investigators. Sometimes normal families, that is families with no history of clinical pathology, constitute the control; sometimes families of patients with non-psychiatric illness; and, sometimes families with non-psychotic but psychologically disturbed or socially deviant members. The findings of many studies, our own included, suggest that families with schizophrenic patients differ in significant ways from each of these other types of families. The first problem in research in a new area— and these studies represent a relatively new line of investigation—is to demonstrate stable and consistent findings, and it is understandable that in assessing research on families of schizophrenics we have until now been concerned primarily with issues of methodology and the comparability and consistency of different findings. These problems are still with us. However, there is now sufficient evidence that these families are different, and we must begin to consider the equally important question of what these differences mean. In essence, how are we to interpret and account for the findings? We would like to share with you our current thinking on this problem particularly as it has developed in our own work around the meaning and interpretation of specific findings.[1]

[1] We learned of Richard Q. Bell's work on the "direction of effects" problem in child development research only after developing our own approach to problems of interpretation in studies of family interaction and schizophrenia. There are close parallels between our respective analyses. (See Bell, 1959–60, 1964, 1968.)

O

The source of the problem is not difficult to find. Most investigators begin with an etiological interest, that is they study family backgrounds and relationships in order to determine some of the causes of schizophrenia. However, with the exception of a few follow-up studies that use clinic records, studies that focus on family relationships are *ex post facto* investigations—that is, data are collected on families only after schizophrenia has been recognized and diagnosed, and the designated family member has been assigned a role as a patient within a psychiatric treatment facility. Thus all the information about those factors that we wish to treat as independent variables in a causal equation is gathered after the dependent variable itself has already appeared. We are faced with the problem of attributing causality to events about which we know only that they exist after the occurrence of the event that we are trying to predict. Further, it is obvious that the variables of central interest, namely family structure and dynamics, may be particularly sensitive to the presence of schizophrenia; they are not independent variables in the sense in which this term is typically used.

We shall turn shortly to some of the ways in which problems of analyzing and interpreting data in *ex post facto* studies have been approached by social researchers engaged in other types of studies, but wish to note in passing that this is a general problem in the study of illness and is not restricted to the study of schizophrenia and the family. Investigators working within biological and psychological traditions tend to assume that their variables are more basic than the symptoms of the illness, and for this reason that they functioned prior to and remained unaffected by the illness. It might be worth while to question whether or not this is always a useful or legitimate assumption in biological and psychological research. In the social sciences we have never been able to afford the luxury of this particular questionable assumption. It may be for this reason, that problems having to do with the interpretation of causality seem to make their first appearance in our work.

The problem may begin to sound familiar, but this should not obscure its importance nor the difficulties in arriving at a reasonable solution. Some of the solutions that have been proposed deserve closer and more critical analysis than they have received. Some investigators, for example, have argued that if marked differences are found between families of schizophrenic patients and other families on significant aspects of family functioning, and where these differences also fit with some theoretically derived hypothesis, that this empirical fact is in itself enough to argue for the etiological relevance of this family variable. The argument seems to run as follows: Important aspects of family relationships do not change easily, the dimensions studied have an obvious and phenomenal stability in everyday experience, therefore, they must have existed prior to the development of schizophrenia. Suppose we find, for example, that mothers and their schizophrenic sons form an intense, interacting dyad that excludes and isolates the father from important important areas of family decision-making. Although there is no *a priori* theoretical or logical justification for assuming that because a relationship is strong after an event that it was strong before it, it is nevertheless argued that the mother–son bind must have existed prior to the onset of schizophrenia. The finding is used in turn to support a particular etiological theory, in this instance, on the importance of the symbiotic attachment to the mother, neglecting the fact that this theory itself was based on similar *post hoc* data.

A few investigators, on the other hand, have countered the etiological explanation with a responsive interpretation of family differences. They point out that parents have had to adapt to a child exhibiting schizophrenic behavior. New ways of relating to each other may emerge. A deviant child's need for control, protection, and support may, for example, pressure the mother into a close and intense relationship with him that results in effectively isolating the father. Over time, these post-illness patterns stabilize and become resistant to change. Thus, findings of a strong mother–child relationship may also be used to provide support for a responsive interpretation. A third locus of explanation is the present situation of the patient and the family. The patient has been hospitalized and familes of patients may define the research situation differently and have different expectations and concerns regarding the possible use to be made of the information than normal control families. The differences in interaction that we find may reflect their differential relationship to the hospital and to the investigator and the research setting rather than the presence of a schizophrenic child.

These contrasting frameworks or models of interpretation—that current patterns of behavior existed prior to the development of schizophrenia, that these behaviors were adaptive responses to the illness, and that families have differential orientations to the research situation—could each provide plausible explanations of experimental findings. The problem is whether there are methodological procedures that would allow us to separate these explanations, to clarify their requirements and implications, and perhaps to assess their relative credibility as explanations.

I must mention still another alternative that attempts to bypass the distinctions we have made and the problems they pose. This is a transactional or field theory of behavior. Causality in this view should be approached in terms of complex feed-back models or sets of interdependent forces; attempts to isolate one factor such as prior family relationships as an etiological agent in schizophrenia are viewed as naïve and unlikely to be productive. This approach marks a different strategy for research and theory-building from our own. We believe that problems of causal analysis are not solved by simply asserting a transactional point of view. Distinctions among variables must still be made, the direction, form, and strength of their relationships must still be determined. The limitations of the simpler causal models that we have compared with each other can be understood only after detailed analysis of their relevance and applicability to various empirical findings. The results of such analyses will help to clarify the requirements of the more complex models that may be necessary, and these may turn out to be transactional ones.

The problems of sorting out and comparing alternative causal models in *ex post facto* research is not restricted to family studies. A number of methodologists in the social sciences have been concerned with this type of study and with the development of techniques of study design and analysis that permit sorting out the effects of different variables. (Greenwood, 1945; Chapin, 1955; Hyman, 1955.) Hyman, in the most recent of these discussions of analytic procedures for sample survey data, defines it as a problem in the time ordering of variables and suggests various criteria and procedures for determining the order in which variables had their effect (pp. 193–226).

We have been exploring these problems of interpretation of *ex post facto* data by trying to develop consistent explanations for differences found in our study between normal families and the families of schizophrenic patients. We have approached the problem by asking, for each of our empirical findings, how the findings could be interpreted within each of three alternative frameworks or models of explanation: an etiological, a responsive and a situational model. This has led us to be explicit about and sensitive to the additional assumptions that must be introduced and the inferences that must be made for each of these to provide an adequate explanation for the data.

Before examining how this was done, a brief description of our study is necessary (details may be found in Mishler and Waxler, 1966, 1968). We used the revealed difference technique to generate discussions among parents and one of their own children. On one occasion the parents participated with their schizophrenic child and on another with a well sibling of the patient of the same sex and approximately the same age. The design of the study included both male and female patients and patients with good and poor premorbid adjustments. There was a normal control group of families in the study which also included paired siblings of the same sex and similar age (Table 1).

TABLE 1. RESEARCH DESIGN: NUMBERS OF EXPERIMENTAL SESSIONS
FOR DIFFERENT TYPES OF FAMILIES*

Type of family	Family of male patient Session		Family of female patient Session	
	Patient	Sibling	Patient	Sibling
Patient				
Good premorbid	5	5	7	3
Poor premorbid	15	14	3	3
	Sibling₁	Sibling₂	Sibling₁	Sibling₂
Normal	10	10	6	7

* A total N of 88 experimental sessions of which 78 are paired sessions where the parents (N = 39) came on two occasions, once with the patient and once with his/her sibling. The remaining 10 sessions are contributed by 10 sets of parents who came only once resulting in 7 unmatched patient sessions and 3 unmatched sibling sessions.

Discussions among these family triads were transcribed and the resultant typescripts analyzed in a blind procedure through the use of an extensive series of code-category systems (Waxler and Mishler, 1967). These produced a large number of quantitative indices of interaction that form the main variables in our analyses. The method of statistical analysis used permits separating the effects that are specific to individual family members, that is fathers, mothers, or children, or to each of the experimental sessions, that is when the patient or his well sibling is present, as well as allowing a determination of effects that apply to the family as a whole across both discussion situations (Mishler and Waxler, 1967). As illustrations, we will be using data that involve comparisons of normal families with the families of patients with good and poor premorbid social adjustments. Our empirical questions are always: Are there significant differences among these three types of families, and what is the order of the relationship among them? Our interpretive questions are: Can we make sense of the empirical findings from the point of view of an etiological, a responsive, and a situational model of interpretation? What additional assumptions and inferences must be introduced to support each of the models?

In asking the interpretive questions, we are interested in comparing the adequacy and relevance of the alternative models. As we noted earlier, they differ primarily in the assumption each makes about the time ordering of variables. The etiological model assumes that the patterns of family interaction displayed in our experimental situation existed prior to the onset of schizophrenia; the responsive model reverses this time order; the situational model shifts the focus to the effects of hospitalization. The problem of sorting out and comparing these explanations with each other is present in all *ex post facto* studies, and the procedures suggested by Hyman are similar to those we have used. Essentially, they involve the use of other variables as statistical controls in the analysis of data, or an assessment of the fit of the data to one or another theoretical expectation, or the introduction into the line of argument of additional inferences and assumptions about the populations studied or the variables measured.

Our research design allows for a number of control analyses. For example, by having two experimental sessions, one of which includes the patient and the other his well sibling, we could control in the analysis of data for the presence of the patient as a factor influencing how the parents interact. If we find that parents behave differently in the two sessions this would support an interpretation based on the status of a child as a patient and would be evidence against a situational interpretation, since the experimental conditions and the relationship of the family to the hospital and to the research setting remain much the same from session to session; in this connection, in order to avoid order effects we varied having the patient come to the first or second family session. In comparing etiological and responsive models with each other, it was necessary to introduce additional assumptions that take into account both the substance of the variable as well as the patterning of findings. In essence, we argued as follows: If there are differences between the normal families and the families of both types of schizophrenic patients, and these differences are consistent with current theories about the etiology of schizophrenia and with our understanding of normal personality development, then this is ground for support for an etiological model. On the other hand, if there are striking differences between the families of the two types of schizophrenic patients on dimensions of behavior that would seem to be sensitive to the severity and recency of disturbance or stress, there would be support for a responsive model.

Let me turn from this general discussion of our approach to some concrete examples drawn from our findings.

One of our measures is an index we have labeled acknowledgment, or responsiveness to others. This is an important variable in a number of theories about the families of schizophrenics. A familiar variant is the notion that the schizogenic mother is impervious to, that is, does not acknowledge, the needs of her child. We found a pattern of findings in the families of female patients where Normal families were most acknowledging, Good families next and Poor premorbid families least acknowledging, a direction of findings that would be consistent with assumptions about the degree of pathology in the children.

These findings are presented in Table 2 in the format developed for presenting the results of the complex statistical analyses undertaken in the study (Mishler and Waxler, 1967, 1968). Briefly, the column labeled "group analysis" refers to a comparison of Acknowledgment scores for the families as social wholes irrespective of member or session differences; these scores are attributes of the family rather than of particular members and provide our most general way of characterizing families. The next column, "roles and sessions", shows the results of partitioning these total family scores in two different ways—the different members and the two sessions. These analyses allow us to examine differences across fathers in the three types of families separately from differences across mothers and children; further we can compare family differences when the patient is present and separately when the well sibling is present. Finally, in the last column, "roles and sessions", there are analyses at the most detailed level, that is the behavior of family members within each of the experimental sessions. These latter analyses show whether or not there are differences, for example

TABLE 2. Acknowledgment: Families of Female Patients

Group analysis				Roles and sessions					Roles within sessions				
H	M	L	p		H	M	L	p		H	M	L	p
Fam_c [N	G	P] ·05		Fa_c	N	P	G	—	Fa₁	N	P	G	—
				Mo_c	N	G	P	·20	Fa₂	N	G	P	—
				Ch_c [N	G	P] ·05			Mo₁ [N	G	P] ·05	
				Fam₁ [N	P	G] ·10			Mo₂.	N	P	G	—
				Fam₂	N	G	P	—	Pt. [N [G	P]] ·10	
									Sib	N	G	P	—

The letters N, G, P refer respectively to the Normal, Good premorbid and Poor premorbid families in the study.

The letters H, M, L refer to High, Middle, and Low Mean rank of the group of families. p values for the Kruskal–Wallis H-test are listed. Brackets between pairs of ranks refer to p-values for the Mann–Whitney U-test: ·10 ⌐‒‒‒¬, ·05 ⌐‒‒‒¬.

across fathers in one, both, or neither experimental session. The argument underlying this approach to the statistical analysis of data is too complex for full presentation here and the reader is referred to the sources noted above. Essentially, the approach allows us to distinguish effects at different levels of conceptual and statistical analysis, that is, group, individual, and situational effects. In turn, this results in a more precise statement of the nature and significance of the differences found between the normal and the two types of patient families.

The findings on Acknowledgment in Table 2 provide a good illustration of the implications of the approach. We noted that there was a general pattern of findings with Normal families being more acknowledging than Good who were more acknowledging than Poor premorbid families. This is evident in the group analysis column. However, it seems both more important and more interesting to discover that the pattern of differences tends to be specific to the schizophrenic daughter and to her mother only in situations where she is interacting with her schizophrenic daughter. (Note the findings in the role-within-session column.) This is a highly specific pattern that seemed to us to be most consistent with an etiological theory. It is specific to particular members of the family interacting with each other, the degree of nonresponsiveness is directly related to the severity of the patient's illness, and the differences are consistent with etiological theories based on other data and observations.

There are also instances where an etiological interpretation of the data appeared to require the introduction of assumptions about more general cultural prescriptions and social norms. For example, we found consistent differences in our analysis of parents in male families in rates of expressiveness, or affective behavior, where Normal fathers and mothers were more expressive than the parents of Poor premorbid patients who in turn were more expressive than the parents of Good premorbid patients. But these differences were present to a statistically significant degree only in experimental sessions where the patient was present and not in the situations with his well sibling. This pattern could be considered as consistent with etiological theories about the relative rigidity and coldness of parents when dealing with their schizophrenic child since the parents do not differ from normal parents when with the well sibling. However, these differences do not appear in our analyses of families of female patients. Here, in our interpretation, we argued that general cultural norms regarding overall levels of expressive behavior from parents to daughters seem to be more potent than specific factors that might be conducive to the development of schizophrenia. In other words, there is a general level of affective behavior expected from parents to daughters whether or not she is schizophrenic.

In each of these instances, where etiological interpretations were introduced, it is clear that a responsive model might also have been used. For example, with regard to differentials in Acknowledgment it seems to us possible to argue that parents faced with a chronic schizophrenic child, with whom they have had to live for a long time, may have learned to ignore, that is fail to acknowledge or respond to his behavior so as to minimize disruption and disturbance within the family. This would mean that they would appear as least responsive. Good premorbid parents faced with a more recent illness remain more responsive but are less so than the normals. With regard to the findings on expressiveness and on other variables where Good premorbid families are found to be most different from the normals, we might argue that the stress of responding to schizophrenia, either as a general illness or in its specific manifestations, is still current for the parents and leads to more rigid non-expressive behavior putting them furthest away from the normals. Here it would be the recency of the stress of the illness that would be introduced as an additional important factor.

In these few examples drawn from our data we have tried to describe the problems and some aspects of our approach to the interpretation of data collected in *ex post facto* studies of families of schizophrenics. We found that even with a relatively large number of control comparisons built into the design of the study—namely, patient and well sibling sessions, two types of schizophrenia, Normal families, and both male and female patients—information external to the pattern of findings such as assumptions about interaction and the nature of the variables, and theories based on other data, had to be introduced to support one or another of the explanatory models. Thus in order to make a judgment about the time order of the major variables—the family interaction patterns and the occurrence of schizophrenia in the child—additional inferences based on other information were always necessary. We found it particularly difficult to sort out an etiological from a responsive explanation. Each has seemed to us overall to be an equally parsimonious and reasonable model, and the data collected at one point in time in an *ex post facto* study do not allow us to decide between them without the addition of other assumptions.

The state of our knowledge about schizophrenia and the role of family processes makes it a foregone conclusion that a study of their relationships must end with suggestions for further research rather than with a catalogue of definitive findings. From our analysis of problems of interpretation, we think certain types of studies take on more importance and therefore that some priorities can be established. In this last section, we shall emphasize various types of research design rather than particular variables. This is because the solution to general interpretative questions, that is to the relative credibility of etiological or responsive models, lies in the area of research design. The usefulness of particular substantive theories for our understanding of families and schizophrenia can be assessed only when these variables are studied empirically within strong research designs focused specifically on these general questions of interpretation.

Given the problems of interpretation that inhere in *ex post facto* designs, it is natural to turn to longitudinal studies. On the face of it, longitudinal studies would seem to solve many of our problems since the time order of variables could be determined directly, and etiological and responsive explanations could than be clearly separated from each other. The benefits of such designs are undoubtedly great and we do not mean to diminish their importance by noting that they are hypothetical and ideal values; the practical and empirical difficulties of longitudinal studies make it likely that *ex post facto* research will continue to have a dominant place in future work. Among the numerous and well-known problems of longitudinal research are: sample attrition over time, the low incidence of schizophrenia with the consequent requirement of large study populations, the critical importance of the variables chosen for initial study, the effects on the data of repeated observation and study leading to complex multi-panel designs, the turnover of members of the research team, and the long delay before the analysis of data can be undertaken and findings generated. In addition, in studying schizophrenia there is the problem of determining its onset; can we state when it begins so that "before" and "after" measures can be separated from each other. (See Bell, 1959–60, for an interesting comparison of the problems of retrospective and prospective research.) We shall return below to some modified longitudinal designs, but these comments provide the grounds for beginning with a discussion of *ex post facto* designs which will continue to have a contribution to make to this area of study.

Our aim is to suggest designs that would help us to evaluate the relative usefulness and validity of situational, responsive and etiological interpretations of differences in interaction between patient and normal families. A situational interpretation assumes that the facts of patienthood and hospitalization have been primary determinants of family behavior. Designs to test this model would be relatively easy to develop since their primary feature would be the inclusion of control groups with illness and treatment histories similar to schizophrenic patient samples. The use of nonschizophrenic psychiatric patients such as character disorders (Reiss, 1966; Stabenau et al., 1965) is focused on this problem of separating out the specific features of schizophrenia from more general effects of patienthood, as is the use of patients with unspecified but nonpsychiatric illnesses (Lerner, 1965) or with a specific nonpsychiatric illness such as tuberculosis (Farina, 1960).

Such designs could be further strengthened if they included two sub-types of schizophrenia since such sub-classification—whether Good and Poor premorbid as in the present study, or chronic and acute or paranoid and nonparanoid as in other studies—has been shown to be of critical importance. In such a design, the nonschizophrenic patient sample should also be divided along a similar dimension so that in the end one would be able to compare, for example, families of chronic and acute schizophrenics with families of chronic and acute nonschizophrenic patients.

One modification of the usual experimental procedures could provide data in support of or counter to a responsive interpretation. If normal parents modified their behavior when with a schizophrenic patient in the direction of the behavior of his real parents, this would be evidence that the patient could evoke such behavior and a responsive interpretation would gain in credibility. One experiment with normal families has been reported (Leik, 1963) where families were rearranged into a number of different three-person groups; the extension of this type of design into the study of schizophrenics and their families would undoubtedly provide important data relevant to the problem of alternative interpretations of the relation of family process to schizophrenia.

Modifications of usual approaches to measurement and data analysis would also be useful in this connection. In particular, more attention to sequential patterns in interaction would allow us to determine whether, for example, parents actually do respond differently to certain types of behavior depending upon whether it is produced by their patient child or his well sibling. One investigator has reported differences in rates of intrusion by third parties into an ongoing two-party discussion (Lennard, 1965) and this is one approach to sequences. We are currently engaged in extended analyses of sequential patterns.

The design modifications suggested above still rely essentially on data collected at one point in time. Even *ex post facto* studies can be extended in time to cover distinct phases in the course of illness such as onset or recognition and diagnosis of the illness, hospitalization, symptom remission, return to the family, relapse or continued recovery. Studies of families through these phases would provide evidence with regard to the functional and adaptive significance for the family of the development of schizophrenia and of hospitaliztion. At this time, alternative hypotheses remain largely speculative—is the patient selected for patienthood and extruded so the family can maintain itself as an ongoing system or can the patient no longer be contained because the system of internal controls and patterns of management has broken down, or does the patient himself initiate and force the process either to escape from the family or as a way of expressing his hostility to his parents. Repeated investigations of families at different points in time would be a recognition of the fact that illness is not a static state but that there are changes over time and these changes are likely to be linked to changes in family behavior.

Such repeated studies of families after the onset of illness offer some of the advantages of longitudinal designs without some of the major practical difficulties, and if they incorporate some of the control groups suggested earlier would help to determine the relative power of a responsive model as an interpretive approach. The use of high-risk groups is a strategy for longitudinal research (cf. Mednick, 1967) that deserves more attention. These and more traditional longitudinal studies would gain from the inclusion of variables that located families within a wider social context. One of the peculiar omissions in the work on family interaction is its isolation from work on the social epidemiology of schizophrenia. Social class, social mobility, migration, and ethnicity, are among the factors found to be associated with differential incidence rates of schizophrenia (cf. Mishler and Scotch, 1963).

Given the high cost and the difficulties of longitudinal studes, it is particularly important that their designs be constructed in ways that permit us to determine the role of these macro-social variables and their relationship to patterns of family interaction in the development of schizophrenia.

We began our work with a number of our basic ideas drawn from the work of those who have been concerned with theories of etiology. Throughout our work, however, we remained somewhat cautious about the extent to which findings from our own and other similar studies could be brought to bear on questions of etiology. At this point, it is instructive to recall discussions at this conference of competing gentic models. Geneticists and researchers concerned with the problem of family concordance for schizophrenia have been at work for a long time, but research directed toward the evaluation of competing models has been difficult to design. I think that it is none too early for those of us studying family interaction to begin this process of clarifying and testing alternative models of explanation.

REFERENCES

BELL, R. Q. (1959–60) Retrospective and prospective views of early personality development, *Merrill–Palmer Quart.* **6**, 131–44.

BELL, R. Q. (1964) The effect on the family of a limitation in coping ability in the child: a research approach and a finding, *Merrill–Palmer Quart.* **10**, 129–42.

BELL, R. Q. (1968) A reinterpretation of the direction of effects in studies of socialization, *Psychol. Rev.* **75**, 81–95.

CHAPIN, F. S. (1955) *Experimental Designs in Sociological Research* (rev. ed.), New York, Harper.

FARINA, A. (1960) Patterns of role dominance and conflict in parents of schizophrenic patients, *J. Abnorm. Soc. Psychol.* **61**, 31–38.

GREENWOOD, E. (1945) *Experimental Sociology: A Study in Method*, New York, King's Crown Press.

HYMAN, H. (1955) *Survey Design and Analysis*, Glencoe, Illinois, Free Press.

LEIK, R. K. (1963) Instrumentality and emotionality in family interaction, *Sociometry* **26**, 131–45.

LENNARD, H. L., BEAULIEU, M. R., and EMBREY, N. G. (1965) Interaction in families with a schizophrenic child, *Arch. Gen. Psychiat.* **12**, 166–84.

LERNER, P. M. (1965) Resolution of intrafamilial role conflict in families of schizophrenic patients: I. Thought disturbance, *J. Nerv. Ment. Dis.* **141**, 342–51.

MEDNICK, S. A. (1967) A longitudinal study of children with a high risk for schizophrenia: first three-year follow-up, in *The Origins of Schizophrenia, Proceedings of the First Rochester International Conference on Schizophrenia, Amsterdam:* Excerpta Medica Foundation.

MISHLER, E. G. and SCOTCH, N. A. (1963) Sociocultural factors in the epidemiology of schizophrenia, *Psychiatry* **26**, 315–53. Also in *Internat. J. Psychiat.* **1**, 258–95 (1965).

MISHLER, E. G. and WAXLER, N. E. (1966) Family interaction and schizophrenia: an approach to the study of family interaction and schizophrenia, *Arch. Gen. Psychiat.* **15**, 64–74.

MISHLER, E. G. and WAXLER, N. E. (1967) Family interaction patterns and schizophrenia: A multi-level analysis, in *The Origins of Schizophrenia, Proceedings of the First Rochester International Conference on Schizophrenia, Amsterdam:* Excerpta Medica Foundation.

MISHLER, E. G. and WAXLER, N. E. (1968) *Interaction in Families: An Experimental Study of Family Processes and Schizophrenia*, New York, John Wiley.

REISS, D. (1967) Individual thinking and family interaction, *Arch. Gen. Psychiat.* **16**, 80–93.

STABENAU, J. R., TUPIN, J., WERNER, M., and POLLIN, W. (1965) A comparative study of families of schizophrenics, delinquents, and normals, *Psychiatry* **28**, 45–59.

WAXLER, N. E. and MISHLER, E. G. (1967) *Interaction Code Book,* mimeo.

FAMILY PROBLEM SOLVING: TWO EXPERIMENTS ON THE RELATIONSHIP BETWEEN FAMILY INTERACTION AND INDIVIDUAL THINKING IN FAMILIES OF SCHIZOPHRENICS, NORMALS AND CHARACTER DISORDERS*

DAVID REISS †

Massachusetts Mental Health Center, Boston, Massachusetts

SEVERAL major theories on the interpersonal origins of schizophrenia place great emphasis on a link between individual thinking and family interaction. For example Theodore Lidz and Lyman C. Wynne, in independent studies, propose that thought disorders of parents of schizophrenics influence interaction of their families and this interaction in turn warps the cognitive development of the offspring who ultimately become schizophrenic patients.[1] The present experiments are not a direct test of the Lidz or Wynne hypotheses of the origins of schizophrenia. They attempt, however, to develop methods and concepts for studying the links between individual thinking and family interaction, and, therefore, explore a central assumption of several major theories on the interpersonal origins of schizophrenia.

The first experiment was the *pattern recognition task*. In this, family members were asked to work together on a task that required them to organize and make inferences from a stream of information coming from an extra-familial source in the person of the experimenter. In the second experiment, the *information exchange task*, each family member worked with his family to organize and make inferences from a flow of information from others in his family. The findings of these experiments suggest a coherent picture of the way our individual subjects worked with their families to experience their environment.

Our sample consisted of five families in each of three groups: families of schizophrenics, normals and character disorders. In each family we used the parents, patient and sibling nearest in age. The normal group was chosen from school and church lists. The patient in the character disorder group had been psychiatrically hospitalized for difficulties in controlling impulsive behavior and was not schizophrenic. The schizophrenic patient had been hospitalized less than a year and had one or more of the following: associational disturbance, hallucinations or delusions or autistic and incoherent speech. The families were matched for age, education and intelligence.

* This research was completed while the author was a Research Fellow in the Laboratory on Social Psychology, Massachusetts Mental Health Center and was supported in part by grants from the Milton Fund, Harvard University and the Medical Foundation, Boston. The assistance of Elliot G. Mishler, Nancy E. Waxler and Lyman C. Wynne is gratefully acknowledged. More detailed descriptions of the current research have been published in *Arch. Gen. Psychiat.* **16**, 80–93 (1967) and *J. Psychiat. Res.* **5**, 193–211 (1967).

† *Present address:* Adult Psychiatry Branch, National Institute of Mental Health, Bethesda, Maryland.

PATTERN RECOGNITION EXPERIMENT

In this experiment we seek to discover how family members make use of each other's experience in gathering and organizing information to gain and give coherence to information they themselves obtain. Some of the experimental methods are derived from those used by Jerome Bruner and George Miller.[2]

When the family enters the laboratory they are seated at a set of booths arranged in a semicircle and shown in Fig. 1.

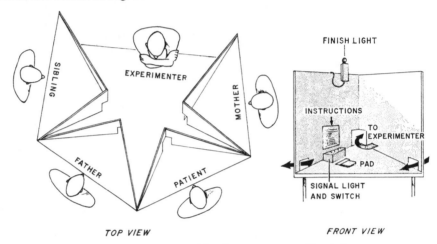

FIG. 1. Apparatus used for the pattern recognition task.

Note that each booth is connected to the others and to the experimenter's station by passageways. There is also a set of signal lights. There are three phases in the procedure.

Phase A. Initial private concept attainment

At first we ask each family member to work alone to form a concept from a small amount of information. We want to be sure that later in the task members will have a chance to learn from each other so we give the parents one kind of information and the children another; the consequences of this will be clear in Phase B. Specifically, in one problem, we gave a sequence of triangles, circles and squares to each member as shown in Fig. 2.

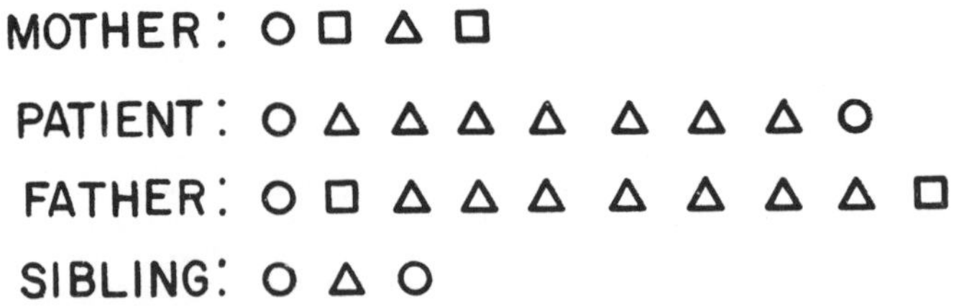

MOTHER: ○ □ △ □

PATIENT: ○ △ △ △ △ △ △ △ ○

FATHER: ○ □ △ △ △ △ △ △ △ □

SIBLING: ○ △ ○

FIG. 2. Example sequences given to the family in problem 2, pattern recognition task.

Note that children get sequences with a circle–triangles–circle pattern whereas parents get sequences with circle–square–triangles–square pattern. We tell each member to discover the sequential pattern in the sequence he is given and to test his recognition he is given a private inventory as shown in Fig. 3. He is asked to check those sequences he thinks have the same sequential pattern as his sample.

_ O △ △ △ △ △ △ △ O	_ □ □ O △ O O
_ O □ △ △ △ □	_ O △ △ O
_ O O △ O O □	_ O □ △ △ △ △ △ △ △ △ △ □
_ △ O O △ O	_ O △ △
_ O □ □ O	_ ⊃ □ △ △ △ △ △ □
_ O △ O O O O O △	_ O △ O △ △ O
_ O □ △ △ △ △ △ △ △ □	_ O □ □ □ □ □ □ □ O
_ O O	_ O □ △ △ □
_ O □ □ □ □ O	_ O △ △ △ △ △ △ O
_ O △ △ △ △ △ △ △ △ △ O	_ O △ O △ △

Fig. 3. Initial private inventory given to the families in problem 2, pattern recognition task.

Most parents checked off a group of sequences like that shown in Fig. 4, and most children like that shown in Fig. 5.

FATHER'S EXAMPLE: O O △ △ △ △ △ △ △ □

O □ △ △ △ □
O □ △ △ △ △ △ △ △ □
O □ △ △ △ △ △ △ △ △ △ □
O □ △ △ △ △ △ □
O □ △ △ □

Fig. 4. In one family a father accepted these sequences on the initial inventory of problem 2, pattern recognition task, and rejected the rest.

SIBLING'S EXAMPLE: O △ O

O △ △ △ △ △ △ △ △ O
O O
O △ △ △ △ △ △ △ △ △ △ O
O △ △ O
O △ △ △ △ △ △ O

Fig. 5. In the same family, sibling accepted these sequences on the initial inventory and rejected the rest.

At this point in the task parents seem to be expressing one pattern concept "circle–square–any number of triangles–square" and children another "circle–triangle–circle".

Phase B.   Collaborative effort by the family to get more information from the experimenter

Family members are now asked to work together to collect more information on the pattern concept they are trying to attain. They make up their own sequences. Each is submitted to the experimenter who rates them right or wong and then each is passed around for the others to see. The experimenter rates as correct any sequence that has the pattern of either the parents' or the children's examples. In most cases parents and children start off by testing sequences like their own examples. And since their examples are different so are their initial test sequences. And since these test sequences are circulated to everyone, parents have a chance to see their children trying something very different from themselves and vice versa. We want to know what use members make of this opportunity to learn from others. Families cannot talk. They learn from each other only by watching what sequences others make up.

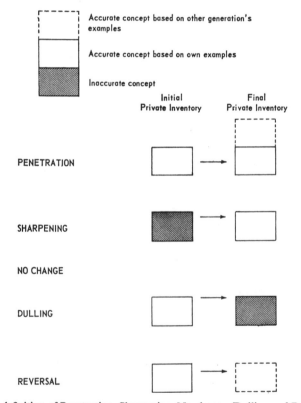

FIG. 6. Graphic definition of Penetration, Sharpening, No change, Dulling and Reversal. Shaded, open and broken boxes represent different kinds of sets of sequences accepted on the initial and final inventories.

Phase C.   Final private concept attainment

Each individual can stop testing whenever he wishes, indicating this by turning on a "finished light". When all have so indicated each is asked to work privately again on second private inventory. He is told to check sequences that have the "correct pattern" according to what he learned from his own initial example and from the testing period in Phase B.

We then can compare initial and final private inventories to see what changes in pattern concept occurred during the task. Five types of change occurred and are illustrated in Fig. 6.

A subject is scored Penetration if on the first inventory he checks sequences with the same pattern as his example and on the second he checks sequences like his example and also checks those like the other generation's. In short, he has recognized and accepted—in one way or another—the pattern initially attained by the other generation by watching them work (the two patterns are so different it is unlikely he would have thought of the

Role and family distribution

		N — M F P S				CD — M F P S				S — M F P S			
	Family number	M	F	P	S	M	F	P	S	M	F	P	S
Penetration	1		o	o				o	o	o			
	2		o	o		o	o	o	o		o		
	3	o	o	o	o					o			
	4									o		o	
	5		o	o	o				o				
Sharpening	1	o	o			o				o		o	o
	2		o							o			
	3					o	o	o				o	
	4	o	o	o	o	o		o	o				
	5	o						o	o				o
No change	1							o					
	2	o										o	
	3												
	4							o				o	
	5												o
Dulling	1							o					
	2												
	3									o			o
	4												
	5					o				o			
Reversal	1												
	2												o
	3							o		o			
	4												o
	5							o		o			

FIG. 7. Distribution of kinds of concepts change, from initial to final inventory, in the three groups of families. Each of the three large columns represents a group of families. Within each large column are four smaller ones representing roles: M=mother; F=father; P=patient and S=sibling. Each of the five large rows represents one of the five kinds of concept change. Within each row are five smaller rows representing each of the families in each group.

second entirely on his own). He is scored Sharpening if, on the first inventory, he checks sequences that are like his example and some others only remotely similar and on the final inventory, accepts only those that are precisely the same as his example. He did not learn from the other generation but he improved his performance nonetheless. No Change speaks for itself and Dulling is the reverse of Sharpening. A subject is scored Reversal if he accepts sequences like his example in the first inventory and rejects all these on the second inventory accepting only sequences like the other generation's examples. Dulling and Reversal both imply that a subject's confidence in his original, and valid, concept has been sorely shaken in the course of the task.

Figure 7 shows results for the three groups of families.

Note that Dulling and Reversal are heavily concentrated in the schizophrenic group whereas Sharpening and Penetration are concentrated in the normal group.

We also measured some characteristics of the sequences tested by each family during Phase B. The Focus-sequence score measures the proportion of sequences that were similar to a preceding sequence tested as shown by an example in Fig. 8.

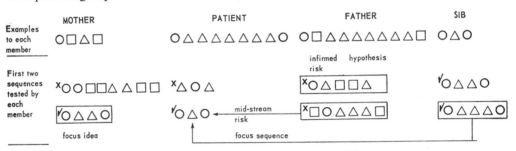

FIG. 8. Graphic definition of focus and risk measures. These are dichotomous measures; every sequence is or is not an instance of focus or risk. Sequences enclosed in boxes are examples of those that were rated as instances of one of the four measures. Two of the measures depend on comparing the characteristic of the sequences being rated with a sequence previously tested. Arrows point from the boxed sequences to the comparison sequences.

The Focus idea score measures the proportion of sequences that were like the other person's example and is illustrated in Fig. 8. The Infirmed Hypothesis Risk score measures the proportion that were rated as wrong by the experimenter. The Mid-stream Risk measures the proportion of sequences that were different from the immediately preceding one if the preceding one was right, i.e. such a sequence represented a willingness to change a good hypothesis in mid-stream. See illustrations in Fig. 8.

Families of schizophrenics rarely tested sequences like the other generation's example. This is probably the reason that they showed very little Penetration, i.e. they did not learn the other generation's concept. Paradoxically, however, they had high Focus-sequence scores and also very low Infirmed Hypothesis Risk scores which implied that they tested many sequences like their own examples and these were frequently rated correct. Thus, although they had much information to support their initial concept, the frequency of Dulling and Reversal in the schizophrenic group implied that members in these families lost rather than gained confidence in their initial concepts. We might wonder if information they gain by testing their own hypotheses is really the basis for validating their own concepts.

Furthermore, subjects who show Reversal, which occurs almost exclusively in the schizophrenic group, give up their own concept despite a great deal of information from sequences they test that it is valid and accept the other generation's concept but rarely test a sequence themselves to prove it is correct. It may be that members in these families are alert to the behavior of the other generation, that they often infer that others have concepts different from their own and that this inference, rather than information they collect themselves, is the basis for validating their concepts. In short they place a low value on their own hypothesis testing which may explain why they seem so unwilling to take risks, as determined by low scores on two risk-taking measures. I propose that often they view wrong hypothesis sequences, like right sequences, as of no particular value. In addition they have the additional liability of being chagrining and are therefore avoided.

On the other hand, normal families test many sequences like the other generation's examples as shown by high Focus idea scores. This implies they notice what the other generation is doing and use it as a basis for their own hypothesis testing strategies. It is not surprising that these families show frequent Penetration. In addition, they show high risk scores. I propose that the normal families view wrong sequences as highly informative, therefore they are well worth whatever chagrin accrues and are not avoided.

The families of character disorders were midway between the normal and schizophrenic groups in the number of sequences they tested that were like the other generation's example —as shown by the Focus-idea score. This would seem to explain why the character disorder group was also between the other two in the frequency of Penetration—the learning of the other generation's concept. They received a good deal of information to support the concepts they formed in the initial private phase—as shown by the Focus scores, and Infirmed Hypothesis Risk score. In contrast to the schizophrenic group they did not ignore this information but used this to validate their initial concepts. This appears to explain the frequency of Sharpening—sticking to the original concept—and the infrequency of Dulling and Reversal—losing confidence in the original. They were also willing to take more risk than the schizophrenic group—as shown in the two risk measures—which also suggests that they placed more value on hypothesis testing.

To summarize at this point, our hypothesis states that members of families of schizophrenics and families of normals place great importance on their inferences of what others in their families are thinking. We have postulated that in the schizophrenic group members use these inferences to validate their initial concepts and tend to ignore any additional information they may collect themselves by hypothesis testing. In the normal group these inferences lead members to test a wider variety of hypotheses which leads in turn to a more complete pattern concept based on information from those hypotheses. I wish to present, briefly, a second experiment that is a more direct test of inferences family members make of what others are thinking.

INFORMATION EXCHANGE TASK

The procedure required that each family member make inferences on the basis of information received from other members only. No information—aside from instructions on how to work the puzzle—was given by the experimenter. This experiment is in the

P

tradition of the studies of communication networks in small groups begun by Alex
Bavelas.[3]

In this experiment the booths are rearranged, significantly, to omit the experimenter.
Each individual has access to the other through a marked passage and the family is left
alone in the laboratory to work on the problem by themselves, as shown in Fig. 9. Each
family member is given a lattice of circles as shown in Fig. 10.

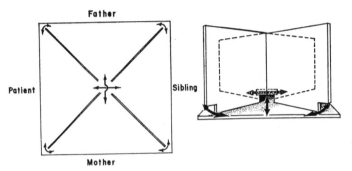

FIG. 9. Apparatus for the information exchange task.

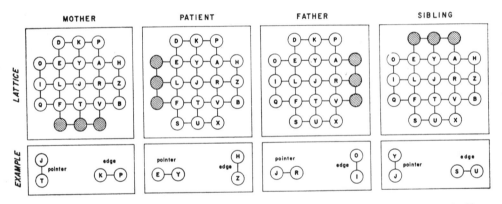

FIG. 10. Lattices for the information exchange task. Each lattice is drawn from a master lattice
so that they are identical except for the position of the empty circles indicated by shading.

Each circle is filled with a letter except for three adjacent circles along one of the edges,
which is empty. The lattices are drawn from a master lattice so that they are all the same
except for the position of the empty circles. Each member knows all the lattices were drawn
from a master lattice but does not know where the others' empty circles are; he does not
even know that they are on an edge. The object of the puzzle is for each member to fill
in his empty circles by learning what the other has in his filled circles in a corresponding
position. Family members were permitted to communicate the contents of their own
lattice to any other member by constructing messages consisting of two adjoining letters.
Each member goes in turn. He sends a message to any other member. Let us call the two
letters in the message x and y. These messages could convey, at the simplest level, the

information "in my lattice x is next to y", where x and y are any two adjoining letters in the sender's lattice. Each time a recipient receives a message he is required to return a message also composed of any two adjoining letters. This message sent to the recipient would be useful to the recipient only if his lattice contained x or y but not both. For instance, if he had x but not y he would fill in the empty circle—adjoining the letter x—with the letter y and be on his way to completing the task. The most critical feature of the procedure is that, in the case illustrated in the slide, there are 32 possible messages. However, only a few of these will be of any use to the others and, if they are sent entirely at random each useful message has only a small chance of being sent to the person who needs it. If communication is conducted by random construction of messages the task extends interminably in time. Thus, subjects are forced to be selective in what messages they send. Senders, to improve their performance, must develop a strategy whereby they either communicate their own informational needs or correctly identify the needs of others.

Our families appeared to use one or both of two strategies. The simpler was the "edge strategy" where members frequently sent messages containing two letters from the edge of the lattice. Examples are shown in Fig. 10. If a member sends a steady stream of messages of this type, it is equivalent to saying "I am sending you nothing but edges because my empty circles are on the edge of my lattice. Please keep this in mind when sending me messages." An understanding recipient of a stream of edge-messages must decode them something like this: "He is sending me lots of edge messages; maybe his empty circles are on his edge." Once members have made this inference it becomes relatively easy for them to quickly supply each other with messages to fill up the empty circles.

A more complicated strategy, successfully used by only a few of our families, is the "pointer–joiner strategy". A subject repeatedly sends messages that point to his empty circles (see Fig. 10 for illustrations) and hopes that a recipient will return messages that

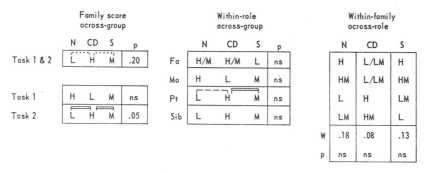

FIG. 11. Turns to completion, information exchange task, relative magnitude of the sums of ranks. Family score analyses use scores derived from the entire family irrespective of the character of the individual contributions of family members; within-role and within-family analyses compare scores derived for individual family members. 1, p-values listed for family scores and within-role comparisons were obtained by Kruskal-Wallis analysis of variance. 2, braces in the family and within-role analyses refer to two-tailed p-values for the Mann–Whitney test: ⌐¬ $=p < 0.02$; ⌐¬ $=p < 0.056$; ⌐ ¬ $=p < 0.10$; ⌐ · ¬ $=p < 0.22$. 3, in the within-family analysis W refers to Kendall's coefficient of concordance and p is its significance. 4, the relative magnitude of the sum of ranks is indicated: H=high; HM=high medium; M=medium; LM=low medium; L=low.

link on to his. For example, father may repeatedly send *Y-A*'s hoping someone will send him an *A*-something. When he gets *A-H,* of course, he can fill in his empty circle.

Figure 11 shows a comparison of the three groups according to the number of turns required by each family to fill in their lattices. The data are presented in a format developed by Elliot Mishler and Nancy Waxler.[4] The relative magnitude of the scores of each group is indicated: H=high; M=middle; L=low. The numbers and braces indicate the results of nonparametric statistical tests; their absence indicates no significant difference was obtained. Note that the schizophrenic and normal families were about the same and used fewer turns than the character disorder group. Thus the schizophrenic and normal group appeared to have exchanged information more efficiently than the character disorder group.

On measures of edge strategy the schizophrenic and normal groups were again about the same and significantly superior to the character disorder group. For the less frequently used pointer–joiner strategy there were no clear differences between the groups.

The superiority of the schizophrenic and normal groups, on turns to completion, implies only that they more efficiently exchanged information. The measure of strategy, it is postulated, provides a critical new dimension. It suggests that their superiority in information exchange is based on the members' ability to infer accurately the informational needs of others, i.e., to develop an accurate schema of the other's lattice.

DISCUSSION

In discussing the findings of both experiments I should like to divide the families in our study into three groups. This grouping is based on how family members seemed to work with others in their family to gain, evaluate and organize information from their environment.

In one group of families individuals can accurately infer the way others organize or perceive information from the environment. This is implied by their performance on the information exchange task. They use these inferences to explore inventively and exhaustively the extrafamilial source of information. They place great value in the information they themselves collect and their final concepts are based on this. The ideas of others in their family influence their hunches and ways they search for information but their final concepts are always based on their own experience. Our normal families appear to be in this group.

In a second group individuals can also accurately infer the ideas others in their family have. But these inferences are used in a way very different from the first group. If they perceive others' ideas as different from their own they will often lose confidence in their own percepts and may surrender them entirely whether information from the extrafamilial source supports this change or not. If they perceive their own concepts and others' to be the same they will retain their initial concept without effectively exploring the extrafamilial source to see if other concepts might also be valid. Thus, the major endeavor of each member is to draw from his family some conviction of being right rather than to use his family's ideas to maintain an accurate and responsive apprehension of a complex and varying stream of information from an extrafamilial source. Our schizophrenic families are probably in this group.[5]

In a third group of families members cannot or will not make accurate inferences of the ideas of other family members. This leads to a relative poverty of hunches and search strategies for exploring the extrafamilial source of information. They seem to use the information they receive, by hypothesis testing, as the basis for the final concepts they attain, unlike the second group. However, because their hypothesis testing lacks diversity and breadth, their final concepts are inferior to the first group. Our character disorder families appear to be in this group.

The procedures of the puzzles were complex and this complexity had two major sources. First, we required each family to use unfamiliar procedures such as the private inventory and the lattices in order to externalize their perceptual and information exchange processes so that they could be objectively measured. Second, we wanted the pathways to puzzle solution to offer a variety of alternatives at each choice point. In this way each family could be observed finding its own path towards a solution. It was hoped that its performance might be uniquely expressive of some of its most characteristic interaction. Puzzles that permitted less lattitude for families might determine only whether the family achieved some criterial performance; whether its performance was "good or "bad". However, complicated procedures require intelligence to learn. In the present studies all families received extensive training in the procedures for each kind of puzzle which included work on sample puzzles. Family members worked on the experimental puzzles only after they grasped the procedures in the sample puzzles. Also, families were matched for intelligence across groups to minimize the effect of individual intelligence on across-group comparisons. Most of the families in the present study were of above average intelligence and modifications in the instructions and puzzle procedures are probably necessary for testing families of below average intelligence.

In the studies I have reported the number of families participating was small. Therefore, the generality of the findings is uncertain. It remains, therefore, to specify, as precisely as possible, what the value of these studies—and a number of similar ones now in progress in Bethesda—are to the study of schizophrenia.

The most fundamental feature of the methods and concepts of the two studies I have described is that they seek to determine the ongoing relationship between individual thinking and family interaction as it is actually occurring at the time of observation. It is not an attempt to infer retrospectively the character of such a relationship as it may have been in the distant past. It holds the promise of finding out by direct observation whether major and ongoing changes in thought and perceptual disorders in schizophrenic patients occur in response to changes in family interaction at the time of observation even months to years after schizophrenia has become manifest. And, conversely, whether major changes in the schizophrenic's thought continue to produce major changes in family interaction and the thought and perception of other family members. Let us suppose that future data support this type of close link between thought disturbances in some or all schizophrenic patients and interaction in each of their families. This still would not explain the origin of schizophrenia for it would remain to account for the development in time of this closely linked system of family interaction and individual thinking. And the origins of this system may be genetic, interpersonal or some other. However, our theories of origin would be required to explain a different set of phenomena. They would not focus exclusively on a self-enclosed, stable thought and perceptual disorder in a single individual but would also attempt to explain the origins of a constantly changing, linked system of family interaction and individual perception.

REFERENCES AND NOTES

1. See T. LIDZ, A. CORNELISON, D. TERRY and S. FLECK, Intrafamilial environment of the schizophrenic patient: VI. The transmission of irrationality, *Arch. Neurol. Psychiat.* **79**, 305–16 (1958). More recent experimental studies of the Lidz group have demonstrated relationships between thought disorder and social interaction in parents of schizophrenics; see C. WILD, M. T. SINGER, B. ROSMAN, J. RICCI and T. LIDZ, Measuring disordered styles of thinking: using the object-sorting test on parents of schizophrenic patients, *Arch. Gen. Psychiat.* **13**, 471–6 (1965). See also L. C. WYNNE and M. T. SINGER, Thought disorder and family relations of schizophrenics: IV. Results and implications, *Arch. Gen. Psychiat.* **12**, 201–12 (1965), and M. T. SINGER and L. C. WYNNE, Communication styles in parents of normals, neurotics and schizophrenics: some findings using a new Rorschach scoring manual, *APA Psychiat. Res. Reports* **20**, January 1966.
2. See J. BRUNER, *A Study of Thinking,* New York, John Wiley, 1956, and GEORGE A. MILLER, *The Psychology of Communication,* New York, Basic Books, 1967, pp. 125–88.
3. See A. BAVELAS, Communication in task oriented groups, *J. Acoust. Soc. Amer.* **22**, 725–30 (1950).
4. See E. G. MISHLER and N. E. WAXLER, Family interaction patterns and schizophrenia: a multi-level analysis, in *The Origins of Schizophrenia, Proceedings of the First Rochester International Conference on Schizophrenia, Amsterdam:* Excerpta Medica Foundation, 1967 (in press).
5. In each family we compared the performance of mother, father, patient and sibling. One of our consistent findings in all three groups was that the patient's performance was not clearly different from the others in his own family. We often found differences between parents and children but not between patient and sibling. This is not surprising for the normal group, since the "patient" is just the child who happens to be on the list we used to locate the family. However, it is a noteworthy finding in the other two groups. It may imply that our experiments failed to capture major differences between family members or that there were no significant differences between family members along the dimensions measured here. It seems important to note that our experimental procedures encourage a great deal of mutual dependence in family members. Particularly, in families of schizophrenics, it was this mutual dependence that seems to have resulted in impaired perceptual discrimination in most family members. It may be that outside the laboratory nonpatient members can partially free themselves from this mutual dependence and retain cognitive and perceptual modes more accurately and quickly responsive to the environment. The patient may remain tied to the most intense processes of mutual dependency in his family, in ways we cannot specify by our methods at present, and thus retain his impaired cognitive and perceptual modes outside the laboratory.

A PSYCHIATRIC ASSESSMENT OF THE ADOPTIVE PARENTS OF SCHIZOPHRENICS

Paul H. Wender, David Rosenthal and Seymour S. Kety

Laboratory of Clinical Science and Laboratory of Psychology,
National Institute of Mental Health, Bethesda, Maryland

In this paper we shall present some preliminary findings from one of a group of studies initiated by Dr. Kety, Dr. Rosenthal and myself. The purpose of these studies is to assess the relative contributions of genetics and experience in the etiology of the schizophrenic syndromes. All three studies depend on the same research strategy: studying persons adopted at an early age. This device allows us to separate and thus unconfound genetic and experiential variables.

Previous studies exploring the etiology of schizophrenia have employed three major lines of approach: (1) consanguinity studies—assessment of the prevalence of mental disease in the relatives of schizophrenic patients; (2) twin studies; (3) psychodynamic and family studies—studies of the psychological environment of schizophrenic patients, their interaction with their parents and the pattern of family interaction to which they have been exposed. All of these approaches have revealed two facts quite clearly. First, that schizophrenics have an increased prevalence of schizophrenic and other psychopathology among their relatives; second, that schizophrenic patients have often been exposed to a variety of deviant psychological experiences during childhood and later life. What makes interpretation of these facts difficult is that the deviant psychological experiences have usually been received at the hands of the patients' biological relatives. It is impossible to decide to what extent the disturbance in the schizophrenic offspring has been genetically or psychologically transmitted, since the deviance in the parents' child rearing techniques may be a manifestation or *forme fruste* of schizophrenic illness in the parents rather than a cause of illness in the child. The data accumulated so far are compatible with both the biological and social transmission of schizophrenia and do not permit an evaluation of the relative contributions of either. Inspecting these data, we are in a position analogous to that of a naïve observer who has found an increased prevalence of red hair and talking Chinese, respectively, in the relatives of redheaded and Chinese-speaking probands; without further knowledge, this observer could not ascertain the mechanism of transmission of these characteristics.

A technique which may permit evaluation of the contributions of social experience and genetic transmission in the etiology of the schizophrenias is one which occurred to each of the authors independently. As mentioned, this technique involves the study of subjects adopted in infancy. In the Adoptive Parents Project we began with schizophrenic patients adopted in infancy and studied their adoptive parents. Since the biological parents are not the parents who rear the children, the transmitters of heredity and social experience are separated. If schizophrenia were transmitted entirely genetically, one might expect at least some of the biological parents to be disordered and the adopting parents to be psychiatrically normal; conversely, if schizophrenia were a purely socially transmitted disorder, one would expect the biological parents to be psychiatrically normal and the adopting parents to be disturbed. However, since adopting parents in general may tend to be disturbed, it was deemed desirable to include a third group of subjects in this study: the adoptive parents of normal persons.

RESEARCH DESIGN

Case finding

Adopted schizophrenic subjects were located by sending letters of inquiry to all American Psychiatric Association psychiatrists and public and private psychiatric in- and out-patient facilities in the eastern portion of the United States, an area which includes a population of approximately 55 million people. All persons meeting the following criteria were accepted as index cases: (1) a diagnosis of acute, chronic or border-line schizophrenia; (2) adopted by a nonrelated couple before one year of age: (3) no clear evidence of organic impairment or intellectual deficiency (IQ less than 80); (4) present age 15 to 35; (5) both parents alive and living together. Twenty-four patients meeting these criteria were found, of whom 11 were willing to come to the NIH for study (in 13 instances the family, and in 1 case the patient, refused to participate). The first 10 of the 11 willing families constitute the Adoptive Parents sample. Sampling biases may well have been introduced by this technique of case finding. In addition to the fact that less than one-half of the cases meeting our criteria cooperated, our overall case finding seems to have been incomplete. If we assume that 1 person in 1000 has been adopted under 1 year of age by nonrelatives (and this is probably a low figure) and if we assume that the prevalance of hospitalized schizophrenia is about 1 %, we would expect to have found about 550 schizophrenic adoptees. We found only 4% of that number and examined just half of those. Therefore we can make no claims about the representativeness of our sample. A summary of the characteristics of these patients is presented in Table 1.

The comparison group of schizophrenics—those reared by their biological parents—was obtained as follows. All schizophrenics admitted to a public and a university psychiatric hospital in the Washington, D.C. area over a period of 2 years had case abstracts prepared. These abstracts noted the sex and age of the patient, the severity of his illness and the relevant parental demographic variables (age, religion, education and socioeconomic status). Another researcher, who had no information regarding pathology in the parents, inspected these abstracts and selected a matched case for each of the adopted schizophrenics. Of the 10 first-choice matches, 8 agreed to participate, 1 could not be located, and 1 refused to participate; second-choice matches were substituted for the latter 2 cases.

The second comparison group—the adoptive parents of nonschizophrenics—was obtained in the following manner. From several public and private adoption agencies we obtained the names of families who had adopted children 20–25 years ago and whose age thus approximated that of our other two samples. That fraction locatable in local telephone, city and county directories (approximately 20%) was contacted. Of those adopted by non-relatives about 23% had to be discarded because of parental reports of psychopathology in the child. Of the remainder, 40% were willing to participate, all on the proviso that the offspring would not be contacted. Willingness to participate was dependent on socioeconomic status; of those meeting our criteria, 100% of those in Hollingshead Social Class II were willing to participate but none in Social Class IV.

As a result, the best match we could obtain still resulted in this group's having a significantly higher SES than either of the other two. Since none of the children could be interviewed, careful histories were obtained about them from their adoptive parents—none gave any evidence by history or current functioning, of falling into the schizophrenic spectrum. It was impossible to obtain enough normal children of one religious group and we were forced to include two families whose children had mild behavior disorders. One was an aggressive 18-year-old boy who had been involved in minor scrapes with the law and who had dropped out of high school; his behavioral difficulties responded to treatment by the Marine Corps. The other was a 15-year-old boy whose school difficulties and rebelliousness with his mother had abated following his transfer to boarding school.

The demographic characteristics of the three groups of parents are summarized in Table 2.

Hypotheses

The questions we are attempting to answer in this study are the following:

1. What is the prevalence and type of psychopathology in these parents?

A high frequency of psychiatric pathology—in addition to clearcut schizophrenia—has been reported in the parents of schizophrenic patients (e.g. Lidz, 1958a, b; Alanen, 1966; Waring and Ricks, 1965). If schizophrenia is socially and psychologically transmitted we would expect a high frequency of psychopathology in the adoptive parents. If schizophrenia is biologically transmitted, we would expect a low frequency of psychopathology in the adoptive parents.

2. What have been the child-rearing characteristics (behavior, attitudes, styles of interaction) of these parents?

If child-rearing practices play an important role in the etiology of schizophrenia, one would expect the characteristics attributed to the biological parents of schizophrenics to be present in the adoptive parents as well (e.g. Gerard and Siegel, 1950; Reichard and Tillman, 1950; Lidz, 1958a, b). Likewise, if some of these patterns are the product of parental reaction to a deviant child we would expect to find them in the adoptive sample. If these characteristics have been a manifestation of a biological abnormality biologically transmitted to schizophrenic children, we would not expect to find them in the adoptive parents.

3. What are the cognitive characteristics of these parents?

Several researchers (e.g. McConaghy, 1959; Wild and Lidz, 1965; Wynne and Singer, 1963a, b; Phillips *et al.,* 1965) have described deviant cognitive functioning in the non-schizophrenic parents of schizophrenic patients. These workers are divided in their interpretation, some claiming that the abnormalities represent a *forme fruste* of the disorder, others claiming that it is an abnormality transmitted by learning. An examination of the

TABLE 1. CHARACTERISTICS OF THE ADOPTED SCHIZOPHRENIC PATIENTS

Patient	Age	Sex	Age of transfer	Premorbid adjustment	Onset of symptoms	Clinical picture	Course	Diagnosis
1	31	M	36 weeks	Shy; a "mamma's boy"	22	Homosexual; transvestite; compulsive and conversion symptoms; clearcut thought disorder, ideas of reference	Multiple hospitalizations over 12 years. Currently an out-patient	Chronic undifferentiated schizophrenia
2	22	M	1 week	Latency: school phobia, inability to complete work. Adolescence: psychopathic behavior	16	Moderate disorganization; extensive paranoid ideation	Multiple hospitalizations. Currently an out-patient	Chronic paranoid schizophrenia
3*	30	M	36 weeks	Shy; withdrawn	About 18	Marked anxiety; apathy; thought disorder; unsystematized delusions	Multiple hospitalizations over 10 years. Currently an out-patient	Chronic undifferentiated schizophrenia
4	18	M	1 week	Shy; dependent; minimal coordination and visual-motor difficulties. No hard neurological findings	15	Gradual deterioration; severe thought disorder and disorganization of behavior	Continuous hospitalization	Hebephrenic schizophrenia
5	20	M	36 weeks	Shy; social isolate; anxiety and phobias	18	Moderate thought disorder; autism; delusions and hallucinations	Out-patient	Chronic undifferentiated schizophrenia
6†	23	F	44 weeks	Latency "a loner". Adolescence: promiscuity; multiple drug use	20	Marked anxiety; multiple suicidal attempts; promiscuous homosexual and heterosexual behavior; moderate thought disorder	Multiple hospitalizations. Currently an out-patient	Pseudo-neurotic schizophrenia

7	15	F	1 week	Pre-school: uneven motor development hyperactivity; ? petit mal—no hard neurological signs. Latency: marked phobias and anxiety	Very gradual	Withdrawn; gradual disorganization of thought and behavior; hallucinations	Not hospitalized before admission to the NIH. Hospitalized since	Chronic undifferentiated schizophrenia
8	19	F	28 weeks	Latency: isolated, shy. Adolescence: promiscuity; multiple drug use	19	Two catatonic episodes with hallucinations; posturing	Hospitalized twice. Currently an out-patient	Catatonic schizophrenia in partial remission
9‡	17	F	5 weeks	Quiet, absentminded	14	Multiple bizarre suicidal attempts; autism; changes in body image; moderate thought disorder; hallucinations	Hospitalized continuously for $1\frac{1}{2}$ years	Chronic undifferentiated schizophrenia
10	20	F	1 week	Socially awkward and shy; easily hurt; very bright academically	15	Severe promiscuity; multiple drug use; flat and inappropriate affect; disorganized repeated suicidal attempts	Multiple hospitalizations; currently an out-patient and employed	Pseudo-neurotic schizophrenic or chronic undifferentiated schizophrenic in fair remission

Biological Family:

*Mother institutionalized psychotic.

†Mother: "dull; evasive; wanted to be left alone; unrealistic and irresponsible".
Brother: "emotionally fragile; avoids coming to grips with reality"—no occupation.

‡Mother: psychotic and (?) mentally retarded.
Sister: chronic undifferentiated schizophrenic.

Table 2. Demographic Characteristics of the Parents

Group	Age			Hollingshead* SES	Religion of parents
	Fathers	Mothers	Children		
Adopted schizophrenics	56·7	54·3	21·9	2·8	5 Protestant 5 Roman Catholic 10 Jewish
Biological schizophrenics	58·0	54·2	23·2	2·8	11 Protestant 1 Roman Catholic 8 Jewish
Adopted normals	55·8	53·8	19·7	1·8	12 Protestant 2 Roman Catholic 6 Jewish

* Adopted schizophrenics or biological schizophrenics *vs.* adopted normals, $p < 0.05$ (*t*-test, two-tailed).

adoptive parents should help to resolve this difficulty: if the abnormalities represent a *forme fruste* of a biologically transmitted disorder they should be absent; if they represent a socially transmitted abnormality they should be present in the adoptive parents as well.

Methods of study

The families were given psychiatric interviews and psychological tests. The parents were interviewed conjointly and individually by two interviewers on several occasions; total time spent with each parent ranged from 3 to 15 hours. All interviews were semi-structured and followed a designated outline specifying topic areas. The conjoint interviews were directed at obtaining a history of the proband and his experience, a history of the relationship between the parents and the child, a history of the relationship between the parents, and a current assessment of the relationship and interaction between the parents. The individual psychiatric interviews were directed at obtaining a detailed history of each parent and an assessment of his present psychological functioning. Particular attention was directed towards detecting minimal soft signs of schizophrenic dysfunction.

The battery of psychological tests administered consisted of those which tend to discriminate schizophrenics from normals and the parents of schizophrenics from the parents of normals. The measures include the Rorschach, TAT, Objects-sorting Test, proverb interpretation, reaction time, and tests of psychophysiological reponsiveness.

RESULTS

Only the interviews with the parents have been subjected to an analysis, albeit still preliminary, and this is the material we report now. The cognitive tests of the parents are being analyzed and will be reported at a later time. Case abstracts—following the format of the structured interviews—were prepared and rated on a global severity of pathology scale. The ratings were made by Dr. Wender who had conducted all the interviews and by Dr. Rosenthal, to whom the same information was presented, with all information deleted which would indicate the adoptive or biological status of the parent or the condition of the child. For this preliminary evaluation the parents were rated on a global 1–7 scale of psychopathology, as were their first-degree relatives. The scale, a slight modification of that employed by Alanen in his evaluation of the parents of schizophrenics, is as Table 3 shows.

TABLE 3. GLOBAL SEVERITY OF PSYCHOPATHOLOGY SCALE
(after Alanen)

I Normal—without any disorder traits.
II Normal—with minor psychoneurotic traits.
III Psychoneurosis or mild character neuroses.
IV Moderate to marked character neuroses.
V *Severe* character neuroses; moderate to marked cyclothymic character; schizoid character; paranoid character.
VI Border-line schizophrenia; other functional psychoses.
VII Schizophrenic psychosis.

Interrater reliability between the two raters was a Pearson product-moment correlation of 0·81. Complete agreement was reached in 42% of the cases, a 1 scale point difference in 57%, and a 2 scale point difference in 1%. The scores used in the analysis of the data are the averages of the two ratings. The frequency distribution of psychopathology within the three groups is shown in Table 4 and Figs. 1 and 2.

The biological parents[1] were rated as more disturbed than the adoptive parents of schizophrenic patients. The difference is highly significant, $p < 0.005$ (*t*-test). Likewise, the

TABLE 4. FREQUENCY AND SEVERITY OF PSYCHOPATHOLOGY IN THE THREE GROUPS OF PARENTS

Group		Severity:						Mean
		1–2	2·5–3	3·5–4	4·5–5	5·5–6	6·5–7	
Adopted schizophrenic	Fathers	1	4	3	2	0	0	3·3
	Mothers	1	3	4	1	1	0	3·5
Biological schizophrenic	Fathers	1	1	1	6	1	0	4·2
	Mothers	0	0	4	3	1	2	4·9
Adopted normals	Fathers	2	6	2	0	0	0	2·6
	Mothers	2	4	4	0	0	0	3·0

Significances, one-tailed t-test
Adoptive schizophrenic parents *vs.* biological schizophrenic parents, $p < 0.005$.
Adoptive schizophrenic parents *vs.* adoptive normal parents, $p < 0.05$.
Adoptive schizophrenic mothers *vs.* biological schizophrenic mothers, $p < 0.05$.
Adoptive schizophrenic mothers *vs.* adoptive normal mothers, NS.
Adoptive schizophrenic fathers *vs.* biological schizophrenic fathers, $p < 0.05$.
Adoptive schizophrenic fathers *vs.* adoptive normal fathers, NS.

---

[1] This terminology tends to be confusing, and it should be remembered that the term "biological parents" refers not to the natural parents of the adopted schizophrenics but to those parents in the comparison group who reared their own schizophrenic offspring.

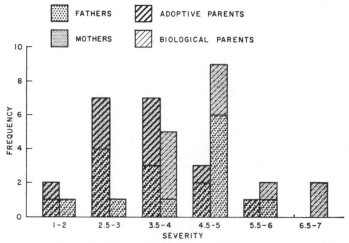

FIG. 1. Frequency and severity of psychopathology: Adoptive parents of schizophrenics *vs.* biological parents of schizophrenics.

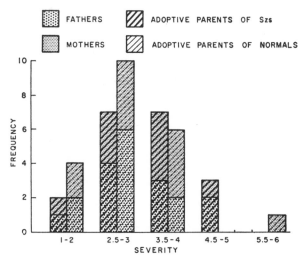

FIG. 2. Frequency and severity of psychopathology: adoptive parents of schizophrenics *vs.* adoptive parents of normals.

adoptive parents of the schizophrenic patients were significantly more disturbed than the adoptive parents of the normal subjects—the difference is significant at a probability between 0·025 and 0·05 (*t*-test).

The families were then compared, employing a cutting point of pathology equal to or greater than scale point 5·0, that is with difficulties more severe than "marked character neuroses", including schizoid, paranoid and cyclothymic characters, border-line schizophrenics and schizophrenic psychoses. The dichotomized analyses are presented in Table 5,

TABLE 5. SEVERITY OF PARENTAL PSYCHOPATHOLOGY

	Global pathology rating	
	One or both parents ≥ 5	Both parents < 5
Adoptive schizophrenic parents	2	8
Biological schizophrenic parents	7	3
Adoptive normal parents	0	10

Significances, Fisher Exact Probability Test:
Adoptive schizophrenic parents *vs.* biological schizophrenic parents, $p < 0.05$.
Adoptive schizophrenic parents *vs.* adoptive normal parents, $p = $ NS.

which shows the number of families in each of the groups having one parent or more with psychopathology of such severity.

Since psychosis—for whatever reason—does have an increased prevalence among the relatives of schizophrenics, we determined from interviews the number of index cases who had at least one schizophrenic relative, who, if he were a biological relative, would have a one-half genetic loading (parent) or a one-quarter genetic loading (aunt, uncle, grandparent). Siblings were excluded since only two of the adopted schizophrenics had adopted siblings. The cutting point was at a severity greater than or equal to scale point 6, that is with pathology at least of border-line schizophrenic severity. The dichotomized analyses are presented in Table 6.

TABLE 6. PSYCHOSIS OR BORDER-LINE PSYCHOSIS IN FIRST OR SECOND DEGREE RELATIVE OF PROBAND

	Relatives with	
	Psychosis or border-line psychosis	No psychosis or border-line psychosis
Adoptive schizophrenics	1	9
Biological schizophrenics	5	5
Adoptive normals	0	10

Significances: Fisher Exact Probability Test:
Adoptive schizophrenic parents *vs.* biological schizophrenic parents, $p < 0.07$.
Adoptive schizophrenic parents *vs.* adoptive normal parents, $p = $ NS.

There is an increased prevalence of schizophrenic pathology among the biological relatives as compared to the adoptive relatives in the two groups of schizophrenics. The difference is significant at the 0·07 level.

We also examined the relationship between severity of illness in the parents and severity of illness in the offspring. If schizophrenia were psychologically transmitted, one might expect the sicker adopting parents to have the sicker offspring. If schizophrenia were genetically transmitted, one might expect, particularly if the transmission were polygenetic, that the sicker biological parents likewise would have the sicker offspring. That is if the psychological hypothesis is true we could expect a positive correlation in the adoptive sample, and if the biological hypothesis is true we could expect a positive correlation in the biological sample. To test both hypotheses, the groups of adopted and biological schizophrenics were separately ranked in severity by the method of paired comparisons. The parents of the two groups were similarly ranked in severity of illness, using the sicker parent of each couple. The child and parent rankings were correlated. The results were as follows: the Spearman rho for the adoptive schizophrenic sample was —0·25, which is not significantly different from zero and in the direction opposite to that predicted by the psychological transmission hypothesis. For the biological schizophrenic sample the correlation between severity of pathology between parent and child was 0·56, which is significant at about the 0·05 level and consistent with the hypothesis of biological transmission.

DISCUSSION

The findings permit a tentative answer to the first of the three questions we hoped to answer in this study: what is the prevalence and severity of psychopathology in the parents of adopted schizophrenics? They suggest that there is a greater prevalence of psychopathology among the biological families of schizoprenics than among the adoptive families of such patients. They also suggest a greater prevalence of psychopathology among the parents of adopted schizophrenics as compared to the parents of a group of adopted normals. In accordance with the logic of the design, the results favor an hypothesis of biological transmission in schizophrenia; however, since the adoptive parents of the schizophrenics are not themselves paragons of mental health, this obviously raises the question of their contribution to the pathology in their offspring. We will return to this question following a methodological critique of the study.

To begin with, we would like to raise the question of the generalizability of the findings. As stated, the sample was acquired in a way that was far from systematic. What manner of bias the sampling generated is difficult to say. The initial selection was made by individual psychiatrists on criteria that shall remain unknown. Of the 24 cases reported, 11 were willing to come. From the letters of the referring physician, it does not seem that refusal to come was indicative of parental pathology. Those refusing often stated that they doubted that we could do much to help them—a realistic judgment—and that they feared rocking an often precarious boat. Contrariwise, many of the adoptive parents who did participate manifested almost magical expectations of help. They came to us as to a Mecca of Mental Health, a treatment source of last resort. Their agreement to come seems often to have been predicated on the childlike hope that the resources of the NIMH could do what those of more parochial facilities could not. In this respect the group may have been biased towards more immature and compliant people. There is, obviously, no way of resolving this question and the conclusion must be a Scotch Verdict. A replication with systematic sampling is necessary. Likewise, we cannot determine whether the participating sample was of lower SES than that of the total population of adoptive schizophrenic parents. We will return to this question later.

A second source of possible methodological error relates to the interviews. This in turn has two components: (a) interviewer bias, and (b) parental reliability and openness in reporting.

(a) To begin with the problem of interviewer bias. The interviewers knew into which group the parents they were interviewing fell and may subtly have altered the intensity of their inquiry in accordance with their own theoretical biases. Likewise, in abstracting the rather voluminous material accumulated, covert emphases and minimizations may have influenced the summaries compiled. The use of a semi-structured interview with a structured case summary format hopefully diminished the effect of such possible biases.

(b) The second issue is that of parental openness and accuracy in self-report. Although a psychiatrist can make meaningful and perhaps even reliable inferences on the basis of an individual's interview behavior (affective contact, cognitive organization, etc.), information capable of being consensually validated depends on openness of self-report, since narrative information may be inspected by other observers. Many of the parents in the adoptive normal group were obviously guarded, withholding and evasive in reporting their subjective experience. The effect of such behavior would be, of course, to minimize their apparent psychopathology. Likewise some of the parents of schizophrenics, both adoptive and biological, were more outspoken and free in self-reporting, possibly because of previous contacts with psychiatrists and social workers: such parents might therefore appear more ill. The overall effect then would be to make the parents of the schizophrenics appear more disturbed than the parents of the adopted normals.

More extensive interviews with parents, particularly if pursued in a therapeutic setting, might produce more abundant and reliable data. There are two limitations to prolonging the length of the inquiry. One is practical. Given a finite amount of time, one must weigh the advantage of a larger, less intensively interviewed sample versus a smaller, more intensively explored one. We were willing and able to make such an investment of time. The parents, many of whom came from considerable distance, were not. The second limitation is epistemological—in the absence of information, one can never be sure that more will not be forthcoming—the quandary of the status of the icebox light when the door is shut.

There is a third source of possible methodological error related to the effect of the child on the parent. Many parents of the schizophrenics, particularly in the adoptive sample, presented pictures of depression, apathy, social withdrawal, preoccupation, anxiety, feelings of futility and guilt. These symptoms, which in about one-half the couples seemed clearly related to the onset of severe problems in the offspring, frequently led to marital difficulties and further individual problems in each parent. It was difficult for the rater to make allowances for these reactive symptoms and interpersonal difficulties which probably led to an attribution of more severe psychopathology than would have been made if these parents had not been faced with, and reacting to, such a stress. The perplexity, confusion and despair of many of the adoptive parents was pathetic. In many instances they had hoped to have children for years, finally and with difficulty obtained a child, and now, at age 60, hoping in the manner of most parents to derive vicarious satisfaction from their children, were faced with a chronic and apparently hopeless illness in the only child they had. Lest the above be considered unduly maudlin, let those who have supervised psychiatric

Q

residents reflect on the amount of self doubt and resignation which these physicians undergo when treating a schizophrenic patient for a few hours per week, and the amount of support these therapists require at first; compare their position with that of the parents who live with the patient 168 hours per week, whose investment is much greater and who often have been told—by therapists more knowledgeable than myself—that they are not only preventing recovery in their children but have probably caused the problem.

Sermonizing aside, it is useful to consider some studies of the effect of a child on the parent. Donnelly (1960) reports observations made of the behavior of the same mother toward her normal and psychotic (often organically impaired) children. As might be expected, the mother reacted differently, treating the disturbed child with more inconsistency, arbitrary restrictiveness, less affection and more involvement. It is easy to see such parental behavior as a reaction to rather than the cause of deviation in the child. Data consistent with this interpretation are reported by Margolis and Wortis (1956) in a study of the parents of children with cerebral palsy. These parents were found to be over-protective, controlled by the child, afraid to thwart him, unduly restrictive of the child's activities, occupied with feelings of guilt and inadequacy, and ambivalent. Like our adoptive parents of schizophrenics, they were obsessed with the question of the child's future and his fate when they died. We do not want to convey the impression that the problems of the adoptive parents of schizophrenics were all reactive. Several couples' difficulties clearly antedated the arrival of their child. These difficulties were reflected in the assessment of their psychopathology, but their effect on their children's early development cannot be determined.

Ideally, we would like to have employed a comparison group of adoptees suffering from a disease as incapacitating as schizophrenia and purely organic in nature, but whose etiology is attributed to the parents. I know of no such disease—unless, of course, it is schizophrenia.

The last methodological questions we should like to discuss relate to the use of adoption as a variable. To begin with, one may argue that, of course, the adoptive parents show less overt psychopathology because they were screened and would not have been allowed to adopt a child if they had manifested gross psychopathology at the time they applied for adoption. Of the adopting families, 3 adopted "independently", not through an agency, and were not screened. The severity of psychopathology of the parents who adopted independently does not differ from that of those parents who adopted through agencies (Mann–Whitney U-Test, $p > 0.10$). With regard to agency adoption, we can be sure that hospitalized chronic mental illness in the parents would have been recognized and such families eliminated. Whether border-line parents would have been recognized 30 years ago and screened is problematical. The one adopting mother who was border-line, successfully concealed her previous hospitalization from the adopting agency. Furthermore, late onset mental illness would, of course, not have been screened. Of the 6 most disturbed biological parents (severity of pathology ≥ 5), 5 had their most prominent symptoms after the arrival of the child, at a median age of 46 when the children's age was 7. If they had been adopting parents, they presumably would have passed agency screening.

A second question pertaining to the use of adoption as a variable relates to the possible pathogenicity of the adoption process itself. The adoptive schizophrenics and adoptive normal groups' mean age of transfer differed because of the comparatively late transfer of 4 adopted schizophrenics (over 8 weeks). Parenthetically, this difference is not significant ($p > 0.10$, Mann–Whitney U-Test). If the experiences attendant on adoption are schizophrenogenic, one might argue that illness in the adopted sample could largely be the product of such experience, and that the greater the delay of transfer to the adoptive parents, the greater would be the pathology. To examine this possibility, the adopted schizophrenics were rank-ordered in severity of pathology, and this severity was correlated with age of transfer to their adoptive parents. The Pearson rho was -0.04, which is not statistically significant. (It should be noted that this hypothesis cannot receive a stringent test from these data since the range of time of transfer is limited: only 4 of the 10 adopted schizophrenics were transferred at an age greater than 8 months.) With regard to this last point, it is worth mentioning that despite strong suggestive evidence of the serious effects in the adult of deviant psychological experience during the first year of life (institutionalization, abnormal mothering, etc.) there are no studies (to the best of our knowledge) that demonstrate its truth but several (Heston, 1966; Roe, 1945; Skeels, 1966) that tend to invalidate it.[2]

The last question to be discussed is that of the possible pathogenic role played by the adopting parents of the schizophrenics. This question must be raised since they were not all perfect specimens of mental health—to be stored when found in Paris, under a bell jar together with the standard meter. To answer this question, one must have specific hypotheses to confirm or refute. Three such hypotheses were presented at the beginning of this paper. One involved the possibility of increased prevalence of psychiatric disorder among the adoptive parents of schizophrenics. We did find that the adoptive parents of the schizophrenics had a significant increase in psychopathology when compared to the adoptive parents of the normals.

It should be noted that in our samples the SES of the adoptive parents of normals was significantly higher than that of the adoptive parents of schizophrenics. What does this mean? This depends on two issues: one, whether SES is correlated with psychopathology; two, whether both these samples were representative ones. If SES is correlated with psychopathology (as it was not in our small sample), and if the two groups' SES differed because of sampling errors (because low SES adoptive parents of normals declined to participate) then one would be justified in partialling out the correlation between SES and psychopathology. If, however, both samples of parents are representative of their respective population (i.e. the adoptive parents of normals and the adoptive parents of schizophrenics) psychopathology associated with SES differences might be an etiological factor. That is, it may be the case that SES and psychopathology are related, and that the lower SES and hence more pathogenic parents, are the only adoptive parents whose offspring become schizophrenic.

The second hypothesis involved is the psychological transmission of cognitive abnormalities; we shall be able to present information relevant to this hypothesis when we finish analyzing the cognitive tests of our groups of parents.

The third hypothesis stated that certain patterns of rearing are the major causative factors in the development of schizophrenia. With a more careful examination of our data, it may be possible to assess the quality and intensity of rearing techniques and shed some

[2] The study of Goldfarb (1955), one of the few long-term follow-ups of institutionalized children, reports adult dysfunction in subjects institutionalized between the ages of 1 and 3. His comparison group had been removed from institutions by the age of 1 year and presumably was normal.

light on this question. And it may not. Retrospective data are often inaccurate and incomplete, and it is difficult to determine which parental behaviors were active and which reactive. This design may not permit an answer to this question. One design which may, suggested by Dr. Rosenthal, involves the study of the offspring of normal biological parents raised by schizophrenic adopting parents. Another difficult but feasible design would involve a longitudinal study of the adopted offspring of nonschizophrenic parents preselected on other theoretical grounds for their rich schizophrenogenic potential.

Before concluding, it would be useful to compare our findings with that of Alanen (1966). This author has evaluated the global severity of psychopathology among two groups, the parents of schizophrenics and the parents of neurotics. His 6-point rating scale served as the basis of our 7-point rating scale, and his ratings were converted to ours by multiplying by a factor of 7/6. The results of the two studies are presented in Table 7.

TABLE 7. A COMPARISON OF THE DATA OF ALANEN (1966) AND THE ADOPTIVE PARENTS STUDY

Alanen		Adoptive parents study	
Group	Mean severity of psychopathology	Group	Mean severity of psychopathology
Fathers of schizophrenics	4·8	Fathers of schizophrenics	4·2
Mothers of schizophrenics	4·8	Mothers of schizophrenics	4·9
Parents of schizophrenics	4·8	Parents of schizophrenics	4·6
Fathers of neurotics	3·2	Adoptive fathers of schizophrenics	3·2
Mothers of neurotics	3·4	Adoptive mothers of schizophrenics	3·5
Parents of neurotics	3·3	Adoptive parents of schizophrenics	3·4
		Adoptive fathers of normals	2·6
		Adoptive mothers of normals	3·0
		Adoptive parents of normals	2·8

As may be seen, the average severity of psychopathology among the biological parents of schizophrenics is virtually identical in the two samples. Likewise, the severity of psychopathology among Alanen's parents of neurotics is virtually identical with the severity of psychopathology among the adoptive parents of schizophrenics in our study.

The inference to be drawn from the comparability of these data depends on how Alanen's data are interpreted; but under the psychological transmission hypothesis the adoptive parents in this sample should not have been capable of generating more than neurotic dysfunction in their offspring. Thus one may conclude that psychopathology in the parents is not a sufficient cause of schizophrenia. How much does it explain? It is possible, using the omega-square estimate of variance accounted for by an independent variable (Hays, 1963), to make a crude estimate of the amount of variance accounted for by the variables of genetic relatedness and parental psychopathology. By application of this statistic to the three groups we find that, roughly, about 18% of the variance is accounted for by the genetic variable and about 6% of the variance is accounted for by the variable of parental psychopathology. It is of interest to compare our results with Heston's. Application of the same statistic shows that 14% of the variance regarding psychopathology in his adopted samples is accountable to biological relatedness. Both studies emphasize the greater weight of genetic factors as compared to those associated with parental psycho-pathology and indicate that a large portion of the variance, of the order of 75%, is un-accounted for. However, it is important to note that the 18% of the variance accounted for by the genetic variable is of the order of magnitude one would expect for a polygenetically transmitted characteristic. Inspecting the morphological variable of height one finds the correlation between parent and offspring to be about 0·5 (Falconer, 1961) so that the parental height accounts for about 25% of the variance in the height of offspring. Parenthetically, this does not imply that 75% of the variance is accountable for by extra-genetic variables. Such a correlation is between parental and filial phenotype. Given a polygenetically determined characteristic and genetic recombination, filial genotype will be correlated, not identical with parental genotype. Therefore, obviously, filial phenotype will be correlated, not identical with parental phenotype, even if environmental influences have no effect on phenotype. Consequently, before attributing variation in the offspring to extra-genetic factors, one must know, as we do not, the correlation between genotype and phenotype in the offspring.

Other possible sources of the remaining variance include: aberrant rearing techniques not associated with parental psychopathology; aberrant parental communication likewise not associated with evident parental psychopathology; biological variation, non-genetic in origin—as is suggested by the findings of signs of minimal brain damage in some schizo-phrenics; and lastly, the fortuitous social experiences of life which are probably as consequential for development as they are difficult to generalize about.

SUMMARY

A preliminary examination of data from the Adoptive Parents Study demonstrates a considerable increase in severity of psychopathology among the biological—as compared with the adoptive—parents of schizophrenics. This finding affords support for a genetic transmission in schizophrenia. We also found a slightly higher level of psychopathology in the adoptive parents of schizophrenics as compared to the adoptive parents of normals, but because of sampling problems, the meaning of this finding is not clear.

ACKNOWLEDGMENT

The authors would like to express their appreciation to Mrs. Yolande Davenport and Mr. Robert Savard, the project social workers, and Mr. John Van Dyke, the project psychologist, for their valuable assistance in the execution of this study.

REFERENCES

ALANEN, Y. O. (1958) The mothers of schizophrenic patients, *Acta psychiat. neurol. scand.,* Suppl. 124.
ALANEN, Y. O. *et al.* (1966) The family in the pathogenesis of schizophrenic and neurotic disorders, *Acta psychiat. neurol. scand.,* Suppl. 189.
DONNELLY, E. M. (1960) The quantitative analysis of parent behavior towards psychotic children and their siblings, *Genetic Psychol. Mono.* **62,** 331–76.

FALCONER, D. S. (1961) *Introduction to Quantitative Genetics,* The Ronald Press, New York, p. 163.

GERARD, D. L. and SIEGEL, J. (1950) The family background of schizophrenia, *Psychiat. Quart.* **24,** 47.

GOLDFARB, W. (1955) Emotional and intellectual consequences of psychologic deprivation in infancy: a revaluation, pp. 105–19 in *Psychopathology of Childhood* (Eds. Paul H. Hoch and Joseph Zubin) Grune & Stratton, New York.

HAYS, W. L. (1963) *Statistics for Psychologists,* Holt, Rinehart & Winston, New York.

HESTON, L. L., DONNEY, D. D., and PAULY, I. B. (1966) The adult adjustment of persons institutionalized as children, *Brit. J. Psychiat.* **112,** 1103–10.

LIDZ, T. *et al.* (1958a) The intrafamilial environment of the schizophrenic patient: IV. Parental personalities and family interaction, *Am. J. Orthopsychiat.* **28,** 764.

LIDZ, T. *et al.* (1958b) The intrafamilial environment of the schizophrenic patient: VI. Transmission of irrationality, *Arch. Neurol. Psychiat.* **79,** 305.

MARGOLIES, J. A. and WORTIS, H. Z. (1956) Parents of children with cerebral palsy, *J. Child Psychiat.* **3,** 105–14.

MCCONAGHY, N. (1959) The use of an Object-sorting Test in elucidating the hereditary factor in schizophrenia, *J. Neurol. Neurosurg. Psychiat.* **22,** 243.

PHILLIPS, J. *et al.* (1965) Conceptual thinking in schizophrenics and their relatives, *Brit. J. Psychiat.* **111,** 823.

REICHARD, S. and TILLMAN, C. (1950) Patterns of parent–child relations in schizophrenia, *Psychiatry* **13,** 247.

ROE, A., BURKS, B., and MITTELMAN, B. (1945) Adult adjustment of foster children of alcoholic and psychotic parentage and the influence of the foster home, *Memoirs Quart. J. Stud. Alcohol,* No. 3.

SKEELS, H. M. (1966) Adult status of children with contrasting life experiences, *Mono. Soc. Res. Child Devel.* **31** (3), 1–65.

WARING, M. and RICKS, D. (1965) Family patterns of children who became adult schizophrenics, *J. Nerv. Mental Dis.* **140,** 351.

WILD, C. *et al.* (1965) Measuring disordered styles of thinking, *Arch. Gen. Psychiat.* **13,** 471.

WYNNE, L. and SINGER, M. (1963a) Thought disorder and family relations of schizophrenics: I. A research strategy, *Arch. Gen. Psychiat.* **9,** 191.

WYNNE, L. and SINGER, M. (1963b) Thought disorder and family relations of schizophrenics: II. A classification of forms of thinking, *Arch. Gen. Psychiat.* **9,** 199.

INTERPERSONAL FACTORS IN THE TRANSMISSION OF SCHIZOPHRENIA

John A. Clausen

Department of Sociology, University of California, Berkeley, California

THE nine papers which comprise the second section of the Conference are concerned with a wide range of interpersonal factors, from the broadest cultural emphases (life patterns available to members of a society) and cultural influences upon family role structure, through the impact of social class on personality development and life experience, to specific aspects of socialization experience and interpersonal dynamics within the family matrix. As contrasted with the papers presented in the first section of the Conference, the second group has been more largely concerned with theoretical perspectives, except for the papers by Drs. Reiss and Wender. Whereas most of the papers presented in Section 1 were concerned with bringing data to bear to test a rather specific hypothesis with respect to hereditary factors in schizophrenia, many of the papers in the second section have been concerned with the conceptualization of interpersonal processes which *seem* to be implicated in the etiology of schizophrenia and in elaborating more adequate hypotheses on the influences of such processes.

As the authors of several papers have made clear, the investigation of interpersonal factors in the transmission of schizophrenia by no means requires that one deny the role of genetic factors. Nevertheless, it is obvious that there are considerable differences in the extent to which the authors of these papers are themselves interested in the genetic hypothesis and in studying the interaction between experiential and genetic factors. None of these papers is directly concerned with that interaction, in part because of the nature of the assignment given and in part because of personal preferences of the authors.

Schizophrenia is manifest not only in cognitive processes but in disruptions of interpersonal relationships. Any attempt to demonstrate the role of interpersonal factors in the genesis of schizophrenia is thereby rendered exquisitely difficult. Genetic predispositions are determined once and for all at conception; it may be possible to index them only very crudely through consanguineal relationships, but at least the genotype will not change. Interpersonal factors, however, are highly variable throughout the life cycle. Individuals *may* change their social class and their cultural allegiance and they *must* change, at least to some degree, their relationships with parents and peers as they move from infancy to adulthood. Moreover, as Dr. Mishler has noted in his paper, and as many students of family crises have demonstrated, family relationship patterns are changed by serious illness or defect in a child or parent. Unless, then, we have relevant data collected prior to the appearance of the illness of the defect, we can never be sure whether particular patterns of relationship represent cause, effect or an interaction between the two.

From the first group of papers it was clear that one can marshal substantial evidence for a genetic component in schizophrenia without having any consensus as to the genetic mechanisms. One might make a similar case for social factors if one could show consistent marked differentials in incidence among social class groups, cultural groups, family climates or other groupings based on sociocultural characteristics or experiences. Unfortunately, the rate differentials found in the occurrence of diagnosed schizophrenia are not so large as to give one confidence that they cannot be attributed to "drift", to differential response to symptoms in different population groups, or to cultural influences on psychiatric decision-making. Indeed, one cannot even rule out the possibility that the differentials among sociocultural groupings are primarily reflections of differential genetic loadings in various parts of the population.

To provide convincing evidence for the importance of interpersonal factors in the etiology of schizophrenia, the mechanisms underlying the transmission or evocation of schizophrenia must be delineated. It is, I think for this reason that one finds the sharp difference in approach between most of the papers given in the first section of the program and those given in the second section. One cannot *prove* the importance of interpersonal factors without very intensive longitudinal data; all that one can hope to do is to demonstrate a high degree of plausibility for a particular formulation. And as we become more sophisticated, theoretically and methodologically, the demonstration of a high degree of plausibility requires very intensive, well conceptualized study of the patient in his social matrix, the delineation of linkages between life experiences and the thoughts and behaviors that manifest schizophrenia, *and* the systematic elimination of alternative explanations that might account for the coexistence of particular life experiences and schizophrenic symptomatology. In general, the papers presented have met the first two of these requirements but have left open the matter of alternative explanations. In order to delineate the mechanisms which may underlie the transmission or evocation of schizophrenia through sociocultural influences, one must have an appropriate conceptualization of schizophrenia. It is not enough to deal with a diagnostic label; one must be able to formulate the schizophrenic process, at least hypothetically, in terms of an aberration or malfunction in the developmental process or in the individual's integration of life experience such as would lead to the specific kinds of disordered thoughts and behaviors that are labeled schizophrenia. One need not hypothesize that all schizophrenia is to be explained in this way. Conceivably, there are a number of pathways to schizophrenic outcomes. Conceivably also, more intensive and measurement-oriented research will permit the delineation of meaningful subcategories of schizophrenia along lines of cognitive development and functioning, modes of coping and defense, etc. But at least some part of what is now called schizophrenia should be explicable in terms of particular kinds of interpersonal influence.

Several of the authors represented in this section of the Conference have, indeed, attempted to delineate more sharply the thought patterns they consider to be the essence of schizophrenia and have attempted to spell out how such patterns are engendered or sustained. Others have not dealt with this issue but have nevertheless offered explanatory models. It may be fruitful to enumerate (while grossly simplifying) the models that attempt to account for the occurrence of schizophrenia in terms of sociocultural or interpersonal factors. Three of these formulations relate primarily to socialization practices and personality development in the family or social milieu. (1) The first stresses the role of early cognitive development: the child exposed to parents whose interpretations of experience are fuzzy, contradictory and irrational is likely to develop serious deficits in his ability to categorize, deficits that may directly engender schizophrenic thought processes later on. (2) A related formulation deals with problems of ego differentiation and ego strength among children involved in symbiotic ties or caught in impossible binds between con- flicting parents. (3) Somewhat less sharply defined is the suggestion that differences in socialization experience that are associated with social class may conceivably help to explain higher rates of schizophrenia in the working class—differences in value orientations, in linguistic styles, in parental modes of support and control of the child. Two of the explana- tory models put primary emphasis on stressful experiences, though the stresses may them- selves be related to socialization influences. (4) The combination of goals engendered within certain cultural groups and the available means of achieving these goals may be such as to envelop the individual in conflict and confusion, thereby evoking schizophrenia in vulner- able persons. Finally, (5) the piling up of noxious experiences in some populations groups may be such as to lead to a higher rate of schizophrenic breakdown within such groups.

It is obvious that these models can readily be interlinked with each other or with genetic models. Indeed, given the evidence for a measure of genetic influence in schizophrenia, it is hard to see how one can construct a reasonably adequate model which leaves genetic pre- dispositions entirely out of the picture. Such predispositions may, of course, be manifest in a number of different ways—in differences of temperament, energy level, biochemical functioning, etc.—and may or may not be manifest early in life. For at least a third and per- haps a much larger proportion of all schizophrenics, such differences do seem to be manifest early. The "poor premorbid" frequently appears different from his siblings almost from the beginning. Where he *is* different, we may expect that the behaviors of others toward him will reflect the fact. Where genetic vulnerability is not manifest, so that the individual is not regarded as unduly problematic until he shows the overt symptomatology of schizophrenia, one can at least try to analyze the nature of the situation confronting him at the time of breakdown.

Let me now turn to a brief consideration of the individual papers, something that could be done only very sketchily at the Conference itself. Dr. Rogler's paper does not deal so much with the transmission of schizophrenia as with its impact upon the family. In the light of the methodological and theoretical issues that must be confronted in attempting to relate family patterns to the evocation or transmission of schizophrenia, however, his presentation is extremely germane. Rogler and Hollingshead established that the impact of schizophrenia upon the family was much more severe if the wife rather than the husband was afflicted. Dr. Rogler has delineated the features of role performance and role segregation in the lower-class Puerto Rican family which make it easier for the family to accommodate to the illness and relative helplessness of the sick husband than to the illness and failure of role performance on the part of the sick wife. The wife can readily incorporate care for an ineffective husband within her role functions; the husband cannot tolerate an ineffective wife. As he notes, family life is chaotic, disorderly, and conflict-ridden when the wife is sick.

One wishes that it had been possible for Dr. Rogler to go into somewhat more detail on the way in which the schizophrenic symptomatology is defined and reacted to within the family. We know from other research that the schizophrenic seldom regards himself as sick until he has been so labeled by coming into treatment, and that he usually comes into treatment through the efforts of others, even if not committed. It would be also helpful to know which role functions are first impaired by the schizophrenic symptomatology and what this impairment does to communication and potential emotional support between husband and wife. Equally relevant would be data on the impact of parental conflict and role changes on the children in these families.

There was considerable agreement among those who have conducted family studies that female schizophrenics tend to be more disorganized than males. This suggested to some an explanation of the greater disorganization found in families where the wife is the patient. It may be observed, however, that in most urban populations the death or long-term illness of a wife–mother is likely to lead to dissolution of the household and to the placing out of children, while the death or long-term illness of a husband–father often more leaves intact the household of mother and children. We may be dealing, then, both with the consequences of a particular cultural constellation and with a more widespread if not universal tendency for the maternal role to be the foundation of family stability.

We turn now to Dr. Murphy's paper in which he has not only reviewed the evidence for significant differences in the incidence of schizophrenia among cultural groups, but has given a cogent perspective for viewing such evidence. First, he notes that pathogenic features will entail a combination of culture and societal conditions. Second, he suggests that culture should not be thought of as a "factor" in schizophrenia, but rather as one of the host of variables that can confront the schizophrenia-prone individual with a particular class of experience able to evoke the disease. It is not, then, the orientation of the culture as such or particular cultural patterns, but rather the meanings that certain patterns or combination of patterns take on for members of particular population groups under particular circumstances.

Cultures provide "designs for living"—shared sets of goals, beliefs, expectations and behavioral repertoires. In all but the simplest societies, cultures embrace considerable heterogeneity. Subcultural patterns, shared by segments of a population, may derive from a variety of historical developments—political, economic, religious, etc. Once developed, such patterns provide new designs for living, having cogency for particular groups. Those who share the subculture still derive many of their beliefs and behaviors from the orientations of the larger culture. The larger culture, at the very least, constitutes a context for the subculture and continues to provide reference points and guidelines, especially for those whose social participation is not confined to their subcultural group.

Each of the groups within which Dr. Murphy has noted higher than average incidence of schizophrenia is subcultural. Each of the sets of circumstances he has delineated either involves competition or conflict between subcultural goals and goals of the larger culture or is associated with subcultural impediments to achieving one set of goals so long as members hold partial allegiance to another set.

As Dr. Murphy notes, the problem of diagnosis in the face of strong cultural coloring of symptoms renders infeasible rate comparisons between markedly differing cultures. Differences in societal response to deviance likewise make it difficult to interpret rate differentials of subcultural groups. With reference to the Tamil-speaking people of South

India, for example, can one be sure that the higher rate of diagnosed schizophrenia is not a consequence of members of this group coming to official attention because of the difficulties with discipline and authority mentioned by Dr. Murphy? Not only do cultural features color symptomatology, but some symptoms are more likely than others to lead to difficulties with associates. Alternatively, of course, it may be that a given, culturally engendered personality constellation leads in certain social situations or cultural contexts to pressures that evoke schizophrenia.

Dr. Kohn's thorough review of the literature in social class and schizophrenia constitutes the most thoughtful sifting of the evidence that I am aware of. The results are, as he says, hardly definitive. I am inclined to the interpretation that there *is* a somewhat higher incidence of schizophrenia at the lowest class levels but more dubious that this reflects a causative factor specifically relevant to schizophrenia. Both the Midtown Manhattan Study (Srole *et al.*, 1962) and data from the longitudinal studies at Berkeley (Haan, 1963) suggest that the psychological functioning of the adult is much more closely related to his adult status than to his social class of origin. Adult social status reflects individual achievement as manifested in educational and occupational attainment, and such attainment is obviously favored by being born to well-educated and occupationally successful parents. Quite apart from any relation to schizophrenia, personal effectiveness in modern society is likely to rest in part on educational opportunity and attainment. Therefore the favored segments of the population should look better, psychologically, than the less favored. What data we have suggest that this is indeed the case, but also suggests that individuals from lower status origins who achieve high status are not appreciably less healthy than those who started with an advantage.

The power of class as a sociological concept derives largely from the breadth of its subcultural correlates. This very power renders it unsatisfactory as an explanatory variable. Class characteristics depend somewhat on migration and population dynamics, on economic conditions and regional subcultures. The meaning of class thus varies somewhat from city to city as well as from nation to nation. This further complicates the task of ascertaining what features or circumstances of life may account for class differences in the occurrence of schizophrenia.

Dr. Kohn has not attempted to formulate the nature of schizophrenia in class-linked terms but has suggested a number of ways in which the life circumstances of lower class populations tend to influence conceptions of reality, styles of thinking and sources of psychological distress, any of which *might* lead to schizophrenia. All are to a degree plausible, but in my opinion that is as far as we can go. I shall comment specifically on only two— the effects of living among persons of a different cultural or ethnic background, and the effects of stress. A number of studies have attested to disproportionately high rates of hospitalization among persons living in areas predominantly occupied by members of other ethnic groups. None of these studies has demonstrated that the choice of residence in such areas is an accidental affair (as it tends to be for waves of new migrants to a city). In other words, it seems to me equally plausible to assume that persons who choose to live in such areas may already be somewhat atypical in outlook, somewhat detached from the dominant patterns of their own ethnic or cultural groups.

One can hardly doubt that the conditions of life in the lower class are "harder" than those in the middle class. They call for different modes of coping and defense. They seem to produce more psychosomatic symptoms, more concern with concrete problems of the here and now, less preoccupation with abstract relationships and with feelings. But there is no evidence that any of these responses is linked with schizophrenia, nor that a hard life is more schizophrenigenic than a soft one. The "stresses" that seem most likely to result in schizophrenia are those that undermine the establishment of identity or self-esteem or that pose insoluble dilemmas for the individual. Here I think our best cues from come the intensive studies of the schizophrenic in the context of the family. There would seem to be more threats to self-esteem in lower class life, yet as long as many people are in the same boat, one's misfortunes do not have to be attributed to personal inadequacies. One can even think of ways in which the high-aspiring, self-conscious middle-class person is subject to greater psychological stress if he does not reach his goals. But again, I would hesitate to predict schizophrenia on this basis.

It is, of course, conceivable that individuals with particular sensitivities or vulnerabilities, subject to the disadvantages and hardships of lower class life would be more likely to develop schizophrenia. The more I learn about life histories, though, the more impressed I am with the resilience of persons at all class levels. Despite all of the deficits and devaluations that go with the life of the lower class segment of American society, then, I doubt that schizophrenia is *directly* engendered by being at the bottom of the heap.

Of the papers relating to family dynamics and schizophrenia, I shall discuss most fully those that attempt to formulate the nature of possible linkages between experience in the family and the development of schizophrenia. Discussion of the individual papers will be followed by a more general examination of the evidence.

Dr. Lidz developed one facet of a theoretical approach which seeks to explain schizophrenia as the outcome of socialization processes and personality development within the family. The essence of schizophrenia lies in distortions of mentation which are seen as a direct reflection, outgrowth, or reaction to the severely disturbed thought processes of the parents. In the many excellent research reports by Dr. Lidz and his co-workers at Yale, a variety of pathological and pathogenic aspects of family interaction have been described in considerable detail. Many of the hypotheses and themes propounded by the Yale group have added provocative new insights to the field of socialization research.

The basic question, of course, is whether these hypotheses and themes do indeed account for the transmission or evocation of schizophrenia. In the present paper, Dr. Lidz focuses attention on the importance of categorization and notes the extent to which faulty or shifting categorization characterizes the families of schizophrenics. Like others who have intensively studied these families, he notes the high prevalence of psychopathology in the parents of schizophrenics. He does not, however, attempt to marshal his data in such a way as to permit him to assess the relative contributions of genetic transmission and transmission through socialization. As he pointed out on several occasions during the conference, Dr. Lidz's strategy has been to analyze as fully as possible the consequences of the disturbed family patterns upon personality development, leaving to others the analysis of genetic-experiential interactions.

Like Dr. Lidz, I believe that language usage and the development of categories constitute critical aspects of cognitive development. At the same time, I must confess to some misgivings about certain of his formulations. For example, Dr. Lidz says that "unless we categorize, we cannot form expectancies, and without expectancies we cannot be intelligent". He appears to suggest that the capacity for categorizing depends entirely upon having words available. This may seem obvious but is belied by experience. Within a matter of weeks the infant about to be picked up by its mother adapts its body posture to facilitate her grasp. Its formation of expectancies is evident in a wide variety of non-verbal transactions between mother and infant. Tensions in the mother–infant relationship can often be observed long before the child has been taught that "love for her child is a critical attribute of the word mother".

To cite another example, deaf children are markedly disadvantaged in achieving category formation, yet they do not appear to develop schizophrenia to an appreciably greater extent than do the non-deaf. I might note that congenitally deaf children or those who become deaf prior to mastery of language tend to create tremendous tensions within the family. The strains deriving from inability of the parents to communicate adequately with the child lead to frequent and often overwhelming frustrations for both parents and child (Meadow, 1967). In this respect, the congenitally deaf child born to deaf parents has a marked advantage over the deaf child born to hearing parents, for the deaf parents early establish communication through signs. During the early years of schooling, deaf children of deaf parents tend to outperform deaf children whose parents can hear, largely because of acquiring this symbol-system. Nevertheless, the differential appears to diminish and the deaf children of hearing parents do not become schizophrenic, even though parental responses to the child's efforts to communicate its needs may very frequently have been inappropriate to the actual needs of the child.

We have almost no systematic data on the antecedents or consequencies of precise language usage in the child. I have the impression that some parents who communicate most obscurely have children who can express themselves quite precisely. It also appears that some persons who use language in imprecise and idiosyncratic ways turn out to have very provocative and novel ideas. There is no question but that people differ in cognitive styles and that some are more preoccupied with being precise and firmly anchored in reality while others are more preoccupied with exploring new realms. In so far as the problem is relevant to schizophrenia, one would like to know whether the child who became schizophrenic showed difficulties in categorization and in language usage prior to the onset of schizophrenia or whether the difficulties only became manifest as part of the general picture of pathology. This question is a difficult one to deal with, but it should be quite feasible to ascertain through limited range longitudinal studies whether early difficulties in categorization and language usage tend to produce severe distortions of mentation at a later date.

The presentation by Lyman Wynne constitutes a general description of his research program and conceptual approach. He emphasizes the importance of trying to identify salient dimensions of schizophrenia and the efforts that he and his co-workers have made to devise methods for the quantitative assessment of such dimensions. Dr. Wynne again places emphasis upon the "structural or core features of the schizophrenic disorder". I am particularly intrigued by the concept of shared focal attention and the efforts to differentiate between "schizophrenicness" and "schizophrenogenicness". The success of Dr. Wynne and

Dr. Singer in training others to differentiate, in blind scoring of protocols, between the parents of schizophrenics and the parents of neurotics or normals indicates that they have developed a powerful tool for research application. Given tools of this sort, one can asses the range of variation among individuals and families classified not only as to psychopathology but also as to cultural background and developmental stage.

One cannot but be impressed with the scope and complexity of the research program that Dr. Wynne described. Yet it is not all clear that the developmental perspective he endorses—with its stress on changing role patterns and on epigenesis—has been utilized in the studies that he enumerated for us. As he notes, these have been cross-sectional studies, using correlational techniques. Longitudinal studies presumably lie ahead. But we are not told how one can analyze the developmental processes antecedent to schizophrenia from longitudinal studies of families that have already produced a schizophrenic. One wishes Dr. Wynne had given an indication of his strategy for applying the developmental perspective.

While he has not given us a model to account for the transmission of schizophrenia, Dr. Wynne has offered a number of hypotheses to account for features in personality development which may predispose an individual to schizophrenia. He does not rule out the possibility that predisposition may also be genetically transmitted, but he makes a case for the occurrence of vulnerabilities through experiential rather than genetic processes. And in a single cryptic sentence he suggests that such vulnerabilities might be responsive "to a number of possible precipitating circumstances". One immediately thinks of the possibility that cultural orientations and demands may to a degree determine whether particular personality patterns constitute sources of vulnerability to schizophrenia, and this may well be what Dr. Wynne has in mind when he talks about the "fit" between the characteristics of the individual and those of his milieu. For further illumination we may have to wait for the findings from the cross-cultural studies now in process.

Dr. Alanen's concise summarization of the findings of his two studies combines the presentation of his most salient findings with a perspective based on a modification of psycho-analytic theory. His assessments of both the parents and the siblings of schizophrenic patients indicate at least as high a prevalence of schizophrenia as has been reported in genetic studies of schizophrenia and a substantially higher prevalence of other functional psychoses or border-line conditions with psychotic traits. In his recent monograph, Dr. Alanen has analyzed the interrelations between parental pathology, family patterns—the chaotic and rigid types described in his paper—and the presence of schizophrenia in other relatives. As he notes, it was in the chaotic families, characterized by an atmosphere of incoherence and irrationality, that he found most of the schizophrenic second-degree relatives. Thus the family environment was most unpromising precisely where genetic vulnerability would seem to have been most manifest. Whether or not both factors interacted to produce a higher rate of schizophrenia than the genetic vulnerability alone would account for we cannot say, though certainly we can say that the environmental effect would be detrimental to normal personality development.

Dr. Alanen does not view schizophrenia as a "specifically different" disorder but rather as the gravest expression of the family's general tendency toward mental disorder. He stresses the defective ego integration of the schizophrenic rather than his symbolic processes, though there is certainly no necessary conflict between his formulation and those of Drs. Lidz and Wynne. To a considerable degree, the problems of the schizophrenic are seen as deriving from identification with disturbed and ineffective parents or from parental intrusiveness that prevents the establishment of self-boundaries. Recent research on the antecedents and correlates of identification suggests that parental warmth and competence tend to maximise identification while authoritarian control and lack of competence militate against such identification once the child is exposed to models outside the home. One wonders to what extent their siblings differed from the schizophrenic children in the identifications made.

Dr. Mishler approached the topic of family interaction from quite a different perspective. He discussed both the potentialities and problems of *ex post facto* study designs to assess the evidence for and against etiological, responsive and situational interpretations of differences (observed in experimental sessions) between families with a schizophrenic patient and other types of families. In his own work he has been concerned with examining the way in which relational and situational features influence manifest patterns of interaction and the extent to which patterns found in families with a schizophrenic child accord with interpretation in terms of the three models he has proposed. He did not elaborate the etiological model but cited as its essential feature "that current patterns of behavior existed prior to the development of schizophrenia". In order to attach causal significance to existing family patterns, they must be in evidence prior to the development of schizophrenia, but this is not, of course, sufficient or even necessarily significant evidence of etiological influence. I suspect that Dr. Mishler did not want to complicate the picture unduly and therefore did not discuss the possibility that parental pathology might account for deviant family patterns while the schizophrenia of a child might be directly attributable to genetic vulnerability. It is likely that in his carefully controlled experimental sessions such parental pathology would be pervasively manifest rather than confined to relationships with the schizophrenic child.

The approach that Dr. Mishler has taken in his own research and his analytic strategies should yield extremely valuable basic data. Yet as he acknowledges, even the most carefully planned *ex post facto* study may leave one unable to choose between the etiological and responsive hypotheses unless one is willing to make certain assumptions. The major alternative to the *ex post facto* study—prospective longitudinal study—apparently seems so formidable to Dr. Mishler, so costly and charged with difficulties, that he tends to dismiss such studies. His points are well taken if one is thinking of cross-sectional samples to be followed up until schizophrenia occurs. But, of course, this is not the only possibility. One can select for study individuals or families known to have a high expectancy for schizophrenia. Whether or not one accepts a genetic interpretation of the data, the family studies conducted by genetically oriented psychiatrists do consistently demonstrate a higher expectancy of schizophrenia among close relatives of a person diagnosed schizophrenic. This has provided a basis for several of the studies reported in the final section of the conference. Equally needed, I believe, are studies that examine the development of personality in families characterized as potentially schizophrenigenic by virtue of interpersonal patterns. It would be more difficult to assemble a sample of such families but not, I think, impossible.

There are many population studies being conducted by social scientists and public health research units that reveal a broad spectrum of family functioning. Measures such as those developed by Dr. Wynne and other students of the family should permit us to locate significant numbers of married couples who show or tend toward the communication patterns and interpersonal binds that characterize the families of schizophrenics. Whether or not schizophrenia materializes, the intensive longitudinal study of such families (along with appropriate controls) should afford a basis for assessing developmental effects on the children, responses to deviance in children and the sequential adaptive efforts of the family group. It should also be possible to look for signs of successful coping and resources that permit children to overcome the detrimental influences of parental pathology and seemingly devastating socialization experiences.

The research in family problem solving reported by Dr. Reiss constitutes a still different approach to the study of family dynamics, with emphasis on non-verbal communication strategies. The tasks confronting the three groups of families were sufficiently formidable so that they could not be successfully accomplished by all five families in any group. One wonders whether such a situation would not be particularly difficult for families already struggling to understand and cope with severe mental illness in a child, even if that child's own performance were not deficient. It would be interesting to know how the different groups of families discussed their performances after the experimental sessions. Was there scapegoating in families unable to achieve success? Were there differences in the ego-involvement of families in the experimental tasks?

Because of the small sample and the possibility of differential situational pressures, one can hardly evaluate the interpretations offered by Dr. Reiss as anything more than suggestive hunches worthy of further study. His concluding paragraph offers a closely reasoned rationale for further work with such experimental techniques, which may serve as one tool for investigating changes in functioning of the family system even though they cannot illuminate the origins of schizophrenia. One suspects, however, that with repeated exposure to such experimental situations families may become "experiment-wise" and perform more successfully.

The paper presented by Dr. Wender is the first report of data from one of a series of studies designed to test alternative hypotheses about the transmission of schizophrenia. At the present status of the analysis, the data bear less on the role of interpersonal relationships and more on the testing of alternative hypotheses as to the role of parental pathology. And of these particular alternatives, the genetic hypothesis received more support. It does not appear that those serving as parents have to manifest extreme psychopathology in order to evoke schizophrenia in their children, despite the fact that half of the biological parents do manifest such psychopathology.

Dr. Wender's own critique of the methodological weaknesses of his study is thorough and incisive. He is aware of potential effects of selective biases in sampling, possible inadequacies in the assessment of the parents' mental health and the influence of the personal dilemmas of these parents upon their presentations of self. He has been candid and ingenious in considering alternative explanations. He leaves little doubt as to his own convictions, but I do not believe that he has in any way let this keep him from searching rigorously for ways of bringing other perspectives to bear on the examination of his data.

One would, however, like more information about the matching of schizophrenic patients, especially with reference to premorbid histories. When dealing with such tiny samples, selective biases become extremely important because one cannot do subgroup analyses. Even the index cases are from homes of somewhat higher social status than would be expected for a cross-section of schizophrenic patients. The normal controls are so much higher still as to suggest serious lack of comparability, as Dr. Wender has recognized. Yet this issue is far less crucial than that of the representativeness of the sample of adoptive families of schizophrenics.

We have in Dr. Wender's paper a graphic illustration of the difficulties to be faced in securing access to defensible samples of subjects and controls. I should like to argue for efforts to secure at least minimal data on all members of a designated sample rather than confining attention to those families that can be studied intensively. When members of a family are unwilling to come in for study, it would be worth going to them and asking relatively non-threatening questions to reveal residential and occupational mobility, the child's school record and developmental history, etc. Some such information can usually be obtained from hospital records, and often one can also secure indications of the nature of parent–child relations. For families that refuse to participate, even minimal data of this sort can be compared with similar evidence for those who do participate, thereby affording cues as to possible biases associated with participation.

A few general comments about the status of knowledge derived from intensive studies of the families of schizophrenics may be in order. There would seem to be virtual consensus that intensive study reveals patterns of communication and role relationships in families that contain a schizophrenic child which are significantly different from those found in "normal" families or families with a neurotic patient. The difficulties and deviations in the families of schizophrenics appear to be linked with severe psychopathology in many of the parents but not in all. Although there is a good deal of evidence to suggest that many of these families were markedly deviant or pathological long before the appearance of schizophrenia in the child, it is not possible to establish whether such deviance is in any way critical to the development of schizophrenia. It is virtually certain that these interpersonal patterns are inimical to normal personality development.

By and large, the studies that have contributed most to the conceptualization of experiences within the family that are most plausibly schizophrenigenic have dealt with relatively small samples. They have been intensive clinical studies not designed to test alternative explanatory hypotheses. Some of them are reaching the scale that should permit such testing, but the findings presently available simply do not lend themselves to this task. There are a number of serious methodological inadequacies in many of these studies. As was true of many of the early genetic studies, the studies of family interaction have not in general been based upon samples constituting a series of successive admissions to treatment or on any other sampling scheme that can be defended as representative. Moreover, there has been relatively little evaluation of influences which lead some parents to participate in such intensive research and others not to participate. Data analysis has been relatively unsophisticated. For example, except for Dr. Alanen's study, data have not been separately reported for families with a high frequency of schizophrenia among close relatives and those where the index patient is the only known schizophrenic. Again, no effort has been made to

R

segregate data for families in which the parents were seriously disturbed from those in which the parents seemed relatively normal. This failure may be attributable to the very small samples, yet typological formulations have been erected by the same investigators on even smaller numbers of cases.

On the grounds of design and methodology, then, this research cannot provide solid support for the hypothesis that family relationships are of etiological significance in schizophrenia. It would, however, be a very serious error if we were to discount the careful conceptualizations and measurement techniques that have been developed in these studies. It is patently unrealistic to expect that the first studies to delineate interpersonal processes in families with a schizophrenic patient should be expected to give an unequivocal answer regarding etiology. It is, I think, unfortunate that the best students of family relationships have sometimes attempted to explain away the findings of genetic studies; it will be equally unfortunate if those who are convinced of the potency of the genetic factor should attempt simply to explain away or dismiss the findings of family studies.

In the discussion that followed each of the papers, issues of fact, theory and interpretation arose. How does it happen that some children learn to categorize correctly even in the most pathological families? Are we dealing with total failure to learn or with retreat or regression to deviant category systems in the face of unresolvable conflict? (The latter.) Normal families seem to show much change over a period of years: Are severely disturbed families less subject to change? (The consensus of those who had studied such families was that many of them showed extreme rigidity.)

Dr. Bleuler noted that he had seen instances of the kind of family pathology described but had seen as many instances of apparently healthy, normal parents of schizophrenics. Investigators of interpersonal patterns, charged with ignoring the genetic component, asked for more adequate models of genetic effect that could be incorporated into subsequent family studies. The fact that only one-tenth of the children in "pathogenic" families became schizophrenic was cited as evidence that family patterns could not be important to etiology. Dr. McMahon quickly rectified this inference, noting that fewer than 10% of heavy cigarette smokers die of lung cancer, yet there can no longer be doubt about the pathogenicity of cigarettes.

Two recurrent themes relating to future research were emphasized throughout the discussion: (1) the desirability of building into future studies of families safeguards against subjective bias and giving more systematic attention to the kinds of data required if one is to choose among alternative explanations; and (2) the desirability of attempting explicitly to develop models which incorporate both genetic and interpersonal factors.

This section of the conference ended with expressions of somewhat discordant views as to where we stand in our knowledge of interpersonal factors in the transmission of schizophrenia. The very term "transmission" suggests a direct mechanism—either genetic or interpersonal—rather than an interaction among influences. For this reason, preference was expressed for Dr. Murphy's term "evocation", which implies an interaction between interpersonal influences and. genetic vulnerability. The section summarizer shared both the tensions that characterized the discussion and the preference for an evocative frame of reference.

REFERENCES

HAAN, N. (1964) The relationship of ego functioning and intelligence to social status and social mobility, *J. Abnormal Social Psychol.* **69** (6).

MEADOW, K. P. (1967) The effect of early manual communication and family climate on the deaf child's development, unpublished doctoral dissertation, University of California, Berkeley.

SROLE, L. *et al.* (1964) *Mental Health in the Metropolis*, New York, McGraw-Hill.

IV. STUDIES EXAMINING THE INTERACTION BETWEEN GENETIC AND EXPERIENTIAL FACTORS

SOME PREMORBID CHARACTERISTICS RELATED TO BREAKDOWN IN CHILDREN WITH SCHIZOPHRENIC MOTHERS*

Sarnoff A. Mednick

Department of Psychology, University of Michigan, Ann Arbor, and
Psykologisk Institut, Department of Psychiatry, Kommunehospitalet, Copenhagen

and

Fini Schulsinger

Department of Psychiatry and Psykologisk Institut, Kommunehospitalet, Copenhagen

Schizophrenics excite a good deal of behavioral research, the goal of much of this research is to produce information concerning the *etiology* of schizophrenia. It may be difficult, however, to isolate such etiological factors through studies carried out with individuals who have lived through the process of becoming and being schizophrenic. The behavior of these individuals may be markedly altered in response to correlates of the illness such as educational, economic and social failure, prehospital, hospital and post-hospital drug regimens, bachelorhood, long term institutionalization, chronic illness and sheer misery. In research with non-schizophrenics, these same factors have been shown to measurably affect behavioral research results. If researchers used control groups which were equated with their schizophrenic groups for all of these correlates of schizophrenia, then any observed differences could reasonably be ascribed to the variable of schizophrenia. But such control groups are apparently not readily available. Consequently, in comparisons of normals and schizophrenics, it is often difficult to judge what portion of the reported differences have unique relevance to schizophrenia. If, for example, comparisons of non-psychiatric prisoners and normals produced identical differences we might tend to attribute the schizophrenic–normal differences to the effects of institutionalization rather than some intrinsic quality of the schizophrenic.

In view of these considerations we decided to attempt to study the schizophrenic before he became ill. We turned to the study of young, high-risk populations (children with schizophrenic mothers). There are certain advantages in examining such subjects:

* This research has been supported by long-term support from the National Association for Mental Health, the Scottish Rite Committee for Research in Schizophrenia, and US PHS grant No. MH 06867. We would like to acknowledge the help of Ekspeditions-sekretaer Karlsen of the Folkeregister, Dr. M. Hauge of the Institute for Human Genetics, Drs. K. H. Fremming and A. Faurbye of Sct. Hans Hospital, Dr. O. Jacobsen of Statshospitalet, Nykøbing Sjaelland, Dr. J. B. Nielsen of Statshospitalet, Vordingborg, Drs. G. Magnussen, and K. Arentsen, Statshospitalet, Glostrup. Our co-workers have been: J. Vive Larsen, MD. Psychologists: Dr. D. Silber, Dr. J. Higgins, M. Kyng, B. Diderichsen. Social Workers: L. Maaløe, G. Skat Andersen, and U. Faltum. Research Assistants: B. Starr, L. Lehd, I. Beck, I. Petersen. Secretaries: K. Scharf, L. Monrad and K. Winther-Petersen.

1. They have not yet experienced many aspects of the schizophrenic life such as hospitalization and drugs. Thus, these factors do not yet color their reactions.
2. The researchers, relatives, teachers and the subject himself do not know that he will become schizophrenic. This relieves the data of a certain part of the burden of bias. The bias is certainly not greater for the future schizophrenic than for other high-risk subjects who do not succumb.
3. The information we gather is current, not retrospective. That part of our inquiry which is retrospective is less so than it would be if the subjects were adults.
4. The data are uniformly and systematically obtained. This is in contrast to retrospective studies which make use of childhood and school records concerning adult schizophrenics.
5. One advantage of this method which may not be immediately apparent is the fact that the ideal controls for the high-risk subjects who become schizophrenic, are the high-risk subjects who develop other deviances and the high-risk subjects who do not become deviant. We consider it an advantage that such controls are an integral part of the design. (See Fig. 1.)

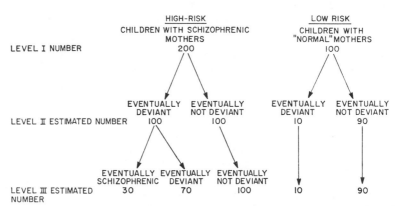

Example of Design of
Study of High-Risk Samples

FIG. 1. This is an illustration of a study using high-risk samples of 200 children with schizophrenic mothers and 100 low-risk control subjects. The design can be conceptualized as developing at three levels. At the first level we can study the distinguishing characteristics of children with schizophrenic mothers in comparison with children with no familial psychiatric background. At the second level we can estimate that about 50% of the high-risk children will become seriously socially deviant. Rather good controls for these deviants are the children with schizophrenic mothers who do not become deviant. At the third level we can estimate that perhaps 30 of the 100 high-risk deviants will be diagnosed schizophrenic. The remaining 70 high-risk deviants may be considered appropriate controls for these 30 schizophrenics, as may the nondeviant, high-risk children and the low-risk children.

Such a study may not be readily or at least easily replicated. Others using even the same design may not be attracted to the same variables. In view of this fact a form of replication can be built into the design. At Level II the 100 eventually deviant individuals may be conceived of as suffering breakdown in five waves of 20 subjects each. Thus, there are four potential replications of the first data analysis. (It should be mentioned that the precision of the replication might be attenuated if the waves differ in age of breakdown or diagnosis.) At Level III, the 30 schizophrenics may be conceived of as suffering breakdown in two waves of 15 subjects each.

Our method involved the intensive examination of 207 "normally functioning" children who had chronic schizophrenic mothers and 104 control children. We estimate that the group of 207 children (high-risk group) contains more than 25 children who will some day be hospitalized for schizophrenia. We intend to follow these 311 children for 20 years from the inception date of the study, 1962.

The study had a number of aims:

Aim 1. An immediate aim was to compare the high-risk and low-risk subjects on a broad range of measures. Since about 50% of the high-risk group seems to be heading for some serious deviancy (Heston, 1966), differences between these two groups may relate to factors predisposing to deviance. Since the schizophrenics will represent a large subgroup of the deviants some of these differentiating characteristics may relate to schizophrenia.

Aim 2. We intend to follow both high- and low-risk samples and periodically retest them. Changes in personal characteristics and/or life conditions or their interactions which instigate or signal developing illness may make themselves evident through such procedures.

Aim 3. As mentioned above, 50% of the high-risk group may be expected to become seriously deviant. At some future time it will be possible to look back at our initial assessment and discover which (if any) of our test variables could have differentiated this deviant group from the high-risk subjects that develop more normally. Of the 50% of the high-risk group expected to become seriously deviant (approximately 100 individuals), about 30% may be expected to develop some form of schizophrenia. It will be of great interest to see which (if any) premorbid characteristics and life circumstances differentiate the schizophrenics from the other varieties of deviance, from the "non deviant" high-risk subjects, and from the low-risk controls. We will give special attention to the interaction of premorbid personal characteristics and life circumstances as possible factors contributing to mental illness.

The aims relating to premorbid differentiating characteristics assume that measures relating to factors predisposing to schizophrenia will be present in our test battery. The test battery was designed to be broad-ranging, tapping areas of function shown by empirical research to be aberrant in the schizophrenic. It is also related to a theory of schizophrenia (Mednick 1958, 1962) which will be referred to below in connection with the discussion of results. Despite our best efforts, the test battery represents a limited realm of variables. It is only too possible that the factors differentiating the preschizophrenic are not directly present in this limited realm. However, even if some of the variables are only indirectly related to variables crucial to the development of schizophrenia, our findings may serve to orient future efforts toward fruitful areas of study.

METHOD OF PROCEDURE

Selection of site for the investigation

The project was first attempted in the State of Michigan in the summer of 1961. It soon became clear that the necessary records in the State were inadequate for our purposes and that following the subject for 20 years would result in an unacceptable rate of loss of subjects (US Bureau of the Census, 1956; Lansing and Mueller, 1967). In contrast to this, a study by Fremming (1951) had 92% success in locating 5500 individuals in Denmark in

60-year follow-up. When this work came to our attention it became clear that our study was possible in Denmark. Denmark also has the advantage of small size and great population concentration in the Copenhagen area.

The excellent follow-up record of the Fremming study is easier to understand in the context of the Danish Folkeregister. These municipal bureaus maintain a lifelong and up-to-date register of the address of every resident of Denmark. Another Danish institution which proved to be of great value to this project is the National Psychiatric Register which maintains a central file on every psychiatric hospitalization in the Kingdom of Denmark. The use of these institutions will be described below.

Reisby study

Our first aim was to check, in Denmark, the frequency of schizophrenia among individuals with schizophrenic mothers. In view of recent apparent disparities between psychiatric genetics investigations in Scandinavia and other countries it is of special value now to have this independent check. In connection with this project, Reisby (1967) investigated the risk of hospitalization for schizophrenia for children of a relatively small, resident hospital, female schizophrenic, Danish population. This risk proved to be 10·4%, which is in the lower range of other estimates, e.g. Kallmann (1946).

SUBJECTS

Selection of schizophrenic mothers

We chose to take children whose *mothers* are *process* schizophrenic for a number of reasons. (1) Allegations of paternity are not always free of challenge. It might be difficult to be quite sure of our major independent variable with alleged fathers, especially if they were schizophrenic. (2) Schizophrenic women have more children than schizophrenic men (Goldfarb, C. and Erlenmeyer-Kimling, L., 1961). In a study of all schizophrenic patients in a Danish state hospital we found schizophrenic women to be five times as fertile as schizophrenic men. (3) Psychodevelopmentally, mothers presumably play a greater role in shaping children. Using mothers has permitted us to carry out research on the effects of being reared by a schizophrenic mother (Higgins, 1966). (4) The offspring of process (typical schizophrenic mothers yield a higher rate of schizophrenia (Schulz, 1939, 1940; Lewis, 1957)).

Diagnosis of mother

Two experienced Danish psychiatrists trained together and then independently tested their reliability in making judgments from hospital records. Their agreement as to diagnosis on 20 test cases was found to be 100%. They merely had to judge whether the mothers were typical schizophrenics. They were instructed to discard *any* questionable cases. Following this reliability check only one psychiatrist checked each record. For each mother a precoded form was filled out which listed her symptoms, provided information concerning her dates of hospitalization and made a summary of her clinical status.

The intent in the selection of the mothers was to choose only cases that would be readily agreed upon in Europe or the United States as being severe and typical schizophrenics. We required at least 5 years of hospitalization, or at least three separate periods of hospitalization, each of at least 3 months' duration, with no sign of improvement during discharge, or an extended hospitalization plus a certified State Invalid Pension for schizophrenia. Excluded, were cases which did not have at least two different types of severe schizophrenic symptoms.

Matching of high-risk and low-risk subjects

Pairs of high-risk (H) subjects were matched on sex, age, father's occupation (the best measure of social class in Denmark; Svalastoga, 1959), rural–urban residence, years of education, and institutional upbringing *vs.* family life. Next, a single low-risk (L) subject was selected who was matched on these same variables individual for individual with each H pair.

In the case that an H child was in a children's home, he would be paired with another H child in a children's home. L children were also sampled from children's homes. In most of these L cases the parents had divorced, died, were alcoholics, suffered from serious somatic illnesses, or criminality. They afford the opportunity of some degree of control for the broken-home aspects of being a child of a schizophrenic mother.

Table 1 presents the mean values for the H and L groups for the matching variables used in this study. As may be seen, the average age of the sample was 15·1 years. There would have been some advantage in testing a younger group; however, it will take 20

TABLE 1. CHARACTERISTICS OF THE EXPERIMENTAL AND CONTROL SAMPLES

	Control	Experimental
Number of cases	104	207
Number of boys	59	121
Number of girls	45	86
Mean age*	15·1	15·1
Mean social class†	2·3	2·2
Mean years education	7·3	7·0
Per cent of group in children's homes (5 years or more)‡	14%	16%
Mean number of years in children's homes (5 years or more)‡	8·5	9·4
Per cent of group with rural residence§	22%	26%

* Defined as age to the nearest whole year.
† The scale runs from 0 (low) to 6 (high) and was adapted from Svalastoga (1959).
‡ We only considered experience in children's homes of 5 years or greater duration. Many of the Experimental children had been to children's homes for brief periods while their mothers were hospitalized. These experiences were seen as quite different from the experience of children who actually had to make a children's home their home until they could go out and earn their own living.
§ A rural residence was defined as living in a town with a population of 2500 persons or fewer.

years for the present sample to pass through a major part of the risk period for schizo-phrenia. The subjects' mean age was selected so as to maximise the probability that the investigators would still be alive at the conclusion of this risk period.

Alarm network

As the subjects of the long-term follow-up begin to breakdown, it will be crucial to be on the spot as soon as possible in order to gain a picture of the circumstances precipitating the breakdown. An alarm network was instituted to deal with this problem. First, through the health insurance system, each of the subjects has a family physician. These physicians are alerted to the fact that their patients are under study and provide information concerning contacts they may have with the subjects.

All hospitals on Zealand and all psychiatric hospitals in Denmark have submitted blank hospital registration cards to us. The 311 subjects have had these registration cards prepared for them using the particular forms of cards for each hospital. Also stamped on each card is a message requesting that the project be informed immediately if the subject presents himself for hospitalization. The secretaries responsible for informing us receive small financial incentives for every notification. The network has been operative for 2 years and seems effective.

Testing procedure

Until testing was complete none of the examiners was informed regarding whether the children tested were H or L subjects. All visits were scheduled by the social worker. The procedures were identical for all subjects.

Subjects arrived at 8 a.m.—height and weight were measured. They were then escorted to the psychophysiology laboratory where they underwent mild stress, conditioning and generalization procedures. They were then tested with a full Wechsler Intelligence Scale for Children (WISC) and the Minnesota Multiphasic Personality Inventory (MMPI). Then came lunch. After lunch they took two Word Association Tests (single word response and continual association) and completed an Adjective Check List describing themselves. They then returned for a second psychophysiology session where they underwent mild stress, semantic conditioning and mediated generalization procedures. Finally, subjects were interviewed by a psychiatrist and given an honorarium.

Psychophysiological procedures

Psychophysiological measures relate to states of cortical activation and emotional arousal. Researchers in the area of schizophrenia have very frequently included these measures in their research designs. Psychophysiological techniques, particularly electro-dermal measures, have revealed significant aberrancies in the schizophrenic (Venables, 1966). In addition, these measures are crucial to aspects of a theory of the etiology of schizo-phrenia proposed by the senior author (Mednick, 1962). Inclusion of these measures in a conditioning paradigm affords us the opportunity to record measures related to the learning and generalization of fear responses. We also wished to observe the psychophysiological response to mild stress.

An Offner–Beckman Type R Dynograph was used to record the physiological variables. After washing and alcohol sponging at points of electrode placement, the subject reclined and was asked to relax. Respiration, heart rate, galvanic skin response (GSR) and electro-myography (EMG) electrodes were attached.

Respiration. An Offner respiration transducer was fastened just above the waistline and below the diaphragm.

Heart rate. Electrodes were attached with rubber straps to the ankles and to the left arm just below the elbow.

EMG. Electrodes were fastened with elastic tape 2 cm above the eyebrows and 5 cm on either side of the nose line.

GSR. A special Wheatstone skin resistance bridge was constructed for the project (Ax and Zacharopolous, 1962). The bridge reversed the polarity of the 1·5 volt reference current every 1·2 sec. The input was processed from the bridge to the pre amplifier via a straight-through coupler. Recording was through high-sensitivity ink penwriters.

When the transducers were attached, recording was started and was continuous until the conclusion of generalization testing. *S* was instructed to relax, and earphones were fitted.

Conditioning, stress and generalization

Approximately 30 sec after the tape recorder was started, *S* heard instructions informing him of the procedure, followed by 8 presentations of the CS (1000 cps tone). These 8 presentations were included to desensitize *S* to the CS and provide information concerning *S*'s orienting response. Nine seconds after the final "desensitization trial", conditioning trials began. UCS was an irritating noise of 96 db presented for $4\frac{1}{2}$ sec following $\frac{1}{2}$ sec after the onset of CS (54 db). There were 14 partial reinforcement trials (9 CS–UCS pairings, and 5 interspersed presentations of the CS alone). Trials were separated by intervals which varied from 17 sec to 77 sec.

Following the final conditioning trial, there was an interval of 3 min, following which conditioning and stimulus generalization testing began. Generalization stimuli were tones of 1311 cps (GS_1) and 1967 cps (GS_2). There were 9 trials, 3 each of CS, GS_1, and GS_2. Duration of CS, GS_1, and GS_2 was 2 sec, and stimuli were separated by intervals which varied from 10 sec to 18 sec. The order of the CS, GS_1, and GS_2 was counterbalanced.

The final conditioning and stimulus generalization-testing trial marked the end of the morning session, which took approximately 50 min. *S* was then disconnected from the apparatus and escorted from the laboratory.

The afternoon psychophysiology session was identical to the morning session except that verbal stimuli and verbal mediation were used for conditioning and generalization (Mednick and Wild, 1962). The verbal materials were taken from Kent-Rosanof word association norms we established on Danish schoolchildren between the ages of 9 and 16 years.

Wechsler intelligence scale for children (WISC)

There has been a considerable amount of research showing an IQ deficit in the childhood school record of adult schizophrenics (Albee and Lane, 1964; Lane and Albee, 1963; Lane and Albee, 1964). Despite limitations in methodology (Mednick and McNeil, in press), the great consistency of the findings prompted us to include the WISC. Added to this is the breadth of the perceptual, reasoning motor and memory functions, which may be examined in a standard manner. The test also yields examples of reasoning and verbal behavior which may be analyzed by existent clinical techniques. A translation of the WISC commonly used in Denmark was administered in accordance with standard instructions.

Minnesota multiphasic personality inventory (MMPI)

A test of personality characteristics was deemed essential. The size of the sample dictated the use of an objective measure. The MMPI has an extensive literature on the schizophrenic for purposes of comparison of results and thus seemed the obvious choice. The MMPI also offers the possibility of the establishment of premorbid scales for the schizophrenic and other deviant outcomes. One drawback of this Danish translation is the lack of corresponding Danish norms. However, Hathaway has pointed out that cross-cultural use of the Inventory has proven it to be quite "robust" in this respect (personal communication). The Inventory was shortened to 304 items by removing items deemed inappropriate or offensive to children. The items were printed on cards and individually administered in the standard manner. In cases where children had difficulty in reading, the examiner read the items aloud.

Word association test (WAT)

The involvement of thought disorder in schizophrenia and the use of associative techniques to isolate and observe these disturbances have been a frequent and fruitful approach to the study of schizophrenia. The Kent-Rosanof Word List was chosen because of the large body of comparison literature available. Danish word association norms did not exist so we gathered and tabulated the word associations of 145 Danish schoolchildren between the ages of 9 and 16. These norms enabled us to evaluate the statistical features of the sample's associations. It will be of great interest to observe changes in associative behavior correlated with changes in psychiatric status and other variables. The list was read to the subject with the instruction to respond to each word with the first single word that came to mind. Response latency was recorded.

Continuous association test (CAT)

In addition to the reasons cited above for inclusion of the WAT, we wished to study the flow of the subject's associations to a single word over a period of one minute. Research has indicated that differences between normals and schizophrenics change qualitatively and quantitatively during the 1-min period.

The 30 stimulus words were each printed on a card which was presented to the subject. He was asked to look at the word during the association period and report all of his associations to the word. Responses and latencies were recorded. If the subject gave multi-word responses or responded to his own associations rather than the stimulus he was cautioned two times.

Adjective check list (ACL)

While the interviewing psychiatrist and the WISC examiner wrote brief clinical sketches of the subjects it was clear that these would be difficult to handle statistically for 311 subjects. Nevertheless, we felt it to be of some importance to be able to summarize the clinical impression the subjects made on the professional personnel. The ACL was chosen because of its objective scoring and because of the large number of scales which have been empirically constructed using this test. The ACL also lends itself to the construction of new scales. The ACL also afforded an opportunity for the subject to describe himself in objective terms.

The ACL of 241 adjectives was handed to the subject with instructions to use it to describe himself. The interviewing psychiatrist, WISC and WAT administrators also used the ACL to describe each subject. Each simply checked all the adjectives that were applicable.

Psychiatric interview

An important reason for the inclusion of the psychiatric interview was to screen children that were already mentally ill. Four children were excluded from the sample on this basis. The interviewer focused on the subject's mental status, social history and attitudes. Parts of the interview were precoded; the interviewer also presented his clinical impression of the subject. The 30–40 min interview was conducted by the junior author in his office.

Parental interview

This interview was meant to give us information concerning the current social, familial and educational status of the subject. The interview also aimed at obtaining information relative to rearing conditions. A social worker interviewed the individual responsible for the child. The interview was highly structured with precoded sections. The interview usually took place in the home of the interviewee and had a duration of $1\frac{1}{2}$–$2\frac{1}{2}$ hr.

School report

Bower et al. (1960) and others have demonstrated the value of school information in delineating characteristics of the preschizophrenic. They obtained their information from teachers; this was our source of data. The teacher is a professional spending many hours with the children. He can make judgments concerning his interactions with them, their peer interactions and their academic achievement. A questionnaire was mailed to each subject's school with the request that the teacher that knows him best respond. Of 311 forms sent out, 310 were returned.

Midwife's report

Many investigators have suggested the possibility that schizophrenia may be a product of damage to the brain occurring during pregnancy or birth. Every birth in Denmark (except under extraordinary circumstances) is attended by a trained midwife who completes a detailed form concerning the pre- and post-birth condition of the mother, the birth process, and the condition of the new born. The forms were located and copied.

RESULTS

The project is now in its fifth year. We shall present two data analyses that will serve to illustrate the manner in which this "follow-up high-risk" design may be exploited. (1) The first analysis compares the behavior and characteristics of the high- and low-risk groups. This comparison is relevant to Aim 1. Due to limitations of space, and in view of the fact that much of this material has appeared earlier (Mednick and Schulsinger, 1965a, 1965b; Mednick, 1966) this presentation will take the form of a narrative summary of some of the significant findings. (2) Twenty of the high-risk subjects have suffered psychiatric breakdown since the inception of the study. The second analysis reports on characteristics which differentiate these individuals from comparable high- and low-risk subjects. These results are relevant to Aim 3.

High-risk vs. low-risk group comparisons

Birth data. There is a general trend for the birth of the H subjects to have been attended with more difficulties. This is in conformance with previous reports on pregnancy and delivery in schizophrenic women. Significantly more of the mothers of the H subjects tended to be unwed. The birth process took much longer for the H subjects and was perhaps therefore attended by significantly more exploratory examinations. Perhaps most significant is the fact that abnormal placentas were evidenced by 11·3% of the H subjects and only 1·2% of the L subjects. Many of the placental disturbances took the form of infarcts.

Psychophysiologic findings. Extremely consistent and highly significant differences were observed in the latency of the galvanic skin response (GSR). These differences, however, seem to be rather complex. Unequivocally and without exception, the H group responds with a shorter period of latency to each of the nine stress stimuli. In every case the differences are significant and marked. This short latency period suggests that the H group is characterized by a volatile autonomic nervous system that is easily and quickly aroused by mild stress.

The differences between the two groups in latency of response to more neutral stimuli are not as marked. Although the H group continues to respond more quickly, there are many instances in which this trend becomes reversed.

We predicted differences in amplitude of response, speed of recovery, and generalization responsiveness. The two predictions concerning amplitude of response and generalization were strongly supported. The H group responds with much greater amplitude to the stress and to the generalization stimuli than does the L group.

In complete contradiction to our prediction is the fairly consistent finding that the H group recovered from its response to the stress stimuli at a relatively greater rate of speed. For the past 10 years our hypothesis in research in schizophrenia has been that the pre-schizophrenic should show slower recovery from stress. Our data seem definitely to contradict this hypothesis. We will discuss some interpretations of this finding below.

The H subject is an individual quick to react with extremely vigorous autonomic responses. His autonomic responses are not discriminating but overgeneralized. (Perhaps the overgeneralization is in part due to the excessively quick latency of the response system.) This very rapid, highly vigorous responding is balanced by an equally labile rate of recovery from autonomic imbalance.

Cognitive findings. The single-word association and intelligence tests yielded few differen-ces between the H and L groups. The H group tended to give more idiosyncratic and frag-mented associations. While the H groups performed a bit more poorly on most of the sub-tests of the WISC, the differences only reached significance on the Arithmetic and Coding subtests.

In a thesis at the University of Copenhagen, Diderichsen (1967) compared the H and L group on the CAT. The H group gave a significantly greater number of responses; they also gave a greater percentage of clang associates, chain associations and repetitions of the response words. These findings suggest that disorders of association are already discernible in the thought processes of some members of the H group. Whether or not these are the individuals slated for schizophrenia remains to be seen. The low magnitude of the single-word association and intelligence test differences probably reflects the fact that no member of either group was mentally ill at the time of the first examination.

Level of adjustment. At the conclusion of the psychiatric interview, the psychiatrist rated the state of adjustment of each subject, taking into consideration personal and environ-mental factors. This resulted in a five-point scale: (1) poor, (2) relatively poor, (3) doubtful, (4) relatively good, (5) good. Twenty-four per cent of the H group was rated 1 or 2; only 1% of the L group fell into these categories.

Social-developmental factors. In the brief narrative summary which follows we will combine many individual findings.

The first characteristic that all of the H subjects have in common, of course, is that they have mothers who are schizophrenic. Their home life has not been harmonious, but has been marked by frequent parental quarrels. The mother has apparently been relatively dominant in the home. However, her influence has not been benign; the child sees her as scolding and unreliable and not worthy of his confidences.

This difficult environment has been imposed upon (or perhaps has been responsible for producing) a child whose autonomic nervous system is highly labile, reacting to threat abnormally quickly and with abnormal amplitude. To make things still more difficult, reactions are not specific, but overgeneralized. This serves to broaden the range of stimuli that are adequate to provoke this sensitive autonomic nervous system.

In school, the child's teachers recognize his tendency to get upset easily. He seems to react to excitement by withdrawing. He handles peer relations and classroom challenges by passivity. Perhaps this mode of reaction is learned, since it is usually followed by the reduc-tion of his anticipatory fear. Despite the use of passivity and withdrawal, the child is still approachable and is performing relatively adequately. He shows his "nervousness" enough for his teacher to remark on it. However, having begun to learn avoidance behavior, it is difficult for the child to stop, since this takes him away from the very social situations in which he might learn more direct means of dealing with his anticipatory anxiety. His auto-nomic recovery being more rapid, his withdrawal is even more effectively rewarded. Since he withdraws, his peers reject him; and the circle gets tighter and more difficult to break.

Although, in general, the child performs adequately, he has already learned to effect momentary withdrawal responses whenever pressures build up. In tasks that require con-tinuous concentration and effort (Arithmetic and Coding the the WISC), his performance will begin to slip.

s

The child is a "loner" much of the time. He does not share associations with his peer group as much as does his schoolmate. In addition, he is beginning to learn to escape from autonomic arousal by drifting off into idiosyncratic thought.

Every statement in the preceding summary is based on a statistically significant finding separating the H and L groups. Two points should be made. First, the groups overlap on all of the measures mentioned. Second, the summary is written as though all of these characteristics were present in a single group of individuals. What is more likely is that different subgroups of the H group were responsible for the significant findings on different items.

Twenty high-risk subjects who succumbed

Since the 1962 assessment the Alarm Network and the follow-up interview have identified 20 H risk subjects who have manifested severely abnormal behavior. We shall call these individuals the Sick Group. Of these, 12 have been admitted to psychiatric facilities or placed under psychiatric care. The remaining 8 are severe schizoids, delinquents, alcoholic or have manifested bizarre symptomatic behavior. Case summaries are presented in Table 2.

Why did these particular H subjects become ill? How are they different from the other H subjects? The answers could lie in certain personal characteristics (physiological, psychological or early experiential) which they already possessed at the time of the 1962 assessment; the answers could lie with the experiences they have had since 1962; the answers could lie in the interaction of these factors. We have recently completed a personal examination and home interview of the H and L samples. Two aims of this personal examination were to obtain information on the course of the subject's recent life and observe the subject interacting with his family in his home. This information may help us to evaluate the role of recent experience in contributing to breakdown. These data are not yet available. In this report we limit ourselves to an attempt to fulfill Aim 3, to "discover which (if any) of our test variables could have differentiated this sick group from the high-risk group that developed more normally".

Selection of comparison groups

At an early stage of this research the H subjects were set off in matched pairs. It was hoped that these matched pairs would provide us with a preselected control for subjects who break down. This strategy failed for two reasons. First, while not ill enough to be in the Sick Group, many of the erstwhile controls are likely candidates and could hardly be said to have "developed more normally". In addition, the original matching variables did not include any indicant of the subject's psychiatric status at the time of the first examination (such as the interviewing psychiatrist's rating of Level of Adjustment). Many of the otherwise matched pairs were widely discrepant for Level of Adjustment. Any differences in the 1962 assessment data between such pairs of subjects might not be prognostic but might simply reflect already existing differences in Level of Adjustment.

In view of these two considerations we rematched each subject in the Sick Group, individual for individual, with one H subject and one L subject. The matching variables

TABLE 2. Descriptions of Conditions of Sick Group

Male, born 16 March 1953; extremely withdrawn, no close contacts, 2 months' psychiatric admission following theft, currently in institution for boys with behavior difficulties, still performing petty thieveries.

Female, born 19 January 1943; married, one child, extremely withdrawn, nervous. Evidence of delusional thinking, pulls her hair out, has large bald area.

Female, born 29 March 1946; promiscuous, highly unstable in work, no close contacts, confused and unrealistic, psychiatric admission for diagnostic reasons, recent abortion, some evidence of thought disorder.

Male, born 1 July 1946; under minor provocation had semipsychotic breakdown in Army, expresses strange distortions of his body image, thought processes vague, immature.

Male, born 2 May 1944; severe difficulties in concentrating; cannot complete tasks; marked schizoid character; marginally adjusted.

Male, born 3 June 1947; lonely in the extreme; spends all spare time at home; manages at home only by virtue of extremely compulsive routines; no heterosexual activity; marked schizoid character.

Male, born 1 October 1953; no close contact with peers, attends class for retarded children, abuses younger children, recently took a little boy out in the forest, undressed him, urinated on him and his clothes, and sent him home.

Male, born 17 January 1954; has history of convulsions, constantly takes antiseizure drug (Dilanthin), nervous, confabulating, unhappy, sees frightening "nightmares" during the day; afraid of going to sleep because of nightmares and fear that people are watching through the window, feels teacher punishes him unjustly.

Female, born 18 March 1944; nervous, quick mood changes; body image distortions, passive, resigned; psychiatric admission, paranoid tendencies revealed, vague train of thought.

Male, born 14 March 1952; arrested for involvement in theft of motorbike; extremely withdrawn, difficulties in concentration; passive, disinterested, father objected to his being institutionalized; consequently he is now out under psychiatric supervision.

Male, born 19 October 1947; level of intellectual performance in apprenticeship decreasing, private life extremely disorderly; abreacts through alcoholism.

Male, born 20 January 1944; severe schizoid character, no heterosexual activity; lives an immature, shy, anhedonic life, thought disturbances revealed in TAT.

Female, born 25 May 1947; psychiatric admission, abortion, hospital report suspects pseudoneurotic or early schizophrenia; association tests betray thought disturbance, tense, guarded, ambivalent. Current difficulties somewhat precipitated by sudden death of boy friend.

Male, born 13 August 1950; sensitive, negativistic, unrealistic; recently stopped working and was referred to a youth guidance clinic for evaluation. Is now under regular supervision of a psychologist.

Male, born 28 May 1947; history of car stealing, unstable, drifting, unemployed, sensitive, easily hurt, one year institutionalization in a reformatory for the worst delinquents in Denmark.

Female, born 1 June 1945; psychotic episode, one year of hospitalization; diagnoses from 2 hospitals: (1) schizophrenia, (2) manic psychosis.

Male, born 3 September 1946; severe schizoid character; psychotic breakdown in Army, preceded by arrest for car thievery. Now hospitalized.

Male, born 28 January 1953; perhaps border-line retarded; psychiatric admission for diagnostic reasons; spells of uncontrolled behavior.

Male, born 23 June 1948; repeatedly apprehended for stealing; severe mood swings, sensitive, restless, unrealistic; fired from job because of financial irregularities.

Female, born 5 July 1941; highly intelligent girl with mystical interests. Very much afflicted by mother's schizophrenia. TAT reveals thought disorder. Receiving psychotherapy.

were: the psychiatrist's rating of Level of Adjustment at the time of the initial assessment, age, sex, and social class. In addition, we imposed the restriction that the H group controls must have either maintained or improved in their Level of Adjustment since the time of the first assessment. This rating was independently obtained by the junior author from the material of the personal follow-up mentioned above. Of the 20 controls from the H Group, 11 had shown definite improvement in Level of Adjustment; 9 had maintained their Level. These controls from the H Group will be called the Well Group. Comparable follow-up

Level of Adjustment ratings are not yet available for the matched L Group control subjects.

The mean values for each of the matching variables may be found in Table 3. "Control Group" refers to the L comparison group. The socioeconomic status (SES) of these groups is somewhat lower than that of the parent H and L groups which had SES scores of 2·2 and 2·3, respectively. This is mainly due to the presence in the Sick Group of a disproportionate

TABLE 3. IDENTIFYING CHARACTERISTICS OF SICK, WELL AND
CONTROL GROUPS

	Sick	Well	Control
Mean age	15·1	15·1	15·1
Mean socio-economic status	1·45	1·05	1·85
Mean level of adjustment	3·0	3·0	3·3
Number of females	5	5	5
Total N	20	20	20

Note: The figures in the table refer to the subjects' status at the time of the initial assessment. The social class scale was adapted from one developed for Denmark by Svalastoga (1959). The scale runs from 0 (Low) to 6 (High). The Level of Adjustment rating is drawn from the Psychiatric Interview.

number of children raised in children's homes. (This factor was matched for both the Well and Control Groups.) SES is zero for such children. Notice also that the Control Group could not be perfectly matched with the Sick and Well Groups for Level of Adjustment because too few L subjects had low enough Level of Adjustment scores for this purpose. We have, however, selected the worst of the L Group for the Control Group.

This matching process yielded three groups. Two of these groups (Sick and Well) are drawn from the H sample, i.e. they have schizophrenic mothers. An experienced psychiatrist found these two groups to be equivalent in Level of Adjustment in 1962. Since that time the members of the Sick Group have suffered severe psychiatric breakdown; the members of the Well Group have tended to maintain or improve their level of adjustment. The matched Control Group, drawn from the L Group, is at the lower end of the "normal" psychiatric spectrum. We will now turn to a consideration of the variables in the 1962 assessment that differentiate these groups.

Results

The latest member of the Sick Group was brought to our attention only 3 weeks before this Conference. Consequently not all variables and tests have been analyzed. This is a preliminary report; more findings may be added in the future. The report of results will concentrate on differences between the Sick and Well Groups.

Birth data

The factors examined included mother's age, marital status, previous pregnancies, time for the birth process, explorations, irregularities, anaesthetic, prematurity, weight, length, and characteristics of the newborn. While there was a slight general tendency for the Sick

Group to have had a more difficult birth, none of the differences reached statistical significance.

Parent interview

Of all the 88 coded items in the Parent Interview only a few significantly differentiated the groups. Most significant is the fact that the Sick Group tended to lose their mothers to a mental hospital quite early and permanently. These figures are shown in Table 4. It is

TABLE 4. PER CENT OF GROUP WITH MOTHER COMPLETELY ABSENT FROM HOME DURING SPECIFIED PERIODS IN THE CHILD'S LIFE

Child's age in years	Sick	Well	Control	χ^2	p
0–1	7	5	0		n.s.
1–2	11	5	5		n.s.
3–5	30	10	10		n.s.
5–10	65	15	30	20·6	<0·01
11–13	81	40	35	15·1	<0·01
14–17	85	42	46	11·8	<0·05

Note: The Sick and Well Groups differ significantly for ages 5–10 ($\chi^2 = 6·5$, 1 *df*, $p < 0·01$), for ages 11–13 ($\chi^2 = 18·63$, 1 *df*, $p < 0·01$), and for ages 14–17 ($\chi^2 = 4·96$, 1 *df*, $p < 0·05$).

important to emphasize that the tabulated percentages refer to the *total* absence of the mother from the home during the specified period. Thus if the mother was in the home for 3 months during the third to fifth year of the child's life and absent thereafter, this absence was first coded in the 5–10 year category. It should be noted that the absence of the mother from the home occurred at about the same time and frequency for the Well and Control Groups. In every case where there is overall significance between the three groups the Sick and Well Group taken by themselves are also significantly different.

For the Sick and Well Groups, the absence of the mother from the home was in every case occasioned by psychiatric hospitalization. On the basis of length of hospitalization, degree of recovery between hospitalizations, and treatment received, the illness of the mother was rated as Very Severe or Moderately Severe. Of the Sick Group mothers, 75% were rated as Very Severe; 33% of the Well Group mothers were rated as Very Severe ($\chi^2 = 6·35$, 1 *df*, $p < 0·05$). The mothers who were Very Severely ill left the home for the hospital at a time when child was significantly younger.

In view of the greater severity of illness of the mothers who left the home early, these data concerning the mothers' absence from the home could be interpreted in relatively environmental or relatively genetic terms. It is also of interest that absence of the mother from the home was correlated with signs of disturbed behavior even in the initial assessment.

School report

The teacher found it characteristic of 67% of the Sick Group that when upset or excited their reaction persisted and they continued to be upset. He reported this for only 22% of the Control Group and 23% of the Well Group ($\chi^2 = 6·69$, 2 *df*, $p < 0·01$).

The Sick Group was also rated by the teacher as being more disturbing to the class. We can identify subjects who were either rated as being class disciplinary problems, domineering, aggressive and creating conflicts, or disturbing the class with chatting. Fifty-three per cent of the Sick Group, 18% of the Well Group and 11% of the Control Group were listed in one or more of these three categories. The frequencies for the three groups are significantly different as are the Sick–Well differences taken by themselves.

WISC and WAT

There were *no* statistically significant differences on these tests between the Sick and Well Groups. On all 12 of the WISC subtests the Well Group achieved a higher mean raw score than did the Sick Group. The three groups differed significantly on the Picture Arrangement Subtest; however, the Sick–Well Group differences were not significant.

Continual association test

In this test where the subject is asked to give multiple single-word associations to a stimulus word, the Sick Group distinguished itself by frequently rattling off a whole series of words which were interrelated but contextually relatively irrelevant. (*Opremsning* in Danish). This series might be given to the stimulus word "Afraid" as follows: "Mother is afraid; father is afraid; brother, sister, aunt, uncle, etc." The mean *Opremsning* scores (corrected for Total Number of Response) for the Sick, Well and Control Groups were 1·33, 0·11, 0·33, respectively ($F = 4·33$, 2/51 df, $p < 0·05$). The Sick *vs.* Well Group differences were also significant ($t = 2·30$, 36 df, $p < 0·05$).

Another characteristic of the associations of the Sick Group is a tendency to slide away from the original stimulus word, despite cautions by the examiner. This characteristic has been named "Drifting"; each of the Sick and Well Groups' sets of associations to each of the 30 stimulus words has been rated on a scale from 1 (no drifting) to 3 (much drifting). The Sick Group had a mean Drifting score of 1·72, the Well Group 1·33 ($t = 2·10$, 38 df, $p < 0·05$).

Electrodermal measures

Basal level

There were no significant differences among the three groups in basal level at any point. The basal levels all hovered around the mean H Group levels. The relatively low basal skin resistance of the Control Group is probably related to their relatively low Level of Adjustment rating.

Responsiveness–stress stimuli

Table 5 presents the mean GSR amplitude for the three groups for the stress stimuli. As can be seen, the Sick Group gives the largest responses to the stress stimuli with the Well Group falling in the middle. On 3 of the 9 trials differences between the Sick and Well Groups were significant. On most of the stress trials the variance for the Sick Group proved to be 5–7 times that of the Well Group. This suggests that a subgroup of the Sick Group

TABLE 5. MEAN AMPLITUDE OF GSR RESPONSE TO STRESS STIMULI,
CONDITIONED STIMULI AND GENERALIZATION STIMULI (COMPARISON
OF SICK, WELL AND CONTROL GROUPS)

Points of measurement	Mean GSR response in ohms			
	Sick	Well	Control	$p*$
UCS Trials				
CS–UCS I	25,859	17,194	9,238	<0·01†
CS–UCS II	14,467	10,472	6,583	<0·05
CS–UCS III	11,128	8,167	4,133	<0·01
CS–UCS IV	10,823	11,567	5,365	n.s.
CS–UCS V	10,759	6,859	4,900	<0·05
CS–ICS VI	10,900	5,494	3,606	<0·05†
CS–UCS VII	8,778	6,728	2,922	n.s.
CS–UCS VIII	10,983	5,761	4,241	<0·05†
CS–UCS IX	9,682	7,217	3,244	<0·05
CS Trials				
CS 1	3,744	2,917	3,189	n.s.
CS 2	5,394	1,959	4,094	n.s.†
CS 3	6,139	1,617	2,853	n.s.†
CS 4	5,694	2,067	1,433	n.s.
CS 5	6,178	3,106	1,711	n.s.
Generalization Trials				
CS (1)	6,611	2,717	1,300	<0·05
GS I (1)	6,189	2,822	422	<0·05†
GS II (1)	3,739	1,422	233	<0·05
GS (2)	5,222	2,389	756	<0·05
GS I (2)	4,400	2,139	50	n.s.
GS II (2)	2,088	1,278	0	<0·05

* Significance of differences was tested in all cases by analysis of
covariance. Basal level just preceding response was the covariance
control.
† Significant t test between Sick and Well.

might have given abnormally large responses which were producing the mean differences in
response amplitude. This point will be discussed below. A count was made of the number
of individuals responding to the stress stimuli. As almost everyone responded on almost
every trial, there were no differences between the groups on this measure.

A comparison of the Sick and Well Groups with the total H Group reveals that on most
trials these two groups fall on either side of the total H Group. However, reversals occur
and the differences are not large.

Responsiveness–conditioned stimuli

There seems to be some evidence that the Sick Group showed more conditioning than
the other groups. This may be seen in Fig. 2. The Well and Control Groups show almost no
evidence of conditioning. The mean summated GSRs to the conditioned stimuli for the
Sick and Well Groups were 5430 and 2311 ohms respectively. This difference was significant

($t = 2 \cdot 15$, 38 df, $p < 0 \cdot 05$). As may be seen in Table 5, the Sick and Well Groups differed significantly on the second and third conditioning trials.

A count was made of the number of CRs per subject. This conditioning score could vary from 0 to 5. The Sick, Well and Control Groups had means of $3 \cdot 28$, $2 \cdot 00$ and $1 \cdot 28$ respectively. These three means were significantly different ($F = 4 \cdot 72$, 2/53 df, $p < 0 \cdot 05$) as were the Sick and Well means ($t = 2 \cdot 00$, 38 df, $p < 0 \cdot 05$).

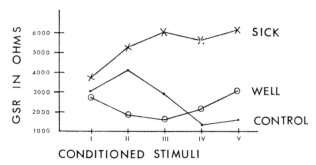

FIG. 2. Amplitude of conditioned responses for 5 test trials with CS alone (for Sick, Well and Control Groups).

Demonstrating a conditioned response with the GSR as a response measure has always proven difficult because of the relatively rapid adaptation of the GSR. This suggests that rapid adaptation could have been a reason for the poor conditioning shown by the Well and Control Groups (see Fig. 2). On the other hand, it could be taken as an indication that the Sick Group is not so much evidencing conditioning as failing to habituate. This argument can be countered by pointing to the fact that from Trials 1 to 5 the CRs of the Sick Group tended to increase in amplitude (unfortunately this increase was not significant). This increase was taking place while their responses to the UCS (among which the CS trials are mixed) were decreasing.

The weight of the evidence slightly favors the conclusion that the Sick Group evidenced superior GSR conditioning. When the conditioning performance of the Sick and Well Groups is compared with that of the total H Group this conclusion is strengthened. The Well Group behaves like a somewhat enfeebled version of the total H Group.

Generalization

The CS and GS_1 and GS_2 were presented in extinction test procedures 3 times each in counterbalanced order at the conclusion of conditioning. Table 5 and Fig. 3 present the mean amplitude of the generalization responses for the first 2 test trials. The third test trial data are not presented since very few subjects were responding.

The generalization responsiveness of the Sick Group is well above the level of the Well and Control Groups; the differences are significant on 5 of the 6 trials. When each subject is given a generalization score by adding together the amplitude of his responses to the first presentations of GS_1 and GS_2, the Sick Group evidences significantly more generalization than the Well Group ($U = 222$, Ns = 18, 18, $p < 0 \cdot 04$). As can be seen in Fig. 3, the Well

Group level of generalization responsiveness is about the same as that of the total H Group. The Sick Group is well up above this level.

It should also be pointed out that the shape of the gradients are approximately the same for the Sick, Well and total H Groups (concave downward) while the gradients for the Control and total L Groups are in the normal concave-upwards form (Mednick and Freedman, 1960). This is also shown in the fact that the amount of relative generalization (ratio of generalization responsiveness to conditioned responsiveness) is about the same

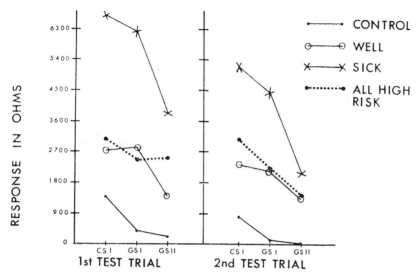

FIG. 3. Generalization gradients for Sick, Well, Control and entire H Groups.

for the Sick and Well Groups. Another way of saying this is that the Sick and Well Group generalization curves are essentially parallel and different from the Control curve. The earlier comparison of the H–L gradients demanded the interpretation of an essential difference between these groups in generalization responsiveness. Both the Sick and the Well Groups continue to evidence this heightened generalization responsiveness. The fact that the Sick and Well Groups evidence parallel curves could suggest that some additional factor might be acting to increase the overall responsiveness of the Sick Group. This factor could either be a higher level of arousal or a failure of habituation or both.

Latency

A summary of the latency data may be found in Fig. 4. The groups differed significantly on all but one of the trials with the UCS (stress stimuli). The mean latencies across all UCS trials were 1·57, 1·77 and 2·47 sec for the Sick, Well and Control Groups respectively (F = 8·63, 2/52*df, p* > 0·005). Of great interest in Fig. 4 is the difference in habituation shown on the one hand by the Control and Well Groups and on the other by the Sick Group.

This difference is especially marked in response to the stress stimuli. The Control and Well Groups' rapid habituation may be seen in the progressive increase in their response latencies from the first to the last of the stress trials. The latencies of the Sick Group progressively decrease suggesting a negative habituation or even increasing irritability. The Sick Group distinguishes itself quite sharply from the Well Group in this regard. Moving from UCS Trials I–IX, 69% of the Well Group exhibits a slowing of response latency; 75% of the Sick Groups actually *increase* the speed of their response. This difference is significant ($\chi^2 = 6\cdot13$, 1 *df*, $p < 0\cdot02$). A tendency for the same failure of habituation of latency in the Sick Group is also shown in response to the conditioned stimuli (Fig. 4).

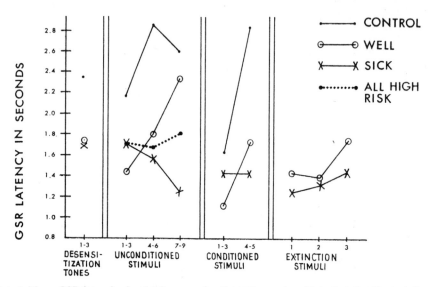

Fig. 4. Mean GSR latencies for the 3 groups for the entire session. Note that the Control Group latencies are omitted for the Extinction Stimuli Trials 1, 2 and 3. These were omitted since there were very few responses and the latencies were completely off the figure. The mean latencies for the Control Group for Trials 1, 2 and 3 were 2·63, 3·12 and 4·83 sec respectively.

As is also indicated in Fig. 4, the Sick and Well Groups were substantially quicker than the Control Group in latency of response. This mirrors the differences between the parent H and L Groups.

Recovery

We devised a rather simple score to analyze the recovery results, the number of ohms recovered per second. We have used the time to *half*-recovery as the score for this index since this initial recovery phase is less likely to be contaminated by intruding external stimuli (such as the next stress stimulus) or internal stimuli. If a response were 1000 ohms and the recovery of half of that response took 10 sec then the subjects' recovery rate was 50 ohms per second.

We have not studied the operating characteristics nor GSR correlates of this measure and to our knowledge neither has anyone else. However, it is possible to guess that it is related to basal level.

Mean ohms recovered per second is reported in Table 6 for the Sick, Well and Control Groups. Because of our interest in evaluating degree of distribution overlap with this measure, the differences were evaluated by the Mann–Whitney U-test. Significance levels were determined by reference to a set of prepared tables (Auble, 1953). All comparisons of the Sick and Control Groups were significant. All comparisons of the Well and Control Groups

TABLE 6. RATE OF RECOVERY OF GSR RESPONSE
TO STRESS STIMULI

UCS trial	Mean ohms recovered per sec.		
	Sick Group	Well Group	Control Group
2	1607	634	521
3	1538	651	595
4	1386	764	394
5	1230	615	582
6	1282	606	331
7	1816	749	401
8	1490	884	392
9	1406	691	590

Notes: (1) The rate of recovery is computed for the first half of the ohms recovered. If a response were 1000 ohms and recovery of half of that response took 10 sec then the recovery rate was 50 ohms/sec.

(2) UCS Trial 1 was omitted since most subjects did not succeed in recovering half of their response to this stimulus before the onset of UCS 2.

were not significant. Comparisons of the Sick and Well Groups were significant for Trials 2, 3, 4, 5, 6 and 9. Trials 7 and 8 were not significantly different. The recovery rate of the Sick Group is substantially greater than that of the Well or Control Groups. The latter two tend to be relatively similar to one another.

The measure separates the groups better than any other in our test battery. The overlap between the Sick and Control Groups is not large. Typically we find 80% of the Sick Group and 20% of the Control Group above the median of the pooled distribution on any one stress stimulus trial. On UCS Trial 6 all but one of the Sick subjects and only two of the Controls are above the median of the pooled distributions. The pooled Sick and Well distributions typically find 70% of the Sick Group and 30% of the Well Group above the median.

DISCUSSION

The outstanding findings in the comparison of the Sick, Well and Control Groups implicate hyperlabile and hypersensitive autonomic functioning, early maternal loss, and disturbed associative behavior as precursors of a variety of psychiatric breakdowns.

The findings of this study relating to autonomic hyperfunctioning are in agreement with certain recent work with both acute and chronic schizophrenics. Zahn (1964) has reported hyperresponsiveness, lower basal skin resistance and a failure of habituation of the GSR for schizophrenic subjects in selected parts of a relatively nonstressful situation. Other recent and methodologically sophisticated studies, in which schizophrenics have been subjected to stress have produced evidence of extremely high autonomic responsiveness in even the chronic schizophrenic (Ax *et al.,* 1962; Malmo *et al.,* 1951; and Ray, 1963). A review by Venables (1966) of recent research in this area seems to place the general form of the hyperresponsiveness hypothesis on a rather firm empirical footing.

When the senior author first advanced the hypothesis of autonomic hyperresponsiveness, as one of several hypothesized etiological precursors of schizophrenia (Mednick, 1958) there were only a few supportive studies that could be cited. "The majority of these studies reported lowered autonomic responsiveness in chronic schizophrenics" (Zahn, 1964, p. 167). The sense of the more recent empirical work on the schizophrenic, and the results of the present study bolster this hypothesis which is central to the theoretical orientation of this project. Two additional preschizophrenic characteristics, which were first hypothesized in 1958, were excessive generalization of autonomic responses and excessively *slower* recovery from stress. The first of these, generalization responsiveness, has found support in the present study. Both the H and Sick Groups evidenced elevated generalization gradients. However, the same cannot be said for the hypothesis of slow recovery. Both H and Sick Groups unequivocally showed abnormally *fast* rates of recovery from autonomic imbalance. It seems clear that this hypothesis of slow recovery merits abandonment. It may be of interest to try to reshape the theory to see what role *quick* autonomic recovery could play in the development of schizophrenia.

The theory identifies schizophrenia as a learned disorder of thought and suggests that there are certain physiological and environmental factors that predispose individuals to such learning.

The thought disorder consists of a set of conditioned avoidance responses which help the schizophrenic to control his autonomic hyperresponsivity. The avoidant responses (associations or thoughts) are learned on those occasions when the preschizophrenic escapes from some arousal-producing stimulus by switching to a thought which interrupts this arousal stimulus. The intruding association may then enable the individual to avoid (perhaps for just a moment) the arousal stimulus. This will automatically result in a momentary reduction in arousal level. (Such a reduction in arousal has been shown to have great reinforcement value.) This reduction in arousal level will reinforce the association between the arousal stimulus and the avoidant thought. This, in turn, will increase the probability of an avoidant associate response to future arousal stimulation. Each time this "arousal-avoidant thought" pairing occurs, it will be automatically reinforced by a reduction in arousal and will increase in probability. Notice that the "avoidant thought-reinforcement" relationship is completely internal to the subject. It is a truly autistic process requiring no physical or social interaction for successful operation. After many such learning trials the individual will have built up a single avoidance response or a small repertoire of responses which will have the ability to remove him from arousal stimulation or at least modulate his arousal stimulation.

This repertoire of avoidant responses will be *automatically* cued whenever the individual senses a stressful stimulus. Perhaps we are observing the beginnings of this process in our Continual Association Test results. This automatic avoidance response will seriously interfere with sustained thought processes and long term sets. It is at the point when these conditioned avoidant responses begin to dominate the individual's thinking that he may be classified as schizophrenic.

According to the earlier version of the theory the preschizophrenic is especially prone to learning this avoidant pattern because of his extreme hyperresponsivity, excessive generalization and slow recovery from autonomic imbalance. However, the hypothesis of slow recovery has always caused critics to point out that this would cause the preschizophrenic to be reinforced more slowly and meagerly for avoidance than even the normal. The finding of an abnormally fast rate of recovery has forced us to alter the theory. It is now our hypothesis that one of the determining features of the preschizophrenic is his abnormally fast recovery; because of this fast rate of recovery he is more easily, quickly and thoroughly reinforced for avoidance than the normal. This taken together with his tendency to chronic hyperarousal will, in a harsh environment, inexorably push him to learn conditioned avoidant thought mechanisms. The revised theory then implicates rapid autonomic recovery from states of autonomic imbalance as a key factor in a complex of factors predisposing individuals to schizophrenia.

As mentioned above the finding of a failure of habituation has been reported by Zahn (1964). At first glance this finding may be seen as antagonistic to the findings on quick recovery. However, the recovery finding refers to single instances of states of imbalance while failure of habituation refers to a tendency to continue to respond to stimuli over an entire experimental session as though they had never been experienced before. Failure of habituation may prove to be an independent factor. Before accepting this assertion, however, we shall explore the relationship between this variable and GSR latency, responsiveness and generalization.

Maternal loss

Early maternal loss through psychiatric hospitalization was a common precursor of breakdown in the Sick Group. This finding might be compared with research which has found a greater frequency of schizophrenics suffering early maternal loss by death (Hilgard and Newman, 1963). Both of these findings suggest an environmental-stress etiological contribution. However, in our sample we found that the mothers of the Sick Group not only were lost to the family earlier but were also more severely schizophrenic. In view of the findings reported here by Kety *et al.* (1968) we cannot disregard the possibility of a heavier genetic burden in the Sick Group as evidenced by the greater severity of their mother's illness. Two findings within the Sick Group reflect on this possibility. First, we found that within the Sick Group the very severely schizophrenic mothers were separated from their children when the children had a mean age of $3 \cdot 75$ years; the children of the moderately severe mothers were $8 \cdot 80$ years of age at separation ($t = 2 \cdot 33$, 18 df, $p < 0 \cdot 025$). The second finding concerns those members of the Sick Group who have been admitted to a psychiatric hospital or who are under psychiatric care. These subjects tend to be the more overtly ill members of the Sick Group with promiscuity and criminality as common symptoms. Eighty-eight per cent of these have very severely schizophrenic mothers; of those Sick Group subjects who have not been hospitalized, 50% have very severely schizophrenic mothers ($\chi^2 = 4 \cdot 40$, 1 df, $p < 0 \cdot 05$). What is suggested tentatively by these results is that the very severely ill schizophrenic mothers (who had less contact with their children) had children with symptom-rich, acutely disturbed, psychiatric involvement. The Sick subjects, who spent more time with their moderately severely schizophrenic mothers tend to be classed as severely schizoid, anhedonic, overconforming, and obsessive. They also tended strongly to manifest more severe associative Drifting ($t = 2·90$, 18 df, $p < 0·005$); these subjects also had significantly poorer Level of Adjustment scores ($\chi^2 = 4·8$, 1 df, $p < 0·05$). They also tended to be in a subgroup of individuals chosen as fast GSR responders, poor in habituation, high in generalization, fast in recovery and high amplitude responders ($\chi^2 = 11·22$, 1 df, $p < 0·005$). These results are highly congruent with those of Reisby (1967). He found that schizophrenics who had spent a relatively long time with their schizophrenic mother tended to develop a more process schizophrenic condition with slow, insidious onset. Schizophrenics having been separated earlier from their schizophrenic mother developed more acute, symptom-rich, reactive schizophrenia.

We present these results on the Sick–Well–Control comparisons with great tentativeness. While the groups are rather well matched and the Sick Group carefully selected, there is a total of only 60 cases. Our tentativeness is even greater regarding the comparisons relating to time spent with the schizophrenic mother. Here our N is only 20. We hope to increase the interpretability of these results by selection of both "relatively sick" and "well" subgroups of the total L Group instead of just a single Control Group. We have one other safeguard built into the research design. As indicated above, we can expect approximately 50% (100 subjects) of the H Group to develop some form of manifest psychiatric disturbance. This means that we have just observed the first wave of 20 disturbed subjects. We can expect four more waves of 20 subjects each. These waves offer opportunities for cross validation. As the number of cases mounts it will be possible to separate out diagnostic groups (such as schizophrenia) for differential data analysis.

REFERENCES

ALBEE, G. W., LANE, E. A. and REUTER, J. M. (1964) Childhood intelligence of future schizophrenics and neighborhood peers, *J. Psychol.* **58**, 141.

AUBLE, D. (1953) Extended tables for the Mann–Whitney statistic, *Bull. Inst. Educ. Res., Indiana University,* **1** (2).

AX, A. F., BECKETT, P. G. S., COHEN, B. D., FROHMAN, C. E., TOURNEY, G. and GOTTLIEB, J. S. (1962) Physiologic patterns in chronic schizophrenia, in Wortis, B. (Ed.), *Recent Advances in Biological Psychiatry,* Vol. IV, Plenum Press, New York.

AX, A. and ZACHAROPOLOUS, G. (1961) Psychophysiological data processing, in P. L. Frommer (Ed.), *Fourth International Conference on Medical Electronics, Fourteenth Annual Conference on Electrical Techniques in Medicine and Biology,* Washington, McGregor & Werner, 1961.

BOWER, E. M., SHELLHAMMER, T. A. and DAILY, J. M. (1960) School characteristics of male adolescents who later became schizophrenic, *Am. J. Orthopsychiat.* **30**, 712–29.

DIDERICHSEN, B. (1967) *Formelle Karakteristika ved Associations-forløbet hos en gruppe børn med høj risiko for schizophreni,* Københavns Universitet.

FREMMING, K. H. (1951) *The Expectation of Mental Infirmity in a Sample of the Danish Population,* Papers on Eugenics, No. 7, London, the Eugenics Society.

GOLDFARB, C. and ERLENMEYER-KIMLING, L. (1961) Changing mating and fertility patterns in schizophrenia, in F. J. Kallmann (Ed.), *Expanding Goals of Genetics in Psychiatry.*

HESTON, L. L. (1966) Psychiatric disorders in foster home reared children of schizophrenic mothers, *Brit. J. Psychiat.* **112**, 819–25.

HIGGINS, J. (1966) Effect of child rearing by schizophrenic mothers, *J. Psychiat. Res.* **4**, 153–67.

HILGARD, J. R. and NEWMAN, M. A. (1963) Parental loss by death in childhood as an etiological factor among schizophrenic and alcoholic patients compared with a non-patient community sample, *J. Nerv. Ment. Dis.* **137**, 14–28.

KALLMANN, F. J. (1946) The genetic theory of schizophrenia, *Am. J. Psychiat.* **103**, 309–22.

KETY, S. S., ROSENTHAL, D., WENDER, P. H. and SCHULSINGER, F. (1968) The types and prevalence of mental illness in the biological and adoptive families of adopted schizophrenics. A preliminary report. These Proceedings, p. 345.

LANE, E. A. and ALBEE, G. W. Childhood intellectual development of adult schizophrenics, *J. Abnorm. Social Psychol.* **67**, 186–9.

LANE, E. A. and ALBEE, G. W. (1964) Early childhood intellectual differences between schizophrenic adults and their siblings, *J. Abnorm. Social Psychol.* **68**, 193–5.

LANSING, J. B. and MUELLER, E. (1967) *Geographic Mobility of Labor,* Institute of Social Research, Ann Arbor.

LEWIS, A. J. (1957) The offspring of parents both mentally ill, *Acta Genet.* **7**, 309–22.

MALMO, R. B., SHAGASS, C. and SMITH, A. A. (1951) Responsiveness in chronic schizophrenia, *J. Personality* **19**, 359–75.

MEDNICK, S. A. (1958) A learning theory approach to research in schizophrenia, *Psychol. Bull.* **55**, 316–27.

MEDNICK, S. A. and FREEDMAN, J. (1960) Stimulus generalization, *Psychol. Bull.* **57**, 169–200.

MEDNICK, S. A. (1962) Schizophrenia: a learned thought disorder, in G. Nielsen (Ed.), *Clinical Psychology,* Proceedings of the XIV International Congress of Applied Psychology, Copenhagen, Munksgaard.

MEDNICK, S. A. and WILD, C. (1962) Reciprocal augmentation of generalization and anxiety, *J. Exp. Psychol.* **63**, 621–6.

MEDNICK, S. A. and SCHULSINGER, F. (1965a) A longitudinal study of children with a high risk for schizophrenia: a preliminary report, in S. Vandenberg (Ed.), *Methods and Goals in Human Behavior Genetics,* New York, Academic Press, pp. 255–96.

MEDNICK, S. A. and SCHULSINGER, F. (1965b) Children of schizophrenic mothers, *Bull. Inter. Assoc. Appl. Psychol.* **14**, 11–27.

MEDNICK, S. A. (1966) A longitudinal study of children with a high risk for schizophrenia, *Ment. Hyg.* **50**, 522–35.

MEDNICK, S. A. and McNEIL, T. F. (in press) Current methodology in research on the etiology of schizophrenia. Serious difficulties which suggest the use of the high-risk group method. *Psychol. Bull.*

RAY, T. S. (1963) Electrodermal indications of levels of psychological disturbance in chronic schizophrenia, *Am. Psychol.* **18**, 393.

REISBY, N. (1967) Psychoses in children of schizophrenic mothers, *Acta psychiat. scand.* **43**, 8–20.

SCHULZ, B. (1939) Empirische Untersuchungen über die beïdseitigen Belastung mit endogenen Psychosen, *Z. Neurol. Psychiat.* **165**, 97–108.

SCHULZ, B. (1940) Kinder schizophrener Elternpaare, *Z. Neurol. Psychiat.* **168**, 332–81.

SVALASTOGA, K. (1959) *Prestige, Class and Mobility,* Copenhagen, Gyldendal.

US BUREAU OF THE CENSUS (1956) *US Census of Population: 1950,* Vol. IV, *Special Reports,* Part 4, Chapter B, Population Mobility—States and State Economic Areas. US Government Printing Office, Washington, DC.

VENABLES, P. (1966) Psychophysiological aspects of schizophrenia, *Brit. J. Med. Psychol.* **39**, 289–97.

ZAHN, T. P. (1964) Autonomic reactivity and behaviour in schizophrenia, *Psychiat. Res. Rep.* **19**, 156–71.

THE DEVELOPMENTAL PRECURSORS OF ADULT
SCHIZOPHRENIA*

E. James Anthony †

William Greenleaf Eliot Division of Child Psychiatry,
Washington University, St. Louis

In addition to a consideration of genetic and environmental factors impinging on the individual, our study was designed to include the aspect of development and allow us to sample the characteristics of schizophrenics' children at different ages. There is thus a preschool group up to 5 years, an elementary school group up to 11 years and a high school group up to 17 years. Since all the children in a given family are included in the study, we are in a position to assess the differential responses of children coming from the same familial environment and to relate them to the ages of the children at the time of the parent's illness.

Two main factors have come under special scrutiny: the degree of *vulnerability* to the genetic factor and the degree of *susceptibility* to the abnormal environmental influences. In our pilot sample, we had been struck by the range and intensity of reactions within the same family from apparently normal to the grossly abnormal and were reminded of an analogy put forward by Jacques May, the disease ecologist, who once discussed vulnerability to stress in the context of three dolls made respectively of glass, plastic and steel exposed to the same standard blow from a hammer. Under impact, the glass doll fragmented, the plastic one showed a dent and the steel one emitted a pleasant musical sound. We concluded that in our investigation, we would be as interested in the "dolls" that gave out "a pleasant musical sound" as in the ones that broke down or scarred. Our overall expectation of morbidity during childhood was based on a careful consideration of the literature. There would be a group of children (10–20%) with a strong diathesis towards schizophrenia, and of these about half would appear relatively normal and half would display manifest indications of predisposition (schizoidness, schizothymia). A second group would show disturbances of varying kinds and degrees brought about through living with one or two schizophrenic parents (about 20–30%). A third group (30–50%) would show relatively normal reactions or even "superphrenic" responses indicative of enhanced qualities of sensitivity and creativity.

* Supported by US PHS Research Grant MH–12043–01 and R01–MH–14052–01. This latter grant is concerned with a system of corrective interventions in the same research population as in the first grant and represents the elaboration of the concept of a specialized "research clinic" set up to deal with problems uncovered by the primary research. The research group in St. Louis is made up of E. James Anthony, Loretta Cass, Norman Corah, Lois Franklin, Rosemary Funderburg, Boaz Kahana, John Lewis, Manon McGinnis, Jon Plapp, John Stern and Marylyn Voerg.

† This paper was not presented at the Conference. Dr. Anthony spoke of his research at length during the discussions. Later, he was invited to prepare this article for inclusion in the published proceedings.

T

THE RESEARCH POPULATION

The research population is drawn from several mental, general and special hospitals in the metropolitan area of St. Louis. The central investigation involves the comparison of a group of children of schizophrenic parents with a matched group of children of parents undergoing hospitalization for some subacute or chronic physical illness. Since the commencement of the project, the design has been expanded in certain ways such as in the inclusion of some manic-depressive parents and of a small control group of 60 parents giving no history of serious or disabling mental or physical illness. As far as the two major comparison groups are concerned, certain of the stresses of illness are the same for both—the concern over a sick parent, the separation as a result of hospitalization, the "broken home" and the disruption of regular home life with substitute care on occasion. It is difficult, however, to control for some of the factors such as the more disruptive impact of the remitting—relapsing type of patient as opposed to the chronically incarcerated one, although the total duration of hospitalization, which is being controlled, may be the same for both. The criteria for the proband cases are the following: a family with both parents alive and living together—apart from the period of hospitalization—having children under the age of 17, and in which the sick parent has been diagnosed unequivocally as suffering from schizophrenia without the contaminating factors of serious physical disability or disease or organic brain syndrome. The diagnosis is made in the first place by the admitting hospital; in the second place by the research psychiatrist assessing the mental status without any recourse to the hospital record; and in the third place by an independent judge reviewing both the hospital record and the findings of the research psychiatrist. The criteria for the main comparison group are almost the same: families in which both parents are alive and living together—apart from the period of hospitalization—having children below the age of 17, and in which the diagnosis of the sick parent is one of subacute or chronic disabling physical illness, excluding organic brain syndrome. There must also be no history or evidence of significant psychiatric disorder requiring treatment or hospitalization either in the sick parent or in the spouse. There is also matching of socioeconomic, educational and racial factors as well as total duration of hospitalization.

The research design is shown in Table 1. The additional control group of children having

TABLE 1

Age and sex of child		Experimental group		Control group		Totals
		Father	Mother	Father	Mother	
Ages 1–5	Boy	10	10	10	10	40
	Girl	10	10	10	10	40
Ages 6–10	Boy	30	30	20	20	100
	Girl	30	30	20	20	100
Ages 11–17	Boy	10	10	10	10	40
	Girl	10	10	10	10	40
Totals		100	100	80	80	360

parents who are neither physically nor mentally ill has not been included in this design, since it includes only children between the ages of 6 and 10, which is the age group at which the main experimental procedures are directed.

METHODOLOGY

The method of investigation is divided into three parts: a field study, a clinical appraisal and an experimental investigation. The three approaches vary in the degree to which the investigator is "blind" in his approach to the subject. The field study is open, the clinical study is relatively blind and the experimental study is rigorously blind.

A. *The field study*

This is based on a week of living-in experience with the family and the worker is necessarily aware that the parent in question is mentally or physically ill. Only 20 families of the total research sample are involved and family life is studied in depth by means of continuous protocols that are tape-recorded at specified periods during the day. The key families are as representative of the total sample as possible and show differences with regard to social class, race, religion, type of illness and sex of the sick parent. The research objectives include an analysis of the disorganization induced by "the culture of psychosis", the mode of encapsulation of the family and the social orbit as made up of relatives and friends. The evaluation of the "culture" is made by a field worker under the supervision of an anthropologist and the criteria are both objective and subjective. On the objective side there is a rating of time schedules, the distribution and arrangement of possessions, the deployment of space, the programming of household tasks, the planning of future events and the systems involved in housekeeping and cleaning. On the subjective side, the observer records as freely and spontaneously as he can the degree of discomfort occasioned in him by the living-in experience.

B. *Clinical appraisal*

Each one of the family members is interviewed and tested in a number of different ways by the team of research psychiatrists and psychologists. The interviewing psychiatrist knows to which group his subject belongs since he is making a systematic study of the ways in which parents and children relate around the problem of the parent's mental or physical illness. At the same time, an examination is made of the mental and physical status. Using the latter information only, and therefore working blindly, the reviewing psychiatrist attempts to make a clinical diagnosis and a general rating of adjustment. The psychiatrist's evaluation of the child includes somatometry, an estimation of physical strength, a short neurological examination and an assessment of physical neglect. A global rating of physical well-being is then made.

1. *Psychiatrist's evaluation of the sick parent*

The sick parent, either mentally or physically sick, is evaluated in terms of observable behavioral characteristics such as might be perceived by the child, so that a "child's-eye view" of the parent's illness is obtained. If the parent is reasonably communicative, an assessment of the relationship with the children is made, especially with regard to the direction of the child's attachments, imitations and identifications. The parent is then rated on the extent to which he is able to differentiate, physically and psychologically, between the children. The examination of the mental status includes the cognitive capacity to deal with proverbs and the categorization of cognitive style in terms of amorphous, concrete, analytical, pseudosystematic and normal, concluding with a global rating of the thought disorder if any. This is followed by an inquiry into the genesis of any delusions and hallucinations with specific reference to type, degree of systematization, strength of conviction and modality of hallucination. A rating is then made of the involvement of the children in either the delusions or hallucinations. The affect is next assessed in terms of a humorous cartoon and the affective style categorized into incongruous, flat, hyperresponsive, depressed and normal. This is followed by a global rating of any affect disorder. Finally, the area of conation is discussed in terms of goals, interests, hobbies and enthusiasms and the conative style categorized as bizarre, plausible but unrealistic, down-to-earth, limited interests and complete apathy. Again, a global rating of a conation disorder, if any, is made. The interviewer then records his impression of how the predominant mode of parental behavior might be perceived by the child in terms of avoidance of contact, constant reproach, distrustfulness and suspicion, sexual manipulation and violent attack. Later, further information about the premorbid adjustment is obtained from the spouse, supplementing what is obtained from the patient, and the psychotic disturbance is then plotted on a continuum ranging from process to reactive depending on scores obtained on a special process-reactive inquiry form. (See Appendix 1.) In general, hebephrenic and catatonic schizophrenias tend to produce low scores, paranoid and simple schizophrenias, intermediate ones, and schizo-affective and pseudoneurotic psychoses relatively high scores. When the child's disturbance is rated simply in terms of severity, it would seem, so far, that the lower the score on the P–R scale, the less

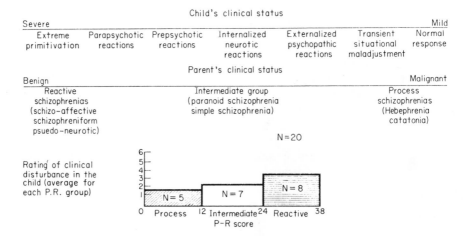

Fig. 1. Parallel morbidity in child and schizophrenic parents.

intense is the disturbance in the child and vice versa. Paradoxically, the more severely psychotic the parent is, the less upset does the child seem.

Further consideration suggests that this may be a matter of timing. The reactive psychoses, especially when a large amount of affect is available, are more likely to involve the child in chaotic interpersonal events and situations and thus create immediate disturbances. The withdrawing, avoidance process cases are less involving, make less impact on the child and, therefore, generate far less immediate disturbance. Later, in maturity, the more insidious, subterranean constitutional tendencies take over and gross disturbances begin to appear. In short, the reactive group elicits current reactions from the child whilst the process group tends to defer its effects until adult life.

2. *Evaluation of the spouse by the psychiatrist*

It has been shown (Kreitman, 1964; Nielsen, 1964) that a higher frequency of mental illness in the spouses of mental patients does exist and that although cumulative and detrimental interaction might be responsible for some of this, assortative mating also appears to be a factor. A psychiatric diagnosis, therefore, is also made on the well parent and, in addition, he is rated on six-point scales for supportiveness, reality orientation and sense of humor. The tendency to transmit insufficient, inaccurate or distorted descriptions and explanations of the spouse's illness to the children is also explored and rated.

3. *The psychiatric examination of the child*

Evidence of pre-psychotic developments are searched for in the child by means of a check list of precursive symptoms, the history of precursive episodes of withdrawal, "microparanoia" or transient panic reactions with primitivization, manifestations of precursive personality developments of a schizoid, paranoid or cycloid pattern and demonstrations of precursive cognitive functioning in terms of amorphous, concretistic, analytical or pseudosystematic styles.

To test for para-psychotic developments due to undue psychotic influencing of the child and manifested in *folie à deux*, Ganser Syndrome, fugues and twilight states, the following measures are used: body sway (suggestibility), unorthodoxed commands (submissiveness), the identification test (identification with the sick parent) and a group of evaluations exploring unusual involvement with the sick parent or his illness. For example, the child is questioned on his knowledge of parental illness, more especially his reactions to the delusions and hallucinations and his degree of conviction about the validity, the three houses test (if you have three houses, one in which you live, a house next door and a faraway house, where would you put people in your family?), the three wishes test (the extent to which they include a wish for the cure and homecoming of the sick parent), the three dreams test (in which the child is presented with a "day residue" and asked to construct a dream; the "day residue" suggested to the child is that he has been sick during that day, that he has been to hospital to visit a sick friend and that he has seen a street accident). Finally, in a doctor game, using miniature figures, he is asked to diagnose, treat and prognosticate regarding a patient. Finally, global ratings of adjustment are made, a similar rating being used by every other investigator receiving the child into a test situation. In making a psychiatric diagnosis on the child, use is made of a special diagnostic form in which the categories have been specially defined for use in the present project. (See Appendix 2.)

It should be emphasized that the children's behavior form and the ratings of adjustment are completed blindly by psychologists, psychophysiologists and teacher. The psychiatrist, on the other hand, is aware of the child's status since his task is to explore the influence of the parent's illness on the thought and feeling of the child.

4. *Evaluation of the family members by the psychologist*

The parents are given a battery of tests that include the WISC, the Rorschach, the TAT and the MMPI. The well parent is also asked to sort a large number of behavior cards (78 items in all) into those that are like and unlike her child. These behavioral items have already been clustered into three groups, after Walker (1963), roughly representing an ectomorphic–introversive syndrome, a mesomorphic–extroverted syndrome and an endomorphic–ambiversive syndrome.

The child is given the WISC, supported by the Binet and Cattel for the younger children, the Bender–Gestalt, the Beery, the Rorschach (scoring for penetration and Fisher's maladjustment index), a modified TAT, a scale for defensiveness (Sarason), the Bene–Anthony Family Relations Test indicating degree of involvement in the family members and the distribution of positive and negative feelings in the family.

5. *Evaluation of the family and family environment by the social worker*

A home visit is made on each family at which time three schedules are completed: an interview schedule devised by Witkin and aimed at eliciting the degree to which psychological growth has been fostered and differentiated. An "indicator system" is built into the interview and "models" are provided of inhibiting and fostering régimes; a family interactional scale devised by Behrens, and the behavior form for children similar to the one completed by other members of the research team.

C. *Experimental investigation*

In the experimental approach, the schizophrenic parent is regarded in three different ways: as a behavioral model which the child attempts to imitate, as a programmer to the child's everyday learning experiences feeding in information that enables it to apprehend and conceptualize the current status of its environment, and as a crucial differentiating agent in the child's growth and development. When such basic human experience is associated with grossly abnormal and inconsistent behavior, incongruous distortions of contact and communication and amorphous, diffuse relatedness, peculiarities and cognition, affect, conation, perception and communication in the child might be anticipated.

There are certain major incongruities in the disordered parent that may determine response behavior in the child in experimental situations designed to tap such responses.

1. *Affect discrimination test*

The test consists of a series of photographs in which actors, male and female, have expressed, in exaggerated form, the common emotions such as happiness, pleasure, anger, sadness, shame, disgust. The child is asked to identify the expressions of the adults and correlate them with given situations that might have brought them into play. The test has already been standardized on normal schoolchildren from 6 to 12 showing a clear, fairly even developmental trend. The normative study delayed its application in the present research and there are insufficient figures to present. However, it does seem that the experimental group of children tend to produce gross errors of identification more frequently than controls.

2. *The double-bind test*

This test has undergone some modification since it was first conceived and administered. In the pilot sample, we made use of simultaneous visual and auditory messages and the child was instructed to disregard one modality and respond to the other. Here again the confused responses were quite striking in some of the experimental group, but the prevalence of reading difficulties made it sometimes difficult to assess the results. In its present form, the child wears earphones and has two dissimilar messages fed in simultaneously through each ear, one in a male and one in a female voice. In the first series, he is asked to respond to the female voice and ignore the male voice and then vice versa and in the third series he is left free to choose his voice. In each instance, the voices instruct him to carry out a series of little concrete activities using play material placed in front of him. An interesting question yet to be answered is whether the children, when free to do so, select the same sex voice as that of the sick parent. It is anticipated that the more disturbed children, showing para-psychotic symptoms and more closely identified with the sick parent will tend to choose in that direction.

3. *The expectation of benevolence or hostility test*

In this play situation, the children are confronted by a bag of golden coins on one hand and a nasty looking plastic spider on the other. They are then asked to predict whether a stranger would be more likely to do them good, that is present them with the money, or do them harm, that is set the spider on them. They are given no data about the stranger or his possible reactions. Next, the children are again asked to predict the stranger's response when his own self-interests are put into direct conflict with theirs. Would he in fact be considerate to them if it also implies choosing badly for himself? An overall appraisal in this particular test situation tries to guage whether the children are sufficiently competent and reality based to dismiss the exercise as lacking sufficient data regarding the stranger's background and response behavior to warrant making any predictions. A normative study has been completed on the test and an early experience with the experimental group appears to justify its inclusion, the reactions in some cases being peculiarly incongruous.

4. *The three mountains test*

This is derived from Piaget's work and has already been used by Anthony (1958) on schizophrenic children. In this experimental situation, the subjects are asked to put themselves into the position of a miniature figure located on some play mountains and to empathize with his perspective. This requires that they have overcome the developmental hazard of egocentrism and appears to be particularly difficult for withdrawn, self-absorbed children.

5. *The "broken bridge" test*

This also derives from Piaget and attempts to assess the degree to which the subjects have overcome a developmental tendency toward magical, pre-causal and pre-logical styles of thinking and to what extent they might relapse into it when confronted with a problem-solving situation. The test consists of a series of pictures which are gradually unfolded and represent a sequence of actions—some children are stealing apples from an orchard—the farmer observes them and gives chase—the children, in escaping, run across an old bridge— it collapses and they fall into the water. Question: Would the bridge have broken if the children had not been doing something wrong and is there, in fact, an "imminent justice" in the nature of things?

6. *The children's embedded figures test*

This is a test, coming from Witkin's laboratory, standardized on normal children and designed to evaluate degrees of differentiation.

7. *Psychophysiological study*

The purpose of the psychophysiological study is to determine where the differences exist between children of mentally ill parents, physically ill parents and parents who have not been ill, mentally or physically, to any significant degree in terms of the following parameters:

(A) *Plethysmographic responsiveness.* Continuous recordings of responses by the vaso-motor system are obtained from the fingers of the subject's left and right hands. The appearance is the adaptation of plethysmographic responses to repetitive stimuli of cool and warm air blown over the arm; differences in responsiveness between the stimulated hand and the non-stimulated hand are of particular interest.

(B) *Electrodermal responsiveness.* Electrodes attached to the palms and ventral surfaces of the forearm of each limb provide continuous recordings of palmar skin potential activity. Again, the initial appearance of responses to air stimulation, the adaptation of these responses, and differences in responsiveness between stimulated and non-stimulated limbs are of major concern. The general expectation is that the high-risk children will show a more immature pattern of responsiveness.

SOME PRELIMINARY RESULTS FROM THE FIRST YEAR OF THE RESEARCH

The various tests in the clinical and experimental approaches were all geared to the series of hypotheses which can be categorized into four sets:

A. The comparison of children of psychotic parents with the children of control parents.
B. The comparison of the disturbed children of psychotic parents with the non-disturbed children of psychotic parents.

C. The comparison of the disturbance in the parents with the disturbance in the children.

D. The comparison of the home environment of the psychotic parents with the home environment of the control parents.

A. *The comparison of children of psychotic parents with the children of control parents*

1. Children of psychotic parents as a group will show a higher prevalence of *clinical disturbance* as compared to children of physically ill parents.

2. Children of psychotic parents will show a greater prevalence of *intrapsychic symptoms* of maladjustment as opposed to *acting out symptoms* as compared to the children of controls.

3. Children of psychotic parents will show a greater impairment of *peer group relations* as compared to the children of controls.

4. The ratings of clinical disturbance being equal, the children of psychotic parents will show a higher frequency of *"precursor" symptoms* as compared to the children of controls.

B. *The comparison of the disturbed children of psychotic parents with the non-disturbed children of psychotic parents*

5. The mean I.Q. of the disturbed children will be lower than the mean I.Q. of the non-disturbed children.

6. The disturbed children will show a greater *variability of intelligence* than the non-disturbed children.

7. The disturbed children will show a greater preponderance of *"organic" features* than the non-disturbed children.

8. The mean *age* of the disturbed children will be lower than the mean age of the non-disturbed children.

9. The *sex* of the disturbed children will be more frequently the same as the sex of the psychotic parent as compared to the non-disturbed children.

10. The disturbed children will more frequently have *mothers* who are psychotic as compared to non-disturbed children.

11. As a corollary to hypotheses 7 and 8, the disturbed children will be more frequently the *daughters of psychotic mothers* as compared to the non-disturbed children.

12. The disturbed children will be more *similar in personality characteristics* to the psychotic parent than the non-disturbed children.

13. The disturbed children will be more *suggestible* than the non-disturbed children.

14. The disturbed children will be less *defensive* than the non-disturbed children.

15. The disturbed children will be *more identified* with the psychotic parent than the non-disturbed children.

C. *The comparison of the disturbance in the parents with the disturbance in the children*

16. The greater the *disturbance* in the sick parent, the greater will be the disturbance in the children.
17. The poorer the *pre-morbid personality* of the sick parent, the greater will be the disturbance in the children.
18. The greater the disturbance in the *"well parent"*, the greater will be the disturbance in the children.
19. The shorter the *time interval* from the onset of the parental psychosis, the greater will be the disturbance in the children.
20. The more the children are *included in the symptomatology* of the sick parent, the more disturbed will they tend to be.
21. The greater the *involvement in the illness* of the parent, the more disturbed will the children be.

D. *The comparison of the home environment of the psychotic parents with the home environment of the control parents*

22. The *child-rearing practices* of the psychotic parents will be more growth-inhibiting as compared to the control parents.
23. The *daily life* of the children in the homes of psychotic parents will be less organized as compared to the homes of control parents.
24. The *degree of disruption following hospitalization* will be greater in the home environment of the psychotic parent as compared to the controls.
25. There will be a greater *incidence of psychiatric disturbance* in the family background of psychotic parents as compared to controls.
26. As compared to control families, the families of the psychotic parents will be low on *sociability*.
27. The *care-taking individuals* deputizing for the hospitalized parents will show a greater degree of disturbance when the hospitalized parent is psychotic than when the parent is physically ill.
28. There will be a higher incidence of *physical illness* (both major and minor) in the children of psychotic parents as compared to controls.

All the tests used in the research are pointed at one or more of these twenty-eight hypotheses and no test is included without a complete rationale regarding its appropriateness to this set of hypotheses.

Measurement techniques

All rating scales used in the research consist of 5 or 6 points with descriptive adjectives of the dimensions to be rated. The judges engaged in making the ratings undergo pre-training to provide necessary conditions for acceptable reliability ratings. As previously stated in the first system of evaluations, the psychiatrist is not "blind" in his evaluation of both adult and child subjects. Subsequently, however, any identifying information about the parent's status as a subject is deleted from the records as independent judges review the material and rerate the subjects on the same scales. Behavioral ratings are made by all researchers to come into contact with the subjects.

RESULTS OF THE CLINICAL STUDY

The results that follow are given to indicate general trends that are appearing at this early stage of the investigation and must be regarded as highly tentative. With regard to intelligence levels on the WISC, it will be noticed that the "high risk" children are apparently doing better than the controls (children with physically ill parents), but this may simply reflect a social class bias, since the control group currently is made up predominantly of lower class Negro children.

TABLE 2. INTELLIGENCE LEVELS AND MEAN SCALE SCORES FOR EACH SUB-TEST OF THE WISC FOR HIGH RISK VS. CONTROL CASES

	Age group	I	C	A	S	V	D	PC	PA	B	O	(01)	Full scale V/P
High risk (N=26)	6–8	10	9	9	11	11	11	11	11	9	12	12	1·060 / 103·8 / 1·073
	9+	10	10	10	11	9	8	10	10	11	11	9	99·7 / 97·3 / 100·7
Control (N=18)	6–8	9	8	8	11	9	9	10	8	8	10	11	96·4 / 94·3 / 99·1
	9+	8	8	7	10	7	8	11	9	8	9	8	89·3 / 88·6 / 92·6

Mean ± one SD for Wechler's normal group: 7–13.

The results in Fig. 1 have already drawn some comment. The parallel morbidities in children and schizophrenic parents is also illustrated in Fig. 1. In the course of the present year, a number of unusual syndromes have come to light under the intensive clinical study. We have observed, for example, four areas of response behavior which we believe to be pre-psychotic, that is prodromata of later psychosis. The genetic, constitutional and environmental factors in these vulnerable children seem to point in one direction. The summation of birth weight, body size, body build and body strength data are already suggestive of constitutional differences between this type of pre-psychotic child and his siblings. In 4 cases out of 5, this child was the most puny in the family. So far, we have not found any major stresses differentiating him from the rest of the family. In order to classify a subject in the pre-psychotic category, the following requirements need to be met:

1. A physical status score (birth weight, body build, body size and body strength) in the lowest quartile.
2. An ectomorphic–introversive listing of behavioral characteristics in the like–unlike my child sorting test carried out by the mother.
3. An occurrence of over 8 items in the check list of precursive symptoms (the list of 24 symptoms include such items as extreme shyness, undue suspiciousness, excessive day-dreaming, extreme apprehensiveness, listlessness, rigidity, etc.).
4. One or more instances of precursive episodes of withdrawal, mistrustfulness or extreme regression. Such episodes are usually clearly remembered by parental inform-ants since they represent a striking departure from the child's habitual mode of behavior.
5. In the check list of precursive symptoms, the parent is asked to give a temporal rating on each item varying from "never present" to "always present". The conjunction of certain precursive symptoms with the "always present" rating allows for a classi-fication of a precursive personality pattern, be it schizoid, paranoid, cycloid, etc.
6. A high rating on the precursive thought disorder in its amorphous, concretistic, analytic or pseudo-systematic form. (In the last named, there is a quasi-systematic approach to causal events with pseudo-associations based on pre-logical argument. An understanding of the child's thought in terms of the developmental stages des-cribed by Piaget help us to understand why it is that fully systematized paranoid delusions do not occur until adolescence. The cognitive style of the younger child allows him only fleeting connections between malevolent ideas, whilst during the middle years of childhood, he is able to link them together through not more than two or three associations. In early adolescence, however, his abstract, propositional type of thinking allows him to weld a coherent, internally consistent group of para-noid ideas together with a firmness that withstands confrontation and challenge.)

Illustration

The precursive, micro-paranoidal episode may last anything from 3 days to 3 months and then seems to disappear almost completely with the child resuming normal reality testing and ego functioning. Peggy, aged 8, is an example of one of these "little madnesses". She is a girl of superior intelligence who is doing extremely well at school. She was always regarded as sensitive, given to taking life over seriously, but at the same time remaining fairly popular with her classmates. She was always extremely well behaved, and her teacher referred to her as "trustworthy". (One would place her in group 4 of the Kasanin groupings of the pre-psychotic state.) One day, on the playground at school, she was asked by a boy to throw him a rock so that he could bat it with a stick. Before she could bring herself to realize that this was against the rules, she had done so, and immediately she was overcome with guilt and remorse. When they went into the classroom again, she felt as if everybody was staring at her and that the teacher was paying special attention to her. All of a sudden, the boy involved in the situation went up to the teacher's desk, whispered to her and went out. (He had asked to go to the bathroom.) She immediately felt that he had taken it upon himself to report her and had been told to go to the headmistress and give a full account of the incident. She became more and more terror stricken until eventually she could bear it no longer and broke into loud wailing. Nothing the teacher could do was able to reassure her. She felt that she was trapped and that they were going to do some-thing terrible to her. She was no better at home, and since she could not be induced to return to school again, I admitted her to hospital. When first seen, she was intensely suspicious and felt that I had been in touch with school and was simply trying to get her to confess. As a result, she was uncommunicative and wary. Naturally, of its own accord, the intensity of the reaction subsided, and within a period of 3 months she resumed her normal, pleasantly cooperative behavior and was even able to laugh at the silly ideas she had once had. She returned to school and continued to do very well. A year and a half later, I saw her for a minor episode involving some pimples on her skin; she felt that some of the children might have been making offensive additions to her diet when she was not looking. This little episode subsided without admission. The relevant information in her case is that her mother had been hospitalized on two occasions with a diagnosis of paranoid schizophrenia.

In order to classify a subject in the para-psychotic category, the following requirements must be met:

1. The subject should be of the same sex as the parent, unduly attached to him, frequently in his company, and very much given to sharing "secrets" and confidences (which include delusional and hallucinatory material) with the parent.
2. The parent in question would most likely be the mother.
3. The familial environment would be highly tolerant of abnormality and eccentricity.
4. The child would fall into the sub-average level of intelligence, mostly in the 80s and below.
5. The subject would score highly on the test for suggestibility (body sway).
6. The child would score highly on the test for submissiveness.
7. In the Identification Test, the child would identify most strongly with the sick parent even against the sex role expectancy.
8. In the Test for Involvement, the child would tend to show a high degree of involvement, both with the sick parent and with his sickness.

This induced psychosis or *folie à deux* may be complete or incomplete, continuous or intermittent, and mild or severe. In general, it mirrors the parent's illness fairly closely and, unlike the pre-psychotic reactions, it tends to disappear altogether when the child is separated permanently from the parent. It has been found to occur most frequently in the mother–daughter dyad.

The impact of a delusional system on a family of children can be roughly predicted from our measures of identification, involvement, suggestibility, and submissiveness. Conviction may at times be as strong as that evinced by the deluded parent, but as the latter's influence is less directly or forcibly applied, the child's conviction, in turn, becomes modifiable. He may, for example, believe in the delusion only at home and not at school, or only in the presence of a deluded parent and not in his absence, or only if alone with the deluded parent and not in a family or extended group where there are good reality-oriented figures about.

Illustration

The variability in the response of a sibship is well shown in the case of a 12-year-old girl who believed completely with her mother that someone was poisoning the food at home and, like her mother, refused to eat except in a restaurant. Her sister, 2 years younger, also refused to take the food but only when the mother ate with the family and not when father was home. A 7-year-old boy, when asked about the problem and why he was able to eat, shrugged his shoulders casually and said, "Well, I'm not dead yet!"

Another para-psychotic reaction is very similar to the adult Ganser syndrome. Here the child does not imitate the parent's psychosis but in fact concocts a psychosis of his own which once again reflects his stage of development and his cognitive and conceptual capacity. It also reflects his own understanding and experience of mental illness and very naturally embodies a certain amount of misconception. The clinical picture, although bizarre, is quite unlike anything that can be met with in childhood psychosis, and wildly approximate answers are given. The mechanism is not an "identification with the crazy one" as with the previous condition but rather, when investigated more closely, a pathetic attempt to relieve magically the psychotic illness of the parent.

Illustration

A boy, aged 8, the only child and youngest son of poor white parents living under very dilapidated circumstances, came into the interview shaking his head from side to side and rolling his eyes upwards. He lurched about the room and eventually sat on the floor in the corner constantly contorting his features or gyrating his limbs. When asked what was the matter, he said, in a silly, simpering way, "You think my brain has bust, but I'm just nutty and fruity!" When asked his name, he would give his telephone number and eventually offered his sister's name. He said that he could not count from 1 to 10 because he was stupid and that he could only count from 10 backwards to 1. His history and test responses indicated a strong involvement with his very psychotic father to whom he had been devoted until the latter's hospitalization with paranoid schizophrenia a year previously. In one of his "saner" responses, the boy said that when he grew up he wanted to become like his dad so that he could fight all of his dad's enemies.

A more frequent response to the psychotic illness is an externalized (often anti-social) disturbance which may last from anywhere between 2 months and 2 years and then tends to subside gradually unless reactivated by a relapse; or an internalized disturbance involving anxiety, depression, phobias, guilt, inhibition and shame.

PRELIMINARY FINDINGS FROM THE FIELD STUDY

The type of disorganization induced by the "cultural psychosis" tends to vary with the sex of the psychotic parent and with the type of psychosis. There is no doubt, so far, that maternal psychosis creates more disorganization, particularly with regard to the children since her hospitalization leads inevitably to surrogation by familiar or unfamiliar caretakers. (The problem of surrogation in this field is a complicated one since the familiar figures, grandparents and others, who come in are often tainted with elements of mental illness which may be as disturbing to the children as the stranger reactions they experience when unrelated homemakers are brought in.) It goes without saying that the outsider is far more impressed by the disorganization than the indweller, so that the first impact is in the nature of a cultural shock. However, even after a week of living in, our workers have reported some degree of acculturation to the strange condition and less officiousness on their part in attempting to reorganize it. The more that they participate intimately in the daily living, the less do they feel alienated from the unusual occurrences. The family itself is governed by the same principle: the longer it has lived in the psychotic culture, the more resistant does it appear to be to all outside intervention attempting change. The index of disorganization (calculated from the various social measures) varies with the size of the family, the number of preschool children, the amount of living space available, and the presence of relatively healthy, reality-oriented adults.

Allowing for these modifying factors, three main types of disorganization can be delineated:

1. A nuclear type where the parent is hebephrenic or catatonic and the household suffers neglect from often extreme degrees of *laissez-faire* and permissiveness. The children begin to lead separate lives of their own, unsupervised and undisciplined, and there is a high incidence of behavior problems.

Illustration

The social investigator arrived at a derelict building, badly in need of repair and found two of the children, a boy aged 9 and a girl aged 7, squatting comfortably on a wall sharing a cigarette. The girl had no pants on and made no postured adjustment to disguise the fact. When asked the whereabouts of their mother, the boy said that "Old Annie" was where she always was, in the backroom. "Take care you don't hurt her when you go in," he added, "she lies on the floor by the door." (There was a curious warmth in his voice and he might have been speaking of a favorite pet.)

2. A paranoidal type, where there is "organized disorganization" in the sense that the family is incorporated into the workings of a delusional system and its whole way of life radically altered to the great bewilderment of the children.

Illustration

In a recent case, a father with paranoid schizophrenia turned his home into a beleaguered fortress in which the family mounted watches against the enemy, and weapon training was rigorously enforced. A great deal of secrecy prevailed, and no one was allowed to come and go without an examination of credentials. A child who went out shopping was closely interrogated on his return. One of the children complained bitterly that he even had to report before going to the bathroom.

3. A reactive type in which inconsistency, made up of contradictory communications, highly ambivalent but powerful affects, chaotic management, and a disturbing degree of intrusiveness into the lives of the children, is the rule. This "environment of irrationality" envelops the family and makes for unpredictable storms and crises that hover over the lives of the children. At one moment they are pulled into intimate closeness and at the next thrust far away with bitter and unjustified recriminations. Belief in the psychotic ideation of the parent becomes a condition for the object relationship so that it is often a case of "love me, love my delusion". In order to keep in with the parent, the children will frequently disguise their doubts and disbeliefs, and the relative pulls of reality and unreality, of rationality and irrationality, of conviction and skepticism can set up peculiar conflicts of loyalty. In these cases, the children are often part of the delusional system and may even be considered among the persecutors. At times they give the impression of floating passively like flotsam in the direction of the pressures exerted upon them.

Illustration

A 5-year-old girl was believed by her father to be a love child of the mother by some other man. At these times he would become furious and, without reason, suddenly seize upon the little girl and start beating her and dragging her across the room by her hair. At other times, he would observe that she was wearing clothes that he had bought her and a bracelet that he had given her and would be overcome by the conviction that she was his daughter and completely like him in every way. He would then proceed to caress her passionately, frightening the child by his vehemence.

As a general rule, the disorganization brought about by a physical illness in the parent such as tuberculosis is not only less intense but also lacks some of the bizarre elements that are present when the parent is mentally ill. The control families seem on the whole more in contact with the outside world, more able to negotiate with agencies for assistance, less loaded with peculiar and unhelpful relatives and friends, and more likely to achieve a satisfactory surrogation. An infectious illness, such as tuberculosis, does create unusual problems for the relationship in that the parents restrict the amount of close physical contact and actually make themselves seem dangerous to the child.

EXPERIMENTAL FINDINGS IN THE FIRST GROUP OF SUBJECTS

1. The CEFT, the "Three Mountains" Test, and the "Broken Bridge" Test
(Data assembled and discussed by Boaz Kahana, Ph.D.)

As expected, the scores on all three tests improve as a function of age in both the experimental and control group. In the 6–8 age range, both groups have similar scores, but in the 9-plus age range, the experimental group performs better despite the fact that their mean age is lower than that of the control.

TABLE 3. THREE TESTS FOR DIFFERENTIATING HIGH RISK AND
CONTROL GROUPS

Test	Group	Mean ages	Mean scores
CEFT*	High Risk (N=15)	(6–8)= 6·9	7·20
		(9+)= 9·6	18·80
		(Total)= 7·8	11·06
	Control (N=9)	(6–8)= 7·7	10·0
		(9+)=10·7	15·0
		(Total)= 9·7	13·3
Three Mountains† (Piaget)	High Risk (N=20)	(6–8)= 6·8	2·11
		(9+)=10·2	2·67
		(Total)= 8·3	2·50
	Control (N=7)	(6–8)= 7·7	2·30
		(9+)=10·7	2·45
		(Total)= 9·7	2·44
Broken Bridge‡ (Piaget)	High Risk (N=14)	(6–8)= 7·0	1·62
		(9+)= 9·9	2·60
		(Total)= 8·0	1·95
	Control (N=9)	(6–8)= 8·0	1·75
		(9+)=10·6	2·2
		(Total)= 9·9	2·1

* Range of score 0–22.   † Range of score 0–3.
‡ Range of score 0–3.

It should be mentioned that much of the "richness" of these tests lies in their content and that the scores themselves tend to iron out important differences. Although the high risk group are able to hit the same score as the controls, they often do so for unusual reasons, so that they differ qualitatively although not quantitatively.

2. *The Psychophysiological Examination*
(*Data assembled and discussed by Jon Plapp, Ph.D.*)

A. *The plethysmographic responses*

Current investigation has shown that there are differences between younger and older normal schoolchildren in the relative aptitude of the plethysmographic dilation responses to warm air given by stimulated and non-stimulated hands. There is a tendency for differentiation to increase over trials, and, in addition, there is a general tendency for younger subjects to show less differentiation during earlier trials.

In Fig. 2, parallel data are presented for the high-risk children and for the children of physically ill parents. The data for the 12 children of physically ill parents (age range 6–12; median age 9 years) does not appear to be different from that of the normal children in terms of absolute magnitudes of responsiveness or tendency for differentiated responding to become more frequent over trials. However, the data for the children of schizophrenic

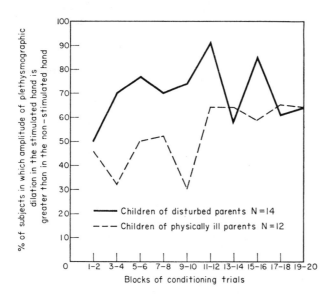

FIG. 2.

parents apparently does differ from that of either the normal children or of the children of physically ill parents. These 14 children (age range 7–13 years; median age 9 years) tend to show rapid initial differentiation which is maintained at high levels, and there is little evidence for a gradual increase in differentiation over the series of trials. The data raised the possibility that these children may show a tendency toward over-differentiation, at least with respect to relative amplitude of responding to heat stimulation in the psychophysiological system being considered here—the vasomotor system. Naturally, a careful examination of this trend, with controls for social class and intelligence, will need to be made before it can be considered more than an interesting trend.

U

In Fig. 3 which deals with absolute frequencies of response rather than amplitude and represents differentiation in terms of higher frequencies of response on the part of the stimulated as opposed to the non-stimulated hand, a further trend may be detected. Here, too, there is evidence that, particularly in early trials, the children of schizophrenic parents respond at higher levels than do the children of physically ill parents. This is true for the responses given by both stimulated and non-stimulated hands.

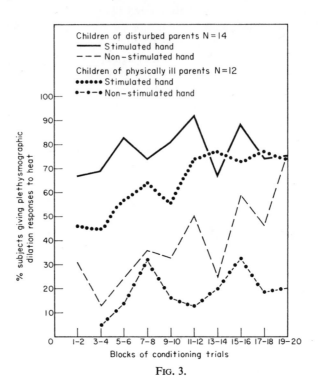

FIG. 3.

Again, looking simply at the frequencies of dilation response in the stimulated hand, there seems to be a more gradual "learning" effect for the children of physically ill parents, whereas the children of schizophrenics apparently reach asymptote almost immediately. Perhaps the most noteworthy feature of these data is, however, to be found in the way in which differentiation, as indicated by low frequencies responding in non-stimulated as opposed to stimulated hands, seems to continually decrease over trials for the children of schizophrenic parents, while for the children of physically ill parents, it seems to remain almost constant. Curves for the two hands eventually meet for the children of schizophrenics but for the children of the physically ill, they remain essentially parallel, although a gradual increase in slope suggests a generally heightened level of responding over trials.

Perhaps what both sets of data reveal is that the child of schizophrenic parents, although functioning initially at a higher (perhaps, too high) level of differentiation, is unable to respond in an increasingly differentiated manner, even though circumstances demand this, as would be the case over a series of specific-stimulation trials. It is as if his ceiling of differentiation were too high to begin with and his situational adaptiveness was therefore impaired. The child of physically ill parents or the normal child, on the other hand, seems able to respond more appropriately, since his level of differentiation increases gradually in response to stimuli which are designed to evoke such differentiation.

B. *Electrodermal responses*

While the electrodermal data have not as yet been analyzed for the children of schizophrenic or physically ill parents, the investigation for normal children and normal young adults has shown a clear-cut difference between the two groups in terms of electrodermal response to the termination of a stimulus complex. The available data and analyses suggest that the maturation and differentiation of psychophysiological responses are likely to be fruitful areas in which to investigate differences in functioning between our comparison groups.

CONCLUSION

Since our investigation has been underway in the past year, there has been one important development that has preoccupied the investigators. We are discovering that a large number of high-risk children never get to see a psychiatrist because they live in relatively encapsulated families manifesting a high degree of symptom tolerance and are, moreover, able to mask their symptoms when dealing with the outside world. It has already been pointed out how these children may conceal shared delusional responses or may believe them at home and forget about them or deny them in school. If the research continues to develop along the same lines, the researchers will soon be faced with a fairly massive mental health problem in the form of significant numbers of children whose subtle and unusual disturbances might otherwise have got by into adult life. It is our hunch that much of the precursive behavior is consolidated during this early period of childhood and that later interventions may be almost too late. From the preventive point of view, it is theoretically possible that certain therapeutic interventions might abort some of this gradual accumulation of disturbance that continues progressively throughout the child's development. Even if it were not possible to affect the pre-psychotic build-up, it should be feasible to counter-influence the para-psychotic cases. We have now been awarded a second grant to establish a special research clinic to study the effects of intervention on these high and intermediate risk children. A research clinic of this kind could have three possible advantages: first, it could point the way to a need for clinical research to look beyond its immediate specific aims and consider the application of the newly-found knowledge, and, secondly, it can orient researchers in the direction of studying interventional measures, and, thirdly, it can help in the preservation of valuable well-studied research subjects so that they become easily available for future follow-up evaluations. It is our hope to demonstrate the importance of establishing these sub-stations in mental hospitals that can help and advise in the prevention and treatment of disorders in the children of admitted parents. It came as a surprise to us, when we began our investigation, that the mental hospitals often have no record at all of the children within the family, let alone details of their adjustment. By and large, they feel that they have enough to cope with in dealing with the patients themselves and to undertake the extensive and intensive investigations and treatments of the children would add an additional burden and responsibility to the already heavy load that they are carrying. Nor have they yet an inkling of the problem and its dimensions and it would take a specialized research clinic serving one mental hospital to demonstrate that such sub-stations in every mental hospital in the country might do a great deal to relieve chronic mental ill health in families and perhaps even effectively cut the frequency of schizophrenic development. There is a growing concern today with the effect of psychosis on family and community life. The new therapeutic measures in the form of tranquilizing drugs, therapeutic communities and "open door" policies are transforming erstwhile custodial institutions into active treatment centers geared to a rapid turnover of patients. This has led to an increase in the incidence of ambulatory and remitted psychosis in the general population. Since the relapse rate has remained relatively constant throughout this time. families are being exposed, more than ever before, to the initial stages of psychotic episodes. Most psychiatrists are in general agreement about the advantages of this new approach for the individual psychotic patient, especially in the mitigation of the institutional influence on the personality, but the potential detriment to the family members resulting from the presence of a psychotic person in their midst has not received the careful scientific scrutiny it deserves. As the traffic between home and hospital multiplies, a point may be reached when the mental health needs of the community as a whole conflict with the mental health needs of individual patients.

VALUE OF THE DEVELOPMENTAL POINT OF VIEW

We are suggesting that a study of the kind we have been describing complements the many genetic and familial studies that are currently being undertaken. Genetic and environmental forces begin their interaction at conception and whatever trait we choose to study is susceptible to change during the life of the individual. As McClearn has pointed out: "Analysis of the long-term development of a characteristic may provide insights into the operation of the hereditary and environmental forces which would be unattainable by study at only one selected developmental period" (1962). It has seemed to us that an epigenetic approach possesses much empirical and theoretical promise for an understanding of abnormal behavior. It does not minimize the degree to which endogenous factors participate in the organization of behavior. It does, however, repudiate the "template" conception which maintains that later response patterns result from the passive translation of genetic factors into behavior through the medium of tissue growth and differentiation. For the epigenologist, the maturational and environmental processes become part of a basic approach seeking to understand the interplay of the two factors within an empirical framework. Perhaps the model that best summarizes the developmental approach is that furnished by Waddington (1957) in which he describes as "a rough and ready picture" an "epigenetic landscape" that resembles a geographical contour in having a background (corresponding to conception) and a foreground (showing different phenotypic values at some point in development). The landscape is thus characterized by valleys and hills, and the particular contour of the landscape may be considered to be determined by genotype. Each individual of different genotype may thus have a different contour. There are regions at upper levels which are almost flat plateaus from which two or three different valleys lead off downwards and which correspond to what are states of competence. If one can imagine a ball rolling downwards, the path as it rolls represents the development of some particular part of the egg, the degree of canalization of any particular path of development. In addition to its heuristic value, Waddington's model provides an instructive summary, for with this scheme in mind, it is difficult to forget the complexity of interaction between genetic and environmental factors and more particularly the great importance of development in the understanding of abnormal clinical states.

APPENDIX 1   PROCESS-REACTIVE CHECK LIST

Item	Rating	Score
1. Premorbid personality	Poor (0), fair (1), good (2)	....
2. Home environment of childhood	Poor (0), fair (1), good (2)	....
3. Incidence of mental disease and defect in the family	None or slight (0), moderate (1), heavy (2)	....
4. School record	Poor (0), fair (1), good (2)	....
5. Work record	Poor (0), fair (1), good (2)	....
6. Marital record	Single (0), divorced/separated (1), married (2)	....
7. Children	None (0), one (1), two and over (2)	....
8. Type of onset of illness	Chronic (0), subacute (1), acute (2)	....
9. Duration of symptoms	Over 5 years (0), 2–4 years (1), less than 1 year (2)	....
10. Age at onset	Under 20 years (0), over 30 years (1), between 20 and 30 years (2)	....
11. Presence of precipitating factors	None apparent (0), vague endogenous conflicts (1), clear psychogenic conflicts, prolonged overstrain, bodily illness (2)	....
12. Suspected etiological factors	Biological only (0), mixed biosocial (1), psychogenic/environmental (2)	....
13. Diagnostic type	Undifferentiated chronic/simple/hebephrenic (0), catatonic/paranoid (1), atypical/schizophreniform/schizoaffective/manic depressive (2)	....
14. Affective response	Flat, incongruous affect (0), congruous but diminished affects (1), good affects in harmony with cognition and conation (2)	....
15. Level of intelligence	IQ below 80 (0), IQ 80–100 with marked scatter (1), IQ over 100 (2)	....
16. Type of symptoms	Process symptoms—massive stupor, depersonalization, derealization and sensation of influence (0), clear cut "secondary" symptoms of delusions and hallucinations integrated into the psychosis (1), presence of confusion and clouding of consciousness (2)	....
17. Body build	Asthenic/leptosomatic (0), dysplastic (1), pyknic/athletic (2)	....
18. Response to tranquilizers	None (0), some response but not maintained (1), good (2)	
19. Course of illness	No remissions (0), infrequent remissions (1), frequent remissions (2)	....
	Process type scores 0–12	
	Mixed type scores 13–25	
	Reactive type scores 26–38	

APPENDIX 2

DIAGNOSTIC CATEGORIES FOR RESEARCH PROJECT MH–12043–01

A. *Psychotic Reactions* (A1, A2, A3)

1. Psychosis of Early Childhood (infantile autism, interactional psychosis, symbiotic psychosis, atypical psychosis, pseudo-defective psychosis).
2. Psychosis of Middle Childhood (childhood schizophrenia, schizophreniform psychosis of childhood).
3. Psychosis of Late Childhood (confusional state, identity diffusion, schizo-affective psychosis, schizophrenia-adult type, pseudo-neurotic psychosis, border-line psychosis).

(None of the cases in Category 1 are ever continuous with Adult Schizophrenia; a few cases in Category 2 have been reported as continuous with Adult Schizophrenia; an appreciable number of cases in Category 3 have been found to be continuous with Adult Schizophrenia).

B. *Pre-psychotic Reactions* (B1, B2, B3)

This diagnosis is based on the occurrence of precursive symptoms, transient, breaks with reality (precurvise episodes of withdrawal, mistrustfulness and panic leading to primitivization), precursive personality patterns, precursive mild continuous or intermittent thought disorder and unusual subjective sensations such as vivid, eidetic imagery. Some of these cases would fall into a border-line category, whereas, with others, the personality pattern would constitute the main feature. Vulnerability would be in large measure genetically determined and tied to other constitutional factors.

1. Schizoid type.
2. Paranoid type.
3. Regressive type.

C. *Para-psychotic or Pseudo-psychotic Reactions* (C1, C2, C3)

This diagnosis is based on involvement with the ill parent and his illness as manifested by a sharing of the symptoms, such as delusions and hallucinations, a close physical and psychological identification and an undue *susceptibility,* to the influence of the ill parent because of such traits as suggestibility, submissiveness and dependency.

1. Induced Para-psychotic Reaction (complete, partial, or intermittent *folie à deux*).
2. Assumed Para-psychotic Reaction (Ganser's syndrome).
3. Dissociative Reactions (fugues, twilight states, multiple personalities, etc.).

The majority of these reactions are based on hysterical identification with the sick parent and tend to diminish or disappear with separation from the sick parent. This is in contrast to the pre-psychotic reactions. *Susceptibility* would be, in large measure, environmentally determined and tied to certain factors in the parent–child and family relationship.

D. *Non-psychotic Reactions* (D1, D2, D3)

This diagnosis is based on the usual diagnostic criteria indicating internalized, externalized or mixed disorders.

1. Internalized Disturbances (as manifested by anxieties, compulsions, obsessions, phobias, conversions, inhibitions, depressions, guilt and other psycho-neurotic reactions).
2. Externalized Disturbances (as manifested by anti-social trends, impulsiveness, sexual deviations, "acting-out", habit disorders and other behavior disorders).
3. Mixed Disturbances (as manifested by both psyhoo-neurotic and behavior disorders, with generally one or the other predominating).

E. *Somatic Reactions* (E1, E2, E3)

This diagnosis is based on the history of physical illness and on the current physical status of the child, and so refers to both past and present illnesses. It indicates both the occurrence as well as the predisposition to physical illness.

1. Chronic Physical Illness (similar to the physical illness of the parent).
2. Chronic Physical Illness (dissimilar to the physical illness of the parent).
3. Chronic Psychosomatic Illness (such as asthma, colitis, peptic ulceration, neurodermatoses, etc.).

It should be noted that a number of chronic physical illnesses such as tuberculosis, and diabetes show roughly the same "inheritance" pattern as schizophrenia, although the causal elements are basically dissimilar. It would therefore be proper to speak of pre-diabetic and pre-tuberculous states analogous to the pre-psychotic state. In the present research, such diagnostic refinements are not included since the primary focus of the investigation is on psychotic and not on physical illness.

F. *Parasomatic or Pseudomatic Reactions* (F1, F2, F3)

This diagnosis is based on involvement with the sick parent and his illness as indicated by a sharing of symptoms, a close identification with the sick parent and an undue susceptibility to the influence of the sick parent because of marked suggestibility, submissiveness and dependency.

1. Induced Parasomatic Reactions (complete, partial or intermittent mirroring of the parent's illness, amounting to a physical *folie à deux*).
2. Assumed Parasomatic Reaction (hypochondriasis or a disposition to imaginary aches and pains leading in severe cases to invalidism).
3. Conversion Symptoms (the somatization of anxiety by means of hysterical mechanisms).

G. *Healthy Reactions* (G1, G2, G3)

This diagnosis is based both on the absence of any abnormal signs and symptoms (other than short-lived, and mild ones, appropriate to the situation in quality and intensity) and on the presence of positive indications of mental health. The reactions are therefore considered to fall within the range of healthy responses.

1. Sub-normal Healthy Reactions (in which the reaction to stress—the stress of parental illness—is healthy but limited by an inferior constitution due to brain damage, mental retardation, etc.).
2. Normal Healthy Reactions (in which an average constitution gives an average reaction to the stress imposed by parental illness).
3. Super-normal Healthy Reaction (in which the individual reacts to the given stress by manifesting superior qualities such as creativity, imagination, talent, artistry, productivity, compassion, etc.).

H. *Underlying Constitutional Factors to Psychological and Somatic Reactions* (H1, H2, H3)

All the reactions in the present nomenclature from A to G can be superimposed on an inferior constitution. In the case of G1, the inferior constitution is already included in the definition of a sub-normal healthy reaction.

1. Mental Retardation (an IQ below 70).
2. Chronic Brain Syndrome (based on both physical and psychological findings),
3. Poor Physical Status (as evident by malnutrition, chronic illness or physical handicap).

It will be noted that combinations of diagnoses can occur, for example, B1, H1, signifying that a schizoid pre-psychotic reaction is imposed on mental retardation or B1, H1, H3, where a poor physical status is added to the total clinical picture.

REFERENCES

ALANEN, Y. O. (1958) The mothers of schizophrenic patients, *Acta psychiat. neurol.* 33, Suppl. 1–4.
ANTHONY, E. J. (1958) An experimental approach to the psychopathology of childhood—autism, *Brit. J. Med. Psychol.* 32 (1) 19–37.

BIRREN, J. E. (1944) Psychological examinations of children who later became psychotic, *J. Abnorm. Soc. Psychol.* **39**, 84–95.

BOWMAN, K. M. (1934) A study of the pre-psychotic personality in certain psychoses, *Am. J. Orthopsychiat.* **4**, 473–98.

ELSÄSSER, G. (1952) *Die Nachkommen geisteskranker Eltenpaare,* G. Thieme, Stuttgart.

FRAZEE, H. E. (1953) Children who later became schizophrenic, *Smith Coll. Stud. Soc. Wk.* **23**, 125–49.

FRIEDLANDER, D. (1945) Personality development of twenty-seven children who later became psychotic, *J. Abnorm. Soc. Psychol.* **40**, 330–5.

KALLMANN, F J., FALEK, A., HURZELLER, M., ERLENMEYER-KIMLING, L. (1964) The developmental aspects of children with two schizophrenic parents, in *Recent Research on Schizophrenia* (Eds. Solomon, P. and Glueck, B. S.), Psychiatric Research Reports of the American Psychiatric Association, No. 19.

KASANIN, J., and VEO, L. (1932) A study of the school adjustments of children who later in life became psychotic, *Am. J. Orthopsychiat.* **2**, 212–27.

KREITMAN, N. (1964) The patient's spouse, *Brit. J. Psychiat.* **110** (465) 159–73.

KUNKEL, C. (1948) Quoted by K. Jaspers in *Allgemeine Psychopathologie,* J. Springer, Berlin.

McCLEARN, G. E. (1962) The inheritance of behavior, in *Psychology in the Making* (Ed. Postman, L.), Alfred A. Knopf, New York.

MICHAEL, C. M., MORRIS, D. P. and SOROKER, E. (1957) Follow-up studies of shy, withdrawn children: II. Relative incidence of schizophrenia, *Am. J. Orthopsychiat.* **27**, 331–7.

NIELSEN, C. (1954) The childhood of schizophrenics, *Acta Psychiat. et Neurol.* **29**, 281–9.

NIELSEN, J. (1964) Mental disorders in married couples (assortative mating), *Brit. J. Psychiat.* **110** (468), 683–97.

O'NEAL, P. and ROBINS, L. N. (1958) Childhood patterns predictive of adult schizophrenia: a 30-year follow-up study, *Am. J. Psychiat.* **114**, 961–9.

SCHULZ, B. (1940) Kinder schizophrener Elternpaare, *Z. Neurol. Psychiat.* **168**, 332–81.

WADDINGTON, C. H. (1957) *The Strategy of the Genes,* Macmillan, New York.

WALKER, R. N. (1963) Body build and behavior in young children: II. Body build and parents' ratings, *Child Develop.* **34**, 1–23.

WITTMAN, M. P. and STEINBERG, D. L. (1944) A study of prodromal factors in mental illness with special reference to schizophrenia, *Am. J. Psychiat.* **100**, 811–16.

BIOLOGICAL, PSYCHOLOGICAL AND HISTORICAL DIFFERENCES IN A SERIES OF MONOZYGOTIC TWINS DISCORDANT FOR SCHIZOPHRENIA

WILLIAM POLLIN and JAMES R. STABENAU

Section on Twin and Sibling Studies, Adult Psychiatry Branch,
National Institute of Mental Health, Bethesda, Maryland

THERE is an old Chinese proverb that says: "The beginning of wisdom is to call things by their right names." To begin with, let us try to make sure that we are using the "right" words, and at a minimum, mutually understood words, by briefly defining our thoughts concerning the two phenomena which together constitute the subject of this meeting: transmission and schizophrenia.

When we use the term schizophrenia, we mean a behavioral syndrome which (a) is a disease process in that there is a demonstrable breakdown of normal function, comfort and effectiveness in a given individual; (b) has a set of common denominator symptoms (thought, affect, and action disorder, delusions, hallucinations and other psychotic manifestations) such that the "typical", hardcore patient presents no diagnostic difficulty to psychiatric workers of many different points of view and nationalities; and (c) a behavioral syndrome which has very unclear limits, so that as one moves away from the hardcore cases there is an increasing degree of difficulty in arriving at diagnostic consensus.

In regard to the other major concept with which we are concerned, i.e. transmission, Webster tells us that transmission is the act, operation or process of sending or transferring from one person to another; or passing on or down to others. Some question may be raised concerning how germane this concept is, at the present stage of our knowledge of schizophrenia. However, if we consider the various models that are implied by the concept of transmission of illness, its usefulness becomes clear. Illness can be transferred from one individual to another by means of the transfer of an active pathogen, as in bacterial infection; or by genetic transmission as in phenylketonuria. There is also a type of social transmission in the sense that children of poverty stricken, socially backward, slum dwellers have a much greater likelihood of coming down with tuberculosis, for example, not necessarily because their parents have transmitted to them a particular bacillus or a given genetic predisposition, but because they have been given a particular social heritage and have been reared in a particular environment which influences the susceptibility to the bacillus which is the prime source of the illness. Another model we need keep in mind demonstrates the fact that though children may very predictably show the behavior of their parents, this need not have any genetic component, as exemplified by the fact that children of French-speaking parents speak French, of English-speaking parents speak English, and so forth.

The two most important issues involved in the question of the transmission of schizo-phrenia would seem to be (a) the extent of such transmission, as manifested, for example, by concordance rates; and (b) the mechanism of such transmission, which may be restated as the question of deciding which of the above types of model might be most applicable. The first issue—that of extent—is one which our study is not designed to investigate. Our work is, however, relevant to the second: the question of mechanism. This issue can be stated in more precise and operational terms as the question of what specific factors or components are transferred or passed on from parents to their children who become schizo-phrenic, and by what processes. Our findings, derived from an intensive study of a series of identical twins discordant for schizophrenia, and their families, suggest the following pat-tern. The intrauterine experience of one twin, relative to the co-twin, tends to be unfavorable or deficient, leading to a relative physiological incompetence and immaturity at birth and in the neonatal period. These differences may induce attitudes and relationship patterns in the family which accentuate dependency and ego identity problems, and retard self-differentiation in the less favored twin. Similar patterns can be set up at a later time for the twin more favored in intrauterine existence, by some major illness or trauma occurring in childhood. The interaction of this slowly increasing relative ego weakness, with certain familial and parental attitudes and personality traits, can lead to the appearance and slow development of excessive anxiety, fearfulness and insecurity. It is in this type of individual and in response to this life situation that schizophrenia subsequently develops.[1,2] We do not feel that we have here the complete sequence of events; there are obviously many steps that remain to be defined. Nor do we feel that the sequence we have found can, at this point, conclusively be considered to be relevant to schizophrenia *per se*; it may instead predispose to a variety of psychopathologies.

The data we wish to present today are primarily concerned with the immediate question of attempting to explain how it comes about that one of a set of identical twins has become schizophrenic and his co-twin has not. Toward this end we have thus far studied 15 families with discordant pairs, focusing on both parents and both twins, but including, in addition, other relatives, teachers, friends, and many additional individuals who knew the family well. (Additional matched families, with normal or concordant pairs, who have been simi-larly studied, will not be considered in this paper.) With the help of a variety of methodo-logical approaches which we will briefly describe, we feel that we have been able to develop a most detailed and reliable set of family history reconstructions. From these there has emerged an apparently consistent pattern of pre-illness differences in the life course of these discordant identical twins, a pattern which we feel casts considerable light upon this ques-tion: why illness in the one and not the other twin. However, for reasons that will become clear during the course of the presentation, we do not feel at this point that our data give any definitive answers as to the role of genetic factors in schizophrenia. Our findings at this point are quite compatible with either genetic, psychodynamic or combined models of the illness.

It is important, at the outset, to emphasize that we have approached the use of twins in the study of schizophrenia from quite a different vantage point than that which has in-fluenced most investigators who have used one variety of twin methodology or another. Rather than being primarily interested in attempting to evaluate the relative role and the nature of the possible interaction between hereditary and environmental factors, we initially were interested in attempting to exclude genetic and biological factors so as to be able to focus upon psychodynamic, interpersonal phenomena that might have some significant etiologic role with respect to schizophrenia. This approach grew out of an earlier study of siblings discordant for schizophrenia.[3] In that design we had compared three matched groups of families; in group one, the same-sexed, approximately same-aged young adult siblings were discordant for schizophrenia; in the second group the siblings were discordant for juvenile delinquency; and in the third group, one of the siblings showed superior adjustment and performance.

Within the psychopathology families a number of features were found that consistently went along with and served to explain the discordance between the siblings. Two of the most prominent of these had to do with differences in identification and in the experience of family crisis. We found a distinctly different pattern of relationships between the parents and each of the two siblings, with consequent identification with different aspects of parental personalities in the psychopathology sib as compared with the control sib. The index sibling was seen more often, and to a greater extent, to be identified with and to have incorporated the conflict-ridden, ambivalent and hostile sectors of the parental personality; in contrast, the control sibs demonstrated more of the conflict-free and functionally effective sectors of their parents' personality structures. A second major difference related to the discordance between the two sibs was the degree of stress encountered during a critical early childhood period ranging from 6 months to 3 years of age.

In the comparative family study, [3a], as shown in Table 1, 17 of the 19 psychopathology siblings as compared to only 2 of 29 control siblings, encountered what was described by their families as "the time" of major or maximal family crisis during this early childhood period. These crises included major economic disasters, a peak of emotional conflict be-

TABLE 1. EARLY POST-NATAL EXPERIENCE OF INDEX (I) AND CONTROL (C) SIBLINGS

	Family crisis "worst time" (age <3 yrs)		Birth of sibling (age <2 yrs)		Depression in mother (age <3 yrs)		Seen as "damaged" (age <6 yrs)	
	I	C	I	C	I	C	I	C
Schizophrenic N = 11	9	1	7	2	9	2	9	0
Delinquent N = 8	8	0	7	3	6	1	2	0
Normal N = 5	X	1	X	2	X	0	X	0
	17/19	2/29	14/19	7/29	15/19	3/29	11/19	0/29

tween the parents, or severe depressive episodes in one parent or the other, particularly in the mother. Suggestive confirmation that these descriptions were not solely the result of retrospective distortion was found in an analysis of the distribution of births of younger siblings. Fourteen of nineteen index subjects had younger siblings born within their first 2 years, whereas only 7 of 29 controls had a similar experience (Table 1). In addition to these two observations, numerous differences in personality, communication and relationship patterns and affects were found that differentiated the three groups of families.[3]

It was on the basis of the interesting and significant findings which emerged from the sibling study that we determined to undertake a similar but more intensive and extensive multidisciplinary evaluation of identical twins discordant for schizophrenia. It was our belief that such a population would represent the optimal controlled sample, in which not only genetic factors but also social, ethnic, chronological and psychological variables were matched to an extent not attainable with any other type of population. Because of such a high degree of matching of many variables which various studies had suggested were relevant to significant aspects of personality formation and the development of schizophrenia, it was our hope that subtle but significant and etiologic factors which otherwise are not possible to define might emerge with more clarity from the study of this group.

We have previously described the procedures involved in locating this type of sample, the criteria employed for zygosity and diagnosis and details of our methodology, and I will only briefly summarize them here.[1, 2] We obtained our sample by means of repeated nationwide mailings describing the type of study we were undertaking and requesting referrals of those identical twins where the diagnosis of schizophrenia in the one twin was clear and certain, the absence of schizophrenia in the other twin seemingly convincing and both parents and both twins were willing and able to come to Bethesda simultaneously as a family group for extensive inpatient multidisciplinary evaluation. Zygosity determination has been primarily based on the evaluation of 28 blood groups in both parents and offspring. With respect to diagnostic issues, we have employed a panel of five psychiatrists and a very strict and narrow concept of schizophrenia. Our hardcore group is composed of those pairs where there has been no doubt whatsoever in any of the five psychiatrists concerning the presence of schizophrenia in the index twin. At the present time we have seen 15 pairs of twins or sets of triplets discordant for schizophrenia.[1] Of these, 10 fall into the hardcore group and 5 which we have very conservatively considered probable schizophrenics. I should like to emphasize how conservative this diagnostic screening has been. The two index twins who score lowest on our scale of certainty with regard to the diagnosis of schizophrenia, in the probable group, are a young woman who had been an inpatient at Michael Reese Hospital over an extended period of time and when seen there during the more active phase of her psychosis was considered schizophrenic by their staff and so signed out; and a young man who had been diagnosed as schizophrenic before admission to NIH, and who, after transfer from NIH to a local university hospital was considered schizophrenic by their staff, and termed typically schizophrenic when presented there to Dr. William Menninger.

The following clinical summary of our first patient gives an indication of the type of patient who makes up our hardcore group:

> *Female, age* 23. At age 4: patient fussier than twin. Age 8–10: had bedtime compulsive rituals. Ages 12–15: preoccupied with sex and body image. Age 15: had two brief episodes of anxiety and uncontrolled crying. Age 16: was given outpatient psychotherapy because of school difficulties; preoccupied with

---

[1] Three of these families (Nos. 5, 8 and 23) include triplets rather than twins. In two of these, two of the three were identical and were the pairs studied; in the third all three were admitted and studied. For purposes of simplicity we will hereafter refer to all 15 as twin pairs.

thoughts of failure. Age 17: became increasingly inappropriate and withdrawn, daydreaming in class, giggling, and failing school work. Preoccupied with religion and God's love, wrath, and punishment. Concerned with sinfulness of sex. After being seen 4 months by outpatient social worker, became deteriorated and required hospitalization. First admission to university hospital characterized by delusions and auditory hallucinations. Responded to voices in a self-destructive manner. Regressed to the point of feces smearing and nudity. *Diagnosis:* acute schizophrenic reaction. Was transferred to state hospital 2 months later. *Diagnosis:* catatonic reaction. Age 18: third admission, characterized by similar giggling, childlike responses, autistic thinking, blocking and poor judgment. *Diagnosis:* schizophrenic reaction, hebephrenic type. Age 20: fourth admission: had symptoms including auditory hallucinations, agitation, combativeness, and argumentative behavior; seemed confused and deluded. *Diagnosis:* schizophrenic reaction, hebephrenic type. *NIH diagnosis:* chronic schizophrenic reaction, undifferentiated type.

The co-twin controls have varied from individuals showing impressive degrees of psychological health and competence to individuals with a substantial amount of psychopathology. At the time of each twin pair's evaluation, none of the controls showed any evidence either in the present, or in their background, of psychosis. During the 5 years that we have been involved in the study, one of the 15 co-twin controls has begun to show substantial paranoid tendencies suggestive of an incipient psychotic process. We know of no others who have shown any similar evidence of psychotic development up to the present. Thus far, the range of time during which the twins have been discordant for psychotic symptomatology is $2\frac{1}{2}$–21 years, mean: 8·8, and for hospitalization $2\frac{1}{2}$–$15\frac{1}{2}$ years, mean: 5·0 years. We anticipate that some of these pairs will in all probability become concordant with the passage of time. However, on the basis of the number of years of discordance which has already elapsed, and the data available from large-scale studies which indicate that some 70% of all concordant pairs become concordant within 4 years,[4] we believe it is likely that the great majority of our discordant pairs will remain discordant. The mean psychopathology ratings of each twin and parent, and the scale employed in such ratings, are shown below in Table 3.

Our study procedures involve a 2–3-week period of very intensive psychiatric and biological evaluation. The multiple procedures and participating collaborative investigators are shown in Table 2 below.

This report will be limited primarily to a discussion of the psychiatric data and that part of the biochemical data which we ourselves have accumulated. Collaborators will be reporting in their own appropriate journals and meetings. Eventually we anticipate that all the data will be integrated in a monograph.

Before describing our results I should like to emphasize our belief in the reliability of the historical reconstructions we have arrived at and to point out the extent to which these differ from the clinical material which heretofore it has been possible to obtain in most twin studies. As far as we know, this is the only twin study in which simultaneous availability of both parents and both twins has been a major criterion for subject selection. During the course of the initial evaluation, over 100 hours of interview time are obtained with family members in both individual and group interviews. These interviews are so structured that there is a continuing exchange, feedback, comparison, review and modification of the recollections and description given by one member of the family by the three other family members. This process, supplemented by extensive use of family photographs, home movies, and objective records of various types, appears to correct substantially for individual family members' distortions. Following the initial evaluation period most of the actively psychotic index twins have stayed on for 6 months to several years of inpatient therapy, which, in two instances, has been intensive analytic therapy. This type of therapeutic relationship has enabled us to re-evaluate and refine our original formulations. Subsequent to

TABLE 2. TWIN STUDY PROCEDURES AND INVESTIGATORS

Procedures	Investigator/consultant
I. *Zygosity* 1. Blood typing	Human Genetics Branch, NIDR, Mr. Webster Leyshon
2. Finger printing 3. Body photos 4. Anthropometric characteristics 5. Taste test	Section on Twin and Sibling Studies Research Assistants*
II. *Psychiatric evaluation*—Individual and group interviews 1. Personal and family histories; formulation	Drs. William Pollin, James Stabenau, Axel Hoffert and Miss Barbara Spillman
2. Home and community visits	Miss Barbara Spillman
3. Diagnostic consultation, inpatient multi-dimensional psychiatric scale	Drs. Donald Burnham, Marvin Adland and Earle Silver
4. Hospital ward observations	Nursing staff
III. *Psychological evaluation* 1. Rorschach, Spouse Rorschach, Family Rorschach	Psychology Unit, APB (Dr. Winfield Scott‡)
2. Sentence completion, draw-a-person, draw-a-house, draw-a-family, Bender, proverbs, Hooper, Shipley-Hartford, TAT, color naming, Binet vocabulary, writing and recall, Harris lateral-dominance, Ishihara	Section on Twin and Sibling Studies Research Assistants*
3. Thought process and intelligence, tell-me thinking test, object sorting, Raven progressive matrices	Drs. Edward Jerome, Marguerite Young and Mr. John Van Dyke
4. WAIS	Mrs. Martha Werner
5. Leary, developmental history, family history, PARI, PBI, CARI, CBI, embedded figures, Gottschalk interviews, Q-sort, moral values, Cornell medical index, Rosenberg ego scales, self-esteem scale, writing sample	Section on Twin and Sibling Studies Research Assistants*
IV. *Polygraph, conditioning and reaction time studies*	Dr. Theodore Zahn
V. *Biological* 1. Physical workup, X-ray, blood and clinical chemistries	Unit of Psychosomatics, LCS (Drs. P. Cardon, H. Mirsky§)
2. Neurological evaluation and EEG	Drs. Richmond Paine and Robert Cohn
3. Auto-immune mechanisms	Drs. J. Philip Welch, G. Solomon and J. Fahey
4. Chromosomal study	Dr. Cecil Jacobson
5. Corticosteroids	Dr. Morton Lipsett
6. Catecholamines	Dr. I. Kopin
3,4-dimethoxyphenylethylamine	Dr. A. Friedhoff

* Mrs. Martha Werner and Miss Christine Walter.
† Formerly Drs. Joe Tupin, Loren Mosher.
‡ Formerly Dr. Nathene Loveland.
§ Formerly Drs. F. Guggenheim, L. Baer.

TABLE 3. PSYCHOPATHOLOGY: GLOBAL RATINGS (Mean)

	Index	Control	Mother	Father
I. DISCORDANT				
8	5·33	3	2	3
18	4·92	3	2·97	2·33
22	4·83	2·67	3	2
9	4·75	2·5	2	3
2	5·15	3·25	2·5	1·5
17	5·6	3·68	3·37	2·97
14	5·5	2·25	2·5	2
7	4·87	1·33	4	1·5
6	5	3·85	4	2
3	6·5	1·25	2	1·5
5	5·25	2·25	3	2·5
4	4·13	3	2·5	1·5
10	4·9	2·75	6	1·5
1	5·4	3·25	3	2
II. CONCORDANT				
20	6·35	5	2·5	2
15	5·6	4·9	4	3
III. "NORMAL"				
11	2	2·25	1·5	1
12	1·25	1·25	1	1·5
16	1·5	2·5	3	1·5
19	1·38	1	1·5	1

Name...

Date ....

Rater...

In comparison with your overall clinical experience, how "sick" or "mentally ill" is this person? Guide lines given should be used only as guides, not absolutes. This should be an overall estimate based on history, mental status, and interpersonal, occupational and social functioning.

1. Normal, not ill at all.
2. Questionably mentally ill. ("Classifiable, but not diagnosable". A few psychologic or psychosomatic complaints.)
3. Mildly ill. ("Diagnosable, no treatment indicated." Distinct psychiatric symptoms, or sees himself as sick.)
4. Moderately ill. ("Diagnosable, treatment indicated." Clearly neurotic or character disordered with functional impairment.)
5. Markedly ill. (Probably psychotic at some time, reactive schizophrenia.)
6. Severely ill. (Prolonged psychosis, process schizophrenia.)
7. Among the most severely ill. (Unremitting severe psychosis, deterioration.)

the inpatient stay at the Clinical Center, a home visit is undertaken by our social worker who visits the home community, lives for a brief time with the family and then interviews a wide number of family relatives, teachers, physicians, and friends. On the last such home visit, 24 individuals were interviewed in connection with the particular family in question. Emerging from this type of workup is an overall picture of the family and specifically of the life course of the two twins which is highly detailed and convincing.

We have been surprised by how consistent the pattern of differentiating life histories for the index and the control twin has become.[5] Four groups of such findings seem to fit together and may be causally related: (a) birth and neonatal constitutional differences in the twins; (b) differential patterns of parent–twin perceptions and relationships; (c) differences in biological and personality development; and (d) a sub-sample of current physical and biochemical observations.

We shall take up each of these categories in turn. The first set of findings has to do with birth and neonatal constitutional differences.

In 12 of 15 of our pairs the index twin was the one who weighed less at birth; in a 13th, the parental memories are contradictory at this point, and the question is being further explored.[2] The great bulk of described episodes of physiological disequilibrium such as respiratory embarrassments, sleep and eating difficulties, and colic are present in the histories of these lighter index twins. The five twins in which there is well-documented evidence of cyanosis at birth are all index schizophrenic twins. The preponderance of neonatal medical complications such as infectious episodes, occurred in the index twins. The one instance

TABLE 4. BIRTH WEIGHT AND PBI

Family number	Birth weight (gm)		PBI (μg%)	
	Index	Control	Index	Control
I. DISCORDANT				
8	1640	1950	4·9	5·1
18	1477	1705	5·5	6·0
22	2216	2159	—	—
9	2460	2550	4·3	6·0
2	1210	1370	3·5	5·1
17	1875	1705	3·7	4·4
14	2180	2460	5·0	6·0
7	3120	3130	5·3	8·6
6	2920	3400	5·0	6·5
3	2640	3120	6·0	6·0
5	1590	2380	5·3	5·7
4	2410	3120	4·2	5·0
10	2270	2500	4·3	5·8
1	2380	2540	5·0	6·3
II. CONCORDANT				
	Ia	Ib	Ia	Ib
20	1918	2017	6·0	7·4
15	2740	2830	5·7	6·9
III. "NORMAL"				
	Ca	Cb	Ca	Cb
11	1590	1930	5·4	5·5
12	1900	1930	4·2	4·5
16	2386	2614	6·3	5·6
19	3324	3565	8·9	7·6

[2] This family, under current study, is not included in Tables 3 or 4.

of suggestive stigmata of birth defect, i.e. an abortive hairlip, occurred in an index twin. It is our impression that the constellation of these findings derive from a common subtle but significant difference in intrauterine experience, where, as a result of differences in fetal circulation, differences in fetal positioning and consequent crowding, and other similar mechanical factors, one twin is born at a different and higher state of physiological and biological maturation and competence than is the other. Later we shall consider the possibility that a part of this sometimes quite slight difference may relate to a CNS difference which may be more directly relevant to subsequent behavioral differences and eventually, in certain cases, to differences in the predilection to psychopathology.

We have become especially interested in those cases which do not show the low birth weight–schizophrenic relationship. Of great interest is the fact that in our last two cases, where the index twins do not definitely show the lower birth weight, there were quite distinctive developmental factors which seemed to bring about similar results. In one pair, the twins were born to an immature 16-year-old mother who was quite unequipped to deal with them. A public health nurse assisting the family reported to us that, on several occasions, the index twin became sufficiently cyanotic because of her positioning in the bedroom close to a defective heater that she had to be returned to the hospital, and that on one occasion it was thought that she had died. Subsequently this twin showed all of the distinguishing features which in the bulk of the series characteristically cluster with the low birth-weight twins. In Family No. 23, the twin heavier at birth had a severe case of Rocky Mountain spotted fever at age $3\frac{1}{2}$. The parents were told he might well die. Subsequent to his recovery, he continued to be the larger of the two (birth weights 4 lb. 4 oz. and 2 lb. 15 oz.) but he showed the developmental pattern and familial relationships characteristic of the lighter birth-weight twins in the series. There was great concern regarding his health, survival and needs, and much conflict within the mother, and between the mother and father, regarding his role in the family. He developed severe and persistent symptoms of phobia and anxiety with increasing hypersensitivity which led to a severe paranoid delusional break at age 25.

A consistent pattern of differences was observed in the way the family, particularly the parents, and especially the mother perceive the two twins and in consequence relate to them in a different manner. The lower birth-weight twin has most often been seen as the vulnerable and weaker of the twins and is the one with whom the mother has become more involved. However, there tends to be a greater degree of ambivalence, frequently reaching levels of conscious rejection, with this greater involvement. The relationship with this twin is also characterized by being a more anxious and uncertain one.

From the first appearance of differences in the development of personality and intra-familial roles, the pattern shown by the indexes in contrast to the controls is most consistent. Repeatedly and almost without exception, the indexes from earliest childhood on were described as the more dependent, more submissive, more fearful, more compliant and more constricted of the two twins. They had less adequate and extensive peer relationships and showed a substantial preponderance of childhood psychopathology. Along with this went a similar difference in biological development so that the indexes tended to be the ones who at successive stages of development were slightly slower than their controls in cutting teeth, learning to walk or talk, and showing signs of puberty. From these differences an overall distinguishing pattern emerges which can be summarized by saying that in contrast to their

v

controls, the indexes from childhood on saw the world as a more stressful and less predictable place and saw themselves as less competent.

One needs to keep in mind, of course, that in almost every pair of identical twins, one twin will weigh less at birth than the other and that in their subsequent development one will show a tendency to be the leader and the other the follower, one more dependent, and so forth. Thus the distinctions we are describing in these pairs are not, of and by themselves, remarkable. However, on the basis of the four non-psychopathology sets of twins we have thus far studied in the same way, and our review of the literature, it is our impression that the pairs discordant for schizophrenia are distinctive in a number of definable respects. To begin with there is a considerable rigidity of the early different roles and postures. This rigidity may result from the fact that subtle but significant constitutional differences are greater in these pairs than in the average pair of twins; or because of differences in the parental personalities and/or relationships, as compared with most parents of twins; or because of an interaction between these two sets of factors. However, whatever the cause, the initial differences between the twins tended to become rigidly fixed and reinforced rather than attenuated. We observed a permanence, and an increasing and consistent pattern to the differences between these twins that is not characteristic of what we have noted in our small number of control twins. Thus though such birth weight and dominance/submission differences between the two twins are in no way unique, it would seem to be highly significant that it has so often been in the one type of twin rather than the other that schizophrenia has developed.

A fourth set of observations appears to fit into the sequences described above and may represent present-day sequelae of some of the earlier differences. One set of such observations has to do with neurological findings.[6] Two neurologists evaluated each of the twins independently and were specifically requested to look for soft neurological signs in addition to characteristic neurological syndromes. Their evaluations were then scored by a third independent observer. A significant preponderance of soft signs, such as difficulties with praxis, hyper- or hypo-reflexia, abortive clonus and the like, was found in the index twins. It is, of course, quite possible that some, if not all of this set of observations with regard to neurological findings may reflect current artifacts such as differences in anxiety level, drug effects, and the like.

A second set of current findings that may relate to some of the previously described distinctions are differences in current protein-bound iodine values. Dr. Stabenau's analysis of the PBI has shown a significant correlation between PBI and birth weight for the whole group of twins. This increases when the non-schizophrenic twins are separately analyzed ($r = 0.65$, $p < 0.001$), suggesting that the relationship is not primarily dependent upon schizophrenia, but is more basically related to the effects of intrauterine experience. Re-analysis of Marks and Man's data, showing a similar correlation between BEI (butanol extractible iodine) and birth weight in 129 new borns, tends to confirm this hypothesis.[7, 8]

Numerous *in vivo* and *in vitro* studies have demonstrated the significant role played by thyroid hormone in the development and differentiation of the CNS in the late uterine and early postnatal stages. Specifically, neuronal branching,[9] learning ability,[10] myelinization,[11, 12] rates of maturation of the pituitary adrenal response to stress, the development of the EEG and the infantile learning of conditioned avoidance responses,[13, 14] have all been related to thyroid activity. Caution is indicated in evaluating the relevance of such data to our findings in view of the fact that (a) most of these are animal studies, (b) they involve differences in thyroid level of a greater magnitude than those found in the twins, and (c) we have not as yet determined to what extent the PBI/birth-weight relationship is dependent upon binding protein, on the one hand, or thyroxine itself, on the other, though current analyses will clarify this issue.

Keeping such qualifications in mind, we note that the apparent relationship between maturity at birth, neonatal thyroid function and CNS development may define one of the specific biological processes which are "passed on" to differing degrees on the two twins, and may thereby constitute one biological basis for differences in subsequent ego capacities, intrafamilial relationships and psychopathology.

Briefly let me mention several other sets of biological data. Our data do not support Fessel's reports of abnormalities in the S-19 macroglobulins in schizophrenics.[15] In 12 pairs of our twins the values were randomly distributed with respect to relationship to schizophrenia. However, we did observe that the S-19 fraction was significantly higher for females as compared to males.[16]

Two procedures which represent efforts to replicate prior observations of presumably abnormal circulating proteins in schizophrenics or psychotics have yielded positive results. One of these is the lactate/pyruvate ratio technique of Frohman et al.[17] using chicken erythrocytes as the experimental preparation, and the other is the agglutination technique of Turner and Chipps[18] using a rabbit preparation. Frohman has been successful at a better than chance level in blind predictions based on his technique and in 10 of the first 12 discordant pairs, the index showed the higher lactate/pyruvate ratio.[19] Turner has shown a similar finding in 5 of the 6 pairs he has thus far studied. To what extent these findings reflect some secondary phenomenon due to medication and/or sequelae of the psychotic process and hospitalization is still unclear.

Another somewhat striking and surprising finding has to do with the incidence of thyroid disease in the mothers of these discordant pairs. Seven of the first fourteen mothers have a well-documented history of some type of significant though variable thyroid pathology, including severe thyrotoxicosis, thyroid CA and hypothyroidism; and one additional mother gives a history of a previous abnormal RAI uptake with subsequent chronic usage of thyroid medication, though thus far we have not been able to document the original pathology. This incidence of thyroid illness is approximately 4 times higher than any reported in any age matched case finding population of women.[20]

In these selected pairs of identical twins so chosen that one twin is schizpohrenic and one not, the twin who becomes schizophrenic is, with great consistency in our series, the one who did less well in intrauterine life, and does less well in childhood and in adolescence, developing more fearfulness and insecurity, less competence and openness, and less successful peer relationships. Clearly this life pattern does not always lead to schizophrenia and is not the only one which leads to schizophrenia. In the two of possibly three cases in our series in which the heavier twin has become the schizophrenic one, this less successful childhood and adolescent pattern has characterized the heavier index following several severe episodes of neonatal cyanosis, in one case; and a severe bout of Rocky Mountain spotted fever, at age $3\frac{1}{2}$, in the other. However, the literature does contain numerous case histories in which the twin who was reportedly heavier at birth, and apparently the leader and the more competent one in childhood, is the one who subsequently becomes schizophrenic. Several possible explanations come to mind as to why this latter pattern which we have thus far not seen in our series is reported at times as the predominant pattern by other investigators. One explanation may derive in whole or in part from the considerable differences in the quantity and detail of the clinical history which we feel we have been able to obtain as compared with that which has been available to most other investigators of similar pairs. So far as we know, we are the only group who have studied only those twins where both parents and both twins are simultaneously available. On the other hand, it may be that this very criterion, and the manner in which we have accumulated our sample, has provided us with a skewed and somewhat atypical population so that the group we are seeing represents only one of several previously not well-defined nor differentiated sub-groups or early pathways to schizophrenia. As we have previously reported,[20] an analysis of our referrals does not suggest any systematic bias that differentiates those families which have accepted, and those which have rejected admission into the study, other than a considerably higher percentage of remission and absence of need for further therapy in the disinterested families. Nonetheless, this possibility of sample bias cannot as yet be eliminated. We may be able to evaluate this possibility during the coming 2 years by means of an evaluation of all of the discordant pairs present in the 15,000-plus pairs of male twins contained in the recently completed National Science Foundation registry of all twin pairs who served in the Armed Services during the period of World War II.

TABLE 5. CASE REPORTS MONOZYGOTIC TWINS DISCORDANT FOR SCHIZOPHRENIA

Investigator	Year	Country	No. of cases	Sex M	Sex F	Sampling* method	Zygocity by blood and/or fingerprints
Grillmayr	1929	Austria	1	—	1	CR	No
Burkhardt	1929	Germany	1	—	1	CR	Yes
Wigers	1934	Norway	1	1	—	CR	Yes
Kasanin	1934	USA	1	1	—	CR	No
Reed	1935	Canada	1	—	1	CR	No
Kallmann	1948	USA	1	—	1	CR	No
Kallmann	1953	USA	1	—	1	CR	No
Hobson	1964	USA	1	—	1	CR	Yes
Total single case reports			8	2	6		
Rosanoff	1934	USA	9	7	2	RH	No
Essen-Möller	1941	Sweden	6	3	3	CA	Yes
Slater	1953	UK	15	8	7	RH and CA	Yes
Kurihara	1959	Japan	26	8	18	R	Yes
Tienari	1963	Finland	16	16	0	BR	Yes
Kringlen	1964	Norway	6	6	0	RH and CA	Yes
Pollin, Stabenau	1966	USA	14	4	10	R	Yes
Total all cases			100	54	46		

* Case report (CR), Resident Hospital Population (RH), Consecutive Hospital Admission (CA), Birth Registry (BR), Referral (R).

Toward the same goal we have also begun during the past year, an intensive evaluation of all cases in the world literature describing identical twins discordant for schizophrenia, in which the evidence for diagnosis and zygosity has appeared reasonably compelling. Including the first 14 cases in the NIMH series, we have thus far analyzed 100 cases with regard to 26 factors, which, on the basis of our own series, have appeared significant in differentiating the life history of the pre-schizophrenic from the non-schizophrenic twin, as shown in Table 5 (Source of Case Reports) and Table 6 (Early Characteristics).[21] Sixteen of these factors show a significant preponderance in the pre-illness life history of the schizophrenic twin, ranging from a ratio of 16 to 1 for "neurotic as a child", to 2·1 to 1 for "lighter at birth". Additional items in which there was a 2 to 1 or greater preponderance in the pre-illness description of the schizophrenic twin included: (a) behavior characteristics: submissive, sensitive, serious-worrier, obedient-gentler, dependent, well behaved, quite-shy, and

TABLE 6. MONOZYGOTIC TWINS DISCORDANT FOR SCHIZOPHRENIA (100 PAIRS)
EARLY CHARACTERISTICS *

Item	Other Studies		NIH Study		Total		Ratio (I/C)
	I†	C‡	I	C	I	C	
Neurotic as child	11	1	5	0	16	1	16·0
Submissive	27	2	10	2	37	4	9·3
Sensitive	26	3	12	2	38	5	7·6
Serious-worrier	10	2	12	2	22	4	5·5
Obedient-gentler	21	2	10	4	31	6	5·2
CNS illness as child	12	2	5	2	17	4	4·3
Birth complication (any)	18	5	6	1	24	6	4·0
Asphyxia at birth	8	3	4	0	12	3	4·0
Dependent	2	0	10	3	12	3	4·0
Well behaved	9	0	7	5	16	5	3·2
Quiet-shy	16	4	9	4	25	8	3·1
Stubborn	14	4	6	3	20	7	2·9
Weaker	16	10	11	1	27	11	2·5
Shorter	27	16	13	1	40	17	2·4
Lighter at birth	29	18	12	2	41	20	2·1
Slower development (walking)	3	1	6	4	9	5	1·8
Somatic illness as child	9	9	9	5	18	14	1·3
Second born	27	29	10	4	37	33	1·1
Fiery	9	5	5	9	14	14	1·0
Athletic	0	4	5	3	5	7	−1·4
Leader	9	—	5	9	14	30	−2·1
Outgoing-lively	8	26	5	9	13	35	−2·7
Spokesman	4	11	3	11	7	22	−3·1
Better at school	6	18	2	11	8	29	−3·6
More intelligent	2	7	2	9	—	16	−4·0
Married, co-twin not married	1	21	0	5	1	26	−26·0

* Number of twins where item clearly differentiated one twin by intrapair co-twin comparison.
† Schizophrenic Index Twin (I).
‡ Non-schizophrenic Monozygotic Co-twin (C).

stubborn; (b) physical characteristics: having had a central nervous system illness as a child, any birth complications (especially neonatal asphyxia), weaker, shorter, and lighter at birth: (c) items favoring the non-schizophrenic co-twin controls by 2 to 1 or better included: more intelligent, better at school, the spokesman, outgoing, lively, the leader, and becoming married. Items which did not discriminate by a ratio of 2 to 1 or better included: slower in development, somatic illnesses as a child, second-born, fiery disposition, and athletic.

This picture of the antecedents of schizophrenia in the discordant twin population is similar in many respects to the results reported in recent studies of non-twin populations. Lane and Albee[22, 23] have reported that the non-schizophrenic siblings of their schizophrenic subjects showed significantly lower birth weights and lower pre-illness IQs. Fleming[24] compared pre-psychotic guidance clinic treatment records of 2 groups of matched subjects one of which became schizophrenic and the other not, and Pollack,[25] among others, has compared schizophrenics and their non-schizophrenic siblings, and they report similar increased childhood levels of fearfulness and anxiety, and dependence in the pre-schizophrenic group. Thus it appears that the pattern which we have described above may be characteristic to some greater or lesser extent of all schizophrenia, rather than applying only to discordant twins. Even in the only-child family we believe that a similar process of comparison may occur, in this instance between the actual child, and the parents' internal mental representations of the ideal child.

If we tentatively accept this pattern as characterizing the life history of some, if not all, schizophrenics what are its implications concerning our central question: What is transmitted? It is our impression that, at this point, our data enable us to more clearly define certain hypothetical models, but not to state with certainty which of these models is indeed the mechanism at work. Clearly these are not incompatible alternative models, and in many respects they have been previously proposed by other investigators.

One such model emphasizes role conflict and focuses particularly on the transmission of contradictory and incompatible role expectations. Originally the constitutionally less favored twin's role as the more vulnerable, more dependent and weaker individual is based on the comparison with his co-twin. However, as this comparison is repeatedly made, with massive repetitive consistency, it becomes generalized to become an essential component of the index twin's self-image and identity, his feeling about himself in comparison to the entire world. This role and self-image are incompatible with the emphasis and demands for accomplishment and independence which are found in these same families. This conflict is exacerbated by the fact that in the same index twins we find a greater identification with and internalization of the conflict-ridden areas of the parents, those aspects of themselves which the parents are troubled by, and which evoke their anger and rejection when they see them appearing in the one twin to a greater extent than in the other.

An alternative model emphasizes constitutional factors. It suggests that a residual, relative, neurological deficiency or instability is transmitted as a result of differences in intrauterine experience, or early postnatal experiences such as episodes of respiratory embarrassment and cyanosis. This relative CNS deficiency constitutes a biological basis for subsequent ego weakness, contributing to greater difficulty in coping with the sequence of customary developmental tasks and environmental stresses and impeding the possibilities and limiting the results of growth experience. As part of, or instead of, CNS deficiency in this hypothetical model, endocrine or enzyme system abnormality might play a major role.

It is our impression that neither our findings nor the models described above constitute evidence pro or con the presence of a possible genetically controlled factor which may play some significant role in the etiology of schizophrenia. Our findings do clarify, we believe, why one of a pair of identical twins would encounter increasingly greater amounts of stress than his co-twin when confronted by customary life situations. And the great bulk of what we know about schizophrenia, from all clinical and research sources, suggests that stress is an essential factor in the development of this disease. At this point, however, it is not clear what the precise etiologic role of stress may be. On one hand it is possible that stress of a certain threshold level is important because it triggers and sets into action some genetically controlled enzyme abnormality which results in the accumulation of a metabolite which in turn causes psychotic symptomatology. Alternatively, the role, if any, of genetic transmission may have to do with the inheritance of certain delimited traits relevant to perceptual differences, or senstitivity to given stimuli, or with the rate of attenuation of certain types of impulses within the CNS, which in turn help to determine the level of stress generated by a given life situation, rather than determining the consequences of stress.

In summary, we have found a consistent and interrelated pattern of life history, psychiatric and biological differences differentiating the index from the control twin in 15 sets of monozygotic twins and triplets discordant for schizophrenia. A similar pattern appears to be present in other studies in the literature which have reported on discordant twin pairs, or looked at matched non-twin populations. We have considered some of the implications of these findings concerning the nature and etiology of schizophrenia, and more specifically, its transmission.

ACKNOWLEDGMENTS

We wish to acknowledge the major contributions to the location, evaluation and treatment of these families, and to the analysis and integration of the materials obtained from them, which have been made by Drs. Joe Tupin, Loren Mosher and Axel Hoffer and Miss Barbara Spillman, M.S.W. Presented in modified form at the Foundations' Fund for Research in Psychiatry Conference, *The Transmission of Schizophrenia*, Dorado, Puerto Rico, 29 June 1967.

REFERENCES

1. POLLIN, W., STABENAU, J. and TUPIN, J., Family studies with identical twins discordant for schizophrenia, *Psychiatry* **28** (1), 60–78 (1965).
2. POLLIN, W. STABENAU, J., MOSHER, L. and TUPIN, J., Life history differences in identical twins discordant for schizophrenia, *Am. J. Orthopsychiat.* **36** (3), 492–509 (1966).
3. STABENAU, J., TUPIN, J., WERNER, M. and POLLIN, W., A comparative study of families of schizophrenics, delinquents and normals, *Psychiatry* **28** (1), 45–59 (1965).
3a. STABENAU, J. and POLLIN, W., Comparative life history differences of families of schizophrenics, delinquents, and "normals", *Amer. J. Psychiat.* **124**, 1526–34 (1968).
4. KALLMANN, F. J., The genetic theory of schizophrenia, *Am. J. Psychiat.* **103**, 309–22 (1946).
5. POLLIN, W., STABENAU, J., MOSHER, L., HOFFER, A. and SPILLMAN, B., The NIH study of a series of monozygotic twins discordant for schizophrenia and their families, Paper presented at the Second Louisville Conference on Human Behavior Genetics, Louisville, April 1966.

5a. POLLIN, W. and STABENAU, J., Findings from the intensive study of a series of identical twins discordant for schizophrenia and their relevance to a theory concerning the etiology of schizophrenia, Symposium presented at the meeting of the IV World Congress of Psychiatry, Madrid, September 1966. To be published by Excerpta Med.

6. MOSHER, L., COHN, R., STABENAU, J., POLLIN, W. and PAINE, R., A neurological study of a series of identical twins discordant for schizophrenia. (In preparation.)

7. STABENAU, J. and POLLIN, W., Maturity at birth and adult protein bound iodine, *Nature,* 1967 (in press).

8. STABENAU, J. and POLLIN, W., Adult protein bound iodine and maturity at birth in monozygotic twins, *J. Clin. Endocr. and Metab.* June 1968 (in press).

9. EAYRS, J., Influence of the thyroid on the central nervous system, *Brit. Med. Bull.* **16,** 122–7 (1960).

10. SMITH, D., BLIZZARD, R. and WILKINS, L., The mental prognosis in hypothyroidism of infancy and childhood: a review of 128 cases, *Pediatrics* **19,** 1011–22 (1957).

11. SCHAPIRO, S., Metabolic and maturational effects of thyroxine on the infant rat, *Endocrinology* **78,** 527–32 (1966).

12. HAMBURGH, M., Evidence for a direct effect of temperature and thyroid hormone on myelinogenesis *in vitro, Develop. Biol.* **13,** 15–30 (1966).

13. ETKIN, W., Metamorphosis—activating system of the frog, *Science* **139,** 810–14 (1963).

14. SCHAPIRO, S. and NORMAN, R., Thyroxine: effects of neonatal administration on maturation, development, and behavior, *Science* **155,** 3767 (1967).

15. FESSEL, W. J., Macroglobulin elevations in functional mental illness, *Nature* **193,** 1005 (1962).

16. STABENAU, J., POLLIN, W. and MOSHER, L. Serum macroglobulin (S–19) in families of monozygotic twins discordant for schizophrenia, *Am. J. Psychiat.* June (1968) (in press).

17. FROHMAN, C. E., CZAJKOWKI, N. P., LUBY, E. P., GOTTLIEB, J. S. and SENF, R., Further evidence of a plasma factor in schizophrenia, *Arch. Gen. Psychiat.* **2,** 263 (1960).

18. TURNER, W. and CHIPPS, H., A heterophil hemolysin in human blood; distribution in schizophrenics and non-schizophrenics, *Arch. Gen. Psychiat.* **15** (4), 373–7 (1966).

19. STABENAU, J., POLLIN, W. and MOSHER, L., A study of monozygotic twins discordant for schizophrenia: some biologic variables, *Arch. Gen. Psychiat.* 1967 (in press).

20. GUGGENHEIM, F., POLLIN, W., STABENAU, J. and MOSHER, L., Prevalence of physical illness in the parents of monozygotic twins discordant for schizophrenia, Presented at the annual meeting of the American Psychosomatic Society, March 1966. (To be published.)

21. STABENAU, J. and POLLIN, W., Early characteristics of monozygotic twins discordant for schizophrenia, *Arch. Gen. Psychiat.* **17,** 723–34 (1967).

22. LANE, E. and ALBEE, G., Comparative birth weights of schizophrenics and their siblings, *J. Psychol.* **64,** 227–31 (1966).

23. LANE, E. and ALBEE, G., Childhood intellectual differences between schizophrenic adults and their siblings, *Am. J. Orthopsychiat.* **35** (4), 747–53 (1965).

24. FLEMING, P., Emotional antecedents of schizophrenia: inner experiences of children and adolescents who were later hospitalized for schizophrenia, Presented at Conference of Life History Research in Psychopathology, New York, 1967.

25. POLLACK, M., WOERNER, M., GOODMAN, W. and GREENBURG, I., Childhood development patterns of hospitalized adult schizophrenic and non-schizophrenic patients and their siblings, *Am. J. Orthopsychiat.* **36,** 510–17 (1966).

THE SUBCLASSIFICATION OF PSYCHOTIC CHILDREN: APPLICATION TO A STUDY OF LONGITUDINAL CHANGE*

WILLIAM GOLDFARB

Henry Ittleson Center for Child Research, Riverdale, New York

My ORIGINAL invitation to participate in this Conference suggested that I discuss the families of autistic children. This was a reasonable request inasmuch as the psychotic children whom we have been studying at the Ittleson Center have included an overwhelming proportion of children who would meet Kanner's diagnostic criteria for infantile autism. All were seriously impaired in their human relationships; were intensely preoccupied with the maintenance of sameness; and were impaired in capacity to communicate. Many showed specific historical symptoms such as failure to show the normal anticipatory response on being reached for during infancy, echolalia and failure to use language for conveying meaning, highly ritualistic and perseverative responses and unusual fascination for objects which contrasted sharply with their detachment from humans.

In the main, psychotic children at the Ittleson Center have represented cases of early childhood psychosis. They generally have been admitted to comprehensive residential or day hospital care at 5–7 years of age; and virtually all have shown insidious developmental deviation since very early in infancy. In such a young group whose disorders were apparent in very early infancy, we have found it difficult to separate the children sharply into precisely differentiated categories such as autistic, symbiotic or undifferentiated schizophrenic psychosis of childhood. Our experience certainly agrees with Eisenberg[1] and others who find that the evidence of clearcut symbiotic psychosis as defined by Mahler is rare. In addition, the Ittleson Center has contained few children with symptoms which would satisfy the criteria of adult schizophrenia. In short, the children would seem to resemble most closely those described by Kanner and Eisenberg as autistic. On the other hand, we have preferred to classify them merely as cases of early childhood psychosis since we have felt that at best the designation of young psychotic children as autistic, schizophrenic, atypical, symbiotic or any one of the non-conventional labels does not result in the classification of homogeneous non-overlapping groups of children.

In any event, we made case studies of the families of our total group of children to compare with Kanner's families of autistic children in mind. We already knew that the parents of Ittleson Center children showed a very high incidence of psychosis and thereby differed sharply from Kanner's parents of autistic children. In a study of the parents of psychotic children at the Ittleson Center,[5] although only one of 45 mothers and one of

* Childhood Schizophrenia Project of the Henry Ittleson Center for Child Research under support of the Ittleson Family Foundation and NIMH Grant No. MH 05753-05.

39 fathers had ever been hospitalized for psychiatric reasons, qualified psychiatric examiners classified 29% of the mothers and 13% of the fathers as schizophrenic on the basis of history and mental status.[1] In contrast Kanner had found that only 3% of 200 mothers and fathers of autistic children showed gross psychiatric abnormalities.[7]

We now asked ourselves whether our data confirmed the remainder of Kanner's remarkable description of his parents. It will be recalled that he noted an extremely high proportion of obsessive, cold, very intelligent parents, far superior to normal in education. Only about 10% of the parents did not fit this parental stereotype. As many as 87% of the fathers and 70% of the mothers had been to college and many of the fathers had achieved professional distinction.

Kanner's descriptions of the parents are clinical descriptions with all the potential hazards and limitations which may arise in the summation of clinical data, such as imprecise and unreliable definitions and the failure to achieve independence of data uncontaminated by a knowledge of the source of the subjects. Any effort to check Kanner's findings by using similar case techniques results in similar limitations. In our own study, using the case method, we found Kanner's parental stereotype in only two of 58 families of psychotic children.

A more precisely defined and reliable source of data is to be found in the social position of the Ittleson Center families of schizophrenic children, using the Hollingshead–Redlich Index of social position.[2] Table 1 summarizes the social position of families of Ittleson Center children suffering with childhood psychosis, and admitted in the past two 5-year intervals. Now it will be noted that these children come from all social classes. Indeed, a majority of the families of psychotic children admitted in the past 5 years come from the two lowest social classes. Here again we fail to confirm Kanner's description of the parents of autistic children.

TABLE 1. SOCIAL CLASS POSITION* OF SCHIZOPHRENIC
CHILDREN ADMITTED TO ITTLESON CENTER,
1956 THROUGH 1965

Social class	Percent of 33 children admitted 1956 through 1960	Percent of 28 children admitted 1961 through 1965
I	9	4
II	12	4
III	36	28
IV	30	39
V	12	25

* Hollingshead–Redlich Two Factor Index of Social Position.

If we assume the accuracy of Kanner's descriptions of his parents, as we probably should, then we must conclude the Kanner and Ittleson Center children represent divergent samples of psychotic children with very early onset of their disorders. Our own experience within the Center has alerted us to the dominant significance of sampling even within the

[1] If the children are further subclassified into those who are free of evidence of neurological impairments ("non-organic") and those who offer evidence of neurological impairment ("organic"), 44% of the mothers and 8% of the fathers of "non-organic" children and 21% of the mothers and 15% of the fathers of "organic" children are diagnosed as schizophrenic.

same treatment installation. For example, we have observed changes in social class position of the families of the psychotic children within the Ittleson Center itself (see Table 1). Thus in the past 5 years, a larger proportion of psychotic and autistic children has come from the lowest social class levels than in the previous 5-year period. Undoubtedly, this class shift merely reflects a new source of referrals to the Ittleson Centre, that is the new anti-poverty agencies. These agencies were suggesting services to families who previously would not have sought assistance on their own initiative.

Similar contradictory findings are usual in studies of childhood psychosis and, in each case, the contradictions would seem to be most easily explained as a reflection of selective sampling. Thus there are differences among the various reports in incidence of serious mental illness in the parents,[3-6] evidence of neurological impairment,[5, 7] ratio of boys to girls,[5, 6] and even in mental patterning.[7, 8] Observers vary in the kind of appraisal techniques they use and in the validity of their techniques. Observers offer contradictory data even where they have employed the same appraisal techniques. We cannot escape the conclusion that while each observer seems to be describing the total universe of childhood psychosis, he is in fact describing only his own sample of children. There is an obvious need for a system of description and subclassification that would enable investigators to define their own samplings of psychotic children and to differentiate them from other samplings. Such subclassification would also permit useful comparisons of comparable groups from different sources.

Subclassification of schizophrenic children which effectively achieves homogeneity of the children in the groups under study is also a prime necessity in longitudinal investigations of schizophrenic children. We have long known that individual psychotic children are highly diversified in patterns of their change over time. Since group trends merely summate individual trends, the group trends are determined by the relative distribution of differing individual trends. Groups of schizophrenic children which differ in the kinds of individual members they contain will show related differences in central tendency. Where individual psychotic children in a group differ significantly among themselves and even show contradictory trends, data representing central tendency of such groups are actually of little significance. On the other hand, every individual certainly represents himself. This undoubtedly explains why the observer experiences understanding and confidence in data representing longitudinal change of individual psychotic children and an equally great uncertainty and lack of confidence in data representing longitudinal changes of undifferentiated groups of pscyhotic children. Nor should undifferentiated groups be considered representative because they are large. The selection of representative cases is more crucial than sample size. However, since the investigator always works with the available sample, he lacks both sampling control and a clearly defined population. In this circumstance, the most practical solution to his dilemma is to define as clearly as possible the individual members of the sample. Subclassification may provide the appropriate description of the individual members of the sample. At least, this procedure permits comparison with similar children in other settings.

My intention, therefore, is to present an approach to subclassification of psychotic children which has evolved out of practical therapeutic management and systematic investigation at the Ittleson Center. Then I shall illustrate the potential contribution of this approach in a study of longitudinal changes in a group of schizophrenic children in the course of a period of residential treatment. In this investigation, it has not been our intention —implicit or explicit—to demonstrate the effects of treatment. Rather our objective has been to portray variations in developmental course of subgroups of schizophrenic children during a period of residential observation.

We have proposed that comprehensive understanding and treatment of the disordered behavior and development of the individual schizophrenic child requires biological and psychological assay in order to spell out his intrinsic needs and adaptive potentialities; and also required is appraisal of the family as a psychosocial unit. The interweaving of biological and social factors and the reciprocating interplay of the schizophrenic child, his parents and his siblings must be comprehended in each case. In practical diagnosis this conceptual model has been implemented by a system of classification embodying the appraisal of level of integrity of the central nervous system, of level of adequacy of the family as a psycho-social climate and of the severity of impairment of the child's adaptive functions. The Ittleson Center has employed an extensive variety of techniques for evaluating the children and their families. For the purposes of subclassifying the psychotic children in the present report, however, we have employed only one technique in each of the three areas of appraisal noted above in order to simplify analytic treatment of the data.

THE APPRAISAL TECHNIQUES FOR SUBCLASSIFYING THE PSYCHOTIC CHILDREN

1. *Ego level and severity of adaptive impairment*

The evaluative technique employed in the present study is a five-step scale for the psychiatric appraisal of ego status. The ratings are highly reliable. (For example, two psychiatrists agreed in 34 out of their 35 ratings.) The scale is based on overt, observable manifestations of adaptive capacity. Each step of the scale summates judgments in a number

1. Very severely impaired	No differentiation of important persons, e.g. mother, from others; makes no contact with anybody; no speech or gestural communication; total or near-total avoidance of looking and listening; indiscriminate mouthing and smelling; near-total absence of self-care; no educability.
2. Severely impaired	Human preferences observable but misidentifications of important persons occur often; limited contact; speech and gestural communication below level of 3-year-old (echoic, pronouns confused, comprehensibility below 90%); mouthing and smelling still prominent; self-care below that of a 3-year-old; minimal educability (at pre-school level).
3. Moderately impaired	Recognition of and responses to important persons; contacting behavior (approaching, talking to others); speech and gestural communication above that of 3-year-old; responds to school education above grade 1; yet gross distortions of reality (body image, capacities, etc.) and psychotic behavior.
4. Mildly impaired	Mild eccentricity and no friends but functions acceptably in relation to school (including community school and with or without special adjustment such as ungraded class or special tutoring) and in relation to the external environment; or no longer manifestly outlandish or bizarre in relationship to people, school, and the external environment but neurotic defenses present (e.g. obsessional or phobic).
5. Normal	By ordinary observation.

FIG. 1. Scale for psychiatric appraisal of ego status of child.

of important functional areas, including human attachment and contacting behavior, differentiation of important persons, speech and communication, receptor behavior, self care and response to schooling. The definitions of each step scale are presented in Fig. 1.

Although a continuum is implied in the scale steps, it is clear that the step intervals are not equal. Thus the movement from level 1 to level 2 is not as large in adaptive import as that between level 2 and level 3. Similarly, the spurt from level 3 to level 4 represents movement into the range of behavior which is acceptable to the community. In our experience, this is a particularly difficult step to consummate. On the other hand, when a child moves from one step in the scale to another, the change represents a sizeable shift in level of adaptive response.

2. *Integrity of central nervous system*

At the Ittleson Center, the child neurologist employs a comprehensive neurological history and examination. He searches for the unequivocal symptoms and signs of central nervous system impairment. Although alert to the "hard" unequivocal localizing signs such as reflex changes, abnormal reflexes, and manifest sensory and motor asymmetries and dysfunctions, he is particularly attentive to "soft" signs of impairment including non-localizing disturbances of gait, posture, balance, coordination, muscle tone, perception and speech. He also notes EEG findings, the presence of congenital stigmata and aberrations in head size. To avoid contamination from other sources, the neurologist conducts his analysis without access to psychiatric or other clinical information.

Using this procedure in a previous study, 65% of a group of 26 schizophrenic children at the Ittleson Center showed evidence of central nervous system, impairment.[7] Neurological study of 48 public school children of comparable age, using the same procedure, revealed no children with unequivocal central nervous impairment and only two children with relatively few "soft" signs.[9]

Neurological study, therefore, may be used operationally to distinguish two clusters of schizophrenic children. One cluster contains children who manifest positive neurological signs, although these are usually "soft" and equivocal in that pathological correlates have not been confirmed ("Organic" cluster). The other cluster does not manifest such neurological signs ("Non-organic" cluster). The dichotomous distribution of schizophrenic children on the basis of neurological impairment or its absence is quite arbitrary although it has been found useful for ordering data. It is a gross method for describing degree of neurological integrity which we actually view as a continuous dimension.

3. *Assay of the family contribution to the child's deviances*

Drawing on therapeutic experience with the child and family, the psychiatrist gages the contribution of the family to the disorders of the children. Ratings of the family contribution to each child's behavioral aberrations range from very marked (1) to slight (5). The ratings correlate significantly with other ratings of the family[10] including ratings of family adequacy based on direct participant observation (rho = 0·88) and clarity of the mothers' communication (rho = 0·58).

RESULTS

Table 2 describes the distribution of 54 schizophrenic children, including 36 boys and 18 girls, in residence at the Ittleson Center with regard to their ego status on admission. All the children fall in the three lowest levels in ego status as defined by our scale. This reflects the unequivocal admission diagnosis of childhood psychosis, embodying defects in all aspects of ego.

TABLE 2. EGO STATUS OF SCHIZOPHRENIC CHILDREN* AT
ADMISSION TO ITTLESON CENTER: TOTAL GROUP

Ego level at admission	Number of children	Percent
Level 1. Very severely impaired	8	15
Level 2. Severely impaired	31	57
Level 3. Moderately impaired	15	28
Total	54	100

* Includes children with at least 2 years of residential treatment.

Nevertheless, it also reflects the broad range of ego deficit among the schizophrenic children at Ittleson Center, for they vary from very severely disordered children—without speech, ability to differentiate people in the environment and with all the other manifestations of the most regressed states—to more moderately impaired children who possess speech and may show superior intelligence and above average school attainments.

Table 3 shows that the most severely impaired children are all "organic" children (with positive neurological findings) and that a larger portion of "non-organic" than "organic" children are at the "moderately impaired" levels of ego status.

TABLE 3. EGO STATUS OF SCHIZOPHRENIC CHILDREN* AT ADMISSION TO
ITTLESON CENTER: BY ORGANICITY†

Ego level at admission	Organic†		Non-organic†	
	Number	Percent	Number	Percent
Level 1. Very severely impaired	8	22	0	00
Level 2. Severely impaired	22	61	9	50
Level 3. Moderately impaired	6	17	9	50
Total	36	100	18	100

* Includes children with at least 2 years of residential treatment.
† "Organic" describes children with positive neurological findings. "Non-organic" describes children who do not show such positive findings.

The psychiatric judgment of the family contribution to the behavioral disorders of the children is summarized in Table 4. Here it is clear that all the children in the "non-organic" category, that is to say all the children free of discernible evidence of neurological impairment, come from the most grossly deviant families. (Qualitatively, these families are so

TABLE 4. FAMILY CONTRIBUTIONS TO DEVIANCY OF
SCHIZOPHRENIC CHILDREN*: BY ORGANICITY†

Family contribution to child's deviancy	Organic		Non-organic	
	Number	Percent	Number	Percent
1. Very marked	19	53	18	100
2.	7	19	0	00
3. Much	5	14	0	00
4.	1	3	0	00
5. Slight	4	11	0	00
Total	36	100	18	100

* Includes children with at least 2 years of residential treatment.

† "Organic" describes children with positive neurological findings. "Non-organic" describes children who do not show such positive findings.

extremely unusual in patterns of organization, communication and interpersonal reaction that there is little doubt of their disturbing impact on the children.) In contrast, the "organic" children come from families in which their psychosocial contribution to the child's deviancy ranges from very marked to slight. (The "organic" children from the most normal families are all severely impaired in ego status, supporting a high degree of intrinsic deficit and primary atypism in the children.)

If we accept as a measure of improvement in adaptive improvement a rise in at least one step interval in our ego status scales, we are now prepared to demonstrate the contribution of our system of subclassification to a study of longitudinal change in the schizophrenic children. In short, longitudinal change will be linked to the diagnosis of neurological impairment and to the severity of ego impairment at admission to the Center. Given the practical limitations of the number of children in the study and the narrow range of family ratings, a study of correlation between longitudinal changes in the children and extent of family contribution to the deviancy of the child is precluded. In the "non-organic" group, for example, all the families are judged to be extremely deviant in their influence on the children. The "organic" group in the present study also contains an excessive number of extremely deviant families and an insufficient number of families at each level of judgment regarding pathogenic influence of the family on the child.

The 54 children in the study have been treated for varying periods of time, ranging between 2 and 6 years. Statements which now follow, therefore, are restricted to longitudinal changes in ego during the first 2 years of treatment, the minimal period of treatment for all 54 children in the study.

It is evident that relatively more "non-organic" children improve in ego status than do "organic" children (Table 5). If we accept levels 4 and 5 of our ego status scales as descriptive of behavior which is acceptably within the range of normal community expectation, then it may be stated that more "non-organic" than "organic" children reach "normalcy" (Table 6). This strengthens the preceding observations that "non-organic" children improve more in ego status than do "organic" children.

TABLE 5. IMPROVEMENT* IN EGO STATUS OF SCHIZOPHRENIC CHILDREN IN FIRST 2 YEARS OF TREATMENT: BY ORGANICITY†

	Organic No. of children	Non-organic No. of children
Improvement	13	11
No improvement	23	7
Total	36	18

Fisher exact probability (1 tailed), 0·004.

* Rise of at least one step interval in Ego Status Scales.

† "Organic" describes children with positive neurological findings. "Non-organic" describes children who do not show such positive findings.

TABLE 6. ATTAINMENT OF "NORMALCY"* IN EGO STATUS OF SCHIZOPHRENIC CHILDREN IN FIRST 2 YEARS OF TREATMENT: BY ORGANICITY†

	Organic No. of children	Non-organic No. of children
Attain "normalcy"	1	4
Do not attain "normalcy"	35	14
Total	36	18

Fisher exact probability (1 tailed), 0·038

* Attainment of levels 4 and 5 on Ego Status Scales.

† "Organic" describes children with positive neurological findings. "Non-organic" describes children who do not show such positive findings.

We now ask when it is that the children who do improve manifest their first signs of ego growth. Do they show immediate signs of growth, or is there a delay? We are able to confirm an observation we have made in previous longitudinal studies. In the "organic" subcluster, the majority of those who improve show their first noticeable signs of improvement in the first year, while the overwhelming majority of the "non-organic" children who improve in the first 2 years of treatment do not begin to show such evidence of improvement before the second year (Table 7).

The significance of the above-noted differentiations of "organic" and "non-organic" subclusters is limited because of group differences between "organic" and "non-organic" children in level of ego at the start of therapeutic observation. For example, all of the lowest order children, rated by the psychiatrists at level 1 in ego status, are in the "organic" subcluster and none are in the "non-organic" subcluster. Previous experience has already taught us that these very primitive children who lack speech, are so low in intelligence that IQs cannot be assigned to them, make no contact with people and cannot distinguish their mothers from other people and who avoid looking and listening, are totally uneducable and show no significant progress in ego organization during treatment. Inclusion of children of such low ego status in a comparison of "non-organic" and "organic" children in regard

TABLE 7. CHANGES IN EGO STATUS IN FIRST AND SECOND YEARS OF
RESIDENTIAL TREATMENT OF SCHIZOPHRENIC CHILDREN WHO IMPROVE:
BY ORGANICITY†

	Organic		Non-organic	
	Number	Percent	Number	Percent
First noticeable improvement in first year	9	69	1	9
First noticeable improvement in second year	4	31	10	91
Total	13	100	11	100

Fisher exact probability (1 tailed), 0·004

† "Organic" describes children with positive neurological findings.
"Non-organic" describes children who do not show such positive
findings.

to ego progress will favor the "non-organic" children. Similarly differences between
"organic" and "non-organic" experimental groups in sex distribution[2] and in duration of
treatment might effect comparison data.

Therefore, a group of "organic" and "non-organic" children were matched in age, sex,
ego status at admission to treatment and in total duration of treatment. Eleven matched
pairs of "organic" and "non-organic" children treated up to 4 years were thereby selected.
In each group, 6 of the children had been rated at level 2 of our ego status scales on admission
and 5 had been rated at level 3.

Now it is still evident that more "non-organic" children improve in ego than do
"organic" children (Table 8). Indeed almost all of "non-organic" children (10 out of 11),
proportionately twice as many as "organic" children, do show ego progress during treatment. It is also of interest that 5 of the "non-organic" children (45%) reach levels 4 and 5

TABLE 8. IMPROVEMENT IN EGO STATUS OF MATCHED*
"ORGANIC" and "NON-ORGANIC"† SCHIZOPHRENIC CHILDREN

	Organic No. of children	Non-organic No. of children
Improvement	5	10
No improvement	6	1
Total	11	11

Fisher exact probability (1 tailed), 0·032

* Duration of treatment ranged from 2 to 4 years. Eleven
pairs matched by sex, ego status at admission and duration of
treatment.

† "Organic" describes children with positive neurological
findings. "Non-organic" describes children who do not show
such positive findings.

---

[2] The ratio of boys to girls in the "organic" and "non-organic" groups is 2·60 and 1·25 respectively.

w

(Table 9), which represent a level of adaptation which is acceptable in the normal community setting. In contrast, only one "organic" child (9%) reaches this level.

TABLE 9. ATTAINMENT OF "NORMALCY"* IN EGO STATUS OF MATCHED†
"ORGANIC" AND "NON-ORGANIC"‡ SCHIZOPHRENIC CHILDREN

	Organic No. of children	Non-organic No. of children
Attain "normalcy"	1	5
Do not attain "normalcy"	10	6
Total	11	11

Fisher exact probability (1 tailed), 0·074

* Attainment of levels 4 and 5 on ego status scales.
† Eleven pairs matched by sex, ego status at admission and duration of treatment. Duration of treatment ranged from two to four years.
‡ "Organic" describes children with positive neurological findings. "Non-organic" describes children who do not show such positive findings.

It should be evident by now that any effort to delineate longitudinal changes in schizophrenic children needs to take into account the heterogeneity of the children included in the population of children we designate as schizophrenic. This position is confirmed by the different patterns and amounts of longitudinal change exhibited by the children who differ in ego level at the start of the therapeutic observation. For example, we have seen virtually no growth in adaptive competence in the most severely ego impaired children who began treatment with no ability to communicate, the most extreme form of mental retardation, the most extreme forms of receptor aberration, and the most minimal expressions of self awareness. Schizophrenic children of higher order of ego do show predictable growth and change. The necessity for achieving homogeneous grouping in studies of longitudinal change is also supported by differences between "organic" and "non-organic" segments of the schizophrenic population. Even when matched in ego status at the beginning of therapeutic observation, more of the "non-organic" children improve and achieve competence for community living than do "organic" children.

Longitudinal study of schizophrenic children is obviously enhanced by subclassification of the children into segments, each of which is homogeneous with reference to one or more key parameter. On the other hand, it is also true that longitudinal study is so complex that unprofitable and unnecessary cross classifications should be avoided. The present report has focused on one approach to subclassification of schizophrenic children which is feasible and utilizes information which becomes available in their clinical management. These psychological, biological and social data derived from therapeutic sources are also significant in the light they cast on the adaptation of each child.

REFERENCES

1. REISENBERG, L., Psychotic disorders in childhood, in Cooke, R. E. (Ed.), *Biologic Basis of Pediatric Practice,* New York, McGraw-Hill, 1966.
2. HOLLINGSHEAD, A. B. and REDLICH, F. C., *Social Class and Mental Illness,* New York, Wiley, 1958.

3. BENDER, L. and GRUGETT, A. E., A study of certain epidemiological factors in a group of children with childhood schizophrenia, *Am. J. Orthopsychiat.* **26**, 131–45 (1956).

4. KALLMANN, F. J. and ROTH, B., Genetic aspects of preadolescent schizophrenia, *Am. J. Psychiat.* **112**, 599–606 (1956).

5. KANNER, L., To what extent is early infantile autism determined by constitutional inadequacies?, *A. Res. Nerv. Ment. Dis. Proc.* (1953) **33**, 378–85 (1954).

6. MEYERS, D. and GOLDFARB, W., Psychiatric appraisals of parents and siblings of schizophrenic children, *Am. J. Psychiat.* **118** (10), 902–8 (1962).

7. GOLDFARB, W., *Childhood Schizophrenia*, Cambridge, Harvard University Press, for Commonwealth Fund, 1961.

8. RUTTER, M., Classification and categorization in child psychiatry, *J. Child Psychol. Psychiat.* **8** (2), 71–83 (1965).

9. GOLDFARB, W., Factors in the development of schizophrenic children: an approach to subclassification, Report to First Rochester Conference on Schizophrenia, Rochester, March 1967.

10. GOLDFARB, W., LEVY, D. and MEYERS, D., The verbal encounter between the schizophrenic child and his mother, In Goldman, G. S. and Shapiro, D., *Developments in Psychoanalysis at Columbia University*, New York, Harper, 1967.

THE TYPES AND PREVALENCE OF MENTAL ILLNESS IN THE BIOLOGICAL AND ADOPTIVE FAMILIES OF ADOPTED SCHIZOPHRENICS

Seymour S. Kety,* David Rosenthal, Paul H. Wender and Fini Schulsinger

From the Laboratories of Clinical Science and Psychology, National Institute of Mental Health, Bethesda, Maryland, and the Psychological Institute, Department of Psychiatry, Kommunehospitalet, Copenhagen, Denmark

Two types of evidence have been the main support of hypotheses which implicate hereditary factors in the etiology of schizophrenia—the significantly higher incidence of schizophrenia in the close relatives of schizophrenic patients[1] and an increasing incidence in such relatives which is correlated with degree of consanguinity, finding its ultimate expression in the high concordance rate for schizophrenia in monozygotic twins.[2-8] Such evidence is inconclusive, however, in that it fails to remove the influence of certain environmental factors. The higher incidence of schizophrenia in the families of schizophrenics does not permit an evaluation of the respective weights of the genetic and environmental factors both of which the family members share with the schizophrenic, while environmental as well as genetic similarity is highly correlated with consanguinity in most circumstances. In the case of monozygotic twins it has been pointed out that such individuals usually share a disproportionate segment of environmental and interpersonal factors in addition to their genetic identity.[9]

In addition, not all of the previous studies have been able to avoid certain methodological and design problems which limit the generalizability of the findings. The question of subjective bias in the diagnosis of schizophrenia or of zygosity[9] has been ruled out in only a few of the studies, while selective bias has undoubtedly affected the sampling in some of the most extensive of the twin studies.[10, 11] Tienari's finding[12] of a low concordance for schizophrenia in a series of monozygotic twins in contrast to studies reporting concordance rates of 60% or more raises the possibility which is supported by the clinical material published in some of the studies, that the concordance rate found was strongly affected by the latitude permitted in the definition of schizophrenia in the co-twin. Much of the discrepancy could be explained if Tienari had chosen too narrow a definition and studies resulting in the highest concordance rates had been too inclusive. It is interesting to note in this connection that Inouye,[6] who employed a spectrum of categories in the diagnosis of mental illness, found a variety of schizophrenic-like illnesses in the co-twins of schizophrenics.

One of us had previously pointed out the possible value of using adopted individuals who developed schizophrenia as a means of separating the hereditary from the environmental contributions to its etiology.[9] Although adopted probands had been employed in evaluating nature and nurture contributions to intelligence and mental retardation,[13] the

* Present address: Department of Psychiatry, Harvard Medical School, Boston, Massachusetts.

peculiar advantages of this approach had not previously been exploited in the psychoses. The present study, the first of three in which we use adoption as a means of disentangling hereditary and genetic influences in schizophrenia,[14, 15] examines the prevalence and nature of mental illness in the biological and adoptive parents, siblings, and half-siblings of adopted individuals who had minimal contact with their biological families and who later became schizophrenic. A number of special precautions were taken to avoid the operation of subjective or selective bias. A diagnostic scheme was adopted with sufficient latitude to allow for a number of possibilities regarding the nature of the transmitted characteristics. For reasons which will become obvious later, the study was carried out in Denmark. By April 1967 practically all of the data originally contemplated had been collected, diagnoses had been made on the relatives who had been identified with evidence of mental illness, the codes broken, and the first analyses begun. The present communication is a first report. Additional data, more detailed analyses and the clinical abstracts upon which the diagnoses were based will be published in a full report at the termination of the study.

METHODS

The study as originally conceived was to be based entirely upon epidemiological information with no resort to personal contact with any of the probands or their families, and that is the nature of the present data. Interviews made by appropriate professional personnel of all probands and family members, if they can be conducted without introducing bias, may considerably increase the richness of the information and are being planned for the future.

The epidemiological study depended upon and was made possible by the existence in Denmark of three registers of remarkable quality and coverage:

Adoption Register of the State Department of Justice[1]

These archives maintained in Copenhagen contain the official records for every adoption granted in Denmark going back well before the period relevant to this study. They are filed separately for the City of Copenhagen and for the rest of Denmark, and chronologically by the date on which the adoption was granted. They contain the name, birth date, and address of the biological mother and the putative biological father. The reliability of the latter information is probably greater than is usually the case since the law requires that the putative father acknowledge paternity and contribute to the costs. In the case of the adopting parents, in addition to names, birth dates and address, they record the income of the adoptive father and his total fortune, his occupation, a description of the adoptive home and of the character of the adoptive parents. They give the name and birth date of the child and the date on which he was introduced to the adoptive home. Relationship between the adoptive and biological parents is noted as are noteworthy features of the child's medical history.

Folkeregister

This is a population register maintained for many years by every community in Denmark and established by law in 1924, giving for each individual (identified by name and birth

---

[1] The authors are grateful to the State Department of Justice for permission to use these files with appropriate safeguards regarding their confidentiality.

date) the address and household in which he has lived from birth to death or emigration. By means of these registers throughout the country it is possible to trace an individual through all changes of address and changes in marital status, deriving information on his parents, children and sibships. Since there are fines for failing to report each change of address shortly after it occurs, these records are remarkably complete. One possible loss, of relevance to the siblings recovered in this study, would be a child born in a hospital and not returned to the mother's household with her.

Psychiatric Register of the Institute of Human Genetics

This Institute of the University of Copenhagen has maintained a register going back to World War I of patients in most of the hospitals in Denmark diagnosed as having certain disorders. All nervous and mental diseases are reportable to the Institute and constitute the Psychiatric Register, which has recently been moved to the Risskov Hospital in Aarhus. Except for the Bispebjerg Hospital in Copenhagen, some departments of child psychiatry, and occasional short periods in the case of some other hospitals, all of the psychiatric hospitals and the psychiatric departments of general hospitals have been reporting all of their admissions quite faithfully. In order to test the completeness of the Psychiatric Register which is crucial to the search for mental illness in the adoptees and family members, a sample of several thousand names has been searched both in this Register and in the individual files of the 14 major psychiatric facilities in Denmark. There is an indication thus far that a search of the Psychiatric Register plus the files of psychiatric admissions to the Bispebjerg Hospital would recover about 95% of the admissions to all psychiatric facilities in the periods covered in the study.

In addition to these major sources of information we made use of the following additional sources, especially in the case of the relatives of the probands, to assure that we had obtained the maximum of recorded information on mental illness or disturbance in the sample:

Records of the Mother's Aid Organization

These contain information on the mental state and socio-economic problems of mothers or prospective mothers and pertinent information on the biological father, the child and other members of the family in applications for abortion, social or financial assistance, or the placing out of a child for adoption. These records were also a valuable source of information on the preadoption history of our probands.

Police and court records

The Psychiatric Register contains some information relevant to delinquency and imprisonment. Prison records and court psychiatric consultations have been used to supplement this information. Although our information regarding simple imprisonment is incomplete, it is likely that most cases in which a psychiatric question has been raised have come to our attention.

Military records

These contain records of discharge from military service for medical or psychiatric reasons and psychiatric evaluation where that has been indicated.

By virtue of the centralization of functions to single organizations and the national scope of the Folke- and Psychiatric Registers, it was felt that there was a unique opportunity for obtaining the maximum of recorded information relevant to our sample of adoptees and their relatives.

Selection of index cases

In order to take advantage of the more complete registers existing after 1920, to assure a substantial number of living parents, and to maximize the yield of index cases by selecting from a pool of adoptees who were within or beyond the period of maximum risk for schizophrenia, it was decided to include all adoptions granted in the City and County of Copenhagen (which at that time comprised 20–25% of the population of Denmark) from the beginning of 1924 to the end of 1947. Thus, the youngest of the adoptees would be more than 17 and the oldest more than 40 years of age at the beginning of the study. From these were excluded those adoptions in which one or both of the adoptive parents was a biological relative of the child. For each of the remaining 5483 adoptees the following information was recorded on a sequentially numbered special "A Form": name, sex, birth date of the adoptee; age in days, weeks or months of first transfer to the adopting parents; age at and date of adoption; name, birth date and address of the biological mother and the putative biological father; name, birth date and address of the adopting mother and father, his occupation and the stated income and fortune. The names of the adoptees were then checked in the Folkeregister to obtain all names acquired by each through life.

The Psychiatric Registers of the Institute of Human Genetics and of the Bispebjerg Hospital were then searched for the names of each of these adoptees, confirmation of identification being made by birth date and, where doubt existed, by ancillary information such as address or names of relatives. When any record was found of admission of an adoptee to a psychiatric facility, regardless of the nature of the illness, a numbered "B Form" was prepared with the following information: adoptee's name, birth date, and A Form number; for each admission to a psychiatric facility: the name of the hospital, the dates of admission and discharge, and the discharge diagnoses. This yielded a total of 507 adoptees who had been admitted to a psychiatric facility for any reason, and it was from this group that the index cases were selected.

The psychiatric hospital records for each of these 507 adoptees were then obtained and examined independently by two Danish psychiatrists. One of these was Dr. Schulsinger, who prepared a brief abstract from the record and classified the individual as definitely schizophrenic, definitely not schizophrenic, or possibly schizophrenic. The other psychiatrist was Dr. Jytte Willadsen who had not been informed of the over-all design of the study and was told simply that the study had as one of its objectives the determination of schizophrenia and other mental illnesses in a group of adoptees. On each B Form she completed a check list which included age at onset of illness, marital status, major clinical features such as: organic signs and symptoms, thought disorder, inappropriateness of mood and affect, delusional thinking, hallucinations, bizarreness, withdrawal, work performance, sexual adjustment, intellectual ability and therapy. She was asked also to record her designation of the most probable diagnosis and also to indicate the likelihood that the patient had schizophrenia. One copy of the B Form, including Dr. Willadsen's entries but not Dr.

Schulsinger's, was sent to Bethesda where, on the basis of the information thus transmitted Drs. Wender and Kety independently rated each of the adoptees with a history of admission to a psychiatric facility as definitely schizophrenic, definitely not schizophrenic or possibly schizophrenic. After that process Dr. Schulsinger's ratings were received and tabulated and the three ratings compared. Where all three had rated an adoptee as definitely schizophrenic, the individual became an index case. Where all three agreed that the adoptee on the basis of the records was definitely not schizophrenic (absence of suggestive symptoms and the ability to form a clear diagnosis of another type of illness), the adoptee was dropped from further consideration as an index case. Where a question of schizophrenia had been raised by one or more of the raters, Dr. Schulsinger was asked to prepare an English summary of the case history as obtained from the hospital records but omitting his own impression. These summaries were then sent to the American authors, and where a consensus on schizophrenia by them and Dr. Schulsinger was reached, these also became schizophrenic index cases. In this way, 34 schizophrenic index cases were selected from the adoptees with a history of admission to a psychiatric facility. Two of these were found to be monozygotic twins but, since they were adopted by the same parents, have been treated as a single case, thus reducing the number of schizophrenic index cases to 33.

Selection of controls

In order to arrive at an estimate of the prevalence of mental illness which would result from our search techniques and diagnostic criteria in the populations of biological and adoptive relatives of adopted children who did not become schizophrenic, a matched control

TABLE 1. SOME CHARACTERISTICS OF THE SCHIZOPHRENIC INDEX CASES
AND THEIR MATCHED CONTROLS

	Index cases	Controls
Number	33	33
Males : Females	18 : 15	18 : 15
With biological parent(s) for:		
less than 1 month	19	20
1 month to 3 months	6	4
3+ months to 6 months	2	2
6+ months to 12 months	5	4
1+ to 2 years	0	2
more than 2 years	1	1
Months spent with biological parent(s)	3·5	4·1
Months spent in children's institution	10·2	8·0
Months spent in foster home	3·6	3·7
Age (months) at transfer to adoptive parents	18·3	16·0
Age (months) at legal adoption	38·0	33·5
Socio-economic class of adoptive parents	3·0	3·0
Mean age, 1 January 1967 (years)	36·1	35·9
Mean year of birth:		
Probands	1931	1931
Biological mother	1906	1909
Biological father	1907	1906
Adoptive mother	1896	1900
Adoptive father	1895	1895

for each index case was selected from the pool of 4976 adoptees without B forms (for whom no admission to a psychiatric facility had been recorded). These were selected as follows:

The file containing the A Forms in sequential order was searched systematically in equal batches before and after the A Form of each index case until at least four other adoptees were found without a history of a psychiatric admission and corresponding to the index case in sex, age, age at transfer to the adoptive parents and socio-economic status of the adoptive family. The latter was determined by occupation of the adoptive father, income, fortune and address, using criteria previously employed for Denmark.[16] Considerably more information was then obtained in Copenhagen relative to the pretransfer history of each of these adoptees. This included: time spent with biological mother, father or other biological relatives, time spent in a children's institution and the nature of the institution, time spent with a foster family other than the adoptive parents. When this information had been returned, Drs. Wender and Kety selected from the tentative controls for each index case one which best approximated the index case in the characteristics noted above and which are summarized for the index cases and the controls in Table 1.

Identification of biological and adoptive relatives

After the probands (index cases and control adoptees) had been selected, their A numbers were mixed together into a single group of probands which was then handled indiscriminately through all the succeeding operations. None of those who made the subsequent searches and diagnoses were given information that would have indicated which were the index cases and which were the controls. From the names and birth dates of the biological and adoptive parents, the subsequent name changes, marital and parental history of each individual was traced through the Folkeregister,[2] thus permitting the identification

TABLE 2. DISTRIBUTION OF IDENTIFIED RELATIVES

	Biological family					Adoptive family				
	Mothers	Fathers	Sibs	Half-sibs	Total	Mothers	Fathers	Sibs	Half-sibs	Total
For 33 index cases: Total identified	33	30	2	85	150	33	30	8	3	74
Lost through: death	9	8	0	3	20	11	13	0	0	24
emigration	1	2	0	1	4	0	0	1	1	2
disappearance	0	0	0	0	0	0	0	0	0	0
Total lost	10	10	0	4	24	11	13	1	1	26
Average age at loss	37	45	—	19	37	56	63	19	22	57
For 33 controls: Total identified	32	31	5	88	156	33	33	17	0	83
Lost through: death	3	6	0	0	9	13	13	0	0	26
emigration	3	2	1	4	10	2	1	0	0	3
disappearance	2	1	0	0	3	0	0	0	0	0
Total lost	8	9	1	4	22	15	14	0	0	29
Average age at loss	38	44	22	30	38	60	53	—	—	57

[2] Additional information for relatives born before 1924 was obtained from old census lists.

by name and birth date of parents, siblings and half-siblings of the proband in both his biological and adoptive families. The dates of death, emigration, or disappearance of any of these family members were also noted, and when this occurred before the age of 15 the individual was not tabulated. Individuals who moved from one part of Denmark to another could readily be followed through the respective Folkeregisters. The number of each type of relative thus identified and remaining beyond age 15 for each of the proband groups is indicated in Table 2. For the 33 schizophrenic probands and their controls, 98% of the biological mothers, 92% of the biological fathers and 98% of the adoptive parents were identified. We cannot with equal certainty establish the percentage of siblings and half-siblings identified. The loss by death, emigration or disappearance of the tabulated identified relatives represented about 6% of the total subject years under examination.

Detection and characterization of mental aberration in the relatives of the probands

The Psychiatric Register of the Institute of Human Genetics and of the Bispebjerg Hospital, the psychiatric admissions of the 14 major psychiatric hospitals, records of the Mother's Aid Organization, police records and military records were now searched for the names of any of the 463 identified relatives of the probands. If check of the birth date and ancillary information confirmed the identity, the individual was placed in a new group of relatives with a history of some mental abnormality. These were described on sequentially numbered forms with admission, discharge and diagnostic information from the Psychiatric Register or other source.

Since the diagnosis of mental illness in the biological and adoptive families of the probands was the crucial determination of the study, every effort was made to insure that this diagnosis was made independently by each of the four raters and in the absence of knowledge which might bias his evaluation. For each of these relatives, the case records were obtained from the respective institutions and an English summary on each was prepared by a Danish psychiatrist, Dr. Erik Glud, who was not aware of the research design or the specific hypotheses being tested (Dr. Schulsinger prepared a few summaries before Dr. Glud joined the project). These summaries were transcribed and the transcriptions edited to delete all personal names, diagnostic opinions by the summarizing psychiatrist, adjectives such as adoptive, biological, etc., and other information which might indicate whether the subject in question was a biological or an adoptive relative and any reference which might indicate whether the subject was the relative of an index case or control. The summaries themselves varied considerably with regard to the amount of information they contained because in some cases we could find only brief notes in the files of the Mother's Aid Organization or the police; but most summaries were sufficiently ample to permit diagnostic assessment with a reasonable degree of confidence.

Four copies of the edited summary were prepared and distributed to the four authors who served as raters and who independently characterized each subject according to the classification described below. The individual ratings were then tabulated and those cases in which there was disagreement among the raters were discussed at a conference of all four authors where an effort was made to review additional edited information which it was possible to obtain and to arrive at a consensus diagnosis acceptable to all. In 4 cases there remained an evenly split opinion regarding the presence of schizophrenia or doubtful schizophrenia, and these were not included in those categories. After the consensus diagnosis was established and recorded for the 67 relatives to whom some mental or behavioral aberration could be attributed, the relationship of each relative to his proband was decoded and the data analyzed.

Diagnostic classification system for the relatives

Before we began to make diagnostic evaluations of the relatives, it had become clear that a system of classification with finer gradations than had been found useful in the selection of index cases would be needed. Whereas we could select only those adoptees as index cases who fulfilled particular criteria, the design of the study required that every relative with a record of mental illness or behavioral aberration be classified without the option of rejecting those who did not fit a particular label. In the diagnosis of the index cases we had found it possible to classify those we would accept as schizophrenia into three

TABLE 3. DIAGNOSTIC CLASSIFICATION SYSTEM EMPLOYED

A. Definitely not schizophrenia (specify diagnosis—see note to Table 4 for diagnoses used).

B. Chronic schizophrenia ("chronic undifferentiated schizophrenia," "true schizophrenia," "process schizophrenia").
Characteristics: (1) Poor pre-psychotic adjustment; introverted; schizoid; shut-in; few peer contacts; few heterosexual contacts; usually unmarried; poor occupational adjustment. (2) Onset—gradual and without clear-cut psychological precipitant. (3) Presenting picture: presence of primary Bleulerian characteristics; presence of clear rather than confused sensorium. (4) Posthospital course—failure to reach previous level of adjustment. (5) Tendency to chronicity.

B2. Acute schizophrenic reaction (acute undifferentiated schizophrenic reaction, schizo-affective psychosis, possible schizophreniform psychosis, [acute] paranoid reaction, homosexual panic).
Characteristics: (1) Relatively good premorbid adjustment. (2) Relatively rapid onset of illness with clear-cut psychological precipitant. (3) Presenting picture: presence of secondary symptoms and comparatively lesser evidence of primary ones; presence of affect (manic-depressive symptoms, feelings of guilt); cloudy rather than clear sensorium. (4) Post-hospital course good. (5) Tendency to relatively brief episode(s) responding to drugs, EST, etc.

B3. Border-line state (pseudoneurotic schizophrenia, border-line, ambulatory schizophrenia questionable simple schizophrenia, "psychotic character", severe schizoid individual).
Characteristics: (1) Thinking: strange or atypical mentation; thought shows tendency to ignore reality, logic and experience (to an excessive degree) resulting in poor adaptation to life experience (despite the presence of a normal IQ); fuzzy, murky, vague speech. (2) Experience: brief episodes of cognitive distortion (the patient can, and does, snap back but during the episode the idea has more the character of a delusion than an ego-alien obsessive thought); feelings of depersonalization, of strangeness or unfamiliarity with or toward the familiar; micropsychosis. (3) Affective: anhedonia—never experiences intense pleasure—never happy; no deep or intense involvement with anyone or anybody. (4) Interpersonal behavior: may appear poised, but lacking in depth ("as if" personality); sexual adjustment: chaotic fluctuation, mixture of hetero- and homosexuality. (5) Psychopathology: multiple neurotic manifestations which shift frequently (obsessive concerns, phobias, conversion, psychosomatic symptoms, etc.); severe widespread anxiety.

C. Inadequate personality.
Characteristics: A somewhat heterogeneous group consisting of individuals who would be classified as either inadequate or schizoid by the *APA Diagnostic Manual*. Persons so classified often had many of the characteristics of the B3 category, but to a considerably milder degree.

D1, 2 or 3. Uncertain B1, 2 or 3 either because information is lacking or because even if enough information is available, the case does not fit clearly into an appropriate B category.

subgroups representing chronic schizophrenia, acute schizophrenic reaction, and border-line or pseudoneurotic schizophrenia. The same three categories could be applied to the probable but not definite schizophrenics. Our experience with possible index cases who were eventually rejected because they did not meet the criteria for classification as schizophrenic caused us to recognize the existence of a group similar in quality to the border-line schizophrenic but of considerably less intensity. This group is best described as inadequate personality in the standard nomenclature. The classification scheme used in making the individual ratings was worked out largely by Dr. Wender and appears as Table 3.

RESULTS

The 66 probands (33 index cases and their controls) on search through the Folkeregister yielded 463 identified relatives who were distributed as indicated in Table 2. Although there is no significant difference in the number or distribution of identified relatives between index cases and controls, there are considerable differences in both characteristics between the biological and adoptive relatives. There are more biological than adoptive half-siblings, and few full biological siblings. This is due in part to many biological parents not being married to one another and having children with other partners. When the adoptive parents acquired additional children, which they did infrequently, they did so usually as a couple. In addition, the biological and adoptive parents differ in age, socio-economic class and in the particular selective processes inherent in their having become biological or adoptive parents, making comparisons difficult between them with respect to the prevalence of mental illness.

On the other hand, none of these differences exist between the families of index cases and controls, whether biological or adoptive. Thus, the prevalence of particular types of mental illness in each group of relatives of the index cases can appropriately be compared with that in the corresponding relatives of the controls, permitting the separate testing of hypotheses based on genetic or environmental factors in the transmission of schizophrenia.

Psychiatric disorders in the biological relatives

Table 4 presents the identified relatives and the consensus diagnosis of mental disorder in them for individual probands. We had recognized certain qualitative similarities in the features that characterized the diagnoses of schizophrenia, uncertain schizophrenia, and inadequate personality, which suggested that these syndromes formed a continuum; this we called the schizophrenia spectrum of disorders. If schizophrenia were to some extent genetically transmitted, there should be a higher prevalence of disorders in the schizophrenia spectrum among the biological relatives of the index cases than in those of their controls. Table 5 presents the data which test that hypothesis. Of 150 biological relatives of index cases 13, or 8·7%, had a diagnosis of schizophrenia, uncertain schizophrenia or inadequate personality compared to 3 of 156, or 1·9%, with such diagnoses among the biological relatives of the controls. The difference is highly significant (p, one sided probability from exact distribution = 0·0072).

TABLE 4A. DIAGNOSED MENTAL ILLNESS IN THE BIOLOGICAL AND ADOPTIVE FAMILIES OF INDEX CASES*

Proband	Diagnosis	Months with biological family	Biological family — Identified relatives				Biological family — Schizophrenia spectrum disorders			Biological family — Other psychiatric diagnoses			Adoptive family — Identified relatives				Adoptive family — Schizophrenia spectrum disorders			Adoptive family — Other psychiatric diagnoses		
			Parents	Siblings	Half-sibs	Total	Parents	Sibs	Half-sibs	Parents	Sibs	Half-sibs	Parents	Siblings	Half-sibs	Total	Parents	Sibs	Half-sibs	Parents	Sibs	Half-sibs
S1	B1	0	2	0	0	2	B3						2	0	0	2				cd+ts		
S2	B2	1	2	0	4	6	D3		D1 B3	p dr		pp dr	2	0	0	2				ca		
S3	B3	0	2	0	3	5		C					2	0	0	2						
S4	B1	8	2	0	1	3							2	0	0	2						
S5	B1	0	2	0	3	6						dr	2	0	0	2						
S6	B1	9	2	0	6	9							2	0	0	4						
S7	B1	0	2	0	0	2	C			su			2	0	0	2						
S8	B1	0	2	0	2	4							2	0	0	2						
S9	B2	1	2	1	1	3							2	1	1	4					mr	
S10	B3	28	2	0	0	2			B3 B3 B3				2	0	0	2						
S11	B1	38	2	0	3	5							2	0	0	2						
S12	B3	0	1	0	0	2							1	0	0	2						
S13	B2	0	2	0	1	2			B1	su su			2	0	0	2	C			lp		
S14	B3	10	2	0	5	7							2	0	0	2						
S15	B1	0	1	0	0	2							1	0	0	2						
S16	B2	0	2	0	1	3			D3				2	0	0	2						
S17	B3	0	2	0	0	2				dr+su dl			2	0	0	2				hc+dr cn+dr cv		
S18	B1	0	1	0	9	11							1	0	0	1						
S19	B2	0	2	0	2	4							2	0	0	2						
S20	B3	0	2	0	3	5							2	0	0	2						
S21	B1	0	2	1	0	2							2	1	0	2						
S22	B1	0	2	0	4	6							2	0	0	2						
S23	B3	0	2	0	3	5							2	1	0	3						
S24	B2	4	2	0	2	4				pp		cd+dr	2	3	0	5						
S25	B1	0	1	0	2	4							1	0	0	1						
S26	B3	2	2	0	0	2				ca+o			2	1	0	3						
S27			1	1	4	6							1	3	0	5						
S28	B2	5	2	0	2	3							2	0	0	2					amp/B2	
S29	B1	1	2	0	15	17							2	0	2	4						
S30	B1	0	2	0	2	4							2	0	0	2						
S31	B1	1	2	0	2	4							2	0	0	2						
S32	B1	0	2	0	1	3							2	0	0	1						
S33	B3	1?	2	0	4	6			B3 D3	cd da cd+ca+su		ppp/B2	1	0	0	1	D3			p sp/md?		
		10																				
Totals			63	2	85	150	3	1	9	12	0	5	63	8	3	74	2	0	0	8	2	0

* For note to Table 4A see p. 356.

TABLE 4B. DIAGNOSED MENTAL ILLNESS IN THE BIOLOGICAL AND ADOPTIVE FAMILIES OF CONTROLS*

Proband	Months with biological family	Biological family — Identified relatives: Parents	Siblings	Half-sibs	Total	Bio. Schizophrenia spectrum disorders: Parents	Sibs	Half-sibs	Bio. Other psychiatric diagnoses: Parents	Sibs	Half-sibs	Adoptive family — Identified relatives: Parents	Siblings	Half-sibs	Total	Adopt. Schizophrenia spectrum disorders: Parents	Sibs	Half-sibs	Adopt. Other psychiatric diagnoses: Parents	Sibs	Half-sibs
C1	0	2	0	1	3							2	0	0	2						
C2	0	2	1	5	8							2	0	0	2						
C3	0	2	0	8	10				cd+ca		cd	2	1	0	3						
C4	4	2	0	1	3	B1			ar / dl			2	0	0	2		B3		sp/B2		
C5	5	2	0	2	4				dr			2	1	0	3						
C6	48	2	0	2	4							2	1	0	3		D3				
C7	0	2	0	3	5							2	0	0	2						
C8	0	2	0	1	3							2	0	0	2						
C9	24	2	0	3	5		B3					2	0	0	2						
C10	0	2	1	4	7							2	0	0	2						
C11	0	2	0	4	6							2	0	0	2						
C12	0	2	0	2	4							2	2	0	4						
C13	0	2	0	3	5				sp		dr	2	0	0	2						
C14	1	2	1	1	4							2	1	0	3						
C15	0	2	0	6	8							2	0	0	2						
C16	1	2	0	8	10							2	0	0	2				hn dl		
C17	0	1	0	0	1						mr	2	1	0	3		B1				
C18	0	2	0	0	2							2	0	0	2						
C19	0	2	0	4	6							2	3	0	5						
C20	14	2	0	4	6	D3			mr / md?			2	0	0	2						
C21	1	2	0	3	5				dr			2	1	0	3						
C22	0	2	0	1	3							2	0	0	2						
C23	0	2	0	4	6							2	2	0	4						
C24	0	2	0	1	3							2	0	0	2						
C25	0	2	0	2	4					ar		2	0	0	2						
C26	2	2	0	1	3							2	0	0	2						
C27	0	2	0	3	5							2	1	0	3						
C28	10	2	2	1	5							2	0	0	2				su		
C29	0	2	0	6	8						o/D3	2	0	0	2						
C30	0	2	0	4	6						pp/D3	2	2	0	4				dr		
C31	12?	1	0	0	1							2	0	0	2						
C32	3?	2	0	1	3							2	0	0	2						
C33	0?	2	0	6	8							2	0	0	2						
C34	8?	2	0	1	3							2	0	0	2						
Totals		63	5	88	156	2	1	0	8	1	5	66	17	0	83	0	3	0	5	0	0

For note to Table 4B, see p. 356.

One troublesome problem was the presence among the 33 index cases of a number who had lived with their biological families for various periods from one month to one year or even more. Although these made the hoped-for separation of hereditary from environmental factors less rigorous, we had decided not to exclude such cases because of the small size of our index group. There are, however, 19 index cases and 20 controls who left their biological families within one month of birth, in most cases within a few days. The prevalence of schizophrenia spectrum disorders is at least as high in the biological relatives of this subsample of index cases (9/93 or 9·7%) as it was in the biological relatives of all 33 index cases, and the difference between them and the biological relatives of the early separated controls (where there were no cases of such disorder in 92 relatives) reaches a higher level of significance ($p=0·002$). The differences for schizophrenia alone and for schizophrenia or uncertain schizophrenia are also significant ($p=0·03$ and $0·01$ respectively). In fact, the difference in prevalence of schizophrenia spectrum disorders noted between the biological relatives of the total sample of index cases and controls derives from the subsample with early separation. The reason for this is a relatively high prevalence of these disorders (4·6%) in the biological families of the controls who were not transferred until late. It is possible that the presence of such illness in the biological family may have been a reason for giving the child for adoption in some cases.

By examining the distribution of schizophrenia spectrum disorders in the biological families and taking family size into consideration, no evidence is found to support the thesis that the high prevalence in the relatives of index cases derives from a few deviant families. The 13 such relatives of the total index sample come from 9 families, the 9 relatives with schizophrenia spectrum disorders among the early transferred cases represent 6 families, and the frequency of affected biological families in each sample of index cases (9/33 or 6/19) is significantly higher ($p=0·028$ or $0·012$) than the frequency of affected families for the corresponding control groups (2/32 or 0/19).[3]

An examination of the prevalence of schizophrenia spectrum disorders among the different relationships indicates that the prevalence is high (10–11%) among the biological half-siblings of both groups of index cases (early and late separated) while these disorders

---

Note to Tables 4A and 4B

* Monozygotic twins concordant for schizophrenia and treated as one case.
Diagnoses in italic type pertain to a father or a paternal half-sibling.
Diagnoses connected by + are diagnoses in the same individual.
Diagnoses separated by a / (as in amp/B2) represent failure to reach a consensus on one or the other diagnosis.

Diagnostic Symbols:

Schizophrenia spectrum disorders:

B1	chronic schizophrenia
D1	chronic schizophrenia (uncertain)
B2	acute schizophrenic reaction
D2	acute schizophrenic reaction (uncertain)
B3	border-line schizophrenia
D3	border-line schizophrenia (uncertain)
C	inadequate personality

Other psychiatric diagnoses:

amp	amphetamine psychosis	dl	delinquency	o	organic psychosis
ar	affective reaction	dr	depressive reaction	p	imprisonment
ca	chronic alcoholism	hc	hysterical character	pp	psychopath
cd	character disorder	hn	hysterical neurosis	ppp	*post partum* psychosis
cn	character neurosis	lp	luetic psychosis	sp	senile psychosis
cv	cerebrovascular disease	md	manic depressive psychosis	su	suicide
da	drug addiction	mr	mental retardation	ts	toxic state

---

[3] In the case of one of the 20 controls, no biological relatives were identified.

are absent among the control half-siblings. The prevalence of these disorders among the parents and the few full siblings of the index cases is not low but is not significantly different from the controls, largely because of their higher prevalence in the parents of late separated controls. The possibility has previously been raised that such illness may have been the basis for delayed adoption. A lower prevalence of schizophrenia is also found in the parents than in the siblings or progeny of schizophrenics reared in their natural families[17] and the same factors may be operating in these and in our series to explain it, i.e. incomplete diagnostic information on older relatives and the decreased rates of marriage and fertility among schizophrenics, so that among an equally genetically vulnerable population those who become parents are less likely to be overtly schizophrenic.

When the index cases are divided according to the type of schizophrenia they displayed, the frequency and type of schizophrenia spectrum disorder in the respective biological families is revealing. In the 82 biological relatives of the 16 probands diagnosed as chronic schizophrenia were found: 1 chronic schizophrenia, 3 border-line schizophrenia, 2 uncertain border-line, and 1 inadequate personality. In the 38 biological relatives of 10 probands diagnosed as border-line schizophrenia were found: 3 border-line schizophrenics, 1 uncertain chronic schizophrenia, 1 uncertain border-line, and 1 inadequate personality. Thus, these families do not differ from each other significantly in type or frequency of disorder in the schizophrenia spectrum. On the other hand, in the 30 biological relatives of 7 probands diagnosed as acute schizophrenic reaction, no instance of schizophrenia spectrum disorder was found. This raises a serious question regarding the validity of classifying that syndrome as a type of schizophrenia, and supports the tendency of European and British psychiatrists to regard it as a disorder *sui generis*. The concept of border-line schizophrenia as a milder variant of schizophrenia is, however, reinforced.

Other mental or behavioral disturbances are, in general, randomly distributed between the biological relatives of index and control probands, 17 and 14 of such disorders being represented in the two populations, respectively. Although the numbers are small and none of the differences significant, it may be interesting to note the diagnoses (other than those previously postulated as constituting the schizophrenia spectrum) which are relatively more and less frequent in the biological families of index cases than in those of the controls. Less frequent are the affective disorders, organic psychoses, senile psychoses and mental retardation. More frequent in the biological relatives of index cases are suicide, psychopathy or delinquency and character disorder. The five discovered cases of suicide among biological relatives all occurred in the index case families, involving both biological parents in the case of one proband.

Some independent considerations suggest a possible relationship between schizophrenia and suicide, psychopathy or character disorder. A relatively high rate of suicide has been found among schizophrenics;[18] Heston[19] has reported a significantly higher incidence of psychopathy and neurotic personality disorders among offspring separated shortly after birth from their schizophrenic mothers; the character disorders in this study exhibit some of the features of border-line schizophrenia or inadequate personality, but in attenuated form. One or another of these three diagnoses occurred 12 times in the biological relatives of index cases as compared with 4 instances in the biological relatives of controls. The difference, though significant ($p=0.034$), emerged retrospectively and permits only the

x

formulation of a hypothesis that character disorder, psychopathy and suicide may represent extensions of the spectrum of schizophrenia-related disorders.

Psychiatric disorders in the adoptive relatives

In contrast to the significant concentration of schizophrenia and related disorders in the biological relatives of index cases, the adoptive families show fewer cases of such illness and these are randomly distributed between the families of index cases and controls (Table 5). Although other psychiatric diagnoses (Table 4) are somewhat more common among the

TABLE 5. DISTRIBUTION OF SCHIZOPHRENIA SPECTRUM DISORDERS AMONG THE BIOLOGICAL AND ADOPTIVE RELATIVES OF SCHIZOPHRENIC INDEX CASES AND CONTROLS

	Biological relatives	Adoptive relatives
Total sample of 33 index cases and 33 controls		
Index cases	$\frac{13}{150}$	$\frac{2}{74}$
Controls	$\frac{3}{156}$	$\frac{3}{83}$
p (one-sided, from exact distribution)	0·0072	N.S.
Subsample of 19 index cases and 20 controls separated from biological family within 1 month of birth		
Index cases	$\frac{9}{93}$	$\frac{2}{45}$
Controls	$\frac{0}{92}$	$\frac{1}{51}$
p	0·0018	N.S.

Numerators = number with schizophrenia, uncertain schizophrenia or inadequate personality.
Denominators = number of identified relatives.

adoptive families of index cases than of controls (10 vs. 5) the difference is not significant and no particular pattern is discernible in the distribution of particular types of illness. The index families compared with control families showed: schizophrenia spectrum disorders (2 vs. 3), character disorder (1 vs. 0), delinquency (1 vs. 1), suicide (0 vs. 1), chronic alcoholism (1 vs. 0), affective disorders (2 vs. 1), neurosis (0 vs. 1), mental retardation (1 vs. 0), senile psychosis (1 vs. 1), and various types of organic psychoses (3 vs. 0). It is possible that the experience of these families with the psychiatric hospitalization of the proband made them more likely to receive psychiatric diagnosis and hospitalization in the case of other members.

DISCUSSION

The relatively high incidence of schizophrenia which is consistently found in the close relatives of naturally reared schizophrenics is compatible with explanations based on either genetic or environmental transmission of these disorders since such families share both types of factors. In the present study, which used adoption to disentangle these variables, 19 of the 33 schizophrenic index cases had been removed from their biological families during the first month and in most cases within a few days after birth and raised by families not biologically related to them. Whereas schizophrenia and related disorders were randomly distributed between the adoptive families of the index cases and their controls, the biological families of the index cases showed a 10% prevalence of such disorders, which is significantly higher than the prevalence in the control biological families. Furthermore, more than half of the schizophrenia spectrum disorders were found in their paternally related half siblings with whom the index cases should have had in common not even an *in utero* environment but only some genetic overlap.

The conclusion appears warranted that the roughly 10% prevalence of schizophrenia found in the families of naturally reared schizophrenics is a manifestation of genetically transmitted factors.

Although this study found little to support the importance of environmental transmission of schizophrenia between family members, it was not designed to evaluate the importance of a large number of environmental factors which may possibly operate in the etiology or pathogenesis of schizophrenic disorders. Besides the presence in the household of an individual seriously enough disturbed to have been admitted to a psychiatric facility and thus registered in our tabulations, there are many more aspects of life experience including subtle personality defects in parents or siblings, deviations in child rearing practices, nutritional peculiarities, and even exposure to toxic or infectious agents, which may serve to evoke and elaborate one or another type of schizophrenia spectrum disorder in a genetically vulnerable individual. If such environmental factors played a significant role in the etiology of schizophrenia they should have tended to make the prevalence of schizophrenia and related disorders in the adoptive siblings of our index cases somewhat higher than in those of the controls, but the number of these relatives in our sample may have been too small to constitute an appropriate test. It is possible that extensions of the present study from Greater Copenhagen to all of Denmark coupled with psychiatric interviews with identified relatives may sufficiently increase the size of the sample and the richness of information on personality and social characteristics of the families to permit a more exhaustive evaluation of possible environmental etiological factors.

The evidence obtained in this study, although strongly supporting the operation of genetic factors in the transmission of schizophrenia, is not readily compatible with any simple genetic model. It is not only schizophrenia which is found in higher prevalence in the biological relatives of schizophrenic index cases, but to an even greater extent, a spectrum of disorders having some features in common with schizophrenia but varying considerably in intensity. Furthermore, the nature and extent of these disorders in the biological families of the clearly schizophrenic and of the border-line index cases are quite indistinguishable.

The 16 index cases with fairly typical chronic schizophrenia (B1) had 82 identified biological relatives of whom 7 were classified in the schizophrenia spectrum (1 chronic schizophrenia, 3 border-line, 2 uncertain border-line, 1 inadequate personality). The 10 probands with border-line schizophrenia (B3) differed considerably from the chronic schizophrenic index cases with respect to type and severity of symptoms and would perhaps not have been called schizophrenic in some places. Yet, of their 38 identified biological relatives, 6 were classified in the schizophrenia spectrum (3 border-line, 1 uncertain chronic, 1 uncertain border-line, 1 inadequate personality). There is nothing to suggest that the biological relatives of the two types of probands are not members of the same population, a finding which is more compatible with the thesis that the schizophrenia in the probands represents some polygenic inadequacy[20] transmitted through heredity but receiving its ultimate expression and differentiation on the basis of a complex interaction among genetic factors or between them and the environment.[21] Intelligence seems more likely to be an appropriate model for the transmission of schizophrenia than does phenylketonuria.

Possible sources of error or bias

It is pertinent to enumerate and discuss the possible errors in selection or diagnosis which might have come into this study despite efforts to avoid them. Some of these possibilities would have operated to decrease the preponderance of schizophrenia spectrum disorders in the biological relatives of the index cases. The enlightened social system in Denmark makes it possible for a pregnant woman to obtain a legal abortion on the basis of a history of schizophrenia in herself or in the father. This, in addition to the relative infertility of overt schizophrenics, could have resulted in the removal from our sample of adoptees of a disproportionate fraction of those with schizophrenia in the biological parents. If, in a similar manner, the adoption process screens out children born of parents with known schizophrenia, this would further have contributed to the possible impoverishment in our adoptee sample of potential index cases with an established incidence in their biological families.

On the other hand, there are biases that could have operated to exaggerate the prevalence of diagnosed schizophrenia spectrum disorder in the biological families of the index cases as compared to the other populations. Possible knowledge of the relationship existing between an index case and a member of his biological family could have affected the tendency to notice, to record, to institutionalize, or to diagnose schizophrenia spectrum disorder in one or the other individual on the part of professional or nonprofessional observers, especially if there were a prevalent belief that schizophrenia was inherited. We believe that this leakage of information was small but are at the present time engaged in determining how often such information appears in the hospital or other records.

The evaluation of mental illness in the relatives was a crucial judgment upon which the results rested, and, being to a large extent subjective, could have been affected by subjective bias in spite of the precautions which were taken to avoid it. Access to and the possibility of retention of salient information varied considerably among the raters. One author (D.R.) was not involved in making the original selection of index cases; another (F.S.) had, one or two years before, read the hospital records of the index cases which may have contained references to affected relatives. He also read and abstracted a few of the relatives' records. The three authors in the United States had available to them only coded abstracts which had been edited to remove any basis for a surmise as to where in the four populations the individual belonged. Analyses of the findings based upon the independent classifications of each of the four authors show little deviation from the analyses based upon their consensus.

There is no evidence of systematic bias and the findings of the study would have remained essentially the same if based upon the independent diagnoses of any one of the raters.

SUMMARY

Adoption has been used as a means of separating genetic from environmental factors in the transmission of schizophrenia. Among the 5483 adoptions granted in the City and County of Copenhagen from the beginning of 1924 through 1947 to adoptive parents not biologically related to the child, 507 adoptees were found who had been admitted to a psychiatric facility. In 33 of these a diagnosis of chronic schizophrenia, border-line schizophrenia, or acute schizophrenic reaction could be agreed upon by independent reviewers of the abstracted case histories. These and an equal number of matched control adoptees with no history of mental hospitalization yielded, by search of the Danish population registers, 306 identified biological parents, siblings or half-siblings and 157 adoptive relatives in similar relationships. Of these 463 relatives, 67 had at some time been admitted to a psychiatric facility. These records were abstracted, edited to remove prejudicial information, and independent and consensus diagnoses made by the four authors.

For the 33 schizophrenic index cases and for a subgroup of 19 who had left their biological families within the first month (usually within the first week) of life, there was a highly significant increased prevalence of schizophrenia and related disorders in the biological families as compared with those of the controls. The prevalence of these disorders in the adoptive families was lower and randomly distributed between the relatives of index cases and controls.

The pattern of schizophrenia-related disorders in the biological families was the same for 16 index cases diagnosed chronic schizophrenia as for 10 probands diagnosed border-line schizophrenia, supporting the inclusion of this syndrome among the schizophrenias. On the other hand, 7 index cases diagnosed acute schizophrenic reaction had no schizophrenia related disorder in the biological relatives, raising some question regarding the relationship of that state to schizophrenia.

The conclusion seems warranted that genetic factors are important in the transmission of schizophrenia; the mode of transmission seems to be polygenic rather than monogenic. The findings are compatible with diathesis-stress hypotheses of the pathogenesis of schizophrenia, although no evidence was found for the operation of one particular environmental influence, i.e. the presence of schizophrenia or related illness in the rearing family.

ACKNOWLEDGMENTS

The authors wish to acknowledge the valuable assistance given by a substantial number of individuals. Dr. Sarnoff Mednick suggested the collaboration with Dr. Schulsinger, offered the facilities of their joint research program in Copenhagen and gave valuable advice in a number of areas, especially with regard to the socio-economic ratings. The Danish psychiatrists who prepared English abstracts of the Danish case histories were Dr. Jytte Willadsen and Dr. Erik Glud. Social workers who abstracted the Danish adoption records

To draw this conclusion is to close on the question of whether or not some schizophrenia disorders — say at the extreme reactive end of the scale — may not involve genetic disability. — This is probably not a productive point of view.

and gathered the data relevant to the pretransfer histories of the probands were Birgit Jacobsen and Grete Skat Andersen. Clerical assistance was given by Ida Bech, Agnete Beck, Susanne Rasmussen and Tove Meier. Kitty Scharf, Copenhagen, and Alice Muth, Bethesda, assisted in the tabulation and analysis of the data.

The authors are especially grateful to Dr. Samuel Greenhouse, Chief of the Epidemiology and Biometry Branch of the National Institute of Child Health and Human Development, for invaluable advice regarding statistical treatment and interpretation of the data.

REFERENCES

1. KALLMANN, F. J., *The Genetics of Schizophrenia,* Augustin, New York, 1938.
2. LUXENBURGER, H., Vorläufiger Bericht über psychiatrische Serienuntersuchungen an Zwillingen, *Z. ges. Neurol. Psychiat.* **116**, 297 (1928).
3. ROSANOFF, A. J., HANDY, L. M., PLESSET, I. R. and BRUSH, S., The etiology of so-called schizophrenic psychoses with special reference to their occurrence in twins, *Am. J. Psychiat.* **91**, 247 (1934).
4. KALLMANN, F. J., The genetic theory of schizophrenia: an analysis of 691 schizophrenic twin index families, *Am. J. Psychiat.* **103**, 309 (1946).
5. SLATER, E., *Psychotic and Neurotic Illnesses in Twins,* Her Majesty's Stationery Office, London, 1953.
6. INOUYE, E., Similarity and dissimilarity of schizophrenia in twins, in *Proceedings of the Third World Congress of Psychiatry,* Vol. 1, p. 524, Univ. Toronto Press, Montreal, 1961.
7. KRINGLEN, E., Schizophrenia in twins: an epidemiological-clinical study, *Psychiatry* **29**, 172 (1966).
8. GOTTESMAN, I. I. and SHIELDS, J., Schizophrenia in twins: 16 years' consecutive admissions to a psychiatric clinic, *Brit. J. Psychiat.* **112**, 809 (1966).
9. KETY, S. S., Biochemical theories of schizophrenia, *Science* **129**, 1528 and 1590 (1959).
10. ROSENTHAL, D., Sex distribution and severity of illness among samples of schizophrenic twins, *J. Psychiat. Res.* **1**, 26 (1961).
11. ROSENTHAL, D., Problems of sampling and diagnosis in the major twin studies of schizophrenia, *J. Psychiat. Res.* **1**, 116 (1962).
12. TIENARI, P., Psychiatric illness in identical twins, *Acta psychiat. scand.* **39**, Suppl. 171, 1 (1963).
13. SKEELS, H. M. and DYE, H. B., A study of the effects of differential stimulation on mentally retarded children, *Proc. Am. Ass. Ment. Def.* **63**, 114 (1939).
14. ROSENTHAL, D., WENDER, P., KETY, S. S., SCHULSINGER, F., WELNER, J. and ØSTERGAARD, L., Schizophrenics' offspring reared in adoptive homes. These Proceedings, p. 377.
15. WENDER, P., ROSENTHAL, D. and KETY, S. S., A psychiatric assessment of the adoptive parents of schizophrenics. These Proceedings, p. 235.
16. MEDNICK, S. A. and SCHULSINGER, F., Some premorbid characteristics related to breakdown in children with schizophrenic mothers. These Proceedings, p. 267.
17. SLATER, E., A review of earlier evidence on genetic factors in schizophrenia. These Proceedings, p. 15.
18. HERMANSEN, L., Schizophrenic patients on a psychiatric ward in a provincial general hospital. A follow-up of schizophrenic first admissions 1956–1966, *Ugeskr. Laeg.* **129**, 1445 (1967) (in Danish).
19. HESTON, L. L., Psychiatric disorders in foster home reared children of schizophrenic mothers, *Brit. J. Psychiat.* **112**, 819 (1966).
20. GOTTESMAN, I. I. and SHIELDS, J., A polygenic theory of schizophrenia, *Proc. Nat. Acad. Sci. USA* **58**, 199 (1967).
21. ROSENTHAL, D., Theoretical overview: a suggested conceptual framework, In *The Genain Quadruplets: A Case Study and Theoretical Analysis of Heredity and Environment in Schizophrenia,* Rosenthal, D. (Ed.), p. 505, Basic Books, Inc., New York, 1963.

INTERACTIONS BETWEEN EARLY LIFE EXPERIENCE
AND BIOLOGICAL FACTORS IN SCHIZOPHRENIA*

Leonard L. Heston

Department of Psychiatry, University of Iowa Medical School, Iowa City, Iowa

and

Duane Denney

Department of Psychiatry, University of Oregon Medical School, Portland, Oregon

This research is based on the life histories of 97 persons who through accident of birth and rearing were eligible for inclusions in a natural experiment bearing on the etiology of schizophrenia. Of these persons, 47 were born to schizophrenic mothers while the remaining 50 were born to mothers with no known history of psychiatric disorder. All mother–child pairs were permanently separated during the first two post-partum weeks. A comparison between these groups allowed assessment of the genetic contribution to schizophrenia where the effects of an environment distorted by the ambivalence and thinking disorder of a schizophrenic parent were separated from the effects of genes from such a parent.

The separation of the children from their mothers entailed special rearing for the children. About one-half were partially reared in foundling homes and most of these subjects were eventually adopted. The remaining half were mostly reared in foster families, usually composed of relatives. This made possible assessment of the effects of several environmental variables.

SELECTION OF SUBJECTS

The experimental subjects

These persons were born between 1915 and 1945 to schizophrenic mothers confined to an Oregon State Psychiatric Hospital. Most of the subjects were born in the psychiatric hospital; however, hospital authorities encouraged confinement in a neighboring general hospital whenever possible, in which case the children were delivered during brief furloughs. All apparently normal children, weighing 5 lb or over, born of such mothers during the above time span were included in the study if the mother's hospital record (1) specified a diagnosis of schizophrenia, dementia praecox, or psychosis; (2) contained sufficient descriptions of a thinking disorder or bizarre regressed behavior to substantiate, beyond reasonable doubt, the diagnosis of schizophrenia; (3) recorded a negative serologic test for syphilis and contained no evidence of a seizure disorder or other coincident disease with

* This research was supported by the Medical Research Foundation of Oregon.

known psychiatric manifestations; and (4) contained presumptive evidence that mother and child had been separated from birth. Such evidence typically consisted of a statement that the mother had yielded the child for adoption, a note that the father was divorcing the mother, the continued hospitalization of the mother for several years, or the death of the mother. In practice these requirements, especially numbers 2 and 4, entailed many disqualifications and meant that the mothers as a group were biased in the direction of severe, chronic disease. No attempt was made to assess the psychiatric status of the father; however, none were known to be hospital patients. The 74 children ascertained as above were retained in the study if subsequent record searches or interviews confirmed that the child had had no contact with its natural mother and never lived with maternal relatives. (The latter restriction was intended to preclude significant exposure to the environment which might have produced the mother's schizophrenia.)

All of the children were discharged from the State hospital within 3 days of birth (in accordance with a strictly applied hospital policy) to the care of family members or to foundling homes. The records of the foundling homes which received some of the children were then reviewed. These records made it possible to follow the subjects through their early life, including, for some, adoption. The early life of those subjects discharged to relatives was less completely known, although considerable information was developed by methods to be described.

Information found in the foundling home records disqualified some of the subjects as shown in Table 1. The remaining 58 subjects were matched to controls.

TABLE 1. LOSSES OF SUBJECTS

	Experimental		Control	
	Male	Female	Male	Female
Number before matching	40	34		
Neo-natal death*	4	2		
Discarded†	3	7		
Total matched with control	33	25	33	25
Died, late infancy or childhood	3	6		5
Lost to follow-up		2		3
Final groups	30	17	33	17

* Fifteen of the 74 Experimental subjects died in infancy or childhood. This rate is greater than that experienced by the general population for the ages and years involved, but not significantly so.

† Contact with natural mother or lived with maternal relatives (8), multiple gastrointestinal anomolies (1), no Control matched (1).

Control subjects

A like number of Control subjects, apparently normal at birth, were selected from the records of the same foundling homes that received some of the Experimental subjects. They were matched individually to experimental subjects for sex, type of eventual placement (adoptive, foster family, or institutional), and for length of time in child care institutions to within $\pm 10\%$, up to 5 years. (Oregon State law prohibited keeping a child in a foundling home more than 5 years. Subjects in institutions up to this maximum were counted as "institutionalized" regardless of final placement.) Control subjects for the Experimental children who went to foundling homes were selected as follows: When the record of an Experimental subject was located, the admission next preceding in time was checked, then the next subsequent, then the second preceding and so on, until a child admitted to the home within a few days of birth and meeting the above criteria was found. The mechanics of this process meant that an approximate match for age was also made. Those Experimental subjects who were never in child care institutions were matched with children who had spent less than 3 months in a foundling home. Goldfarb (1947) found that up to 6 months of such care had no measurable effect. Nearly all of these children were placed in foundling homes because of the death or desertion of their mother. The restrictions regarding maternal contacts were applied to the Control group. Oregon State Psychiatric Hospital records were searched for the names of the natural parents (where known) of the Control subjects. In 2 cases a psychiatric hospital record was located and the children of these persons were replaced by others.

Exact matching was complicated by the subsequent admission of several subjects to other child care institutions and by changes of foster or even adoptive homes. However, these disruptions occurred with equal frequency and intensity in the 2 groups and are considered random.

All subjects were Caucasian, apparently normal at birth, and went to homes in which both parental figures were represented.

After the final groups had been formed there were further losses of subjects as shown in Table 1.

Grouping of subjects

About half (25/47) of the children from the psychiatric hospitals went to foundling homes while the remaining half went directly to families. This distribution was nearly duplicated among their Controls. Thus a second major variable, institutional care during childhood, was introduced into the study. Children partially reared in foundling homes have been reported to suffer from major personality and character disturbances. Bowlby (1952), Yarrow (1961), and Ainsworth et al. (1962) have reviewed this subject. Table 2 shows how

TABLE 2. GROUPING OF SUBJECTS

Genetic	Early environments		
	Child care institution	Family rearing	
Schizophrenic mother	25	22	Experimental group: N = 47
Mother with no psychiatric illness recorded	22	28	Control group: N = 50
	Institutional group: N = 47	Family group: N = 50	

the Experimental and Control groups are subdivided and 2 new groups; the Family and Institutional were formed.

EARLY ENVIRONMENTS

The foundling home group

Those children who were in foundling homes, the Institutional group, spent a mean period of 24·7 months in group care. The distribution of these time periods is presented in Table 3. However, these time spans are certainly an underestimate of the actual period during which the Institutional children underwent environmental disruptions. Ten subjects

TABLE 3. TIME IN FOUNDLING HOME

Months	No. subjects
–6	4
–12	10
–18	8
–24	5
–36	8
–48	4
–60	1
>60	7
Mean = 24·7 months	47

were known to have been readmitted to the same or other foundling homes. Several others changed foster homes one or more times. On the other hand, 2 subjects were visited regularly by close relatives while they were in a foundling home. These events were found to be impossible to measure quantitatively.

The actual extent to which these children were deprived of maternal or emotional nurture beyond that implicit in group care must be inferred largely from indirect evidence. The four foundling homes from which subjects were selected operated as group care institutions with common eating, play, and sleeping areas. Each home cared for between 20 and 50 children aged 0–5 years. No reliable information was obtained bearing on the personality characteristics of the nursery personnel or specific nursery routine. However, the later history of the children strongly supports the hypothesis that significant deprivation did occur. Random observations recorded in school or nursery records and recollections of foster parents and subjects describe several children as shy, withdrawn, demanding excessive attention, or sad; few as happy, spontaneous, or normal. Some are recorded as requiring sedation at night. More systematic evidence is available from test scores. Twelve institutionalized children were given intelligence tests as part of a pre-adoption evaluation. Later school-administered test results were available for 9 of these 12 subjects. In 4 cases, the score did not significantly change, although all were higher on the second test. The remaining 5, all originally with IQs below 80, showed striking increases of from 21 to 32 points. It is certain that most of these children were unhappy and probable that there was significant deprivation of emotional nurture.

Most of the children who stayed in foundling homes more than 3 months were adopted. The adoptive parents knew of the psychiatric illness of the biologic mothers. However, the records mention only one instance of a refusal to adopt on these grounds.

The family group

Most of the children who did not go to foundling homes plus those who were in such homes for less than 3 months started life in foster families which were usually composed of relatives. In one typical pattern the child went with his father to the home of the paternal grandparents where both stayed until the father remarried. Other children went with or without their fathers to paternal aunts, uncles, etc. Although many of these children were shifted about, the environmental disruptions within the Family group were trivial as compared to the Institutional group.

FOLLOW-UP METHODS

Starting in 1964, it proved possible to locate or account for all of the original subjects except 5 persons, all females. During this phase of the research, considerable background information of psychiatric import was developed. The records of all subjects known to police agencies and to the Veterans' Administration were examined. Retail credit reports were obtained for most subjects. School records, civil and criminal court actions, and newspaper files were reviewed. The records of all public psychiatric hospitals in the three West Coast States were screened for the names of the subjects and the records located were reviewed. Inquiries were directed to psychiatric facilities serving other areas where subjects were living, and to probation departments, private physicians, and various social service agencies with which the subjects were involved. Finally, relatives, friends, and employers of most subjects were contacted.

In addition to information obtained from the above sources, for most subjects the psychiatric assessment included a personal interview, a Minnesota Multiphasic Personality Inventory (MMPI). an IQ test score, the social class of the subject's first home, and the subject's current social class. As the subjects were located, they were contacted by letter and asked to participate in a personal interview. The interview was standardized, although all promising leads were followed. It was structured as a general medical and environmental questionnaire which explored all important psychosocial dimensions in considerable depth. Nearly all of the interviews were conducted in the homes of the subjects, which added to the range of possible observations. The short form of the MMPI was given after the interview. The results of an IQ test were available from school or other records for nearly all subjects. If a test score was not available, the Information, Similarities, and Vocabulary subtests of the Wechsler Adult Intelligence Scale (WAIS) was administered and the IQ derived from the results. Two social class values were assigned according to the occupational classification system of Hollingshead (1958). One value was based on the occupation of the father or surrogate father of the subject's first family at the time of placement, and a second on the subject's present occupational status or, for married females, the occupation of the husband.

All of the investigations and interviews were conducted by one of the authors (L.L.H.) in fourteen States and in Canada.

EVALUATION OF SUBJECTS

The dossier compiled on each subject excluding genetic and foundling home information, was evaluated blindly and independently by two psychiatrists, one of whom is a co-author (D.D.). A third evaluation was made by the senior author (L.L.H.). Two evaluative measures were used. A numerical score moving from 100 to 0 with increasing psychosocial disability was assigned for each subject. The scoring was based on the landmarks of the Menninger Mental Health Sickness Rating Scale (MHSRS) (Luborsky, 1962). Where indicated, the raters also assigned a psychiatric diagnosis from the American Psychiatric Association nomenclature.

The MHSRS proved highly reliable as a measure of degree of incapacity. The Intraclass Correlation Coefficient between the scores assigned by the respective raters was 0·94, indicating a high degree of accuracy. As expected, several differences arose in the assignment of specific diagnoses. In disputed cases a fourth psychiatrist was asked for an opinion and differences were discussed in conference. The only differences not easily resolved involved distinctions such as obsessive–compulsive personality or mixed neurosis versus emotionally unstable personality. All differences were within three diagnostic categories: Psychoneurotic disorders, personality trait or personality pattern disturbances. The raters decided to merge these categories into one: "Neurotic personality disorder". This category included all persons with MHSRS scores less than 75—the point on the scale where psychiatric symptoms become troublesome—who received various combinations of the above three diagnoses. In this way, complete agreement on four diagnoses was achieved: schizophrenia, mental deficiency, sociopathic personality, and neurotic personality disorder.

Evaluations of 97 persons were done. Seventy-two subjects were interviewed. Of the remaining 25 persons, 6 refused the interview (7·6% of those asked to participate), 8 were deceased, 7 were inaccessible (active in Armed Forces, abroad, etc.), and 4 were not approached because of risk of exposure on the subject's adoption. It did not seem reasonable to drop all of these 25 persons from the study, since considerable information was available for most of them. For instance, one man was killed in prison after intermittently spending most of his life there. His behavioral and social record was available in prison records plus the results of recent psychological evaluations. A man who refused the interview was a known overt, practising homosexual who had a recent felony conviction for selling narcotics. All persons in the Armed Forces were known through letters from their commanding officers or medical officers to have been serving honorably without psychiatric or serious behavioral problems. One 21-year-old man, the least known of any of the subjects, had been in Europe for the preceding 18 months in an uncertain capacity. He is known to have graduated from high school and to have no adverse behavioral record. In a conference the raters agreed that it would be misleading to discard any cases, and that all subjects should be rated by forced choice. One mental defective was also diagnosed schizophrenic and another sociopathic. Only one diagnosis was made for all other subjects.

RESULTS

Genetic

Psychiatric disability was heavily concentrated in the Experimental group. Table 4 summarizes the results.

TABLE 4. COMPARISON OF CONTROL AND EXPERIMENTAL GROUPS

	Control	Experimental	Exact probability
Number	50	47	
Males	33	30	
Age, mean	36·3	35·8	
Adopted	19	22	
MHSRS, means			
(Total group mean = 72·8. SD = 18·4)	80·1	65·2	0·0006
Schizophrenia	0	5	0·024
Mental deficiency (IQ < 70)	0	4	0·052
Sociopathic personality	2	9	0·017
Neurotic personality disorder	7	13	0·052
Persons spending more than 1 year in			
penal or psychiatric institution	2	11	0·006
Total years incarcerated	15	112	
Felons	2	7	0·054
Armed forces, number serving	17	21	
Discharged from armed forces on			
psychiatric or behavioral grounds	1	8	0·021
Social group, first home, mean	4·2	4·5	
Social group, present, mean	4·7	5·4	
IQ, mean	103·7	94·0	
Years in school, mean	12·4	11·6	
Children, total	84	71	
Divorces, total	7	6	
Never married, > 30 years of age	4	9	

One mental defective was also schizophrenic.
Another was sociopathic.
Considerable duplication occurs in the entries below "neurotic personality disorder".

The MHSRS scores assess the cumulative psychosocial disability in the 2 groups. The difference is highly significant, with the Experimental group the more disabled by this measure. However, the difference is attributable to the low scores achieved by about one-half (26/47) of the Experimental subjects rather than a general lowering of all their scores.

The diagnosis of schizophrenia was used conservatively. Four Experimental subjects were regarded as schizophrenic or as borderline by one or two of the raters, but these subjects were finally given other diagnoses. In addition to the unanimous opinion of the 3 raters, all subjects were similarly diagnosed in psychiatric hospitals. One female and four males comprised the schizophrenic group. Three were chronic deteriorated patients who had been hospitalized for several years. The other 2 had been hospitalized and were taking anti-psychotic drugs.

The age-corrected rate for schizophrenia is 16·6%, a finding consistent with Kallmann's 16·4%. (Weinberg's short method, age of risk 15–45 years.) Hoffman (1921) and Oppler

(1932) reported rates of from 7% to 10·8% of schizophrenia in children of schizophrenics. No relationship between the severity and subtype of the disease in the mother–child pairs was evident.

Mental deficiency was diagnosed when a subject's IQ was consistently less than 70. All of these persons were in homes for mental defectives at some time during their life and one was continuously institutionalized. His IQ was 35. The other mentally deficient subjects had IQs between 50 and 65. No history of CNS disease or trauma of possible causal importance was obtained for any of these subjects. The mothers of the mentally defective subjects were not different from the other mothers and none were mentally defective.

Three behavioral traits were found almost exclusively within the Experimental group. These were: (1) significant musical ability, 7 persons; (2) expression of unusually strong religious feelings, 6 persons; and (3) problem drinking, 8 persons.

Two sub-groups of Experimental subjects exhibited roughly delineable symptom-behavior complexes other than schizophrenia or mental deficiency. The personalities of the persons composing these groups are summarized below.

The first group is composed of subjects who fit the older diagnostic category, "schizoid psychopath". This term was used by Kallmann (1938) to describe a significant sub-group of his relatives of schizophrenic persons. Eight males from the present study fall into this group, all of whom received a diagnosis of sociopathic personality. These persons are distinguished by antisocial behavior of an impulsive, illogical nature. Multiple arrests for assault, battery, poorly planned impulsive thefts dot their police records. Two were homosexual, four alcoholic, and one person, also homosexual, was a narcotics addict. These subjects tended to live alone—only one was married—in deteriorated hotels and rooming houses in large cities, and locating them would have been impossible without the cooperation of the police. They worked at irregular casual jobs such as dishwasher, race-track tout, parking attendants. When interviewed they did not acknowledge or exhibit evidence of anxiety. Usually secretive about their own life and circumstances, they expressed very definite though general opinions regarding social and political ills. In spite of their suggestive life histories, no evidence of schizophrenia was elicited in interviews. No similar personalities were found among the control subjects.

A second sub-group was characterized by emotional lability and may correspond to the neurotic sibs of schizophrenics described by Alanen et al. (1963). Six females and two males from the Experimental group as opposed to two control subjects were in this category. These persons complained of anxiety or panic attacks, hyper-irritability, and depression. The most frequent complaint was panic when in groups of people as in church or at parties. Most subjects described their problems as occurring episodically; a situation that they might tolerate with ease on one occasion was intolerable on another. The women reported life-long difficulty with menses, especially hyper-irritability or crying spells, and depressions coincident with pregnancy. These subjects described themselves as "moody", stating that they usually could not relate their mood swings to temporal events. Four such subjects referred to their strong religious beliefs much more frequently than other respondents. Psychophysiological gastrointestinal symptoms were prominent in 5 subjects. The most frequent diagnoses advanced by the raters were emotionally unstable personality and cyclothymic personality, with neurosis a strong third.

Of the 9 persons in the control group who were seriously disabled, 2 were professional criminals, careful and methodical in their work, 2 were classed with the emotionally labile group described above, one was a compulsive phobia-ridden neurotic, and 4 were inadequate or passive personalities.

One further result deserves special emphasis. The 21 Experimental subjects who exhibited no significant psychosocial impairment were not only successful adults but in comparison to the Control group were more spontaneous when interviewed and had more colorful life histories. They held the more creative jobs: musician, teacher, home-designer; and followed the more imaginative hobbies: oil painting, music, antique aircraft. It must be emphasized that the finding of what may be especially adaptive personality traits among persons in the Experimental groups was noticed only in retrospect as the material compiled on each person was being reviewed. Such traits were not systematically investigated: Most psychiatric studies focus on pathology, not on the delineation of degrees of normal psychological health and this study was not an exception. Also it is uncertain what influence the known greater variability in intelligence among the relatives of schizophrenics might have had. We wish to report a strong *impression* that within the Experimental group there was much more variability of personality and behavior but more evidence is required before this can be regarded as confirmed.

Environmental: The first among the assessable environmental variables that might have influenced the above results is foundling home care. Table 5 exhibits most of the demographic and psychosocial measures previously shown in Table 4. In contrast to Table 4 in which the groups were divided genetically, Table 5 shows that the total load of disability was evenly divided between the Institutional and Family groups.

TABLE 5. COMPARISON OF INSTITUTIONAL AND FAMILY GROUPS

	Institutional	Family
Number	47	50
Male	31	32
Age, mean	34·1	38·0
Schizophrenic mother	25	22
MHSRS, mean	73·0	72·7
Schizophrenia	3	2
Mental deficiency	2	2
Sociopathic personality	5	6
Neurotic personality disorder	9	11
Persons spending more than 1 year in psychiatric or penal institution	8	5
Total years incarcerated	79	48
Felons	6	3
Armed forces, number serving	24	14
Discharged from armed forces on psychiatric or behavioral grounds	4	5
Social group, first home, mean	3·9	4·6
Social group, present, mean	5·1	5·0
IQ, mean	98·4	99·3
Years schooling, mean	12·1	12·0
Children, total	74	81
Divorces, total	5	8
Never married, > 30 years of age	7	6

Several other measures confirm that Institutional care had no appreciable effect. Table 6 demonstrates that the mean raw MMPI scale scores of the 2 groups were nearly identical.[1]

TABLE 6. MEAN MMPI RAW SCALE SCORES

Scale	L	F	K	1 (Hs)	2 (D)	3 (Hy)	4 (Pd)	5 (MF)	6 (Pa)	7 (Pt)	8 (Sc)	9 (Ma)	0 (Si)
Family N = 34 Male = 21	4	5	14	13	22	21	23	29	10	27	23	19	25
Institutional N = 35 Male = 22	5	4	16	14	20	22	22	29	10	27	25	20	25

Looking now within the Institutional group, the length of time these subjects were in child care institutions was not correlated with adult adjustment as measured by the MHSRS. The Spearman Rank Order Correlation Coefficient (r_s) between these variables was $-0\cdot028$. Adult IQ was only weakly correlated with length of foundling home care: The r_s was $0\cdot15$ which does not approach significance.

There was no evidence from the present study that institutional care during childhood had any effect on adult psychosocial adjustment. It should be noted that this was the first follow-up of foundling home children into adulthood and the first lengthy follow-up which utilized a control group.

Social class

Another environmental variable that might have influenced the results is the social class of the subjects' childhood homes.

Before looking at the results with respect to social class, some reservations regarding scoring, especially the score assigned to the subject's first home, should be noted. Where information was available from hospital and foundling home records, the assignment of a score for the home of the first placement was probably accurate; but some scores were derived from old city directories or other contemporary sources, and this made some decisions, e.g. estimating the value of a farm, subject to significant possible error. Also, the years 1915–45 saw socio-economic revolutions which make interpretation of the scores difficult. Nevertheless, the social class values probably provide an adequate though rough estimate of the relative social ranking of the subject's first childhood home. The social class values assigned to the subject's status at the time of follow-up is more reliable. The scores range from 1 to 7 with *decreasing* social class.

---

[1] In a similar comparison of mean raw MMPI scale scores of the Control and Experimental groups the scores were nearly as close. However, many of the most disabled subjects, i.e. the deteriorated schizophrenics, could not be given the MMPI. These subjects were all from the Experimental group so the comparison between the Control and Experimental groups was considered biased. The same disabled subjects were divided evenly between the Institutional and Family groups.

Table 7 compares the social class of the subject's *first childhood home* with the psychosocial outcome as measured by the MHSRS score achieved by these persons as *adults*. There is no consistent relationship between these measures. The same comparison is made in Table 7 for children who were adopted. These children were reared in homes of considerably higher social standing than were other subjects. However, the outcome is the same.

TABLE 7. RELATION BETWEEN SOCIAL CLASS AND ADULT ADJUSTMENT

Social classes	I	II	III	IV	V	VI	VII	Mean
First childhood home								
Number of subjects*	6	6	12	15	21	22	8	
Adult adjustment: mean MHSRS	79·0	70·3	60·1	77·1	75·3	77·9	69·5	73·6
First childhood home, adopted S's								
Number of subjects	5	6	8	12	9	1	0	
Adult adjustment: mean MHSRS	80·3	70·3	56·8	84·6	80·3	71·4	—	75·2
Adult social class								
Number of subjects	0	9	7	22	17	17	25	
Adult adjustment: mean MHSRS	—	85·5	85·9	76·1	77·8	74·2	57·7	72·8

* Excluding the 7 subjects reared largely in institutions.

Several large surveys (Hollingshead and Redlich, 1958; Srole *et al.*, 1962) suggest that the presence of psychiatric disorder is related to social class. Table 7 demonstrates a clearly positive relationship between the subjects' *adult* social class and psychiatric disability. This finding is consistent with the above studies, but the whole of the date on social class suggest that the psychiatric disability produced a secondary lowering of social class rather than that low social class produced psychiatric disability.

The results of this study provide no evidence that the social class of the childhood home affected adult adjustment.

Still another environmental variable that could be assessed was the type of placement. The 41 subjects who were adopted achieved a mean MHSRS score of 75·2; the subjects reared in foster families (49) had a mean score of 72·2 and the 7 subjects who were in foundling homes 5 years or longer, 63·7. The latter group includes 2 subjects who were mentally deficient and who were clearly in institutions for long periods solely for that reason. The other 5 subjects in this group had a mean score of 79·1, well above the mean score for all subjects. The type of placement was without significant effect on adult psychosocial status. It is important to note that this finding tends to exclude factors such as differential treatment in the foundling homes or selective factors in adoptive placement since the outcome for the foster family and adoptive groups was the same.

DISCUSSION

The results of this study support a genetic etiology of schizophrenia. Schizophrenia was found only in the offspring of schizophrenic mothers. The probability of this segregation being effected by chance is less than 0·025.

Y

This finding is consistent with the results obtained by Kallmann (1938), Slater (1953), and many others: Schizophrenia occurs more often than expected in relatives of schizophrenics. And the evidence from the present study indicates that being reared with the schizophrenic relative has no effect on this outcome. Karlsson (1966) reports similar findings as one result of his study from Iceland.

It is unlikely that these results are peculiar to being born to a schizophrenic mother and thus be explainable as resulting from possible biochemical or other prenatal factors found in the pregnant schizophrenic mother. The children of schizophrenic fathers by normal mothers develop schizophrenia in about the same proportion as found in this study (Kallmann, 1938; Sheldon Reed, unpublished). (This was pointed out to us through a personal communication of Dr. Reed to Dr. Curt Stern which Dr. Stern forwarded.)

The association of mental deficiency with schizophrenia has been reported by Hallgren and Sjögren (1959) who noted an incidence of low-grade mental deficiency (IQ 50–55) in schizophrenic subjects of about 10·5%. Kallmann (1938) found from 5% to 10% mental defectives among descendants of schizophrenic persons, but he did not consider the finding significant. The association of mental deficiency with schizophrenia—if such an association exists—remains uncertain.

About one-half of the Experimental group exhibited major psychosocial disability. The segregation of so much of the total disability into the Experimental group is uncomfortably close to the discredited familial "taint" or "degeneracy" theories. Yet the finding of a significant group of psychiatrically notable persons is a persistent result of studies of relatives of schizophrenics. Kallmann's (1938) rate for first-degree relatives and Slater's (1953) for dizygotic twins of schizophrenic persons who developed significant psychosocial disability other than schizophrenia are slightly lower, though in the same range, as those found in the present study. Two of several possible explanations are: (1) schizophrenia is a polygenetic disorder. A subcritical dose of the pathological genes produces or predisposes to disabilities other than schizophrenia and perhaps in other combinations to especially adaptive personality traits; or it could equally well be maintained that a single gene responsible for schizophrenia is modified by other genes. Genes controlling intelligence and somatotype would be likely possibilities. (2) Schizophrenia as a biologic entity is broader than our present clinical entity. Biologic schizophrenia may, in fact, include persons who are presently placed in other diagnostic categories, the differing manifestations being due to modifying genes or life experiences.

It is clearly premature to stake a comprehensive theory on the available evidence. Much more work is needed. However, it is also clear that the consistent finding of serious disorder in persons related to schizophrenics has at least one important practical consequence: The selection of control groups for biochemical or other studies of schizophrenics will have to be done in view of this fact.

The consistently negative findings with respect to the environmental features investigated was totally unexpected. It was also disappointing as it was hoped that some interaction between genes and environment could be demonstrated. (However, the findings should be of considerable comfort to social agencies who must deal with parentless children.)

The failure to demonstrate environmental effects must be evaluated in view of the following: (1) None of the subjects were reared in typical or "normal" circumstances. (2) This study looked at a few broad features of the environments, e.g. institutional care and social class. Although these variables, which have been thought to be of great importance in the etiology of psychiatric disorders, did not affect the results significantly, there remains tremendous scope for other environmental variables of a less obvious kind which must have been active in shaping the lives of the subjects. Given this, could environmental factors account for the differences between the Experimental and Control groups? Absolute exclusion of this possibility is impossible in principle. Doing so would require the delineation and exhaustive elimination of all elements and combinations of elements in the experience of the subjects. However, it must be regarded as extremely unlikely that any such element(s) could have been distributed so unevenly between the Experimental and Control groups.

The evidence presented relates the development of schizophrenia to a single variable, being born to a schizophrenic mother. However, this variable was related to other psychosocial outcomes too, some equally disabling, but also including having more special talents and being more variable and interesting in personality.

ACKNOWLEDGMENTS

The authors are greatly indebted to Drs. Ira B. Pauly and Arlen Quan, who evaluated the case histories and provided invaluable advice and encouragement. Drs. Paul Blachly, John Kangas, Harold Osterud, and Richard Thompson provided advice and/or facilities which greatly contributed to the success of the project. All of the above are faculty or staff members of the University of Oregon Medical School.

This research could not have been completed without the splendid cooperation of numerous officials of various agencies who provided indispensable information. The Honorable Wayne Morse, Senior United States Senator from Oregon was most helpful in enlisting the cooperation of several federal agencies. We are especially indebted to the following: Dean R. Mathews, Waverly Baby Home; Elda Russell, Albertina Kerr Nurseries; Stuart R. Stimmel and Esther Rankin, Boys' and Girls' Aid Society of Oregon; Reverend Morton E. Park, Catholic Charities; George K. Robbins, Jewish Family and Child Services; Miss Marian Martin, State of Oregon, Department of Vital Statistics, all of Portland, Oregon. Drs. Dean K. Brooks, E. I. Silk, Russel M. Guiss, J. M. Pomeroy, Superintendents of Oregon State Hospital, Eastern Oregon State Hospital, Dammasch State Hospital, and Oregon Fairview Home, respectively. David G. Berger, Research Coordinator, Oregon State Board of Control; Stewart Adams, Research Director, Los Angeles County Probation Department; Robert Tyler, Research Information Director, California Bureau of Corrections; Evan Iverson, State of Washington, Department of Institutions; Anthony Hordern, Chief of Research, California Department of Mental Hygiene; Captain George Kanz, Oregon State Police; J. S. Gleason, Administrator, Veterans' Administration; and Lt.-General Leonard D. Heaton, Rear-Admiral E. C. Kenney, and Major-General R. L. Bohannon, Chief Medical Officers of the Army, Navy, and Air Force respectively. James Shields and Eliot Slater of the Psychiatric Genetics Research Unit, Maudsley Hospital, London helped greatly in the organization of the material presented.

Finally, we wish gratefully to acknowledge the contribution made by the subjects of this research project, most of whom freely gave of themselves in the interest of furthering medical science.

REFERENCES

Ainsworth, M. *et al.* (1962) *Deprivation of Maternal Care: A Reassessment of its Effects,* Public Health Papers No. 14, World Health Organization, Geneva.

Alanen, T. O., Rekola, J., Staven, A., Tuovinen, M., Takala, K. and Rutanen, E. (1963) Mental disorders in the siblings of schizophrenic patients, *Acta psychiat. scand.,* Suppl. 169, 39, 167–75.

Bowlby, J. (1952) *Maternal Care and Mental Health,* Monograph Series No. 2, World Health Organization, Geneva.

Goldfarb, W. (1947) Variation in adolescent adjustment of institutionally reared children, *Am. J. Orthopsychiat.* 17, 449–57.

Hallgren, B. and Sjögren, T. (1959) A clinical and genetico-statistical study of schizophrenia and low grade mental deficiency in a large Swedish rural population, *Acta psychiat. neurol. scand.,* Suppl. 140, 35.

Hoffman, H. (1921) *Studien über Vererbung und Entstehung geistiger Störungen. II. Die Nachkommenschaft bei endogenen Psychosen,* Berlin, Springer.

Hollingshead, A. B. and Redlich, F. C. (1958) *Social Class and Mental Illness: A Community Study,* New York, Wiley.

Kallmann, F. J. (1938) *The Genetics of Schizophrenia,* New York, Augustin.

Karlsson, J. L. (1966) *The Biologic Basis of Schizophrenia,* Springfield, Illinois, Charles C. Thomas.

Luborsky, L. (1962) Clinicians' judgments of mental health; a proposed scale, *Arch. Gen. Psychiat. (Chicago)* 7, 407.

Oppler, W. (1932) Zum Problem der Erbprognosebestimmung, *Z. Neurol.* 141, 549–616.

Slater, E., with Shields, J. (1953) *Psychotic and Neurotic Illness in Twins,* Medical Research Council Special Report Series, No. 278, London, H.M. Stationery Office.

Srole, L., Langner, T. S., Michael, S. T., Opler, M. K. and Rennie, T. A. C. (1962) *Mental Health in the Metropolis: The Midtown Manhattan Study,* New York, McGraw-Hill.

Yarrow, L. J. (1961) Maternal deprivation: toward an empirical and conceptual re-evaluation, *Psychol. Bull.* 58, 459–90.

SCHIZOPHRENICS' OFFSPRING REARED IN ADOPTIVE HOMES

David Rosenthal,* Paul H. Wender,* Seymour S. Kety,*

Fini Schulsinger,† Joseph Welner,† and Lise Østergaard‡

This is the first of a projected series of reports on what Dr. Kety, Dr. Wender and I call the Adoptees Study.[1] The one that Dr. Kety presented we call the Extended Family Study and the one that Dr. Wender presented we call the Adoptive Parents Study. The names may help to distinguish the studies in future discussions of them.

This is a preliminary as well as a first report, since we are still very much in the midst of our extensive research activities. We will be finding and examining subjects for at least another year. In June 1967 we began the third year of this project.

The reader will observe a strong resemblance, as well as important differences in conception and method, between the Adoptees Study and the study reported by Heston. We want to point out that our study was conceived and planned years before we learned of Heston's remarkable feat, and it was well under way for some time before Heston's report appeared.

Although all our studies attempt to assess the relative contributions of heredity and environment to schizophrenia, the major focus of the Adoptees Study is somewhat different. Here we are trying to obtain evidence that a diathesis-stress theory of schizophrenia is correct. What we would like to do is to detect and describe some behavioral and psychological aspects of that inherited diathesis. Paul Meehl would call it the "schizotype", which is a perfectly good name for it.

* National Institute of Mental Health, Department of Health, Education and Welfare, Public Health Service, Bethesda, Maryland.

† Psychological Institute, Department of Psychiatry, Kommunehospitalet, Copenhagen, Denmark.

‡ Laboratory of Psychology, Copenhagen University, Denmark.

[1] The American authors originally formulated the principal strategy of this study together. Our Danish collaborators include: Dr. Fini Schulsinger, who did much to implement the strategy of the study, to enlist the cooperation of Danish authorities, to provide the facilities for the examinations, to supervise the on-the-scene administrative aspects of the study, and who did the psychiatric interviews when Dr. Welner was ill; Dr. Joseph Welner, who performed the psychiatric examinations and evaluations of subjects, and who supervised the day to day administration of the study's research aspects; and Prof. Lise Østergaard, who helped to choose some of the tests used and who selected and supervised the project psychologists. Other participating professional personnel include: Psychiatrists who prepared the R-forms and assisted in the diagnoses of the parents: Dr. Hans Søvsø, Dr. Harriet Thieme, Dr. P. Freitag, Dr. Kirsten Bjerke, Dr. B. Jacobsen; Psychologists: Mr. Vestberg Rasmussen, Mrs. Kirsten Boman, Mr. Rasmus Jordan, Mrs. Ulla Praetorius and Mrs. Brita Jørgensen; Social workers: Mrs. Birgit Jacobsen and Mrs. Skat Andersen. Secretaries and clerks: Lene Monrad Hansen, Agnathe Beck, Ida Bech and Kitty Scharf. Dr. Sarnoff A. Mednick suggested that we carry out our studies in Denmark and use the facilities of the Psychological Institute, of which he is Director. Mr. John L. Van Dyke, Bethesda, assisted in the analysis of the data and in the selection of Control subjects.

Another way to get at this assumed diathesis is to examine the non-schizophrenic twin in discordant monozygotic pairs. Several investigators are taking a closer look at such twins and, hopefully, the various studies will support and complement one another. In twins, one has the task of evaluating the effects, both prenatal and experiential, of the twinship *per se*. We do not run into such problems in the Adoptees Study.

A research design such as Mednick and Schulsinger's hinges on the deliberate selection of what they correctly call high-risk subjects. These are children born of schizophrenic mothers. Most of them were reared in the parental home, or in various institutions or foster-homes. From the usual environmentalist point of view as well as the genetic, these are indeed high-risk subjects. Therefore, behavioral differences between them and a control group could reflect both genetic and environmental effects. For this reason their subjects are less useful in the search for the schizotype, but are very well suited to their main purpose, viz. the delineation of behavioral precursors of schizophrenia.

SELECTION OF SUBJECTS

We begin with a pool of subjects who were given up for nonfamilial adoption at an early age. These are the same adoptees that were found, identified and coded by number in the Extended Family Study reported by Dr. Kety. There were slightly less than 5500 such children in the years 1924 to 1947. The number-coding that identified each adoptee was done sequentially on special forms, which we call A-forms. The A could stand for *Adoptee*. On each A-form was listed the names of, and other identifying information about, the biological and adoptive parents.

It is the approximately 11,000 biological parents who now become our focus of attention. Unfortunately, in about 25% of the cases, the biological father was not known. This leaves us with about 10,000 known biological parents. We want to find out who among them was schizophrenic.

To begin this search, clerks compare the parents' names and birth dates listed on the A-forms with the names in the Psychiatric Register of the Institute of Human Genetics. The same search is made at the Bispebjerg Hospital, which does not report to the Human Genetics Institute. A large number of biological mothers must first be screened in the Folke-register in order to learn all their changes of names. When a parent's name is found in the Register, the information in his file is copied. We then request his case record from every psychiatric hospital or other facility that he attended.

Psychiatrists read through the case records and dictate a summary of the case in English, emphasizing the main areas stipulated on another prepared form, which we call the R-form. The R could stand for the parent's case Record. The R-forms are number-coded sequentially, and the A-form number of the corresponding adopted child is recorded on each. The psychiatrist preparing the R-form reports the parent's name(s), birthdate and sex; all institutional admissions, including the dates, length of stay, and discharge diagnoses; behavior leading to admission; major features of life history; major features of the pre-morbid personality; known precipitating factors; major features of the illness noted at the first admission; additional major symptoms noted in the subsequent course of the illness; and clinical course and outcome. The psychiatrist then makes his own final diagnosis and another according to a code which was worked out primarily by Dr. Wender, with some minor assists from Dr. Kety, Dr. Schulsinger and myself. This is the same code described by Dr. Kety in his report on the Extended Family Study.

The R-forms are then sent to Bethesda as soon as they are completed and typed. Initially, Dr. Kety, Dr. Wender and I reviewed each R-form independently and made our separate coded diagnoses. Subsequently, since Dr. Kety left for a year in Paris, Dr. Wender and I have been making the diagnoses without him. In each case where we have a full consensus that the parent is in the schizophrenic range (coded B_1, B_2 or B_3), the child he or she gave up for adoption is selected as an Index Case.

Now, the A-form number of the Index child is copied from the R-form. We then enter a file where we keep all the A-forms, which are arranged in number sequence. We find the A-form and record from it the adoptee's name, sex, birthdate, age of transfer to his adoptive parents, age at formal adoption, and the adoptive parent's occupation, income and "fortune", as it is called in Denmark. Beginning at the place in the file occupied by this A-form, we search systematically forward and backward in the file until we find at least four other adoptees who are of the same sex as the Index Case, and who have approximately the same age, age of transfer, age at adoption, socio-economic status of their adoptive or rearing parents, and who do *not* have a parent with an R-form or known psychiatric diagnosis. These data for the four or more subjects are recorded on another form. I and one other person, Dr. Wender or a psychologically trained research assistant, independently rank the four or more subjects according to how closely each resembles the Index Case in these several respects weighed together. The subject with the highest summed rank is selected as the Control. If he refuses to or cannot participate in the study, the subject with the next highest rank is substituted as the Control, and so on down the list.

The mingled A-form numbers of both Index and Control subjects are then sent to Copenhagen. Of course, we send only the numbers. We do not say which numbers represent Index Cases or which represent Controls. We say only that these are new subjects. The examining staff never knows if the subject before them is an Index Case or not. Even the psychiatrist who obtains a history from the subject cannot know, since the adoptee himself does not know about his biological parents,[2] and the psychiatrist does not actively seek this information, though he is permitted to pursue the matter if the adoptee himself volunteers to talk about it. To date, the examining psychiatrist has not known whether any subject was an Index Case or not. The psychologists do not even have the possibility of finding out. It is especially this aspect of the study which makes it so esthetically appealing, as well as scientifically sound.

The social worker who receives the A-form numbers first sends a specially prepared form letter to the prospective subjects and then contacts them by telephone to try to arrange an examination date or to make an appointment for a personal visit to discuss the matter further. The subjects are told that a scientific study is being conducted on the relation between environment and health, that all strata of the population are included, and that such studies require that all subjects selected participate since the results might otherwise be invalidated. The social worker uses all her skills to persuade the subjects to come to

[2] One subject said that her adoptive father had told her that he was also her biological father. We rechecked the records. They gave different names for adoptive and biological fathers.

Copenhagen's Kommunehospitalet to participate in the study. An examination lasts 2 days. The subject is offered compensatory pay for salary he may be missing, or for the cost of a baby sitter. His transportation is paid, as are his hotel bills if he must stay at an hotel. If he wishes to have another person accompany him, that person's transportation is paid as well. In addition, each subject is given a modest sum of money as a bonus or added incentive.

SELECTION OF EXAMINATION PROCEDURES

Let us assume now that the subject has agreed to come. We have 2 precious days in which to examine this scientifically precious person. What should we do in this time?

If one has a specific theory in mind, the question is easily answered. Mednick, for example, could tailor his procedures so that each one would bear on one or more aspects of his neatly formulated theory. We, on the other hand, were more or less committed to a broad conceptual framework which, in *The Genain Quadruplets* (Rosenthal, 1963), I called diathesis-stress theory. This is less a theory than a designation for a class of theories. It says nothing specific about either the nature of the diathesis or of the stress.

We were making a series of assumptions. The first was that heredity was an important contributor to schizophrenia. The second was that this inherited factor manifested itself in the behavior or personality of persons who were not frankly schizophrenic. The third was that these manifestations could be detected by tests or in one or two interviews. The fourth was that we would know which questions to ask or which tests to use to detect these manifestations.

Lacking a clearcut theory, we had recourse to three broad strategies to guide our decisions about what or what not to do. The first was that differences found between schizophrenics and normal controls on various psychological or behavioral tests might reflect inherited differences, and that we should therefore use these tests in hopes of finding similar differences, but perhaps of lesser degree, between our two groups of subjects. This strategy is a shaky one since the differences found in the schizophrenia studies may simply reflect the clinical condition itself, the consequences of being ill rather than the causes. Nevertheless, when a simple task such as reaction time discriminates schizophrenics and normals so well, and when one considers that reaction time may indeed reflect hereditary influences, one feels almost compelled to include such a procedure. Actually, a few of our tests are based on this strategy, including reaction time.

The second strategy seemed more promising. It was based on the idea that we should find the same kinds of traits and aberrations in our Index group as in the premorbid personality of known schizophrenics. Of course, those who become schizophrenic must be different in some way from those who do not, and since we could expect only a few of our subjects to become schizophrenic, we might be focusing on the wrong traits. Moreover, the literature on the premorbid personality of schizophrenics was hardly exciting. It was based on retrospection, or on past clinical records prepared in service settings for reasons not necessarily coinciding with ours.[3] Formulations thus derived emphasized traits like shyness,

---

[3] The Judge Baker Guidance Center reports (Fleming, 1967; Waring and Ricks, 1965) had not appeared or were not known to us when we began this study.

timidity, passivity, sex difficulties, introversion, and others. We would, of course, look for such traits, but we hoped for a more fine-grained description of the inherited diathesis than that. We included a self-assessment procedure whose items were based on such literature and on our own clinical observations or impressions as well.

A third strategy was simply to emulate success. Mednick, for example, was able to discriminate his Index and Control groups using autonomic indices in a conditioning procedure. However, the possibility existed that environmental factors were contributing significantly to this discrimination. Would it occur as well when rearing factors were more balanced between the two groups? It was a question worth asking in our study. Moreover, to the extent that heredity plays a role at all in Mednick's theory, it implies that it is the propensity for high anxiety levels that is inherited in, and is critical for, the development of schizophrenia. An alternative hypothesis would be that the critical inherited factor is cognitive rather than affective, if one can make this conceptual distinction at the inherited level. Nevertheless, we included a conditioning procedure similar to Mednick's but with a few tactical modifications, and we added an habituation and "demandingness" procedure used successfully at the NIMH to discriminate schizophrenic and control groups (Zahn *et al.*, in press).

In emulating success, we attended especially to the work of Wynne and Singer. They were able to discriminate relatives of schizophrenic and neurotic subjects with respect to cognitive, attentional and transactional factors elicited by projective tests. The possibility existed that it was exactly such moderately deviant behaviors that were inherited. We invited Dr. Singer to Denmark where she spent 2 weeks lecturing to our psychologists (and others) and consulting intensively with Dr. Lise Østergaard, who is the senior psychologist in the Adoptees Study and who is a leading authority on cognitive disturbances in border-line schizophrenics. Dr. Østergaard has since worked out a system for evaluating cognitive and projective test performance, combining in it features of both her own and Dr. Singer's approach to such test evaluation. Consequently, we included several such tests in our battery.

In addition, we were not above playing hunches, and a few tests were included on that basis. It would take much too long to describe all the tests and procedures selected; and of course there were many others that we would like to have included, but could not.

Dr. Joseph Welner and I hammered out together the nature and orientation of the psychiatric interview he would employ. The interview is taped. The subject is encouraged to speak freely, and to set his own pace and direction. However, there are 26 categories of information that the interview is supposed to cover, and if the subject does not lead into them himself, Dr. Welner at opportune moments guides the interview towards those categories still not covered. The interviews have lasted from 3 to 5 hours. Afterward, Dr. Welner dictates a psychiatric summary in which he not only formulates his characterization and diagnosis of the subject, but also describes the information elicited for each category separately. In this way, we can compare our Index and Control subjects category by category.

Before we began the actual examination of our own subjects, we ran several known border-line schizophrenics through the entire 2-day examination on a dry run basis. This was done to synchronize all procedures, to trim the timing so that we could stay within our limited schedule, and to help each examiner develop familiarity and skill with the procedures he would use.

THE SAMPLE

The diagnoses and sex of the sick parents of our Index Cases are shown in Table 1.

TABLE 1. CONSENSUS DIAGNOSES AND
SEX OF THE SICK PARENTS

Diagnosis*	N	Sex	
		♂	♀
B_1	36	8	28
B_2	7	2	5
B_3	3	1	2
B_1/B_3	2	2	0
B_1/B_2	6	2	4
B_2/B_3	2	0	2
D	1	1	0
B_1/D_1	1	0	1
B/M	1	0	1
D/M	1	1	0
M?	1	1	0
M	8	5	3
Total	69	23	46

* B_1 = chronic schizophrenia. B_2 = acute schizophrenic reaction. B_3 = border-line or pseudoneurotic schizophrenic. D = doubtful schizophrenia. M = manic-depressive psychosis.

You will be surprised to learn that a number of Index Cases had parents who carried a diagnosis of verified or possible manic-depressive psychosis. We did not want to bring up this point when we were describing our method of case finding, which was already complicated enough. These cases were included for two reasons. The first was one of expediency. There were periods when we simply did not have enough schizophrenic parents processed and the staff in Copenhagen had no subjects to examine. The second and more important reason derived from this question: What if we should find differences between our Index and Control groups; how could we know that these differences were specific to a schizophrenic genotype? Might they not represent the severity dimension of a general factor of mental illness? If we had a comparison pathology group, we might be able to learn something about the specificity problem. As a bonus, we might also learn something about the possible genetic relationship between schizophrenia and manic-depressive psychosis, and about the nature of the assumed inherited diathesis for manic-depressive psychosis.

In 56 cases, the parent was clearly schizophrenic by our criteria, although in 10 of these we differed as to the subcategory of schizophrenia in which he belonged. In 2 cases we could not decide between schizophrenia or doubtful schizophrenia and manic-depressive psychosis.

Among the 56 schizophrenic cases, the ratio of mothers to fathers is about $2\frac{1}{2}$ to 1. There is a slight excess above expectancy of mothers over fathers, and it could result from the fact that about 25 % of all biological fathers were not known. In the main, this distribution speaks well for the representativeness of the sample. Among the manic-depressive parents, there are actually more fathers than mothers, but the numbers are small. They do suggest, however, that this is indeed a different diagnostic group.

Among the Index adoptees, we find 31 males and 38 females. The difference from expectancy is small, but the possibility exists that there may have been a slight preference for adopting girls in past years.

It may be important to know whether the sick parent was psychotic before the adoptee was born, or if the illness had its onset after the birth and transfer of the child. Some data relevant to this point are shown in Fig. 1. in which the date of the parent's first admission for psychosis has been subtracted from the birthdate of the child. If the parent's admission occurred first, the difference is negative.

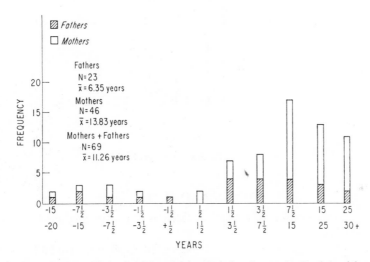

FIG. 1. Years between birth of child and first admission for psychosis of the sick parent.

Of the 69 parent–child pairs, in only 11 instances (16 %) had the parent been admitted before the child's birth, and of the 11, only 5 were mothers. In this respect, then, our sample differs strikingly from Heston's, since all his schizophrenic mothers were actively psychotic and hospitalized when his Index children were born. Is it possible that the active psychosis, with concomitant hospitalization and treatment, provided gestational conditions detrimental to the subsequent mental health of the offspring, apart from genetic factors? It is at least a point worth keeping in mind. Although 84 % of our parents were not hospitalized until after the child's birth, it is of course still possible that a number of them may have been ambulatory psychotics for years before their first admission. We will look at such temporal relationships carefully in the future and check on their possible bearing on mental illness in our adoptees.

The age distribution of our Index Cases is shown in Fig. 2. The sample is still a young one. The mean age is 31·51 years, the standard deviation 7·81 years.

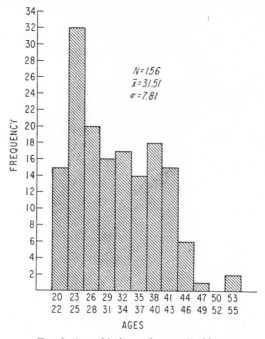

FIG. 2. Age of index and control subjects.

FINDINGS AND DISCUSSION

Now let us show you some of the salient features characterizing our Index and Control groups (see Table 2).

As of the day we began to prepare this paper, 28 April 1967, we had sent the A-form numbers of 155 adoptees to Copenhagen to be subjects in this study. The reason we have more Controls than Index Cases is that when a selected Control cannot or will not participate, we send another Control to replace him. When an Index Case refuses to participate, no replacement is possible.

We had reason to expect that most refusals would occur among the Index group. In fact, the refusals are evenly distributed among the two groups. The possibility exists, however, that those who refuse are a particularly pathological group whom it would be important for us to examine. We will obtain as much data as possible from other sources about these people to check this possibility. However, since in the Extended Family Study the name of every adoptee was searched in the Psychiatric Register and in the files of the 12 major mental hospitals in Denmark, we are reasonably certain that only four of the persons who refused had ever been seen at a psychiatric facility. Three of these were Control subjects, and none was in the schizophrenic spectrum.

The possibility remains, too, that the reasons underlying the refusals differ between the

TABLE 2. SOME DEMOGRAPHIC CHARACTERISTICS OF THE
ADOPTEES SAMPLE

	Index cases	Control subjects
Number sent	69	86
Refused to participate	14	15
Number of refusals who have had contact with a psychiatric facility	1	3
Died	2	4
Congenital idiot	1	0
Living in Norway or Sweden	2	1
Migrated elsewhere	1	5
Could not locate	0	2
Hospitalized for schizophrenia	1	0
Incarcerated for crimes	0	1
Other psychiatric hospitalization	2	1
Suicidal attempts	0	2
Examined	39	47

two groups. We examined the first 25 refusals to check this possibility, but could see no obvious pattern differentiating the two groups. Perhaps the Controls on the whole were less ambivalent in their refusals. One Control thought she was selected because she was living with a man to whom she was not married, and she was opposed to speaking of personal matters. One Index Case said he had simulated disease in military service and was fearful of being found out. One Control was a 41-year-old woman who still lived with her mother and kept an unlisted telephone number. One 37-year-old Index male lived with his parents, and his mother said he would refuse. He had been admitted to the Kommunehospitalet at age 11 because of behavior problems in school. Now he is a travel guide. The total group of refusals included about twice as many women as men. The Index refusals included proportionately more people in their young twenties. It is difficult to say what these figures mean. We will continue to try to persuade these people to come for examination, but will in any case learn as much as possible about them.

Not as many Index children died as Control children. The figures, however, throw no light on the question of possible increased mortality among the offspring of schizophrenic parents. Not only are the figures small, but it is usually *infant* mortality that is at issue, and it is clear that most of such cases, if they did indeed exist, would have died before they could have been adopted. The one congenital CNS syndrome that occurs in the sample is in fact an Index Case.

One might have expected the Index subjects to be more migrant, but the opposite seems to be the case. We do not know to where one of the Index Cases migrated. The 5 subjects who definitely left Scandinavia were all Controls. They migrated to England, France, Spain, Switzerland and Singapore. Maybe Index Cases are less bold and adventurous. Of the 2 Controls who could not be located, 1 disappeared from view during the war.

Among the entire sample of 155 subjects, only 1 had ever been hospitalized for schizophrenia. This is a low rate, of course, and is consistent with the rate for the general Danish population. The 1 hospitalized schizophrenic was an Index Case. We should expect a greater number of such cases, based on Heston's findings. Our sample is about 5 years younger than Heston's but that is probably not an important factor. We will soon show you why our data are in good agreement with his in regard to schizophrenic psychopathology.

Where our data *dis*agree with his is in the area of criminality and psychopathy, which occurred with high frequency in his non-schizophrenic Index Cases. In our sample, the only instance of criminality occurs in a Control subject who served 6 years at the Horsens psychopathic hospital for 4 petty crimes that he committed as a young man. He was the only subject in our sample diagnosed as a frank psychopath. We should pay close attention to this difference between Heston's study and ours because it suggests that whether an individual with the assumed diathesis that we are talking about becomes psychopathically antisocial or not is determined in overriding fashion by environmental factors. And it suggests that such factors are much more prevalent in the United States than in Denmark. It is also possible that prenatal factors among Heston's hospitalized mothers may have somehow contributed to psychopathy in their children.

There is one other point in Table 2 that warrants comment. Two of our examined Index Cases who were not schizophrenic had been admitted at some time in their lives to a psychiatric hospital. In each case, the issue was relatively minor and transient, involving affective or depressive reactions to unhappy personal affairs, and very brief hospital stays. These are counterbalanced by one similar episode and two suicidal attempts among the Control subjects, who also had what could be described as affective reactions. Thus, there are no appreciable differences between the groups in these respects.

Now, let us return to the question of schizophrenic psychopathology. Dr. Welner made a carefully formulated diagnostic evaluation of each case examined. Both he and Dr. Schulsinger, who pinch-hit for him when Dr. Welner was ill, have an appreciation of the nuances of diagnosis which is too often discounted in the United States. In addition, both have had training and supervision in psycho-analysis, and both have been psycho-analyzed. Thus, they are attuned to both the symptomatic and dynamic factors in each case they examine. We would like to present their detailed diagnostic formulations regarding every case in the study, but that would take much too long. If we did, the reader would have a better appreciation of the richness of the material and of the wide variety of symptoms and personalities represented in both groups of subjects. Some time in the future, Dr. Welner will present much of this material himself. For now, however, we will present only those thumbnail diagnostic formulations which we may consider to be in the realm of schizoid–schizophrenic psychopathology (Table 3).

First, note that 3 subjects are diagnosed as schizophrenic, and all 3 are Index Cases. Seven cases are called clear border-line schizophrenics. Six of the seven are Index Cases. There are 13 Index Cases in the schizophrenic spectrum as compared to 7 Control subjects. Note, too, that among the Controls the diagnoses tend to be more qualified, as though the

TABLE 3. Diagnoses in the Schizophrenia Spectrum (by Dr. Joseph Welner)

Parent D_x	Index (N = 39)	Control (N = 47)
B_1/D_1	Schizophrenia, hospitalized	Border-line Sz
B_1	Schizophrenia, never hospitalized	Pre-Sz character, near border-line
B_1/B_2	Schizophrenia, never hospitalized	*Schizoid or premorbid Sz personality
B_1	Border-line Sz	Probable border-line paranoid
B_1	Border-line Sz	*Moderately schizoid
B_1	Border-line Sz	Not too vulnerable schizoid
B_2	Border-line Sz	Subparanoid personality
B_1	Border-line Sz or pervert	
M	Border-line pseudoneurotic Sz	
B_1	Schizoid, paranoid border-line	
M?	Schizoid	
B_1/B_3	*Vague schizoid tendencies	
B_3	Paranoid character	

* These diagnoses were made by Dr. Fini Schulsinger.

examiner sees the psychopathology as not quite so severe. For example, 1 case is said to be "near border-line", but not quite. Another is "probable" borderline, but not surely. The 2 schizoid subjects are said to be "moderately" or "not too vulnerably" schizoid. And the subject in the paranoid spectrum is called "subparanoid". The two qualifications in the Index group include 1 case called "border-line schizophrenia or pervert", a matter of some indecision regarding the differential diagnosis although the emphasis was on border-line schizophrenia, and the second case was said to have "tendencies" that are vague and schizoid. Since the 13 Index Cases were so diagnosed from among 39 Index Cases examined, one-third fall in the schizoid–schizophrenic spectrum. This is a high proportion indeed. Since the 7 Controls were so diagnosed from among 47 subjects, or about 1 in 7, the rate is more than two times as great for the Index group. Moreover, the more severe disorders cluster primarily among the Index subjects.

It is worth pointing out that if such findings were reported in the usual study, where the diagnostician knows which subjects are Index Cases and which are Controls, they would be mighty suspect indeed. Here there is no question of the diagnostician being influenced by such information.

Does the particular form of the diagnosis in the parent make any difference with respect to the frequency of schizophrenic spectrum diagnoses in the children?

We can read the answer to this question in Table 4. The frequency among the B_1 offspring, where we are dealing with hard-core schizophrenia, seems to be no higher than for the less severe types of schizophrenia. Moreover, the rate for the offspring of manic-depressives seems to be in the same range. Among the other three offspring of manic-depressives, one was called repressive, with alcohol bouts and a bad memory, a second was said to be slightly overreactive but functioning well, and the third had some mild neurotic features but was also functioning well. Such data suggest that the inherited core diathesis is the same for both schizophrenia and manic-depressive psychosis, but that manic-depressives may have other modifying genes or life experiences which direct the clinical manifestations of the diathesis in a different way.

Table 4. The Percent of Schizophrenia Spectrum
Diagnoses in the Offspring according to the
Subcategory Diagnosis of the Parent

Parental diagnosis	Number of cases examined	Number in the schizophrenia spectrum	Percent in the schizophrenia spectrum
B_1	24	7	29
B_2	5	1	20
B_3	2	1	50
B/	3	2	67
M or M?	5	2	40
None	47	7	15
Total	86	20	23

It is important, too, to note that the rate of schizophrenic spectrum diagnoses among the Controls is 15%, a figure which is not negligible and which is actually half the rate found in the offspring of B_1 parents, although the disturbances among the latter tended to be more severe. It is possible that a number of the biological parents of Controls might have been called psychiatrically ill if they had been personally examined in the same way as the Adoptees. Since many of these parents are now old or dead, it is questionable whether there would be any appreciable value in trying to bring them in for such examination. All we know is that they probably have never had contact with a psychiatric facility.

There are two other questions we must ask ourselves. One concerns the events in the life of the Adoptees that occurred between birth and transfer to the adoptive family. The Index and Control adoptees are matched for age of transfer, but perhaps that is not enough. We are now in process of collecting as much information as possible about birth, time spent with biological parents or in institutions, and some other data relevant to this question. We should eventually be in a position to determine whether the length of time spent with a psychotic or pre-psychotic parent during this earliest phase of life is related to degree or type of psychopathology.

The other question concerns the possibility that the rearing of the Index Cases differed from that of the Controls. Possibly, for some reason not clear, those people who adopted children of schizophrenics may have themselves been more psychopathological or more psychonoxious to the child. We have left this factor uncontrolled and assumed randomness across both groups in regard to it. However, we will in the near future control the factor of psychopathology in the rearing parents and evaluate its contribution to possible psychopathology in their adopted children.

One inference ought to be drawn from these data: that is, if we are going to learn anything more about the genetics of schizophrenic disorders, we can no longer rely on statistics based only on hospitalized cases. Had we done so in this study, we would have concluded that heredity did not contribute significantly to schizophrenia, or that, if it did, the gene was probably recessive. Moreover, such data imply what many of us have long recognized, that the dichotomy of schizophrenia vs. non-schizophrenia is artificial and masks an underlying continuity of severity of pathology in this spectrum of disorders. Although such continuity of symptomatology suggests a polygenic theory with respect to the probably inherited diathesis, we should have a better appreciation of the contribution of environmental agents of various kinds before we accept this theory unqualifiedly.

It is probably not necessary, but let us remind you that the figures presented today are not final. We are still collecting subjects. The patterns we have seen so far could change. In a year or two we will be able to present the final figures, with somewhat larger N's and a more complete assessment of the material.

We would have liked to present many results from our testing program. Unfortunately, we are able to present only fragments of findings from two of our procedures. These are really self-assessments rather than tests. One involves a widely used and studied set of such assessments, the MMPI. The other involves a set of items that we thought might have particular relevance to the assumed diathesis. We call them the Self-rating Scales.

There are 52 such scales. Each has 7 points. The midpoint is assigned a score of 4 and represents an evaluation of self as average with respect to that item. Scores 5, 6 and 7 represent the more-than-average direction, scores 3, 2 and 1 the below-average direction.

We had misgivings about self-assessments, for many reasons, but we thought that the self-concept might be a readily visible reflection of the inherited diathesis, and a harbinger as well of a trend toward clinical schizophrenia. The confronting problems were again methodological. Could subjects see themselves as they really were, i.e. could they represent their true self-concept accurately? And if they could, would they? We could do nothing about the first question, except to hope that the self-assessments would not be too distorted. To maximize cooperativeness and candor, the Self-rating Scales were administered during the first morning of the 2-day examination. The subject was told to answer all items as best he could and that later that afternoon a psychiatrist would discuss his ratings with him. In fact, the psychiatrist did so, as part of his interview. Whether the anticipation of an inquiry about their ratings loosened subjects' defenses in this respect, we cannot say. In any case, the statistically significant results are shown in Table 5.

One item is significant at the 0·01 level, two at the 0·025 level, and three at the 0·05 level. Three items go in the predicted direction, and their t values are printed in italic figures; three go in the reverse direction. Such findings could be due to chance. Nevertheless, we ought not

TABLE 5. COMPARISON OF INDEX AND CONTROL SUBJECTS ON SELF-RATING SCALES

Item	Group means		Difference	t
	Index (N = 30)	Control (N = 29)		
Shy	3·53	4·24	−0·71	2·342
Close friends	4·50	3·90	0·60	2·376
Feel things are unreal	4·00	3·24	0·76	*2·721*
Feel I'm not master of my own fate	3·83	3·24	0·59	*2·029*
A good talker	4·70	4·07	0·63	2·184
Sense of humor	4·33	4·79	−0·46	*2·239*

At $p = 0·05$, $t = 2·000$, two-tailed.
At $p = 0·025$, $t = 2·299$, two-tailed.
At $p = 0·01$, $t = 2·660$, two-tailed.

z

dismiss them out of hand. They may be meaningful. We do not want to spend too much time with possible explanations of these findings. The N's are about half of what we expect the final N's to be, and the significant items could change. There are no extreme scores here; all mean values hover around average, ranging from over 3 to less than 5. The mean differences are not large. The three predicted items indicate that the Index Subjects have more feelings of unreality, feel that they are less in control of their own destiny, and have less of a sense of humor. The fact that they say they are less shy, have more close friends and are better conversationalists than the Controls suggests that they may have a distorted self-image or are over-defensive with respect to such traits. It is difficult to explain such self-assessments, and we leave the matter open for now.

How does the MMPI discriminate the two groups? The answer is found in Table 6.

TABLE 6. COMPARISON OF 24 PAIRS OF MATCHED
INDEX AND CONTROL SUBJECTS ON MMPI SCALES

Scale	Mean T score		Difference	t
	Index	Control		
K	57·96	57·38	0·58	0·092
F	56·83	55·67	1·16	0·158
L	59·38	59·13	0·25	0·183
HS	63·67	59·21	4·46	1·451
D	61·13	61·92	−0·79	0·071
Hy	65·67	60·96	4·71	1·451
PD	55·83	54·17	1·66	0·656
PA	57·00	53·75	3·25	0·605
PT	54·04	53·63	0·41	0·265
SC	61·33	57·29	4·04	0·913
MA	55·83	54·71	1·12	0·477
SI	51·75	52·93	−1·17	1·085
ES	53·92	55·38	−1·46	0·697

At $p = 0.05$, $t = 2.07$, two-tailed.
At $p = 0.05$, $t = 1.71$, one-tailed.

We see that the groups are very similar with respect to their K, F and L scale scores, which are all acceptable. With respect to the 8 pathology scales, not one reaches a statistically significant difference, but the Index group is higher on 7 of them, the Controls scoring slightly higher on Depression. The difference between the groups on the Schizophrenia scale is in the predicted direction, but it is not large and not significant statistically. The Index group scores highest on Hysteria and Hypochondriasis, not Schizophrenia, and scores slightly *lower* than Controls on Social Introversion. The latter finding is again contrary to expectation.

Again, we do not want to dwell on these findings. Here, the N is small and will increase considerably. We may see many changes. The time to discuss theoretical implications will be when all the data are in and analyzed in more ways, and in more sophisticated ways, than we were able to marshal for this presentation.

What we have done primarily is to sketch the research design we have used to get some leverage on the possible contribution of heredity to schizophrenia and the nature of that contribution. We have presented some preliminary findings so that readers can obtain some idea of the potential usefulness of such a design. At this point, the story we hope to tell has only begun to unfold. We look forward to learning the full story with all the anticipation that we hope any interested professional audience will feel when it learns about such a study.

REFERENCES

FLEMING, P. (1967) Emotional antecedents of schizophrenia: inner experiences of children and adolescents who were later hospitalized for schizophrenia, Lecture at NIMH, 19 May 1967.

ROSENTHAL, D. (Ed.), *et al.* (1963) Theoretical overview, in *The Genain Quadruplets,* Basic Books, New York.

WARING, M. and RICKS, D. (1965) Family patterns of children who became adult schizophrenics, *J. Nerv. Ment. Dis.* **140,** 351–64.

ZAHN, T. P., ROSENTHAL, D. and LAWLOR, W. G. (1968) Electrodermal and heart rate orienting reactions in chronic schizophrenia, *J. Psychiat. Res.* (in press).

GENE-ENVIRONMENT INTERACTION
IN HUMAN DISEASE

Brian MacMahon

Department of Epidemiology, Harvard School of Public Health, Boston, Massachusetts

My objectives in this paper are to illustrate the great complexity and variability of gene-environment interactions in human disease, and to mention some of the investigative methods that have contributed to our understanding of these relationships in diseases other than schizophrenia. A second part of my assignment was to suggest how these matters might have relevance to research in schizophrenia. It will become apparent, I am afraid, that I have been unable to make more than token gestures towards this portion of my task.

THE COMPLEXITY OF GENE-ENVIRONMENT INTERACTION

First, I should like to note that there are at least four senses in which the nature–nurture distinction is becoming more and more blurred as our understanding of disease etiology increases:

(1) It has become clear that there is no disease which is determined entirely by either genetic or environmental factors.
(2) There is, evidently, more overlap in the time of operation of genetic and environmental factors than was previously suspected.
(3) Just as the environment may exert its effect through the genetic mechanism of mutation, so may genetic factors operate by changing the environment.
(4) The roles of gene and environment, and the nature of the specific factors involved, may be quite different in individuals with identical manifestations.

"Genetic" and "environmental" diseases

With respect to the first sense—that no disease is determined entirely by either genetic or environmental factors—recent discoveries provide examples for which only laboratory animal models were available a few years ago.

In 1933, Hogben[1] pointed out that, even when the simplest of genetic or environmental agents is involved, one cannot describe a trait as either genetically or environmentally determined. His point was illustrated by the trait "yellow shanks"—a characteristic produced in certain strains of fowl when fed on yellow corn. He noted that a farmer using only yellow corn as feed and owning several strains of fowl would observe that the trait appeared only in certain strains; he would therefore regard it as genetically determined. Another farmer, feeding some of his flock on yellow and some on white corn, would note that the trait appeared only in those fed yellow corn; he would conclude that the condition was environmentally determined. Thus neither "genetic" nor "environmental" accurately describes the etiology of this condition; an accurate statement would be that within a specified range of genetic background environmental factors determine its occurrence, and, within a specified range of environment, the trait is genetically determined. Logical as this position seemed to be, its relevance to man was not immediately apparent (particularly in the light of knowledge of many human traits and diseases associated with single fully penetrant genes, the expression of which seemed to be dependent on environment only to the extent that an environment compatible with life was required).

Now, phenylketonuria and other metabolic errors dependent on single major genes are in all our minds as exactly comparable models in man. Within our present environment, in which phenylalanine is a universal component of the diet, phenylketonuria appears as a purely genetic trait, dependent on the action of a single autosomal recessive gene. However, in a population homozygous for the recessive allele and having a more varied diet than present human populations, the occurrence of phenylketonuria would be determined by the level of phenylalanine in the diet. Indeed, the creation of such an exotic circumstance is the basis of our method of treating the homozygous members of our present population. Thus, our characterization of phenylketonuria as a genetic trait depends on the particular environment in which we find ourselves, and the search for the limits of the environmental circumstances within which the trait is genetically determined has, in this particular case, been rewarding.

If the concept of a normal human population not exposed to phenylalanine is so exotic that this argument seems to be only a semantic quibble, we might turn to the case of the fava bean. Here is a specific dietary component which produces a severe illness in genetically susceptible individuals; susceptibility is determined by a single sex-linked recessive gene. Frequency of the relevant gene, as well as of consumption of the bean, varies greatly from one population to another. Thus, we have ethnic groups that have high rates of favism because they have a high frequency of the gene and others whose high rates result from high rates of consumption of the bean. We have populations that can eat the bean with impunity and others whose genetic constitution, because they do not eat the bean, is irrelevant. The gene–bean interaction provides a very close analogy to Hogben's "yellow shanks".

It is true that environmental limits have not been identified for most of the human diseases in which single major genes are involved, but this does not mean that they do not exist. Fifteen years ago there was nothing to distinguish phenylketonuria from hundreds of other "genetic" diseases in this respect. Every gene is dependent on the environment for provision of its building materials. The issue is not whether environmental factors are involved, but whether they can be identified, and whether any essential component can be modified without damage to the organism. The relevance of this point to schizophrenia is fairly obvious: even if the concordance of monozygous twins were 100% and that of dizygous twins close to zero, we should not give up the search for environmental determinants that have preventive significance. Furthermore, there is nothing in the rules which says that the environmental limits must be biochemical, merely because these are the only types so far identified.

In the laboratory animal, the converse situation—the presence of genetic limits within which a condition appears to be environmentally determined—can be demonstrated readily. In all species susceptible to particular cancerogenic viruses there are some genetic strains which are not affected; environmental agents that readily produce congenital malformations in some strains do not do so in other strains of the same species. I know of no completely satisfactory example of this in man, for, although we know of many instances in which genetic background modifies the effects of environment, these do not amount to the complete suppression of effect that can be achieved in the pure-bred laboratory animal.

An intriguing example of a simple genetic modifier in man is the attenuation of malaria seen in persons heterozygous for the gene for hemoglobin S. By comparison with the homozygous normal individual, persons heterozygous for the sickling gene, although as frequently infected with the malaria parasite, are more resistant to it. The mechanism of genetic selection in favor of persons with the sickling trait probably accounts, at least in part, for the high frequency of sickle cell disease in areas of high malaria prevalence. Neel[2] views this situation as an example of "balanced polymorphism", in which the loss of abnormal genes through death of children with sickle cell disease is balanced by loss of normal genes in the greater mortality from malaria of homozygous normal individuals. "Children with sickle cell anemia are the price the population pays for the ability of a substantial proportion of its members to resist malaria." Neel believes that this mechanism, in more complex form, may be common and account, for example, for a substantial proportion of human congenital defects.

The concept of balanced polymorphism is a common one in discussions of mental illness, although the factors thought of as being in balance are more frequently psychological than genetic. For example, there is the view that mental symptomatology may be the price paid, either by the individual or the community, for the privileges of free will, individualism, creativity and other desired characteristics. A status of genetic balance in schizophrenia has been postulated as depending on an increased resistance of affected persons and their relatives to trauma, infections and intoxications.[3] The postulate is, as yet, not supported by data.

Another clear-cut example of a single major gene modifying environmental effects is provided by the sex-linked recessive gene associated with congenital agammaglobulinemia. Here the gene effect is substantial. Unless given frequent injections of gamma globulin, affected individuals almost invariably die of infection. The condition illustrates once again that a phenomenon, in this instance death from infection in a person with agammaglobulinemia, cannot be regarded as either genetically or environmentally determined; it results from a particular combination of gene and environment, either component of which can be modified to eliminate the undesirable outcome.

The results of two twin studies, of poliomyelitis and tuberculosis, are shown in Table 1. The pattern is quite reminiscent of that reported in studies of schizophrenia. For our purposes, the important point is not whether or not these studies reflect the real situation— the same methodologic difficulties that are now well recognized in the earlier twin studies of schizophrenia are present in many studies of other diseases—the point is that these differences *could* be real, and reflect major genetic components of these diseases, and still our faith would not be shaken in the possibility of controlling tuberculosis and poliomyelitis by manipulation of the environment.

Table 1. Concordance Rates of Infectious Diseases in Two Series of Twins

Type of twin	Tuberculosis[4]		Poliomyelitis[5]	
	No. of pairs	Percent both affected	No. of pairs	Percent both affected
Monozygous	78	67	14	36
Dizygous	230	23	33	6

These two diseases are, in fact, interesting to reflect on. In former days, the situation was quite comparable to the present status with respect to phenylketonuria—in both diseases, infection with the responsible organism was almost as common as exposure to a high phenylalanine diet is now. Morbidity from the infection was determined by factors other than internalization of the micro-organism. We still do not know what these factors were—probably some were environmental and some genetic—but nevertheless the diseases were successfully attacked by specific measures directed against the micro-organisms—reduction in exposure to the tubercle bacillus, on the one hand, and the use of a vaccine, on the other. It is as if phenylketonuria were a sufficiently prevalent condition to warrant a major change in the diet of the entire population, so that genetic differences with respect to ability to metabolise phenylalanine became irrelevant.

It is apparent that whether we regard a condition as being due to "genetic factors modified by environment" or "environmental factors modified by genes" depends not so much on the biologic relationships involved, but on the priority of discovery of genetic or environmental agents and on a strictly anthropomorphic view of the utility of knowledge of particular relationships. These considerations make nonsense of supposed quantitative estimates of heritability and other comparisons of the "relative importance" of gene and environment in any particular disease.

In no field are there more complex examples of the gene-environment relationship than in experimental cancer research. The effects of carcinogenic viruses, chemicals and physical agents are specific for species, strain, and sometimes sex. Viruses that cause the common cold in man produce cancer in other species—the cancer researcher is currently intrigued by the possibility that the converse may also be true. In strains in which manifestation of specific tumors is close to 100%, major modifications of incidence, including virtual elimination of the tumor, can be achieved by a variety of environmental manipulations. These modifications are also strain-specific—for example, removal of the thymus will protect certain strains of mice against radiation-induced leukemia, but will not protect other strains. Maternal age is associated with incidence of certain tumors in the offspring in some strains, but not in others. In what is perhaps the most perfect union between gene and environment yet observed, we have examples of tumors resulting from the incorporation of virus particles into the cell genome in a relationship so intimate that we can no longer separate them or even distinguish what was formerly gene from what was formerly environment.

Time of action of etiologic agents

I turn now to the second sense in which the nature–nurture distinction is becoming blurred. As knowledge of environmental mechanisms of mutation increases, it becomes clear that the distinction between genetic and environmental agents is basically one of time at which the agent exerted its effect, for the individual's genotype is itself the end result of his ancestor's accumulated environments—from those which induced the original mutations through those which selectively determined which mutations would survive. Again, until recently, this rather obvious point of view seemed, to the human biologist, to be of more philosophical than practical interest, for the two time spans involved seemed so grossly different that it was useful to maintain the distinction by the use of two separate terms: perhaps "genetic" might have been more aptly named "ancient environmental", but the conventional term had the advantage of brevity.

However, recent discoveries in cytogenetics indicate that there is more overlap in the time spans than was thought. For example, Down's syndrome due to trisomy 21 has quite definite genetic components. Yet this genetic damage did not arise until the final stages of the meiotic divisions of oogenesis (at the time of ovulation and fertilization), or conceivably even during one of the earliest divisions of the fertilized ovum that subsequently becomes the mongol child. The responsible environmental factor—revealed by the association with maternal age—may be something active around the time of ovulation and fertilization, or it may be something to which the mother was exposed earlier in her life and of which the residua do not become manifest until this time. Whichever is the case in Down's syndrome, it is clear that the environment at the time of ovulation and fertilization could have an important influence on the genotype of the conceptus. Thus, we see the possibility of environmental determination of an individual's genotype in the days immediately prior to his conception, or in fact after his conception.

Indeed, the occurrence of genetic mosaicism and of a variety of chromosomally aberrant cells in adults makes it clear that genetic change is constantly in process from the time of conception until death. Those mutations which occur at a sufficiently early stage to become incorporated into the individual's own germ cells we refer to as genetic, and those which occur later as somatic. The distinction is important from the point of view of the individual's descendants, but from the point of view of his own health it may be less so. A mutant which becomes incorporated into his genetic material may have less significance to the individual than a somatic mutation occurring in a stem cell in his bone marrow.

Environmental mechanisms for genetic effects

To turn to the opposite side of the coin—genetic effects operated through environmental mechanism—we might take another intriguing model from phenylketonuria. A few cases have recently been reported of pregnancies in women with unrecognized phenylketonuria. Phenylalanine readily crosses the placenta, and high maternal blood levels produce in the child the mental retardation and other manifestations of the disease, regardless of the genotype of the child. Here, then, is a defect virtually independent of the genotype of the affected individual but highly dependent on the genotype of another person who is providing the environment of the affected person.

The model is interesting in the context of some of the discussions at this meeting, for the hypothesis that the abnormality of schizophrenia depends on abnormalities in the parents in a sense only pushes the issue back a generation—what causes the parental abnormality?

Manifestational and etiologic entities

We must also refer to the old problem of concordance, or lack of concordance, of entities structured on the basis of signs, symptoms and other findings with those based on etiologic criteria.

Schizophrenia is, of course, a manifestational entity. The restructuring of disease classification around newly-discovered etiologic agents, such as micro-organisms, has usually led to major revisions in concepts of what manifestations belong together in a "disease entity". Mongolism provides an example of a manifestational entity that contains several etiologically quite distinct groups. Thus, while mongolism due to trisomy 21 probably originates about the time of conception, that due to translocation is passed from generation to generation in the manner of a classical single gene. The manifestations of the trisomy and the translocation cannot be distinguished.

You are all highly conscious of the possibility that schizophrenia may be similarly divisible from the point of view of etiology. Perhaps indeed a little too conscious. It is of interest that, in psychiatry, with all its preoccupation with the validity and reliability of diagnosis, the revisions of nosology following etiologic discoveries have so far been less marked than in many categories of physical illness. For example, prior to the discovery of their etiology, general paralysis of the insane and pellagra were both regarded as entities on the basis of manifestational criteria, and the change to classification on the basis of exposure to a specific micro-organism and a vitamin deficiency, respectively, led to the reclassification of relatively few patients. Compare this with, for example, the tremendous changes consequent on creation of the entities "tuberculosis" or "vitamin A deficiency".

The success of psychiatrists in distinguishing pellagra and general paralysis on the basis of manifestational criteria encourages the belief that the cases now grouped under schizophrenia—at least those cases on which there is general psychiatric agreement—may be found to have etiologic factors in common.

IMPLICATIONS TO PREVENTION

The complexity of interaction between gene and environment often leads to expressions of pessimism as to the possibility of man's ever understanding the relationship in any depth, which in turn may lead to a fatalistic attitude towards preventive possibilities. A similar aura of pessimism frequently surrounds the term "multifactorial etiology" which, for some reason that is not apparent to me, is often applied as though it had greater relevance to the chronc diseases of unknown etiology than to, for example, the acute infectious diseases. One cannot quarrel with the concept of multifactorial etiology, for the complexity of the gene-environment interaction is often matched only by that of the separate variables within the two broad categories. One can, however, quarrel with the pessimism.

The identification of breakable threads does not require an unravelling of the entire web of causation. While diseases do not have single causes, epidemics often, and perhaps usually, do. The etiology of carcinoma of the lung is no doubt extremely complex, involving both genetic and environmental factors, but the cause of this century's remarkable epidemic is simple and singular—it is cigarette smoking. The cause of the now-declining epidemic of general paralysis of the insane was infection with the *Treponema pallidum*, although many other unidentified factors were important in determining which individuals became affected. Much can be achieved by reversion to the non-epidemic state of affairs through action against the (single) cause of the epidemic, recognizing that this is only one component of the causal complex of the disease.

The same is true whether "epidemic" is defined in terms of time or other demographic variables. The Puerto Rican population of New York City has approximately six times the incidence of carcinoma of the cervix as does the non-Jewish white population; this difference probably has a single cause. While believing in the complex etiology of schizophrenia, I also believe that the familial clustering observed in this disease will be explained in terms of a single factor.

These statements require qualification, since there are exceptions to the single difference–single cause hypothesis. The high mortality from tuberculosis of American Negroes probably has both genetic and socio-economic components. Familial similarity with respect to height probably has both genetic and nutritional determinants. However, the exceptions do not sufficiently outnumber the conformities to warrant rejection of the single cause as a first working hypothesis.

INVESTIGATION OF GENE-ENVIRONMENT INTERACTION

Accepting the single difference–single cause as a working hypothesis, the investigator is often first concerned to determine whether the single cause of an observed difference is more likely of a genetic or environmental nature. In this, he usually has the classical concept of "genetic" in mind. The distinction is seen primarily as a useful step in identifying the cause more specifically, since the determination influences the type and design of the next logical steps of the investigation. The distinction is usually not thought of as a useful end in itself— as has been implied by some previous speakers.

There are two primary arguments:

(a) A difference in disease incidence between two groups that have similar environments but different genetic constitutions is probably due to genetic factors. Some of the differences that can be interpreted as genetically determined under this argument are listed in Table 2. The inferences regarding differences in genetic constitution between groups can usually be supported. The assumption of lack of environmental difference is more difficult. The listing is given in the approximate order in which this assumption seems realistic. The argument is, of course, valid only to the extent that this assumption is sound.

TABLE 2. HUMAN GROUPS THAT ARE FREQUENTLY COMPARED BECAUSE OF
SUPPOSED DIFFERENCES IN GENETIC CONSTITUTION

Compared groups		Supposed degree of similarity of environment of the two groups
Index	Comparison	
MZ twins of affected individuals	(a) DZ twins of affected (b) non-twin siblings of affected	Close Variable
Offspring of con- sanguineous matings	General population*	Usually close
Carriers of a known genetic marker	General population*	Variable
First degree relatives of affected persons	General population*	Poor
An ethnic group	General population*	Poor
Males	Females	Poor

* Greater similarity of environment is obtained by consideration of geographic, social, economic and other obvious sources of difference.

(b) A difference between groups that have similar genetic backgrounds but different
environments is probably due to environmental factors. Some of the comparisons
frequently made under this argument are listed in Table 3. Here, the soundness of
the argument depends on the validity of the assumption of comparability of genetic
background. Again, the listing is in approximate order of confidence in this assumption.

TABLE 3. HUMAN GROUPS THAT ARE FREQUENTLY COMPARED BECAUSE OF
SUPPOSED DIFFERENCES IN ENVIRONMENT

Compared groups		Supposed degree of similarity of genetic background
Index	Comparison	
A population	Same population, different time	Complete, if time short
Affected MZ twins	Discordant members, same sets	Almost complete
Children born in early birth orders or maternal ages	Later-born	Close
Persons exposed to a specific agent	General population	Usually close*
A socio-economic, occu- pational or geographic subgroup	General population	Usually close*
An ethnic group	General population	Poor
Males	Females	Poor
Members of affected families	General population	Poor

* If groups are of similar ethnicity.

Sometimes, the genetic or environmental nature of a cause is evident from the placing of the observed differences on one of these lists, and on the level on each list at which the individual interpreter draws the line between a "reasonable" assumption and an unreasonable one. This level may depend on the investigator's personality, the number of times that he has been wrong (or right) in the past, and many other intangibles. I have noted that geneticists tend to draw the line further down the "genetic" list than do epidemiologists, and vice versa. Sooner or later, however, everybody reaches a level at which he becomes uncertain as to the interpretation, if for no other reason than, as you have no doubt noted, some observations appear on both lists. In this event, a particular observation may be interpretable by reference to other studies of variables at a higher level in the hierarchy.

In considering how these methods might have relevance to the separation of environmental and genetic factors in schizophrenia, one is struck by the number of techniques which in most diseases lead to fairly clear interpretations but which in schizophrenia, because of the nature of the illness, are considerably less helpful. For example, the observation of a disease concordance rate between spouses of the same order as that between other family members would generally be considered as evidence of environmental determination of familial clustering. In the case of schizophrenia an interpretation of such an observation would be complicated by the psychological and other factors entering into spouse selection. Sibship clustering resulting from common infection and other acute episodes can sometimes be detected by examination for common exposure periods of affected members. If sibship clustering in schizophrenia is environmentally determined, it is likely that the responsible environment is a relatively long-lasting one not susceptible to pin-pointing in time. Inferences regarding environmental etiology, including suggestions as to time of action of possible agents, have been made from studies of migrant populations. In the case of schizophrenia such inferences are complicated by knowledge of the role of migration itself as a pertinent variable. The disease is too common to expect that studies of the role of consanguinity will be informative.

I recognize the irony of my expounding to this audience on the difficulties of investigating schizophrenia. Perhaps I can make amends, to some extent, by reminding you that the investigator in schizophrenia need not be concerned that he has a monopoly, either of methodologic problems or of inadequate data. In fact, those methodologic problems that seem to preoccupy investigators in this field—definition and diagnosis of the disease, its "true" incidence, and the significance of other pathology seen in affected individuals and their families—are those which seem to an outsider to be the least unique to the field. They constitute, for example, a considerable proportion of any critical discussion of the etiology of diabetes and hypertension.

To take only one example that has been mentioned at this conference, the interpretation of twin studies in diabetes mellitus is open to all the problems that have been discussed in connection with schizophrenia. Whether the higher rate of concordance among MZ than among DZ twins reflects the influence of genetic factors is as problematic in one disease as in the other. Furthermore, the *data* on diabetes in twins do not begin to compare, either in quantity or in quality, with those available for schizophrenia.

Indeed the general recognition of the problems of twin studies and the development of methodology for their solution has received considerable impetus from work in schizophrenia. The method of detailed investigation of discordant monozygous twins (item 2 in Table 2) was applied by Planansky and Allen[6] to tuberculosis some time ago, but otherwise has received little attention. The potential importance of differences in birth weight between the members of twin pairs, as indicative of differences in prenatal environment, is suggested by a recent study showing significant physical and mental retardation among the lighter members of pairs in which major discrepancies in birth weights occurred.[7] Hopefully, the successful use of the method of twin discordancy in schizophrenia will stimulate its application on a much wider scale.

It does seem that there is still room in the investigation of schizophrenia for well-controlled studies of objective criteria of environmental effects early in life, using adequate numbers of representative cases. Variables still needing investigation include order of birth, maternal age, and even parental loss. One can sympathize with the impatience of investigators to identify the specific nature of environmental factors influencing the development of schizophrenia, but still wish that someone would develop the broader, although less specific, evidence that such factors exist.

In general, however, a marked impression left by the 5 days of this conference is that the volume and quality of work under way in schizophrenia is such that success in the interpretation of the curious phenomena so far observed in this disease is more likely to shed light on gene-environment interactions in other diseases, than vice versa. It is not for me to say whether this should give investigators in this field cause for satisfaction or concern.

REFERENCES

1. HOGBEN, L., *Nature and Nurture,* Williams & Norgate, London, 1933.
2. NEEL, J. V., Some genetic aspects of congenital defect, in *Congenital Malformations, First International Conference,* Lippincott, Philadelphia, 1961.
3. HUXLEY, J., MAYR, E., OSMOND, H. and HOFFER, A., Schizophrenia as a genetic morphism, *Nature* **204,** 220 (1964).
4. KALLMANN, F. J. and REISNER, D., Twin studies on the significance of genetic factors in tuberculosis, *Am. Rev. Tuberc.* **47,** 549 (1943).
5. HERNDON, C. N. and JENNINGS, R. G., A twin-family study of susceptibility to poliomyelitis, *Am. J. Hum. Genet.* **3,** 17 (1951).
6. PLANANSKY, K. and ALLEN, G., Heredity in relation to variable resistance to pulmonary tuberculosis, *Am. J. Hum. Genet.* **5,** 322 (1953).
7. BABSON, S. G., KANGAS, J., YOUNG, N. and BRAMHALL, J. L., Growth and development of twins of dissimilar size at birth, *Pediatrics* **33,** 327 (1964).

THE INTERACTION OF BIOLOGICAL AND EXPERIENTIAL FACTORS IN SCHIZOPHRENIA

LEON EISENBERG*

Department of Child Psychiatry,
Johns Hopkins School of Medicine, Baltimore

A DISCUSSANT's lot is not a happy one, more so when he must comment on a group of papers so excellent as these than when quality is poor and he can content himself with displaying his own erudition and superiority. Despite the common theme that informs these contributions, they employ such disparate methods and deal with such different issues that an integrated summary exceeds my grasp. I must content myself with a few remarks about individual papers followed by a more general discussion of underlying conceptual problems.

Dr. Goldfarb is certainly correct in attributing to skewed samples the remarkable differences in the characteristics of psychotic children and their families as described by different investigators. I can attest from my own experience, while assisting Dr. Kanner, to the frequency with which his autistic families were marked by parents of high intellectual and scientific attainment but it is also noteworthy that these patients were referred privately to Dr. Kanner from all over the country. It is also true that less affluent families in large numbers were seen at the clinic. However, given the rarity of the disorder and the likelihood that the poor child with grossly aberrant behavior was managed quite differently in the community (i.e. referred to the facility for defectives), no conclusions can be drawn from the fact that few such children were seen at our Service. Indeed, one recalls the story of the two elderly Jews who were sitting in a café in the lower East Side. The first asked the number of Jews in the world and was told there were 6 million. He then asked the number of Chinese and was told there might be 700 million. He then addressed the following philosophic question to his colleague: "How come, then, all I see when I walk down the street are Jews?" Each of us has been at his own East Side café and has described the people walking through the door as though they were a representative population.

I would further agree that a neutral term like "autism" or "childhood psychosis" is to be preferred to "childhood schizophrenia" except for that small group of children, first observed clinically at age 8 or 9 who show in microcosm all the symptoms we would recognize as schizophrenic in an adult. Our follow-up study on autistic children did *not* indicate that the clinical picture in adulthood was identical with that of schizophrenia. Other follow-up studies of psychotic children have encountered increasing evidence as follow-up time lengthened that children originally described as "psychotic" or "schizophrenic" later presented frank evidence of neurological impairment.

* *Present address:* Department of Psychiatry, Harvard Medical School, Boston, Massachusetts, 02115.

403

Dr. Goldfarb's separation of his psychotic patients into an organic and a non-organic group has the virtue of specifying characteristics and permitting a first level differentiation of a very heterogeneous population. The follow-up studies by Rutter, Pollack, and our group, are in accord with the observations reported here that children with limited IQ and/or limited speech have a poor prognosis with any of the currently available treatment methods. In fact, so different is the prognosis for these two groups (whether one takes an IQ cut-off point or some measure of verbal ability) that it is difficult to believe that they are variants of a single entity.

Other recent studies, such as that of Hertzig and Birch, report a high proportion of "soft" neurological signs among adolescent patients admitted to a city hospital with a diagnosis of schizophrenia.

Thus, there is accumulating evidence that children and adolescents with disorders of behavior gross enough to be termed psychotic are quite heterogeneous and include a significant proportion with convincing or presumptive evidence of central nervous system dysfunction.

This leads us to Dr. Pollin's remarkable finding that in almost every instance the psychotic twin of the discordant monozygotic pair was lighter in weight at birth as well as the one likely to have been exposed to other hazards to CNS development. He, too, finds the preponderance of "soft" neurological signs in the index cases. Equally unexpected is the lower protein bound iodine values in the index cases and the correlation between PBI and birth weight. While it is tempting to speculate that these findings might relate to faulty brain development in the index cases, our knowledge of thyroid function in relation to brain development is too imprecise for firm conclusions. Athyroid states in infancy clearly impair brain development. The original optimism that early treatment would prevent damage altogether has not been borne out clinically, though treatment is clearly effective. Moreover, the measured IQ of children treated late shows a surprising degree of instability with no clear relationship between vigor of treatment and final outcome. Hyperthyroidism produces unequivocal mental symptoms. However, we as yet have no evidence that levels of circulating thyroid hormones above a given minimum but below a certain maximum show any dose-effect relationship to brain function.

Dr. Pollin proposes an interesting and eminently reasonable model for the interrelationship between biological vulnerability, parent–child transactions, and individual psychological development. That it is reasonable does not establish that it is true.

The papers by Drs. Kety, Rosenthal, Wender and Schulsinger present, individually and in tandem, a most impressive body of data that there is a heritable factor in schizophrenia. These findings, taken together with the other twin studies, persuade me—and I trust most of you—not only that there is a genetic component in the transmission of schizophrenia (a position no more controversial than the defense of motherhood) but that it is a *significant* determinant of the occurrence of the disease.

We are told that the idea for these studies occurred independently to Kety, Rosenthal and Wender. Now that it has been described to us, we can all agree that the idea is simple and obvious. Its obviousness after it has been described is the hallmark of the originality of its creators. To have thought of it was a contribution. But to have worked through the innumerable administrative and methodologic details necessary to get the studies done is an even more outstanding accomplishment. Having heard brief reports on the research as it progressed, I have been waiting impatiently for the findings, all the time nursing a secret pessimism that the number of cases would just miss statistical "significance" or that inter-action effects would obscure the main findings or that the administrative problems would finally prove insuperable. I cannot restrain my delight at the consistency of the accumulated evidence which firmly argues for a major hereditary component and which is free of the methodologic uncertainties that have plagued many of the older studies.

At the same time, I confess to discomfort with the notion of a "spectrum of schizo-phrenic disorders" when it extends so widely. One hears in it echoes of the nineteenth century theory of hereditary "taint". Perhaps I am responding like an old fire horse to the alarm bell. The concepts employed by these authors do not carry with them the baggage of mystical philosophic concepts implicit in the "taint" proposition. However, once one includes psychopathology in a continuum from process to reactive schizophrenia to per-sonality disorder, alcoholism, eccentricity and even talent (as Dr. Karlsson is willing to do), one faces a formidable problem in differentiating environmental phenocopies which surely must occur the more frequently the further out on the spectrum we search.

We all feel we know what schizophrenia is even though we find it hard to agree on a definition. I hold no brief for the failure to attempt a definition but I would argue that our inability to agree does not necessarily mean that we are not recognizing a real phenomenon. Pattern recognition is far easier for the human eye than it is for the computer, at least at present levels of computer technology; this statement, translated, means that we cannot yet specify for the computer what we do intuitively. A field study by an anthropologist in the South Pacific uncovered the remarkable fact that the native system for naming and classify-ing birds corresponded remarkably well with the Linnean one. Perhaps even more striking is the observation that the native informants, when shown specimens thay had never before seen (from neighboring islands), assigned to them families that corresponded with what the scientific system required. This is a notable feat, for simple variables like size, color and shape do not suffice for classification and the classifier must recognize a trait complex. Yet, these expert classifiers could not specify just what they were responding to. I offer this *obiter dicta* merely to suggest that it is legitimate to rely on clinical intuition even as we attempt to refine it.

The paper by Dr. Heston excites my admiration, not only for his ingenuity in taking advantage of a natural experiment, but his remarkable tenacity and capacity for work in singlehandedly following and obtaining data on such a high proportion of a nomadic population. Indeed, he puts the rest of us to shame. If one were to insist on so high a yield of scientific data from so limited an expenditure of professional manhours, very few of us would qualify for research grants. His findings do *not* establish that rearing has no effect upon adult personality but rather that schizophrenia occurs much more commonly among the children of schizophrenic parents, even when they have been separated from their parents and have been reared in environments similar to those of a comparison group.

The lack of an effect from early institutional experience, not on schizophrenia (which orphanages have never been shown to produce) but on IQ and other measures of social adjustment, is discordant with the expectations generated by other studies. It suggests both that the effects of an early orphanage experience are more reversible than has been believed

AA

and that the post-orphanage experience was more beneficent than that provided children described in earlier studies. The ominous and irreversible post-institutional psychopathology described by earlier investigators may have resulted from not merely the initial but subsequent life experiences of the patients. Psychiatrists have been far too ready to extrapolate the theoretical model of "imprinting" provided by ethologists. Their demonstration in *certain* species of birds and ungulates that very early experiences could be remarkably determinative of adult behavior has led to far too loose a generalization across phylogenetic lines. It should be noted that there is not any data for primates and certainly none for man that would justify imprinting *sensu strictu* as a major factor in human development.

The only possibility of explaining Dr. Heston's findings on other than a genetic basis would be the presence of a serum factor in the pregnant mothers that produced central nervous system lesions in their offspring. You will recall that these children were born to mothers who were state hospital patients and thus were presumably psychotic at the time of pregnancy. However, this factor could not have applied in the case of the Kety, Rosenthal and Wender studies and I therefore do not offer it as a likely explanation of Heston's findings.

The high rates of familial psychopathology in both the Danish and the Oregon studies would suggest that the genetic trait for this spectrum of disorders is widely distributed. This raises an evolutionary question that genetic theorists must deal with. In what sense might the heterozygous state be advantageous, if one is to follow the model of sicklemia and resistance to malaria? Dr. Karlsson suggests that it may be associated with creativity. The evidence from genealogies is unconvincing and other studies have shown no true association between intellectual gifts and psychopathology. Other have suggested that heterozygosity may be associated with protection against infectious disease and that schizophrenia is simply the price paid, but the evidence is yet to be presented. Is it possible that there might *not* be a selective advantage because (1) schizophrenia did not appear until late in the evolutionary scale, say in the past 50,000 years, after human culture had developed; (2) culture protected the schizophrenic (by assigning him a role as shaman or priest) as it does the myopic; and (3) until recently fertility was not much affected because child bearing occurred early in adult life and thus the mid-life schizophrenic was not excluded from the competition for mates. I do not argue for any or all of these speculations but I do suggest that the geneticist must address himself to such questions as one way of grappling with the nature of the genetic mechanisms and its biological meaning.

Dr. Mednick is to be congratulated on having embarked on a longitudinal study by employing a high risk population. It is not to minimize his contribution to suggest that longitudinal studies have long been recognized as a crying need but he is to be applauded for having started the work while the rest of us have merely discussed it. The longitudinal study does however not necessarily answer etiologic questions. It should be free of the antecedent-consequent-social field confusion which confounds cross-sectional studies but it will not ascertain causes unless specific etiologic theories are tested as part of the longitudinal design. (For example, such a population would provide an ideal group on which to test the Singer–Wynne or Lidz family interaction models by studying family interaction before disease appears in the child.) Moreover, there are very special problems in the collection of large amounts of data unless specific hypotheses are formulated in advance of the study.

We are all familiar with the probability that random differences will attain a statistical level of "significance" by chance alone if one simply collects enough data. One faces an enormous task in reducing data to proportions that the investigator can handle conceptually even if the computer can tangle with them numerically. Here again Dr. Mednick is ahead of us in having a theory which he is putting to test. It is no dishonor that his findings so far seem to run in a direction contrary to prediction. If his findings hold up, it would still suggest that he has sensed a significant variable even if he has not predicted the precise mode of its influence. I take him to task only for disdaining the cross-sectional study in his preference for the longitudinal one. The latter is our greatest area of deficit but it is not a panacea and it has its own hazards.

Let me now turn to some general comments. After 5 days of data presentation and discussion, it would appear that our methodologies are not sufficiently exact to permit a critical test of hypotheses that still do not generate precisely testable predictions. As Dr. Mishler pointed out, the findings from the family interaction studies, even if they are accepted as valid, still leave us in a quandary as to whether the associations are causal in one direction or another (i.e. from parent to child or child to parent) or reflect the common action of an independent factor. The findings from the genetic studies, though they seem convincing as to the presence of a hereditary factor, still leave us in the dark as to the nature of that factor. To call it "polygenetic inheritance" is not necessarily to say very much since in the end every attribute ultimately must be polygenetic.

The questions each of us has asked reflect his bias or set. To get effective dialogue (dialogue that would lead to a change of opinion) has seemed singularly difficult. Might it be fruitful in another conference to ask opponents of a given theory to design a study intended to provide a critical challenge for it, a design which would have to be simultaneously acceptable to the proponents of the theory? I am not suggesting that research can be done by committees but rather that such an effort might force each side to specify its premises and its methods in such a way as to lead to confrontation on the critical points of dispute.

If we understand the implications of what we all have agreed upon (namely, that there is a gene-environment interaction in the production of schizophrenia) then it follows that genetic effects will be detectible only in environments that permit their manifestation, and, conversely, that environmental effects will be detectible only in populations whose genetic characteristics are not so loaded as to wash out environmental factors. Moreover, it follows that certain levels of genetic loading or environmental pathology will be far more appropriate for detecting the effects we seek than others. Whether one chooses to concentrate his efforts on genetic or family studies, he would be well advised to examine and specify the other parameter if only in order to increase the efficiency of his research design. Let me suggest a few simple examples.

In the first, let us imagine ourselves in the position of an investigator studying the manifestations of pellagra. We know today that the symptom complex of diarrhea, dermatitis, dementia and death can occur as a result of a diet deficient in tryptophan and nicotinic acid, but also as well in children with Hartnup's disease, a rare autosomal recessive disease reported thus far in 23 patients in 14 families. Pellagra appears in normals only when the diet is grossly deficient. In Hartnup's disease, it occurs on a normal diet but apparently can be corrected by an excess of these essential nutrients. Table 1 contrasts the number of cases

Table 1. Distribution of Pellagrins

| Genetic status | Rich | Metabolites in diet | |
		Moderate	Poor
Normal	0	0	+++ (familial)
H-Homozygote	0	+++ (familial)	++++ (familial)

found in normals and in Hartnup homozygotes, under circumstances of three different diets, one rich, one moderate, and one poor in the nutrients in question. Under the conditions of rich diet, no cases appear in either group. Under conditions of a moderate diet, the disease appears only in homozygotes and it shows familial aggregation. Under conditions of a poor diet, it occurs in both normals *and* homozygotes and in both it shows a familial aggregation, not because of genetic but because of social factors. You will recall that pellagra was considered to be an hereditary disorder by many thoughtful physicians because of familial aggregation.

Hartnup's disease was discovered only because dietary causes of pellagra had been excluded. Such patients would never have been discriminated in an area where pellagra was endemic because of malnutrition.

Table 2. Mean IQ

| | Social class | |
	Middle	Low
Normal	111	89
Hydrocephalic	20	19

The second example contrasts a normal population of children with a population of children suffering from severe hydrocephalus (Table 2). It supposes that the investigator is interested in the effects of social class on IQ. In the normal population, middle class is associated with an IQ of 111 and low class with an IQ of 89, a difference highly significant in the population of 300 children from whom it was obtained (these are actual figures from a recent study of our own undertaken for different purposes). On the other hand, hydrocephalics show no significant difference in IQ in relation to social class. (The latter figures are hypothetical.) Now none of us would have looked for social class effects on hydrocephalus because the hydrocephalic is so grossly abnormal in appearance. But nature is not always kind in giving us physical stigmata to identify a group at high risk for some disorder. We daily confront instances in which our failure to find either genetic or environmental effects stems from our disregard for the second variable as we examine the first. The range of variability permitted by genetic constitution (or environment) must be wide enough for the effects of one or the other to be manifested.

My third example is a hypothetical model for schizophrenia. Let me suppose, for purposes of argument only, that there are family environments so positive in their capacity to promote personal development that schizophrenia rarely occurs except in the presence of overwhelming genetic loading. Let me suppose a second group of families so traumatic in their effects on offspring that psychosis is produced almost universally even in non-carriers. In average families, I suppose that schizophrenia is largely determined by genetic effects and rarely by unusual concatenations of environmental events. The outcome of such a state of affairs is indicated in Table 3.

TABLE 3. DISTRIBUTION OF SCHIZOPHRENIA

Genetic status	Family life		
	Optimal	Average	Abysmal
Carrier	±	+++	++++
Normal	0	±	+++

Table 3 indicates that the student of genetic factors who chose either optimal or abysmal families would be hard put to it to differentiate the carriers from the normals. Differences in rates would be marginal. He might incorrectly conclude that there was no hereditary factor. Had he excluded the extremes of family pathology and concentrated on average families, he would have obtained very conclusive evidence for his thesis.

On the other hand, the student of environmental factors, were he to study a genetically vulnerable population and to contrast only average and abysmal families would find rather weak evidence for a family contribution. Were he to have a population without genetic loading, then the contrast between average and abysmal families would be striking.

The data of course have been cooked to suit my example. They illustrate a strong interaction effect. They were designed on the thesis that a protective environment can limit the manifestation of the disease but that it appears frankly in an average environment and that there is not much room for increase in its manifestations in the worst environment; contrariwise, they assume that schizophrenia can occur even in the absence of a genetic component but that it only occurs to an appreciable extent under such a condition when the environment is particularly savage.

What I am trying to suggest is that the allegiance of a theorist to a particular position should not blind him to the importance of controlling for the other factor if only in order to enable himself the best chance of demonstrating the validity of his own hypothesis.

V. RECAPITULATION AND CRITICAL OVERVIEW

THE HEREDITY-ENVIRONMENT ISSUE IN SCHIZOPHRENIA: SUMMARY OF THE CONFERENCE AND PRESENT STATUS OF OUR KNOWLEDGE*

David Rosenthal

Laboratory of Psychology, National Institute of Mental Health, Bethesda, Maryland

This past April, while I was in Copenhagen, an affair of honor took place in France that most of you probably will remember. It was a duel between two members of the French Parliament, Monsieur Deffere and Monsieur Ribière. Monsieur Deffere had called Monsieur Ribière a cretin, and then, to emphasize his point, a congenital cretin. It is not quite clear whether Monsieur Ribière interpreted this to mean his IQ has been underestimated or that his parents had been maligned, but he must have concluded that he had been insulted. He decided to challenge Monsieur Deffere to a duel. It is not clear how a duel would have proved he was not a cretin. As a matter of fact, it was well known that Monsieur Deffere was a skilled swordsman, whereas Monsieur Ribière had no knowledge of the art at all. The challenge itself undoubtedly increased many people's suspicions that Monsieur Deffere may have been a shrewd diagnostician. A photograph of the duelists in action was made and published in newspapers around the world. I am sure that most of you have seen it, but I am not sure how clearly you remember it. It captures the grace and awkwardness of the combatants as they poised for thrust and parry. More important, it reveals that both were dressed in elegant white shirts. The French code of honor calls for duels to be fought bare-chested. However, the duelists had agreed to wear the shirts to protect themselves against the greatest danger of French dueling, catching a cold.

In several respects, the heredity–environment controversy with regard to schizophrenia is reminiscent of that white-shirted French duel. In times past, the participants in the controversy usually managed to avoid each other so thoroughly that they never exposed themselves even to the danger of catching cold. The fact that we have been able to convene this Conference reflects the great change in the nature of the controversy that has occurred during the past decade. This week we have been able to sit here day after day and listen to people expounding ideas both compatible and contrary to our own, and far from catching any dread affliction, the only thing we have caught, I hope, is the spirit of earnest concern about the other man's data and opinions. From now on, we may all be a little more diligent about doing our homework in the other fellow's field, as Dr. Slater put it, and perhaps even redesigning our research or adopting new research models.

---

* The paper is printed as it was given, except for a few minor changes. At the end of the Conference, all participants were asked to submit for inclusion in this summary the main points they made during the long and warm discussions. Not all submitted statements. I have tried to include as many of those submitted as fitted into an appropriate place in the paper. They are shown as footnotes.

My job is to summarize the Conference. We have heard twenty-three papers and three formal discussants. In addition, many hours have been spent in reviewing points and issues, reworking and reinterpreting data old and new, challenging and defending positions, and generally trying to act civilized all through the give and take of open debate. We may not have always succeeded, but as far as I know, nobody has challenged anybody to a duel. The talk did not end at the Conference table but continued at the dining tables, the beaches, and of course, the hospitality room. So much ground has been covered, so many ideas put forth, and so many data presented that it is impossible to include them all in a summary. I will confine my remarks to what I think are some of the main issues about which we would all like to draw conclusions. This means that I will omit reference to hundreds of points raised that deserve discussion, many of which are simply beyond my competence.

Basically, we were trying to achieve a clearer understanding of the contributions of genes and experiences in the transmission of schizophrenia. The question had most often been formulated in this way: Is schizophrenia an inherited disease, or is it not? How can the hereditarians and the environmentalists in years past have taken such opposite positions when both sought with equal sincerity to provide a valid understanding of this disorder?

One can divide the investigators in this field into two main types: those who like to look at numbers and those who like to look at patients. The former tend to be hereditarians, the latter environmentalists. The hereditarians like to produce and analyze statistics, citing concordance rates in twins and incidences in populations and in blood relatives of different degree. They believe that such data are more scientific. The environmentalists like to look at the "meanings" of the symptoms they observe in their patients; they point to the rearing and experiential difficulties that the patient has undergone during his formative and developmental years; and they point to the relationship between many of his life experiences and the particular form of the syndrome which afflicts him. They believe that such data are more immediate, relevant and compelling. The opposing groups of proponents, however, have had one trait in common: they have shared a passion for generating a host of hypotheses, frequently untestable, and too often based on data that have been unsystematically selected or of dubious validity.

The answers the opposing groups gave to our question at issue were based on radically different views of the nature of the illness. We can still hear their reverberations in the conceptions of and attitudes towards schizophrenia held by our two eminent senior participants, Dr. Slater and Professor Bleuler. Both began their excellent studies with hard-core, clearly-defined schizophrenics. Dr. Slater says: "Schizophrenia is an illness affecting the mind and the personality of the patient in a way which is seldom completely resolved; after an attack of illness there is nearly always some degree of permanent change of personality, and if there are several attacks this change will become more and more marked. This change is one that de-individualizes and de-humanizes the patient, and leaves him above all with impaired capacities for normal affective responses."

Professor Bleuler says, in contrast: "More than twenty or thirty years after the onset of a severe schizophrenic psychosis, the general tendencies go towards an improvement . . . It is true that it is mostly a partial improvement, but it consists of a real reappearance of both healthy intellectual life and very warm-hearted, very human emotional life in certain situations and in the contact with certain persons."

I doubt that such opposing views of the illness can be reconciled or even modified by a week in conference, but it is well to keep these contrasting orientations in mind as we attempt to gain some perspective on the historical background of the problem. Dr. Slater believes that the two views are basically not as dissimilar as they might appear.[1]

Probably, our first order of business here was to determine whether we had enough evidence to decide whether a specific kind of heredity definitely does or does not play a role in the etiology of schizophrenia. In the past, all genetic studies were at least consistent with a broad genetic hypothesis: the consanguinity studies, the incidence studies and the twin studies. Positive affirmation of the heredity hypothesis was withheld by many because they mistrusted the data collected, because no Mendelian distribution could be found, or because they believed that the data could as well be explained by nongenetic factors.

These objections do not stand up well today. In the past decade, the data of the older genetics studies have been intensively examined and analyzed, their error margins estimated and the implications of these errors evaluated. The hunt for a Mendelian distribution of the phenotype has become less determined as the field of quantitative genetics has developed and become better understood. And during this Conference we have heard the findings of four studies which used adoption to tease apart the genetic and rearing factors that have been so intensely debated in the genetic–nongenetic controversy. Although each study has its own methodological problems, these differ from one study to another, yet all four studies taken together point strongly to the conclusion that heredity contributes to a schizophrenic outcome. When we add these studies to the masterful review of the field by Shields, it appears that, unless we can find legitimate objections not raised before, all the reasonable doubts that had been raised in past years have now been answered, and the case for heredity has held up convincingly. At the moment, I can see no grounds for withholding affirmation any longer. As a matter of fact, I could find no one at this meeting who openly disagreed with this point of view, and some indicated that they had long held it, although the fact that they did may not have been generally known.[2]

It is in this sense, as well as in the fact that we are meeting at all, that our Conference may have historic significance. It could be remembered as the time when it was definitely and openly agreed by our foremost students of family interaction that heredity is implicated in the development of schizophrenia.[3]

---

[1] Professor Bleuler agreed with Dr. Slater that, as a rule, the personality is changed after a real schizophrenic psychosis. However, he believed that the change was a natural consequence of the stress of the psychosis itself. He could not imagine anyone going through all the experiences of being psychotic without some reactive personality changes, and emphasized that such changes were psychologically intelligible. Dr. Wynne thought that the Conference as a whole neglected sufficient consideration of principles and methods for describing, classifying and differentiating schizophrenics. He pointed out that European and American psychiatrists differed not only from one another, but among themselves as well in both diagnostic criteria and methods of studying patients. Moreover, the specific points of disagreement—and agreement—remain largely unknown. As a result, when a second-order problem such as the transmission of schizophrenia is discussed, there is considerable ambiguity and vagueness about what it is that a given investigator thinks may be transmitted.

[2] Dr. Lidz said that he and his colleagues had repeatedly pointed out in their papers that they had more reason to believe that a genetic factor was involved in schizophrenia than did any of the earlier genetic studies, but that they were unable to differentiate the genetic and environmental influences, and chose to focus their attention on the environmental aspects in the familial transmission of the disorder.

[3] Dr. Slater said that the acceptance of a role for genetics in the causation of schizophrenia was much

However, as we move away from this question, we learn that there were really more gnawing issues underlying it. One, I think, has to do with the question, is schizophrenia an inherited disease, or is it not? First, we should recognize that the question itself leads us into difficulties because of the way it is phrased. In the strictest sense, it is clearly not schizophrenia that is inherited. The genes that are implicated produce an effect whose nature we have not yet been able to fathom. It is clear that not everybody who harbors the genes develops schizophrenia. We know this from the twin studies. We heard Drs. Kringlen, Gottesman and Tienari tell us that their systematically sampled studies have actually been turning up as many or more *dis*cordant than *con*cordant monozygotic pairs. Dr. Margit Fischer in Denmark reports similar findings. Dr. Kringlen once pointedly asked: If schizophrenia is an inherited disease, how can we explain even one MZ pair where one twin is clearly schizophrenic and the other is clearly normal? It is for such reasons, and perhaps others, that many people have maintained and may continue to maintain that schizophrenia is *not* an inherited disease. They might nevertheless acknowledge a contribution of heredity but would be inclined to minimize its importance.

Others look at the question in a different way. They say that it is a secondary matter whether any particular individual does or does not develop clinical schizophrenia. What is primary is that if he has the implicated hereditary factors, he is either basically or potentially schizophrenic. They would be inclined to say, for example, that the discordant MZ twin of a schizophrenic has a *forme fruste* of the disease, whether we can detect it clinically or not. It is not necessary to know whether a single genotype is involved, but the belief is that no one will develop true schizophrenia if he does not harbor the implicated gene(s). People who interpret the question in this way will assert that schizophrenia *is* an inherited disease, and they will minimize the importance of environmental factors.

There is a third way of looking at the question, one which is really a modification or amplification of the first. People holding this view would say that whether or not a potentially identifiable genotype eventually leads to a clinically schizophrenic illness depends primarily on environmental factors, among them the kinds of life experiences the gene carrier encounters. However, according to this argument, individuals with this genotype may develop many other phenotypical patterns as well, not all of them bad. For example, in Heston's study we heard that a number of such affected people might develop antisocial traits and become criminals or psychopaths, and that others may show talents and interest in the fine arts. Some showed creative abilities and were more spontaneous and lived more colorful lives. Karlsson also found talented and creative people intermingled with schizophrenics in his genealogies. In this sense, the genes could, through interaction with the right kind of environment as well as with other genes, be compatible with highly desirable

more important for the climate of psychiatric opinion in America than in Europe; that European psychiatrists had accepted the fact that genetics played some part in such causation and had been more interested in measuring the magnitude of the contribution and to distinguish the ways in which it shows itself, to clarify the interaction between genetical and environmental factors, and to exploit genetical information for a better understanding of the nature of the schizophrenic syndrome, its taxonomic status and its biological function. He added that if American psychiatric opinion can be moved to the point of admitting that human genetics has a contribution to make to the behavioral sciences, we can hope that many gaps will be bridged between psychiatry, medicine and biology, and between Europe and America. He could imagine fantastic changes taking place over a very wide front, including psychology, sociology and educational theory.

characteristics as well as morbid ones. Moreover, those who develop clinical schizophrenia may constitute only a fraction of the total number of individuals who harbor the genotype. People who hold such a viewpoint would *not* say that the MZ twin of a schizophrenic has a *forme fruste* of schizophrenia. Rather, it is the schizophrenic twin who has unfortunately developed a clinical phenotype which was primarily the consequence of psychonoxious life experiences, but perhaps secondarily abetted by some biologically influenced factors. Proponents of this view would be inclined to say that schizophrenia is *not* an inherited disease.

In contrast, a polygenic point of view would hold that the qualitatively different outcomes just noted are the results of different combinations of genes, none of which by itself would necessarily be clinically pathogenic, and that schizophrenia must therefore be considered an inherited disease. Karlsson, using a two gene model, would come to the same conclusion.

This brief review suggests the possibility that the heredity–environment controversy may have resulted in part from semantic confusion as well as from genuinely opposed points of view. In the various theoretical positions I have just listed, all agreed that both heredity and environment were implicated in the development of schizophrenia, yet they would have replied differently to the question: Is schizophrenia an inherited disease? Perhaps much of the argument might be avoided if we refrained from asking the question in this way, since it is capable of being interpreted so differently.

We have heard many arguments in the past that heredity or environment was more important. It should be clear by now that since both hereditary and environmental factors are implicated in schizophrenia, they must both be important. Dr. MacMahon pointed out that which of the two appears to be the more important will vary with both the range of genotypes and the range of environmental factors that are implicated in any given study. His illustration of *yellow shanks* in fowl was an extreme example. There he pointed out that "within a specified range of genetic background, environmental factors determine occurrence of the trait, and that, within a specified range of the environment, the trait is genetically determined."

In all earlier genetic studies of schizophrenia that I know, the environment has been left to vary randomly. We have no idea at this point as to the limits of particular environmental influences regarding the prevention of schizophrenic outcomes in individuals with the implicated genotype.

I think that Dr. Erlenmeyer-Kimling came closest to formulating the issue in a way that is compatible with current knowledge and conducive to developing productive research in the future. She says: "The question to be asked is not: 'What are the relative contributions of heredity and environment' but rather 'What kinds of environmental input trigger manifestations of the disorder in genotypically vulnerable persons, and why are these important, in a psychophysiological sense?' " I myself would have phrased the same point in this way: How do the implicated hereditary and environmental variables interact or coact to make for various kinds of schizophrenic and nonschizophrenic outcomes? The level at which the analysis of interaction would be conducted, i.e. physiological, psychological, or psychophysiological, would be left to the individual investigators, but all such analyses could be informative.

Everyone agreed that it is the *interaction* which must be our major future concern, but differences of opinion existed regarding the implications of this view. Dr. Lidz thought that the geneticists should specify the implicated genotype in a way that would make it possible to know what it was and how it was manifested, so that behavioral transmissionists could recognize it and deal with it accordingly. The Adoptees study aims to make a beginning in providing such information. Some people expressed the idea that it might not be possible at all to recognize either the hereditary or the environmental factors separately, and that they could be identified only through their interaction in the first place. The Mednick–Schulsinger study loads its subjects with the implicated genotype and then looks at environmental differences between those who become ill and those who do not. This might be the kind of sample that could provide indications of when the two variables are interacting. Since they do not study the daily lives and familial behavior of their subjects, however, the family transmission people would be inclined to believe that this study cannot identify the important environmental variables with sufficient specificity. Some people believe that it might really be an academic problem anyway, since all you need to know that you can do anything about are the environmental variables. Some raised the question of the level at which the interaction occurs. We will have to wait to see the kinds of studies that investigators design to study this interaction. Some have been liberal with suggestions and models for research that others should carry out. Maybe there will be some takers.

What is the most accurate concordance rate for schizophrenia in MZ twins? If I understand these matters correctly, there *is* no most accurate concordance rate. There does seem to be a *modal* concordance rate among the most recent studies, and that value lies in the neighborhood of 40–50%. But as we know, past studies have reported rates varying from 6% to 86%, and although all the studies confronted methodological difficulties of one kind or another, there is no reason to preclude the possibility that such a range of concordance rates could indeed occur, and that each rate could be entirely accurate. Such discrepant rates could be partially explained by postulating a polygenic transmission of schizophrenia, and by adding a corollary postulate that more of these genes, or the more virulent genes, prevail in New York, for example, as compared to Finland. Since Finnish twins would have fewer of these genes, or the less noxious ones, one twin would have a better chance of warding off the expected development of clinical symptoms than would a twin in New York, who would harbor more of the nastier genes. To render this formulation even less parsimonious, environmental factors would still have to be brought in to explain why, in any given pair of MZ twins, one twin developed clinical schizophrenia whereas the other did not.

I want to footnote this last sentence by saying that, although we ought to prize parsimony highly in theorizing about these matters, we should be prepared to accept the fact that the true state of affairs may indeed be a complex one at many levels, and that parsimony may prove to be more an ideal than an actuality. Dr. Gottesman expressed this view. Yet, when we compare two alternative explanations for a set of data, we should cling to parsimony as an important criterion for choosing between them.

In explaining discrepant discordance rates it may be simpler to postulate that the genetic factors implicated in schizophrenia are not too differently distributed through different populations, that environmental factors vary from country to country in regard to the magnitude of intrapair differences in the experiences of twins, or in regard to intrauterine differences between them, and that the differences found in concordance rates reflect such differences. The consensus here, I believe, was that either or both of these factors *are* involved with respect to discordances already found. It would involve no great stretching on our part to admit simply that these factors could vary from place to place and time to time. Conceivably, should world culture and the range of human experience become more homogenized, we might find a modal concordance rate that is even more constant than the rates already found. This would reflect the fact that the range of possible environmental influences had narrowed to an even greater extent than currently exists.

What about genetic transmission theories? Among the relatively few people who have discussed this issue here, we find quite a variety of such theories. Dr. Slater has long been a leading advocate of monogenic theory, holding that the gene is a partial dominant. He still holds to this theory, although he is weighing it against polygenic theory. Dr. Karlsson likes a two-gene theory, one dominant, the other recessive. Several, led by Gottesman and Shields, but now including many new converts, lean toward a polygenic theory. Dr. Erlenmeyer-Kimling prefers a heterogeneity model. Professor Bleuler believes that no specific pathogenic genes are involved, but rather that genes implicated in normal traits that are incompatible happen to be transmitted to the same individual.[4] I myself have stayed out of the controversy by saying only that a core diathesis is inherited, but that the continuity of symptomatic severity in the schizophrenic spectrum disorders among our Index Adoptees favors a polygenic theory of some sort.

Previous attempts to validate such theories have been based on hospitalized cases. If the Adoptees study, the Extended Family study, and Heston's study are correct, and if the high incidence of psychopathology in the parents and sibs of schizophrenics reported here represents genetic effects in good part, then the hospitalized cases may comprise only the small part of the iceberg that is plainly visible. The bulk of genetically affected cases may be missing from the statistical configurations on which the genetic transmission theories are based. In the Adoptees Study, only 1 of the 20 subjects with schizophrenic spectrum diagnoses had been hospitalized for schizophrenia. Moreover, the figures may vary sufficiently from study to study, time to time, and place to place that one may have considerable latitude in selecting the figures he prefers to fit his theory. Future theorizing about transmission will have to come to grips with such factors. If the geneticists include only *Echt*schizophrenia based on hospitalization, the issue of transmission is likely to remain where it has been for many years. Usually a single gene plus modifiers has been postulated, although we have also had two-gene theories before. Dr. Karlsson has presented a new two-gene theory that is attractive in many ways, but like everything in this field, it confronts big problems. Should incidence for sibs be 16% or 8%? Should the penetrance be 80% or 40%? Is it compatible

---

[4] Professor Bleuler indicated that his theory of genetic dis-harmony is very similar to the multifactorial genetic model. He said that if many genes are harmless in most constellations and harmful only in an exceptional constellation, it is better to speak of the importance of the harmony of the genetic tendencies. However, in another view of polygenic theory, the effects of the implicated genes are summative rather than conflictual, i.e. these separate genes are thought in fact to be pathogenic, and to lead to disturbances of varying degree depending only on the number present. If only one or two such genes are present, the phenotypic effect may be small and not necessarily detectable. Dr. Wynne thought the phrase "transmission of schizophrenia" was unfortunate because it did not emphasize sufficiently the possible heterogeneity or multiplicity of entities that might be subsumed by this term, or that these entities might be dimensional and continuously graded. Also, the term "transmission" implies that the *same* entity and/or characteristics are passed on, but he believes that, in addition, *new and different* characteristics are evoked or induced through the transactional impact of persons on one another.

with the supposedly constant incidence of schizophrenia though schizophrenics have reduced fertility?[5] How will he decide when a subject meets the criteria for being creative or when he will not?[6] And what will he do with the schizoids and the border-lines that abound in the families?

If geneticists do intensive diagnostic evaluations of families, they may be led to a polygenic theory. Dr. Eisenberg warns that if the number of genes is not finite and their effects not major, the polygenic model could prove to be trivial. We could in fact be leading ourselves back to the days of hereditary taint.

The great promise of psychiatric genetics was that it led to specificity, specific genes for specific disorders. If we give that up, what will we have left? Yet how can we ignore the findings of the adoption studies, and the twin studies as well? The discordant MZ twins usually have some psychiatric disorder, presumably due to the same genotype. Assigning grades of concordance to them does not solve the problem, since, when these same clinical pictures occur in other family members, they are ignored, i.e. not counted, in genetic studies of schizophrenia.

Our only hope of escaping this dilemma is to identify either the genotype itself or its core manifestation in a biochemical, physiological, or core behavioral characteristic. Then we will know what to count in genetic studies.

The advancement of knowledge in this field will be no better than the methods and designs we use to achieve it. My orthopedist tells me that a bad or ill-fitting backbrace is worse than none at all. Similarly, bad data that do not really fit the facts may be worse than none at all. Of course, methodological sophistication has increased considerably during the last decade, and we have seen many examples of it in the papers presented in this Conference.[7] It would be impossible in the time available to review each study and to present a detailed analysis of the many methodological issues that could be raised in all of them, including those of my colleagues and myself. Clearly, the ideal study will never be achieved. We can only hope to approximate it as best we can.

Nevertheless, I would like to reinforce this increasing interest in research methods. The most frequently discussed methodological issue this week involved the dependability of

---

[5] Dr. Erlenmeyer-Kimling asked Dr. Karlsson whether he had data on the differential fertility of the superphrenic (the supposedly creative group) relative to the general population and to other members of the kinship, since according to his genetic scheme these would be the portion of the population responsible for maintaining polymorphism with respect to the s gene. Dr. Karlsson said that he had not examined the fertility of this group, but he liked to think that, at least until recent times, these superphrenics had been maintained through superior intellectual and creative abilities. Dr. Erlenmeyer-Kimling said that if he meant that this led to differential viability, it would be impossible to assess, since the creative potentials of those who died before reaching maturity would probably have been unknown.

[6] Dr. Naiman and others pointed out that Dr. Karlsson had not presented clear criteria for defining his superphrenic type, nor data concerning the prevalence of such individuals in those branches of the families studied that were not afflicted with schizophrenia.

[7] Dr. Wynne pointed out that all these valuable research procedures fall short of describing and standardizing the most essential part of the diagnostic process—the actual interviewing and other means of obtaining the data from and about the patients and other subjects. To him, this was analogous to making and reporting linear measurements without specifying the methods or units of measurements or whether the individual measured was in a sitting or standing posture. The World Health Organization, with Dr. Tsung-yi Lin as principal investigator, is working toward the standardization of psychiatric diagnosis through the use of a standardized set of interview schedules. This study may not be completed until 1970.

diagnostic assessments when the investigator had prior information relating both to the patient and to the hypothesis under study. Let me quote a man named Churchman, who is a professor of business administration and who writes a review on extra-sensory perception for a psychiatric journal (1967):

> ... Much of the time we accept the ridiculous assumption that if the investigator knows in his own heart that he is honest and objective, self-deception cannot occur. And yet over and over again in experimental science one can detect hidden deceptions. I well remember the shock I had as a young statistician when I began checking physical measurements to see if they were in "statistical control" and found that they were far from it; for example, that there were significant differences between runs in the measurement of the velocity of light, the same indented steel bar received Rockwell hardness readings ranging from steel as soft as lead to the hardest possible, and so on.

If such variability can be obtained in the physical sciences with instruments presumably much keener than our own senses, and if that variability reflects self-deception, how much more careful we need to be than the supposedly objective physicist.

Professor Churchman is obviously not out on an offbeat limb all by himself. Dr. Eisenberg and others referred to the work of Robert Rosenthal, with whom, as far as I know, I share no familial genes. Rosenthal examines experimenter–subject transactions that occur in supposedly well-controlled psychological experiments. I would like to quote to you the Summary from his most recent article (Rosenthal, 1967).

> Unintended covert communication by E to S appears to be the norm in psychological experiments. Such communication can (a) affect S's response to the experimental task, and (b) be partially predicted from a knowledge of various E attributes. The nature of E's unintended messages can be affected by (a) E's experience as E, (b) the behavior of his S, (c) the physical scene in which E conducts his research, and (d) E's perception of a relationship with the principal investigator. One particular type of unintended communication is the process whereby E covertly influences S to respond in accordance with E's hypothesis or expectation. Such unintended fulfillments of interpersonal prophecies have also been found beyond the E–S dyad, as when schoolchildren show significant IQ gains simply by virtue of their teachers' expectations that such gains will be made.

Now, it occurs to me that Rosenthal has put himself in a ridiculous bind because, if he is correct, we have every reason to believe that he has influenced his own experiments so that his results would be in accord with his own hypotheses, and we therefore cannot believe what he tells us. Nevertheless, despite Rosenthal's extreme and almost nihilistic position, we should exercise every possible precaution with regard to how we influence and are influenced by our subjects.

In the twin studies, the investigator who makes the diagnostic evaluation of the twins usually knows their zygosity or has some idea about it, or a judge makes the diagnostic determination based on records written by someone else who may well have known the twins' zygosity or family history. It is of course difficult or expensive to avoid such contingencies, and most investigators might be inclined to feel, like Dr. Slater, that any additional gain achieved in scientific precision would be negligible, and not worth the additional burden and cost. Yet, even should this belief prove true, we are obliged to impose all possible controls and to rule out as many possible confounding factors as we can. If we do not, we will not completely allay our own doubts, let alone those of others; we will not have met the best scientific standards; and we may well be infusing needless error into our studies.

The situation with regard to the family studies is at least as questionable, and probably more so, since these investigators interact more with their subjects, have greater opportunity

BB

to influence their subjects' general behavior or specific responses, and must make judgments about the behavior of patients' *relatives,* who are likely to be less ill and more varied in manner, verbal and facial expression, and in their interactions with the investigator. Add a strong theoretical preference to these ingredients and one could be brewing all kinds of errors.

I would like now to turn to those studies that focus on possible environmental factors in the transmission of schizophrenia. Though we know from the twin studies that such factors *must* be involved, Dr. MacMahon reminds us that "the issue is not whether environmental factors are involved, but whether they can be identified". The speakers here have pointed to four kinds of such factors: biological, familial, social class, and cultural.[8]

With respect to biological factors, Dr. Pollin finds that the schizophrenic twin in his discordant MZ pairs is more often than not the one who is smaller at birth, has more "soft" neurological signs, lower protein-bound iodine levels,[9] higher lactate/pyruvate ratios, and more episodes of neonatal cyanosis, colic, disturbed sleep and motility patterns. He reasons from such data that some biological deficit, not genetic, contributes to the development of schizophrenia. Unfortunately, the studies by Kringlen, Tienari and Fischer do not find consistent differences in birth weight or physical fitness between their sick and non-schizophrenic twins. Their findings dull the point of Pollin's theory, but these investigators did not make the other biological assessments that Pollin reports, and their birth-weight data may be less reliable. Moreover, in an assessment of all discordant twins reported in the literature, Pollin finds increased support for his position. Others suggested that some biological factors not genetic might be transmitted by actively schizophrenic mothers to their as yet unborn offspring. It was thought that these factors could have influenced Heston's findings. Presumably, the same possibility might apply to some of the high-risk children in the Mednick–Schulsinger study. In any case, the deficit postulated would have to be a secondary factor in the genesis of schizophrenia rather than a primary one, since it would not alone account for the clustering of schizophrenic-spectrum disorders in families. Pollin himself believes that the deficit is a contributing but not a major cause, and that it leads to a familial behavioral pattern involving the smaller twin which in turn reinforces a noxious role assigned to him in accord with unresolved family conflicts, pushing him toward subsequent schizophrenia. Dr. Goldfarb urges us to screen *all* our schizophrenic subjects for various neurological signs, and to use this information to generate more homogeneous groups in our research.

Pollin finds that the weaker twin is overprotected, develops a marked dependency relationship to his mother and becomes submissive to his cotwin. The submissiveness was originally noted by Slater to occur mostly in the sicker twin, and this finding has been confirmed by Kringlen and emphasized by Tienari. The finding itself cannot be doubted,

---

[8] Dr. Murphy thought the viewpoints of social psychiatry would have been better represented at the Conference if we had invited more papers dealing with variations in incidence rates that could not be accounted for by genetic theory, e.g. differences in incidence of schizophrenia between males and females in some populations, or differences between generations.

[9] Professor Bleuler held that hypothyroidism in the mother does not increase the risk of schizophrenia in her children, and that, except in some individual cases, thyroid function has nothing to do with the genesis of schizophrenic psychoses.

but the manner in which it is *related* to the development of severer forms of schizophrenia is still in question. We do not know if it is the psychological character of submissiveness within the context of the twin relationship which breeds the morbidity, or if the submissiveness is itself merely a symptomatic expression of a weaker constitution which is itself predisposing. We might some day get a partial answer to this question if we could find enough cases of schizophrenia in twins reared apart. If the sicker twin in such separated pairs was found to be more submissive in his peer relationships generally, and if the submissiveness was not related to physical debility, this could support the belief that submissiveness is itself a pathogenic as well as a pathological trait, and that it does not have to occur in the context of a relationship to an identical twin.

With respect to the family interaction studies, all the investigators are sensitive to the problem of whether the unusual, bizarre, or even irrational behavior that occurs within the families of schizophrenics may not itself be a milder expression of the same genetic factors which have led to full-blown illness in the schizophrenic member. They are also aware of the possibility that the pathological behavior is itself a reaction by the family to the irrational behavior of the schizophrenic in its midst. Although the investigators have struggled with these questions, they have not yet found a solution to them.

Dr. Mishler has made a special effort to separate and define the issues involved in interpreting a family's pathological behavior and has developed models to guide him.

Despite agreement among all the investigators regarding the very large amount of psychopathology in the families of schizophrenics, and the plausibility of their belief that such family pathology helps to cause schizophrenia in the child, they have yet to marshall clear evidence that their view is valid. The adoption studies suggest that they may have overstated their case. The Adoptive Parents study indicates that the adoptive children who became schizophrenic did so even when the extent of psychopathology in their adoptive parents was considerably less than that found in biological parents of schizophrenics.[10] This study, however, needs to be replicated, with more systematic selection of subjects and better control of procedures. Moreover, we have heard that it is not parental psychopathology *per se* that produces the noxious effects in the offspring, but a constellation of familial interaction or role patterns classified into two main types. Dr. Rogler has given us a poignant picture of how the disruptive effects upon the family in lower class Puerto Rico may vary, depending on whether it is the mother or the father who is the schizophrenic member of the family. Although the pictures he presents are clearly culturally determined to a marked degree, they give us reason to believe that in a more fluid culture the responses

---

[10] This study was criticized on the grounds that potentially adopting parents with more severe psychopathology would have been screened out by adoption agencies. Dr. Wender pointed out that some of the adoptive parents had adopted "independently", not through an adoption agency, and that they were actually a little *less* disturbed than those who adopted through agencies. He also pointed out that, among the latter, appreciable psychiatric illness developed *after* adoption, suggesting that their disturbances may have been partly reactive. Critics also stated that it was not psychopathology *per se* in the rearing parents that was pathogenic, but some rearing practices that were correlated, but only imperfectly, with parental psychopathology. Both Dr. Wender and Dr. Hunt pointed out that it was important to know the prevalence of such rearing practices in families where children did not become schizophrenic. Dr. Naiman, who is studying mothers of children born out of wedlock who are given up for adoption, pointed out that such mothers differed from a control group of married mothers in a number of respects, and that this fact had to be taken into account in any study involving adoptees.

of the families harboring a schizophrenic member would vary to a much greater extent, some being far more disruptive than others. Whether this disruption is by itself sufficient to produce schizophrenic illness is, however, still an unsettled matter.[11]

The study of intrafamilial behavior is a much newer field than psychiatric genetics, and those who are not themselves investigators in this area have found much to complain about. However, a field must begin somewhere. Dr. Lidz chose to begin by observing his families intensively and describing his observations. This is the way most fields begin. The fact that he continues to do so after all these years was the cause of concern expressed by a number of people, but Dr. Lidz and others find the method to be one of continuing value.

These investigators now seem to be singling out for concentrated study different aspects of their families' behavior. Alanen, for example, seems to focus on the total family atmosphere. Lidz, in his presentation, focuses on linguistic disturbances, and Wynne focuses on the way in which the family destroys the child's efforts to maintain a focus of attention.

However, the need for greater clarification of these complex processes has already been felt for some time, and we have begun to see the application of more controlled methods to the original observational studies. Almost all the investigators have been using tests to supplement their observations in recent years. Comparison groups are now more often employed. Dr. Reiss has devised or adapted a rather ingenious, although complicated experimental procedure, to evaluate family roles, communication styles, and decision making processes in families. Wynne and Singer are developing research strategies that may yet help them to demonstrate that parental behavior can produce schizophrenia. Mishler has devoted much of his thought and energy to the research problems and issues in this field and is trying to inaugurate objective procedures for their analysis. All in all, we have reason to be hopeful that these investigations, and ones yet to come, will further our understanding of familial behavior and any possible role it might play with respect to the development of psychopathology in its members. But the consensus of the Conference, if I infer it correctly, is that so far the case for familial transmission is not proved.[12]

---

[11] Based on his extensive family studies, Professor Bleuler pointed out that the influence of parents' schizophrenic psychoses on their children is, as a rule, very severe, contributing toward neurotic development, lack of good education and unstable family life. However, some children adapt to the parent's psychosis in a wonderful way. Even small children can realize early what is psychotic or not psychotic, and can maintain a very warm contact with the patient while quite aware of his morbid nature. Some see the proper nursing of the parent as a great task for their own life, and sometimes the whole family unites to nurse the patient and to combat successfully the tremendous threat instigated by having a psychotic member. As a rule, he added, the social standard of families with schizophrenic members is not diminished. Dr. Lidz questioned whether even some of Professor Bleuler's families were reasonably satisfactory. Dr. Lidz said that he and Dr. Alanen, as well as other investigators in many different countries had sought seriously and even painstakingly to find families in which the family environment was not seriously disturbed. He pointed out that Professor Bleuler had not provided us with evidence that such reasonably salubrious environments exist after careful study; that in an earlier study conducted at the Bürgholzli itself, a small proportion of the families of schizophrenic patients seemed to be reasonably good, but after more careful study were found to be just as disturbed as the others. Dr. Lidz expressed disappointment in not being able to find less disturbed families since he had hoped that they might provide the key to what specifically might be wrong in the families that gave rise to schizophrenic offspring.

[12] Dr. Lidz protested strongly against this inference. Even with the new evidence from the adoption studies, he said, there is more than ample room for the findings that the family is one of the essential determinants of schizophrenia. In fact, he added, one could say that family disorganization of certain types is necessary to the etiology or transmission of schizophrenia but that the condition will only occur in clear-cut form in those

With respect to social class factors in schizophrenia, I think that we must all have appreciated greatly Dr. Kohn's review of this issue. He gave us a thorough, scholarly, critical, and well-balanced analysis of the extensive literature published in this field. He concluded that, although the higher prevalence of schizophrenia in lower classes is well-documented, the relationship between social class and schizophrenia is not clear. Nevertheless, he was clearly attracted to the hypothesis that social class does seem to play some etiological role. He also pointed out that there has not been a single well-controlled study that demonstrates any substantial difference between the family relationships of schizophrenics and those of normal persons from lower- and working-class backgrounds. Most agreed with Dr. Kohn's strong appeal that we "bring all these variables—social class, early family relationships, genetics, stress—into the same investigations, so that we can examine their interactive effects."[13]

With respect to the possible contribution of cultural factors to schizophrenia, Dr. Murphy gave us an eloquent and incisive summary of the best studies that support such a view. He pointed out the enormous difficulties one has in trying to get unequivocal results in such studies. The genetic and cultural variables are so closely intertwined that it is almost impossible to rule out altogether the possible contribution of heredity. Yet Dr. Murphy presented an unusual body of data, fascinating and provocative by itself, which must prompt us to keep the issue alive and to heed the possible reality of a culturally induced increase in the rate of schizophrenia in certain populations. Even if the differences in such rates are real, the attempted explanations of them, almost inevitably *post hoc,* will be difficult to substantiate.

Dr. Murphy has elsewhere presented data purporting to show in fair detail how sociocultural factors can influence the *symptomatic* expression of schizophrenic illness. These data are equally provocative, and their validity may be more readily demonstrable. It requires no great leap in inference to suppose that if culture can influence the expression of the illness, it can influence the rate of illness as well. But the inference cannot be taken for granted. If the symptom differences are comparable to the differences between a delusion in French and a delusion in English, they are trivial. If they involve having delusions of persecution rather than periods of excitement, anxiety, obsessive rituals, or depressive reactions, they could more readily be regarded as possible contributors to different schizophrenic rates.

Both Dr. Murphy and Dr. Slater presented rates of schizophrenia in different peoples. Dr. Slater looked for constancy in the figures he cited, and found it. Dr. Murphy looked for contrasts in the figures he cited, and found them. In point of fact, the highest rate that Dr. Slater cited was 150% greater than the lowest rate. In Dr. Murphy's tables, the largest

---

individuals who have a genetic predisposition to it; that anyone wishing to discard this proposition must show that schizophrenia appears in stable families; and that the adoption studies particularly should pay attention to the adoptive homes in which the schizophrenic patients were raised.

[13] In this context, and especially in regard to the proposed study by Dr. Erlenmeyer-Kimling, Dr. Murphy and many others raised ethical *caveats* regarding such investigations. The greatest concern, of course, was to avoid disturbing children. Some proposed incorporating into the research design ways of protecting or providing special services for the children.

such difference was about 200%, but the general order of differences between the two sets of figures seems to be approximately the same.

Dr. Slater pointed out that the time of study did not influence the admission rates in the table he showed. There are, however, other factors that have often been said to influence hospitalization, viz. the number of hospital beds available in relation to the total population, the accessibility of hospitals, attitudes to mental illness and hospitalization, and others, all of which could conceivably average out or combine to yield approximately similar admission rates in relatively broad geographical areas. We know that many schizophrenics are never admitted to hospitals, so that the rates themselves are minimal figures rather than true ones in studies where the entire population has not been personally examined.

Dr. Murphy devoted a good part of his paper to examining the several possible factors that could have led to the significantly different admission rates he found, but ruled out all of them except culture. He also made the interesting observation that cultural traditions are themselves adaptive, and that aspects of such traditions that might lead to schizophrenia are likely to be modified, leading to a more even distribution of incidence rates among cultural groups. Thus, he proposes a theory based on the evolution of culture rather than on genetic evolution. Clearly, there are at least two ways to look at such data.

Having considered the four kinds of environmental factors covered at the Conference that might be implicated in schizophrenia, viz. biological, intrafamilial, social class, and cultural, we are led to the conclusion that all are suggestive and none of them proved. Regarding our task to *identify* the environmental variables, we must admit that we have not as yet been able to do so in any convincing way.[14] Some pointed out that we should look beyond the family for such factors. A few cited peer relations as one of them, and one pointed to a Harlow monkey study as suggestive in this regard. Others also suggested that we might look at animal studies for clues, but some, notably Dr. Hunt, raised some question about the interpretation of such studies. Some even suggested considering whether the relevant environmental factors might be ubiquitous, but this would not account for the high discordance rate in MZ twins.

What shall we say about the concept of schizophrenia itself? Let me mention two studies. The first is the Adoptees Study. Recall that our index biological parents included four basic diagnostic groups: clearcut chronic schizophrenics, acute or reactive schizophrenics, border-line or pseudoneurotic schizophrenics, and manic-depressive psychotics. The numbers for most of the groups are still small, but they suggest that the incidence of schizophrenic–spectrum disorders in their respective offspring is approximately the same. Traditionally, a great deal of emphasis has been laid on the clinical, genetic and dynamic differences between these groups. This study suggests that, at least from the genetic side, we must pay more attention to their similarities. Moreover, if we consider Heston's findings, and the findings of the Extended Family study and Karlsson, we should include the psycho-

---

[14] Professor Bleuler expressed the opinion that therapeutic experiences with schizophrenics had to be considered when the nature of the psychosis was discussed. Dr. Naiman amplified this point by saying that since such treatment involved interpersonal contact, this constituted evidence in favor of interpersonal factors having etiological significance. Dr. Wender retorted that heart failure responds to digitalis but is not caused by a deficiency of digitalis. Dr. Naiman replied that a model based on the role of phenylalanine in phenylketonuria is as compatible with data on psychotherapy as a model based on digitalis in heart failure.

pathies or severe character disorders in this genetic family, and at least some artistic and creative people as well. From the twin studies, we learn that some people with the genotype for schizophrenia may even be called just plain normal.

Now, recall the first study you heard reported this week, the one by Professor Bleuler. It is unique in its goal, its scope, its time span, its breadth of view, and its personal involvement with the subjects under study. Professor Bleuler begins his study with 216 hard-core cases of classical schizophrenia. Yet over the decades he finds that this is not a homogeneous group. He is able to distinguish 7 groups among them in terms of their onset, course and outcome. He points out that the expression of schizophrenic illness is changing. Whereas the old catastrophe–schizophrenia occurred with high frequency, not a single one of his subjects developed this form of illness, even though the modern drug therapies were not introduced until more than a decade after his study began. One-third of this subjects recovered. Of patients who reached an *Endzustand* described as petrified, incorrigible, and hopeless, approximately 40% showed definite improvement in this very late phase of the psychosis. He could find no absolute deterioration, even in the worst chronic cases. In all he could find signs of normality, both intellectual and emotional.

Thus, even among hard-core cases, the rule is heterogeneity of manifestation rather than homogeneity, ranging from terminal chronicity through definite improvement to recovery. It is this heterogeneity of manifestation in all phases and aspects of the illness that makes the evaluation of etiological factors such a precarious enterprise. It also serves as a challenge, not to a duel, fortunately, but to our ability to solve complex problems. That we are at least inching along toward a fuller appreciation of the problem itself, there can be no doubt.

REFERENCES

CHURCHMAN, C. W. (1967) Perception or deception, review of ESP: a scientific evaluation by C. E. M. Hansel, *Psychiat. Social Sci. Rev.* **1**, 7–11.
ROSENTHAL, R. (1967) Covert communication in the psychological experiment, *Psychol. Bull.* **67**, 356–67.

AUTHOR INDEX

Abe, K.   100, 124
Achte, K. A.   157, 170
Ainsworth, M.   365, 376
Alanen, T. O.   370, 376
Alanen, Y. O.   55, 62, 202, 204, 209, 211, 212, 237, 248, 249, 315
Albee, G.   330, 332
Albee, G. W.   273, 297
Allen, G.   39, 47, 57, 63, 65, 82, 108, 109, 125, 402
Angst, J.   118, 126
Anthony, E. J.   299, 315
Arensberg, C. M.   145, 152
Arlow, J. A.   210, 212
Arnold, O. H.   119, 126
Astrup, C.   160, 171
Atkinson, G. F.   106, 124
Atkinson, M. W.   209, 212
Auble, D.   287, 290
Ax, A. F.   273, 288

Babigian, H. M.   157, 169
Babson, S. G.   402
Bahn, A. K.   157, 170
Bateson, G.   166, 172, 179, 184
Bavelas, A.   230, 234
Beaulieu, M. R.   221, 222
Beckett, P. G. S.   287, 290
Behrens, M. I.   194, 195, 196, 198
Bell, R. Q.   213, 220, 222
Bender, L.   335, 343
Benedetti, G.   12
Benjamin, J. D.   188, 198
Bentley, A. F.   185, 198
Bhattacharjya, B.   141, 152
Birren, J. E.   316
Bleuler, E.   47, 176, 184, 185, 186, 198
Bleuler, M.   12, 95, 123
Blizzard, R.   326
Böök, J. A.   16, 25, 85, 94, 124
Boszormenyi-Nagy, I.   210, 212
Bower, E. M.   275, 290
Bowlby, J.   365, 376
Bowman, K. M.   316
Bramhall, J. L.   402
Brenner, C.   210, 212
Brown, A. C.   99, 124
Brown, R.   183, 184
Bruner, J.   224, 234
Brush, S.   54, 55, 63, 68, 83, 107, 125, 345, 362
Bruun, K.   27, 36

Buchsbaum, M.   189, 198
Buck, C.   157, 171
Burks, B.   250
Burruss, G.   111, 125

Camps, F. E.   117, 126
Chapin, F. S.   215, 222
Chapman, T. S.   76, 83
Churchman, C. W.   421, 427
Clark, J. A.   47
Clark, R. E.   156, 169
Clausen, J. A.   155, 157, 159, 162, 163, 169, 170, 171, 172, 173
Cohen, B. D.   287, 290
Cohn, R.   326
Connell, P. H.   25
Cooper, B.   99, 124
Cooper, M.   157, 160, 170
Cornelison, A.   176, 179, 184, 189, 198, 223, 234
Cornelison, A. R.   110, 114, 122, 125, 204, 207, 212
Cowie, J.   98, 124
Cowie, V. A.   98, 124
Crocetti, G. M.   142, 152
Czajkowski, N. P.   327, 332

Daily, J. M.   275, 290
Day, J.   166, 172
Dee, W. C. J.   157, 169
Demerath, N. J.   156, 169
Deming, W. E.   68, 69, 72, 82
Dewey, J.   185, 198
Diderichsen, B.   277, 290
Dodd, B. E.   117, 126
Dohrenwend, B. P.   161, 164, 172
Dohrenwend, B. S.   161, 164, 172
Donnelly, E. M.   246, 249
Donney, D. D.   250
Dunham, 155, 156, 157, 158, 159, 168, 169, 171
Dye, H. B.   345, 362

Eaton, J. W.   139, 152, 156, 169
Eayrs, J.   326
Edwards, J. H.   82, 116, 125
Eisenberg, L.   333, 342
Elliot, G.   155, 168
Elsässer, G.   66, 71, 82, 97, 115, 123, 316

429